THE LETTERS OF
DAVID HUME

Edited by
J. Y. T. GREIG

Volume II
1766–1776

OXFORD
UNIVERSITY PRESS

OXFORD
UNIVERSITY PRESS
Great Clarendon Street, Oxford, OX2 6DP

Oxford University Press is a department of the University of Oxford.
It furthers the University's objective of excellence in research,
scholarship, and education by publishing worldwide in

Oxford New York

Auckland Cape Town Dar es Salaam Hong Kong Karachi
Kuala Lumpur Madrid Melbourne Mexico City
Nairobi New Delhi Shanghai Taipei Toronto

With offices in
Argentina Austria Brazil Chile Czech Republic France Greece
Guatemala Hungary Italy Japan Poland Portugal Singapore
South Korea Switzerland Thailand Turkey Ukraine Vietnam

Oxford is a registered trade mark of Oxford University Press
in the UK and in certain other countries

Published in the United States
by Oxford University Press Inc., New York

First published 1932
First published in paperback 2011

British Library Cataloguing in Publication Data
Data available

Library of Congress Cataloging in Publication Data
Data available

Printed in Great Britain
on acid-free paper by
MPG Biddles, Bodmin and King's Lynn

ISBN 978-0-19-969325-2 (Pbk)

1 3 5 7 9 10 8 6 4 2

CONTENTS

VOLUME II

NOTE

SINCE this volume was printed, Volume XV of *Correspondance générale de Rousseau* has appeared. Letters 297, 305, 306, 308, 310, 311, 313, 315, 316, 320, 323, 324, 328, 333, and 341 from Hume to Rousseau appear in that volume, as well as Rousseau's Letters, Appendix G III, IV and Appendix H I–III, to Hume; and also Hume's Letters to Richard Davenport—Nos. 325, 327, 329, 331, 332, 335, 339, 340.

* 297. *To* JEAN-JACQUES DE LUZE [1]

M. Hume est convenu avec M. Rousseau de se rendre au Temple Samedi[2] a onze heures et de partir tout suite. Il prie M. de Luze d'etre pret a cette heure-la. Le Temple est dans le chemin, pour aller a Bourget, qui est la premiere poste. Il vaut mieux sortir de Paris ensemble, de peur des meprises.

Jeudi matin.

[2 janvier 1766]

A Monsieur Monsieur de Luze chez Briel, Baigneur rue de Richelieu a Paris.

† 298. *To the* COMTESSE DE BOUFFLERS

London, 19 January, 1766.

My pupil and I, dear Madam, arrived safely in this place,[3] both of us in good health, and also in good humour, after the first melancholy of my separation from you was a little dissipated.

My companion is very amiable, always polite, gay often, commonly sociable. He does not know himself when he thinks he is made for entire solitude. I exhorted him on the road to write his Memoirs. He told me, that he had already done it with an intention of publishing them.[4]

At present, says he, it may be affirmed, that nobody knows me perfectly any more than himself; but I shall describe myself

* MS. in Bibliothèque publique de Neuchâtel; hitherto unpublished in England.

† *Priv. Corr.*, 125 ff.; Burton, ii. 303 ff. (incomplete).

[1] Jean-Jacques de Luze (born 1728), succeeded his father, of the same name, in 1763, as Président de la Chambre de Blés and as member of the Large and Small Councils, at Neuchâtel. He accompanied Hume and Rousseau from Paris to London.

[2] Writing to Du Peyrou on 1 Jan. 1766, Rousseau says: '. . . je pars demain pour le public, et samedi réellement' (*Œuvres*, 1826, xxiii. 244).

[3] From a letter of Rousseau to Mme de Boufflers, dated 18 Jan., it appears that they arrived in London on Monday, 13 Jan., having taken eight days on the journey.

[4] Writing to Du Peyrou on 1 Jan. 1766, Rousseau says: 'Tâchez, je vous en prie, de m'envoyer par mademoiselle Le Vasseur toutes les lettres, mémoires, brouillons, etc., depuis 1758 jusqu'à 1762, mois de juin inclusivement, c'est-à-dire jusqu'à mon départ de Paris, attendu que la première chose que je vais faire sera de mettre au net toute cette suite de pièces, de peur d'en perdre la trace' (*Œuvres*, 1826, xxiii. 245).

in such plain colours, that henceforth every one may boast that he knows himself, and Jean-Jacques Rousseau. I believe, that he intends seriously to draw his own picture in its true colours: but I believe at the same time that nobody knows himself less. For instance; even with regard to his health, a point in which few people can be mistaken, he is very fanciful. He imagines himself very infirm. He is one of the most robust men I have ever known. He passed ten hours in the night time above deck during the most severe weather, when all the seamen were almost frozen to death, and he caught no harm. He says that his infirmity always increases upon a journey, yet was it almost imperceptible on the road from Paris to London.[1]

His wearing the Armenian dress is a pure whim, which, however, he is resolved never to abandon. He has an excellent warm heart; and, in conversation, kindles often to a degree of heat which looks like inspiration. I love him much, and hope that I have some share in his affections.

I find, that we shall have many ways of settling him to his satisfaction,[2] and as he is learning the English very fast, he will afterwards be able to choose for himself. There is a gentleman, of the name of Townsend, a man of four or five thousand a year, who lives very privately, within fifteen miles of London, and is a great admirer of our philosopher, as is also his wife. He has desired him to live with him, and offers to take any board he pleases. M. Rousseau was much pleased with this proposal, and is inclined to accept of it. The only difficulty is, that he insists positively on his gouvernante's [3] sitting at table, a proposal which is not to be made to Mr and Mrs Townsend.

[1] The sentimental appeal which Rousseau made to the eminent ladies of his day is well illustrated by Mme de Boufflers's reply to this paragraph. In an undated letter, written either at the end of Jan. or at the beginning of Feb., she says: 'Vous pretendes que Rousseau n'a pas souffert, parce quil ne s'est pas plaint, et quil n'a pas de maladie parce quil est de constitution robuste. Oserois-je vous demander si c'est ainsi quon raisonne a Edimbourg! J'aurois cru que la force etoit dautant plus grande qu'on n'apercevoit moins ses efforts, et que le courage etant la force morale, il suivoit les memes regles. Il y a bien de l'audace a moy de reprendre ainsi mon maitre' (MS., R.S.E.; an unpublished passage of the letter given in *Eminent Persons*, 232 ff.).

[2] The original proposal of a gardener's house at Fulham was dropped after Hume and Rousseau went to see the house, which was found to be very dirty, and too small.

[3] Mlle Le Vasseur, who had now arrived in Paris from Switzerland and was to follow Rousseau to England at the first opportunity.

This woman forms the chief encumbrance to his settlement. M. de Luze, our companion, says, that she passes for wicked, and quarrelsome, and tattling, and is thought to be the chief cause of his quitting Neufchatel.[1] He himself owns her to be so dull, that she never knows in what year of the Lord she is, nor in what month of the year, nor in what day of the month or week; and that she can never learn the different value of the pieces of money in any country. Yet she governs him as absolutely as a nurse does a child. In her absence his dog has acquired that ascendant. His affection for that creature is beyond all expression or conception.

I have as yet scarce seen anybody except Mr Conway and Lady Aylesbury. Both of them told me, they would visit Jean-Jacques, if I thought their company would not be disagreeable. I encouraged them to show him that mark of distinction. Here I must also tell you of a good action which I did; not but that it is better to conceal our good actions. But I consider not my seeking your approbation as an effect of vanity: your suffrage is to me something like the satisfaction of my own conscience. While we were at Calais, I asked him whether, in case the King of England thought proper to gratify him with a pension, he would accept of it. I told him, that the case was widely different from that of the King of Prussia; and I endeavoured to point out to him the difference, particularly in this circumstance, that a gratuity from the King of England could never in the least endanger his independence. He replied: 'But would it not be using ill the King of Prussia, to whom I have since been much obliged?[2] However, on this head,' added he, 'in case the offer be made me, I shall consult my father'; meaning Lord Marischal. I told this story to General Conway, who seemed to embrace with zeal the motion of giving him a pension, as honourable both to the King and nation. I shall suggest the same idea to other men in power whom I may meet with, and I do not despair of succeeding.

[1] The result of these remarks about Mlle Le Vasseur was that Mme de Boufflers, who had always patronized the woman before, now found it more difficult to do so. In her undated reply, she says: 'J'ay vu Mlle Le Vasseur mais pas daussi bon oeil qu'a l'ordinaire a cause de ce que vous m'avez mandé. Je me le reproche pourtant, car si elle est accusée elle n'est pas jugée' (MS., R.S.E., unpublished).

[2] It will be recalled that Rousseau at Neuchâtel had declined the pension and other favours offered him by Lord Marischal Keith in the King of Prussia's name.

Permit me to finish by mentioning, in one word, my warm and indissoluble attachment to you, an attachment founded both on esteem and affection, not to mention gratitude. I speak not of my acknowledgments to the Prince of Conti, because I should never finish were I to enter on that subject.

Please remember me to Madame de Vierville and Madame de Barbentane: tell the latter that Rousseau says, no French author could have wrote in a more elegant style than the letter which he received from me at Strasburgh.

I write this the day after my arrival, so that I can give you no account of any of your friends, except Lady Hervey, who is well, and remembers you very kindly.

Please direct to me to the care of James Coutts, Esq. Banker, in the Strand.

P.S.

Since I wrote the above, I have received your obliging letter, directed to Calais.[1] M. Rousseau says, the letter of the King of Prussia is a forgery; and he suspects it to come from M. de Voltaire.[2]

[1] A short letter (MS., R.S.E.; *Eminent Persons*, 231 f.) asking for news of the journey, and asking also whether the supposed letter from the King of Prussia which was current in Paris was genuine or not.

[2] This supposed letter, constantly referred to in the letters that follow, and which had so disastrous an effect on the relations of Hume and Rousseau, was a joke of Horace Walpole's. Writing to General Conway from Paris on 12 Jan. 1766, he says: '. . . my present fame is owing to a very trifling composition, but which has made incredible noise. I was one evening at Madame Geoffrin's joking on Rousseau's affectations and contradictions, and said some things that diverted them. When I came home, I put them into a letter, and showed it next day to Helvetius and the Duc de Nivernois; who were so pleased with it, that, after telling me some faults in the language, which you may be sure there were, they encouraged me to let it be seen. As you know I willingly laugh at mountebanks, *political* or literary, let their talents be ever so great, I was not averse. The copies have spread like wild-fire; *et me voici à la mode!* I expect the end of my reign at the end of the week with great composure. Here is the letter:—

"LE ROI DE PRUSSE À MONSIEUR ROUSSEAU.

"Mon cher Jean Jacques,

"Vous avez renoncé à Genève votre patrie; vous vous êtes fait chasser de la Suisse, pays tant vanté dans vos écrits; la France vous a décrété. Venez donc chez moi; j'admire vos talens; je m'amuse de vos rêveries, qui (soit dit en passant) vous occupent trop, et trop long tems. Il faut à la fin être sage et heureux. Vous avez fait assez parler de vous par des singularités peu convenables à un veritable grand homme. Démontrez à vos ennemis que vous pouvez avoir quelquefois le sens commun: cela les fâchera, sans vous faire tort. Mes états vous offrent une retraite paisible; je vous veux du bien,

The project of Mr Townsend, to my great mortification, has totally vanished, on account of Mademoiselle Le Vasseur. Send all his letters under my cover.

* 299. *To* WILLIAM STRAHAN

Dear Strahan

Is it not strange that you and I have not yet met? I have been so hurry'd both with my own Affairs and with Mons[r] Rousseau's, that I can excuse myself: But I own that I hopd your Leizure woud allow you to come hither. I go out of town to morrow and Sunday: As soon as I come back I propose to beat up your Quarters. My Compliments to Mrs Strahan.

Yours sincerely
DAVID HUME.

Buckingham Street, York Buildings,
Mrs Adams's. Friday [end of Jan. 1766].[1]

† 300. *To* ADAM SMITH

[London, ? end of January 1766]

Dear Smith

I can write as seldom and as Short as you—I am sorry I did not see you before I left Paris. I am also sorry I shall not see you there soon. I shall not be able to fix Rousseau to his Mind

* MS. at Barnbougle Castle; Hill, 73.
† MS., R.S.E.; Burton, ii. 392 (incomplete).

et je vous en ferai, si vous le trouvez bon. Mais si vous vous obstiniez à rejeter mon secours, attendez-vous que je ne le dirai à personne. Si vous persistez à vous creuser l'esprit pour trouver de nouveaux malheurs, choisissez-les tels que vous voudrez. Je suis roi, je puis vous en procurer au gré de vos souhaits: et ce qui sûrement ne vous arrivera pas vis-à-vis de vos ennemis, je cesserai de vous persécuter quand vous cesserez de mettre votre gloire à l'être.

"Votre bon ami,
"FRÉDÉRIC".'

(*Letters*, vi. 396 f.)

[1] William Rouet, writing to William Mure from London on 25 Jan. 1766, says: 'David Hume, and J. J. Rousseau, are in Buckingham Street, next door to J. Stuart's [John Stewart's, the wine merchant], where many go from civility to see him; and our friend David is made the shower of the Lion. He is confoundedly weary of his pupil, as he calls him; he is full of oddities and even absurdities . . .' (*Caldwell Papers*, II, ii. 63). L. J. Courtois (*Le Séjour de J.-J. Rousseau en Angleterre*, 30) suggests that Hume's letter ought to be dated 7 March 1766, but long before that date Hume had gone to live at his old quarters in Lisle Street, Leicester Fields.

for some Weeks yet: He is a little variable & fanciful, tho' very agreeable. Lord Hertford is to be over some time in April. I must then wait for him; and afterwards must be dispos'd of, for some time, by his Commands. I recommended my Servant St Jean to you: If he be with you or the Duke, I am sure you will like him and keep him on; and you need say nothing of this to him. But if you did not engage him, please send to him and tell him, that as I cannot promise on my Return to Paris soon, I do not wish he woud deprive himself of any other good Service that offers. He lives at Collet's, a Hirer of Coaches in the Rue des vieux Augustins, a few Doors from the Hotel du Parc roiale where you intended to lodge. He is known either by the Name of St Jean or Jean Garneaux——Some push me to continue my History. Millar offers me any Price: All the Marlborough Papers are offerd me:[1] And I believe no body woud venture to refuse me: But cui bono? Why shoud I forgo Idleness and Sauntering and Society; and expose myself again to the Clamours of a stupid, factious Public? I am not yet tir'd of doing nothing; and am become too wise either to mind Censure or Applause. By & bye I shall be too old to undergo so much Labour: Adieu

David Hume.

A Monsieur Monsieur Adam Smith Chez Mons[r] Foley, Banquier a Paris

* 301. *To* John Home of Ninewells

Dear Brother

I hope you will excuse my not writing, immediatly upon my Arrival. I knew, that the Papers wou'd inform you of that Event; and I had nothing to say, but what was Matter of mere Curiosity and might be delay'd till our meeting. You are acquainted with my usual Indolence in writing, to which the Hurry of my removal and coming into a new Scene gave some Excuse. As you know, that I never left any place without Regreat, you may imagine, that I did not leave Paris altogether willingly, after having been so long accustomd to it. I do not find this new Scene near so much to my Taste, and I shall be long ere I am reconcil'd to it. Perhaps, Edinburgh may please me better: I promise myself at least some Satisfaction in my

* MS., R.S.E.; Burton, ii. 308 ff. (incomplete).

[1] Presumably the papers which Mallet had had for more than twenty years and had done nothing with.

Nephews, of whom I hear a very good Account: And it is surely more suitable to one of my Years to seek a Retreat in my native Country, than to pass the Dregs of Life, among the Great and among People, who, tho' they seem to have a Friendship for me, are still Strangers. I accustom myself, therefore, to this Idea without Reluctance; and since I have cross'd the Seas, I find my Regreat for the good Company I left behind me, less pungent and uneasy.

You give me bad Accounts of the Loss of my Money: This is a Favour I owe that Rascal, Tom Cockburn, who coud not but know something of Haliburton's Affairs.[1] I doubt not but Davie Anderson[2] will do all he can to save something, if possible. I have sold out my four per cents in the Stocks, at 1545 pounds. I keep only the long Annuities, which I coud sell for between 4 & 500 pounds; so that I am a Gainer near 500 Pounds by the Stockjobbing. I have remitted the Money to Scotland, and shall imitate your Example in settling it.

Tell Lady Stewart,[3] that I wrote her an Answer by Jemmy Coutts, who did not go to Scotland, as he intended. I coud give her Friend no Encouragement to go to Paris. I shall write to the Bishop of Downe and Connor[4] about Wilson[5]; but my Success is very little to be depended on, as I know the Government in Ireland is as much straiten'd as that of England. His Money is too little to buy a Chaplaincy. On the whole, Carlysle writes me, that Wilson is for the present very well with him, if he coud be contented; but this shall not hinder me from doing him all the Service in my power.

You will have heard by this time, that I have brought over with me the famous Rousseau, the most singular Man surely in the World. He applyd to me last Summer to take him under

[1] I do not know who Tom Cockburn was. Haliburton seems to have been a merchant in Edinburgh.

[2] David Anderson seems to have had charge of some of Hume's financial business. There is one letter, dated from Edinburgh, 30 Oct. 1767, from him to Hume among the MSS., R.S.E. He says: 'You are turning so fast rich we must conceal it, as being inconsistent with a Philosopher, if Rousseau knew it, he might make a bad use of it against you. But Philosophers must alter with the times, and in that view you are a very sensible Philosopher.'

[3] Possibly Lady Frances Wemyss, sister of Lord Elcho, and wife (1743) of Sir James Steuart of Coltness. But there is no letter from her extant among the MSS., R.S.E.

[4] Trail, formerly Chaplain at the Paris Embassy.

[5] The young minister who had acted for a time as tutor to John Home's sons, and was now assistant to Alexander Carlyle of Inveresk.

my Protection in England, as he calld it; but in the mean while, he was chac'd out of Switzerland, and came to Strasbourg, with an Intention of going to the King of Prussia, who pressd him earnestly to live with him. At Strasbourg my Letter reachd him, making him an Offer of all my Services, upon which he turn'd short, and having obtaind the King of France's Passport came and joind me at Paris. I have liv'd with him ever since: He is a very modest, mild, well-bred, gentle-spirited and warm-hearted Man, as ever I knew in my Life: He is also in appearance very sociable: I never saw a man who seems better calculated for good Company nor who seems to take more Pleasure in it; yet is he absolutely determind to retire and board himself in a Farmer's House among the Mountains of Wales for the sake of Solitude. He has refus'd a Pension from the King of Prussia and Presents from hundreds: I have been offerd great Sums for him, if I cou'd have prevaild on him to accept of them: Yet till within these three Months he was in absolute Beggary: He has now about 70 pounds a [year] which he has acquird by a Bargain, for his Works. It is incredible the Enthusiasm for him in Paris and the Curiosity in London. I prevaild on him to go to the Play-house, in order to see Garrick, who placd him in a Box opposite the King and Queen. I observd their Majestys to look at him, more than at the Players. I shoud desire no better Fortune than to have the Privilege of showing him to all I please. The hereditary Prince[1] payd him a Visit a few days ago; and I imagine the Duke of York calld on him one Evening when he was abroad. I love him much and shall separate from him with much Regreat.

I am Dear Brother

Yours sincerely

London 2^{d} Feby 1766 DAVID HUME

To John Home of Ninewells Esqr at Ninewells near Berwick

* 302. *To the* COMTESSE DE BOUFFLERS

12[2] of January, 1766.

I have the satisfaction to tell you, that the project which I had formed for our friend's service, has succeeded. You

* *Priv. Corr.*, 129 ff.; Burton, ii. 307 f. (incomplete).

[1] Charles William Ferdinand (1735–1806), Hereditary Prince of Brunswick, brother-in-law of George III.

[2] *Sic* in printed text, and apparently in the autograph also; for Mme de Boufflers begins her reply, which is dated 'ce 18 [février?]':

'J'ay receu avant hier votre seconde lettre datée du 12 de janvier, ce qui remember the conversation between him and me at Calais, of which I gave you an account. I found means to have that conversation related to the King, by a friend of mine, who possesses much of his confidence. He was pleased with it; promised our philosopher a pension, without naming the sum; and there now wants only Lord Marischal's consent to his accepting it. We have wrote to Berlin for that purpose; and I entertain no doubt of our obtaining it. You know that our Sovereign is extremely prudent and decent, and careful not to give offence. For which reason, he requires that this act of generosity may be an entire secret. As I am sensible it would give you great pleasure, and as I am well acquainted with your secrecy and discretion, I would not conceal it from you; allowing you to inform the Prince of Conti alone, who, I know, will take part in this success. I pretend also, that you are to like me a little better, on account of the share I have had in it.

Our friend is surprised he does not hear either from you or Mademoiselle Le Vasseur.[1] I persuade him, that she is on the road; otherwise you would have sent me by the post the letters which you mentioned to me. If any accident has happened, please to relieve his anxiety by a line or two. I should be glad to know how your inquiries at Rougemont's have turned out.[2]

est une meprise assurément, mais je ne puis comprendre de quelle datte elle est reellement' (MS., R.S.E.; *Eminent Persons*, 235).

On internal evidence, and after comparing it with the letters of Rousseau written about the same time, I should date it in the first week of February.

[1] Writing to Mme de Boufflers from Chiswick on 6 Feb. 1766, Rousseau says: 'J'ai changé d'habitation, Madame, depuis que j'ai eu l'honneur de vous écrire. M. de Luze, qui aura celui de vous remettre cette lettre, et qui m'est venu voir dans ma nouvelle habitation, pourra vous en rendre compte; quelque agréable qu'elle soit, j'espère n'y demeurer que jusqu'après l'arrivée de Mademoiselle Le Vasseur, dont je n'ai aucune nouvelle et dont je suis fort en peine, ayant calculé, sur le jour de son départ et sur l'empressement que je lui connois, qu'elle devroit naturellement être arrivée . . .' (*Œuvres*, 1826, xxiii. 257).

[2] M. de Rougemont was a banker in Paris with whom Rousseau had been more or less closely associated about 1762; his name occurs often in Rousseau's correspondence about that time. It would seem that Hume, with the assistance of Mme de Boufflers and Mme de Barbentane, was trying to find out from de Rougemont whether Rousseau's much-vaunted indigence was genuine or not; and that he did at last find out that it was not. There is nothing definite on this subject among the MSS., R.S.E., but in his *Concise Account* Hume says: 'It is with reluctance I say it, but I am compelled to it; I now know of a certainty that this affectation of extreme poverty and distress was a mere pretence, a petty kind of imposture which M. Rousseau

It is only matter of mere curiosity. For, even if the fact should prove against him, which is very improbable, I should only regard it as one weakness more, and do not make my good opinion of him to depend on a single incident. I shall write, this post or next, to Madame de Barbantane; and as she is one of the numerous enthusiasts of our modern Socrates, I shall amuse her by an account of several particulars concerning him.[1]

I suppose, that by this time you have learned it was Horace Walpole who wrote the Prussian letter you mentioned to me. It is a strange inclination we have to be wits, preferably to every thing else. He is a very worthy man; he esteems and even admires Rousseau; yet he could not forbear, for the sake of a very indifferent joke, the turning him into ridicule, and saying harsh things against him. I am a little angry with him; and I hear you are a great deal:[2] but the matter ought to be treated only as a piece of levity.

I find, that I might have spared myself the trouble of a journey to London, and that other foreign ministers, of a higher rank, have, without scruple, remained in the place of their mission. As I shall not get back as soon as I intended, I sometimes wish that I had taken this party.

The method of living is not near so agreeable in London as in Paris. The best company are usually, and more so at present,

successfully employed to excite the compassion of the public: but I was then very far from suspecting any such artifice.'

Burton, in dealing with this subject (*Life*, ii. 329 f.) made a mistake. He stated that there was one letter from de Rougemont among the MSS., R.S.E., but that much of the letter was devoted to literary gossip and none of it to money matters. There is *no* letter from de Rougemont among the MSS., R.S.E. The letter that Burton had before him, which is unsigned, is unmistakably from Mme de Barbentane. It ends: 'Nous ne savons encor rien de M. de Rougemont'—and that seems to have been the reason why Burton attributed it to the banker.

[1] Mme de Boufflers, replying to this paragraph, protested: 'Je ne say pourquoi vous aves reservé pour Me de Barbentane les particularités qui concernent notre ami. Depeches-vous du moins de les lui mander car j'ay une impatience que je ne puis vous exprimer, de sçavoir comment il se conduit en Angleterre, s'il s'y plait, et quel opinion le peuple prend de lui' (MS., R.S.E.; *Eminent Persons*, 235).

[2] Walpole himself, writing to Gray on 25 Jan. 1766, says: 'Madame de Boufflers, with a tone of sentiment, and the accents of lamenting humanity, abused me heartily, and then complained to myself with the utmost softness. I acted contrition, but had like to have spoiled all, by growing dreadfully tired of a second lecture from the Prince of Conti, who took up the ball, and made himself the hero of a history wherein he had nothing to do' (*Letters*, vi. 409).

in a flame of politics: the men of letters are few, and not very sociable: the women are not in general very conversible. Many a sigh escapes me for your sweet and amiable conversation: I paint you to myself all serenity, and cannot believe that ever I had the misfortune to displease you. I often steal an hour's chat with you: *Sic mihi contingat vivere, sicque mori.* As often as I see Lady Hervey, or Lord Tavistock, or the Holdernesse family, I have the satisfaction of hearing your name mentioned, which is some consolation in this land of banishment.

Adieu, my amiable friend!

P.S.

Since I wrote the above, I have seen General Conway, who tells me that the King has spoke to him on the same subject, and that the sum intended is a hundred pounds a year; a mighty accession to our friend's slender revenue.

A letter has also come to me open from Guy the bookseller,[1] by which I learn that Mademoiselle sets out post, in company with a friend of mine; a young gentleman, very good-humoured, very agreeable, and very mad.[2] He visited Rousseau in his mountains, who gave him a recommendation to Paoli,[3] the King of Corsica; where this gentleman, whose name is Boswell, went last summer, in search of adventures. He has such a rage for literature, that I dread some event fatal to our friend's honour. You remember the story of Terentia, who was first married to Cicero, then to Sallust, and at last, in her old age, married a young nobleman, who imagined that she must possess some secret, which would convey to him eloquence and genius.

* 303. *To the* Rev. Hugh Blair

Dear Doctor

I have perus'd Ferguson's Papers[4] more than once, which had been put into my hands, some time ago, at his desire. I sat

* MS., R.S.E.; Burton, ii. 310 (incomplete).

[1] Partner of Duchesne. They published some of Rousseau's work.

[2] James Boswell (1740–95), the biographer of Johnson. He was first introduced to Hume in Edinburgh in July 1758. He then thought Hume 'a very proper person for a young man to cultivate an acquaintance with' (*Letters of Boswell*, i. 2).

[3] Pascal Paoli (1725–1807), who led the Corsicans in their struggles for independence. Boswell published in 1768 *An Account of Corsica, the Journal of a Tour to that Island; and Memoirs of Pascal Paoli.*

[4] The MS. of the *Essay on the History of Civil Society*, which appeared in the following year.

down to read them with great Prepossession, founded on my good Opinion of him, on a Small Specimen I had seen of them some Years ago, and on yours & Dr Robertson's Esteem of them: But I am sorry to say it, they have no-wise answer'd my Expectation. I do not think them fit to be given to the Public, neither on account of the Style nor the Reasoning; the Form nor the Matter. My Concern for his Reputation obliges me to tell you my Opinion; which I find also to be Elliots, as well as Dr Lowthe's,[1] a very candid & ingenious Critic. I beseech you and Robertson to give them another Perusal, with more Severity and less Prepossession. This is a very serious Matter: Any Failure of Success in this particular, besides the Mortification attending it, operates backwards, and discredits his Class, which is at present in so flourishing a Situation. He has not wrote a word to me about the Subject, so that I cannot with any Propriety give him my Judgement; and I demand of you & Dr Robertson the strictest Secrecy. Remember that you two forc'd out *the Siege of Aquileia* [2] upon the Public, in spite of my Judgement. It is not natural to imagine, that these Sections, which he has sent as a Specimen, are the worst parts of the Performance: Yet surely, what I saw was much better. It is needless to enter into a Detail, where almost every thing appears to me exceptionable. If I come down to Scotland next Summer, I shoud concur in any Method to prevent or retard the Publication; but they are now put into General Clerk & Lord Shelburne's hands, who are not the most proper Judges in the World; and if you do not interpose, they will certainly be printed. I shall be agreeably disappointed, if the Success prove contrary to my Opinion.[3]

I did not answer Yours, which Oswald [4] delivered me; because I take it for granted that you receivd mine, which I wrote from Paris, under Lord Kaims's Cover. You have seen

[1] Robert Lowth (1710–87), Bishop of St. David's, 1766, of Oxford, 1766–77, and of London, 1777–87.

[2] John Home's play, which was produced by Garrick in 1760.

[3] In answering this letter on 24 Feb. 1766, Blair says that he thinks Hume too severe in his criticisms of Ferguson's book, and that, whether or no, it is impossible to do anything about it now; since both he himself and Robertson have given a favourable opinion to the author, and so cannot retract it. He adds: 'You know too the nature of the author: not overmuch given to submit' (MS., R.S.E., unpublished).

[4] Oswald's son was now living with Blair in Edinburgh as a pupil, in Hume's house.

in the News papers enow of Particulars concerning my Pupil, who has now left me and retir'd to Chiswick.[1] He is impatient to get into the Mountains of Wales.[2] He is a very agreeable, amiable Man; but a great Humourist. The Philosophers of Paris fortold to me, that I coud not conduct him to Calais without a Quarrel;[3] but I think I cou'd live with him all my Life, in mutual Friendship and Esteem. I am very sorry, that the Matter is not likely to be put to a Trial. I believe one great Source of our Concord, is, that neither he nor I are disputatious, which is not the Case with any of them. They are also displeas'd with him, because they think he over-abounds in Religion; and it is indeed remarkable, that the Philosopher of this Age, who has been the most persecuted, is by far the most devout. I do not comprehend such Philosophers as are invested with the sacerdotal Character. I am Dear Dr Yours usque ad aras

DAVID HUME.

Lisle Street
11 of Feby 1766
To The Reverend D[r] Hugh Blair at Edinburgh.

* 304. *To the* MARQUISE DE BARBENTANE

Lisle Street, Leicester Fields, 16 of Feb. 1766

You have sometimes, dear Madam, been embarassed between opposite opinions, with regard to the personal character of M. Rousseau: his enemies have sometimes made you doubt of his sincerity; and you have been pleased to ask my opinion on this head. After having lived so long with him, and seen him

* *Priv. Corr.*, 142 ff.

[1] William Rouet, writing on 6 Feb. 1766 to William Mure, says: 'Rousseau is boarded at a small house in Chiswick; his landlady is a grocer. He sitts in the shop and learns English words, which brings many customers to the house' (*Caldwell Papers*, II, ii. 71).

[2] It appears that a friend of Rouet's, a farmer in Wales, offered Rousseau a lodging. Rousseau was enthusiastic about this offer for a time, but on 2 March he writes to Du Peyrou: 'Certaines instructions m'ont un peu dégouté, non du pays de Galles, mais de la maison que j'y devois habiter' (*Œuvres*, 1826, xxiii. 270).

[3] Morellet says that just before Hume left Paris d'Holbach said to him: 'Mon cher M. Hume, je suis fâché de vous ôter des espérances et des illusions qui vous flattent; mais je vous annonce que vous ne tarderez pas à être douleureusement détrompé. Vous ne connoissez pas l'homme [Rousseau]. Je vous le dis franchement, vous allez rechauffer un serpent dans votre sein' (*Mémoires*, 109). This story is confirmed, almost in the same words, by Marmontel.

in a variety of lights, I am now better enabled to judge; and I declare to you, that I have never known a man more amiable and more virtuous than he appears to me: he is mild, gentle, modest, affectionate, disinterested; and, above all, endowed with a sensibility of heart in a supreme degree. Were I to seek for his faults, I should say, that they consisted in a little hasty impatience, which, as I am told, inclines him sometimes to say disobliging things to people that trouble him: he is also too delicate in the commerce of life: he is apt to entertain groundless suspicions of his best friends; and his lively imagination, working upon them, feigns chimeras, and pushes him to great extremes. I have seen no instance of this disposition; but I cannot otherwise account for the violent animosities which have arisen between him and several men of merit, with whom he was once intimately connected; and some who love him much have told me, that it is difficult to live much with him, and preserve his friendship; but for my part, I think I could pass all my life in his company, without any danger of our quarrelling.

There is one circumstance, that renders him very amiable, and may serve to abate the envy arising from his superior parts; which is, that he is endowed with a singular simplicity of manners, and is, indeed, a perfect child in the ordinary occurrences of life. This quality, joined to his great sensibility of heart, makes him be easily governed by those who live with him; and his maid, in particular, has an uncontrolled authority over him. Shall I give you an instance? He showed me the letter which he had received from the Corsicans, in which he is invited to come among them, to frame them a body of laws, and to be the Solon or Lycurgus of this new commonwealth. He told me, that he had once intended to comply with this invitation, but, on consulting Mademoiselle Le Vasseur, he found she did not approve of the journey; upon which he laid aside all thoughts of it. His dog also has great influence with him; of which I shall give you an instance that may amuse you. Soon after our arrival, I prevailed on him to go to the playhouse, and see Garrick. Mrs Garrick gave him her box, which is much concealed from the audience, but opposite to that of the King and Queen; and their Majesties were privately informed, that they might there expect to see M. Rousseau. When the hour came, he told me, that he had changed his resolution, and would not go: for——what shall I do with Sultan? That is the name of his dog. You must leave him behind, said I. But the first person, replied he, who opens the door, Sultan will run into the streets in search of me, and will be lost. You must then, said I, lock him up in your room, and put the key in your pocket. This was accordingly done: but as we went downstairs, the dog howled and made a noise; his master turned back, and said he had not resolution to leave him in that condition; but I caught him in my arms and told him, that Mrs Garrick had dismissed another company in order to make room for him; that the King and Queen were expecting to see him; and without a better reason than Sultan's impatience, it would be ridiculous to disappoint them. Partly by these reasons and partly by force, I engaged him to proceed. The King and Queen looked more at him than at the players.

When I have proposed to him schemes for enriching him, he has told me, that he dreads the inconvenience of changing his manner of life; particularly, said he, I should be tempted, if I were richer, to take another servant, which, I know, is taking another master; and I should in that case have my will in nothing.

The public here has taken a great interest in M. Rousseau; and though we are now in the hottest time of our hottest factions, he is not forgot. Every circumstance, the most minute, that concerns him, is put in the newspapers. Unfortunately, one day, he lost his dog: this incident was in the papers next morning. Soon after, I recovered Sultan very surprizingly: this intelligence was communicated to the public immediately, as a piece of good news. Hundreds of persons have offered me their assistance to settle him; you would think that all the purses and all the houses of England were open to him. Did he understand the language, he would live very happily in this country. He is particularly pleased that no body makes him speeches or compliments.

What has chiefly begot a doubt of his sincerity, are his great singularities, which some people take for affectation, and an art to gain celebrity: but his greatest singularity is the love of solitude, which, in a man so well calculated for the entertainment of company, and seemingly so sociable, appears very extraordinary. I can however answer for his sincerity in this particular. He would not stay in London above a fortnight. I settled him in a village about six miles from it: he is impatient to remove from thence, though the place and the house are both very agreeable to him; and, of a great variety of schemes which

I propose to him, the most solitary, the most remote, the most savage place is always that which he prefers. In a few weeks he will certainly remove to Wales, and will board with a substantial farmer, who inhabits a lonely house amid forests and rivulets, and rocks and mountains. I have endeavoured to throw a hundred obstacles in the way, but nothing can divert him; his obstinacy is here an invincible proof of his sincerity. I must, however, confess, that I think he has an inclination to complain of his health, more than I imagine he has reason for: he is not insincere, but fanciful, in that particular. I know not how your enquiries with regard to M. Rougemont have turned out.

Please tell Madame de Boufflers that I received her letter the day after I wrote mine. Assure her that Horace Walpole's letter was not founded on any pleasantry of mine: the only pleasantry in that letter came from his own mouth, in my company, at Lord Ossory's [1] table; which my Lord remembers very well. Tell her also that I like Mademoiselle Le Vasseur, upon acquaintance. She appears to me a good creature, more clever than she had been represented. She is only somewhat of a gossip, or what you call *une commère*.

Thus, dear Madam, I have wrote you a long letter concerning a third person; and have left myself neither room nor leisure to say any thing either of you or of myself. I must therefore be the more concise on that head. What can I say, but that I esteem and love you, and regret my being absent from you? I am more a stranger in this place than in Paris, and the manners are by no means so agreeable to me. There is a hardness in most characters, of which I now become more sensible than before. You have spoiled me for this country; and are obliged in conscience to be good to me when I shall return to you, which I hope will be soon. Remember me to Madame de Vierville and Madame de Maury,[2] and to M. de Puiségur,[3] as well as to M. de Barbentane. Embrace Madame de Boufflers in my name. I have only wrote to you and her since my arrival in London; which is a great crime I have been guilty of.

I have the honour to be with great sincerity,

Your most obedient humble servant,

David Hume.

[1] John Fitzpatrick (1745–1818), 2nd Earl of Upper Ossory. He was in Paris in the autumn of 1765. In 1769 he married Anne Liddell, the divorced wife of the Duke of Grafton.

[2] I do not know who this was (see also p. 159 below).

[3] Pierre-Louis de Chastenet (born 1727), comte de Puységur.

* 305. *To* JEAN-JACQUES ROUSSEAU

Dear Sir

I shall call on you to morrow half an hour past two in the Afternoon, in order to attend you to Town.

I have made Enquiries concerning the Viscount d'Ars.[1] I find, he is alive and in health. He is a Widower: and engaged in a Law-suit, which seems of a very delicate Nature, and of an uncertain Issue: It is of Importance; but a full Explication of it, as it wou'd be difficult for me, is not material to M^{de} de Verdelin.

I hope you remember your Promise, that you are to give me the Receit for playing the Trick of Hocus Pocus, which you mention in your *Lettres de la Montagne* and which you play'd when at Venice. I have already promised it, on your Faith, to the Countess of Ailesbury, who is impatient to know it. I am, with the greatest Sincerity Dear Sir Your most obedient Servant

DAVID HUME

Friday morning.
[February 1766.]
To Mr Rousseau at Mr Pulleyn's Grocer in Chiswick

† 306. *To* JEAN-JACQUES ROUSSEAU

Mr Hume presents his best Respects to Mr Rousseau. He will have the Honour of waiting on him to morrow forenoon, and of presenting to him Mrs Boscowen,[2] Widow of the Admiral, and Sister in law to Mr Price[3]

Tuesday forenoon
[Feb. 1766.]
To Mr Rousseau at Mr Pulleyn's Grocer in Chiswick

* MS. in Bibliothèque publique de Neuchâtel; Streckeisen-Moultou, ii. 278 (in French translation); hitherto unpublished in England.

† MS. in Bibliothèque publique de Neuchâtel; Streckeisen-Moultou, ii. 277 f. (in French translation); hitherto unpublished in England.

[1] An uncle of Mme de Verdelin (see note 1 on p. 526 of vol. i).

[2] Frances (died 1805), daughter of William Evelyn Glanville, of St. Clair, Kent, m. (1744) the Hon. Edward Boscawen, afterwards Admiral Boscawen (1711–61). She was afterwards a particular friend of Hannah More.

[3] Richard Price (1723–91), Nonconformist minister at Newington Green; author of *Review of the Principal Questions in Morals*, 1757, which criticized Hume. Hume was on good terms with him.

* 307. *To the* Earl of Hertford

Lisle Street, Leicester Fields,
27 February, 1766.

As I seldom have occasion to hear of gentlemen's setting out for Ireland, I have checked my inclination of writing to your Lordship concerning the late transactions, which are certainly very curious, and seemingly unaccountable. For what can be more extraordinary, than an Opposition which insists on the rigorous support of Government, and a Ministry which recommends lenity towards resistance? We have seen the King's favorite [1] and his Ministers vote on different sides; and men uncertain which was the surest way of paying court to his Majesty. Some wags have remarked that the Bench of Bishops itself was obliged to vote according to conscience, for want of better direction; and their numbers were in one vote pretty equally divided. As the causes of these events are now pretty generally known, or at least publicly talked of, it may be less imprudent to write to your Lordship what is no longer mentioned in a whisper.

The first day after reassembling, the Parliament opened by a very extraordinary speech of Mr. Pit's. Besides asserting that England had no right to her Colonies, and that it was unconstitutional to take money from free-born subjects without their consent, he ran into many other topics, which much astonished his audience. He seemed even to treat the Parliament with contempt; he used many severe expressions against the last Ministry; he employed some unkind ones towards the present: and men were thrown into such wonder at the lofty and intrepid style of his discourse, that nobody had courage or presence enough of mind to answer him. But when gentlemen were retired to their private societies, they began to compare their sentiments and to find that they had rather been ill used by the orator. The effects of this general indignation appeared two days after, when Sir Fletcher Norton [2] attacked him with great severity, and even threatened to move that he should be sent to the Tower. He was heard with infinite applause by the House; and when Mr Pit answered him, his discourse was received with a cold and universal silence. He soon perceived

* Morrison, *Catalogue of . . . Autograph Letters*, ii. 315 ff.

[1] Lord Bute.

[2] Sir Fletcher Norton (1716–89), afterwards 1st Baron Grantley. He became Speaker in 1770.

that he had gone too far, and like an able man, he has ever since lowered his tone, and talked with great submission and deference to the House, so that he has entirely recovered the good will of his audience.

Meanwhile the question which he had started, was brought on in the House of Peers: it was disputed, whether the English Parliament had a right to tax the Colonies. Lord Camden[1] in a long and artful speech maintained the contrary; and was answered by Lord Mansfield, who spoke two hours, in the most masterly manner: it is agreed on all hands that nobody ever remembers such a discourse for matter, for style, and for delivery. On the division of the House, there were only found to be four with Lord Camden, among whom was Lord Shelburn. The debate was maintained on the same subject in the House of Commons by Mr Pit almost alone: the House did not divide, but it was thought that not above five would have followed him in the vote. But these events were not esteemed any way decisive on the state of parties; because Mr Pit had carried the matter farther than almost anybody was inclined to follow him. There soon came on in the House of Peers a more trying vote. It was proposed by the Ministry that the House should address his Majesty to *recommend* to the Assemblies of the Colonies the making reparation to such persons as had suffered from the populace on account of the Stamp Act: the Opposition insisted that the word *require* should be used instead of *recommend.* The difference seemed not very material; but as the word *recommend* suited the lenity of the ministerial measures, and the other word was more agreeable to the intended rigor of the Opposition, the two parties chose to make trial of their force on this occasion. Lord Bute spoke on the anti-ministerial side; and his example had such influence that the word *require* was carried by four voices. But matters went otherwise in the House of Commons. It was moved by Mr Grenville that the House should address his Majesty to inforce the laws in America. The previous question was carried against him by a majority of 140; a number which surprised the Ministers themselves, who expected to prevail only by a small majority. There are three reasons assigned

[1] Charles Pratt (1714–94), created Baron Camden, 1765, and Earl Camden, 1786; Attorney-General, 1757; Lord Chief Justice of the Common Pleas, 1762; Lord Chancellor in the Ministry formed originally by Pitt, 1766–70. He was a particular friend of Pitt, and followed him in all his political manœuvres.

for the great success, First, Lord Rockingham published everywhere that the King had said to him that he was for the repeal of the Stamp Act, which was understood to be a general declaration in favour of his Ministers, and brought them an accession of force. The King has since said, that this was a mistake in Lord Rockingham; for that the question between them was only whether the law should be strictly inforced in its present shape or be repealed; in which case, his Majesty declared for the repeal: but there was no mention made of lenitives and mediums, which he would rather approve of.[1] *Secondly*, Lord Bute in his speech to the House of Lords had said, that in doing his duty as a Lord of Parliament he would lie under no influence; he would not be swayed even by the opinion of a Master whom he loved and adored. This was understood as if the King and he entertained different sentiments on the present question; tho Lord Bute has since declared that he meant nothing but to express in general the independence of his conduct. The third reason, which brought the Ministry such an accession of force, was the general cry of the public, which loudly demanded a repeal of the Stamp Act. It was foreseen, that the countenance given the Americans by Mr Pit and Lord Camden's appearance for them would increase, if possible, their obstinacy. The bad effects on trade began already to be sensibly felt. Many manufacturers all over England had threatened to dismiss a half or two-thirds of their tradesmen, which must have produced infinite confusion, and been dangerous to Government itself. These motives were so strong, that I am persuaded no one voted

[1] Cf. Walpole's account in *Memoirs of George III*, 1894 edit., ii. 205: The King, Walpole says, told Lord Strange that he was not in favour of the repeal of the Stamp Act. 'So extraordinary a tale soon reached the ear of Lord Rockingham, who immediately asked Lord Strange if it was true what the King was reported to have said to him? The other confirmed it. On that, Lord Rockingham desired the other to meet him at Court, when they both went into the closet together. Lord Strange began, and repeated the King's words; and asked if he had been mistaken? The King said, "No". Lord Rockingham then pulled out a paper, and begged to know, if on such a day (which was minuted down on the paper) his Majesty had not determined for the repeal? Lord Rockingham then stopped. The King replied, "My Lord, this is but half"; and taking out a pencil, wrote on the bottom of Lord Rockingham's paper words to this effect: "The question asked me by my ministers, was, whether I was for enforcing the Act by the sword, or for the repeal? Of the two extremes I was for the repeal; but most certainly preferred modification to either."' Cf. also memorandum by George III in *Corr. of George III*, i. 268 f.

against the repeal but from party and in full hopes and confidence of being out-voted. Some have confessed it to me.[1] The repeal was carried by a majority of 104, which in subsequent votes mounted to 107. It is not doubted but the House of Peers will concur with the Commons, notwithstanding the former majority of the anti-ministerial party. Every one is sensible, that an invidious law, repealed by one branch of the legislature, can never possibly be carried into execution.

Thus I have endeavoured to give your Lordship a sketch of the public transactions of Parliament, in which it is universally acknowledged that Mr Conway did his duty as an able speaker and statesman. The intrigues of the Cabinet ought to have been more mysterious and more uncertain; but according to the genius of this country, everything is talked of and nothing remains long a secret: sometimes indeed matters are misrepresented; and I shall not affirm but this may sometimes be the case, in what I am going to add to your Lordship, tho I think I draw my intelligence from good sources. It is known, that Lord Bute was extremely dissatisfied with a considerable part of the present Ministry, from their first entry into power. They not only declared publicly, that they had no connexions with him, and would not in anything be subjected to his influence: but what is worse, this public declaration (which might only be meant to avoid the odium of these connexions) they actually carried into execution: his brother[2] was not restored to his office: his friends, Lord Despenser,[3] Sir Fletcher Norton, and Dr Hay,[4] were turned out: it was supposed to be a sufficient reason for refusing any competitor that he was known to be Lord Bute's friend: and some of the Ministers had even publicly refused to drink his health when it was proposed at their table. Meanwhile they courted Mr Pit with all the assiduity imaginable, who kept aloof from any particular connexions with them. These measures which are ascribed to the younger part of the

[1] I suspect that Gilbert Elliot was one of these. As one of the 'King's Friends', he voted against the repeal.

[2] Stuart-Mackenzie.

[3] Sir Francis Dashwood (1708–81), Chancellor of the Exchequer, 1762–3; succeeded as 15th Baron Le Despencer, 1763. As Chancellor of the Exchequer he was notorious, even in the eighteenth century, for his inability to understand finance.

[4] Dr. George Hay (1715–78), M.P. for Stockbridge; Lord of Admiralty, 1756–65; Dean of the Arches, Judge of the Prerogative Court of Canterbury, and Chancellor of the Diocese of London, 1764; knighted 1773.

Ministry are thought to have been imprudent; both because they could never reasonably expect to support themselves by popularity alone, contrary to the Cabinet; and because the taking in Mr Pit was receiving a master still more domineering than, it was likely, Lord Bute would prove. However this may be, it is esteemed certain that Lord Bute projected to overthrow the Ministry, tho without having concerted any plan for a new administration, and without any formal alliance with the late Ministry. If he could, by his interest, have prevented the repeal in the House of Commons, it was supposed that the present ministers would have thrown up and a new plan would have been instantly formed. Men began to lay wagers, whether the frost[1] or the Ministry would last longest, but the great majority in the House of Commons suspended these projects, tho it is not doubted that they are still in agitation. It is known that the Duke of Bedford and Mr Grenville met Lord Bute at Lord Eglinton's, where they made acknowledgements to him of their past errors, and begged the return of his friendship. He answered that he was glad to stand well in their good opinion, but nothing was concluded. I am assured that the present Ministry have also made advances to him, tho with no greater success, and every thing appears still doubtful and uncertain. It seems happy that the Stamp Act is repealed, for if the motion for that repeal had been rejected, and if the Ministry had thereupon been changed, the Americans, seeing all their friends turned out merely from friendship to them, would have been reduced to despair, and would probably have made an obstinate resistance, attended with the most fatal consequences. The frightful idea they have been taught to entertain of the old Ministry would have made them expect nothing but blood and slaughter, and the most severe executions.

It is remarkable that Lord Chesterfield, who had never gone to the House of late years and had not even taken the oaths during this reign, qualified himself a few days ago in order to vote for the repeal. He said he was a non-juror, and repented of his disaffection. It is equally remarkable that the Dukes of

[1] Rousseau, writing to Du Peyrou on 15 Feb. 1766, complains of this frost. He says: 'La Tamise a été prise, la gelée est terrible; nous avons eu l'un des plus rudes hivers dont j'aie connoissance' (*Œuvres*, 1826, xxiii. 259). Horace Walpole, writing from Paris to Mann on 9 Feb. 1766, says: 'We are again up to the ears in snow' (*Letters*, vi. 418).

York and Gloucester[1] voted against the King's ministers, in the only trying vote that has been in the House of Peers that session. There is however no manner of doubt that the repeal will pass that House; because, among others, I hear that the Chancellor[2] and Lord Mansfield have strongly declared for it, since it has passed the Commons.

I give your Lordship and Lady Hertford joy upon this agreeable incident in your family.[3] I learn from Lady Aylesbury that another of the same kind is soon expected.[4] Some mention a third:[5] but I should be sorry to find your Lordship robbed at once of so considerable and so agreeable a part of your family, tho in so agreeable a manner. In all cases, I take part most sincerely in whatever incident can interest your Lordship.

* 308. *To* Jean-Jacques Rousseau

Mr Hume presents his Respects to Monsr Rousseau. He sends him Mr Malthus's[6] Letter. He wishes Monsr Rousseau had asked Mr Malthus's Direction; but if Monsr Rousseau will be pleased to write an Answer, and deliver it to Mr Hume on Saturday, he will find means to convey it to Mr Malthus.

Mr Davenport[7] has been with Mr Hume, and is very happy

* MS. in Bibliothèque publique de Neuchâtel; Streckeisen-Moultou, ii. 278 f. (in French translation); hitherto unpublished in England.

[1] Prince William Henry (1743–1805), younger brother of George III; created Duke of Gloucester, 1764; married (1766) Horace Walpole's niece, the Dowager Countess Waldegrave.

[2] Sir Robert Henley (1708–72), created Baron Henley, 1760, and Earl of Northington, 1764; Attorney-General, 1756–7; Lord Keeper, 1757–61; Lord Chancellor, 1761–6; Lord President of the Council, 1766–7.

[3] Lord Hertford's eldest daughter Anne (died 1767) married Charles, 1st Marquis of Drogheda on 15 Feb. 1766.

[4] Sarah Frances, the second daughter (died 1770) married Robert, 1st Marquis of Londonderry on 3 June 1766.

[5] The third daughter, Gertrude, was not married till 1772.

[6] Daniel Malthus (1730–1800) entered Queen's College, Oxford, 1747, but left without taking his degree, and from 1759–68 lived quietly among his books at the Rookery, Guildford; superintended the education of his son, T. R. Malthus, author of the *Essay on Population*, on somewhat original lines, said to have been derived in part from Rousseau's *Émile*. Courtois (*Le Séjour de J.-J. Rousseau en Angleterre*) has printed a number of Malthus's letters to Rousseau; and from these it appears that Malthus busied himself in trying to find a habitation for Rousseau in Surrey. See also next Letter.

[7] Richard Davenport (? 1705–71). Little more is known of him than appears from Hume's and Rousseau's letters at this time.

with the Prospect of receiving Monsr Rousseau at his Country House. He proposes to wait on Monsr Rousseau at Mr Ramsay's[1] on Saturday. He is an elderly Man, of a considerable Fortune and a good Character. His Proposals appear to Mr Hume very inviting; and he hopes that they will appear so to Monsr Rousseau.

Mr Hume has had a long Letter from the President Malesherbes,[2] which he will communicate to Monsr Rousseau at meeting.

Mr Stewart tells Mr Hume, that Monsr Rousseau's Trunk is arrived; tho' he has not yet been able to get it from the Custom-house. But Monsr Rousseau need have no anxiety on that head.

Thursday evening
[Feb. or March 1766.]
To Mr Rousseau at Mr Pulleyn's Grocer in *Chiswick*

* 309. *To* [*the* Rev. Richard Penneck] [3]

Lisle Street Leicester Fields
Sunday Evening [? 2 March 1766][4]

Sir

I find, that Mon^r^ Rousseau is as yet undecided as to the place in which he will settle himself. Several (and I am of the Number) advise him to prefer your Neighbourhood in Surrey; and Mr Stewart tells me, that you have been so good as to offer him your good Offices. He has also a Friend very near you, Mr Malthus, who is desirous of doing him every kind of Service.

* MS. in J. Pierpont Morgan Lib., New York City; *Annales de la Soc. J.-J. Rousseau*, xvii (1926); hitherto unpublished in England.

[1] Allan Ramsay, who was painting his portrait of Rousseau at this time, at Hume's request.

[2] Chrétien-Guillaume de Lamoignon de Malesherbes (1721–94), son of the Chancellor, and Directeur de la Librarie, 1750–63. Morley calls him 'a Turgot of the second rank' (*Rousseau*, ii. 62 n.).

The letter in question, which is undated, and which is the only one from Malesherbes among the MSS., R.S.E., is given in Appendix C below.

[3] A guess. Richard Penneck (died 1803), Rector of Abinger, Surrey, and St. John's, Bermondsey; Keeper of the Reading Room, British Museum, 1761–1803. (See Rousseau's reference to him on p. 389 below.)

[4] On Saturday, 8 March, Rousseau, Hume, and Thérèse Le Vasseur went down into Surrey and spent the night with Col. R. Webb (1715–85). The next day they visited Daniel Malthus at the Rookery, near Wootton. He pressed them to stay the night with him, but Rousseau declined, and hurried back to Chiswick instead. I conjecture that this letter must have been written the previous Sunday.

Be so kind as to write to any Correspondent in that Country; and try whether you cou'd not find a Place, where he coud board at reasonable Rate, he and his Gouvernante: He wishes, that the Price cou'd be fixed for Bed, boarding, washing and firing; or for as many of these Circumstances as possible. As he is impatient to leave London, he wishes also to know, whether there be not a tolerable Inn, in the Neighbourhood, where he coud settle till he find a Place to his Mind. It is probable you know Mr Malthus's Direction. Be so good as to put it on the enclosd, and send it to the Post. He wishes to have your Answer as soon as you receive this, and also as soon as you hear from your Parish. I am

Sir

Your most obedient humble Servant

David Hume

P.S.

Mr Rousseau lives at Chiswick; but be pleasd to direct your Letter to me in this Place.

* 310. *To* Jean-Jacques Rousseau

[10–17 March, 1766]

Dear Sir

The Bearer, Mr Gosset,[1] an ingenious Artist, is desirous to have a Model of you, at the earnest Application of several Gentlemen, who wish to adorn their Closets with it. He assures me, that it will not cost you above half an hour to sit to him. I coud not refuse so reasonable a Request; and I hope you will excuse this Liberty. I am Dear Sir

Your most obedient humble Servant,

David Hume

P.S.

Mr Davenport tells me, that there is a Retour Chaise for Ashburn. He has made a Bargain for you and Mlle Le Vasseur. It goes off on Wednesday Morning; and he will send his Coach for you on Tuesday Evening.

To Mr Rousseau at Mr Pulleyn's Grocer in Chiswick

* MS. in Bibliothèque publique de Neuchâtel; Streckeisen-Moultou, ii. 279 (in French translation); hitherto unpublished in England.

[1] Isaac Gosset the Elder (1713–99), a modeller of portraits in wax. He made models of Francis Hutcheson; Frederick, Prince of Wales; Charles Townshend; General Wolfe, &c.

* 311. *To* JEAN-JACQUES ROUSSEAU

Dear Sir

I am desired by Lady Ailesbury and General Conway to propose to you to do them the Favour of dining with them to morrow, along with Mlle le Vasseur. If you accept, Mr Davenport's Coach will bring you to Town before Dinner, with all your Baggage. If you decline the Invitation, from whatever Reason, I shall endeavour to make your excuses. It is not necessary, that you constrain Yourself the least in this Affair. I am Yours, with great Sincerity

DAVID HUME[1]

Monday Afternoon
[17 March 1766.]
To Mr Rousseau at Mr Pulleyn's Grocer in Chiswick

† 312. *To* JOHN HOME OF NINEWELLS

Dear Brother.

I do not think it likely, that you and Mr Robertson[2] will agree about the Price after differing so widely. I remember the Place you mention, which did not appear very fertile; but I know that Improvements succeed best on such light Soils. I shoud be pleas'd that at your Leizure you made Enquiry about the Price; and as I know you to be cautious, I shall be directed by you in the Offer. Mean-while Davie Anderson may be seeking out a hand for my Money.

As most of my Money is now getting into heritable Security, I must alter the Mode of my Settlement. Be so good, therefore, as to send me my Will and Testament, which I left with you.

Rousseau left me four days ago. He goes to live in a House of Mr Davenport, a worthy Gentleman of 5 or 6000 pounds a year, who gives him one of his houses in Derbyshire, in which he himself seldom lives, and takes 30 pounds a Year of board for him and his Gouvernante. Surely Rousseau is one of the most singular of all human Beings, and one of the most unhappy. His extreme Sensibility of Temper is his Torment; as he is much more susceptible of Pain than Pleasure. His Aversion to Society

* MS. in Bibliothèque publique de Neuchâtel; Streckeisen-Moultou, ii. 280 (in French translation); hitherto unpublished in England.

† MS., R.S.E.; Hill, 79 (extract only).

[1] Rousseau replied the same day (see his letter in Appendix G).

[2] Apparently a neighbour in Berwickshire.

is not Affectation as is commonly believd: When in it, he is commonly very amiable, but often very unhappy. And tho' he be also unhappy in Solitude, he prefers that Species of suffering to the other. He is surely a very fine Genius: And of all the Writers that are or ever were in Europe, he is the man who has acquird the most enthusiastic and most passionate Admirers. I have seen many extraordinary Scenes of this Nature. He sat for his Picture at my Desire: It was to Allan Ramsay, who has succeeded to Admiration, and has made me a most valuable Portrait.

I am very sorry for Lord Nisbet:[1] His Family has made a great Loss. Were his Projects all finish'd and to Advantage. I beg my Compliments to Mrs Home. I am now longing much to be at home. Your affectionate Brother

DAVID HUME

Lisle Street Leicester Fields
22 of March 1766
To John Home of Ninewells Esqr at Ninewells near Berwick

* 313. *To* JEAN-JACQUES ROUSSEAU

My dear Sir

I am very anxious to hear of your safe Arrival at Wooton; and above all, that the Place answers our expectation. Mr Davenport has been with me this morning. He expresses the same Anxiety: He still insists on your Promise, that you are to tell freely every Circumstance, that displeases you. It shall be remedy'd if in his power; If Wooton in general displeases you, he hopes that a small farm-house, near his other House in Cheshire, may be more to your Mind. If that shou'd not be agreeable, he will lend his Assistance to settle you to your mind in some other place; and he says, that he will never lose sight of you, till he see you contented and easy. The same is the great Object of my Ambition.

Mr Stewart sent me his Account the Morning after your Departure. He made an Apology for not sending it the Evening before. He was so busy that he cou'd not wait on you before your Departure. I have pay'd the Account and have received payment from Mr Davenport. I send it enclos'd.

* MS. in Bibliothèque publique de Neuchâtel; Streckeisen-Moultou, ii. 280 f. (in French translation); hitherto unpublished in England.

[1] George Carre, Lord Nisbet, died 1766.

Adieu, My Dear Friend: May Health and Happiness ever attend you. My Compliments to Mlle le Vasseur. I am yours with great Sincerity

DAVID HUME

Lisle Street Leicester Fields.
22[d] of March 1766

P.S.

Mr Gosset has brought me one of your Models, which, he says, you intended as a Present.[1] Pray, inform me to whom I must send it.

*314. *To the* REV. HUGH BLAIR

Dear Doctor.

I had askd M. Rousseau the Question you propose to me: He answer'd, that the Story of his Heloise had some general and distant Resemblance to Reality; such as was sufficient to warm his Imagination and assist his Invention: But that all the chief Circumstances were fictitious. I have heard in France, that he had been employ'd to teach Music to a young Lady, a Boarder in a Convent at Lyons; and that the Master & Scholar fell mutually in love with each other, but the Affair was not attended with any Consequences. I think this Work his Master-piece; tho' he himself told me, that he valu'd most his *Contrat sociale*; which is as preposterous a Judgement as that of Milton, who preferd the Paradise regaind to all his other Performances.

This Man, the most singular of all human Beings, has at last left me; and I have very little hopes of ever being able for the

* MS., R.S.E.; *Lit. Gazette*, 1821, pp. 731 f.; Burton, ii. 312 ff.

[1] Rousseau misunderstood this sentence. Replying on 29 March, he says: 'Il n'est point vrai du tout que je sois convenu avec M. Gosset de recevoir un modéle en present. Au contraire, je lui en demandai le prix qu'il me dit être d'une Guinée et demie, ajoutant qu'il m'en vouloit faire la galanterie; ce que je n'ai point accepté. Je vous prie donc de vouloir bien lui payer le modéle en question dont M. Davenport aura la bonté de vous rembourser. S'il n'y consent pas il faut le lui rendre et le faire achetter par une autre main. Il est destiné pour M. Du Peyrou qui depuis longtems desire avoir mon portrait et en a fait faire un en miniature qui n'est point du tout ressemblant. Vous étes pourvu mieux que lui mais je suis fâché que vous m'ayez ôté par une diligence aussi flatteuse le plaisir de remplir le même devoir envers vous. Ayez la bonté, mon cher Patron de faire remettre ce modelle à Mrs. *Guinand et Hankey Little St Hellens Bishopsgate Street* pour l'envoyer à M. Du Peyrou par la prémiére occasion sure . . .' (MS., R.S.E.; *Corr. gén. de Rousseau*, xv. 128 f.).

future to enjoy much of his Company; tho' he says, that, if I settle either in London or Edinburgh, he will take a Journey on foot every Year to visit me. Mr Davenport, a Gentleman of 5 or 6000 pounds in the North of England, and a Man of great Humanity and of a good Understanding, has taken the Charge of him. He has a House, called Wooton, in the Peake of Derby, situated amidst Mountains and Rocks and Streams and Forrests, which pleases the wild Imagination and solitary Humour of Rousseau; and as the Master seldom inhabited it, and only kept there a plain Table for some Servants, he offer'd me to give it up to my Friend: I accepted, on condition that he wou'd take from him 30 pounds a Year of Board, for himself and his Gouvernante, which he was so good natur'd as to agree to. Rousseau has about 80 pounds a Year, which he has acquird by Contracts with his Booksellers, and by a Liferent Annuity of 25 pounds a Year, which he accepted from Lord Mareschal. This is the only Man who has yet been able to make him accept of Money.

He was desperately resolv'd to rush into this Solitude, notwithstanding all my Remonstrances; and I forsee, that he will be unhappy in that Situation, as he has indeed been always, in all Situations. He will be entirely without Occupation, without Company, and almost without Amusement of any kind. He has read very little during the Course of his Life, and has now totally renounc'd all Reading: He has seen very little, and has no manner of Curiosity to see or remark: He has reflected, properly speaking, and study'd very little; and has not indeed much Knowlege: He has only felt, during the whole Course of his Life; and in this Respect, his Sensibility rises to a Pitch beyond what I have seen any Example of: But it still gives him a more acute Feeling of Pain than of Pleasure. He is like a Man who were stript not only of his Cloaths but of his Skin, and turn'd out in that Situation to combat with the rude and boisterous Elements, such as perpetually disturb this lower World. I shall give you a remarkable Instance of his turn of Character in this respect. It passd in my Room, the Evening before his Departure.

He had resolv'd to set out with his Gouvernante in a Post chaise; but Davenport, willing to cheat him and save him some Money, told him, that he had found a Retour Chaise for the Place, which he might have for a Trifle, and that luckily, it set out the very day in which Rousseau intended to depart: His Purpose was to hire a Chaise, and make him believe this Story.

He succeeded at first; but Rousseau, afterwards ruminating on the Circumstances, began to entertain a Suspicion of the Trick. He communicated his Doubts to me, complaining that he was treated like a Child, that tho' he was poor he chose rather to conform himself to his Circumstances than live like a Beggar, on alms, and that he was very unhappy in not speaking the Language familiarly, so as to guard himself against these Impositions. I told him, that I was ignorant of the Matter, and knew nothing more of it than I was told by Mr Davenport; but if he pleas'd I shou'd make Enquiry about it. *Never tell me that,* reply'd he, *if this be really a Contrivance of Davenports, you are acquainted with it, and consenting to it; and you cou'd not possibly have done me a greater Displeasure.* Upon which he sate down very sullen and silent; and all my Attempts were in vain to revive the Conversation and to turn it on other Subjects: He still answerd me very dryly & coldly. At last, after passing near an Hour in this ill-humour, he rose up and took a Turn about the Room: But Judge of my Surprize, when he sat down suddenly on my Knee, threw his hands about my Neck, kiss'd me with the greatest Warmth, and bedewing all my Face with Tears, exclaim'd, *Is it possible you can ever forgive me, my Dear Friend: After all the Testimonies of Affection I have receivd from you, I reward you at last with this Folly & ill Behaviour: But I have notwithstanding a Heart worthy of your Friendship: I love you, I esteem you; and not an Instance of your Kindness is thrown away upon me.* I hope you have not so bad an Opinion of me as to think I was not melted on this Occasion: I assure you I kissd him and embrac'd him twenty times, with a plentiful Effusion of Tears. I think no Scene of my Life was ever more affecting.

I now understand perfectly his Aversion to company, which appears so surprizing in a Man well qualify'd for the Entertainment of Company, and which the greatest Part of the World takes for Affectation. He has frequent and long Fits of the Spleen, from the State of his Mind or Body, call it which you please, and from his extreme Sensibility of Temper. During that Disposition, Company is a Torment to him. When his Spirits and Health & good Humour return, his Fancy affords him so much & such agreeable Occupation that to call him off from it gives him Uneasyness; and even the writing of Books, he tells me, as it limits and restrains his Fancy to one Subject, is not an agreeable Entertainment. He never will write any more; and never shou'd have wrote at all, coud he have slept a nights. But he lies awake commonly, and to keep himself from tiring he usually compos'd something which he wrote down when he arose. He assures me, that he composes very slowly and with great Labour and Difficulty.

He is naturally very modest, and even ignorant of his own Superiority: His Fire, which frequently rises in Conversation, is gentle and temperate; he is never, in the least, arrogant & domineering, and is indeed one of the best bred Men I ever knew. I shall give you such an Instance of his Modesty as must necessarily be sincere. When we were on the Road I recommended to him the learning of English, without which, I told him, he wou'd never enjoy entire Liberty, nor be fully independant, and at his own Disposal. He was sensible I was in the right; and said, that he heard there were two English Translations of his *Emile* or Treatise of Education: He woud get them, as soon as he arriv'd in London; and as he knew the Subject, he woud have no other Trouble than to learn or guess the Words: This woud save him some Pains in consulting the Dictionary; and as he improvd, it woud amuse him to compare the Translations, and judge which was the best. Accordingly, soon after our Arrival, I procurd him the Books; but he returnd them in a few days, saying that they coud be of no Use to him. *What is the Matter*, reply'd I. *I cannot endure them*, said he, *they are my own Work; and ever since I deliverd my Books to the Press, I never coud open them or read a Page of them without Disgust. That is Strange*, said I, *I wonder the good Reception they have met with from the World has not put you more in conceit with them. Why!* said he, *if I were to count Suffrages, there are perhaps more against them than for them. But*, rejoind I, *it is impossible but the Style & Eloquence and Ornaments must please you. To tell the Truth*, said he, *I am not displeasd with myself in that particular: But I still dread, that my Writings are good for nothing at the bottom, and that all my Theories are full of Extragance.*[1] Je craigne toujours que je peche par le fond, et que touts mes systemes ne sont que des extravagances. You see, that this is judging himself with the utmost Severity, and censuring his Writings on the Side where they are most expos'd to Criticism. No feign'd Modesty is ever capable of this Courage. I never heard Robertson reproach himself with the godly Strain of his History: No body ever heard you express any Remorse for having put Ossian on the same footing with Homer.

Have I tir'd you, or will you have any more Anecdotes of this

[1] *Sic* in MS.

singular Personage? I think I hear you desire me to go on. He attempted once to justify to me the Moral of his new Heloisa, which, he knew, was blam'd, as instructing young People in the Art of gratifying their Passions, under the Cover of Virtue and noble refind Sentiments. *You may observe*, said he, *that my Julia is faithful to her Husband's Bed, tho she is seduc'd from her Duty during her single State. But this last Circumstance can be of no Consequence in France, where all the young Ladies are shut up in Convents & have it not in their power to transgress: It might indeed have a bad Effect in a protestant Country*. But notwithstanding this Reflection, he told me, that he has wrote a Continuation of his Emilius, which may soon be publishd:[1] He there attempts to show the Effect of his Plan of Education, by representing Emilius in all the most trying Situations, and still extricating himself with Courage & Virtue. Among the rest, he discovers that Sophia, the amiable, the virtuous, the estimable Sophia is unfaithful to his Bed, which fatal Accident he bears with a manly, superior Spirit. *In this Work*, added he, *I have endeavourd to represent Sophia in such a light that she will appear equally amiable, equally virtuous, & equally estimable, as if she had no such Frailty. You take a Pleasure, I see*, said I, *to combat with Difficulties in all your Works. Yes*, said he, *I hate marvellous & supernatural Events in Novels. The only thing that can give pleasure in such Performances is to place the Personages in Situations difficult and singular*. Thus you see, that nothing remains for him but to write a Book for the Instruction of Widows; unless perhaps he imagines that they can learn their Lesson without Instruction.

Adieu, Dear Doctor: You say that you sometimes read my Letters to our common Friends; but you must read this only to the initiated. Yours, usque ad aras

DAVID HUME

Lisle Street, Leicester Fields
25 of March 1766
To The Reverend Dr Hugh Blair at Edinburgh

*315. *To* JEAN-JACQUES ROUSSEAU

My dear Sir

We have had very bad Weather for some time past, which has made me uneasy with regard to you.[2] I hope you was able

* MS. in Bibliothèque publique de Neuchâtel; Streckeisen-Moultou, ii. 291 (in French translation); hitherto unpublished in England.

[1] It never was published; probably it never was written.

[2] Writing on 29 March, Rousseau says: 'Il gèle ici depuis que j'y suis; il

to get thro' the Mountains of Derbyshire without any bad Accident.

The Artist has brought me a Model of your Bust, and told me, that you intended it for a Friend. Pray tell me to whom I shall deliver it.

Mr Malthus was with me to day, who desires his Compliments to you. He regreats very much your Change of Resolution. I am

Yours sincerely

27 of March 1766 DAVID HUME

*316. *To* JEAN-JACQUES ROUSSEAU

Lisle Street Leicester Fields
30 of March 1766

I ask you ten thousand pardons, my dear Friend, for the Cheat attempted to be put upon you: I had not, however, any hand in it; except concealing it. Mr Davenport himself repents of it, and by my Advice is resolved never more to form such a Project: So that you need not be any farther apprehensive on that head.[1]

Nothing can make me Happier, than to find, that your Situation is to your Mind. I hope it will long continue so. Mr Davenport insists on your promise, that you are to inform him, if any Circumstance displease you, that he may endeavour to correct it. You cannot better correspond to his friendly Intentions than by using this Freedom. My good wishes attend you, to whatever place of the World you may retreat; mixed with regreat, that I am so far distant from you.

I have sent you two Letters by the post, under two Covers franked by a Member of Parliament, which pay no postage. If you have refused them, please send for them again, because they may contain Business. I think, that you ought to receive all Letters, that are franked; because they will probably be transmitted either by Mr Davenport or me. I am My dear Sir

Yours, with the greatest Sincerity,

DAVID HUME

* MS. in Bibliothèque publique de Neuchâtel; Streckeisen-Moultou, ii. 291 f. (in French translation); hitherto unpublished in England.

---

a neigé tous les jours; le vent coupe le visage; malgré cela j'aimerois mieux habiter le trou d'un des lapins de cette garenne que le plus bel appartement de Londres . . .' (MS., R.S.E.; *Œuvres*, 1826, xxiii. 277).

[1] The affair of the post-chaise. See Rousseau's letter of 22 March in Appendix G below.

* 317. *To the* COMTESSE DE BOUFFLERS

Lisle Street, Leicester Fields, April 3, 1766.

It is impossible for me, dear Madam, to express the difficulty which I have to bear your absence, and the continual want which I feel of your society. I had accustomed myself, of a long time, to think of you as a friend from whom I was never to be separated during any considerable time; and I had flattered myself that we were peculiarly fitted to pass our lives in intimacy and cordiality with each other. Age and a natural equability of temper were in danger of reducing my heart to too great indifference about every thing: it was enlivened by the charms of your conversation, and the vivacity of your character. Your mind, more agitated both by unhappy circumstances in your situation and by your natural disposition, could repose itself in the more calm sympathy which you found with me. But behold! three months are elapsed since I left you; and it is impossible for me to assign a time when I can hope to join you. Lord Hertford has wrote me, that he expects to quit Ireland in a few weeks, and that he hopes to find me in London. I know that he proposed to be in France this summer; and he may probably desire me to delay my journey, that we may go together. I still return to my wish, that I had never left Paris, and that I had kept out of the reach of all other duties, except that which was so sweet and agreeable to fulfil, the cultivating your friendship, and enjoying your society. Your obliging expressions revive this regret in the strongest degree; especially where you mention the wounds which, though skinned over, still fester at the bottom.[1]

* *Priv. Corr.*, 147 ff.

[1] In her letter of 18 [Feb.] Mme de Boufflers says: 'J'aurois bien besoin de vous a present mon cher Maitre, je suis malade d'un rhume assez violent, je sors malgré cela tous les jours. Mais si j'avois votre compagnie je ne sortirois pas; si vous saviez jusqu'ou va mon courage, et combien cette vertu est penible a exercer a la longue! Je me trouve dans une situation extraordinaire, je ne desire rien et tout m'est ennuyeux. Cependant qui que ce soit ne pourroit juger par les apparences de ma disposition interieure je remplis tous les devoirs de la societé je me prete a ses amusemens je donne a souper trois fois de la semaine, jamais je n'eus plus de *serenité* parce que jamais je n'eus plus d'indifference. Je ne say si c'est un simptome de guerison ou d'exces d'abattement. Mais au nom de dieu ne retardez pas votre retour car voila ce qui me mettroit au desespoir. Votre appartement sera pret, il est comode suffisament grand, et tout meublé, il a la vue sur un jardin. Vous n'aurez nulle contrainte nul assujettissement, et nous serons tres proche l'un de l'autre' (MS., R.S.E.; *Eminent Persons*, 236).

Oh, my dear friend, how I dread that it may still be long ere you reach a state of tranquillity, in a distress which so little admits of any remedy, and which the natural elevation of your character, instead of putting you above it, makes you feel with greater sensibility. I could only wish to administer the temporary consolation, which the presence of a friend never fails to afford.

The chief circumstance which hinders me from repenting of my journey, is the use I have been to poor Rousseau, the most singular, and often the most amiable man in the world.

I have now settled him in a manner entirely to my satisfaction, and to his own. There is one Mr Davenport, a worthy man, a man of letters, and sense, and humanity, and of an ample fortune, about 6 or 7000 pounds a year, an elderly man, and a widower. Among several country seats which belong to him, he has one in the county of Derby, situated amid rocks and mountains, and rivulets and forests, and surrounded with the most beautiful savage country in England. As he seldom lives there, he proposed to me to give an apartment to our friend; and as he has there a gardener and other servants, for whom he must keep a table, he told me that he could easily supply him with his diet, and all other conveniences. I accepted of the offer, provided that he would take thirty pounds a year of board for M. Rousseau and Mademoiselle Le Vasseur. He laughed very heartily, but had the good nature to agree to my proposal. It is a fortnight since poor Rousseau left me, and here is a paragraph of a letter he writes me. . . .[1]

I must however confess, that I have not the consolation to think he will long be happy there. Never was man, who so well deserves happiness, so little calculated by nature to attain it. The extreme sensibility of his character is one great cause; but still more, the frequent and violent fits of spleen and discontent and impatience, to which, either from the constitution of his mind or body, he is so subject. These disqualify him for society, and are the chief reason why he so much affects solitude. When his health and good-humour return, his lively imagination gives him so much entertainment, that company, by disturbing his musing and meditation, is rather troublesome to him; so that, in either case, he is not framed for society. He is commonly however the best company in the world, when he will submit to live with men. Every one who saw him here, admires the

[1] Hume then quotes the opening of Rousseau's letter of 22 March 1766 (see Appendix G below).

simplicity of his manners, his natural unaffected politeness, the gaiety and finesse of his conversation. For my part, I never saw a man, and very few women, of a more agreeable commerce.

I shall tell you a very singular story of him, which proves his extreme sensibility and good heart. Mr Davenport had thought of a contrivance to save him part of the expenses of his journey. He hired a chaise, and told him that it was a retour chaise, which would only cost a trifle. He succeeded at first; but M. Rousseau, the evening before his departure, began to entertain suspicions from some circumstances which had escaped Mr Davenport's attention. He complained to me grievously of the trick, and said that, though he was poor, he chose rather to conform himself to his circumstances, than live like a beggar upon alms; and such pretended favours were real injuries. I replied, that I was ignorant of the matter, but should inform myself of Mr Davenport. No, cried he, no; if this be a contrivance, you are not ignorant of it: it has not been executed without your connivance and consent; but nothing could possibly be more disagreeable to me. Upon which he sate down in a very sullen humour; and all attempts which I could make, to revive the conversation and turn it on other subjects, were in vain. After near an hour, he rose up, and walked a little about the room. Judge of my surprise when, all of a sudden, he sat down upon my knee, threw his arms about my neck, kissed me with the greatest ardour, and bedewed all my face with tears! Ah, my dear friend, exclaimed he, is it possible you can ever forgive my folly? This ill humour is the return I make you for all the instances of your kindness towards me. But notwithstanding all my faults and follies, I have a heart worthy of your friendship, because it knows both to love and to esteem you.

I hope, dear Madam, that you have not so bad an opinion of me as not to think I was extremely affected with this scene. I confess that my tears flowed as plentifully as his; and that I embraced him with no less cordiality.

Please to tell this story to Madame la Maréchale de Luxembourg, to whom I desire that my sincere respects be presented. I also allow you to tell it to Madame de Barbantane, and to such of her female friends as you think worthy of it. I scarce know a male who would not think it childish. Ask Madame [1] L'Espinasse, whether she can venture to tell it to D'Alembert. I own that I am ashamed to mention that lady's name, as I

[1] *Sic* in printed text, but Hume probably wrote 'M^{le}' or something like that.

have not yet answered the letter with which she honoured me.[1] What do you think also of my ingratitude, when I tell you that I have not yet wrote to Madame Geoffrin?[2] I thank God, however, that I have not the impudence to desire you to make my apology, when I know that no apology can possibly be made. I am at a loss in what terms to express my acknowledgments to the Prince of Conti. Nothing can be more honourable as well as agreeable to me, than the offer which he is pleased to make me.[3] I leave you to judge what addition the pleasure of living in your company must make to all the other inviting circumstances that attend it. But there is only one particular which we must weigh together, when we meet.

When I return to Paris, it will be necessary for me to lay a plan of life more conformable to my character and usual habits: I must resolve to pass a great part of my time among my books, and in retreat. How far will such a plan be consistent with the situation projected?

I forgot to tell you, that Lord Marischal has given an answer such as I expected:[4] but General Conway has been ill, so that we have not yet attained the warrant for the pension; though there is no doubt to be entertained of it.

I must add, that Davenport told me he intended to leave our friend, by will, the life-rent of the house in which he lives, if he finds that his attachment to it continues. You see, then, that in point of circumstances he is not to be pitied: for I have also discovered, that he has some little resources beyond what he mentioned to the President Malesherbes and to me. It is one

[1] Mlle de Lespinasse's letter is dated from Paris on 23 Feb. 1766 (see Appendix C below).

[2] Mme Geoffrin wrote to Hume on 1 Feb. 1766:

'je ne peut pas laisser partire Le Colonel gordon sans luy donner un petit mot pour mon gros Drole.

'et ce petit mot est, que je l'aime bien, et que j'ay beaucoup D'impassiance de Le revoir.

'Monsieur Le Colonel gordon est aimable, il paroit contant de nous, je le vois partire avec regret.

'A Monsieur Monsieur Hume a Londres de la part de M^{de} Geoffrin.' (MS., R.S.E.; *Eminent Persons*, 288 f.)

[3] A reference, presumably, to the 'appartement' which is ready for Hume in the Temple.

[4] Earl Marischal Keith wrote to Hume on 4 March 1766:

'J'admire le bon coeur du Roy d'Angleterre, il faut qu'il soit veritablement bon pour n'etre pas endurci par la devotion envers notre ami. Je lui ay écris, qu'il n'y a pas a balancer. Ainsi je le conte a l'aise pour le reste de ses jours . . .' (MS., R.E.S.; *Eminent Persons*, 69).

of his weaknesses, that he likes to complain. The truth is, he is unhappy, and he is better pleased to throw the reason on his health, and circumstances and misfortunes, than on his melancholy humour and disposition.

Please to make my compliments to Miss Becket:[1] Lord Tavistock was so good as to execute her commission. I kiss your hands, with all the devotion possible.

* 318. *To the* Hon. Henry Seymour Conway

April 5 [1766].

Mr Hume presents his respects to General Conway. He cannot forbear thanking him, in the name of all that is ingenious in Europe, for the favours he has conferred on Monsieur Rousseau. He will keep it a secret, tho one of the most laudable actions in the world. He has informed Monsieur Rousseau, who, as he has the greatest sensibility imaginable, must feel the proper gratitude for the obliging manner in which he is treated.

Mr Hume desires to know how that pension is to be paid; whether it is to pass through the Treasury, or is to be paid secretly from the Privy Purse. If the former is the case, he apprehends that M. Rousseau must write to the Secretary of the Treasury, desiring him to pay the money to some banker whom he shall appoint. If the latter, he must choose some friend into whose hands it must be secretly paid.

† 319. *To* [C. G. de Lamoignon de Malesherbes] [2]

Lisle Street, Leicester Fields, ce 2 de mai, 1766.

J'ai besoin de bien d'apologies, Monsieur, auprès de vous, d'avoir tardé si long-tems de reconnoître l'honneur que vous

* *Rockingham Memoirs*, i. 316 f.

† *Priv. Corr.*, 160 ff.; an English version appeared in *Original Letters of J. J. Rousseau . . . Butta Fuoco and David Hume, Translated from the French*, 1799, and new edit., 1820. It is impossible to be sure that Hume originally wrote this letter in French, but the English version reads like a translation and not like a transcript of Hume's own English. For example, 'Je ne serois pas surpris qu'il quittât bientot cette retraite' appears as 'I should not be surprised that he had soon quitted this retreat'.

[1] Lydia Becquet. There are two rather hysterical letters from her to Hume among the MSS., R.S.E., dated 5 and 8 Aug. 1765, and showing that the position of companion to a lady so *sensible* as Mme de Boufflers was not altogether to be envied. What her commission was, which Lord Tavistock executed, I do not know.

[2] This is a pure conjecture. The letter appears to be a belated answer

m'avez fait; mais j'ai différé de vous répondre jusqu'au tems que notre ami seroit établi et auroit eu quelque expérience de sa situation. Il paroît être à present dans la situation la plus heureuse, ayant égard à son caractère singulier, et il m'écrit qu'il en est parfaitement content. Il est à 50 lieus éloigné de Londres, dans la province de Derby, pays célèbre pour ses beautés naturelles et sauvages. M. Davenport, très honnête homme et très riche, lui donne une maison qu'il habite fort rarement lui-même; et comme il y entretient une table pour ses domestiques, qui ont soin de la maison et des jardins, il ne lui est pas difficile d'accommoder notre ami et sa gouvernante de tout ce que des personnes si sobres et si modérées peuvent souhaiter. Il a la bonté de prendre 30 livres sterling par an de pension, car sans cela notre ami n'auroit mis le pied à la maison. S'il est possible qu'un homme peut vivre sans occupation, sans livres, sans société et sans sommeil, il ne quittera pas ce lieu sauvage et solitaire, ou toutes les circonstances qu'il a jamais demandées semblent concourir pour le rendre heureux. Mais je crains la foiblesse et l'inquiétude naturelles à tout homme, surtout à un homme de son caractère. Je ne serois pas surpris qu'il quittât bientôt cette retraite; mais en ce cas-là il sera obligé d'avouer qu'il n'a pas connu ses propres forces, et que l'homme n'est pas fait pour être seul. Au reste, il a été reçu parfaitement bien dans ce pays-ci. Tout le monde s'est empressé de lui montrer des politesses; et la curiosité publique lui étoit même à charge.

Madame de Boufflers vous a sans doute appris les bontés que le Roi d'Angleterre a eues pour lui. Le secret qu'on veut garder sur cette affaire est une circonstance bien agréable à notre ami. Il a un peu de foiblesse de vouloir se rendre intéressant en se plaignant de sa pauvreté et de sa mauvaise santé; mais j'ai découvert par hasard qu'il a quelques ressources d'argent, petites à la verité, mais qu'il nous a cachées quand il nous a rendu compte de ses biens.[1] Pour ce qui regarde sa santé, elle me paroit plutot robuste qu'infirme, à moins que vous ne vouliez compter les accès de melancolie et de *spleen* auxquels il est sujet. C'est grand dommage: il est fort aimable par ses manières; il est d'un cœur honnête et sensible; mais ces accès

to the one from Malesherbes referred to in Letter 308 above and given in Appendix C below. On the other hand it may have been to Daniel-Charles de Trudaine (1703–69), father of Trudaine de Montigny.

[1] Cf. the statement in Letter 317 above to Mme de Boufflers.

l'éloignent de la société, le remplissent d'humeur, et donnent quelquefois à sa conduite un air de bizarrerie et de violence, qualités qui ne lui sont pas naturelles.

Je vous prie, mon cher Monsieur, de me garder une place dans votre souvenir. Je me flatte de profiter, l'été prochain, de l'amitié que vous avez la bonté de me marquer. Des accidens ont retardé jusqu'ici mon retour en France.

J'ai l'honneur d'être &c.

* 320. *To* JEAN-JACQUES ROUSSEAU

It is but a few days ago, since General Conway recovered His Health so well as to come to town. Immediatly upon his arrival, I informed Him of Lord Mareschal's Answer, and reminded him of renewing his Applications to his Majesty. I received this Letter from him yesterday, which I transmit to you.[1] I fancy, that it will be necessary for you to write to Mr Conway, both to notify to him your Acceptance of his Majesty's Bounty, and to thank him for his good Offices. As the Characters of our Ministers may probably be unknown to you, I must inform you, that there is no man in the Kingdom of more approved morals than Mr Conway, and more noted for Probity and Honour; so that you need not fear, lest any Marks of Esteem you may give him, will be prostitute or be dishonourable to you.

I shall inform myself of Mr Conway concerning the proper

* MS. in Bibliothèque publique de Neuchâtel; Streckeisen-Moultou, ii. 282 ff. (in French translation); hitherto unpublished in England.

[1] The letter is as follows:

'Little Warwick Street
2d May 1766

'Gen: Conway's compliments to Mr Hume & acquaints him that in consequence of what he heard from him he has this day spoke to his Majesty on the subject of Monsr Rousseau, & that his M: is pleas'd to consent to give him a Pension of one hundred pounds per An:—desiring only it might be a private one.

'G.C. does not know Monsr Rousseau's direction & therefore begs Mr Hume to inform him in his name that he has his M's orders to make him this Offer & that if it is agreable to him he shall think himself extremely happy to have been an instrument in providing him any convenience or satisfaction, & in having contributed to procure for one of his distinguish'd Genius & Merit these marks of favour & protection which will do honour to this Country & in a particular manner to the Royal hand from whom this bounty flows.'

(MS. in Bibliothèque publique de Neuchâtel; *Corr. gén. de Rousseau,* xv. 197.)

Methods of your receiving this Pension, and shall inform you. Mean-while you may think of some Banker or other person into whose hands you will choose to consign the Money.

It gives me great Satisfaction, My Dear Friend, to hear, that your present Situation is agreeable to you. I cou'd only have wished, that you and Mad^lle^ le Vasseur had taken the Management of your Family into your own hands. It wou'd have been an Amusement to you: You wou'd have had every thing more to your mind: And as Mr Davenport had taken his Measures for that purpose, it wou'd have been no Inconvenience to him. But as he is to be with you in a few days, I shall say nothing farther on that head.

Permit me to express, in a few words, my Regreat of a Passage in one of your Letters to Mr Davenport: You suppose, that there are Calumnies spread concerning your Morals in London, and that these Calumnies gain Credit.[1] I cannot imagine who gave you this Intelligence, but be assured, that it is entirely groundless. There is indeed a satyrical Letter of Voltaire's very incorrectly printed,[2] which probably you have seen: But even that Letter contains nothing against your Morals, except a hint of your loving Wine, which is founded only on a Passage of your Letter to M. Dalembert. But, my dear Friend, if you must fly from Mankind, do not at once renounce the Amusement and Consolation of Society, and feel all the Pain which may result from the idle Opinions of Men and those mis-represented. The Expressions contained in this Letter of General Conway may convince you in what Estimation you are held by all Men of Character in England. We only wish, that you wou'd like our Company as well as we do yours.

Lord Mareschal has sent me the enclos'd, which is a piece of Raillery of the King of Prussia's and seems to me but an indifferent Performance.

[1] Rousseau was by this time fully convinced of the plot to ruin him in England, and of Hume's share in it. He was filling his letters to D'Ivernois, Mme de Boufflers, his cousin, and others, with his delusions on this subject.

[2] Probably a 12mo pamphlet entitled *A Letter from Mr Voltaire to M. Jean Jacques Rousseau* (in both French and English) published in London in April; it was not Voltaire's at all, though it was afterwards reprinted in Paris along with Voltaire's letter to Hume of 24 Oct. 1766. Or possibly the reference is only to a letter signed 'Z. A.', one of 'the People called Quakers', which appeared in the *St. James's Chronicle* for 17–19 April, and which was a kind of parody of Voltaire's *Lettre d'un Quaker à Jean-Georges*. Hume may have been for a time deceived into thinking this written by Voltaire.

I had a Letter lately from M^de^ de Boufflers, who is well, and desires to be remembered to you. My Compliments to Mlle Le Vasseur.

Lisle Street, Leicester Fields
3 of May 1766

* 321. *To* [*the* Earl of Hertford] [1]

My Lord

I am assur'd, that there arriv'd yesterday an Express from New York to the board of Trade, which is kept Secret, and contains the most interesting Articles of Intelligence. I was told, that the general Assembly of the Provinces, when they first heard of Mr Pitt's Declaration in their Favour,[2] were so much encourag'd, that they pass'd the most extraordinary Votes and Resolutions, much beyond the Principles avow'd by that Gentleman. They voted that the Parliament of England had no Right to impose on them any Taxes whatsoever; that they had no Right to make any Laws for them without their Consent; that the Colonies had a Right to trade freely to any Part of the World where they found their Advantage; that they were determin'd to maintain these Principles to the last Drop of their Blood; and that the whole Militia and Arms be carefully inspected, in order to maintain the Colonies in a State of Defence against all Invaders. A Gentleman of very good Sense told me these Circumstances, which he heard from a Person who had perus'd the Letters in the board of Trade. If this Intelligence hold to the Extent here related, there will certainly be a considerable Revolution in the Ministry. Mr Pitt will be sent for and receiv'd on his own Terms, as the only Person who has Authority sufficient to extricate us from so dangerous a Situation.

At present, even before the Arrival of this surprizing Piece of News, the Ministry seem to be in great Perplexity. The Duke of Grafton [3] has in effect, resignd, and goes no longer near the Office, except for the Dispatch of such necessary Business as cannot wait, till his Successor be appointed. There are three Noblemen commonly namd for that Office Lord Hardwicke,

* MS. in Henry E. Huntington Library, San Marino, California; hitherto unpublished.

[1] A guess. The autograph is endorsed in a hand very like Hertford's.

[2] In his famous speech of 14 January 1766, in which he declared: 'I rejoice that America has resisted.'

[3] He was Secretary of State.

Lord Egmont,[1] and the Duke of Richmond. Many People think Lord Egmont will be Secretary and that the Duke of Richmond will succeed him in the Admiralty. In all cases, it is not thought probable, that the Duke of Richmond will return to France: It is believ'd that Lord Holdernesse will succeed him in that Employment.

Mr Pitt's Politics, in the End of the Sessions, appear to have been as remarkable and peculiar as during the whole Course of it. He threw out Appearances of a Union with his Brothers, the Greenvilles, in order to alarm the Ministry; he attack'd all the Measures of Administration with great Vehemence; sometimes he voted differently from George Grenville, in order to show that the Union was not entirely cemented, and that the Court need not despair of gaining him; and having thrown all the Ministers into Confusion by these Proceedings, he retires to Bath at the very Instant when the Supplies came before the House, and when he had it in his Power to perplex still more all the public Measures. The Meaning of this Conduct is commonly understood to be, that he wants to be Minister with full Power of modelling the Administration as he pleases: Had he routed the Ministry entirely, the Grenvilles and the Duke of Bedford must have come in, Men whom he regards as the least obsequious and pliable in England. He therefore keeps aloof from all positive Engagements with them; he lets the Ministry see, that, if his Terms be not comply'd with, this Union must in time have place; he knows that such a Union must overwhelm them as every one sees visibly that they enjoy not the King's Confidence or rather are exposd to his secret ill-will; so that a Pretence is only wanted to turn them all out of office, and the first considerable Vote they lost wou'd serve to that Purpose. Mr Pitt concluded, that these Considerations woud soon open the Door to him on his own Terms; and his Opinion appears very probable: But these Events in America, if true, as I believe, they are, must quicken extremely the Operation of all those Causes. He seems to be the only Man, who can either bring the Americans to submit peacably by his Authority; or subdue them by his Vigour. It does not seem probable that the Repeal alone of the Stamp Act will suffice.

[1] John (1711–72), 2nd Earl of Egmont, First Lord of the Admiralty, 1762–6. He spent most of his time in the early part of 1766 in carrying secret messages between the King and Lord Bute; and resigned when Pitt came into power later in the year.

Lord Holdernesse had an Intention of taking soon a Journey to France in order to visit his Friends, and he press'd me much to be of the Party: But I declind it, in order to have the Honour of accompanying your Lordship thither: These late Events have made him delay his Journey: As far as one can see thro such a misty Air, it appears to me very probable, that he will be our Ambassador at that Court. He has Connexions with Mr Pitt, as far as any one can have with that Gentleman, which at all Adventures will facilitate his Nomination; and it woud be difficult to find in England a Person more fit for the Office or who woud be more acceptable to the Court of France.

I hope we may now flatter ourselves with the hopes of seeing your Lordship soon in this Part of the World. I am with the utmost Regard My Lord

Your Lordship's

Most obedient & most humble Servant

DAVID HUME

Lisle Street Leicester Fields
8th of May 1766.

* 322. *To the* COMTESSE DE BOUFFLERS

Lisle Street, Leicester Fields, 16 May, 1766.

Nothing could have given me more pleasure than your letter.[1] Though I never doubted of your friendship, every instance of it affords me new satisfaction; especially one which opens to me the prospect of passing most of my time in your company. I could not wish for a more happy situation, nor one more conformable to my inclination. The objections appear to me, at this distance, very light in comparison of the advantages. But I reserve the forming a full judgment till our next meeting, which, I hope, will be after your return from Pougues.

I have sent you Addison's Travels to Italy,[2] by Mr Ainslie, a young gentleman, who is known to Miss Becket, and who seems to be very agreeable.[3] He would think himself much

* *Priv. Corr.*, 168 ff.; Burton, ii. 324 (incomplete).

[1] Mme de Boufflers's letter of 18 April [1766] is given in Appendix E below.

[2] She had asked for this book in her letter of 18 April.

[3] Fortescue has printed (*Corr. of George III*, ii, p. 311 ff.) a document copied in the King's handwriting, entitled 'Anecdotes of the Court of France by Mr Ainslie', and dated from Paris, 3 Jan. 1772. It is an interesting, gossipy document, showing that Mr Ainslie, whoever he was, had good opportunities for picking up details about all the latest scandals. I suspect that this was the man Hume refers to.

honoured by any notice you would please to take of him. He will also deliver to you six prints of Rousseau, done from an admirable portrait, which Ramsay drew for me. I desire you to accept one of these prints for yourself; to beg Madame de Luxembourg, in my name, to accept of another; Madame de Barbantane of a third; Mademoiselle de L'Espinasse of a fourth; M. de Malesherbes of a fifth; and Madame de Montigny[1] of a sixth. This lady lives in your neighbourhood, in the Rue des Vieilles Andriettes. All these are enthusiasts for our friend, and this trifle will give them satisfaction.

I am afraid, my dear Madam, that notwithstanding our friendship, and our enthusiasm for this philosopher, he has been guilty of an extravagance the most unaccountable and most blameable that is possible to be imagined. You know what steps I took, with his knowledge and consent, towards obtaining him a pension from the King, and the success I had met with. As soon as I got an answer from Lord Marischal, approving the acceptance of the pension, I informed General Conway, whose bad health detained him in the country several weeks. When he came to town, he renewed his application to the King, who renewed his consent. The General informed me of this matter in a letter, where he expressed his satisfaction of being serviceable to a man of so much genius and merit; and he added, that, if he had known his direction, he would have wrote to himself. I sent immediately this letter to Rousseau. I waited yesterday on Mr Conway, who put into my hands a letter of which the enclosed is a copy.[2] He is so good-humoured as not to be angry; but begs me to use every expedient to overcome this objection. You see that our friend objects to the pension's being a secret; whereas, in his letter to Lord Marischal, he said, that he liked it the better on that account, as it was a testimony of esteem from his Majesty, without any mixture or suspicion of vanity. I shall write to him, and tell him that the affair is no longer an object of deliberation: he had already taken his resolution, when he allowed me to apply to the minister; and again, when he allowed the minister to apply to the King; and again, when

[1] Mme Trudaine de Montigny (died 1776), daughter of Bouvard de Fourqueux. Mme du Deffand sneers at her 'remarques fines' (*Lettres à Walpole*, i. 196), but was a frequent enough guest at her house all the same.

[2] Rousseau's letter to Conway (*Priv. Corr.*, 165 f.; and *Œuvres de R.*, 1826, xxiii. 334 f., where the date, 12 May, is incorrectly given as 22 May). It is given in Appendix H below.

he wrote to Lord Marischal; and again, when he allowed me to notify Lord Marischal's answer to the minister; and again, when he acquiesced two months in this determination; and that the King, General Conway, Lord Marischal, and I, shall all have reason to complain of him. Was ever any thing in the world so unaccountable? For the purposes of life and conduct, and society, a little good sense is surely better than all this genius, and a little good humour than this extreme sensibility.

As to the deep calamity of which he complains, it is impossible for me to imagine it. I suppose it is some trifle, aggravated by his melancholy temper and lively fancy. I shall endeavour to learn from Mr Davenport, who is just gone to that neighbourhood. Lady Aylesbury and General Conway believe, that it is Horace Walpole's letter which still torments him. That letter was put into our newspapers; which produced an answer, full of passion, and indeed of extravagance, complaining in the most tragical terms of the forgery, and lamenting that the imposter should find any abettors and partizans in England.[1] Mr Walpole has wrote a reply, full of vivacity and wit, but sacrifices it to his humanity, and is resolved that no copy of it shall get abroad.[2] He assures me that he, as well as Madame du Deffan, were entirely innocent of that publication at Paris: it was a lady, a friend of yours, who gave the first copy.

You have probably seen Voltaire's letter to our exotic philosopher. I fancy it will rouse him from his lethargy. These two gladiators are very well matched: it is like the combat of Dares and Entellus, in Virgil. The sprightliness and grace, and irony and pleasantry of the one, will be a good contrast to the force and vehemence of the other.

It is universally believed that the Duke of Richmond will not return to Paris.[3] Lord Holdernesse, it was thought, would

[1] Rousseau's letter of 7 April 1766 (*Œuvres*, 1826, xxiii. 297; *St. James's Chronicle*, April 8–10, 1766). (See Appendix H below.)

[2] This reply, which is entitled 'Lettre d'Émile à Jean-Jacques Rousseau', has now been published in a footnote to Mme du Deffand's Letters to Horace Walpole (i. 3 f.). It deserves the description Hume gives it. It begins: 'Hélas! mon cher gouverneur, j'arrive dans ce pays-ci, et pour première nouvelle on me dit que vous perdez l'esprit, que vous courez le spectacle en habit de masque et que vous vous emportez contre un homme qui en badinant vous avait donné de forts bons conseils.'

[3] And neither he did. He was appointed Secretary of State, Southern Dept., in succession to the Duke of Grafton, and kissed hands on 23 May 1766.

succeed him; which would be a great satisfaction to us all: but this report vanishes, and it is now believed that Lord Townshend[1] will be our Ambassador. He passes for a great wit, in our London style. I am not personally acquainted with him; but I am much mistaken, if his wit succeeds at Paris. He will be much surprised at first to find that he is no wit at all; but will discover at last that it is entirely your fault. He passes for a man of worth and honour.

You are happy that while your son[2] shall be at Florence, he will have the company and the protection of M. and Madame de Barbantane;[3] but surely you and I shall much regret the want of the lady's company at Paris. Please to make my compliments to her and to Madame de Vierville. I have a project of accompanying you to Lyons.[4] Would to God it were possible for us to take our flight thence into Italy; and from thence, if you would, into Greece. A friend of mine, who has been long settled in Smyrna, returns thither next spring, and urges me to take the journey along with him.[5] What do you think of the project? The idea of it is not altogether extravagant. Might we not settle in some Greek island, and breathe the air of Homer, or Sappho, or Anacreon, in tranquillity and great opulence? And might we not carry thither our philosopher of Derby, who will surely prefer that sunny situation to the mountains and clouds of this northern climate? Perhaps Madame de Bussy[6] might consent to be of the party. Please remember to me that lady's situation, which is not indifferent to me, both on her own

[1] George (1724–1807), 4th Viscount, and 1st Marquis, Townshend; A.D.C. to Duke of Cumberland, 1747–50, and to George II, 1758; received the surrender of Quebec, 17 Sept. 1759; Lieut.-Gen. of the Ordnance, 1763–7; Lord Lieutenant of Ireland, 1767–72; Field-Marshal, 1796. Instead of going to Paris, as Hume anticipated, he succeeded Lord Hertford at Dublin. It was the Earl of Rochford who went to Paris as Ambassador.

[2] His Christian names are not known. He was born in 1746. Horace Walpole gave him a letter of introduction to Sir Horace Mann, British Envoy at Florence, on 11 July 1766 (*Letters*, vii. 17 f.).

[3] The Marquis de Barbentane had just been appointed French Envoy at Florence, but Mme de Barbentane did not go there, being employed at Paris in chaperoning Princess Louise-Marie-Thérèse-Bathilde (died 1822), daughter of the Duc d'Orléans.

[4] When her son set off for Italy.

[5] I do not know who this was.

[6] Wife (1765) of Charles de Bussy (1718–85), Marquis de Bussy-Castelnau, who had served with distinction in the French armies in India.

account, and on account of the interest you take in it. I kiss your hands, with great regard and attachment.

P.S.

Since I wrote the above, my Lady Hervey tells me, that she has been beforehand with me, in sending you a print. If you have one to spare, please send it to M. Turgot, who is an enthusiast of the same sect. Mademoiselle L'Espinasse could convey it.

* 323. *To* JEAN-JACQUES ROUSSEAU

I send you, My Dear Sir, the Copy of the King of Prussia's Rescript, which was sent me by your Friend, Mons[r] Peyrou.[1] He tells me, that this Piece was printed by Voltaire, who, however, cou'd not forbear making one Alteration in it. For in Page 2, Line 14, instead of *au Sieur Rousseau*, he has substituted *a un homme*. Such a Reluctance he had to name you in any particular that might be to your Honour or Advantage.

Your Letter to General Conway has given me great Uneasyness; as it did also to the General. We can see no Reason why you shoud retract the Consent you had once given, to accept this Testimony of His Majesty's Goodness towards you. You said in your Letter to Lord Mareschal, that the Secrecy of the Pension was rather an agreeable Circumstance to you, as it showed that the Pension was merely the Effect of Esteem in the King, not of Vanity, in affecting to appear an Encourager of Letters. General Conway hopes, that you will return to the same way of thinking, and that you will write to him to notify your Acceptance.

But there was another Circumstance of your Letter, which

* MS. in Bibliothèque publique de Neuchâtel; Streckeisen-Moultou, ii. 284 f. (in French translation); hitherto unpublished in England.

[1] Pierre-Alexandre Du Peyrou (1729–94), the well-known friend of Rousseau in Neuchâtel, about whom see the *Confessions*, and Rousseau's Correspondence, *passim*. His letter to Hume (B.M. MSS. Add. 29626, printed by Courtois, 288 ff.) is dated from Neuchâtel, 4 May 1766. One paragraph reads: 'Il a paru ici une petite pièce que je vous envoye cy incluse. C'est la réponse du Roy de Prusse à son cher clergé de Neufchâtel, qui s'étoit plaint des arrêts du Conseil d'Etat relatif à l'affaire de Mr Rousseau. Vous comprenez bien, Monsieur, que ce ne sont pas nos Prêtres qui ont publié cette réponse. On en attribue l'impression à leur adversaire le plus redoutable, Mr de Voltaire. La pièce est bien conforme à l'original, excepté à la ligne 14 de la page 2 où au lieu de *à un homme*, étoit *au Sr Rousseau*. Je vous en envoye cy inclus un exemplaire.'

gave me still greater Uneasyness: You mention some great Calamity or Affliction which you have met with, and which has thrown you into the most profound Melancholy. General Conway and My Lady Aylesbury fancy, that this is the Letter of Mr Walpole: If so, they desire me to inform you, that Mr Walpole is very sorry to have given you so much Offence; and that that idle Piece of Pleasantry was meant to be entirely secret, and the publication of it was contrary to his Intention and came from Accident. Mr Walpole has expressed the same Sentiments to me. I have this Moment received a letter from Lord Mareschal,[1] who seems to be in good Health. I am Yours with great Sincerity

DAVID HUME

Lisle Street Leicester Fields
17 of May 1766
To M[r] Rousseau

* 324. *To* JEAN-JACQUES ROUSSEAU

Mr Hume presents his Compliments to M. Rousseau. He has received the enclosed from the English Minister at the Court of Turin.[2] He begs to be remembered to Mr Davenport.

Lisle Street Leicester Fields
26 of May 1766

† 325. *To* RICHARD DAVENPORT

Dear Sir

About ten days ago, I wrote both to you and Monsr Rousseau; tho' I fancy my Letters have miscarry'd. The Reason of my Suspicion [is], that some of the Covers you left me are wrong directed by Mistake; and I am afraid I might thro inadvertance

* MS. in Bibliothèque publique de Neuchâtel; Streckeisen-Moultou, ii. 285; hitherto unpublished in England.

† B.M. Addit. MSS. 32491; Courtois, 275 f.; hitherto unpublished in England.

[1] The letter is dated 'April 29'. It was wrongly ascribed by Burton (*Life*, ii. 104 f.) to the year 1762. Apart from its references to Rousseau it is of importance; for it shows unmistakably that Hume was at this time seriously thinking of continuing his *History*, and had suggested getting information about the Jacobite rebellions from the Earl Marischal. (See Appendix F.)

[2] Louis Dutens (1730–1812), a French Huguenot who took orders in the Church of England; author of *Mémoires d'un Voyageur qui se repose*, 1805; sometime Secretary to the British Embassy at Turin, and, in 1766, *Chargé d'affaires* there.

have made use of one of these. If so, be so good as to inform me, that I may correct the Mistake, and write him again on the the same Subject. I am with great Sincerity

Dear Sir

Your most obedient & most humble Servant

DAVID HUME

Lisle Street Leicester Fields
27 of May 1766

To Richard Davenport Esqr

* 326. *To the* REV. HUGH BLAIR

My dear Sir

I cannot begin my Letter without lamenting most sincerely the Death of our Friend, Dr Jardine:[1] I do not aggravate it by the Circumstance of its being sudden; for that is very desirable: But surely we shall ever regreat the Loss of a very pleasant Companion and of a very friendly honest Man. It makes a blank which you must all feel, and which I in particular will sensibly feel, when I come amongst you. I need not ask you, whether the Miscreants of the opposite Party did not rejoice. For I take it for granted.

As soon as I receiv'd yours, I put it into Mr Dodwell's [2] hands, who said that he woud deliberate with his Wife about it. I did not hear of him till to day, when he told me, that he desir'd much to settle his Son with Dr Drysdale,[3] and woud give a hundred a Year with him, beginning with the first of November next. I told him, that I wishd he had informd me

* MS., R.S.E.; Burton, ii. 318 (incomplete).

[1] John Jardine dropped dead in the General Assembly on 28 or 29 May 1766. The story is graphically told by Alexander Carlyle in his *Autobiography*, 466 ff.

[2] The Rev. William Dodwell, D.D. (1709–85), theological writer and controversialist. He was considering whether to send his son to Edinburgh for education, in accordance with a custom that was growing in popularity at this time; and Blair having no more room in his house for such pupils, it was suggested that the boy should be put under the care of the Rev. John Drysdale.

[3] Rev. John Drysdale (died 1788), a contemporary and fellow-townsman of Adam Smith; minister of Lady Yester's, Edinburgh, 1763; translated to the Tron Church in succession to Jardine, 1766; Moderator of the General Assembly, 1773 and again in 1784; Clerk to the General Assembly, 1778. He was a faithful adherent of Robertson in ecclesiastical affairs, and both Blair and Carlyle thought Robertson favoured him unduly.

sooner, for I was afraid, that it woud be too late for Dr Drysdale to find a House. I added, that you had desird in your Letter to have an Answer immediatly: He told me, that he had not observed that Clause. I beseech you to engage Dr Drysdale, if it be possible, to take the Boy on these Terms. I am Dear S^{r}

Yours sincerely

DAVID HUME.

Lisle Street Leicester Fields
5 of June 1766
To the Revd Dr Hugh Blair at Edinburgh

* 327. *To* RICHARD DAVENPORT

Dear Sir

Your Guest is not a little whimsical. He made me no Reply, when I endeavour'd to perswade him to accept of His Majesty's Bounty, even tho a Secret: Upon which I made a new Application to General Conway, that he wou'd prevail on his Majesty to depart from this Condition. The General only requires, as is reasonable, that Mr Rousseau shou'd promise to accept, in case the King be pleas'd to bestow on him a Pension publickly. I have wrote him the enclos'd[1] for that Purpose, in case he be with you at Davenport. I have also wrote to Wooton under Direction to your Steward, in case he be at that Place. If he be at Wooton, you may open & read & burn the enclosd.

I am Dear Sir

Your most obedient & most humble Servant

DAVID HUME

Lisle Street
Leicester Fields
19 June 1766

† 328. *To* JEAN-JACQUES ROUSSEAU

As I have not received any Answer from you, I conclude, that you persevere in the same Resolution of refusing all Marks of His Majesty's Goodness, as long as they must remain a Secret.

* B.M. Addit. MSS. 32491; Courtois, 276; hitherto unpublished in England.

† MS. in Bibliothèque publique de Neuchâtel; *Concise Account*, 28; Burton, ii. 325 f. (date incorrectly given as 16 June); Streckeisen-Moultou, ii. 286 f. (in French translation).

[1] The enclosure, a copy of the next letter, is not with the autograph.

I have therefore apply'd to General Conway to have this Condition removed; and I was so fortunate as to obtain his Promise, that he wou'd speak to the King for that Purpose. It will only be requisite, said he, that we know previously from M. Rousseau whether he wou'd accept of a Pension publickly granted him, that His Majesty may not be exposed to a Second Refusal. He gave me Authority to write to you on that Subject; and I beg to hear your Resolution as soon as possible. If you give your consent, which I earnestly entreat you to do, I know, that I cou'd depend on the good Offices of the Duke of Richmond, to second General Conway's Application; so that I have no doubt of Success. I am, My Dear Sir, Yours with great Sincerity

DAVID HUME.

Lisle Street Leicester Fields.
19 of June 1766.
To Mr Rousseau

* 329. *To* RICHARD DAVENPORT

Dear Sir

I have a Friend,[1] who has a considerable Estate in the County of Suffolk, and who is esteem'd one of the most judicious Farmers and Improvers in that part of England. I gave him an Account of your Machine for levelling Ridges; and as he tells me, that high Ridges abound very much in Suffolk, and are as destructive there as elsewhere, he has a great Desire of having that Machine both for his own Benefit and that of his Neighbours. He askd me, whether I coud use the Freedom of desiring you to order one to be made for him, and have it sent up to London, with some general Directions for using it. I said, that I knew enough of your beneficent Disposition to be certain you woud do every thing to promote so useful an Art as Agriculture: I beg, therefore, the Favour of you, that you woud order your Tradesman to make a Machine similar to yours, and to send it up by the Waggon, directed to Mr Mure in Nicholas Lane Lombard Street. He will order the Carriage and the Price to be pay'd on receiving it. He is a Gentleman of a very mechanical Head; so that the Machine itself and a short Description of its Use will be sufficient for his Understanding it. Lord Holdernesse told me, that, towards the End of Autumn, he intended to

* B.M. Addit. MSS. 32491; Courtois, 276 f.; hitherto unpublished in England.

[1] Hutchinson Mure of Saxham Hall, Baron Mure's uncle.

send his Steward across the Country, in order to learn the Use of this Machine. I doubt not but you will give your People Orders to communicate to him all the Instruction possible.

I am very anxious that I have receivd no Answer from your Guest to my second Letter,[1] containing the Offer of which I gave you an Account. Were he not the most unaccountable Man in the World, I shoud be very much scandalizd and very much offended at this long Silence. After his Arrival at Wooton, I receivd a Letter from him full of the highest Expressions of Esteem and Affection; and as there has been since no Intercourse between us, except in this Affair, where he sees the strongest Proof of my Friendship, it is impossible for me to imagine, that he can be any way disgusted with me: Yet perhaps something has struck his Fancy, which I shall never be able to guess or imagine. Did you ever hear from him any Surmises of that kind? Or have you ever discoverd what that deep Affliction was, which he said overwhelmed him about the time of your Arrival at Wooton? Coud your People ever discover it from Mademoiselle? Or was there really any Affliction at all? Your Letters about that time assurd me, that he was in the best humour and the best Health in the World; and he is not surely a Man who can cover with a fair Appearance his Spleen and Peevishness. If he be with you at Davenport, be so good as to tell him, that I, having occasion to write to you of another Affair, had express'd my Surprize at not hearing from him. He woud not choose, I fancy, that you shou'd enter farther into this Matter. I am Dear S^r^, with great Regard

Your most obedient and most humble Servant

DAVID HUME

[Lisle][2] Street Leicester Fields
[ ][2] June 1766

To Richard Davenport Esq at Davenport, Brereton Green Cheshire.

* 330. *To* JEAN-JACQUES ROUSSEAU

Mr Hume's Compliments to M. Rousseau. He sends him a Letter from M^de^ de Boufflers;[3] and begs, as soon as convenient,

* MS. in Bibliothèque publique de Neuchâtel; Streckeisen-Moultou, ii. 286 (in French translation); hitherto unpublished in England.

[1] The preceding letter.

[2] In breaking the seal, a piece has been torn out of the autograph.

[3] Mme de Boufflers's letter from Montmorency, dated 4 May 1766 (Streckeisen-Moultou, ii. 57 f.). It begins: 'M. Hume me donne des

an Answer to his last; as he shall be obliged to leave London soon; and shall not then have it in his Power to be any longer of Service to him.

Lisle Street Leicester Fields
21 of June 1766

* 331. *To* Richard Davenport

My Dear Sir

You and you alone can aid me in the most critical Affair, which, during the Course of my whole Life, I have been engaged in. I send you a Copy of Rousseau's Answer[1] to that friendly Letter, which I wrote him, and of which I sent a Duplicate to you at Davenport. You will be astonishd, as I was, at the monstrous Ingratitude, Ferocity, and Frenzy of the Man. I send you also enclos'd my Answer,[2] which I beg you to peruse before you deliver it. You must certainly think, that, after this Provocation, I have treated him with sufficient Temper, and that my Demand is extremely reasonable. I can insist on no less, than that he specify the Points of which I am accus'd and name the Accuser. If it were necessary, I shoud conjure you by all your Regards to Truth and Justice to second my Demand, and make him sensible of the Necessity he lies under of agreeing to it. He must himself pass for the Lyar and Calumniator, if he does not comply. Be so good, therefore, since Matters have come to this Extremity to deliver to him this Letter, and tell me his Behaviour on perusing it. You will here have Occasion to become acquainted with the Morals and Character of your Guest. I am Dear Sir

Your most obedient & most humble Servant
David Hume

Lisle Street Leicester Fields
26 of June 1766
PS.

Pray observe in what manner he disguises the Story, which I told you preceded the day of his Departure from London.

* B.M. Addit. MSS. 32491; Courtois, 278; hitherto unpublished in England.

nouvelles de vous, Monsieur, qui m'inquiètent à un point inexprimable. Il dit que vous êtes actuellement accablé du plus violent chagrin dans l'asile où vous êtes. Je n'en puis imaginer la cause. . . .'

1 Rousseau's letter of 23 June 1766 (see Appendix G below).

2 Letter 333.

I shoud be very unhappy were I engag'd with a man of less Probity and Morals than yourself.[1]

* 332. *To* Richard Davenport

My dear Sir

I write you both to Davenport and to Wooton; but my chief Letter goes to Wooton; because, from your Account, I have best Reason to think you are there. I beseech you keep the Duplicate of my last Letter[2] to Rousseau, which I desird you to open and to read at Davenport; and I wish you woud either send it to me or a Copy of it by the first Post. I shall not have Peace of Mind till you have met with this Man, and have given me an Account of your Conference with him. Have Compassion, I beseech you, on the most signal Beneficence, exposd to the blackest Ingratitude. You have a heart formd for feeling that cruel Situation. I am Dear Sir

Your most obedient humble Servant

David Hume

Lisle Street Leicester Fields
26 of June 1766

To Richard Davenport Esqr at Davenport Brereton Green Cheshire

† 333. *To* Jean-Jacques Rousseau

Sir

As I am conscious of having ever acted towards you the most friendly part, of having ever given you the most tender, the most active Proofs of sincere Affection, you may judge of my extreme Surprize on perusing your Epistle:[3] Such violent Accusations, confined altogether to Generals, it is as impossible to answer as to comprehend them. But Affairs cannot, must not remain on that Footing. I shall charitably suppose, that some

* B.M. MSS. Add. 29626; Courtois, 278 f.; hitherto unpublished in England.

† MS. in Bibliothèque publique de Neuchâtel; *Concise Account*, 31 ff.; Ritchie, 196 ff. and 470 ff.; Burton, ii. 326 ff.; Streckeisen-Moultou, ii. 287 ff. (in French translation).

[1] Accompanying this letter is one from Rousseau to Davenport (see Appendix H below).

[2] That is, the letter of 19 June (No. 328 above).

[3] Rousseau's letter of 23 June 1766 (see Appendix G below).

infamous Calumniator has belyed me to you: But in that Case, it is your Duty, and I am perswaded it will be your Inclination, to give me an Opportunity of detecting him, and of justifying myself, which can only be done by your mentioning the Particulars, of which I am accused. You say, that I myself know, that I have been false to you; but I say it loudly, and will say it to the whole World that I know the contrary, that I know my Friendship towards you has been unbounded and uninterrupted, and that tho' the Instances of it have been very generally remarked both in France and England, the smallest part of it only has as yet come to the Knowledge of the Public. I demand that you will produce me the Man who will assert the contrary; and above all I demand that he will mention any one particular, in which I have been wanting to you. You owe this to me, you owe it to yourself, you owe it to Truth and Honour and Justice, and to every thing that can be deemed sacred among men. As an innocent Man; I will not say, as your Friend; I will not say, as your Benefactor; but I repeat it, as an innocent Man, I claim the Privilege of proving my Innocence, and of refuting any scandalous Lye which may have been invented against me. Mr Davenport, to whom I have sent a Copy of your Letter, and who will read this before he delivers it, I am confident will second my Demand, and will tell you, that nothing possibly can be more equitable. Happily, I have preserved the Letter you wrote me after your Arrival at Wooton; and you there express, in the strongest Terms, indeed in Terms too strong, your Satisfaction in my poor Endeavours to serve you: The little epistolary Intercourse, which afterwards passed between us, has been all employed on my Side to the most friendly Purposes: Tell me what has since given you Offence: Tell me, of what am I accused: Tell me the man who accuses me. Even after you have fulfilled all these Conditions to my Satisfaction and to that of Mr Davenport, you will have great Difficulty to justify the employing such outrageous Terms towards a Man, with whom you have been so intimately connected, and whom on many accounts you ought to have treated with some Regard and Decency.

Mr Davenport knows the whole Transaction about your Pension, because I thought it necessary, that the Person, who had undertaken your Settlement, shoud be fully acquainted with your Circumstances; lest he shou'd be tempted to perform towards you concealed Acts of Generosity, which, if they came to your Knowlege, might give you some Grounds of Offence. I am Sir

Your most humble Servant,
DAVID HUME

Lisle Street Leicester Fields
26 of June 1766
To Mr Rousseau

* 334. *To the* REV. HUGH BLAIR

Dear Doctor

I did not apply, in your Favour, to any Minister of State, because any small Interest I may be suppos'd to possess was already bespoke for Mr Drysdale, who wants it much more than you, and whom you yourself seem'd not willing to enter into Competition with.[1] I shou'd willingly have seconded Dr Wallace's [2] Application for the Thistle; but as the Dr had, of himself, appeald to me for a Character, which I coud with Pleasure have given him in the amplest Manner, I expected every day that Mr Conway wou'd have spoke to me of the Matter, which he never did: The Secretary told me yesterday that for these two small Offices more Applications had been made to him by able and learned Divines than if Canterbury & Durham had been both vacant: a Proof what poor Prizes you in Scotland have to contend for.

You will be surprizd, dear Doctor, when I desire you most earnestly never in your Life to show to any mortal creature the Letters I wrote you with Regard to Rousseau: He is surely the blackest and most atrocious Villain, beyond comparison, that now exists in the World; and I am heartily asham'd of any thing I ever wrote in his Favour. I know you will pity me, when I tell you, that I am afraid I must publish this to the world in a Pamphlet, which must contain an account of the whole

* MS., R.S.E.; Burton, ii. 344 f. (incomplete).

[1] Jardine had been Dean of the Chapel Royal, and Dean of the Order of the Thistle. On 12 June Blair wrote to Hume asking his help towards securing the former office. He says: 'You know I have nothing from the Government but the salary of my College office which I work for. Others without doing any work have much greater & better things; and as I have been always upon the side of Government, I have some title to be taken notice of, amongst others in the distribution of these Favours.' (MS., R.S.E.) Through Robertson's interest Drysdale secured the office, being translated from Lady Yester's to the Tron.

[2] The Rev. Robert Wallace.

Transaction between us. My only Comfort is, that the Matter will be so clear as not to leave to any mortal the smallest possibility of Doubt: You know how dangerous any Controversy on a disputable Point woud be with a man of his Talents. I know not where the Miscreant will now retire to, in order [to] hide his Head from this Infamy. I am Dear Dr

Yours most sincerely
DAVID HUME

Lisle Street Leicester Fields
1 of July 1766.

P.S.

If you suspect any body took any Copies of any part of my Letters, employ all your Address and Influence to recover them. I suspect Mrs Cockburn:[1] You was so imprudent as even to lend her my Letters.

To The Rev^{d} Dr Hugh Blair at Edinburgh

* 335. *To* RICHARD DAVENPORT

Dear Sir

I conjecture from your Letter, that Rousseau had sent you the Copies of some of my Letters to him, since he went to Wootton. I wish heartily you coud get Copies of all them, and wou'd send them to me. You wou'd find every one of them extreme friendly, and even wrote with the greatest Discretion as well as Civility. It wou'd be of no Consequence for me to have Copies of them, were he not the most dangerous Man in the World, on account of his Malice and his Talents: I cannot take too many Precautions against him. I doubt not but you have long ago deliverd to him my Letter, which I sent you open; and that you have carefully remarked the Effects of it. I pray heartily on all Accounts that your Grandson may be thoroughly recover'd. You see how innocent I am; yet I assure you I feel Uneasyness from the Pain which you must feel on this Occasion.

If he denies, that he ever gave his Consent to the solliciting

* B.M. MSS. Add. 29626; Courtois, 279; hitherto unpublished in England.

[1] Alison Rutherford (1712–94), m. (1731) Patrick Cockburn of Ormiston, advocate (died 1753); authoress of one of the versions of 'The Flowers of the Forest'. She was a lively and charming figure in Edinburgh society and a great friend of Hume's. There are three sprightly letters from her to Hume among the MSS., R.S.E. which were printed (with omissions) by Burton in *Eminent Persons*.

this Pension, tell him of his Letter to Lord Mareschal, and his thanking General Conway and General Græme [1] for their Friendship in this Affair. I am

Dear Sir

Your most obedient & most humble Servant

DAVID HUME

Lisle Street Leicester Fields
4 of July 1766

To

Richard Davenport Esqr at Wootton, Ashborne Derbyshire

Readdressed in another hand:

To

Richard Davenport Esqre att Davenport near Holmes Chaple Cheshire To be left at Brereton Green

* 336. *To the* COMTESSE DE BOUFFLERS

Lisle Street, Leicester Fields, 15 July, 1766.

After an instance of your friendship, dear Madam, so charming, so agreeable to me, I should not have delayed a moment the making you the warmest acknowledgments;[2] but before I have ended this letter, you will find me but too well justified in my long silence. I shall only say, therefore, that, if I can find fault with any thing, it is a circumstance which renders your method of proceeding the more obliging; I mean, your going

* *Priv. Corr.*, 173 ff.

[1] David Graeme (died 1797), ex-Jacobite, but a protégé of Lord Bute; negotiated George III's marriage with Sophia Charlotte of Mecklenburg-Strelitz; Secretary to the Queen, 1761; Maj.-Gen., 1763; Controller of the Queen's Household, 1765. Horace Walpole (*George III*, i. 65) says that Hume once congratulated Graeme on having exchanged the dangerous employment of making (Jacobite) kings for the lucrative trade of making (Hanoverian) queens.

[2] Mme de Boufflers wrote on 6 May [1766]:

'Vous pouvez arriver quand il vous plaira. Votre appartement est tout prest, tout meublé, gay joli et comode. Vous aurez outre ce qui est necessaire, comme antichambres chambres &c une bibliotheque suffisante. Et si vous ne travailles pas ce sera votre faute . . .' (MS., R.S.E.; *Eminent Persons*, 237). For other extracts, concerning Rousseau, from this letter, see Appendix K below.

I suspect that Hume had in fact received this letter before he wrote his of 16 May (No. 322 above), but that he now pretended he had not, without actually saying so. He seems to have found Mme de Boufflers's importunity over his return to Paris a little irksome.

too far and too hastily in your arrangements for me. How many accidents might have deprived me of all means of profiting by them! I have twice thought myself on the brink of returning to Paris, in the same station which I occupied before: and it was for this reason I told you, that this was a subject on which it were better for us to converse together, when I should have the happiness to see you. I now continue my narration with regard to Rousseau.

I left off by telling you, that I intended, by Mr Conway's advice, to remonstrate with him on account of his bad usage of the King, of Lord Marischal, of General Conway, and above all of me, whom he had allowed to solicit a pension merely that he might have the ostentatious glory of refusing it. But when I reflected further on the strange character and unaccountable proceedings of the man, I thought that the pressing him so hard might with him be a sufficient ground of quarrel; and I therefore contented myself with remarking to him, that this circumstance of secrecy, to which he now seemed to object, was once most agreeable to him; that I hoped he would return to the same way of thinking, and that, if ever he did, he might inform Mr Conway, who would endeavour to keep the matter still open for him. To this prudent and cautious letter I received no answer for three weeks, upon which I began to suspect that he was really ashamed to write to me; and being determined to take nothing amiss, and being desirous of consummating my good work, I went to General Conway, and persuaded him to engage the King to depart from the circumstance of secrecy, which seemed to give offence. He consented at my request to humour this whimsical man in his whimsies; only, said he, let us be sure beforehand, that he will accept of the pension in this form.

I immediately wrote to Rousseau to that purpose; and in four days, I received the following answer, dated at Wootton, the 23d of June. . . .[1] This letter needs no commentary; I only desire you to remark with what impudence and malice he has perverted that story which I formerly told you, and which I then thought to his advantage. I mean the disgust about the hiring of his chaise. I immediately wrote him the following answer, dated 26th of June. . . .[2]

I shall now for your satisfaction transcribe to you his letter

[1] Here follows a transcript of Rousseau's letter (see Appendix G below).

[2] Here follows a transcript of Hume's letter of 26 June (No. 333 above).

to me, wrote immediately on his arrival in the country: you will see in what a friendly strain it is composed, and how lucky it is that I have kept it. . . .[1]

The whole interval between this friendly letter and the other outrageous one was filled up by repeated and successful acts of friendship on my part. Though I have, from decency, supposed in my letters to him, that some calumniator had belied me, I know it could not be so, both because he receives no letters by the post, and because he could receive no letters from any part of the world which would not give him new proofs of my friendship towards him. What is worse, this is a deliberate and a cool plan to stab me; for here is the great distress which he mentioned to General Conway, and which neither you nor I could understand.

This distress and affliction was entirely a counterfeit and a lie; for Mr Davenport wrote me at the very same instant, that he was very cheerful, and gay, and sociable, and enjoyed himself extremely, and was in no distress at all. But to return to my narration; Mr Davenport delivered him my letter: he was in the utmost confusion; but upon that gentleman urging to him the absolute necessity of his giving me an answer, he promised to do it. He attempted also to tell him the story, but the only thing which he could understand was, that I lived in friendship with some philosophers at Paris who were his enemies. Several posts have since passed, and I have received no answer,[2] nor do I indeed expect any. It is impossible that he can make me any apology for so black a proceeding. I should have wrote you of this matter sooner, had I not been desirous of sparing you the vexation of it till all was finished. You was besides absent from Paris. But as you may now be returned, and perhaps may have heard some surmises of the story from other hands, I was willing to give you a perfect account of it.

I must now, my dear friend, apply to you for consolation and advice in this affair, which both distresses and perplexes me. Should I give the whole account to the public, as I am advised by several of my friends, particularly Lord Hertford and General Conway, I utterly ruin this unhappy man. Every one must turn

[1] Here follows a transcript of most of Rousseau's letter of 22 March (see Appendix G below).

[2] Cf. three succeeding letters. Either this letter is wrongly dated (which is very probable) or Rousseau's epistle of 10 July did not arrive till late in the day; by which time Hume had written and sent away his to Mme de Boufflers.

their back on so false, so ungrateful, so malicious, and so dangerous a mortal. I know not indeed any place above ground where he could hide his shame; and such a situation must run him into madness and despair.

Notwithstanding his monstrous offences towards me, I cannot resolve to commit such a piece of cruelty even against a man who has but too long deceived a great part of mankind. But on the other hand, it is extremely dangerous for me to be entirely silent. He is at present composing a book, in which it is very likely he may fall on me with some atrocious lie. I know that he is writing his memoirs, in which I am sure to make a fine figure. Suppose that these memoirs are wrote, and are published after his death. My justification must lose a great part of its authenticity, both because several of the persons concerned may then be no more, and because every one may say, that it is easy to advance any thing against a dead man.

My present intention, therefore, is to write a narrative of the whole affair, and to insert all the letters and original papers: to draw this in the form of a letter to General Conway: to make several copies of this narrative: to leave one in your hands, one with Lord Marischal, one with General Conway, one with Mr Davenport, and perhaps one or two with other persons: to send also a copy to Rousseau, and tell him in what hands the other copies are consigned; that if he can contradict any one fact, he may have it in his power. These copies then will lie safe, till he attack me in some way or other, and then, whether he be dead or alive, whether I be dead or alive, they will be published with all the authenticity, as if they had been committed to the press instantly. This is my present idea, which I hope you will approve of. But is it not very hard that I should be put to all this trouble, and undergo all this vexation, merely on account of my singular friendship and attention to this most atrocious *scélérat*? Was there ever another instance in human nature that obligations alone, without other pretences, became a ground of quarrel? Surely such diabolical pride was never seen in any other mortal.

You need not be surprized to hear rumours of this story flying about Paris. I told it to all my friends here, which I thought necessary for my own justification against so dangerous a man: and I wrote some hint of it to Baron d'Holbach, whom I desired to examine Rougemont's books with his own eyes.[1] I

[1] For d'Holbach's reply on this matter see his letter in Appendix K below.

know not but the inserting that story may be to my purpose. You always forget to execute your intention on this head; or perhaps you have done it, but have concealed the issue from me, as not being willing to disgust me with my good friend. I must beg of you to communicate this whole affair to the Prince of Conti, and desire his advice and orders for my conduct in it. If the Maréchale de Luxembourg's health and spirits permit her to enter into it, I should not be displeased that she were acquainted with it.

I know that I shall have Madame de Barbantane's sympathy and compassion, if she be at Paris; and should be glad to have her opinion.

I have not yet wrote to Lord Marischal; but must soon. I am glad you have taken my friend Smith[1] under your protection: you will find him a man of true merit; though perhaps his sedentary recluse life may have hurt his air and appearance, as a man of the world.

* 337. *To the* REV. HUGH BLAIR

Dear Dr

I go in a few hours to Woburn;[2] so can only give you the Outline of my History. Thro many Difficulties I obtain'd a Pension for Rousseau. The Application was made with his own Consent & Knowlege. I write him, that all is happily compleated, and he needs only draw for the Money. He answers me, that I am a Rogue and a Rascal; and have brought him into England, merely to dishonour him. I demand the Reason of this strange Language; and Mr Davenport, the Gentleman with whom he lives, tells him, that he must necessarily satisfy me. To day, I receiv'd a Letter from him,[3] which is perfect Frenzy: It woud make a good eighteen-penny Pamphlet; and I fancy he intends to publish it. He there tells me, that D'Alembert, Horace Walpole and I had from the first enterd into a Combination to ruin him; and had ruin'd him: That the first Suspicion of my Treachery arose in him, while we lay together in the same Room of an Inn in France: I there spoke in my Sleep and betray'd my Intention of ruining him: That young Troncin lodg'd in the same House with me at London; and

* MS., R.S.E.; Burton, ii. 345 f.

[1] Adam Smith.

[2] The country house of the Duke of Bedford.

[3] Rousseau's enormous letter of 10 July 1766 (see Appendix G below).

Annie Elliot lookd very coldly at him as he went by her in the Passage: That I am also in a close Confederacy with Lord Lyttleton, who he hears is his mortal Enemy: That the English Nation were very fond of him on his first Arrival; but that Horace Walpole & I had totally alienated them from him. He owns, however, that his Belief of my Treachery went no higher than Suspicion while he was in London; but it rose to Certainty after he arrivd in the Country: For that there were several Publications in the Papers against him, which coud have proceeded from no body but me or my Confederate Horace Walpole. The rest is all of a like Strain, intermix'd with many Lyes and much Malice. I own, that I was very anxious about this Affair but this Letter has totally reliev'd me. I write in a hurry, merely to satisfy your Curiosity. I hope soon to see you; and am Dear Sir

Yours most sincerely

15^t^ of July 1766 DAVID HUME

To The Reverend Dr Hugh Blair at Edinburgh

* 338. *To* WILLIAM STRAHAN

[London, July 15, 1766.]

All I can say of Sir David Dalrymple is that he is now a Lord of the Session, and passes by the Name of Lord Hales or Newhales, I know not which. He is a godly Man; feareth the Lord and escheweth Evil, And works out his Salvation with Fear and Trembling. None of the Books Sir David publishes are of his writing: They are all historical Manuscripts, of little or no Consequence.[1] I go to Woburn for three or four days.

I have got a Letter from Rousseau, which woud make a good eighteen penny Pamphlet. I fancy he intends to publish it. It is perfect Frenzy; consequently sets my Mind quite at ease.

Yours

D. H.

† 339. *To* RICHARD DAVENPORT

Dear Sir

I receiv'd to day a Letter from Rousseau, which is as long as wou'd make a two Shillings Pamphlet; and I fancy he intends

* MS. at Barnbougle Castle; Hill, 74.

† B.M. MSS. Add. 29626; Courtois, 280 f.; hitherto unpublished in England.

[1] Lord Hailes had still to publish his *Annals of Scotland*.

to publish it. It is a perfect Frenzy. He says . . . .[1] I am really sorry for him; so that, tho' I intended to be very severe on him in my Answer, I have been very sparing; as you may see. I wou'd not, however, have you imagine that he has such an extreme Sensibility as he pretends. He wrote to General Conway, that he was oppress'd with such a grievous Calamity as deprivd him of the Use of his Senses and Understanding: This was about the time of your first Arrival at Wootton; when you wrote me, that he was perfectly gay, good-humourd and sociable: So that these Complaints of his Misery and Sufferings are a mere Artifice. I find in many other Respects that he lies like the Devil: You cannot imagine what a false and malicious Account he has the Assurance to give me of the Transaction between him and me the last Evening he was in Town, which I related to you. I am afraid indeed you have a very bad Pennyworth of him; but if I may venture to give my Advice, it is, that you wou'd continue the charitable Work you have begun, till he be shut up altogether in Bedlam, or till he quarrel with you and run away from you. If he show any Disposition to write me a penitential Letter, you may encourage it; not that I think it of any Consequence to me, but because it will ease his Mind and set him at rest. I write you in some hurry, as I set out to day for the Duke of Bedford's. I shall, if possible, pay my Respects to you in my way North. I am Dear Sir

Your most obedient humble Servant

David Hume

15 of July 1766

P.S.

The grievous Calamity, which he spoke of to General Conway, he now tells me was his Discovery of my Treachery.

I thought to have wrote to him by this Post; but really have not Leizure and scarce Patience. I shall perhaps write him some time after.

* 340. *To* Richard Davenport

Dear Sir

I must beg to take the Trouble of sending the enclos'd [2] to your Guest, after having read it. It is the last Trouble of the

* B.M. MSS. Add. 29626; Courtois, 281; hitherto unpublished in England.

[1] He then summarizes Rousseau's letter of 10 July, in much the same words as to Blair in Letter 337 above.

[2] The next letter.

kind, which I shall ever give you; so I hope for your Excuse. As he will receive no Letters by the Post,[1] this is the only Method by which I cou'd reach him; and I am besides well pleas'd that you shoud be well acquainted with every Step of my Behaviour, in hope of your Approbation. This Man's Composition is such a Composition of Wickedness and Frenzy, that one does not know whether they are to be angry at him for the one or to pity him for the other. I flatter myself, that you will think my Letter sufficiently temperate and decent.

I propose soon to be at your Fire-side or rather in your shady Grove: For I think the Weather more suitable to the latter than the former. You will allow me to bring my Friend along with me: It is Dr Armstrong, Author of the Art of preserving Health, and of many other fine Pieces: He is besides a very worthy Man. I shall use the Freedom to inform you some time before we set out. I am Dear Sir

Your most obedient & most humble Servant

DAVID HUME

Lisle Street Leicester Fields
22 of July 1766

*341. *To* JEAN-JACQUES ROUSSEAU

Sir — Lisle Street Leicester Fields 22^d^ of July 1766

I shall answer onely one Article of your long Letter:[2] It is that which regards the Conversation between us the Evening before your Departure. Mr Davenport had imagined a good natured Artifice, to make you believe, that a Retour Chaise had cast up for Wooton; and I believe he made an Advertisement be put into the Papers, in order to deceive you. His Purpose only was to save you some Expences in the Journey; which I thought a laudable Project, tho' I had no hand either in contriving or conducting it. You entertained however, Suspicions of his Design, while we were sitting alone by my Fire-side; and you reproached me with concurring in it. I endeavoured to pacify you and to divert the Discourse; but to no

* MS. in Bibliothèque publique de Neuchâtel; *Concise Account*, 84 ff.; Ritchie, 240 ff. and 510 ff.; Burton, ii. 341 f.; Streckeisen-Moultou, ii. 289 ff. (in French translation).

[1] Rousseau, by his own account, had been so much troubled, and put to so much expense, by receiving letters through the post from unknown and often impertinent correspondents, that he had warned his friends he would decline to accept any letters delivered to him in this way.

[2] Of 10 July (see Appendix G below).

purpose: You sate sullen and was either silent or made me very peevish Answers. At last, you rose up, and took a Turn or two about the Room; when, all of a sudden and to my great Surprize, you claped yourself on my Knee, threw your Arms about my Neck, kissed me with seeming Ardour, and bedewed my Face with Tears. You exclaimed, 'My Dear Friend, can you ever pardon this Folly? After all the Pains you have taken to serve me, after the numberless Instances of Friendship you have given me, here I reward you with this ill-humour and Sullenness. But your Forgiveness of me will be a new Instance of your Friendship and I hope you will find at bottom that my Heart is not unworthy of you.' I own, that I was very much affected; and I believe there passed a very tender Scene between us. You added, by way of Compliment that tho' I had many better Titles to recommend me to Posterity; yet perhaps my uncommon Attachment and Friendship to a poor unhappy persecuted Man would not altogether be overlooked.

This Incident, Sir, was somewhat remarkable; and it is impossible, that either you or I cou'd so soon have forgot it. But you have had the Assurance to tell the Story to me twice in a manner so different or rather so opposite, that when I persist, as I do, in this Account, it necessarily follows, that either you or I are Lyar. You imagine, perhaps, that because the Incident passed privately, without any witness, the Question will lie between the Credibility of your Assertion and of mine; But you shall not have this Advantage or Disadvantage, which ever you are pleased to call it. I shall produce against you other Proofs, which will put the Matter beyond all controversy.

(1) You are not aware, that I have a Letter under your hand, which is totally irreconcileable with your Account and confirms mine.[1]

(2) I told the Story next day or the day after to Mr Davenport, with a friendly View, of preventing any such good-natured Artifices for the future. He surely remembers it.

(3) As I thought the Story much to your honour, I told it to several of my Friends here: I even wrote it to M^{de} de Boufflers at Paris. I believe no one will imagine, that I was at that time preparing beforehand an Apology, in case of a Rupture with you; which, of all human Events I shou'd then have thought the most incredible, especially, as we were separated almost for ever, and I still continued to render you the most essential Services.

[1] Rousseau's letter of 22 March (see Appendix G below).

(4) The Story, as I tell it, is consistent and rational. There is not common Sense in your Account. What! because sometimes, when absent in thought, I have a fixed Look or Stare, you suspect me to be a Traytor, and you have the Assurance to tell me of such black and ridiculous Suspicions! Are not most studious Men (and many of them more than I) subject to like Reveries or Fits of Absence, without being exposed to such Suspicions? You do not even pretend, that, before you left London, you had any other Ground of Suspicion against me.

I shall not enter into any Detail with regard to your Letter. The other Articles of it are as much without Foundation as you know this to be. I shall only add in general, that I enjoyed, about a month ago, an uncommon Pleasure, when I reflected, that, thro' many Difficulties and by most assiduous Care and Pains, I had, beyond my most sanguine Expectations, provided for your Repose, Honour, and Fortune. But I soon felt a very sensible Uneasyness, when I found, that you had, wantonly and voluntarily, thrown away all these Advantages, and was the declared Enemy of your own Repose, Fortune, and Honour. I cannot be surprized after this, that you are my Enemy. Adieu, and for ever.

DAVID HUME

P.S.

I send you enclosed a Letter from Mr Boswel, which came to my hand about three Weeks ago. He complains to me very much of your Silence.

* 342. *To* MME LA PRÉSIDENTE DE MEINIÈRES [1]

Lisle Street Leicester Fields 25 of July 1766

Tho' I have great Reason, Madam, to be ashamed, when I am prevented by you, in writing, I own, that your Letter [2]

* MS. in J. Pierpont Morgan Library, New York City; *Annales de la Soc. J.-J. Rousseau*, xvii. 1926; hitherto unpublished in England.

Prof. Albert Schinz, who discovered this letter in the Morgan Library and who made it the basis of an article, *La querelle Rousseau-Hume*, in loc. cit., prints also a contemporary translation of it into French, which is also in the Morgan Library. He discusses the authorship of this translation at some length, and concludes that it must have been made by Mme de Meinières herself. The matter is put beyond all reasonable doubt by her letter in reply to Hume, printed as XIV in Appendix K below, in which she says: 'J'ai communiqué . . . la lettre que vous m'avés fait l'honneur de m'écrire, à M. de Montigny . . . je l'ai donc traduite le plus litteralement qu'il m'a été possible, et je l'ai fait lire à plusieurs personnes. . . .'

[1] Formerly Mme Belot.

[2] No. V in Appendix K below.

gave me a sensible Pleasure: I am happy in retaining some Share in your Memory and Friendship; and I hope, that the same Disposition will incline you to have Indulgence for me in my very culpable Silence. But my Indolence in this particular is unaccountable even to myself. You know, I lived almost with M. de Montigny and his Family and that there are no Persons in the World for whom I have a greater Value: Yet except one Letter to M^{de} Dupré, I have given them no Testimony of my Gratitude or Esteem. I cannot possibly tell a stronger Instance of my ill Behaviour in this particular.

You desire an Account of my Transactions with M. Rousseau, which are certainly the most unexpected and most extraordinary in the World. I shall endeavour to abridge them as much as possible. It is needless to give you a long Detail of my Behaviour towards him while he lived here and in this Neighbourhood, the Marks of Affection and Attachment which I gave him, my Compliance with all his Humours, my constant Occupation in his Service. I was blamed by all my Friends for giving him so much of my Time and Care, and was laughed at by others. All the Letters, which I wrote to any part of the World, were honourable and friendly for him; and he, on his part, gave me the warmest Testimonies of Gratitude, seemed transported whenever he saw me, and after he went to the Country, he wrote me Letters, which I have happily preserved, and which contain Expressions of Friendship that even the Energy of his Pen cou'd not carry farther. I settled him in a most beautiful Country. . . .[1] I received no Answer for above three Weeks, tho' the Post cou'd have brought me the return of my Letter in four Days. It was then I broke out, and told the Affair to my Friends: I needed but to have told it to one Person: The Account flew like Wildfire all over London in a Moment. Every body's Surprize at his Ingratitude to me, whose Friendship towards him had been so generally remarked; the Singularity of the Man and of his Conduct; his Celebrity itself and any Degree of Reputation I may have attained; all these Circumstances made the Story the Subject of general Conversation. I find the same thing has happened at Paris from my Letter to the Baron, which I never desired him to conceal. I have also sent to M. D'Alembert a Copy of Rousseau's Letters and of mine. I had many Reasons

[1] Hume then tells of the settlement of Rousseau with Davenport, the misunderstanding over the pension, Rousseau's letter of 10 June, and his own reply of 26 June.

for not concealing the Affair. I know Rousseau is writing very busily at present, and I have Grounds to think that he intends to fall equally on Voltaire & on me. He himself had told me, that he was composing his Memoirs, in which Justice wou'd be equally done to his own Character, to that of his Friends, and to that of his Enemies. As I had passed so wonderfully from the former Class to the latter, I must expect to make a fine Figure: And what, thought I, if these Memoirs be published after his Death or after mine? In the latter Case, there will be no-one to vindicate my Memory: In the former case, my Vindication will have much less Authenticity. For these Reasons I had once entertained Thoughts of giving the whole instantly to the public; but more mature Reflection made me depart from this Resolution, and I am glad to find, that you concur in the same Opinion.

When I had come to this Part of my Narration, I receive unexpectedly a Letter from Rousseau which had been extorted from him by the Authority of Mr Davenport, the Gentleman with whom he lives. It consists of 18 Folio Pages, in a very small hand, and wou'd make a large Pamphlet. Never was there such a heap of Frenzy and Wickedness united. . . .[1] This is the Substance of the Letter: But wou'd you believe it, that in a Piece so full of Frenzy, Malice, Impertinence & Lyes, there are many Strokes of Genius and Eloquence; and the Conclusion of it is remarkably sublime. The whole is wrote with great Care, and I fancy he intends it for the Press. This gives me no manner of Concern: The Letter will really be a high Panegyric on me; because there is no-one who will not distinguish between the Facts which he acknowledges, and the Chimeras which his Madness & Malice have invented: He even says, that, if my Services were sincere, my Conduct was above human Nature; if they were the Result of a Conspiracy against him, it was below. I own, that I was somewhat anxious about the Affair till I received this mad Letter; but now I am quite at my ease. I do not however find, that, in other Respects he is madder than usual; nor is his Conduct towards me much worse than toward M. Diderot about seven Years ago. I beg my Compliments to Monsr de Menieres to whom I wish you woud explain this Letter. The President de Brosses [2] can read

[1] Hume then summarizes Rousseau's letter of 10 July.

[2] Charles de Brosses (1709–77), first President of the Parlement de Bourgoyne; author of works on geography, history, etymology, and of an edition

it in the Original: Please mark to him my Respects. I coud wish also that Mons[r] de Montigny saw it. I have not room to subscribe myself regularly as I ought.

DAVID HUME

A Madame Madame la Presidente de Meinieres rue Poissoniere pres le Rampart a PARIS.

*343. *To* HORACE WALPOLE

Saturday Forenoon [26 July 1766].

Dear Sir,

When I came home last night, I found on my table a very long letter from D'Alembert,[1] who tells me, that, on receiving from me an account of my affair with Rousseau, he summoned a meeting of all my literary friends at Paris, and found them all unanimously of the same opinion with himself, and of a contrary opinion to me, with regard to my conduct. They all think I ought to give to the public a narrative of the whole. However, I persist still more closely in my first opinion, especially after receiving the last mad letter. D'Alembert tells me, that it is of great importance for me to justify myself from having any hand in the letter from the King of Prussia: I am told by Crawford[2] that you had wrote it a fortnight before I left Paris, but did not show it to a mortal, for fear of hurting me; a delicacy of which I am very sensible. Pray recollect, if it was so. Tho I do not intend to publish, I am collecting all the original pieces, and shall connect them by a concise narrative. It is necessary for me to have that letter and Rousseau's answer. Pray assist me in this work. About what time, do you think, were they printed?

I am, dear Sir,

Your most obedient humble servant,

DAVID HUME.[3]

* Walpole, *Works*, iv. 257; Burton, ii. 355.

of Sallust. There are two letters from him to Hume among the MSS., R.S.E., which were printed by Burton in *Eminent Persons*.

[1] Dated 21 July 1766 (No. VIII in Appendix K below).

[2] John Crawford (died 1814), son of Patrick Crawford of Auchenaimes, William Mure's friend; often known as 'Fish' Crawford; a young man about town, and a particular friend of Horace Walpole and Mme du Deffand; M.P. Renfrewshire, 1774.

[3] For Walpole's reply to this letter see No. XII in Appendix K below.

* 344. *To the* Marquise du Deffand [1]

Lisle Street, Leicester Fields,
5me d'Août 1766.

Je me suis senti fort emu à la lecture d'un passage de votre lettre à M. Crawford. Non! Madame, ce ne fut qu'avec un déplaisir mortel que je perdis le moindre terrein auprès de vous, et que je me vis reduit à changer le titre de votre ami, pour celui d'être simplement une de vos connoissances. Vous sçavez que j'ai fait tous mes efforts pour résister au courant qui m'entraînoit. Je vous ai même tendu la main, en vous appellant à mon secours. Combien de fois vous ai-je dit que j'étois prêt à épouser les affections de mon amie, mais que j'avois de la répugnance à adopter ses animosités? Je vous conjure, ma chère Dame, de peser, encore une fois, ces sentimens dans les ballances de votre jugement exquis et de l'usage ordinaire du monde; et quand même elles ne pancheroient pas du côté qui me seroit le plus favorable, que le désir ardent que j'ai de recouvrer votre amitié l'emporte.[2]

Vous aurez sans doute appris la querelle dans laquelle je me

* Formerly among the Waller MSS.; *Times Lit. Supp.*, 3 June 1920 (published by Dr. Paget Toynbee).

[1] Marie de Vichy-Chamrond (1697–1780), m. (1718) Jean-Baptiste de la Lande (died 1750), marquis du Deffand; mistress of the Regent Duke of Orleans for a fortnight only, *c.* 1722, and of the President Hénault, *c.* 1730–70; installed herself in the Convent of S. Joseph, Rue Saint-Dominique, 1747, and there for the next thirty years figured as the most distinguished salonnière of the century; became totally blind, 1752. Horace Walpole met her first in Oct. 1765, and was not very favourably impressed; he called her 'an old blind *débauchée* of wit' (*Letters*, vi. 312). But soon after, he became her devoted admirer, while on her side there commenced that strange sentiment for him, which lasted till her death, and which has been called 'une tendresse exaltée . . . dont le vrai nom échappe, tant celui d'amitié serait faible et celui d'amour dérisoire.' (Quoted in footnote to Walpole's *Letters*, vi. 312.) There are four letters from her to Hume among the MSS., R.S.E. His relations with her are sufficiently indicated in the text above, and in the notes that follow. (See also article by Dr. Paget Toynbee, *Modern Language Review*, Oct. 1929.)

[2] As I understand this paragraph it means that Hume had tried to take no side in the quarrel between d'Alembert and Mlle de Lespinasse on the one side and Mme du Deffand on the other, which broke out shortly after he arrived in Paris in 1763; but that he had found it impossible to remain good friends with Mme du Deffand if he continued to frequent Mlle de Lespinasse's salon; and so had been reluctantly excluded from Mme du Deffand's salon in the later portion of his stay in Paris.

trouve engagé avec un fou et un méchant, du caractère duquel vous avez toujours mieux jugé que moi.[1] Toute sorte de querelle est désagréable, mais celle-ci est moins que d'ordinaire; les fondemens en sont trop claires pour qu'aucune personne puisse suspendre son jugement là-dessus. Notre ami, M. Walpole, est compromis dans la querelle, ainsi que M. Dalembert. Rousseau dit que je suis entré dans un complot avec ces deux Messieurs à Paris pour le perdre; que M. Dalembert est auteur de la lettre du Roi de Prusse; et que M. Walpole n'est que le prête-nom. Il dit qu'il connoit ce fait par conviction intérieure aussi clairement que s'il l'avoit vu. Tous le reste de ses accusations, dont on pourroit faire une ample brochure, est également extravagant. Surtout, la méthode que j'ai mis en usage pour le ruiner est un peu extraordinaire: Elle consiste en l'avoir placé chez un Gentilhomme, fort honnête homme, qui jouit de 7000 livres sterling de rente, auquel il ne paye que 30 livres sterling pour sa pension et pour celle de sa gouvernante, et en lui avoir procuré une pension du Roi. J'enverrai une copie de tous les papiers à D'Alembert, puisqu'il est compris dans la dispute. M. Walpole en rit; et il a raison.

Votre ami, le petit Crawford, n'est qu'un vaut-rien: Rendez-moi, je vous supplie, cette part de vos affections, qu'il mérite de perdre et dont il m'a privé. Assurez de mon souvenir votre *ancien et féal ami*; titre que j'ambitionne et que je ne désespère pas, un jour ou l'autre, de posséder. Agréez, Madame, mes respects très assurez: J'ai l'honneur detre, Madame,

Votre très humble et très obéissant Serviteur,

David Hume.[2]

[1] Mme du Deffand's attitude to the Hume-Rousseau quarrel, as revealed in her letters to Walpole, was fairly impartial: she blamed both. Writing to Walpole on 5 Aug. 1766, she says: 'Où prenez-vous que je ne condamne pas extrèmement Jean-Jacques? Je l'ai toujours si méprisé, que ce dernier trait ne m'a point surprise; c'est un coquin, c'est un fou. Mais je n'estime guere le Paysan [her nickname for Hume].' She was also rather maliciously amused at the disturbance which the quarrel made among the Temple group—the Prince of Conti, Mme de Boufflers, Mme de Luxembourg, &c.

[2] Writing to Walpole on 18 Aug. 1766 Mme du Deffand says: 'Je vais vous apprendre quelque chose qui m'a bien surprise et qui vous surprendra peut-être aussi. J'ai reçu avant-hier une lettre du Paysan, la plus honnête et la plus tendre; il s'excuse de sa conduite, il tâche de la justifier; il parle de sa querelle, il vous nomme en disant "notre ami M. Walpole", il est jaloux du petit Craufurd, il désire d'être aussi bien avec moi à son retour qu'il l'était à son arrivée en France. Je ne me presserai point de lui faire réponse; dites-moi quel ton je dois prendre avec lui; j'attendrai vos conseils

* 345. *To* ANNE-ROBERT-JACQUES TURGOT [1]

5 of Augst 1766

Do not entertain the least Suspicion, My Dear Sir, that your Letters [2] were not extremely acceptable and agreeable to me; tho' they have been occasioned by a disagreeable Subject and tho' you differ sometimes in Opinion from me. My Friends to whom I have shown the Letters of this .... (I leave you to fill the blank) are also of different Sentiments among themselves: All of them allow that there is a strong Mixture of Frenzy and of Wickedness in them; but some maintain, that the former Ingredient prevails and some the latter. But on the whole, what Epithet cou'd you give to a Man like this, when you must allow, that it is safer to take a Basilisk or a Rattle-Snake into your Bosom than to have the least Intercourse with him; and that above all things it is sovereignly dangerous to lay him under Obligations? He now allows, that it is above four months since he put into the public Papers the most atrocious Article against me, tho' neither I, nor any body else then understood it. This long Letter itself which he wrote after near a month Deliberation is full of the utmost Malice, Violence and Impertinence. What think you of this Passage near the beginning? 'Le premier soin de ceux qui trainent des noirceurs est de se mettre a couvert des preuves juridiques. Il ne serait pas bon leur intenter des procés. La conviction intérieure admet un autre genre de preuves qui réglent les sentiments d'un honnete homme: vous scaurez sur quoi sont fondés les miens.' You see then that he

* MS. in archives du château de Lantheuil; hitherto unpublished in England.

---

et je m'y conformerai. . . . Je vous mandai hier que j'attendrais vos conseils pour répondre à M. Hume. Je change d'avis, et je lui écrirai par cet ordinaire-ci.' (*Lettres à Walpole*, i. 104 and 108.)

Her letter to Hume is given in Appendix K below.

[1] Anne-Robert-Jacques Turgot (1727–81), baron de l'Aulne, economist and statesman, who has been called the one sane Frenchman of the first eminence in the eighteenth century; a friend of d'Alembert, Mlle de Lespinasse, the Trudaines, and the physiocrats; Intendant of Limoges, 1761–74; Minister of Marine, 1774; Contrôleur-Général des Finances, 1774–6; dismissed, 1776.

[2] The earliest letter of Turgot to Hume extant among the MSS., R.S.E. is dated 23 July [1766]. It is printed in full in *Eminent Persons*, 130 ff., and in *Œuvres de Turgot*, 1914, ii. 495 ff. Extracts relating to Rousseau are given in Appendix K below.

has never had a Moment's relenting with regard to me. For he proceeds, in very good Language, to prove, from his internal Conviction that I am a perfidious Traitor, and a Villain, and one of the deepest Rascals in the World. You wou'd think it were as easy for me to have had an internal as well as external Conviction of the contrary: No! but he hates me; and he sees every thing about me in the blackest Colours. But why? For no other reason, but because I have laid him under the greatest Obligations. I need not mention about a dozen of palpable Lyes, which he had inserted in his Letter in order to help out his internal Convictions. But I shall not anticipate your Judgement: I send the whole to D'Alembert with a short Narrative to connect the Letters; and if he and my Friends at Paris think fit to publish them, they shall be very welcome. The Pacquet will probably arrive before the first of September. I beg you to peruse it with care, and your Sentiments will have a great Weight with me.

I agree with you, that a little Precipitation after such Injuries, is but a slight Fault, yet really I cannot reproach myself even with that Fault. I immediatly saw with what a dangerous Man I had to do, on account of his Talents, his Malice and his lying, and I determined not to keep Silence, till he shou'd give the Blow. I was indeed anxious till I received this long Letter, as not knowing the Extent nor Grounds of his Imputations; but now I am perfectly at Ease: The partizans of Rousseau have only to chuse whether he is a Villain or a Madman, or a Mixture of both, which is my own Opinion.

Horace Walpole is perfectly innocent as well as M. D'Alembert and I, in this whole Affair. He always acknowleged that Letter as soon as Copies of it were dispersed. He has now acknowleged it under his hand, as D'Alembert wou'd tell you. When you see D'Alembert desire him to show you all my Letters: For there is nothing which needs be kept a Secret. I wou'd not have any Secret in this whole Affair: It concerns too much my Character, to have it buryed in Darkness. And on all accounts I am extremely anxious to stand well in your Judgement. You imagine, that I had employed some Pleasantry against Rousseau while he was in Paris; and that this gave Occasion to Walpole's Letter. But surely, there never was any such thing; and Mr Walpole informs me that his Letter was wrote before Rousseau's Arrival at Paris, tho' totally unknown to me. In this long list of Grievances, Rousseau mentions no such things.

But to turn the Discourse to something more agreable, tho' I find I must still have the Misfortune to differ from you. I approve however very much of your Premium;[1] but why limit so much the Discourse of the Memorialists by taking it for granted as a certain Truth, that all Taxes fall upon the Proprietors of Land? You know, that no Government in any Age or any Country of the World, ever went upon that Supposition: Taxes have always been supposed to rest upon those who pay them by consuming the Commodity; and this universal Practice joined to the obvious Appearances of things leaves at least room for Doubt. Perhaps it would not have been amiss to have proposed the Question itself as an Object of Dispute.

I am very sensible of the Bishop of Lavaur's [2] Attention in sending me his Sermon. I have heard much good of it, and shall read it with Attention and Curiosity. His Subject is better for Eloquence than that of his Friend the Archbishop of Tholouse.[3]

I am very sorry to hear, on all hands, such bad Accounts of Sir James Macdonald. There is little Reason, I fear, to expect his Recovery, and surely we shall lose in him a very extraordinary young Man in all Respects.[4]

I coud wish that M^de^ Du Pré and M. Trudaine had just Notions of my Conduct in this strange Affair with Rousseau. I trusted to their being in Paris about this time and have not wrote to them about it, being mortally tired of the Subject. If M^de^ du Pré comes to Town, be so good as to carry her my Letters to D'Alembert or at least explain to her and M. Tru-

[1] In his letter of 23 July Turgot enclosed the particulars of a prize offered in July 1765 by La Société d'Agriculture du Limousin (of which he was president) for the best 'Mémoire dans lequel on aurait le mieux démontré et apprécié l'effet de l'impôt indirect sur le revenu des propriétaires des biens-fonds'. The competition was to close in January 1767, and Turgot says that essays written in English will be accepted. He seems to have hoped that Hume would compete.

[2] Jean-de-Dieu-Raimond de Boisgelin de Cucé (1732–1804), Bishop of Lavaur, 1765–70; Archbishop of Aix, 1770–90. On 12 June 1766 he pronounced the Funeral Sermon on Stanislas, King of Poland, who had died at Lunéville in February. Mme du Deffand called the Bishop 'un petit farfadet, métaphysicien, rhéteur, analyseur, sophiste, etc., etc.' (*Lettres à Walpole*, i. 66), and of the sermon itself said, 'ce n'est que du verbiage, des galimatias d'un petit bel esprit' (ibid., i. 71). But then she was prejudiced, for he was a partisan of Mlle de Lespinasse.

[3] Étienne-Charles de Loménie de Brienne (1727–94), Archbishop of Toulouse, 1763–88. His *Oraison funèbre du Dauphin* had just been published.

[4] He died in Rome about a week after the date of this letter.

daine the Contents of them. A Friend of mine has, I believe, wrote something of the Subject to M. de Montigny. I beg very sincerely the Continuance of your Friendship and promise you a very sincere return. I am Dear Sir

Your most obedient and most humble Servant

DAVID HUME

P.S. Mr Smith was entirely mistaken in his Conjecture. Rousseau's Letter to General Conway was a plain Refusal, and was so understood both by the General and by me; and is confessed to be so meant by himself. You will find when you see all the Papers that every Circumstance of this Affair is more atrocious one than another.

* 346. *To the* COMTESSE DE BOUFFLERS

Lisle Street Leicester Fields, 12 Aug., 1766.

Nothing could more rejoice me than the sight of your handwriting after such long silence.[1] My pleasure was not diminished by the contents of your letter: for though you reprove me with some vehemence, it is at the same time in so friendly and so reasonable a manner, that I kiss the rod which beats me, and give you as sincere thanks for your admonitions, as I ever did for any of your civilities and services. I am sensible that nothing could be more unsuitable to my attachment towards you, and my respect towards the Prince of Conti, than to have conducted myself so as that this story should have come to your ears by any other canal than through myself. But I considered you as one hundred leagues distant from Paris. I wrote indeed to Baron d'Olbach, without either recommending or expecting secrecy: but I thought this story, like others, would be told to eight or ten people; in a week or two, twenty or thirty more might hear of it, and it would require three months before it would reach you at Pougues. I little imagined, that a private story, told to a private gentleman, could run over a whole kingdom in a moment: if the King of England had declared war against the King of France, it could not have been more suddenly the subject of conversation. This, I own, misled me; I delayed writing to you a few posts, expecting every day to

* *Priv. Corr.*, 204.

[1] Her letter begun on 22 July and continued on 25 July 1766 (No. IX in Appendix K below).

hear something that would enable me to give you a more decisive view of the affair, and at the same time might enable you to give me that counsel on which I so much depended. I ask you ten thousand pardons. You see my error proceeded only from a blunder in my reasoning. I beg it of you to make the Prince of Conti sensible of my contrition, after you have yourself pardoned me.

As to the other point, more material than any failure of civility even towards you, I mean my too great violence and precipitation in accusing Rousseau, I beg of you to weigh the following considerations:—Think of the effect of such an outrageous letter, wrote after a long train of civilities and services, and wrote at the very moment that I had consummated all these and brought them to a happy period. Consider also, that I immediately discovered, that this rage, if real, was not the result of a sudden passion in him, but had been secretly boiling in his breast during near three months, and had never relented a moment, even while I was rendering him the greatest services.

Reflect likewise, that his letter contained a most studied premeditated lie against me, viz. his account of our evening conversation the last time I saw him in London. You know I wrote you an account of that conversation, very opposite to that which he delivers. It was impossible that any report or mistake could mislead him in that particular: and nothing could aggravate the atrocity of such a lie; of a lie invented by him against me. But what chiefly determined me at once to break all measures with him and to make our rupture as public as possible, was, the consideration of his memoirs; in which I was, no doubt, to make a fine figure. I have mentioned this circumstance to you already. You see it is always uppermost in his thoughts. He flatters me obliquely with his panegyrics in his letter of the 22d of March: he threatens me with his satire in that of the 23d of June. What could I do in that situation? If I was to keep our rupture a secret, he would multiply his lies without number; and these would certainly gain the attention, and might gain the belief of the world, if supposed to come from a man who was living in friendship with me. The quarrel, you say, might have been made up: but a quarrel without the least pretence or reasons, never could be made up; for the cause still remained, viz. his obligations to me, which he never could forgive. There could not surely be less occasion of quarrel, if he had had common sense or gratitude, than when I was one hundred and fifty miles distant from him, and was occupying myself continually in his service.

Allow me to tell you, my dear friend, that the event has justified my reasoning. Though I wrote him a very decent letter, as you saw, I got back a studied oration, or invective, against me, of eighteen folio pages, full of the same virulence and lies contained in his short epistle. I have given some accounts of it to D'Alembert, who will communicate them to you. I should have wrote the same to you; but I knew not where you was, nor how to direct to you, nor when you was expected in Paris. I have drawn up the whole story in a short narrative, and have inserted all the letters and papers; and have delivered the pacquet to General Conway, to be sent by the first courier to M. D'Alembert. It is not with a view of having it published, which both he and I are averse to, but to lie by him in case of need, as he is so unexpectedly and absurdly brought into the quarrel. I have struck out your name in one place, as suspecting that you would not care to be mentioned in such an affair. When you peruse this long letter of Rousseau, you will think that it aggravates extremely his guilt, except only in one particular, that it gives us reason to suspect him an arrant madman.

All the conjectures that have been formed at Paris, are without foundation. No mortal ever gave him false information against me: he never heard of any such pleasantry as that you mention, if such a thing ever existed. He acknowledges I behaved always towards him with perfect civility while we lived together; but yet I was all along a perfidious traitor, in the manner you shall see, but never, I am sure, will be able to conjecture.

But, dear Madam, I find, that imperceptibly I owe him still a greater grudge than any I have mentioned: he occupies all my thoughts while I am writing to you, and gives me no leisure either to speak to you of myself, or any of our common friends. I hope the waters of Pougues agreed perfectly with the Prince of Conti. I hear Madame de Barbantane does not go to Florence, which pleases me very much. I ought to have wrote to her about this unhappy affair; but in desiring you to communicate to her my letter, I considered myself as writing to you in common. Lord Tavistock is very happy, as is also the Duke of Bedford, on account of the increase of his family by the accession of a new boy. I passed some days at Woburn lately. You know that every thing is decided here by bets. The Duke has taken My Lady Tavistock for a third son, against any woman in England who is not pregnant. I passed yesterday with Lord Holdernesse at Zion Hill: you may conjecture that you was mentioned at least once or twice by us. I was much satisfied with his account of the state of your health. The Bishop of Lavaur was so kind as to send me a copy of his sermon, which is as good as a sermon and a panegyric can well be. Your son still leaves [1] you soon for Italy; and you are probably at this moment occupied in more worthy and more interesting details than any which can come to you from this part of the world. Write me, however, a short note, after you have perused my narrative. Believe me to be ever yours, with the greatest sincerity.

* 347. *To* JEAN-CHARLES TRUDAINE DE MONTIGNY [2]

Lisle Street, Leicester Fields, 12 of Augt 1766

My dear Sir

I have used the Freedom to send to you in two Pacquets by this Post the whole Train of my Correspondence with Rousseau, connected by a short Narrative. I hope you will have Leizure to peruse it. The Story is incredible as well as inconceivable, were it not founded on such authentic Documents: Surely never was there so much Wickedness and Madness combined in one human Creature; nor did ever any one meet with such a Return for such signal Services, as those I performed towards him. But I am told, that he used to say to Duclos and others, that he hated all those to whom he owed any Obligations: In that Case, I am fully entitled to his Animosity.

I am really at a Loss what use to make of this Collection. The Story, I am told, is very much the Object of Conversation at Paris: Tho' my Conduct has been entirely innocent, or rather indeed very meritorious, it happens, no doubt, as is usual in such Ruptures, that I will bear a Part of the blame; from which a Publication of these Papers woud entirely free me: Yet I own

* MS. in J. Pierpont Morgan Library, New York City; Morrison, *Catalogue of Autographs*, ii. 318; Burton, ii. 347 f.

[1] *Sic* in printed text, but probably a misprint for 'will leave'.

[2] This letter was supposed by Burton (following Henry Brougham) to have been addressed to the Abbé Le Blanc, but a comparison of it with Trudaine de Montigny's reply dated 23 Aug. 1766 (see No. XXI in Appendix K below) shows that it must have been addressed to him.

I have an Antipathy and Reluctance to appeal to the Public; and fear that such a Publication woud be the only Blame I cou'd incur in this Affair. You know that no-body's Judgement weighs farther with me than Yours: Think a little of the Matter: if M^de^ Dupré were in Town, I wou'd desire her to give these Papers a Perusal, and tell me her Opinion. Unhappily Mon^r^ Trudaine woud only understand the French Part, which is by far the most considerable. What wou'd his Friend, Fontenelle,[1] have done in this Situation? I am as great a Lover of Peace as he, and have kept myself as free from all literary Quarrels: But surely, neither he nor any other Person was ever engaged in a Controversy with a Man of so much Malice, of such a profligate Disposition to Lyes, and such great Talents. It is nothing to dispute my Style or my Abilities as an Historian or a Philosopher; My Books ought to answer for themselves, or they are not worth the defending: To fifty Writers, who have attacked me on this head, I never made the least Reply: But this is a different Case: Imputations are here thrown on my Morals and my Conduct; and tho' my Case is so clear as not to admit of the least Controversy, yet it is only clear to those who know it, and I am uncertain how far the Public in Paris are in the Case. At London, a Publication woud be regarded as entirely superfluous.

I must desire you to send these Papers to D'Alembert after you have read them. M. Turgot will get them from him: I shoud desire that *he* saw them before he sets out for his Government.

Does not M^de^ de Montigny laugh at me, that I shoud have sent her but a few Weeks ago the Portrait of Rousseau done from an Original in my Possession and shoud now send you these Papers, which prove him to be one of the worst Men that perhaps ever existed; if his Frenzy be not some Apology for him. I beg my Compliments to M. & M^de^ de Fourqueux:[2] And am with great Truth & Sincerity My Dear Sir

Your most affectionate humble Servant

DAVID HUME

P.S.

I am sorry to tell you, that our Accounts of the poor Chevalier Macdonald are very bad.

[1] Bernard le Bovier de Fontenelle (1657–1757).

[2] Bouvard de Fourqueux, a friend of Turgot's, and sometime Contrôleur-Général de Finances under Louis XVI. Trudaine de Montigny married his daughter.

* 348. *To* Adam Smith

[Lisle Street, Leicester Fields,
August, 1766]

Dear Smith

There is a Bookseller at Paris, one Dessain,[1] who has some Character, but has play'd me a very ugly Trick. I bought of him two Volumes of Buffon's Natural History and paid him thirty Livres [2] for them; but as M. Buffon made me a Present of them afterwards, Dessain took them back. I gave him a pretty large Commission of Books to be sent to me to the Care of David Wilson;[3] and I left among the rest, these two Volumes of Buffon, together with Mrs Macaulay's History [4] and some other Books. He has sent over several Parcels to Mr Wilson, but will neither send over my Books, nor answer my Letters nor take any Notice of me. He lives on the Quay des Augustins, not far from you: I wish you woud speak to him and threaten him a little. Tell him I shall prosecute him either myself on my Return to Paris or by Order, if he do not send over my Books & Money. I wonder he acts so foolishly: For my Commission woud be more profitable to him, than so small a Pittance as this sum.

You may see in M. Dalembert's hands the whole Narrative of my Affair with Rousseau along with the whole Train of Correspondence. Pray is it not a nice Problem, whether he be not an arrant Villain or an arrant Madman or both: The last is my Opinion; but the Villain seems to me to predominate most in his Character. I shall not publish them unless forc'd, which you will own to be a very great Degree of Self denial. My Conduct, in this Affair, woud do me a great deal of Honour;

* MS., R.S.E.; Burton, ii. 348 f. (incomplete).

[1] For references to Messrs. Dessaint and Sailland, booksellers in Paris, see Rousseau's *Correspondence*, *passim*.

[2] The livre at this period was worth about 1*s*.

[3] The London bookseller (see note 3 on p. 465 of vol. i).

[4] Catherine Sawbridge (1731–91), m. (1) Dr. George Macaulay, and (2) William Graham. Her *History of England* was published in 1763, and her then husband (Macaulay) sent a copy to Hume in Paris. Hume does not seem to have acknowledged receipt of it, for Macaulay wrote on 22 March 1764, telling Hume that it had been sent some five months before, and adding, rather ironically: 'I now thought proper to send you this intelligence, least you shou'd imagine that we were chargeable with any want of punctuality.' (MS., R.S.E.; *Eminent Persons*, 111 f.)

and his woud blast him for ever; and blast his Writings at the same time: For as these have been exalted much above their Merit, when his personal Character falls, they woud of Course fall below their Merit. I am however apprehensive that in the End I shall be oblig'd to publish. About two or three days ago, there was an Article in the St James's Chronicle copyd from the Brussels Gazette, which pointed at this Dispute. This may probably put Rousseau in a Rage; he will publish something, which may oblige me for my own Honour to give the Narrative to the Public. There will be no Reason to dread a long Train of disagreeable Controversy: One Publication begins and ends it on my Side. Pray, tell me your Judgement of my Work, if it deserves the Name: Tell D'alembert I make him absolute Master to retrench or alter what he thinks proper, in order to suit it to the Latitude of Paris.

Were you & I together Dear Smith we shoud shed Tears at present for the Death of poor Sir James Macdonald. We coud not possibly have sufferd a greater Loss than in that valuable young Man.

I am

Yours most sincerely

DAVID HUME

P.S.

In a little time, I go down to pass a few Weeks with my Friends in Scotland but direct still to me at Miss Elliots: My Letters will follow me. I wish I had a strong unanswerable Motive to determine me whether I shall live henceforth in London or in Paris. My Inclination and indeed my Resolutions lead me to the latter place; but my Reason points out the former. I for [ ][1] :ar, that I woud have a great Facility to continue my History [ ][1] Clamour of Faction on both Sides seems to have subsided: But c[ ][1]me a good Reason, why I shoud put myself to that Trouble? [ ][1] Compliments to Baron D Holbach.

A Monsieur Monsieur Smith Gentilhomme Anglois Hotel du Parc roiale, Fauxbourg St Germain a ~~Paris~~[2] a compiegne a compiegne

[1] Autograph torn.

[2] Struck through, and 'a Compiegne' added twice, in another hand.

* 349. *To the* Marquise de Barbentane

Lisle Street, Leicester Fields,
29 of August, 1766.

It is not easy for you, dear Madam, to imagine the pleasure which your letter gave me.[1] Nothing could be more obliging than your writing to me on this occasion, and in such obliging terms. It was the true method of making me compensation for all the vexations occasioned by so strange and surprizing an incident, which surely never had its parallel in the world. But though I have long ago forgot all the uneasiness which it gave me, and still more when I find that you take part in it, I have suffered a real loss, which I cannot easily repair. I was just ready to set out for Scotland, in order to visit my friends, and take leave of them, when I received that horrible letter, accusing me of the blackest crimes, in return for all my favours and good offices. I was then necessarily detained at London, in order to clear up so capital a charge. I was engaged in a correspondence with Paris, which I could not in honour neglect, and thus a great deal of time has been uselessly and disagreeably lost. But it is with pleasure I hear from Lord Tavistock, that you are not to attend M. de Barbantane into Italy, and that we may still hope to enjoy your company at Paris. I should have been sorry to hear of your setting out for Florence at all; but much more without my being able to bid you adieu.

I am very well satisfied, that you think with regard to this quarrel in the same manner with Madame de Boufflers; but I am persuaded both you and she will change somewhat your sentiments after you have seen the suite of papers which I have desired her to communicate to you, after she has received them from M. D'Alembert. You will see that the only possible alleviation of this man's crime is, that he is entirely mad; and even then, he will be allowed a dangerous and pernicious madman, and of the blackest and most atrocious mind.

The King and Queen of England expressed a strong desire to see these papers, and I was obliged to put them into their hand. They read them with avidity, and entertain the same sentiments that must strike every one. The King's opinion confirms me in the resolution not to give them to the public,

* *Priv. Corr.*, 209 ff.

[1] For extracts from Mme de Barbentane's letter of 3 Aug. 1766 see No. XV in Appendix K below.

unless I be forced to it by some attack on the side of my adversary, which it will therefore be wisdom in him to avoid.

We hear that you was much alarmed in France with the prospect of war, upon Mr Pitt's being taken into the ministry.[1] That apprehension was always without foundation; but now more than ever, on account of his losing all his popularity, merely on account of his accepting a peerage.[2] Of all the caprices of the people, in all ages, never was any more ridiculous and surprizing. Lord Chatham is as much detested as ever Mr Pitt was adored, without its being possible to assign any reason for this alteration. The folly, it is true, will probably pass in time; but this minister will never fully recover his former consideration, on account of his leaving the House of Commons, which is the great scene of business.

We have heard lately very strange stories from France, which excite horror in every one, and give me a sensible concern. You conjecture that I mean the atrocious punishment of the Chevalier de la Barre by the Parliament of Paris, on account of some youthful levities.[3] Such of my friends as are not over favourable to France, insult me on this occasion; and surely, if our accounts be true, nothing can do less honour to the country. It is strange, that such cruelty should be found among a people so celebrated for humanity, and so much bigotry amid so much knowledge and philosophy. I am pleased to hear, that the indignation was as general in Paris as it is in all foreign countries.

I saw to-day an Italian abbé, and talked to him about the Court of Florence. He says that it has become a very disagreeable place, and that nothing can exceed the narrowness of mind in the Archduke[4] and Archduchess.[5] That princess rubs off,

[1] Pitt came into the Ministry as Lord Privy Seal in July 1766. The Duke of Grafton became First Lord of the Treasury and nominally Prime Minister.

[2] Writing to Mann on 1 Aug. 1766, Horace Walpole says: 'Well! Europe must have done talking of Mr Pitt; there is no longer such a man. He is Lord Privy Seal, and Earl of Chatham. I don't know how Europe will like it, but the City and the mob are very angry.' (*Letters*, vii. 32.)

[3] Jean-François Lefèvre, chevalier de la Barre (1747–66), was beheaded at Abbeville for alleged sacrilege. Voltaire wrote a famous pamphlet on the subject, *Relation de la mort du chevalier de la Barre*.

[4] Peter Leopold (1747–92), afterwards the Emperor Leopold II; succeeded his father as Grand Duke of Tuscany, 1765; and as Emperor, 1790. He was no favourite with his Italian subjects, being cold and reserved in manner.

[5] Maria Louisa, daughter of Charles III of Spain, married to Leopold, 1764.

with her own hands, the paint and patches from the faces of the ladies, and makes them presents of tippets to cover their bosoms. I beseech you, never go to a place where you must be virtuous by constraint, lest you should take an inclination to become otherwise. You may, perhaps be allowed, as Ambassadress from France, to keep your *rouge*; but are you sure that you may not take a quarrel with virtue, when you see it accompanied with so much folly and ridicule? I beg my compliments to Madame de Vierville, and that you will believe me, with the greatest regard,

Madam,

Your most obedient humble servant,

DAVID HUME.

* 350. *To* RICHARD DAVENPORT

Dear Sir

I have been detain'd so long in London, that Dr Armstrong has left me above a fortnight ago;[1] and now I am hurryd down to Scotland, and by another Road & in another Company; so that it will be impossible for me to pay you a Visit at Davenport. I assure you, that I regreat this Accident very sincerely; I proposd to myself a great deal of Pleasure in passing some days with you in your Country Seat; and I wanted very much to show you the whole Train of Correspondence between your Guest & me. I am sorry, that that Affair has made so great a Noise all over Europe: But I found myself obligd to make the Rupture public, in order to prevent the Effects of his Malice against me: He is writing his Memoirs, and intends to blacken me, as much as possible: He threatens me in a Letter with this Vengeance; and I forsaw, that these Memoirs might be published either after my Death or after his. In the former Case, there wou'd be no body to tell the Story or to vindicate my Memory. In the second Case, my Apology, being wrote against a dead Man, woud lose much of its Authenticity. For this Reason, I have drawn a Narrative of the whole Transaction, inserting all the Letters on both Sides, which indeed compose the far greatest part of the Piece: Among the rest, I insert that long

* B.M. MSS. Add. 29626; Courtois, 281 ff.; hitherto unpublished in England.

[1] See Letter 340 above.

Letter of Rousseau, which contains a full Detail of his Grievances against me, and which I have already mentiond to you. I intended to have shown you the whole Narrative. I have made one Copy, which I have deposited in a sure hand at Paris: I have given another to Lord Hertford, and I keep another to myself. These will remain in Reserve, till Rousseau attacks me, which I expect every day; and I wonder indeed he has delay'd it so long. I know not whether so much Precaution on my part be not superfluous; tho' the Malignity and Talents of your Guest render him very dangerous. There is scarce, however, a Person in Europe, who does not look upon him at present as very mad or very wicked or as both; and if the public Voice were not apt to be soon obliterated, I might safely rest my Defence upon it.

When I say, that he is a very dangerous Man, I do not mean, that he is likely to prove so to you: As you have been so happy as never to make yourself known to the Public as an Author, he is less likely to entertain any Jealousy against you; and he may submit with the less Repugnance to the great Obligations, which he owes you. Your living at such a Distance from him will also serve not a little to preserve your mutual Friendship. For these Reasons, I shall use the Freedom to repeat my Exhortations to you, that you continue, as long as possible, the same good Offices towards him, which you have so charitably begun. Notwithstanding his atrocious Conduct towards me, I shoud be very sorry to see him abandoned by all the World: Your Knowlege of his Character will only serve you to use the greater Precautions against him: And he is now a better Object of your generous Humanity, that he has been, in this Instance, so unfortunate in his Behaviour.

He must now expect to live altogether on his own Funds without any Pension. Unhappy Man! to deprive me so cruelly of the delicious Pleasure I felt in serving him; and at the same time to oppose so violently his own Interest. I was oblig'd to show the whole Train of the Correspondence to General Conway, which cuts off all his hopes from that Quarter. But what is worse, the King has heard of the Affair, and express'd a great Curiosity to know the whole of it; so that I was oblig'd to send my Narrative to His Majesty. Rousseau needs not complain, that only one Side is shown: For as his long Letter is inserted, his Pleading is very fully heard against me.

If you do me the Favour to write me, please to direct to me as usual. For I shall not probably be long in Scotland; and my

Landladies have Directions to send my Letters after me. I am Dear Sir with great Sincerity Your most obedient humble Servant

DAVID HUME

Lisle Street Leicester Fields,
2 Septr 1766

* 351. *To* ANNE-ROBERT-JACQUES TURGOT

[London, late in September 1766.][1]

I agree heartily with you, My Dear Sir, that M. Rousseau is a Madman and I shall add, if you please, that he always was so; but this will, by no means, excuse him, or save him from more black Imputations. On the contrary it is by means of his Madness that his other bad Qualities appear in their full Light, and perhaps become more dangerous on that account and can less be guarded against. For Instance What can be more blameable than his Conduct with regard to M. Dalembert? There was no manner of Connexion, which led from M. Walpole to him; and Rousseau was only carry'd to suspect him as an Accomplice in that Piece of Pleasantry, on account of his own Rage and Malignity against him. But on what was this Malignity founded? Plainly on nothing, as he himself, in a manner confesses, but because d'Alembert did not pay him a Visit when he was at Paris. The Truth is: d'Alembert intended to have waited on him, but I innocently prevented him by telling him, that Rousseau complained so bitterly of being harrassed with Company, that I thought it better to let him alone. Think then of the Atrocity of that Man's Mind, who could treasure up such a Stock of Malice from so slight an Offence; and think of his Falshood and Quackery in continually pretending to fly into Solitude while he is watching with the most anxious Sollicitude, the Honour of Visits, and resenting the smallest Neglects of this kind.

But the extreme Depravity of his Heart appears the more strongly in his Conduct towards me: For not only there was not the smallest Chain that led from Mr Walpole to me, not the smallest Thread, not the smallest Hair; but there was an infinite reason to exempt me from all Suspicion: What then induced

* MS. in archives du château de Lantheuil; Léon Say, *Turgot* (Eng. trans.), 53 ff. (incomplete).

[1] This undated letter is written in answer to Turgot's of 27 July and 7 Sept. 1766 (see Appendix K below).

him to suspect me? His Rage and Malignity against me. And on what founded? It is needless to explain it. He has said to M. Duclos, to Baron d'Holback and to many others as I am now certainly informed, that he hates all those to whom he owes Obligations, and surely, in this Light, I was fully entitled to his Hatred. But, I ask, was such a Perversity of Mind ever before known in any human or indeed in any animal Being? A Tyger or a Hyæna, if you feed him in his Den, will abate of his Fury while you approach him; and will lick the beneficent hand which nourishes and caresses him. But this Prodigy of Pride and Ferocity interprets every Favour into an Injury, and meditates your Ruin even while you are serving him with the greatest Zeal and Industry. It is no Apology to say that his Madness made him believe me guilty of a Confederacy with Mr Walpole against him. He himself pretends not the smallest Reason for believing it. He had no such Indication; he had no such Information; even amidst his greatest Folly he hesitates and scruples to affirm it: He has only, as he confesses, an internal Conviction of it. That is his Rage against me suggested such an Opinion. For the Passion plainly arose not from the Opinion, but produced it.

Consider also, Dear Sir, the other Scene which opens at the same time. You now see, that, even while we were living together in seeming Intimacy, his Heart, amidst all his Caresses and Professions of Fondness was full of Malignity against me; and he was watching every Look and Gesture and Accent, not to say, Word and Sentence, whether I was sleeping or awake, in order to put a malicious Interpretation upon them. Judge of the Innocence of my Conduct, when, in three Months' Intercourse, he cou'd, properly speaking, find nothing but an Excess in Civility and Attention to object.

I hope also, you will not forget the palpable and absurd Lyes with which he interlards his Invective against me. He was sensible, mad as he is, that, if we had so long lived together in Friendship and had parted amicably, it was absurd in him, while dwelling in the Mountains of Derbyshire, to burst into Rage against an absent Person who was continually employ'd in his Service and against whom he could not bring the smallest Shadow of Evidence. He pretends therefore, very cunningly (for nothing so cunning as a Madman) that he had formerly reproached me with Perfidy, and that I had not attempted to justify myself. But happily, this Lye is refuted, as well by his own Letters, as by the whole Tenor of my Conduct. For surely, I shoud never have given myself so much Trouble to serve a Man who had thrown out such an absurd Suspicion against me. I omit the other numerous Falshoods contained in his Letter.

It is needless, by vain Rhetoric, especially to you, to aggravate the Atrocity of deliberate Lyes and Calumnies, or to remark how much this Guilt, already great, may be augmented by particular Connexions with the Person who is attacked by these poysoned Weapons. Were you a less zealous Friend of this Man, I shoud only desire you to divert yourself on this Occasion with the Magnificence and Ostentation of his usual Pretentions on the head of Veracity, and compare them to his Practice. You know, that he has even engraved a Seal with this Motto 'Vitam impendere vero' and that he never seals any Letter, not even those to me with any other Device. The Life of such a Man is to be regarded as one continu'd Lye and Imposture.

You say indeed, that he cannot properly deserve the severe Epithets with which I have honoured him; because it is probable that he had not calmly formed the deliberate Purpose of quarrelling with me and calumniating me: He was only actuated by the Sourness and Melancholy of his Temper. Add, by the Pride and Malignity of his Heart: Add, that he sacrifices every regard to Truth and Honour, in order to gratify his Malice; add, that his Ferocity is directed not only against a Man who is his Benefactor, but because he is so; all Villains are not calm ones: Catiline and Caligula and Nero were not the Men of the coolest Dispositions in the World.

You see, therefore, that I am far from pleading, as an Apology for my Letter to Baron d'Holbach the natural Vivacity of a first Movement, on receiving such violent Outrage from Rousseau in return for so many Favours. I really believe him one of the worst and most depraved of Men; and tho' his Conduct towards many others besides me will justify this Opinion; it is needless for me to go any farther than myself. The only Apology, which any part of my Conduct requires is, my engaging so far in Friendship with a Man who was in a manner personally unknown to me. But I was acquainted with his Genius and his Misfortunes, and besides his applying to me himself, he was put into my hands by those in Paris, with whom I lived in great Intimacy, and to whose Civilities I had been extremely beholden. Tho' some prudent Persons gave me

Warning of his black and dangerous Character, I was still inclined rather to believe those who spoke favourably of him; and while we lived together, his Behaviour was such as gave me no reason to repent it. I contracted a real Affection and Friendship for him; and endless is the Raillery which I now sustain from my Acquaintance, on account of what I said and wrote in his Favour. But I shall never be much ashamed of Mistakes of this Nature.

I wonder you shou'd regard the breaking out of this Affair as a Misfortune. I think rather that nothing can be more fortunate than the Detection of such a Mountebank: For I am willing to soften my Epithets, in Complaisance to you. I wish, that all other Cheats and Impostors in all Professions were as fairly exposed. You know, that I always esteemed his Writings for their Eloquence alone and that I looked on them, at the bottom, as full of Extravagance and of Sophystry. I found many good Judges in France and all in England, of a like Opinion. Is there any Harm that the Public in general shou'd adopt the same Sentiments, and shou'd appreciate at their just Value Compositions whose general Tendency is surely rather to do hurt than Service to Mankind?

You judge Mr Walpole with great Severity when you blame his Pleasantry against Rousseau. Is every Epigram or Stroke of Satyre against an Author so great a Crime? On the contrary it seems to me that Authors alone or such as exhibit themselves on the public Stage of the World are fairly exposed to those Darts and must expect Applause or Hisses, according to their own Merit or the Humour of their Audience. In vain you say that Mr Walpole's Pleasantry was the Cause of all this Mischief. I see little Mischief, except to those who deserve it. And it was quite necessary that Rousseau's secret Rage against d'Alembert and me shou'd burst out on some Occasion or other. Indeed, it was not easy for him to find a less favourable Occasion or less plausible Pretence, than that which he has laid hold of; besides, I beg you to consider, that Mr Walpole never intended to publish that Piece of Pleasantry, and that a Copy of it was stolen from him.

But, My Dear Sir, at the same time, that I cannot forbear wondering at your great Partiality in favour of Rousseau, I acknowlege, with the most lively Sense, your Candour and Friendship towards me, in delivering it as your Opinion that it will be necessary to publish for my own Vindication, the whole

Train of Correspondence between us. I have heard of the Challenges and Defiances thrown out in several of his Letters; and these have been so publicly handed about that Translations of two of them have already got into the English News papers. It is with the utmost Reluctance, I own that I shall proceed to this Extremity; and herein consists the only real Injury, that this Man has been able to do me. I may boast, that, among all the Authors now alive, I am, perhaps, the most remarkable, for my continued and uninterrupted Love of Peace; and no Provocation has yet been able to engage me in any Controversy either personal or literary. I cou'd cover the Floor of a large Room with Books and Pamphlets wrote against me, to none of which I ever made the least Reply, not from Disdain (for the Authors of some of them, I respect) but from my Desire of Ease and Tranquillity. There is a Prelate,[1] in England, noted for his illiberal Insolence and Scurrility, who has also formed a Confederacy of Authors, as remarkable for these Qualities, as any School of Painters ever was for their peculiar Style and Manner. The Master and the Scholars have all of them successively honoured me with their Insults and Outrages. I never gave them the least Sign of Life: But this Silence, I own, proceeded as much from Disdain as from my Love of Peace; and I pretend not to make a Merit of it.

If I be at last obliged to publish my own Vindication in this Affair (which indeed will consist of little more than my Adversary's Accusation) I shall reap this Advantage, that I shall be ever after secure from any Calumny, that he may be tempted to throw out against me. Dead or alive, his Testimony will never have any Authority to defame me. I own, that this Consideration chiefly induced me to inform my Friends, both in London and Paris, of my Rupture with Rousseau, and diverted me from that Secrecy which I intended at first to have kept with regard to it. I knew, that he, and even perhaps the World, might regard this Silence as a Presumption of Guilt, and that nothing cou'd more carry the Face of Innocence than an open Indignation at this Treatment which I had met with. You say, that the Letter, which, at that Moment, I wrote to Baron d'Holbach, was not sufficiently moderate: but, besides that it was only a private Letter, tho' not wrote with any View of Secrecy, I think I have fully vindicated it at present and shown

[1] Bishop Warburton.

my Imputations to be well founded. It cannot surely be interpreted as Want of Temper if, at any time, but much more in the first Movement of Surprize and Indignation, I bestow on a Man the same Epithet, which, upon mature Deliberation, he had to my Face and without any Provocation, thrown on me, after receiving from me the strongest Proofs of Friendship and Attachment.

But his letter to me did me no hurt, and my Complaints against him have done him an irreparable damage in his Character. To this I reply that the Case is similar as if an Assassin had fired a Pistol at me, and missed me; while I, to prevent his firing another Pistol, run him thro the Body. It is always happy when the harm falls on the first Aggressor.

We are told that Sophocles in his old Age was supposed to have lost his Senses; and his Family for that Reason apply'd for a Commission of Lunacy against him. But the Poet, as his only Answer, read some Scenes of his Tragedy of Œdipus Colonnus which he was at that time composing. And he was unanimously acquitted by the Judges. The Public will probably have soon an Opportunity of giving a Verdict of a like kind with regard to Rousseau. When he publishes what he has composed since his Arrival in England, I dare venture to prophesy that he will be found as much in his Senses as ever he was in his life, and no-one, at least, will say, that, if his Heart was not depraved, he wants Understanding sufficient to conduct him in the ordinary Offices of Life.

But I am heartily tired of this Subject, as you very well conjecture; and I shall here take my Leave of it, I hope for ever. Tho' you must be tired too of my Letter, I am tempted to say a Word to the political Question, which has been often agitated between us, viz the Method of laying on Taxes, Whether it is better to impose them on landed Possessions or on Consumptions. You will own, that, as the public Revenue is employ'd for the Defence of the whole Community, it is more equitable to levy it from the whole; but you say, that this is impracticable: It will fall on the Land at last; and it is better to lay it on there directly. You suppose then that the Labourers always raise the Price of their Labour in proportion to the Taxes. But this is contrary to Experience. Labour is dearer in Neuf-chatel and other parts of Swisserland, where there are no Taxes, than in the neighbouring Provinces of France, where there are a great many. There are almost no Taxes on the English Colonies; yet Labour is three times dearer there than in any Country of Europe. There are great Taxes on Consumptions in Holland, but the Republic possesses no Land, on which they can fall. The Price of Labour will always depend on the Quantity of Labour and the Quantity of Demand; not on the Taxes. The Tradesmen who work in Cloath, that is exported, cannot raise the Price of their Labour; because in that Case the Price of the Cloath wou'd become too dear to be sold in foreign Markets: Neither can the Tradesmen who work in Cloath for home Consumption raise their Prices; since there cannot be two Prices for the same Species of Labour. This extends to all Commodities of which there is any part exported, that is, to almost every Commodity. Even were there some Commodities of which no part is exported, the Price of Labour employ'd in them, cou'd not rise; for this high Price wou'd tempt so many hands to go into that Species of Industry as must immediatly bring down the Prices. It appears to me that where a Tax is laid on Consumption, the immediate Consequence is that either the Tradesmen consume less or work more. No Man is so industrious but he may add some Hours more in the Week to his Labour: And scarce any one is so poor but he can retrench something of his Expence. What happens when the Corn rises in its Prices? Do not the poor both live worse and labour more? A Tax has the same effect. I beg you also to consider, that, besides the Proprietors of Land and the labouring Poor, there is in every civilized Community a very large and a very opulent Body who employ their Stocks in Commerce and who enjoy a great Revenue from their giving Labour to the poorer sort. I am perswaded that in France and England the Revenue of this kind is much greater than that which arises from Land: For besides Merchants, properly speaking, I comprehend in this Class all Shop-Keepers and Master-Tradesmen of every Species. Now it is very just, that these shoud pay for the Support of the Community, which can only be where Taxes are lay'd on Consumptions. There seems to me no Pretence for saying that this order of Men are necessitated to throw their Taxes on the Proprietors of Land, since their Profits and Income can surely bear Retrenchment.[1] After so long a Letter, you will surely excuse my concluding without any Ceremony or Compliment. Be only assured that

[1] Hume had already developed these principles in his essay *Of Taxes*, and *passim* in others of the *Political Discourses*. But he never succeeded in converting Turgot.

no Man puts a higher and juster Value on your Friendship than I do.

DAVID HUME.

* 352. *To* JAMES OSWALD OF DUNNIKIER

Ninewells, 1 of Oct. 1766

My dear Oswald,

As your friend Mr Charteris [1] intends to be only a few weeks in Paris, he will be sufficiently occupied in seeing the Palace and gardens and houses and pictures, and other curiosities which are commonly shown to strangers: it would be an absurdity in me to recommend to any French family a young man who proposes to make so short a stay among them; and I have always kept myself carefully from making such a return for the civilities I myself met with. Our friend, Smith, is at present at Paris; and the properest person to put Mr Charteris in a proper way of gratifying his curiosity in those particulars. He will be very fond of an opportunity to oblige you.

I shall probably be in town, that is Edinburgh, next week: I intend to pay you a visit at Kirkaldy. Oh that horrid sea-sickness! Are there no chairs from the ferry to your house?

I am, my dear Oswald,
Yours sincerely,
DAVID HUME.

† 353. *To* WILLIAM STRAHAN

[Edinburgh, Oct. 1766.]

Dear Sir

My Friends at Paris have thought it absolutely necessary to publish an Account which I sent them, of my Transactions with Rousseau, together with the original Papers:[2] The Affair had made a great Noise every where, and he had been such a Fool, as to write Defiances against me to all parts of Europe; so that the Justification of my Character they thought requir'd a

* MS., R.S.E. (copy only); hitherto unpublished.
† MS. at Barnbougle Castle; Hill, 84 ff.

[1] From a letter of Blair's dated 27 March [1767] it appears that this was the eldest son of —— Charteris, Solicitor to the Customs.

[2] *Exposé succinct de la contestation qui s'est élevée entre M. Hume et M. Rousseau, avec les pieces justificatives*, Londres [Paris], 1766 (12mo).

Publication, which, however, is very much against my Will, coud it have been prevented. The whole will compose a pretty large Pamphlet,[1] which, I fancy, the Curiosity of the Public will make tolerably saleable. I desire you to take upon you the printing and publishing of it; and if any Profit result from it to you, I shall be very happy; reserving the after property and Disposal of the Pamphlet to myself. You will take in what Bookseller you please; Becket or Caddel[2] or any other: For Mr Millar woud not think such a Trifle worthy of his Attention.

I shall immediatly send you up a Copy of the original Manuscript, which is partly English, partly French; but more of the latter Language, which must be translated. I shall employ Mr Coutts's Cover.[3] The Method the Translator must proceed is this: My Friends at Paris are to send me over in a Parcel ten Copies, which will be deliverd to Miss Elliot. I have desird her to send them to you; open the Parcel and take out one Copy for your own Use. Get a discreet and careful Translator:[4] Let him compare exactly the French Narration with my English: Where they agree, let him insert my English: Where they differ, let him follow the French and translate it: The Reason of this is, that I allowd my Friends at Paris to make what alterations they thought proper; and I am desirous of following exactly the Paris Edition. All my letters must be printed verbatim, conformable to the Manuscript I send you.

My Parisian Friends are to add a Preface of their own composing, which must be translated: Add, by way of Nota bene, that the Original Letters will all be deposited in the Musæum. The Reason of this is, that Rousseau has been so audacious as to write, that I dare not publish his Letters without falsifying them.

If you think, that a Republication of the French Edition will answer the Expence, I am also willing you should do it.

[1] The English version ran to 96 8vo pages.

[2] Thomas Cadell (1742–1802), apprenticed to Andrew Millar, 1758; taken into partnership, 1765; succeeded to the business, 1767. When he retired in 1793 his business was considered 'the first in Great Britain'.

[3] James Coutts the banker, who was M.P. for Edinburgh.

[4] The translator was neither discreet nor careful: the footnotes he added on his own initiative are generally uncalled-for and sometimes irritating; and his knowledge of French was limited. For example, Rousseau, in his letter of 10 July 1766, says: 'Peu de tems après notre arrivée à Londres, j'y remarquai dans les esprits à mon égard un changement sourd qui bientôt devient très sensible.' The translator rendered this as: 'A very short time after our arrival in London I observed an absurd change in the minds of the people regarding me, which soon became very apparent.'

Of the remaining nine Copies, send one to Lord Hertford, lower Grosvenor Street, another to Mr Secretary Conway, another to Horace Walpole, Arlington Street, another to Lady Hervey, St James Place. Send the remaining five to me by any private hand or by the Waggon.

Mr Kincaid tells me, that two Years ago he sent enclosd in a Parcel of Yours a corrected Quarto Copy of my History to be deliverd to Mr Millar.[1] Yet Mr Millar told me in London that he had never seen any such thing. I suppose he has forgot and will be able to find it upon Search. Try, if you can recollect and put him in mind of it.

I am Dear Sir Your most obedient humble Servant

David Hume.

* 354. *To* Andrew Millar

Dear Sir

I fancy Mr Macleane's Questions are by this time answerd to his Satisfaction:[2] For my Friends at Paris have thought it absolutely necessary to publish a Narrative of the whole Affair between Rousseau and me, translated from an Account I sent them. I believe the World never heard of so ridiculous and absurd an Affair.

Allan Ramsay is in this Country but I have not yet seen him. I spoke to him in London of the Affair you mention;[3] but he says, that there is no Engraver here (I suppose he excepts Strange, who is otherwise employ'd) that is capable of doing a head tolerably. I am much, much better pleasd to have the

* MS., R.S.E.; *Englische Studien*, Band 63, Heft 3 (1929); hitherto unpublished in England.

[1] See next Letter.

[2] Writing to Hume from Kew Green on 4 Oct. 1766, Millar says he has had a letter from Maclaine at The Hague asking for details of the Hume-Rousseau quarrel. He quotes passages from Maclaine's letter, such as: 'Everybody, however, except a few foaming partisans of Rousseau, is perswaded that Mr Hume has been ill repaid for his generosity and friendship. ...For my own part I am of this way of thinking, tho at the same time, I cannot say it was highly prudent in Mr Hume to bring w[t] him such an *ouran-outang* into England . . .' (MS., R.S.E., unpublished). Alexander Maclaine (1722–1804), a Scotsman, was minister of the English church at The Hague and translator of Mosheim's *Ecclesiastical History*. He was also a brother of 'The Gentleman Highwayman', who was executed at Tyburn in 1752.

[3] In the same letter Millar says, 'Did not you promise y[t] Allan Ramsay sh[d] fix on an engraver for y[r] head? He and y[o] are both gone without doing this. . . . All this delays time and y[r] new Edition sh[d] appear this Winter. . . .'

Edition come out without it: I am indeed averse to the prefixing a Print of the Author, as savouring of Vanity.

I am just now recovering myself of my Habits of Dissipation, and returning to my old Habits of Study & Retreat. I shall not lose Sight of the Object you mention,[1] as soon as I think Affairs are ripe for it. I woud fain see the Prejudices of Faction a little more abated, in order to smooth the way for my Access to the Cabinets of the Great: For really I am not qualify'd for overcoming any Difficulties of that Nature.

About two Years ago, I wrote you, that I had left with my Sister a corrected Copy of my History, which I woud desire her to send you. You wrote to Kincaid who sent for it, and sent it to you in a Parcel of Strahan's. This Circumstance is enterd by Kincaid in his Minute Book of 16 of Octr 1764. When in London, I asked you about this Copy; and you told me, that you had never heard of it. I suppose this is only a Defect of Memory. I shoud be very vext it was lost. Please enquire about it; and if you recover it, be so good as to send it me by the Waggon. I beg my sincere Compliments to Mrs Millar. I hope to be often merry with you & her in your House in Pall-Mall; and I wish both of you much Health & Satisfaction in enjoying it. I am Dear Sir

Your most obedient humble Servant

Edinburgh DAVID HUME

21 of Octr 1766

To Mr Andrew Millar Bookseller opposite Catherine Street in the Strand

* 355. *To* HORACE WALPOLE

Edinburgh, 30 of Oct. 1766.

Dear Sir,

A few posts ago I had a letter from M. D'Alembert,[2] by which I learn, that he and my other friends at Paris had determined to publish an account of my rupture with Rousseau, in consequence of a general discretionary power which I had given them. The narrative they publish is the same with that which

* Walpole, *Works*, iv. 259; Ritchie, 256 f.

[1] Millar was again urging him to continue his *History* to the death of George I. 'You have got into such a track of dissipation that you do not know how to break of,' Millar says. 'But *Begin* once and resolve to continue, and the business will be done.'

[2] Letter of 6 Oct. 1766 (No. XXIX in Appendix K below).

I left with Lord Hertford, and which I believe you have seen. It consists chiefly of original papers, connected by a short recital of facts. I made a few alterations, and M. D'Alembert tells me he has made a few more, with my permission and at my desire. Among the papers published is your letter to me, justifying my innocence with regard to the King of Prussia's letter. You permitted me to make what use of it I pleased for my own apology; and as I knew that you could have no reason for concealing it, I inserted it without scruple in the narrative. My Parisian friends are to accompany the whole with a preface, giving an account of my reluctance to this publication, but of the necessity which they found of extorting my consent. It appears particularly, that my antagonist had wrote letters of defiance against me all over Europe, and said, that the letter he wrote me was so confounding to me, that I would not dare to show it to any one without falsifying it. These letters were likely to make impression, and my silence might be construed into a proof of guilt. I am sure that my friends have judged impartially in this affair, and without being actuated by any prejudice or passion of their own; for almost all of them were at first as averse as I was to the publication, and only proceeded to it upon the apparent necessity which they discovered. I have not seen the preface; but the book will probably be soon in London, and I hope you will find that the reasons assigned by my friends are satisfactory. They have taken upon them the blame, if any appears to lie in this measure.

I am with great truth and sincerity, Dear Sir
Your most obedient and most humble servant,
DAVID HUME.

* 356. *To* WILLIAM STRAHAN

Dear Sir

I have receiv'd by the Post a Copy of the Paris Edition of the Pamphlet I mention'd to you. I wish it were possible not to print an Edition in London, because the whole Affair will appear perfectly ridiculous to the English: But as I am afraid this is impossible, I believe it is better for me to take care, that a true Edition be printed. I committ that matter to your Care.

Contrary to my former Directions, I now desire you not to follow the Paris Edition in my Narrative; but exactly the

* MS. at Barnbougle Castle; Hill, 97 f.

English Copy which I sent you in Manuscript. There is only one Passage, where I desire a Sentence to be inserted: It is a little before the Copy of the King of Prussia's letter to Rousseau. I there say, 'But I little expected, at the Distance of 150 Miles and employing myself constantly in his Service, to be the Victim of his Rage and Malevolence'. Add, 'An Incident happened about this time, which set this Disposition of M. Rousseau in a full Light. There had been a feigned Letter of the King of Prussia's', etc.

There is a very material Note, ommitted by the Editors of the Paris Edition, which I desire you to insert.[1] I send you a Copy of it, with Directions for inserting it. I suppose all along, that you have receivd the Paris Edition by this time: Otherwise I woud have sent it you.

I am Dr Sir Yours sincerely

Edinburgh
4 of Novr 1766.

DAVID HUME.

P.S. I need not tell you that Rousseau's long Letter to me is to be translated from the Paris Edition with all the Notes. The other Letters may be translated indifferently either from that Edition or from my Manuscript.

* 357. *To* HORACE WALPOLE

Edinburgh, 4 of Nov. 1766.

Dear Sir,

Yesterday I received by the post a copy of the edition, printed at Paris, of my narrative of this ridiculous affair between Rousseau and me. There is an introduction in the name of my friends, giving an account of the necessity under which they found themselves to publish this narrative; and an appendix in D'Alembert's name, protesting his innocence with regard to all the imputations thrown on him by Rousseau. I have no objection with regard to the first, but the second contains a clause which displeases me very much, but which you will probably only laugh at: it is that where he blames the King of Prussia's

* Walpole, *Works*, iv. 262.

[1] The note in answer to Rousseau's accusation that his letters had been opened while passing through Hume's hands. It appears on p. 51 of the *Concise and Genuine Account*, whereas in the corresponding passage of the *Exposé succinct* all that is said is: 'Ces imputations d'indiscretion et d'infidélité sont si odieuses, et les preuves en sont si ridicules, que je me crois dispensé d'y repondre' (p. 68).

letter as cruel.[1] What could engage D'Alembert to use this freedom, I cannot imagine. Is it possible that a man of his superior parts can bear you ill will because you are the friend of his enemy, Madame du Deffand?[2] What makes me suspect that there may be something true of this suspicion, is, that several passages in my narrative, in which I mention you and that letter, are all altered in the translation, and rendered much less obliging than I wrote them: for my narrative sent to Paris was an exact copy of that left in Lord Hertford's hands. I would give any thing to prevent a publication in London (for surely the whole affair will appear perfectly ridiculous); but I am afraid that a book printed at Paris will be translated in London, if there be hopes of selling a hundred copies of it. For this reason, I fancy it will be better for me to take care that a proper edition be published, in which case I shall give orders that all the passages altered in my narrative shall be restored.

Since I came here I have been told that you have had a severe fit of sickness, but that you are now recovered: I hope you are perfectly so. I am anxious to hear of your welfare; being with great sincerity,

Dear Sir,

Your most obedient and most humble servant,

DAVID HUME.

* 358. *To* JEAN-BAPTISTE-ANTOINE SUARD [3]

I cannot sufficiently express, My Dear Sir, all the Acknowlegements, which I owe you, for the Pains you have taken in

* MS. in J. Pierpont Morgan Library, New York City; *New Monthly Mag. & Universal Register*, Vol. xiii, Pt. I (Jan. to June, 1820), pp. 5 f.; Burton, ii. 357 f. (incomplete).

[1] D'Alembert was consistent in this attitude throughout. See his letters in Appendix K below.

[2] What d'Alembert felt about Mme du Deffand may be gathered from the following extract from his letter of 1 Sept. [1766] to Hume: 'A l'égard de ma voisine la Vipere, (car c'est ainsi que je l'appelle) je persiste aussi à dire que c'est une carogne, qui vous flagorne aujourd'hui, non par amitié pour vous, mais uniquement par haine pour Rousseau. Vous êtes la dupe de sa platte fausseté, mais croyez qu'elle vous hait, premièrement parce qu'elle hait tout le monde, et surtout les gens de merite, secondement parce qu'elle sait que vous aimez des gens qu'elle n'aime pas, et qui à la verité le lui rendent bien, ou plutôt qui lui rendent en mépris la monnoye de sa haine' (MS., R.S.E.; *Eminent Persons*, 201). The particular reference here is to Mme du Deffand's letter of 13 Aug. 1766 (see Appendix K below).

[3] Jean-Baptiste-Antoine Suard (1734–1817), journalist and translator;

translating a Work, which so little merited your Attention or the Attention of the public. It is done entirely to my Satisfaction; and the Introduction in particular is wrote with great Prudence & Discretion, in every point except where your Partiality to me appears too strongly.[1] I accept of it, however, very willingly as a Pledge of your Friendship. You and M. Dalembert did well in softening some Expressions, especially in the Notes; and I shall take care to follow these Corrections in the English Edition. My Paper, indeed, was not wrote for the public Eye; and nothing but a Train of unforeseen Accidents cou'd have engaged me to give it to the Press. I am not surprized, that those, who do not consider nor weigh those Circumstances, shou'd blame this Appeal to the Public; but it is certain, that, if I had persevered in keeping Silence, I shou'd have passed for the guilty Person, and those very People, who blame me at present, wou'd, with the Appearance of Reason, have thrown a much greater Blame upon me. This whole Adventure I must regard as a Misfortune in my Life; and yet even after all is past, when it is easy to correct any Errors, I am not sensible, that I can accuse myself of any Imprudence; except in accepting of this Man when he threw himself into my Arms: And yet it wou'd then have appeared cruel to refuse him. I am excusable for not expecting to meet with such a Prodigy of Pride and Ferocity, because such a one never before existed. But after he had declared War against me in so violent a Manner, it cou'd not have been prudent in me to keep Silence towards my Friends, and to wait till he shou'd find a proper time to stab my Reputation. From my Friends, the Affair passed to the Public, who interested themselves more in a private Story, than it was possible to imagine; and rendered it quite necessary to lay the whole before them. Yet after all, if any one be pleased to think, that by greater Prudence I cou'd have avoided this disagreeable Extremity, I am very willing to

sometime editor of the *Gazette de France* (an official publication), and joint editor of the *Gazette littéraire de France*; admitted to the Academy, 1773; translator of Robertson's *History of Charles V*.

[1] The opening paragraph of the Advertisement written by the French editors and translated for the *Concise and Genuine Account* reads: 'The name and writings of Mr. Hume have been long since well known throughout Europe. At the same time, his personal acquaintance have remarked, in the candour and simplicity of his manners, that impartiality and ingenuousness of disposition which distinguishes his character, and is sufficiently indicated in his writings.'

submit: It is not surely the first Imprudence I have been guilty of.

I agree with you, that Rousseau will probably reply, and yet it is very difficult to imagine what he can possibly say, after having already entered into so long and minute and tedious a Detail. It will be ridiculous for him to bring out any new Facts of Consequence, which he may pretend to have omitted; after he has already mentioned the Looks of my Land-ladies and my own, as Grounds of Complaint. But whatever he may say, I am resolute to keep an absolute Silence for the rest of my Life; and allow everyone to entertain what Opinion they please with regard to this Story. I fancy the only Dispute in the World will be whether Rousseau is more wicked or mad, or whether he be not both in nearly equal proportions. You say that he has Enthusiasts, who still pretend to excuse him. Do they pretend then, that Dalembert, Horace Walpole, and I entered into a Conspiracy against him to lead him into England, and ruin him, by settling him in a most commodious and agreeable Manner, and by doubling his Income? For if this be not asserted, how can his outrageous Behaviour towards me admit of any Apology?

Cou'd I look on Rousseau as one of the Classics of your Language, I shou'd imagine, that this Story, silly as it is, might go to Posterity, and interest them as much as it has done our Contemporaries: But really his Writings are so full of Extravagance, that I cannot believe their Eloquence alone will be able to support them. He has a Suspicion himself, that this is the Case: I shall tell you the Story because I think it for his Credit: For otherwise I wou'd not repeat any thing that passed between us during the time of our Familiarity. When we were on the Road, he told me, that he was resolved to improve himself in English: and as he heard, that there were two English Translations of his *Emile*, he wou'd procure them, he said, & read them, and compare them: His Knowlege of the Subject wou'd facilitate his Advances in the Language. Immediatly on our Arrival, I procured the Books for him. He kept them two or three days, and then returned them, by telling me, that they cou'd be of no Use to him. He had not patience, he said, to read them; he was in the same Case with regard to the Original and all his other Writings, which, after their Publication, he cou'd never take into his hand without Disgust. It is strange, I reply'd, that Pieces so much admired for their Eloquence cou'd give no

Satisfaction to their Author: Why! said he, with regard to their Style & Eloquence, I am not altogether dissatisfy'd with them; but I dread always *qu'ils pechent par le fond*; and that their Lustre is only the Blaze of a day.

I am sensible of your great Partiality & Friendship, in offering to become my Translator for any Work, which I may hereafter give to the Public: Surely I cou'd not desire to be introduced to foreign Countries in a more advantageous Manner, than I shou'd be by your elegant Pen. But my Scritoire is at present exhausted, and I have no Prospect of filling it: I am even unsettled as to my Views of establishing myself; and I indulge myself in the humour of living from day to day, partly in Reading, partly in Company, partly in Indolence. I am afraid, that you indulge yourself too much in this last Enjoyment: Otherwise, why do you, who have Taste & Knowlege in so eminent a Degree, desire to translate the Works of any other Person, and not rather give some original Performance to the Public? You say, perhaps, that the Constraints, under which you labour in France, discourages you; and you envy the Liberty of England. But be assured, that the Indifference and I may say, Barbarism of England is more discouraging than all the Persecutions of France, which sometimes tend only to give a Lustre to an Author, and to render him more interesting.

I beg my Compliments to all my Friends of your Society: They may be assured that I shall never give up the Thoughts of revisiting them but with my Life. I am with the greatest Sincerity My Dear Sir Your most obedient and most humble Servant

DAVID HUME

Edinburgh
5 of November
1766

* 359. *To* RICHARD DAVENPORT

Dear Sir

You wou'd see by the News Papers, that my Friends at Paris have found it necessary to publish an Account of this strange and ridiculous Affair between Rousseau and me, together with all the original Letters. He had wrote Defiances against me to the different Parts of Europe: His Friends had been very industrious in showing these Letters: Some of them had even got

* MS. in Bibliothèque publique de Neuchâtel; hitherto unpublished.

into the public Papers: And on the whole, things had come to that Extremity, that my Silence wou'd universally have been interpreted as a Sign of Guilt. There will, no doubt, be an English Translation soon publishd; & the Affair, tho' very little worthy of the public Attention, will be in every body's hands. Your Name is often mention'd, but always with the Regard that is due to it. Among other particulars of Rousseau's Letters to his Friends, he says, that, if I ever publish our Correspondence, it will be with enormous Falsifications: I doubt not, but he will now have Recourse to that Shift: But please to let him know, that I have all his original Letters and will deposit them in the Musæum, to prevent such a Calumny. I am Dear Sir

Your most obedient & most humble Servant,

DAVID HUME

Edinburgh
8 of Novr 1766

To Richard Davenport Esqr at Davenport, Brereton Green Cheshire

* 360. *To* ANDREW MILLAR

Dear Sir

Your Letter gave me a great deal of Uneasyness; by letting me see, that I had, innocently and undesignedly given you Uneasyness.[1] I assure you, that I believe I have made a very trifling Present to Mr Strahan and what will scarce be worth his Acceptance. I fancy, that 500 Copies of the Account of that ridiculous Affair between Rousseau and me will be more than sufficient to satisfy the Curiosity of the Public at London: The Pamphlet will not appear as coming from my hand but as a Translation of the Paris Edition; and as Becket has commonly the first Copies of French Books, it will be thought quite natural to come from his Press If I had imagin'd, that it wou'd have given you the least Satisfaction to be the Publisher, it shoud never had been sent to any other hand.

I shall endeavour to render the next Edition of my History as correct as possible; tho' I do not expect to see it necessary

* MS., R.S.E.; Burton, ii. 393 (incomplete).

[1] Millar was hurt at Hume's having handed over the publishing of the *Concise and Genuine Account* to Strahan and Becket instead of to himself. 'Can you imagine anything however so trifling in which your name is concerned, not worth my while?' he asks in his letter of 2 Nov. (MS., R.S.E.).

for several Years.[1] Your last Edition was certainly too numerous; but that cannot now be prevented. Mr Bell & Mr Donaldson tell me, that they are quite out of Copies of my philosophical Pieces. The former assurd me that he sold but a few of his Quota at London; the second none at all. But this last, I doubt of a little. I own, that the quick sale of my Philosophy surprizes me as much as the slow sale of my History. You have scarce dispos'd of 2000 Copies in three Years.

I shall probably do as you advise; and Sketch out the Outlines of the two or three subsequent Reigns, which I may finish at London, after I find, that there remains no farther Obstacles to this Work, and that it is favour'd, I do not say, by every body (for that is impossible) but by the Generality of the World. I beg my Compliments to Mrs Millar.

I am Dear Sir
Yours sincerely
DAVID HUME

Edinburgh
8 of Octr 1766[2]

P.S.

Dr Robertson talks of being ready Winter after this.[3] He is just now finishing an Introduction.

To Mr Andrew Millar Bookseller

*361. *To* WILLIAM STRAHAN

[Nov. 1766]

Dear Sir

I had a Letter from Mr Millar, complaining of my giving to any other besides him the Publication of my Account of this ridiculous Affair, between Rousseau and me. I am certainly in the wrong, not to have conjoind him, if I coud have imagind,

* MS. at Barnbougle Castle; Hill, 99 f.

[1] In the same letter Millar urges Hume to run through all the *History* and make such corrections as he wished; 'for depend on it, It will be to be reprinted and that soon, and I am sure in opposition to all faction, it will be as Lord Chesterfield often said to me, The only History of England that will go down to Posterity. I have sold since Augt 60 Setts, and it continues every week to sell.' But Hume no longer trusted Millar's statements; and in point of fact the next edition of the *History* did not appear till 1770, two years after Millar's death.

[2] Hume misdated this letter 'Oct^r', but it must have been written in Nov., since it answers one of Millar's dated 2 Nov. 1766.

[3] With his *Charles V*, which he had now been engaged on for six and a half years.

that he woud have thought it worthy of his Attention. I wish you may find it worth while;[1] but I fancy 500 Copies will be more than sufficient to gratify the Curiosity of the Public. It is necessity, not choice, that forces me on this Publication.

If it be not too late, add the following short Note to Page 59 of the Paris Edition, at these words: Des ce moment les imprimés ne parlerent plus de moi que d'une maniere equivoque ou malhonnete. *So then, I find I am to answer for every Article of every Magazine and Newspaper printed in England: I assure Mr Rousseau I woud rather answer for every Robbery committed on the high way; and I am entirely as innocent of the one as the other.* If you have already printed the Page to which this Note refers, print the Note apart, as an Ommission or Erratum.[2] I doubt not but you have already got the Paris Edition otherwise I coud send it you.

I am Yours etc.

D. H.

* 362. *To* WILLIAM STRAHAN

Dear Sir

As I have not heard from you; I suspect that you have not yet got the Paris Edition of my Pamphlet. I have therefore sent you the Manuscript of Rousseau's long Letter with all the Notes such as I wish them to be printed; excepting the Note which I sent you in a Paper apart, and which must be inserted. Mr Rousseau's Notes must be printed in Italics to distinguish them from mine;[3] and you must advertise the Reader of this Precaution, in order to prevent Confusion. Even tho' you shoud have got the Paris Edition rather follow the Manuscript, if it be not too late. The Paris Editors have added a Preface and a Declaration of M. D'Alembert, and a Latin Motto[4] at the end. You

* MS. at Barnbougle Castle; Hill, 101.

[1] From a letter of Millar's to Hume dated 22 Nov. 1766 (MS., R.S.E.) it appears that he felt strongly enough about the *Concise and Genuine Account* to ask Strahan to add his name to Becket's and De Hondt's on the title-page. Strahan agreed, but Becket did not.

[2] This unnecessary and rather stupid note was duly added as an Erratum on the back page of the *Concise and Genuine Account*.

[3] This was not done, but the authorship of each note was indicated by the author's name printed at the end of it.

[4] Perdidi beneficium. Numquid quæ consecravimus perdidisse nos dicimus? Inter consecrata beneficium est; etiamsi male respondit, bene collocatum. Non est ille qualem speravimus; simus nos quales fuimus, ei dissimiles. Seneca, *De Beneficiis*, lib. vii, cap. 29.

must not publish the Pamphlet without these. If you have not got that Edition I shall send it you; tho' I wish you coud rather get it in London.

I am Dear Sr Yours sincerely
DAVID HUME.

13 Novr 1766.

* 363. *To* HORACE WALPOLE

Edinburgh, 20 of Nov. 1766.

I readily agree with you, my dear Sir, that it is a great misfortune to be reduced to the necessity of consenting to this publication; but it had certainly become necessary. Even those who at first joined me in rejecting all idea of it, wrote to me and represented, that this strange man's defiances had made such impression, that I should pass universally for the guilty person, if I suppressed the story. Some of his greatest admirers and partisans, who had read my manuscript, concurred in the same sentiments with the rest. I never consented to anything with greater reluctance in my life. Had I found one man of my opinion, I should have persevered in my refusal. One reason of my reluctance was, that I saw this publication, if necessary at Paris, was yet superfluous, not to say worse, at London. But I hope it will be considered that the publication is not, properly speaking, my deed, but that of my friends, in consequence of a discretionary power which I gave them, and which it was natural for me to give them, as I was at too great a distance to form a judgment in this case.

I am as sensible as you are of the ridicule to which men of letters have exposed themselves, by running every moment to the public with all their private squabbles and altercations; but surely there has been something very unexpected and peculiar in this affair. My antagonist, by his genius, his singularities, his quackery, his misfortunes, and his adventures, had become more the subject of general conversation in Europe (for I venture again on the word) than any person in it. I do not even except Voltaire, much less the King of Prussia and Mr Pitt. How else could it have happened, that a clause of a private letter, which I wrote somewhat thoughtlessly to a private gentleman at Paris, should in three days' time have been the only subject of conversation in that capital, and should thence have propagated

* Walpole, *Works*, iv. 266 ff.; Ritchie, 268 ff.

itself every where as fast as the post could carry it? You know, that at first I was so little inclined to make a noise about this story, that I had entertained thoughts of giving no reply at all to the insult, which was really so ridiculous: but you very properly dissuaded me from this resolution; and by your advice I wrote that letter, which certainly nobody will find fault with.

Having made this apology for myself (where, however, I expect to be absolved as much by your compassion as your judgment), I proceed to say something in favour of my friends. Allow me then to inform you, that it was not D'Alembert who suppressed that clause of your letter,[1] but me, who did not transcribe it in the copy I sent to Paris. I was afraid of engaging you needlessly in a quarrel with these literati; and as that clause had no reference to the business in hand, I thought I might fairly secrete it. I wish I could excuse him as well on another head. He sent me above two months ago something like that declaration, and desired me to convey it to Rousseau; which I refused to do, and gave him some reasons of my refusal: but he replied to me, that he was sure my true secret reason was my regard to you. He ought thence to have known, that it would be disagreeable to me to see such a piece annexed to mine. I have remarked also the omission of a phrase in the translation; and this omission could not be altogether by accident: it was where I mention your suppressing the King of Prussia's letter, while we lived together at Paris. I said it was *agreeable to your usual politeness and humanity*. I have wrote to Becket the bookseller to restore this passage, which is so conformable to my real sentiments: but whether my orders have come in time, I do not know as yet.[2] Before I saw the Paris edition, I had desired Becket to follow it wherever it departed from my original. The difference, I find, was in other respects inconsiderable.

It is only by conjecture I imagine, that D'Alembert's malevolence to you (if he has any malevolence) proceeds from your friendship with Madame du Deffand; because I can find no other ground for it. I see also, that in his declaration there is a stroke obliquely levelled at her, which perhaps you do not understand, but I do; because he wrote me that he heard she was your corrector.[3] I found these two persons in great and

[1] The first paragraph of Walpole's letter of 26 July 1766 (No. XII in Appendix K below).

[2] They did not come in time.

[3] Speaking of Horace Walpole's letter to Rousseau in the King of Prussia's

intimate friendship when I arrived at Paris: but it is strange how intemperate they are both become in their animosity; tho perhaps it is more excusable in her, on account of her age, sex, and bodily infirmities. I am very sensible of your discretion in not citing me on this occasion; I might otherwise have a new quarrel on my hands.[1]

With regard to D'Alembert I believe I said he was a man of *superior parts*, not a *superior genius*; which are words, if I mistake not, of a very different import. He is surely entitled to the former character, from the works which you and I have read: I do not mean his translation of Tacitus, but his other pieces. But I believe he is more entitled to it from the works which I suppose neither you nor I have read, his Geometry and Algebra. I agree with you, that in some respects Rousseau may more properly be called a superior genius; yet is he so full of extravagance, that I am inclined to deny even him that appellation. I fancy D'Alembert's talents and Rousseau's united might fully merit such a eulogy.

In other respects, D'Alembert is a very agreeable companion, and of irreproachable morals. By refusing great offers from the Czarina and the King of Prussia, he has shown himself above interest and vain ambition. He lives in an agreeable retreat at Paris, suitable to a man of letters. He has five pensions: one from the King of Prussia, one from the French King, one as member of the Academy of Sciences, one as member of the French Academy, and one from his own family. The whole amount of these is not 6000 livres a year; on the half of which he lives decently, and gives the other half to poor people with whom he is connected. In a word, I scarce know a man, who, with some few exceptions (for there must always be some exceptions), is a better model of a *virtuous* and *philosophical* character.

You see I venture still to join these epithets as inseparable and almost synonymous; tho you seem to regard them almost as incompatible. And here I have a strong inclination to say a few

name, d'Alembert in his Declaration says: 'He acknowledges only that he was a little assisted in regard to the stile, by a person he does not name, and whom perhaps he ought to name' (*Concise and Genuine Account*, 94).

[1] In a postscript of his letter to Hume of 11 Nov. 1766 Walpole says: 'It occurs to me that you may be apprehensive of my being indiscreet enough to let Dalembert learn your suspicions of him on Mad. du Deffand's account; but you may be perfectly easy on that head.'

words in vindication both of myself and of my friends, venturing even to comprehend you in the number. What new prepossession has seized you to beat in so outrageous a manner your nurses of Mount Helicon, and to join the outcry of the ignorant multitude against science and literature? For my part, I can scarce acknowledge any other ground of distinction between one age and another, between one nation and another, than their different progress in learning and the arts. I do not say between one man and another; because the qualities of the heart and temper and natural understanding are the most essential to the personal character; but being, I suppose, almost equal among nations and ages, do not serve to throw a peculiar lustre on any. You blame France for its fond admiration of men of genius; and there may no doubt be, in particular instances, a great ridicule in these affectations: but the sentiment in general was equally conspicuous in ancient Greece, in Rome during its flourishing period, in modern Italy, and even perhaps in England about the beginning of this century. If the case be now otherwise, it is what we are to lament and be ashamed of. Our enemies will only infer, that we are a nation which was once at best but half civilised, and is now relapsing fast into barbarism, ignorance, and superstition. I beg you also to consider the great difference in point of morals between uncultivated and civilized ages.—But I find I am launching out insensibly into an immense ocean of commonplace; I cut the matter therefore short, by declaring it as my opinion, that if you had been born a barbarian, and had every day cooked your dinner of horseflesh by riding on it fifty miles between your breech and the shoulder of your horse, you had certainly been an obliging, good-natured, friendly man; but at the same time, that reading, conversation, and travel have detracted nothing from those virtues, and have made a considerable addition of other valuable and agreeable qualities to them. I remain, not with ancient sincerity, which was only roguery and hypocrisy, but very sincerely, Dear Sir,

Your most obedient and most humble servant,

David Hume.

P.S.

The French translation of this strange piece of mine (for I must certainly give it that epithet) was not made by D'Alembert, but by one under his direction.

* 364. *To* William Strahan

Nothing could more surprize me, Dear Strahan, than your Negligence with regard to this silly Pamphlet I sent you. You have never been at the Pains once to answer one of my Letters with regard to it; tho' certainly I intended you a Friendship by sending it to you: You never informd me, that Becket had got over a Copy from Paris; You have never conveyd any of my Directions to the English Translator; but the greatest Enormity of all, and what covers me with Shame and Confusion, is your printing the Name of two Ladies, who had expressly forbid it; and that under Pretence, that the same Reason did not hold for concealing them in London as in Paris: As if it were impossible, that any Piece of Intelligence coud pass from the one Place to the other.[1] How your Compositor came so much as to know the Name of M[de] de Boufflers I cannot so much as imagine: He has surely read it thro my Razure and so has inserted it. What do you think of that Practice? I have scarce met with anything that has given me more Displeasure.

I am Dear Sir Your most obedient Servant

David Hume.

Edinburgh
25 of Nov[r] 1766

† 365. *To* Richard Davenport

Dear Sir

I doubt not but you have already got a Copy of that Pamphlet, which with great Reluctance I was obliged to allow my Friends at Paris to publish with regard to this miserable Affair between Rousseau and me; and I cannot doubt of the Judgement you wou'd form of it. Two days ago, I received a Letter of which

* MS. at Barnbougle Castle; Hill, 102.

† MS. in Bibliothèque publique de Neuchâtel; hitherto unpublished.

[1] Rousseau in his letter of 4 Dec. 1765 to Hume mentioned Mme de Verdelin. In the *Concise and Genuine Account* the name is indicated by 'Madam ***', but the following footnotes are inserted: '†The person here mentioned desired her name might be suppressed. *French Editor*.

'As the motive to the suppression of the lady's name can hardly be supposed to extend to this country, the *English translator* takes the liberty to mention the name of the Marchioness of Verdelin.'

Later in the pamphlet Mme de Boufflers's name is printed as that of one of Hume's correspondents.

I send you a Copy enclosed.[1] The References are to the Paris Edition; but the English Translation has the same Passages. The pages 85, 86 of the Paris Edition correspond to 65, 66 of the Translation; and the pages 92–96 to 70–74 of the Translation; I beg of you to transmit the enclos'd to Rousseau.[2] The Reason is, that my Friends imagine, he is mad enough to think of replying and continuing the Controversy: He will see, from this Instance, what weapons I have still in my hand to confound him, if he shoud make such an Attempt, and if I shoud think it worth while to take any farther Notice of it.

I am Dear Sir

Your most obedient humble Servant

DAVID HUME

Edinburgh

27 of Novr 1766

To Richard Davenport Esqr at Davenport, Brereton Green Cheshire

* 366. *To the* COMTESSE DE BOUFFLERS

Edinburgh, 2d December, 1766.

I have had one of your letters, dear Madam, too long before me unanswered.[3] I have been of late in a way of life somewhat unsettled: I came down to visit my friends here and put some affairs in order; but find myself so entangled with friends and affairs, that I know not when I shall get rid of them. I agree heartily to what you say, when you wish you had not allowed me to depart from Paris: it was not so necessary as I imagined to depart from it; and notwithstanding my inclination, I find unexpected difficulties in returning. I am confined here for the greater part of this winter.

I had a letter from Miss Becket, wrote by your order, concerning a Negro, who called himself son to an African king at

* *Priv. Corr.*, 228 ff.

[1] A letter from George de Yverdun dated from London, 18 Nov. 1766 (MS., R.S.E.; *Eminent Persons*, 297 ff.), in which he confesses having written two articles in the *St. James's Chronicle*, about the first of which Rousseau had said that he was convinced Hume had furnished the materials for it.

[2] Davenport did so, and Hume's transcript of de Yverdun's letter is now among the Rousseau MSS. at Neuchâtel.

[3] Mme de Boufflers's letter of 6 Aug. 1766 (see extract in Appendix K below).

Annamaboüe. I wrote to a gentleman[1] who had been governor of an English fort on that coast; and having transmitted him Miss Becket's letter, desired him to tell the truth of the matter. His answer only came to me lately. He says, that it is an abuse to call any of these miserable heads of tribes, kings; but even allowing them to be such, the person in question is not the son of a king; his mother only, after his birth, was married to a king, that is, was one in fifty slaves, whom he lay with, when his caprice led him. His black Majesty gave his son-in-law as a pledge to one Hamilton, captain of a trading vessel on that coast, and received some goods in exchange. As he afterwards refused to ransom the young man, Captain Hamilton had a right to do as he did: he carried him off, and sold him with the rest of his slaves at Barbadoes. He was there found by a projecting fellow, one Creighton, or Creiton, a surgeon, who purchased him, brought him over to London, passed him for the son of a king, and got a small pension for his subsistence. The pension was afterwards withdrawn, and the young man sent back to his own country. This is the only story of note, which has passed of late years on the coast of Annamaboüe. The person you mean, either is this young man, or desires to pass himself for such. The time, the place, and some circumstances of his adventures, all concur: but as far as I can learn, he never had any thing to do with the Secretary of the Royal Society.

Thanks to God, my affair with Rousseau is now finally and totally at an end, at least on my part: for I never surely shall publish another line on that subject. It was with infinite reluctance I consented to the last publication. I lay my account that many people will condemn me for it, and will question the propriety or necessity of it: but if I had not published, many people would have condemned me as a calumniator, and as a treacherous and false friend. There is no comparison between these species of blame; and I underwent the one, to save me from the other.

There is a concluding circumstance in this affair, which has given me some vexation: you are named, as well as Madame de Verdelin, in the English translation. I sent up to a bookseller in London copies of my original letters, that they might be inserted in the English translation. I had erased your name; but it seems not so, but that it was legible; and it is accordingly printed. The bookseller, the printer, and the compositor, all

[1] J. Roberts by name. His letter is extant among the MSS., R.S.E.

throw the blame on each other, for this accident. I ask you ten thousand pardons: but as I had the delicacy on your account to erase your name even from the manuscript copy you sent over to my friends at Paris; you may easily believe, that I would never willingly have allowed it to be printed contrary to your orders.

A few posts ago I received a very curious letter from a Swiss gentleman, who resides in London, but whom I never either saw or heard of before: his name is Deyverdun, and he calls himself a native of Lausanne. He says, that he was extremely surprized to find that Rousseau had, in page 85–86, and in page 92–96, accused me for being the author or accomplice of the two libels wrote against him; and he says, with regard to the last, that he has an intimate and a certain conviction of it: I was not able to give any other answer, than that I had never so much as seen either of these pretended libels. Now the Swiss gentleman tells me, that he himself was the author of them; and gives me leave to publish his letter for that purpose to the whole world. But my aversion to farther publications on that head is so great, that I shall not give this letter to the press. I have only sent a copy of it to Mr Davenport, to be delivered to Rousseau. If he has the least remains of a sentiment of honour, he must fall on his face before me, upon the perusal of this letter.

I have not heard any thing, of a long time, that has given me more pleasure than what you write me, that you are perfectly satisfied with the character and conduct of your son. It is a delicious sentiment, and will be a consolation to you through life. Adieu, my dear friend: my regrets for parting with you are as lively as they were at the first moment. Please to direct to me as before—to the care of Mr Coutts, banker, in the Strand, London.

* 367. *To* Thomas Becket

[Edinburgh, December 1766]

Sir

I have no objection to your joining M. de Voltaire's Letters to mine:[1] You have certainly a Right to dispose of them as you think Proper.

* MS. in Seligman Collection, Columbia Univ. Library, New York City; hitherto unpublished.

[1] Voltaire's letter to Hume about Rousseau, dated from Ferney, 24 Oct. 1766. It was published in London by S. Bladon in Nov. 1766. In the same

I cannot imagine that a Piece wrote on so silly a Subject as mine will ever come to a second Edition; but if it shoud, please order the following Corrections to be made.

Page viii of the Advertisement, in the Note say The original Letters of M. Rousseau will be lodged &c.[1]

Page 4 Read *Hic domus, hac patria est.*[2]

Page 6 The Passage of the Note which names M^de^ de Verdelin must be suppress'd.

Page 18 read *on condition only that the Affair shoud remain a kind of Secret.*[3]

Page 21 instead of *out of regard to me*, read, *agreeably to the usual Politeness & Humanity of his Character.*[4]

Page 34 There is a Note ommitted here, which shoud be restord from the French Edition.[5]

Page 38 In the Note instead of *is equally contemptible* read, *is equally mistaken.*[6]

Page 70 Add to my Note, these Words: *Since the publication of the first Edition, I receivd a Letter from a Foreigner, residing in London, who expresses his extreme Surprize at Mr Rousseau's ascribing this Piece to me, together with that mentiond in page 65. For this Gentleman, whom I never saw, confesses that he wrote both for his Amusement: He then conceal'd his Name, because he did not care to appear as the Author of such trifles: But he very genteely offers to allow me to publish his Letter, if I think it necessary for the Vindication of my Character: But really I do not think it necessary, and I do not judge it proper to*

month there appeared at Paris a 12mo pamphlet of 44 pages entitled *Le Docteur Pansophe ou Lettres de M. de Voltaire.* This contained: i. Voltaire's letter to Hume above-mentioned, and, ii. *Lettre de M. de Voltaire au docteur Jean-Jacques Pansophe.* The latter had previously been published in England, in English and French, as *A Letter from Mr Voltaire to M. Jean Jacques Rousseau.* Voltaire categorically denied having written it, and it has been attributed by his editors to various other hands.

[1] the 1st edit. reads: 'The Original letters of both parties will be lodged . . .', which was absurd, since Rousseau had the originals of Hume's letters.

[2] The 1st edit. reads: 'Haec domus, haec patria est.'

[3] The 1st edit. reads: 'On condition only that the affair should not be made publick.'

[4] The reference is to Horace Walpole.

[5] 'M. Rousseau ne m'a assurément jamais donné lieu de lui demander une explication. Si, pendant que nous avons vecu ensemble, il a eu quelques-uns des indignes soupçons dont cette Lettre est remplie, il les a tenus bien secrets.'

[6] The reference is to Rousseau and Allan Ramsay's portrait of him. The English translator had mistranslated 'M. Rousseau s'est donc également mépris . . .'.

take the Gentleman from his Retreat by giving his Name to the Public. Nothing but new Defiances on the part of M. Rousseau shall oblige me to make use of the Freedom, which the Gentleman allows me.

Page 71 Ommitt the Translator's Note.[1]

Page 79 Add to my Note, these Words. *If M. Rousseau consult his Plutarch, he will find, that when Themistocles fled into Persia, Xerxes was so pleas'd with this Event, that he was heard to exclaim several times in his sleep, I have Themistocles, I have Themistocles. Why will not M. Rousseau understand my Exclamation in the same Sense?*

Page 86 Ommitt M^{de} de Boufflers Name.

Page 94 read *on whom the public Suspicions have never fallen.*[2]

I am Sir Your most humble Servant

DAVID HUME

* 368. *To* MATTHEW MATY [3]

Sir

As M. Rousseau had wrote to several of his Correspondents abroad, that I never dared to publish the Letters, which he had wrote me; or if I published them, they wou'd be so falsify'd, that they wou'd not be the same, I was obliged to say in my Preface, that the Originals wou'd be consigned in the Musæum: I hope you have no Objection to the receiving them. I send them by my Friend, Mr Ramsay.[4] Be so good as to give them the Corner of any Drawer: I fancy few people will trouble you by desiring a Sight of them: All the World seem to be satisfyed concerning the Foundation of that unhappy Affair: Yet notwithstanding, I own, that I never in my Life took a Step with so much Reluctance as the consenting to that Publication; but as it appeared absolutely necessary to all my Friends at Paris, I cou'd not withstand their united Opinion. I have also sent

* MS., R.S.E.; Burton, ii. 359 f.

1 A particularly fatuous addition by the English translator to one of Hume's notes. It is not worth quoting.

2 This is part of D'Alembert's Declaration. The 1st edit. reads: 'As to my part, on whom the public suspicions have fallen in this affair . . . '.

3 Matthew Maty (1718–76), one of the librarians of the British Museum; Principal Librarian, 1772; editor of *Memoirs and Miscellaneous Works of Lord Chesterfield*, 1777. He figured in a minor role in the Hume-Rousseau quarrel, being dragged in by Rousseau (see Rousseau's letter of 10 July 1766, in Appendix G below).

4 Allan Ramsay.

the Original of Mr Walpole's Letter to me, which enters into the Collection.[1]

I am Sir

Your most obedient and most humble Servant

DAVID HUME

Edinburgh

23 of January 1767.

* 369. *To the* COMTESSE DE BOUFFLERS

Edinburgh, 2 of February, 1767.

Mr Ainslie [2] was mistaken.[3] The house in which I live, was purchased by me five or six years ago. I was prevented by a singular accident from disposing of it a very little before I left Paris. Do you not remember, that I set out to pass the Christmas with you at L'Isle Adam, but could get no farther than Moselle, where I staid all night, and returned next day, with great difficulty, to Paris? There was a great fall of snow, which rendered the roads quite impracticable. I had wrote a letter, to dispose of my house, and I had left this letter with my landlord at Paris, to be sent to the post-house on the post-day. Happily, or rather, I believe, unhappily, the letter had not gone off; upon which I kept it, as thinking that if any affair called me to this country, it would be very inconvenient for me not to have a house to retire to. Had not this unexpected accident happened, my house would have been disposed of; and as this is a growing town, where it is very difficult to find lodgings, I should never more have thought of returning to it.

I kept, however, my resolution of establishing myself at Paris; and for that purpose, I hired no less than two houses; one was in the Fauxbourg St. Germain, which Madame Geoffrin was so good as to undertake to furnish for me. But this I found, on reflection, too small; and though I paid rent for it, I was resolved not to make use of it. I hired another house in the quarter of the Palais-Royal, which Baron d'Holbach undertook to furnish before I could return from London. Had this bargain

* *Priv. Corr.*, 231 ff.

[1] Dr. Maty returned the papers, saying that the Trustees did not think proper to receive them (Letter dated 22 April 1767, MS., R.S.E.).

[2] See note 3 on p. 44 above.

[3] The letter to which this of Hume appears to be an answer is not extant among the MSS., R.S.E.

taken place, I should at this time have been established at Paris, and probably for life. But the proprietor of the house was absent, being the head of the commission sent down to Brittany: I made the contract with his agent, who had a power from him; but in the mean time, somebody had wrote to the proprietor himself, and had hired the house immediately from him. This event happened only two days before my departure; and being hurried by the Duke of Choiseul's order to M. Rousseau,[1] I had not time to look for another house.

You see then, dear Madam, what a complication of accidents has prevented me from being at present a Parisian, and I hope your constant guest and attendant.

But I am now in Edinburgh, and finding myself at my own fire-side, amid my books, conversing with company who are both estimable and agreeable, my former passion for study, derived both from nature and habit, has seized me with greater violence, by reason of so long an interruption, and I am so occupied with present things, that I form no distant resolution; at least, none that I shall speak of, lest I should not be believed, and lest my not executing it should expose me to the reproach of levity.

But what terms shall I employ to express my gratitude and acknowledgments to the Prince of Conti, for the honour which he intends me? You must here come to my assistance, and aid me with your usual eloquence, otherwise I shall never be able to do justice to my internal sentiments. But unfortunately, instead of corresponding to marks of distinction so honourable to me, I may even be thought wanting in my due regard to the Prince.

It was certainly my duty to have fixed sooner my resolution, and to have notified it to you; but by the letters which passed between us when I was at London, it appeared to me that I had sufficiently explained my passion for retreat and solitude, and that you had made the Prince sensible that nothing but my sincere regard for him made me worthy of the honour he intended me. In other respects, my habits of life disqualified me from profiting by it. I beseech you, dear Madam, give me your aid, where you can do it so much justice, and where I stand so much in need of it.

I am almost vexed to find, that my Fridays are too well supplied, and still more that I myself cannot enjoy the good

[1] See note 2 on p. 529 of vol. i.

company which assemble with you on that day. I desire to be remembered to all and sundry of them. Please to tell M. D'Alembert, that if I were not as lazy as he is at writing letters, I should certainly have taken care not to allow our correspondence to drop. I am right in my conjecture, that we are not to expect any answer from Rousseau: Mr Davenport writes me, that he is entirely occupied in writing his Memoirs, which will be a very bulky book, where M. D'Alembert and I will probably make a great figure. But that affair is now so totally ridiculous, that it can no longer give us the least shadow of anxiety. Agreeably to the licence of this country, there has been a great deal of raillery on the incident, thrown out in the public papers, but all against that unhappy man. There is even a print engraved of it: M. Rousseau is represented as a Yahoo, newly caught in the woods; I am represented as a farmer, who caresses him and offers him some oats to eat, which he refuses in a rage; Voltaire and D'Alembert are whipping him up behind; and Horace Walpole making him horns of *papier maché*. The idea is not altogether absurd.[1]

I interest myself very much in Madame de Barbantane. I fancy that the way of life you mention will not be disagreeable to her, considering the sobriety of her disposition and character. I am obliged to you for the intelligence you give me of our other common friends and acquaintances, by whom I have a great ambition to be remembered. I need not tell you what share you have in my attachment and regard.

* 370. *To* Adam Ferguson

[London, 24 February, 1767][2]

Dear Ferguson

I happen'd yesterday to visit a Person three hours after a Copy of your Performance [3] was open'd for the first time in London. It was by Lord Mansfield. I accept the Omen of its future Success. He was extremely pleas'd with it; said it was perfectly well wrote; assurd me, that he woud not stop a moment

* MS. in possession of Mr. W. S. Lewis, Farmington, Conn., U.S.A.; hitherto unpublished.

[1] This print, entitled 'The Savage Man', the design for which was Boswell's, is reproduced in Tinker's *The Young Boswell* and in my *David Hume*.

[2] This letter can be dated by the next letter.

[3] *Essay on the History of Civil Society*. For Hume's private opinion on this book see Letter 303 above.

till he had finishd it, and recommended it strongly to the Perusal of the Archbishop of Yorke,[1] who was present.

Tho' I set out with Reluctance I do not regreat my Journey. Direct to me at Miss Elliots in Brewer's Street. I have not seen Smith: judge of my Hurry.

Yours sincerely
DAVID HUME

*371. *To the* REV. HUGH BLAIR

Dear Sir

I happend yesterday to visit a Person three hours after a Copy of Ferguson's Performance was open'd for the first time in London. It was by Lord Mansfield. I accept this Omen of its future Success. He was extremely pleas'd with it; said it was very agreeable and perfectly well wrote; assur'd me, that he wou'd not stop a Moment till he had finishd it; and recommended it strongly to the Perusal of the Archbishop of Yorke who was present. I have wrote the same Article of Intelligence to Ferguson himself; but as he is the likeliest Person in the World to suppress it, I thought it safest to put it into your hands, in order to circulate it.

General Conway told me on my Arrival, that Rousseau had made an Application to him, thro' the Canal of Mr Davenport, to have his Pension granted to him. The General's Answer was, that I was to be in town in a few days; and without my Consent and even full Approbation he woud take no Step in that Affair. You may believe, that I exhorted him to do so charitable an Action. I wish he may not find a Difficulty with the King, who is very much prejudicd against Rousseau. This Step of my old Friend confirms the Suspicion which I always entertain'd, that he thought he had Interest enough to obtain the Pension of himself, and that he had only pick'd a Quarrel with me in order to free himself from the humiliating Burthen of Gratitude towards me. His Motives, therefore, were much blacker than many seem to apprehend them.

A Gentleman told me, that he heard from the French Ambassador, that His Most Christian Majesty had given an Arret

* MS., R.S.E.; Burton, ii. 365 and 386.

[1] Robert Drummond (1711–76), 2nd son of Viscount Dupplin, afterwards 7th Earl of Kinnoul; Bishop of St. Asaph, 1748; Bishop of Salisbury, 1761; Archbishop of York, 1761.

prohibiting under the severest Penalties the printing, vending or dispersing any Paper of Rousseau or his Partizans against me. I dine with the Ambassador to day; so shall know the Truth of the Matter, which scarce appears credible. It is surely very honourable for me; but yet will occasion that strange Man to complain, that he is oppressd with Power all over the World. I am Dear D[r] Yours sincerely

DAVID HUME

London
24th of Feby 1767

Mrs. Montague [1] desires her Compliments to you.

* 372. *To* WILLIAM STRAHAN

Dear Sir

I was sorry not to be at home, when you did me the Favour to call on me the other day: My Occupations [2] prevent my calling on you: But if you be any day at this End of the Town, the best way is to call on me at Mr Conway's House, where I am every forenoon, and commonly between 10 and 3: It is in Little Warwick Street: You'll do me a Pleasure in allowing me at any time half an hour's Conversation with you.

I am Dear Sir Yours sincerely
DAVID HUME.

Friday Forenoon
[? February 1767.]

† 373. *To* WILLIAM STRAHAN

Mr Hume asks Mr Strahan ten thousand Pardons: When Mr Strahan was so kind as to ask him to dine with him on Monday, he was already engagd several days before, but had forgot it. Meeting yesterday with the Gentleman, he put him in mind of it, and insisted that the prior Engagement was to him. So that he hopes Mr Strahan will be so good as to excuse him.

Sunday
[? February 1767.]

* MS. at Barnbougle Castle; Hill, 103.
† MS. at Barnbougle Castle; Hill, 112.

1 Mrs. Montagu had paid a visit to Scotland and met all the celebrities there in 1766.

2 As Under-Secretary of State, Northern Department.

* 374. *To the* Comtesse de Boufflers

London, 1 March, 1767

There has happened, dear Madam, a small change in my situation and fortune since I wrote to you. I was then very deeply immersed in study, and thought of nothing but of retreat and indolence for the rest of my life, when I was surprized with a letter from Lord Hertford, urging me to come to London, and accept of the office of Depute[1]-Secretary of State under his brother. As my Lord knew that this step was contrary to the maxims which I had laid down to myself, he engaged my Lady Hertford to write me at the same time, and to inform me how much she and my Lord desired my compliance. I sate down, once or twice, to excuse myself; but I own I could not find terms to express my refusal of a request made by persons, to whose friendship I had been so much obliged. I foresaw also, that a place was offered me of credit and confidence; that it connected me with General Conway, one of the best men, in every respect, of this country; and that my continuance in place was likely to be very short, both because of the usual fluctuations of power in this country, and because the General, I know, was only waiting an opportunity of returning from the civil, to his usual military line. Behold me, then, embarked for some time in state affairs;[2] and my former chains, from old friends and family connexions, exchanged for others, of a less durable nature. For I do not suspect myself, at my years, and after such established habits of retreat, of being ensnared by this glimpse of court favour to commence a new course of life, and relinquish my literary ambition for the pursuit of riches and honours in the state. On the contrary, I feel myself at present like a banished man in a strange country; I mean, not as I was while with

* *Priv. Corr.*, 235 f.

[1] A regular Scottish form of *Deputy*.

[2] The two Secretaries of State divided foreign affairs between them somewhat as follows:

Southern Department: France, Spain, Italy, Portugal, Switzerland, Turkey (and generally the American Colonies).

Northern Department: Austria, Germany, Poland, Russia, Denmark, Scandinavia, the Low Countries.

They divided Home affairs too, though seldom on any recognizable principle. In Hume's period of office Scotland came under the Northern Department.

you at Paris, but as I should be in Westphalia or Lithuania, or any place, the least to my fancy in the world.

I have seen Lord Holdernesse since I came to London, and immediately commenced a conversation about you: I think it is a cement of friendship between his Lordship and me, that we are of the same sentiments on that head.

* 375. *To* WILLIAM STRAHAN

Dear Strahan

It was not possible for me to get an Opportunity last Night of speaking to Lord Hertford;[1] I shall try if I can be more fortunate this Evening; and I shall as soon as possible, give you Information: A Moment will be sufficient, as I have only to put him in Mind of his Engagements. Yours

D. H.

Sunday Forenoon
[? 8 March 1767.]

† 376. *To* WILLIAM STRAHAN

[? 10 March 1767.][2]

Dear Sir

I spoke to Lord Hertford on Sunday Evening: I know not if what I said woud have any Influence; but he seemd to think, that the Determination of that Question woud depend on the Lords who had been active in conducting the Affair, viz: Marchmont, Sandes [3] and Bautitout:[4] I know not by what means you can have Access to them.

* MS. at Barnbougle Castle; Hill, 111.

† MS. at Barnbougle Castle; Hill, 106.

[1] Lord Hertford was now Lord Chamberlain. What Strahan wanted from him is not definitely known, but probably he was trying to secure the appointment of Printer for the Rolls of Parliament and the Journals of the House of Lords, which was vacant at this time. The three peers mentioned in the next Letter were appointed, on 9 March 1767, on a committee of the House of Lords that was given power to make the appointment. Actually, it went to William Bowyer, principally owing to Lord Marchmont's influence (Nichols, *Lit. Anecdotes*, iii. 39).

[2] The dating of this and the previous letter is mere guesswork, but they must have been written some time in the spring of 1767.

[3] Samuel Sandys (died 1770), 1st Baron Sandys, President of the Board of Trade.

[4] Norborne Berkeley (died 1776), created Baron Botetourt, 1764; Groom of the Bedchamber, 1760; Governor-General of Virginia, 1768.

I send you a Volume of Olivet's Cicero [1] at Mr Millar's Desire, who proposes instantly to begin an Edition of my Essays in that Form,[2] as a Forerunner to the like Edition of my History.[3] Let us see a Sample of your English Press: I do not believe you can make such a Book; and I give you a Defiance. Pray return the Book carefully, after you have carefully survey'd it.

If Becket has a few Copies to spare of the French Edition of my Controversy with Rousseau, I shoud be glad to have three or four of them.

There was a good pleasant Paper, inserted, I believe in your Chronicle, about three months ago. It containd Rousseau's Articles of Charge against me, and then some good humourd Raillery against him and Voltaire and me.[4] I should be glad to have two or three Copies of it, if you can readily find them.

I know not if Becket printed Voltaire's Letter to me, but if he did he may perhaps have two or three Copies to spare, which woud oblige me.

I am Dr Sir Yours sincerely

D. H.

* 377. *To* ADAM FERGUSON

London 10 of March 1767

Dear Ferguson

It is with a sincere Pleasure I inform you of the general Success of your Book. I had almost said universal Success; and the Expression would have been proper, as far as a Book can be suppos'd to be diffus'd in a Fortnight, amidst this Hurry of Politics and Faction. I may safely say, that I have met with no body, that has read it, who does not praise it, and these are the People, who by their Reputation and Rank commonly give the Tone on these Occasions. Lord Mansfield encreas'd his

* MS. in possession of Captain F. L. Pleadwell, U.S. Navy; hitherto unpublished.

[1] A beautiful edition of Cicero, edited by Joseph Olivet and published at Paris in 9 vols., large 4to, 1740–2.

[2] A new edition of the *Essays and Treatises*, in 2 vols., L.P. 4to, appeared in 1768.

[3] A new edition of the *History*, in 8 vols., L.P. 4to, appeared in 1770.

[4] Possibly the skit on the Hume-Rousseau quarrel entitled 'Heads of an Indictment laid by J.J. Rousseau, philosopher, against David Hume, Esq.', quoted by Burton, ii. 340 (see pp. 446–8 below).

Style of Approbation; and is very loud to that Purpose in his Sunday Societies. I heard Lord Chesterfield and Lord Lyttleton express the same Sentiments; and what is above all, Caddel, I am told, is very happy; and is already projecting a second Edition of the same Quarto Size. You ought to have up more Copies to this Place; tho' I doubt not but you will easily dispose of all those which you retained for Edinburgh.

Lord Shelburn is in the southern Department: I shall have no Difficulty by his means of sending over your Copy to Paris. I had almost forgot to tell you, that this noble Lord, as well as Lord Bute, are among your most zealous Partizans. The last says, that your Book is one of the best he ever read.

Last night, Horace Walpole desir'd me to make his Compliments to you: He has receiv'd your Book, in a Present from you, as he supposes. He gives you many thanks, approves extremely of what he has read, but delays writing you till he has read the whole.

I shall tell you all our domestic Politics, in which there is no Secret. The Ministry on Friday was Sennight lost the Vote of the Land tax by a Majority of eighteen, very unexpectedly both to themselves and to their antagonists. The Country Gentlemen, to save themselves a shilling a pound, and to please the Counties whom they represent joined the Opposition. Every body blames extremely the Measure. Even many of those who voted for it, are frank in declaring their Disapprobation; and some scruple not to say, that if they had thought it possible for them to have prevailed, they would not have been on that Side.[1] But tho' these were unlucky Circumstances for the Opposition, and their Majority had proceeded merely from an Accident, they were extremely elated with their Success; and express'd their Confidence of finally prevailing. The general Opinion of Dissensions among the Ministry encreas'd their Hopes; and as it was universally known that my Patron and Charles Townsend differ'd in opinion from the rest with regard to the Conduct of

[1] Writing on the same subject to Mann on 2 March 1767, Horace Walpole says: 'The causes of this event were the absence of Lord Chatham, who has lingered at Bath and Marlborough till so ill, that he could not come to town. No business was done: the other ministers were uneasy or inactive. The opposition seized the moment, and collected all their strength. Still this would not have signified; but the friends of the court were so inapprehensive of any defeat, that many of them privately and separately consulted their own popularity, and were actually engaged in the division, before they had any notion of being in the minority' (*Letters*, vii. 87).

the East Indian Affairs,[1] they muster'd up all their Force on Friday last, in order to make a Trial of Parties. But it then appear'd that the Difference was only of Opinion, not of Affections. The General & the Chancellor of the Exchequer supported the Measures of Administration and the Opposition did not think proper to call a Vote. But yesterday they thought to have stolen a March on us. They introduced into the House a small Branch of the same East Indian Affair; and had given the Rendesvous to each other. Mr Townsend was accidentally absent: But Mr Conway (and this I tell you from universal Testimony) exerted himself with so much Eloquence and Ability that he retain'd the Majority to the Number of thirty-three. This is thought a great and deserv'd Victory for the present Session; and the Majority, it is believ'd, will be daily encreasing. Sir Gilbert Elliot also spoke admirably as I am told. But Burke did very ill, which I am sorry for. It is pretended, that he rather sinks in Reputation.

Wedderburn is always in Opposition, but rises in Character.

I am not hurry'd with Business. I commonly attend on the Secretary from ten to three; but often read a Book of my own, and see Company there, and have indeed no more Business than would be requisite for my Amusement in this place, while I am not engag'd in any literary Occupation.

* 378. *To* William Strahan

Dear Strahan

I have been so happy as to prevail in my Applications both to Lord Hertford and to General Conway: I doubt not but Charles Townsend will be favourable to you. Pray, are you thinking of this new Dress in which you promis'd to put me?[2] Shall I pretend to rival Cicero in Garb and Accoutrements.

Yours

D. H.

Monday Forenoon
[March 1767.]

* MS. at Barnbougle Castle; Hill, 111.

[1] Chatham was determined to mulct the East India Company of some of their ill-gotten gains. Conway and Townshend thought he was going too far.

[2] See Letter 376 above.

* 379. *To the* MARQUISE DE BARBENTANE

London, 13th of March, 1767.

You may probably, dear Madam, have heard of the Disaster that has happened to Lord Tavistoke,[1] and may have heard it represented in more dismal colours than the true; which is the reason that I now take the Liberty to write to you. I know that your Friendship for him wou'd give you the most real Concern, and as there are great Hopes of his Recovery, I was willing to convey them to you. Four Days ago, he fell from his Horse at hunting. He was taken up for Dead; and on Examination was found to have his Skull (sa crane) fractured in a most violent manner. A surgeon was immediatly sent for; a difficult Operation was successfully performed; and he was brought to his Senses. The Symptoms have ever since been very favourable; tho' his Situation is still very dangerous. It is impossible to conceive any one more universally regretted. No body believes that the Duke would survive his Son's Death: His Condition is in a great Measure concealed from Lady Tavistoke, who is six months gone with child. I sent about an hour ago to Bedford House that I might give you the most recent Account, and had a very favourable Answer. As it is thought, that the four first Days were most critical, there are now good hopes entertained of his Recovery.

Mde de Boufflers wou'd probably tell you, that I am now, from a Philosopher, degenerated into a petty Statesman, and am entirely occupyed in Politics. I am too well acquainted with our usual Fluctuations and Revolutions to believe that this Avocation will be durable. But whatever I am or wherever I live, believe me to be, with great Sincerity, Dear Madam,

Your most obedient humble Servant

DAVID HUME.

To Madame la Marquise de Barbentane au Palais roiale a Paris

† 380. *To the* COMTESSE DE BOUFFLERS

London, 17 March, 1767.

Your letter, dear Madam, for the first time in my life, gave me uneasiness and no less surprize.[2] Surely, whenever the offer

* MS. in possession of R. N. Carew Hunt, Esq., London; *Priv. Corr.*, 237 f.

† *Priv. Corr.*, 238 ff.

[1] See note 4 on p. 470 of vol. i.

[2] It is significant that none of Mme de Boufflers's letters belonging to this

of your friend[1] was mentioned, at the same time that I expressed the highest sense of his goodness, I never spoke of any thing but difficulties and objections. I was conscious how little qualified I am for that course of life pointed out to me, and how much the habits of study and indolence, and liberty, prevailed over me, to admit of such an attachment as was proposed. Your exhortation, and, still more, the prospect of passing much of my time in your company, had great influence over me, but were never able to overcome the internal conviction which I retained, that I should be extremely misplaced in such a situation. You will please to remember, that very early after my return to London, I wrote you a letter to this purpose, and you had the compliance to yield to my reluctance, and even to make me another proposal, the most charming and most obliging in the world, which however I delayed accepting, till I should see how far it was inconvenient to you. I mentioned the arrangements which I had taken before I left Paris, in order to convince you that I was quite serious in my resolutions of returning; resolutions in which you cannot doubt but my attachment to you had a considerable share. How it happens that you was not at the time acquainted with these arrangements, I cannot imagine: I cannot but think you have forgot. Perhaps your absence from Paris till within a few days of our departure, was the reason why I never mentioned them to you. Surely, the two persons who were so good as to promise me their assistance, live in so public a manner, that, as I never desired them to conceal the matter, they were the most likely to spread the knowledge of it among my friends and acquaintance. On the whole then, I hope to be entirely justified in your eyes; or if that should fail me, I hope to be forgiven. Provided I be restored to your favour and good opinion, I am the more indifferent about the means.

To think that I have incurred your displeasure, is too grievous to be borne; even though it should happen, as you say, that my absence from you were to be eternal. But I prognosticate better of my good fortune than to think so. Sure I am that my present

period are extant among the MSS., R.S.E. From the tone of Hume's replies it is clear that she was angry and hurt at his not returning to France. Probably he thought her letters too intimate, or too compromising, to be preserved. The next letter of hers extant is dated 25 May 1768.

[1] Probably the Prince of Conti, who had offered Hume quarters in the Temple.

connexions are rather likely to forward our re-union. This situation will not probably be durable, much less perpetual. It was only in the prospect of its terminating soon, that I accepted of it.

Last post, I informed Madame de Barbantane of this terrible accident that has happened to Lord Tavistock. I have now the pleasure to tell you that he is in a very promising way, and great hopes are entertained of his recovery.[1]

I beg it of you, not to be long in answering me.

*381. *To* William Robertson

London, 19 March, 1767.

My dear Sir,

You do extremely right in applying to me wherever it is the least likely I can serve you or any of your friends. I consulted immediately with General Conway, who told me, as I suspected, that the chaplains to forts and garrisons were appointed by the War Office, and did not belong to his department. Unhappily I have but a slight acquaintance with Lord Barrington,[2] and cannot venture to ask him any favour; but I shall call on Pryce Campbell,[3] tho not of my acquaintance, and shall enquire of him the canals through which this affair may be conducted: perhaps it may lie in my power to facilitate it by some means or other.

I shall endeavour to find out the unhappy philosopher you mention,[4] tho it will be difficult for me to do him any service. He is an ingenious man, but unfortunate in his conduct, particularly in the early part of his life. The world is so cruel as never to overlook these flaws; and nothing but hypocrisy can fully cover them from observation. There is not so effectual a scourer of reputations in the world. I wish that I had never parted with that *Lixivium*, in case I should at any future time have occasion for it. . . .

* Stewart, *Robertson*, 355 f.; Burton, ii. 365 (fragment).

[1] He died, however, on 22 March.

[2] William Wildman (1717–93), 2nd Viscount Barrington; Secretary-at-War, 1755–61 and 1765–78; Chancellor of the Exchequer, 1761–2; Treasurer of the Navy, 1762–5.

[3] M.P. for Cromarty and Nairn, 1762–8; Commissioner of the Treasury, 1766; an amateur engraver of some talent.

[4] I suspect that the reference is to Archibald Campbell, for whose history see Letter 442 below.

A few days before my arrival in London, Mr Davenport had carried to Mr Conway a letter of Rousseau's, in which that philosopher says, that he had never meant to refuse the King's bounty, that he would be proud of accepting it, but that he would owe it entirely to His Majesty's generosity and that of his ministers, and would refuse it if it came through any other canal whatsoever, even that of Mr Davenport.[1] Mr Davenport then addressed himself to Mr Conway, and asked whether it was not possible to recover what this man's madness had thrown away? The Secretary replied, that I should be in London in a few days, and that he would take no steps in the affair but at my desire and with my approbation. When the matter was proposed to me, I exhorted the General to do this act of charity to a man of genius, however wild and extravagant. The King, when applied to, said, that since the pension had once been promised, it should be granted, notwithstanding all that had passed in the interval. And thus the affair is happily finished, unless some new extravagance come across the philosopher, and engage him to reject what he has anew applied for. If he knew my situation with General Conway he probably would; for he must then conjecture that the affair could not be done without my consent.

Ferguson's book goes on here with great success. A few days ago I saw Mrs Montague, who had just finished it with great pleasure: I mean, she was sorry to finish it, but had read it with great pleasure. I asked her, whether she was satisfied with the

[1] Rousseau's letter to Davenport, dated [?] Feb. 1767, opens with the following paragraph:

'Bien loin, Monsieur, qu'il puisse jamais m'être entré dans l'esprit d'être assez vain, assez sot, et assez mal appris pour refuser les grâces du Roi, je les ai toujours regardées et les regarderai toujours comme le plus grand honneur qui me puisse arriver. Quand je consultai milord Maréchal si je les accepterois, ce n'étoit certainement pas que je fusse là-dessus en doute, mais c'est qu'un devoir particulier et indispensable ne me permettoit pas de le faire que je n'eusse son agrément. J'étois bien sûr qu'il ne le refuseroit pas. Mais, Monsieur, quand le Roi d'Angleterre et tous les souverains de l'univers mettroient à mes pieds tous leurs trésors et toutes leurs couronnes, par les mains de David Hume, ou de quelque autre homme de son espèce, s'il en existe, je les rejetterois toujours avec autant d'indignation que, dans tout autre cas, je les recevrois avec respect et reconnoissance. Voilà mes sentiments, dont rien ne me fera départir. J'ignore à quel sort, à quels malheurs la Providence me reserve encore; mais ce que je sais, c'est que les sentiments de droiture et d'honneur qui sont gravés dans mon cœur n'en sortiront jamais qu'avec mon dernier soupir. J'espère, pour cette fois, que je me serai exprimé clairement' (*Œuvres*, 1826, vol. xxiv. 100 f.).

style? Whether it did not savour somewhat of the country? Oh yes, said she, a great deal: it seems almost impossible that anyone could write such a style except a Scotsman.

I find you prognosticate a very short date to my administration; I really believe that few (but not evil) will be my days. My absence will not probably allow my claret time to ripen, much less to sour. However that may be, I hope to drink out the remainder of it with you in mirth and jollity.

I am,

Sincerely yours, usque ad aras,

David Hume.

* 382. *To the* Earl of Eglintoun [1]

Wednesday [Spring 1767].

My Lord

Not finding an Opportunity yesterday of speaking to Lord Hertford in favour of Mr Burney,[2] I spoke to My Lady, and told her the whole Case. She already knows Mr Burney and has an Esteem for him. She said it gave her great Uneasyness & she was sure, woud do so, to my Lord, that he was already engag'd; and she believd, to the Duke of York. It occur'd to me, that his royal Highness's Application might also be in favour of Burney; in which Case, the Matter is easy. If not, it is probable your Lordship may engage him to depart from his Application: For really Mr Burney's Case, independant of his Merit, is very hard and cruel.

I have the Honour to be

My Lord

Your Lordships Most humble & most obedient Servant

David Hume

P.S.

If your Lordship honour me with an Answer in the Forenoon, please send it to Gen[l] Conways in Little Warwick Street, if in the Afternoon, at Miss Elliots Brewer Street Golden Square.

To The Earl of Eglinton Piccadilly

* MS. in J. Pierpont Morgan Library, New York City; hitherto unpublished.

[1] Lord Eglintoun was Lord of the Bedchamber, 1760–7.

[2] Charles Burney (1726–1814), author of *History of Music*, 4 vols., 1776–89; father of Fanny Burney. He was first introduced to Hume in Paris in 1764 by Hume's friend Michael Ramsay, who had been tutor to Lord Eglintoun.

* 383. *To the* Rev. Hugh Blair

The success of the Book,[1] Dear D^{r}, which you mention, gives me great Satisfaction, on account of my sincere Friendship for the Author; and so much the rather, as this Success was to me unexpected. I have since begun to hope, and even to believe, that I was mistaken; and in this Perswasion have several times taken it up and read Chapters of it: But to my great Mortification and Sorrow, I have not been able to change my Sentiments. We shall see, by the Duration of its Fame, whether or not I am mistaken. Helvetius & Saurin [2] both told me at Paris, that they had been consulted by Montesquieu about his *Esprit des loix*: They us'd the Freedom to tell him, as their fix'd Opinion, that he ought to suppress the Book; which, they forsaw, wou'd very much injure his Reputation. They said to me, that, no doubt, I thought, they had reason to be ashamd of their Judgement: But still, added they, you may observe, that the public are very much returnd from their first Admiration of that Book, and we are perswaded, that they will daily return still more. I hope, that I shall be found a false Prophet as much as these Gentlemen: For tho' the Esprit des loix be considerably sunk in Vogue, & will probably still sink farther, it maintains a high Reputation, and probably will never be totally neglected. It has considerable Merit, notwithstanding the Glare of its pointed Wit, and notwithstanding its false Refinements and its rash and crude Positions.

Helvetius and Saurin assurd me, that this Freedom of theirs never lost them any thing of Montesquieu's Friendship: I believe the like woud be my Case; but it is better not to put it to a Trial. On that Account, as well as others, I recommend to you Secresy, towards every Person, except Robertson.

My way of Life here is very uniform, and by no means disagreeable. I pass all the Forenoon in the Secretary's House from ten till three, where there arrives from time to time Messengers, that bring me all the Secrets of this Kingdom, and indeed of Europe, Asia, Africa and America. I am seldom

* MS., R.S.E.; Burton, ii. 384 and 387 f. (incomplete).

[1] Ferguson's *Civil Society*. Blair, writing to Hume on 24 March [1767], and referring to the success of this book, says: 'I must take a little credit to my critical Sagacity' (MS., R.S.E.).

[2] Bernard-Joseph Saurin (1706–81), dramatist and poet; author of *Spartacus*, 1760, *Les Mœurs du Temps*, 1760, &c.

hurry'd; but have Leizure at Intervals to take up a Book, or write a private Letter, or converse with any Friend that may call for me: And from Dinner to Bed-time is all my own. If you add to this, that the Person, with whom I have the chief, if not only Transactions is the most reasonable, equal temperd, and gentlemanlike man imaginable, and Lady Aylesbury the same, you will certainly think I have no reason to complain: And I am far from complaining. I only shall not regreat when my Duty is over; because to me the Situation can lead to nothing; at least, in all Probability; and reading and sauntering and lownging and dozing, which I call thinking, is my supreme Happiness, I mean my full Contentment.

I send you a Pamphlet, which was publishd near three Months ago; but I never heard of it till last Week, nor saw it till two days ago. Neither Mr Walpole nor I know any thing of the Author; tho' I am told the public ascribd it to himself, which he positively denies, and I entirely acquit him, tho the piece is not ill-wrote.[1]

I thank you for the Acquaintaince you offer me of Mr Percy:[2] But it woud be impracticable for me to cultivate his Friendship, as Men of Letters have here no Place of Rendesvous, and are indeed sunk and forgot in the general Torrent of the World. If you can therefore decline without harshness any Letter of Recommendation, it woud save Trouble both to him and me.

Direct to me as under-Secretary of State, at the Secretarys Office.

1 of April
1767

[1] *A Letter to the Hon. Mr. Horace Walpole, concerning the Dispute between Mr. Hume and Mr. Rousseau.* It is among the list of books for Dec. 1766 in the *Gentleman's Mag.*; which describes it as 'a mere fungus, the excrescence of a popular subject'. It takes Hume's part throughout, and is not badly written. The author, according to Nichols (*Anecdotes*, iii. 531 ff.), was the Rev. Ralph Heathcote, D.D. (1721–95), a Leicestershire vicar, author of pamphlets against Middleton, of *A Sketch of Lord Bolingbroke's Philosophy*, and of numerous other pamphlets, &c.

[2] Thomas Percy (1729–1811), afterwards Bishop of Dromore; editor of *Reliques of Ancient English Poetry.* In his letter of 24 March Blair says: 'There is a Mr Thomas Percy, Chaplain & Secretary to the Duke [of Northumberland] who would be very glad to be acquainted with you; he is a man of letters, and some Taste, . . . a good sort of man, of no very enlarged views however.' Though Hume declined Blair's introduction, he seems to have met Percy in London; for Percy begins a letter to him on 5 Jan. 1772: 'As I had the honour to be not unknown to you, when you resided in London; I flatter myself . . .' (MS., R.S.E.; *Eminent Persons*, 317).

* 384. *To the* REV. HUGH BLAIR

My dear Sir

I had yesterday a Conference with the Chief Baron[1] upon your Affair.[2] He is of Opinion, that I shoud apply to Lowndes[3] for an Order of Payment, notwithstanding this Informality; but he says, that Lowndes is a difficult Man, and it is a Chance whether I shall be able to perswade him. I shall however give him a Trial to day: For tho' I be not acquainted with him, our common Situation, as Sub-ministers gives us a Connexion together. The Chief Baron thinks, as well as I do, that it will be impossible to engraft any Advantages on this Blunder. Why, the Devil, woud you not take 100 pounds Sallary, when you might have had it?

You may perhaps have heard, that Rousseau has elop'd from Mr Davenport without giving any Warning; leaving all his Baggage except Mad^{lle}, about thirty pounds in Davenport's hands, and a Letter on the Table abusing him in the most violent Terms, insinuating that he was in a Conspiracy with me to ruin him.[4] He took the Road to London; but was missing for about a Fortnight: At last he emerges at Spalding in Lincolnshire; whence he writes a Letter to the Chancellor, informing him that the bad Usage he had met with in England made it absolutely necessary for him to evacuate the Kingdom,

* MS., R.S.E.; hitherto unpublished.

[1] Robert Orde (died 1778), a Novocastrian, and Chief Baron of the Scottish Exchequer. Hume was afterwards on very friendly terms with him and his daughters in Edinburgh.

[2] I do not know what this affair was. Blair's letter about it is not extant among the MSS., R.S.E. Probably Hume passed it on to somebody else in the course of trying to get the business put through.

[3] Charles Lowndes, M.P., was, like his more distinguished father, William Lowndes, Secretary to the Treasury.

[4] In this letter, dated 30 April 1767, Rousseau says: '. . . Demain, Monsieur, je quitte votre maison. J'y laisse mon petit équipage, et celui de Mademoiselle Le Vasseur, et j'y laisse le produit de mes estampes et livres pour sûreté des frais faits pour ma dépense depuis Noël. Je n'ignore ni les embûches qui m'attendent, ni l'impuissance où je suis de m'en garantir; mais, Monsieur, j'ai vécu; il ne me reste qu'à finir avec courage une carrière passée avec honneur. Il est aisé de m'opprimer, mais difficile de m'avilir. Voilà ce qui me rassure contre les dangers que je vais courir. Recevez derechef mes vifs et sincères remerciements de la noble hospitalité que vous m'avez accordée. Si elle avoit fini comme elle a commencé, j'emporterois de vous un souvenir bien tendre, qui ne s'effaceroit jamais de mon cœur . . .' (*Œuvres*, 1826, vol. xxiv. 146).

and desiring his Lordship to send him a Guard to escort him in Safety to Dover; this being the last Act of Hospitality, he will desire of the Nation. He is plainly mad; tho I believe not more so, than he has been all his Life. The Pamphlet you mention was wrote by one as mad as himself, and it was believd at first to be Tristram Shandy, but proves to be one Fuseli, an Engraver.[1] He is a fanatical Admirer of Rousseau, but owns he was in the wrong to me. The Pamphlet I sent you was wrote by an English Clergyman whom I never saw;[2] a man of Character, and rising in the Church: For which Reason, it is more prudent in me to conceal his Name. When woud *you* have done so much for me?

I hear good things said of Ferguson's Book every day. Lord Holdernesse showd me a Letter from the Archbishop of Yorke, where his Grace says, that in many things it surpasses Montesquieu. My Friend Mr Dodwell[3] says, that it is an admirable Book, elegantly wrote, and with great Purity of Language. Pray tell to Ferguson and to others all these things.

I remember I said to John Home, that I was anxious for its Success because the Success of all philosophical Writings was peculiarly precarious. This was all I said to him.

I am told the Pamphlet is very near the genuine Speech of L. Mansfield.[4]

I am Dear Sir
Yours sincerely
DAVID HUME

London. 20 of May
1767.

To The Revd Dr Blair Minister of the Gospel at Edinburgh

Free
Da: Hume

[1] Johann Heinrich Fuessli (or Fuseli) (1741–1825), painter and man of letters; member of a Zurich family rich in artists; author of a translation of Winckelmann's *Reflections on the Painting and Sculpture of the Greeks*, 1765. He was induced to come to England by Sir Andrew Mitchell, and became a friend of Andrew Millar, James Coutts, John Armstrong, &c. It is said that most of the copies of his pamphlet on the Hume-Rousseau quarrel were accidentally destroyed by fire in the bookseller's warehouse, and that he did not much regret the loss.

[2] See note 1 on p. 134 above.

[3] See note 2 on p. 50 above.

[4] I have not been able to trace the pamphlet here referred to.

* 385. *To* Anne-Robert-Jacques Turgot

[22 May 1767.]

I never sollicited, My Dear Sir, nor even desired to have a Share in public Business.[1] This last Employment was offered me in such a way by those to whom I had the highest Obligations, that having no good Excuse to give, I must have lain under the Imputation of Ingratitude if I had declined it. Upon Trial, my Situation appears far from disagreeable, and I find, that to a Man of a literary turn, who has no great undertaking in view, Business, especially public Business, is the best Ressource of his declining Years. Learning requires the Ardor of Youth, the full Vigour of Imagination, a Fund of Vanity, and often an unrelenting Application, of all which, men past middle Age are generally incapable. The Notion of Retreat and Solitude which often seizes people when disgusted with Business, is commonly unhappy; because old men, having few Ressources in their Passions and none in their future Hopes, require more Support from Company or Amusement or Affairs, and ought least to be left to their own Reflections. After the Course of hard Study in which I have been engaged, Business is rather a Relaxation than a Labour to me.

I know not, whether you have heard of the late Incidents which have happened to the poor unfortunate Rousseau, who is now plainly delirious and an Object of the greatest Compassion. About three Weeks ago, he ran off, without giving the least Warning, from Mr Davenport's, carrying only his Gouvernante along with him, leaving most of his Baggage, and above thirty Guineas of Money: There was also a Letter found on his Table, abusing his Land-lord, and reproaching him as an Accomplice with me in the Project of ruining and affronting him. He took the Road towards London; and Mr Davenport begged me to find him out, and to discover how his Money and Baggage might be sent after him. He was never heard of for a fortnight; till at last a most extravagant Letter of his was delivered to the Chancellor, dated at Spalding in the County of Lincoln. He there tells the Magistrate that he was on his

* MS. in archives du château de Lantheuil; *Priv. Corr.*, 220 ff. (incomplete and in French translation).

[1] This is in answer to a letter from Turgot dated 25 March [1767] congratulating Hume on his new appointment, discussing Rousseau, and continuing the argument on the best method of taxation (MS., R.S.E.; *Eminent Persons*, 149 ff.; Turgot, *Œuvres*, ii. 658 ff.).

Road to Dover, in order to leave the Kingdom (tho' Spalding is entirely out of the Road). But he dares not proceed a Step farther, nor stir out of the House; for fear of his Enemies: He entreats therefore the Chancellor to send him an authorized Guide to conduct him; and this he demands as the last Act of Hospitality from the Nation towards him. A few days after, I learned from Mr Davenport that he had received a new Letter from Rousseau dated still at Spalding, in which he expresses great Contrition, speaks of his miserable and unhappy Condition, and marks his Intention of returning to his former Retreat at Wootton. I was then hopeful, that he had now recovered his Senses; when behold! a few hours after, General Conway received a Letter from him dated at Dover [1] above two hundred Miles distant from Spalding: This great Journey he had made in about two days. Nothing can be more frenzical than this Letter: He supposes himself to be a Prisoner of State in the hands of the General at my Suggestion, entreats for Leave to depart the Kingdom, represents the Danger of assassinating him in private, and while he owns that he has been rendered infamous in England during his Life he fortells that his Memory will be justifyed after his Death. He says that he has composed a Volume of Memoirs, chiefly with regard to the Treatment he has met with in England, and the State of Captivity, in which he has been detained; and if the General will fairly give him Permission to depart, this Volume, which is deposited in safe hands, shall be delivered to him, and nothing ever appear to the Disgrace of the Nation or of its Ministers. He adds, as if a Ray of Reason then broke in upon his Soul, speaking of himself in the third Person: 'Il abandonne pour toujours le projet d'écrire sa vie et ses mémoires; mais qu'il ne lui échappera jamais ni de bouche ni par écrit un seul mot de plainte sur les malheurs, qui lui sont arrivés en Angleterre; qu'il ne parlera jamais de M. Hume ou qu'il n'en parlera qu'avec honneur; et que lorsqu'il sera pressé de s'expliquer sur quelques indiscrètes plaintes qui lui sont quelquefois échappées dans le fort de ses peines, il les rejettera sans mystère sur son humeur aigrie et portée à la défiance et aux ombrages par ce malheureux penchant, ouvrage de ses malheurs, et qui maintenant y met le comble.'[2]

I inform you of all these particulars, that you may see the

[1] This letter is printed in *Œuvres*, 1826, vol. xxiv. 147 ff.

[2] The printed version, taken, presumably, from the rough copy retained by Rousseau, differs from this extract in phrasing, but not in sense.

poor Man is absolutely lunatic and consequently cannot be the Object of any Laws or civil Punishment: He has certainly passed over to Calais;[1] and being within the Jurisdiction of the Parliament of Paris, he will probably be seized and may be treated without any Regard to his unhappy Condition. When I was at Paris, I saw Instances of the uncommon Animosity borne against him by several Members of that illustrious Body; and I am afraid that his Appearance may again revive the same zealous Spirit among them. It appeared to me, therefore, of Importance that a Person of your Weight and Merit shoud be acquainted from the first hand, with the true State of the Case; and that the Enemies of this unhappy Man may have their Vengeance fully satiated by his past Misfortunes, and may no longer aggravate Afflictions too heavy to be borne. I have spoke to Mr de Guerchy that he may represent Matters in this Light if he writes any thing concerning them to his Court: This letter I have sent under a flying Seal to M. de Montigny, in case you shoud have left Paris and gone to your Intendance. Either you or he will inform the President de Malesherbes. M. de Trudaine will join his good Offices; and I doubt not but your united Endeavours added to the plain Reason of the Case woud procure him Security. If he coud be settled in any safe and quiet Retreat, under a discreet Keeper, he has wherewithall to bear all Charges for his Support: He has, if I conjecture right, about a hundred pounds a Year of his own: The King of England has granted him lately a hundred a Year more, and some Person might be found in a private Place in France who from regard to his Genius wou'd treat him tenderly and keep him from doing any harm either to himself or others. It would be proper that his Gouvernante shoud enter into the Scheme, tho' I find that Mr Davenport had entertained no very advantageous Idea of her Character or Conduct while they lived with him.[2] But he has been accustomed to her and she knows better to humour him than any other Person can do. It is suspected that she has nourished all his Chimeras in order to chace him out of a Country where having no Person to speak to, she tired most desperatly. I beg you to believe me with the most sincere Attachment, My Dear Sir,

Your most obedient humble Servt

David Hume

[1] He arrived at Calais on 22 May.

[2] It seems clear from the documents printed or referred to by Courtois that Thérèse Le Vasseur quarrelled with Davenport's servants at Wootton.

* 386. *To the* Comtesse de Boufflers

London, 22 May, 1767.

Madam,

I find you are desirous to hear no more of me, which, I own, is one of the greatest surprizes, and none of the least afflictions I have met with in the course of my life. However, I could not forbear writing to you, because I shall put it in your power to do an act of generosity, which, unless you be, indeed, totally changed in every respect, must give you pleasure. . . .[1]

It is evident, from all these contrarieties and extravagances, that he [2] is quite disordered in his judgment; yet are his letters, particularly that to Mr Conway, still wrote with beauty and elegance. He laments his being alive, and regrets his being obliged to leave England, but says that he finds every body prepossessed against him; for what reason he cannot imagine, unless it be on account of his conduct towards me, in which he owns he may be to blame. He accepts, however, with gratitude the King's pension; and says he will again write to the General from Calais. He is not in his Armenian dress,[3] so that he may perhaps pass unnoticed: but if he be discovered, as is more probable, there is nothing he has not to dread from the violence of the Parliament; and little relief can be expected from the good will of the ministers towards him. I thought it proper to inform you, that if you hear of his being discovered and arrested, you may employ your credit in restoring him to his liberty, by representing him in his true colours, as a real and complete madman, who is an object of compassion, and can be dangerous to nobody. I find myself much inclined to say a great deal more to you about other subjects, but much check my inclination; and therefore desire only my compliments to Madame de Vierville and Madame de Barbantane, and to Miss Becket; and am

Madam,

Your most obedient and most humble servant,

David Hume.

* *Priv. Corr.*, 240 ff.

[1] He then tells the story of Rousseau's flight to Dover in substantially the same words as in the preceding Letter.

[2] That is, Rousseau.

[3] He had a blue coat made for him at Spalding.

* 387. *To the* Rev. Hugh Blair

Dear Doctor London. 27 of May 1767

I find you have got your Affair done without me, and that the Chief Baron has anticipated my Endeavours and deprivd me of the Merit of obeying your Commands. I am glad, however, it is done.

Since you are curious to hear Rousseau's Story, I shall tell you the Sequel of it. . . .[1]

We hear that notwithstanding his imagined Captivity he has passd over to Calais; where he is likely to experience what real Captivity is. I have however us'd my Perswasion with Monsr de Guerchi to represent him to his Court as a real Madman, more an Object of Compassion than of Anger. We shall no doubt see his Memoirs in a little time which will be full of Eloquence & Extravagance; tho' perhaps as reasonable as any of his past Productions. For I do not imagine he was ever much more in his Senses than at present. I think I may be entirely without Anxiety concerning all his future Productions.

Pray how has the General Assembly passd? I have had a long Letter from Mass David Dickson [2] complaining of your Injustice. Has John Home any Thoughts of coming up?

Tell Robertson, that the Compliment at the End of General Conway's Letter to him was of my composing, without any Orders from him. He smild when he read it; but said it was very proper, and signd it. These are not bad Puffs from Ministers of State, as the silly World goes.[3]

To The Revd Dr Hugh Blair Minister of the Gospel at Edinburgh

Free Da: Hume

* MS., R.S.E.; Burton, ii. 371 ff. and 383 (incomplete).

[1] He then tells the story of Rousseau's flight to Dover in substantially the same words as in Letter 384 above.

[2] The Rev. David Dickson (died 1780) was ordained minister of Newlands, Peebles, in 1756; deposed by the Presbytery, 1763; reponed by the General Assembly, 1763, but suspended from exercising his ministry; finally deposed, 1767. At the General Assembly in 1767 he protested against his deposition, but without effect. His letter to Hume (MS., R.S.E.) is a rather incoherent document, and not of much interest.

[3] Replying on 4 June [1767], Blair says: 'This General Assembly has pass'd extremely well; we had the strength & the numbers, but to the conviction of our adversaries were very moderate. Your friend D. Dickson told the Assembly that he had writ to you; & that he expected by your assistance to have an Assembly called *pro re nata* to do him justice. I suppose

Dear Smith

* 388. *To* Adam Smith

The Count de Sarsfield[1] is a good Acquaintance of mine from the time I saw him at Paris; and as he is really a Man of Merit, I have great Pleasure whenever I meet him here: My Occupations keep me from cultivating his Friendship as much as I shoud incline. I did not introduce him to Elliot, because I knew that this Gentleman's Reserve and Indolence wou'd make him neglect the Acquaintance, and I did not introduce him to Oswald, because I fear that he and I are broke for ever: At least, he does not seem inclined to take any Steps towards an Accommodation with me. I am to tell you the strangest Story you ever heard of. I was dining with him above two Months ago, where among other Company was the Bishop of Raphoe.[2] After dinner, we were disposed to me[3] merry; I said to the Company that I had been very ill us'd by Lord Hertford: For that I always expected to be made a Bishop by him during his Lieutenancy, but he had given away two Sees from me, to my great Vexation & Disappointment. The Right Reverend, without any farther Provocation, burst out into the most furious, and indecent, and orthodox Rage, that ever was seen: Told me that I was most impertinent; that if he did not wear a Gown I durst not, no, I durst not have us'd him so; that none but a Coward woud treat a Clergyman in that manner; that henceforth he must either abstain from his Brother's House or I must; and that this was not the first time he had heard this stupid Joke from my Mouth. With the utmost Tranquillity and Temper, I askd his Pardon; assurd him upon my honour that I did not mean him the least Offence; if I had imagind he coud possibly have been displeas'd I never shoud have mentiond the Subject; but the Joke was not in the least against him, but entirely against myself, as if I were capable of such an Expecta-

* MS., R.S.E.; Burton, ii. 388 ff.

you writ the King's Letter, and I make the Commissioner's speeches—but this *entre nous*. Robertson has got Mr Conway's Letter; and is very well pleased with the close of it. He enjoined me to keep the secret strictly, of its composition' (MS., R.S.E.).

[1] It was at one time thought that he would succeed M. de Guerchy as Ambassador in London in 1767; but he did not. Adam Smith had recommended him to Hume in a letter from Kirkcaldy dated 7 June 1767 (MS., R.S.E.).

[2] John Oswald (died 1780), younger brother of James Oswald of Dunnikier; a school friend of Adam Smith; Bishop of Clonfert and Kilmacduagh, 1762, of Dromore, 1763, and of Raphoe, 1763.

[3] *Sic* in MS.

tion as that of being a Bishop; my Regard for himself and still more for his Brother, with whom I had long been more particularly connected, wou'd certainly restrain me from either Joke or Earnest, which coud be offensive to him: And that if I had ever touchd on the same Topick before, I had entirely forgot it; and it must have been above a twelvemonth ago. He was no wise appeas'd, ravd on in the same Style for a long time: At last, I got the Discourse diverted and took my Leave seemingly with great Indifference & even good humour. I was no wise surprizd nor concernd about his Lordship; because I had on other Occasions observ'd the same orthodox Zeal swell within him, and it was often difficult for him to converse with Temper when I was in the Company: But what really surprizd and vexd me, was, that his Brother kept Silence all the time; I met him in the Passage when I went away, and he made me no Apology; he has never since calld on me; and tho he sees, that I never come near his House, tho formerly I us'd to be three or four times a week with him, he never takes the least Notice of it: I own this gives me Vexation, because I have a sincere Value and Affection for him: It is only some Satisfaction to me to find, that I am so palpably in the right, as not to leave the least Room for Doubt or Ambiguity. Dr Pitcairne,[1] who was in the Company, says, that he never saw such a Scene in his Life time. If I were sure Dear Smith that you and I shoud not one day quarrel in some such manner, I shoud tell you, that I am Yours very affectionately & sincerely

D. H.

London
13 of June
1767

*389. *To the* REV. HUGH BLAIR

Dear Doctor

I write you as long as I can frank a Letter:[2] I believe the Kirk of Humbie will go by Sir Gilbert Elliot's Recommendation, not to your Friend; tho' I am not sure.[3]

* MS., R.S.E.; Burton, ii. 395 (incomplete).

[1] William Pitcairne (1711–91), another Fife man; M.D. Oxford, 1749; began practice in London, 1750; President, Royal College of Physicians, 1775–85.

[2] Hume expected Conway to be out of office any day. See subsequent letters.

[3] In his letter of 4 June [1767] Blair had recommended one Clarke for presentation to the parish of Humbie in East Lothian. Blair was under the impression that the right of presentation in this parish lay with the Crown.

We are all again in Confusion: Negotiations for a new Ministry: The fatal month of July approaching: A new Settlement to be made, which will be no Settlement: I fancy I return in a few Weeks to my former Situation: Yours D. H.

London.
18 of June 1767

To The Rev[d] D[r] Blair, Minister of the Gospel Edinburgh
Free Da: Hume

* 390. *To the* Comtesse de Boufflers

London, 19 of June, 1767.

It was not surely, dear Madam, with indifference that I regarded your displeasure against me. Nothing could have given me more uneasiness; and I was more afraid of the coolness of your reproaches than even of your anger. But your last letter has brought me great relief. Though our commerce should never go beyond letters (an idea however which I will never allow myself to entertain) your friendship would still be dear to me, and I should regard the loss of it as a great calamity.

Happily my dread of that event proceeded more from my own anxiety than from any reality on your part. You are only unkind not to have told me so sooner.

You ask the present state of our politics. Why, in a word, we are all in confusion. This, you'll say, is telling you nothing new; for when were we otherwise? But we are in greater confusion than usual; because of the strange condition of Lord Chatham, who was regarded as our first minister. The public here, as well as with you, believe him wholly mad; but I am assured it is not so. He is only fallen into extreme low spirits and into nervous disorders, which render him totally unfit for business, make him shun all company, and, as I am told, set him weeping like a child, upon the least accident.[1] Is not this a melancholy situation for so lofty and vehement a spirit as his? And is it not even an addition to his unhappiness that he retains his senses? It was a rash experiment, that of repelling the gout, which threw him into this state of mind; and perhaps a hearty

* *Priv. Corr.*, 243 ff.

[1] From early in 1767 till the summer of 1769 Chatham was too ill to take any effective part in public business. He was suffering from diffused gout, which brought on a very acute degree of mental depression that was little removed from insanity. The aloofness of the man and the obscurity of his illness made many people (including the King) believe that what he was really suffering from was 'political gout'.

fit of it may again prove a cure to him. Meanwhile, the public suffers extremely by his present imbecility: no affairs advance: the ministers fall in variance: and the King entertains thoughts of forming a new administration. The first person, whom he addresses himself to, is your friend the Duke of Bedford, whose consideration is very great, on account of his quality and riches, and friends, and above all, of his personal character. It was very happy for the Duke that, at the time of poor Tavistock's death, there were public transactions of moment before the Parliament, in which his friends urged him to take part. The natural fervour of his character insensibly engaged him in the scene. He was diverted from his own melancholy reflections, and business thus proved to him the best consolation. He has not however recovered thoroughly that terrible shock; and the Duchess, to whom the world did not ascribe so great a degree of sensibility, is still more inconsolable. On the whole, you see, that we are at present in a crisis. The Duke of Bedford would be received with open arms; but he has formed some connexions, particularly with Mr Greenville,[1] which are not so acceptable; and it is uncertain, whether we are to have a change of ministry or not, though the former is much more probable.

But pray, who are you to give us as Ambassador from France, in place of M. de Guerchi, who has succeeded very well among us? I think I know more or less all your *grands seigneurs*; and I amuse myself by forming conjectures on that head. M. de Chatelet,[2] it is said, might be the man; but he did not like us enough, when he made us a visit, to be willing to pass years among us. M. de Castries [3] is named, and I believe he would succeed perfectly, except only that he has not a wife whom he could bring along with him; but he is not on such cordial terms with your Minister,[4] as to make him hope for this employment. I believe the Count d'Ayen [5] aspires to that embassy: but he is

[1] George Grenville.

[2] Louis-Marie-Florent (1727–93), comte, and afterwards duc, du Châtelet. His mother having been a patroness of Voltaire for years, he believed himself Voltaire's son. If so, he inherited none of his father's gifts. He was appointed Ambassador to England in July 1767.

[3] Charles-Eugène-Gabriel de la Croix (1727–1801), marquis de Castries.

[4] The duc de Choiseul. There was an undying feud between him and de Castries, because when the latter was promoted Lieut.-General out of his turn, de Choiseul had the promotion cancelled and the Prince de Beauvau (who was senior) promoted instead.

[5] Jean-Louis-François-Paul de Noailles (born 1739), duc (not comte) d'Ayen.

perhaps too young, and has besides something of the pedant about him. Would the Prince of Beauveau wish for this station? He is not supple nor pliable enough: though the Princess is likely to succeed extremely, could she submit to the drudgery of being affable to all the world, as Madame de Guerchi is. The other day I was talking of this subject to the Prince of Masserane;[1] who said, that he knew not whom your Court would choose; but surely, added he, they ought to choose the wisest man in France, for a station so delicate, and so essential towards preserving the general tranquillity. I wish the choice may fall on the Prince and Princess of Beauveau, and that you may come over with them. I should like to have affairs of state to transact with you and her.

General Conway will not allow that Rousseau is mad: he says, he is only whimsical and capricious. I know not whether I told you, that he had wrote from Dover a long letter to the General, in which he entreats him to give him his liberty; warns him of the danger of assassinating him in private; promises never to publish his memoirs, nor complain of the ministers and people of England, if he may be allowed to go abroad; and even engages in that case to speak well of me. All this, you'll say, is mad enough: but yet the letter is coherent and seemingly rational, and so probably will his memoirs be; and perhaps as full of genius as any others of his writings. So strange a prodigy is he! The affair of his pension was entirely settled; but as he has given authority to nobody to receive payment, he may perhaps meet with difficulties in case of a change of ministry.

You know that ministerial falls are very light accidents in this country: a fallen minister immediately rises a patriot, and perhaps mounts up to greater consideration than before. For this reason, our tottering situation does not hinder us in this family from being in great joy, by the marriage of Miss Conway[2] to Mr Damer.[3] They are both your acquaintance, and seem to make a very proper marriage.

You say, that you have many interesting matters to tell me, but do not care to trust them by the common post. If they

[1] Victor Amé Philip (1713–78), Prince de Masseran, Spanish Ambassador in London.

[2] Anne Seymour Conway (1749–1828), only child of General Conway and Lady Ailesbury. She inherited Strawberry Hill on Horace Walpole's death.

[3] Hon. John Damer (died 1776), eldest son of Lord Milton. He was a spendthrift, contracted huge debts, and when his father refused to pay them, shot himself in a tavern in Covent Garden.

interest you, they cannot be indifferent to me. Give me some hint of them. Do they concern yourself in particular? Are there any new prospects opening to ——? You know my meaning; or what is next best, have you lost all hopes, and laid aside all desire of that object?

You made me very happy by telling me, that your young gentleman in Florence pleased as well as interested you very much. I hope the accounts you receive of him are still satisfactory.

Adieu, my dear friend.

* 391. *To* Richard Davenport

Dear Sir

You seem'd desirous of knowing what may have become of your old Guest, the wild Philosopher: I heard by a Letter yesterday from Paris, that he had appeard at Meudon, in the neighbourhood of that City, and had there shown himself in a pretty public manner: My Friend adds, that from the late Transactions, all the World looks on him as absolutely mad; yet it was to be fear'd if he continu'd to appear publickly, he wou'd either be put in arrest, or banish'd the Kingdom. However, if you have any thing to write to him, I believe I cou'd find the means of conveying it; and you will therefore be so good as to send it to me. He is much to be pity'd, particularly from the strange unhappy Turn that his Madness has taken: And I doubt he may remain long in his present melancholy Situation, too wise to be confind, too mad to govern himself. Some People will even question, whether he ever was otherwise, notwithstanding the great Genius and Talents, that appear in his writings.

I know not, what can be done with regard to his Pension: It has pass'd all the Forms in the Treasury; but unless he appoint some Person to receive it, it never can be pay'd. Be so good as to mention that Matter to him, and desire him to write a Letter to Charles Lowndes Esqr Secretary to the Treasury, appointing him to pay the Money to some Person, whom he, Rousseau, shall chuse.

I shall be glad to have a Copy of his Letter to you on leaving you. I do not know, if you heard, that he said to a Gentleman in Lincolnshire, that your Housekeeper had quarreld with his

* B.M. MSS. Add. 29626; Courtois, 283 f.; hitherto unpublished in England.

Gouvernante, and that the former threw Cinders and Ashes into his Pot, which was the Reason of his leaving you. By all Accounts, the same Demoiselle is a very mischievous Creature: I have been assur'd, that she was the Cause of all the Fray between him and me.

We shall, no doubt, have his Memoirs soon publish'd, which will be a curious Performance. But you think his chief Occupation while at Wootton was of a different Nature. Have you any Notion what it was?

Lord Holdernesse has thank'd me much for your Civility to his Steward, who is much satisfy'd with your Machine. Yesterday, I was giving to Charles Turner of Yorkshire [1] an Account of its Operation: He stands much in Need of such a Machine in his part of the World; and I may perhaps have occasion to give you the same Trouble with regard to him. But I know that you do not regard the Propagation of Improvements in Husbandry as a Trouble.

You will probably see in a few Posts an Account of General Conway's Resignation: However, I shall not immediatly leave London; and shall be glad to hear from you. I am Dear Sir Your most obedient and most humble Servant

London DAVID HUME

1 of July 1767

P.S.

Please direct to me at Miss Elliots in Brewer Street.

* 392. *To* BARON MURE OF CALDWELL

Dear Baron

I believe you knew, before you left London, that I had wrote to Dr Smith of Oxford,[2] desiring him to look out for a young Man, who might be Usher to Graffigni:[3] He sent up one, whom he recommended strongly, and who seemd to me a Man of Sense and Knowledge; but he coud not come to any Agreement with Graffigni, because he desird six Weeks or two Months

* MS. in possession of William Mure, Esq., London; MS., R.S.E. (copy); *Caldwell Papers*, II. ii. 115 f.; Burton, ii. 390 f. (incomplete).

[1] Charles Turner of Kirkleatham Park, M.P. for York City.

[2] Probably John Smith (1721–97), a Scotsman, who entered Balliol College in 1744. He was Savilian Professor of Geometry from 1766 to 1797.

[3] A Frenchman and the head master of a newly established school at Norlands, near Kensington. It appears that the school had been set up under the patronage of Lord Hertford, Lord Bute, &c. The two Mure boys had been sent to it, and Hume was exercising a general supervision over them.

Vacation, in order to keep his Degrees in the University, which Graffigni refus'd. The young Man told me, that it woud be impossible for Graffigni to find any body fit for his Purpose on these Conditions; since no one of Spirit woud lay a plan to be a Schoolmaster all his Life, and give up every other Pretension. However this may be, here is Graffigni without either a French or Latin Master; and likely so to continue for some time.

But this is not the worst Circumstance. I believe I told you, that D'alembert disclaimd all sort of Acquaintance with him: I have this Moment receiv'd a Letter from Helvetius doing the same.[1] It was in Answer to one I wrote him at Lord Hertford's Desire. I know not from what Quarter we had heard, that he had given a good given[2] to Lord Harcourt[3] or Lord Newnam[4] a good Character of Graffigni; but it must have been a Mistake. For to me he says, that he knows no such Man; that his Wife, who was Niece to the famous M^{de} de Graffigni[5] and educated with her never saw or heard of such a Man; nor can they imagine who he may be. After this second Imposture, it is certain that Lord Hertford will not put his Sons to him; nor do I think it fit yours shoud longer remain. He is an empty, conceited Fellow; full of Chimeras and Pretensions; and I think you are at no great Loss for parting with him.

The Question [is] what to do next. Sir Gilbert had an Idea of proposing to Rose[6] to diminish the Number of his Boarders: I shall mention the same think[2] to Lord Hertford: What do you think of it? I am very anxious to hear of the Hamilton Cause. I have laid my Account with the worst. My Compliments to Mrs Mure and your Sister. I am Dear Baron

Yours sincerely

London DAVID HUME

7 of July. 1767.

P.S.

We know nothing of the Ministry. Some People now say,

[1] Helvétius's letter, dated 28 June 1767, is printed in *Eminent Persons*, 14 f.

[2] *Sic* in MS.

[3] Simon Harcourt (died 1777), 2nd Viscount and 1st Earl Harcourt; Lord Chamberlain to the Queen, 1763; Ambassador at Paris, 1768–9.

[4] George Simon Harcourt (1736–1809), Viscount Nuneham; succeeded as 2nd Earl Harcourt, 1777.

[5] Françoise d'Issembourg d'Apponcourt, dame de Graffigny (1694–1758), novelist, author of *Lettres d'une Péruvienne*, &c.

[6] Dr. William Rose (1719–86), who kept a boarding-school at Chiswick. He translated Sallust.

that, instead of our being the only Part of the Ministry that will turn out, we are the only that will remain. I believe no body knows.[1]

* 393. *To* ADAM SMITH

Dear Smith

I send you the enclosd with a large Packet for Count Sarsfield. This is the last ministerial Act, which I shall probably perform; and with this Exertion I finish my Functions. I shall not leave this Country presently: Perhaps I may go over to France. Our Ressignation[2] is a very extraordinary Incident; and will probably occasion a total Change of Ministry. Are you busy? Yours

DAVID HUME.

London 14 of July 1767

You must keep Count Sarsfield's Papers till a proper Method of returning them be pointed out to you. Have you read Lord Lyttleton?[3] Do you not admire his Whiggery and his Piety; Qualities so useful both for this World & the next?

† 394. *To* ANDREW MILLAR

Dear Sir

I was sorry I did not see you before you left this Place. But I cou'd not possibly call on you in the Evening of Tuesday; and you was abroad in the Forenoon when I calld.

We are still in as unsettled a Condition as when you left us: There will certainly be a considerable Alteration in the Ministry; and I do not at present reckon my Principal's Situation more

* MS., R.S.E.; *Lit. Gazette*, 1821, p. 745; Burton, ii. 395 f. (incomplete).

† MS., R.S.E.; Burton, ii. 393 f. (incomplete).

[1] Replying from Edinburgh on 13 July [1767] Mure says: 'I thank you, My Dear David, for your information about Grafigni, tho 'tis far from being agreeable. Every thing relating to these Boys affects me intimately. This second Detection is very bad, and tends to confirm all our former suspicions. Yet still I would wish more than negative evidence. . . . You know Sir Gilbert and you may dispose of my two youths. I trust them to you as my two best Friends, and the most capable to direct a matter of that kind . . .' (MS., R.S.E.; *Caldwell Papers*, II. ii. 116 f.).

[2] That is, General Conway's, which carried Hume's along with it.

[3] The long-delayed *History of Henry II*, the first three vols. of which had just appeared.

precarious than that of any other Minister. He speaks, however, like a Man who is to be out of Office in a few days. I have also taken the Precaution to desire him to request of the King in my Name the Liberty, after my Dismission, of inspecting all the public Records and all the Papers in the Paper-Office: His Majesty was pleasd to say that he very willingly comply'd with my Request, and was glad to hear of my Intentions. But my chief View is to run over such Papers as belong to the Period which I have already wrote, in order to render that part of my History as little imperfect as possible. It woud be folly to think of writing any more; and even as to correcting, were it not an Amusement, to what purpose woud it serve; since I shall certainly never live to see a new Edition? I beg my Compliments to Mrs Millar: I hope the Waters agree with all of you. I am Dear Sir

Your most obedient & most humble Servant
DAVID HUME

London
17 of July 1767

* 395. *To* TOBIAS SMOLLETT [1]

London, July 18, 1767.

Dear Sir,

I have had a conversation with Lord Shelburne concerning your affairs: he told me that he had long been pre-engaged for the consulship of Nice to the Spanish Ambassador,[2] and could not possibly get free of that obligation. I then mentioned the consulship of Leghorn; but he said he was already engaged for that office to a friend of Mr Dunning, the lawyer.[3] On the whole, I cannot flatter you with any hopes of success from that quarter; even supposing his Lordship were to remain in office, which is very uncertain, considering the present state of our ministry. For of all our annual confusions, the present seems to be the most violent, and to threaten the most entire revolution, and the most important events. As Lord Chatham's state

* *Scots Mag.*, 1807, p. 248; Burton, ii. 405 f.

[1] Tobias George Smollett (1721–71), the novelist.

[2] Prince Masseran.

[3] John Dunning (1731–83), afterwards 1st Baron Ashburton; Solicitor-General, 1768–70. He did not enter Parliament till 1768. Horace Walpole, writing to Lord Hertford on 3 Dec. 1764, mentions him as 'a lawyer lately started up, who makes a great noise' (*Letters*, vi. 154).

of health appears totally desperate, and as Lord Shelburne's connexion is supposed to be chiefly, if not solely, with him, many people foretell a short duration to the greatness of the last-named minister. Every thing is uncertain: there is a mighty combination to overpower the King. The force of the Crown is great; but is not employed with that steadiness which its friends would wish. I pretend not to foresee, much less to foretell, the consequences.

I am, dear Sir,

Your most obedient and most humble servant,

David Hume.

* 396. *To* Baron Mure of Caldwell

Dear Baron

I wrote Mrs Mure an ostensible Letter, which however, contain'd nothing but Truth:[1] Lord Hertford is not decided, but intends to ask of Lord Harcourt, who are the Persons that recommended Graffigni, since it now appears, that Helvetius was none of them, as he had apprehended: We shall then make farther Enquiries. I see no Inconvenience in your boys remaining till that time: For they are really well in every thing that concerns Health and Exercise: They seem to be improving in English and also in French, and will now go on in Latin. Graffigni's Conceits, tho' they appear to me nonsensical, can do them no hurt. I fancy it was only Vanity, which engag'd him to cite those two celebrated Philosophers. Lord Hertford intends to inform Lord Bute of this Incident.

We are still in Confusion: The Report is, that the Grenvilles, the Rockinghams, and the Bedfords, have enterd into a sworn Confederacy to adhere to each other, till Lord Bute be banish'd from his Majesty's Person and Councils, for ever, and all his Friends turn'd out of all Offices, as a Pledge of His Majesty's entire Submission. It is certain, that my Principal, who has great Credit and Authority with all Parties, is the most moderate Man of the whole. From the present Aspect of things (which I own is very changeable) he is the most likely Person of the present Ministry to remain in power, and even to gain Ground.

* MS. in possession of William Mure, Esq., London; MS., R.S.E. (copy); *Caldwell Papers*, II. ii. 118 f.

[1] In his letter of 13 July Mure had said: 'You did well to send your letter under a friend's cover, that it might not fall into the hands of a too anxious mother.' Mrs. Mure seems to have thought very ill of the Norlands school.

You may easily conceive my Satisfaction on Hamilton's Victory:[1] This incident puts you in entire Security, whatever becomes of the Decision here. But I think you run very little Chance to lose it in the House of Peers. The Triumph of Reason over Prejudice was very signal even in that small Majority among your Judges; but things having once taken a Turn, such strong Reason, aided by time, must certainly overcome weaker Prejudices. Lord Mansfield, the same day he heard of the Presidents Declaration, gave him very high Praises to a Friend of mine; and protested, that he himself was as yet totally ignorant of the Merits of the Cause. I am Dear Baron

Yours sincerely,
DAVID HUME.

London. 18. of July
1767

* 397. *To* JOHN HOME OF NINEWELLS

Dear Brother

Were my present Situation any Object of Anxiety, I shoud have been very unhappy of late; so uncertain has my Continuance appeard every Moment, and so near did my ministerial Functions seem to draw towards their Conclusion. But as the Matter was very nearly indifferent to me, I neither felt Anxiety for my past danger, nor so I experience any Joy from my present Establishment. For we are now establishd, for some time at least; and all Apprehensions of a Change are remov'd to a Distance. The History of our late Transactions is in short, as follows. About this time twelvemonth, when the last Revolution of Ministry took place, Mr Conway stay'd in, tho' Lord Rockingham and most of his Friends were turn'd out; but it was with Reluctance, and only on the earnest Entreaties of the King & Lord Chatham, and on their giving him a Promise, that several of his Friends & Party shou'd still continue to hold their places. This Engagement was broke last Winter: Some of these Gentlemen were turn'd out:[2] And Mr Conway, after

* MS., R.S.E.; Burton, ii. 396 f. and 403 f.

[1] The judgement given by the Court of Session in favour of the Hamiltons in the Douglas Cause.

[2] In Nov. 1766 Chatham suddenly turned out Lord Edgcumbe, a Rockingham Whig and Treasurer of the Household, and put Mr., afterwards Sir John, Shelley in his place. The Rockingham Whigs sent Conway to

protesting against this Usage, declard, that, tho' he wou'd keep his Office during the Session, not to disturb the King's Business, he wou'd resign as soon as the Parliament shoud rise. He accordingly desird the King, about six Weeks ago, to provide him a Successor, and was entreated only to keep the Seals, till a proper Person shou'd be thought of. When the Matter came to be discuss'd, it was found very difficult. The Duke of Grafton declard, that, being deprivd of Lord Chatham's Support, he coud not continue to serve without Mr Conway; and a total Dissolution of the Ministry seemd to be the Effect of this Incident. Negotiations were accordingly set on foot with the Leaders of the Opposition; and a great Meeting of them was held last Week at Bedford House: It was found, that they cou'd not by any means agree in their Demands; and they separated in mutual Discontent. Every body thinks, that Mr Conway has now satisfy'd to the full the point of Honour, in which he is very scrupulous; and that he will cordially resume his Functions; especially as he stands so well with the King and his Fellow Ministers, and has brought it within the Choice of his old Friends to accept of the Ministry, if they had thought proper. I was beginning to wish for our Dissolution; but upon this turn of Affairs, I resume my Occupations with Cheerfulness.

My present Situation revives those Reflections, which have frequently occurr'd to me, concerning the Education of your Son's, particularly of Josey, whose Age now advances, and seems to approach towards a Crisis. The Question is, whether he had better continue his Education in Scotland or in England. There are several Advantages of a Scots Education; but the Question is whether that of the Language does not counterballance them, and determine the Preference to the English. He is now of an Age to learn it perfectly; but if a few Years elapse, he may acquire such an Accent, as he will never be able to cure of. It is not yet determin'd what Profession he shall be of; but it must always be of great Advantage to speak properly; especially, if it shou'd prove, as we have reason to hope, that his good Parts will open him the Road of Ambition. The only Inconvenience is, that few Scotsmen, that have had an English Education, have ever settled cordially in their own Country,

Chatham to ask for an explanation of 'the affronts put upon them'; and when Chatham answered that he would not treat with any set of men as a party, seven members of his ministry resigned, including the Lord Chamberlain and the First Lord of the Admiralty.

and they have been commonly lost ever after to their Friends. However, as this Consequence is not necessary, the superior Recommendations of an English Education ought not to be neglected. I have been making Enquiries for some time; and on the whole, I find Eton the best Place for the Education of Youth. He woud there be able to form Connexions with many young People of Distinction; tho' the whole Expence woud scarcely exceed 70 pounds a Year, which I fancy is little more than he costs you at present. I suggest, therefore, this Idea to you, that you may weigh it at Leizure, and determine upon it: I know you do not like to be hurry'd, and therefore, the more time for Reflection the better. His Friend & Companion, young Adam,[1] is coming up soon; but is going to Westminster School, which is a place I find some Objections to.

I hope Mrs Home is perfectly recoverd: I am glad to hear such good News of Jock.[2] I had a Letter from Davie[3] last Week, which gave me Pleasure. I am Dear Brother Yours sincerely

DAVID HUME

London 28 of July
1767

* 398. *To* BARON MURE OF CALDWELL

[London, summer 1767.]

Dear Baron

I have seen your young Folks twice at Norlands since I wrote to you and Mrs Mure, and I see Graffigni from time to time. They are as well in their Health as can be imagind, are happy and contented, and are us'd well. But still the School does not encrease, and it is impossible it can continue long on its present Footing. The poor Devil must be a considerable Loser, with such a House and Family on his hands, and with so slender an Income. I am afraid Lord Hertford's Children will not go to him. My Lord was inclind to pass over that disagreeable

* Caldwell MSS.; MS., R.S.E. (copy only); *Caldwell Papers*, II., ii. 120 f.; Burton, ii. 391 (incomplete).

[1] Probably a son of John Adam.

[2] John Home, the 3rd son of David Hume's brother, became a W.S., and died in 1786.

[3] David Hume (for he afterwards followed his uncle's example in the spelling of the family name) (1757–1839), the 2nd son; admitted advocate, 1779; Professor of Scots Law, Edinburgh, 1786; Baron of the Exchequer, 1822; succeeded to the family estates on the death of his brother Joseph, 1832.

Circumstance of Graffigni's giving himself Airs of Acquaintance with Men to whom he was an utter Stranger; but asking me if I really thought his Method of teaching Latin was the most proper for advancing young People, I coud not say it; upon which he seems determind to send his Boys elsewhere. This is a severe Blow to Graffigni's School. He is indeed a conceited Man, full of Whims and Affectations; reasoning always in the Clouds about the most obvious things, and hunting after Novelties and Singularities of which his Genius is incapable. What, for Instance, can be more whimsical than his Method of teaching Latin? He gives his Boys a long List of Words, which they are to get by heart like the Muster-Roll of a Regiment, and a great Heap of Grammar Rules, which are to them unintelligible. After he has laid this Foundation of a Language, as he imagines, he begins them with the most difficult of all the Latin Poets: And for this plan of Education he will give you a Galimatias of Reasons, cloathd in the smoothest Language, and deliverd with the softest Accent. But his Latin Master [1] really seems to me a sensible young Fellow, and very fit for his Business, were he allowd to go on his own way, tho' I have never been able to get a private and confidential Conversation with him. But as Graffigni professes a Resolution to follow my Advice, and to alter every thing that displeases me (tho' probably this is only an empty Compliment), yet, if you have any Intention to continue your Sons there, I shall desire to have a private Conference with the Latin Master, and shall know his real Sentiments of the Matter, and insist upon such Alterations as may be thought proper.[2] I think, besides the Difficulty of changing Masters, to you especially, who are at a Distance, the Boys are so well in other respects, that it may be worth while to try what can be done before you determine to seek another Place. Pray, is Andrew Steuart likely to succeed in his Elections?[3] Compliments to your Wife, Sisters, Uncle, &c. Yours

DAVID HUME.

[1] One Elin by name, who eventually succeeded Graffigny as head master.

[2] Mure had his own rather rigid notions about the importance of Latin; and later, when Elin was in charge of the school and trying to introduce some modern methods in the teaching, Mure insisted that his sons should have extra Latin (up to five hours a day) and forgo other diversions and other less important subjects of instruction. (Unpublished materials among the Caldwell MSS., kindly communicated by Miss B. G. Mure of Oxford.)

[3] Andrew Stuart was standing for the county of Lanark. He failed to get in.

* 399. *To* BARON MURE OF CALDWELL

[London, end of July 1767]

Dear Baron

It will be some time before Lord Hertford come to a Resolution because he does not expect to see Lord Harcourt soon, and till then he shall not be able to know who they were that recommended Graffigni. In my Conversation with your young Folks yesterday, I endeavoured to inform myself concerning their Progress in Latin. I find that they are not taught any Latin Grammar: They are only instructed in the Sense of single detachd Words, which they learn both in Greek and Latin at once: Accordingly they told me Water, aqua, and ὕδωρ but tho' I tryd them in about half a dozen more Words, I coud not find their Learning extended so far. All this appears to me very whimsical; and I doubt a dead Language can never be learnt in this manner without Grammar. In a living Language the continual Application of the Words and Phrazes teaches at the same time the Sense of the Words and their Reference to each other; but a List of Words got by heart, without any connected Sense, easily escapes the Memory, and is but a small Part of the Language. But tho' I suspect this Man in general to be empty and conceited, as your boys are so very young, their time is not very precious; and provided they be well in point of Health and Morals or rather manners (which seem to me unexceptionable) you may allow them to remain there some time without Anxiety. I am deliberating myself about my Nephews; and shall communicate to you the Result of my Enquiries and Reflections. Yours

D. HUME.

† 400. *To the* ABBÉ MORELLET

Je vous suis extrêmement obligé, mon cher abbé, de la traduction de Lucien que vous m'avez envoyée au commencement de l'hiver dernier.[1] Je suis honteux d'avoir différé si long-temps à vous en remercier, mais je puis excuser mon silence. J'ai com-

* MS. in possession of William Mure, Esq., London; M.S., R.S.E. (copy); *Caldwell Papers*, II. ii. 119 f.; Burton, ii. 391 f. (incomplete). The letter is endorsed 'Rec[d] 4th Aug[t]'.

† Morellet, *Mémoires*, 1821, i. 169 f. (incomplete). Morellet prints only the beginning of Hume's letter, with no date except 1767.

[1] On 8 Sept. 1766 Morellet sent Hume a copy of a dialogue of Lucian that

paré votre traduction avec Lucien, et j'ai trouvé que vous avez fait une copie élégante et pleine de vie d'un original élégant et animé. Mais j'ai cru voir aussi quelque négligence à rendre exactement le sens de l'auteur grec, et je me proposais de déployer à vos yeux toute mon érudition grecque par une critique de votre traduction.

Je me disposais même à cette entreprise, lorsque j'ai été appelé au service de l'état, comme vous l'aurez su peut-être; j'ai laissé là mon Lucien et votre traduction, et j'ai perdu malheureusement cette occasion de vous montrer toute l'étendue de mon savoir. . . .[1]

*401. *To the* Marquise de Barbentane

London, 4 of August, 1767.

As Lady Tavistoke, Dear Madam, receives no Company, I was obliged to employ Lord Ossory [2] to make Enquiries about M. de Barbantane's Commissions: He told me, that they were found in the House after poor Lord Tavistoke's Death; and no-body knowing what to do with them, they were restored to the Joiner.[3] Ossory left the Town next day: the Duke and Dutchess of Bedford are in the Country: But as they will come to Town next Month to attend Lady Tavistoke's Lying-in, I shall then endeavour, if possible, to recover these pieces of

* MS. in possession of R. N. Carew Hunt, Esq., London; *Priv. Corr.*, 247 f.

he had translated into French and published in the *Gazette littéraire*. He says: 'Comme Lucien est votre auteur favori et que vous scaves que je l'aime bien autant que vous si vous êtes content de cet echantillon je ne suis point eloigné de le donner tout entier' (MS., R.S.E.; *Eminent Persons*, 308).

[1] Morellet quotes no more, but adds that in the rest of the letter Hume doubted if any single man could carry through the task Morellet had set himself, the compilation of a dictionary of commerce; announced that he was sending a large book by Sir James Steuart [*Inquiry into the Principles of Political Economy*, 2 vols., 1767], which contained good materials but was written in a prolix manner and hardly deserved praise for either form or style; and finally, promised to send Morellet the best English books on political economy as they appeared.

[2] John Fitzpatrick (1745–1818), 2nd Earl of Upper Ossory.

[3] Writing to Hume on 8 June 1767, Mme de Barbentane asked him to inquire about a tea-table and some other small commissions which the late Lord Tavistock had undertaken to procure for, and send to, M. de Barbentane in Florence (MS., R.S.E.).

Furniture, and to find a method of conveying them to Italy; that is, provided you at present desire it. I am happy in the most trifling Occasion to mark my Attachment to you.

Your present retired Life,[1] you say, is not disagreable to you: But do you know, that it is not likely to continue long, and that your Pupil may probably be Empress?[2] If you have not heard of this design before, say not a Word of it to her, or any body else. I hope in God such an Event, shou'd it happen, will not carry you to Vienna, to pass your life there in tiresome State and Dignity. It would be a great Disappointment to me to come to Paris, and find you a thousand Miles distant.

I believe that M^{de} de Verdelin is in the same Convent with you. Please make my Compliments to her. Tell her, that the reason of my not answering her Letter last Summer was, that a Report then prevailed, that Mr Melville, Governor of the Granades,[3] was dead; and before that mistake was cleared up, I had left London. But if I can do any thing for her Service at present, she may command me.

I hope I am not lost altogether to M^{de} de Mauri's memory.[4] If so, she is very ungrateful.

You have heard probably that our Ministry was on the Eve of a Revolution. We were so; I thought once that I shou'd have been out of Office in two days: But all is come about again; and we seem to be more settled than ever. I had made a Party with the Chevalier Darcy[5] to pay you a visit at Paris, if I had been an Ex-Minister. That journey would have been sufficient to comfort me from much greater Affliction. Believe me to be, Dear Madam, with the most sincere Regard and Attachment, Your most obedient and humble Servant

DAVID HUME.

To Madame la Marquise de Barbantane A L'abbaie de Pantemont rue de Grenelle, Fauxbourg St Germain a Paris

[1] In a convent, as guardian or chaperon to Princess Louise-Marie-Thérèse d'Orléans (1750–1822).

[2] This came to nothing. Mlle d'Orléans married Louis-Henri-Joseph de Bourbon, duc de Bourbon, in 1770.

[3] Unidentified.

[4] See Note 2 on p. 16 above.

[5] Probably Patrick Darcy (1725–79), an Irish Jacobite, educated in France and serving in the French army; a mathematician and a friend of Clairaut. He is known to have visited London, though the date is uncertain.

* 402. *To* SIR GILBERT ELLIOT OF MINTO

London 13 of August 1767.

Dear Sir Gilbert

I am told that the Minister of Kirkton, in the Presbytery of Jedburgh, is either dying, or is to be remov'd, and that the Living is in the Gift of the Crown. I have spoke to General Conway desiring that, in case no unexpected Difficulties occur, he may give it to my Nephew's Tutor; and he has agreed to it. I have since heard, that the Living, tho' it stands in our List as a Crown Presentation, is alternately in the Gift of Sir John Elliot of Stobs,[1] and Cavers Douglas.[2] I shall be much obligd to you, if, without mentioning the Reason, you coud make Enquiries and give me Information.

You have heard, no doubt, that all our Negotiations have vanishd, and that our present Ministry is settled on a firmer Basis than ever. Mr Conway's Delicacy of Honour was satisfy'd, by bringing his old Friends, the Rockinghams, to have an Offer; and as it was impossible for them to concert a Ministry, he has agreed to act cordially with the Duke of Grafton. The King is very happy that no Changes are to have place. I do not reckon the Change in Ireland for anything, because Lord Bristol [3] goes out at his own earnest and repeated Desire. I am told that Lord Townsend [4] openly ascribes his own Promotion entirely to the Friendship of Lord Bute. Charles Fitzroy [5] lately, in a great Meeting, proposd Lord Bute's Health in a Bumper. It will be no Surprize to you certainly, if that noble Lord shoud again come into Fashion, and openly avow his Share of Influence, and be openly courted by all the World. I am Dear Sir Gilbert

Yours sincerely
DAVID HUME.

* MS. at Minto House; Burton, ii. 406 f.

[1] Sir John Elliot of Stobs (1705–67), 4th Bart.

[2] Sir Archibald Douglas of Cavers (died 1774), Postmaster-General for Scotland.

[3] George William Hervey (1721–75), 2nd Earl of Bristol; Ambassador at Madrid, 1758–61; Lord Lieutenant of Ireland, 1766–7. Chatham had appointed him to Ireland and insisted that he should go and live there. But he never did, though he drew the allowance for his equipage.

[4] See note 1 on p. 47 above. He continued in the Lord-Lieutenancy till 1772.

[5] Colonel Charles Fitzroy (1737–97), the Duke of Grafton's brother; Vice-Chamberlain to the Queen, 1768; created Baron Southampton, 1780.

* 403. *To* Sir Gilbert Elliot of Minto

10 Sept[r] 1767

Dear Sir Gilbert

Lord North [1] has refusd the Office of Chancellor of the Exchequer,[2] tho' it was earnestly press'd upon him, and tho' he professes an entire Satisfaction with every Person in the Administration. He dreads the Labour of the Office, especially as it obliges him to take so great a part in the Business of the House of Commons. It will not probably be offer'd to any Scotsman, for Fear of popular Reflections concerning the Influence of the Thane.[3] The same Objection, as well as others, lie against Dyson, who has been thought of. I see the Ministry in some Perplexity: Perhaps this Incident may draw on new Resignations and Negotiations and Cabals. I think one Defect of the present Situation of our Government is, that nobody desires much to have any Share in the Administration, except Adventurers, of whom the Public is naturally distrustful. The pecuniary Emoluments are of no Consideration to Men of Rank & Fortune: You have often more personal Regard from being in the Opposition: The Protection of the Law is at all times sufficient for your Security: And by acquiring Authority, you are expos'd to Insults, instead of gaining the Power to revenge them. Why then shoud a Man of Birth, Fortune, and Parts, sacrifice his Fame and Peace to an ungrateful Public? Such is the Defect that arises from the Perfection of the most perfect Government.

† 404. *To* Sir Gilbert Elliot of Minto

London 19 Sept 1767

No: Sir Gilbert: With your leave, I did not say, that the Ministry had attaind some sort of Appearance of a kind of Stability, *because* one Minister was indifferent about Power and

* MS. at Minto House; Burton, ii. 407 f.

† MS. at Minto House; hitherto unpublished.

1 Frederick North (1732–92), generally known as Lord North; Lord of the Treasury, 1759–65; Joint Paymaster-General, 1766; Chancellor of the Exchequer, 1767; First Lord of the Treasury and Prime Minister, 1770–82; succeeded his father as 2nd Earl of Guilford, 1790.

2 Rendered vacant by the death on 4 Sept. of the Hon. Charles Townshend. Lord North first refused the office, as Hume states; but later in the month accepted it.

3 Lord Bute.

another desirous of Retreat, but *notwithstanding* that Circumstance.

I have many very important and very interesting Events to communicate to you; but shall omitt it, as you have treated my last Intelligence so ludicrously.[1]

* 405. *To* John Home of Ninewells

Dear Brother

I write to you because it is long since we had any Correspondence, tho' I have nothing particular to say to you. The time of your going to Edinburgh approaches, which makes a great Change in your way of Life, and will naturally make Yourself, as well as all your Friends, anxious about the Issue of it. However, I cannot but think, that you will there live more cheerfully with all your Children about you, than in the Country during the Winter, when your Boys were absent. At first only, as your Spirits are not very strong at present, you may feel uneasy at the Alteration; as you are at present somewhat apprehensive about it.

As to myself I pass my time as I told you, in an agreeable enough kind of Business, and not too much of it. My Income also is at present very considerable, over 1100 Pounds a Year, of which I shall not spend much above the half. Notwithstanding, I sometimes wish to be out of Employment, in order to prosecute my History, to which every body urges me. When Mr Conway was on the Point of resigning, I desird him to propose to the King that I might afterwards have the Liberty of inspecting all the public Offices for such Papers as might serve to my Purpose: His Majesty said that he was glad that I had that Object in my Eye; and I shoud certainly have all the Assistance in his Power. He was also pleasd some time after to send to me the Baron Behr, Minister for Hanover, to tell me that he had orderd over some Papers from Hanover, to be put into my hands, because he believd they woud be of Use to me. I believe I have told you, that the Use of the Marlborough Papers had been promisd me by Lord and Lady Spencer[2] but

* MS., R.S.E.; Burton, ii. 394 and 397 (incomplete).

[1] The letter from Elliot which provoked this outburst is not extant among the MSS., R.S.E.

[2] John Spencer (died 1783), great-grandson of the 1st Duke of Marlborough; created Viscount Spencer, 1761, and Earl Spencer, 1765; married (1755) Margaret Georgiana (died 1814), eldest daughter of Stephen Poyntz.

Marchmont, who had some Pretence of Authority over them, as Trustee, delay'd giving them up, suspecting, I suppose, the Use they intended to make of them. But I know, that a Word from the King must immediatly determine him: For however malicious he be, he is still more servile. I am told, that he is wonderfully broken of late both in his Health and Spirits,[1] and is even falling fast into a State of Imbecillity which is strange at his Years. But I suppose Rage and Malignity have worn all the Fibres of his Constitution. I desire to be rememberd to Mrs Home and Katy; as likewise to my three young Friends. I take it for granted that Jock is quite recoverd. You say nothing to me about Aby Home,[2] whom I am much concernd for. Pray is this a good Crop with you? The Accounts we have from different Parts of England are so various, that there is no forming a Judgement of it, till more of it be threshd out. I am

Dear Brother Yours sincerely

London
DAVID HUME

6 Oct[r] 1767

* 406. *To* ADAM SMITH

[London, Oct. 1767]

Dear Smith,

I thank you for your friendly Resentment against the Right Reverend.[3] I easily forgive our Friend for not making me any Apology. Tis with great Concern I observe, that he has not Spirits enough for such an Effort,[4] and perhaps is fetterd by some kind of Dependance on his Brute of a Brother. I have receivd two Letters from him in our usual friendly Style and have answerd him in the same. Yours

D. H.

* MS., R.S.E.; hitherto unpublished.

[1] He lived till 1794.

[2] Probably the Rev. Abraham Home, Hume's first cousin; he became assistant to his father, the Rev. George Home, at Chirnside in 1741; was translated to Whittinghame in 1748; and died on 2 Oct. 1768.

[3] Adam Smith wrote to Hume from Dalkeith House on 12 Sept. 1767, expressing indignation at the behaviour of John Oswald, Bishop of Raphoe. He says: 'The Bishop is a brute & a beast & unmerited preferment has rendered him, it seems, still more so. . . . He was at Kirkaldy since I received your letter & I was obliged to see him, but I did not behave to him as I otherwise would have done' (MS., R.S.E.).

[4] James Oswald was in failing health. He resigned his seat in Parliament and retired from public life in 1768.

* 407. *To* Adam Smith

Dear Smith

I shall give you an Account of the late heteroclite Exploits of Rousseau, as far as I can recollect them: There is no Need of any Secrecy: They are most of them pretty public, and are well known to every body that had Curiosity to observe the Actions of that strange, undefineable Existence, whom one woud be apt to imagine an imaginary Being, tho' surely not an *Ens rationis*.

I believe you know, that in Spring last, Rousseau apply'd to General Conway to have his Pension. The General answered to Mr Davenport, who carry'd the Application, that I was expected to Town in a few days; and without my Consent and Approbation he woud take no Steps in that Affair. You may believe I readily gave my Consent: I also sollicited the Affair thro' the Treasury; and the whole being finish'd, I wrote to Mr Davenport and desir'd him to inform his Guest that he needed only appoint any Person to receive Payment. Mr Davenport answerd me that it was out of his Power to execute my Commission: For that his wild Philosopher, as he calld him, had elop'd of a sudden, leaving a great Part of his Baggage behind him, some Money in Davenports hands, and a Letter on the Table, as odd, he says, as the one he wrote to me, and implying that Mr Davenport was engag'd with me in a treacherous Conspiracy against him. He was not heard of for a fortnight; till the Chancellor receiv'd a Letter from him, dated at Spalding in Lincolnshire; in which he said, that he had been seduc'd into this Country by a Promise of Hospitality, that he had met with the worst Usage, that he was in Danger of his Life from the Plots of his Enemies, and that he apply'd to the Chancellor, as the first civil Magistrate of the Kingdom, desiring him to appoint a Guard at his own (Rousseau's) Expence, who might safely conduct him out of the Kingdom. The Chancellor made his Secretary reply to him that he was mistaken in the Nature of the Country, for that the first Post-boy he coud apply to was as safe a Guide as the Chancellor coud appoint. At the very same time, that Rousseau wrote this Letter to the Chancellor, he wrote to Davenport, that he had elop'd from him, actuated by a very natural Desire, that of recovering his Liberty, but finding he must still be in Captivity, he preferd that at Wootton:

* MS., R.S.E.; *Lit. Gazette*, 1821, pp. 649 f.; Burton, ii. 374 ff. (incomplete).

For his Captivity at Spalding was intolerable beyond all human Patience; and he was at present the most wretched being on the Face of the Globe: He wou'd therefore return to Wootton, if he were assur'd that Davenport wou'd receive him. Here I must tell you, that the Parson of Spalding was about two Months ago in London, and told Mr Fitzherbert,[1] from whom I had it, that he had passd several Hours every day with Rousseau while he was in that Place; that he was chearful, good-humourd, easy, and enjoyd himself perfectly well, without the least Fear or Complaint of any kind. However, this may be, our Hero, without waiting for any Answer either from the Chancellor or Mr Davenport, decamps on a sudden from Spalding, and takes the Road directly to Dover; whence he writes a Letter to General Conway seven Pages long, and full of the wildest Extravagance in the World. He says. . . .[2] This Letter is very well wrote, so far as regards the Style and Composition; and the Author is so vain of it, that he has given about Copies as of a rare Production. It is indeed, as General Conway says, the Composition of a whimsical Man; not of a Madman. But what is more remarkable, the very same Post he wrote to Davenport, that having arrivd within Sight of the Sea, and finding he was really at Liberty to go or stay, as he pleas'd, he had intended voluntarily to return to him; but seeing in a News Paper an account of his Departure from Wootton, and concluding his Offences were too great to be forgiven, he was resolvd to depart for France. Accordingly, without any farther Preparation and without waiting General Conway's Answer, he took his Passage in a Packet Boat, and went off that very Evening. Thus you see, he is a Composition of Whim, Affectation, Wickedness, Vanity and Inquietude, with a very small, if any Ingredient of Madness. He is always complaining of his Health; yet I have scarce ever seen a more robust little Man of his Years: He was tird in England, where he was neither persecuted nor caress'd, and where, he was sensible, he had expos'd himself: He resolvd therefore to leave it; and having no Pretence, he is oblig'd to contrive all those Absurdities, which, he himself, extravagant as he is, gives no Credit to. At least, this is the only Key I can devise to his Character. The ruling Qualities abovementioned, together

[1] William Fitzherbert (died 1772), of Tissington, Derbyshire; M.P. for Derby; Lord of Trade, 1765–72.

[2] Hume then gives the gist of Rousseau's letter in substantially the same words as in Letters 384–5 above.

with Ingratitude, Ferocity, and Lying, I need not mention, Eloquence and Invention, form the whole of the Composition.

When he arrivd at Paris, all my Friends, who were likewise all his, agreed totally to neglect him: The Public too disgusted with his multiplyd and indeed criminal Extravagancies, showd no manner of concern about him. Never was such a Fall from the time I took him up, about a Year and a half before. I am told by DAlembert and Horace Walpole, that, sensible of this great Alteration, he endeavourd to regain his Credit by acknowledging to every body his Fault with regard to me: But all in vain. He has retird to a Village in the Mountains of Auvergne, as M. Durand[1] tells me; where no body enquires after him.[2] He will probably endeavour to recover his Fame by new Publications; and I expect with some Curiosity the Reading of his Memoirs, which will I suppose suffice to justify me in every body's Eyes, and in my own, for the Publication of his Letters and my Narrative of the Case. You will see by the Papers, that a new Letter of his to M. D, which I imagine to be Davenport, is publishd. This Letter was probably wrote immediatly on his Arrival at Paris; or perhaps is an Effect of his usual Inconsistance: I do not much concern myself which: Thus he has had the Satisfaction, during a time, of being much talkd of, for his late Transactions; the thing in the World he most desires: But it has been at the Expence of being consign'd to perpetual Neglect and Oblivion. My Compliments to Mr Oswald; and also to Mrs Smith.[3] I am Dear Smith Yours sincerely

DAVID HUME

London 8 of Oct^r
1767

P.S. Will you be in Town next Winter.

* 408. *To* JOHN HOME OF NINEWELLS

Dear Brother

I never prognosticated well of Josey's Genius for the Mathematics from his great Slowness in learning Arithmetic; and I am not surpriz'd to find, that his Progress in Euclid has not been so great as might have been expected from his Quickness and

* MS., R.S.E.; Burton, ii. 404 f. (incomplete).

[1] Durand was 'Ministre et résident' of the French Embassy in London.

[2] Actually Rousseau was at this time at Trye, one of the Prince of Conti's country houses, near Gisors, and living under the name of Renou.

[3] Adam Smith's mother.

his Capacity in other particulars. There is indeed something very unaccountable in his Turn; so childish in many Cases, and yet so manly and quick and sensible in others. The Presence of Strangers, above all, seems to make him recollect himself, and he is exceedingly taking among them. His Address in particular is remarkably good, and he seems to have a Turn for the World and for Company: However, I do not think him by any means deficient in his Talents for Literature: It appeard to me that he always read his Books with a very good Taste, Latin as well as French and English, and I imagine that he will make at least a very Gentleman like Scholar. I wish therefore he had a farther Trial of the Greek; and if that will not do, I think with you that the Italian is an easy and genteel Acquisition, which will furnish him with Occupation for this Winter.[1]

I shall send down two or three hundred Pounds to be joind to Haliburtons Money,[2] as soon as it can be got; with such Interest as shall be pay'd it may all be put in a Bond together. Meanwhile, you may put such Money as comes to be, into the hands of Coutts's House. I am of your Opinion, that Macbyehills[3] Bond shoud be registerd.

Paty Home of Wedderburn[4] has just now left me. I askd him what he was doing with regard to his Fishery at Paxton: He desird me to recollect that last Winter I told him he must make me Referee, and he had promisd to do so, and he woud stand to his Word. I do recollect it; but scarce thought he was in earnest. However, he assures me he will not stir a Step in the Affair, till I shoud come down and coud examine the Question. My Compliments to all your Family.

London
13 Oct 1767

I am Your affectionate Brother
DAVID HUME

P.S.

I need not tell you that you are welcome to the use of my Books or any thing my House can afford.

[1] From the only complete letter of John Home of Ninewells to his brother that is extant among the MSS., R.S.E., and which is dated 21 Nov. 1768, it would appear that he was somewhat concerned about his eldest son, who was not applying himself very seriously to study, and who did not seem fitted for any learned profession. Joseph was ultimately sent into the army.

[2] Haliburton seems to have been an Edinburgh merchant. (See p. 7 above.)

[3] This sounds like the name of a farm or an estate.

[4] A neighbour from the Merse. Paxton is a village close to Berwick.

* 409. *To* ADAM SMITH

London, 17 Octr 1767.

Dear Smith.

I sit down to correct a Mistake or two, in the former Account which I gave you of Rousseau. I saw Davenport a few days ago, who tells me, that the Letter, inserted in all the News Papers, was never addressd to him: He even doubts its being genuine; both because he knows it to be opposite to all his Sentiments with regard to me, to whom he desires earnestly to be reconcild, and because it is too absurd and extravagant, and seems to be contriv'd rather as a Banter upon him. Davenport added, that Rousseau was retir'd to some Place in France, and had chang'd his Name and his Dress; but wrote to him, that he was the most miserable of all Beings; that it was impossible for him to stay where he was; and that he wou'd return to his old Hermitage, if Davenport wou'd accept of him. Indeed, he has some Reason to be mortify'd with his Reception in France: For Horace Walpole, who has very lately returnd thence, tells me, that, tho' Rousseau is settled at Cliché,[1] within a League of Paris, no body enquires after him, no body visits him, no body talks of him, every one has agreed to neglect and disregard him: A more sudden Revolution of Fortune than almost ever happend to any man, at least to any man of Letters.

I ask'd Mr Davenport about those Memoirs, which Rousseau said he was writing, and whether he had ever seen them: He said Yes, he had: It was projected to be a Work in twelve Volumes; but he has as yet gone no farther than the first Volume, which he had entirely compos'd at Wootton. It was charmingly wrote, and concluded with a very particular and interesting Account of his first Love, the Object of which was a Person, whose first Love it also was. Davenport, who is no bad Judge, says, that these Memoirs will be the most taking of all his Works; and indeed, you may easily imagine what such a Pen wou'd make of such a Subject as that I mentiond. Mean-while, it appears clearly, what I told you before, that he is no more mad at present, than he has been during the whole Course of his Life, and that he is capable of the same Efforts of Genius. I think I may wait in Security his Account of the

* MS., R.S.E.; Burton, ii. 378 ff. (incomplete).

[1] Rousseau was not at Clichy (a suburb of Paris), but at Trye.

Transactions between us: But however, this Incident, which I forsaw, is some Justification of me for publishing his Letters, and may apologize for a Step, which you, and even myself, have been inclind sometimes to blame and always to regreat.

Tell Mr Oswald, that I saw yesterday young Fitz-patrick,[1] Lord Ossory's Brother, who is just returnd from Caen, and who gave me very good Accounts of Jemmy[2] in every Respect.

*410. *To* [RICHARD DAVENPORT]

Dear Sir

I doubt not but you are desirous of hearing Accounts of your wild Philosopher, as you us'd to call him: Mr Walpole has return'd from France a few days ago, who tells me, that he left him at Cliché, a Place within a League of Paris, where he liv'd in a very retir'd and obscure manner. I fancy he may pay you another Visit: For this Tranquillity is not what he desires; and if he cannot get Persecution, he will at least seek after Variety. May I use the Freedom to put you in mind of bringing up with you all the Letters he wrote on his Departure from you and afterwards? There are some who are of Opinion, that the Letter lately publishd is not genuine, but is rather contriv'd as a Banter upon him. I am Dear Sir

Your most obedient and most humble Servant

DAVID HUME.

London
17 of Octr 1767

†411. *To* ANDREW MILLAR

Dear Sir

The Picture which Donaldson[3] has done for me is a Drawing; and in every body's Opinion, as well as my own, is the likest that has been done for me, as well as the best Likeness. Since

* MS. in J. Pierpont Morgan Lib., New York City; hitherto unpublished.
† MS., R.S.E.; Burton, ii. 408 f. (incomplete).

[1] The Hon. Richard Fitzpatrick (1747–1813), entered the army and saw service in America; Secretary-at-War, 1783.

[2] James Townsend Oswald, son of Hume's friend. He had been a pupil with Hugh Blair in Edinburgh, and in 1768 succeeded his father in the House of Commons.

[3] John Donaldson (1737–1801), miniature painter and etcher. An engraving of the author, bearing the legend 'Donaldson pinxit, Ravenet sculpsit', forms a frontispiece to vol. i in both the 1768 edit. of Hume's *Essays and Treatises* and the 1770 edit. of the *History*.

you still insist that an Engraving shoud be made from it, we are more likely to have a good Engraving made than by any other Means. I shall however be glad to sit to Ferguson.[1]

I intend to give up all my Leizure time to the Correction of my History, and to contrive more Leizure than I have possessd since I came into public Office. I had run over four Volumes; but I shall give them a second Perusal, and employ the same or greater Accuracy in correcting the other four. I shall read carefully all the Records in the Paper Office, as far back as they go, and shall leave nothing untry'd that may bestow the greatest Exactness upon it. For this Reason, as well as many others, I woud not have you precipitate this Edition, which is probably the last, that I may have occasion to make. I woud wish to leave that Work as little imperfect as possible to Posterity.

I shoud be glad to see you when you come to Town. But why do you out again? It is time that you & Mrs Millar shoud be taking Shelter in this Metropolis.

I am Dear Sir
Yours sincerely
DAVID HUME

Monday
19 of Oct[r] 1767
To Andrew Millar Esq[r] at Kew Green

* 412. *To* EDWARD GIBBON [2]

Sir,

It is but a few days ago since Mr Deyverdun[3] put your manuscript[4] into my hands, and I have perused it with great pleasure and satisfaction. I have only one objection, derived from the language in which it is written. Why do you compose in French, and carry faggots into the wood, as Horace says with regard to the Romans who wrote in Greek? I grant that you

* Gibbon, *Autobiographies*, 277 n.; Ritchie, 289 f.; Burton, ii. 411 f.

[1] James Ferguson (1710–76), better known as an astronomer. For several years he gained a living by drawing miniature portraits.

[2] Edward Gibbon (1737–94), the historian. He had now returned from his travels, and was settled at Buriton, whence he made occasional visits to London.

[3] This is the George de Yverdun who wrote the letters to the *St. James's Chronicle* about Rousseau (see note 1 on p. 113 above). He was a clerk in the Secretary of State's office, and therefore under Hume. He was also a personal friend of Gibbon's, and along with Gibbon was engaged in writing *Mémoires littéraires de la Grande Bretagne*, of which only two issues appeared, in 1767 and 1768.

[4] The beginning of a History of the Swiss Revolution, written in French. It was dropped.

have a like motive to those Romans, and adopt a language much more generally diffused than your native tongue: but have you not remarked the fate of those two ancient languages in following ages? The Latin, though then less celebrated, and confined to more narrow limits, has in some measure outlived the Greek, and is now more generally understood by men of letters. Let the French, therefore, triumph in the present diffusion of their tongue. Our solid and increasing establishments in America, where we need less dread the inundation of Barbarians, promise a superior stability and duration to the English language.

Your use of the French tongue has also led you into a style more poetical and figurative, and more highly coloured, than our language seems to admit of in historical productions: for such is the practice of French writers, particularly the more recent ones, who illuminate their pictures more than custom will permit us. On the whole, your History, in my opinion, is written with spirit and judgment; and I exhort you very earnestly to continue it. The objections that occurred to me on reading it were so frivolous that I shall not trouble you with them, and should, I believe, have a difficulty to recollect them.

I am, with great esteem, Sir, Your most obedient and most humble Servant,

David Hume

London
24th of Oct. 1767

*413. *To the* Comtesse de Boufflers

London, 27 of November, 1767.

I was always sensible, dear Madam, that there were several inconveniences attending one's settlement in a foreign country: but I was never much alarmed with any of them, except that of wars breaking out between France and England; an event which, from the opposite interests, and still more the contrary humours of the two nations, is always to be dreaded. In this respect, it must be owned, that France has not usually adopted such a liberal practice as that of England. No Frenchman is ever expelled this country even when the sovereigns are at war; but this is almost always the case in France; and on the commencement of the last hostilities, some Englishmen, who had great protection, and who earnestly desired to remain, were yet

* *Priv. Corr.*, 249 ff.

obliged to leave the country. I suppose the reason of this difference in conduct proceeds from the difference in our governments: for as we cannot pretend to secrecy, we care not who is acquainted with our measures; which is not precisely the case with you. This prospect, I own, always gave me uneasiness. A man, in the decline of life, to be expelled a country, which he had chosen for the place of his residence, and where he had formed a number of agreeable connexions, must suffer a violent shock; especially, if he is to return to company less suited to him, and who are perhaps disgusted with the preference given to foreigners. But I was willing to shut my eyes to this inconvenience, which was distant, and depended on accident: I could more easily bear this prospect, than the immediate and final separation from friends whom I loved; and I shall not name to you the person who had the chief hand in my taking this determination. But here, another office has been conferred upon me, which, though I did not desire it, I could not avoid; and if I should return to settle in France, after being twice employed by the English ministry in places of trust and confidence, could I hope that, in case of a war, I should be allowed to remain unmolested; when, even considered in the light of a man of letters, I could scarcely flatter myself with enjoying that privilege? Add to this that, when I shall get rid of this office (which I hope will be soon) I am almost universally exhorted to continue my History; and all imaginable assistance has been promised me. The King himself has been pleased to order that all the records and public offices shall be open to me, and has even sent for some papers from Hanover, which he thought would be useful. You see then, my dear friend, what reason I have to remain in suspense: for even though a permission should be granted me to remain at Paris, in case of a rupture, the most unexceptionable conduct could not free me from suspicion; and I must tremble at every mark of jealousy or ill-will from every clerk in office. However, I cannot yet renounce the idea, which was long so agreeable to me, of ending my days in a society which I love, and which I found peculiarly fitted to my humour and disposition. I can only delay the taking any determination till the event shall require it of me.

I saw here with Lord Holdernesse, an architect recommended to him by you and the Prince of Conti: you may believe, that these names were not indifferent to me. I immediately gave him a letter to my friend, Mr Adam, a man of genius, and allowed to be the best architect in this country, or perhaps in Europe. He delivered the letter; but some affairs called him suddenly from this country; so that Adam had not an opportunity to be so serviceable to him as he intended.

Horace Walpole told me he was so happy as to see you several times at Paris. I was much pleased with the account he gave me of your state of health and spirits and way of life. I hope he was not deceived. Next to this I should be happy to hear good accounts, or rather the continuance of good accounts, of the Count de Boufflers:[1] I foresee that the satisfaction of your future life is likely to depend much on his conduct.

There is an affair broke out, which makes a great noise, between Lady Bolingbroke [2] and your friend Beauclerc.[3] This lady was separated from her husband some time ago; but 'tis pretended, bore a child lately to Mr Beauclerc; and it is certain her husband has begun a process for a divorce, in which nobody doubts of his success. It is a great pity: she is handsome, and agreeable, and ingenious, far beyond the ordinary rate. I know not whether she was of your acquaintance.

Pray remember me in the kindest and most respectful manner to Madame de Barbantane: let her know that I answered her letter long ago. This I mention, not that I looked for any answer from her; for mine required no answer. But I am really afraid that my letter might have miscarried; because I put, somewhat imprudently, an article of news in it,[4] which might have been the cause of its being intercepted; in which case, she would naturally be inclined to blame my negligence.

I hope you remember, that the new year is approaching; and that you think of your promise at that time.

* 414. *To the* REV. ROBERT WALLACE

Dear Sir

Certainly it is impossible for any body to object to this Scheme of a Book; and he must be very captious indeed who woud

* Laing MSS. (Univ. of Edin.), ii. 96; hitherto unpublished.

1 Her son.

2 Lady Diana Spencer (1734–1808), m. (1757) Frederick St. John, 2nd Viscount Bolingbroke, who divorced her in March 1768.

3 Topham Beauclerk (1739–80), son of Lord Sidney Beauclerk, and friend of Dr. Johnson. He married Lady Diana two days after she was divorced.

4 See Letter 401 above.

pretend to find fault with it.[1] I return it with many Thanks for your Goodness in allowing me to peruse it. I shoud have returnd it sooner; but really it is wrote in so small a hand, that it was with Difficulty I coud read it, and it was some time before I cou'd fully decypher it. I beg my Compliments to your Son; and I am very sincerely Dear Sir

Your most obedient and most humble
Servant
DAVID HUME

London 15 of Dec[r] 1767
To The Rev[d] D[r] Wallace Minister of the Gospel
at Edinburgh.
Free Da: Hume.

* 415. *To the* COMTESSE DE BOUFFLERS

26 April, 1768.

I should have sooner replied, dear Madam, to your most obliging letter, had I not been prevented by an accident. Soon after, General Conway demitted his office,[2] and my commission expired of course. Lord Hertford then told me, that he and his brother had made a point with the King and the ministers, that in consideration of my services, I should have some farther provision made for me, which was immediately assented to, only loaded with this condition, by the King, that I should seriously apply myself to the consummation of my History. I replied to my Lord, that I did not think I had any farther claim, either on the public or his family; and that for a man of letters and a good economist, I had reason to esteem myself very rich. He said, that this was a more proper way of thinking for me than for my friends; but he could not yet tell me what was the provision intended, because nothing was fixed. Ever

* *Priv. Corr.*, 257 ff.

[1] The letter from Wallace, to which this is an answer, is also in the same bundle of the Laing MSS. It is of 5½ foolscap pages, very closely written and very fatiguing to read, and is accompanied by the scheme of the book Hume refers to, viz., *Advice to all True Patriots, or Proposals to promote the Grandeur and Prosperity of Great Britain.*

[2] On 20 Jan. 1768. At the same time the conduct of American affairs was taken out of Shelburne's hands and entrusted to the Earl of Hillsborough, as 3rd Secretary of State. Viscount Weymouth succeeded Conway in the Northern Department.

since, the ministry have been so occupied by the elections,[1] that nothing has been done; and our politics have been in such perpetual fluctuation, that every prospect of this nature that is delayed, must be looked on as uncertain; but, luckily, a disappointment will give me no great vexation. Meanwhile I delayed writing to you from week to week, in hopes of communicating to you this mark of goodness of my Sovereign, in return for what you was so good as to tell me of your Sovereign's goodness towards you. I suppose it was not proper for you to enter into particulars, otherwise you would have done so; as you must be sensible, that nothing can interest me more than every thing that concerns you. I do not find that this sentiment diminishes by time or absence; and even the loss of those once flattering ideas, that I was to pass my latter days with you, gives me the same sting of regret as formerly. You cannot imagine with what satisfaction I heard lately of the Count de Bouffler's marriage:[2] I hope it is as advantageous for him, as it is represented to me.[3] I foresee, that he and his family are to be the consolation of your future life: I hear him mightily well spoken of; and as he is in every respect put into a flourishing situation by your care and attention, you will better be able to compensate the injustice of fortune in one particular, by her favour in another.

I salute and embrace M. de Pont de Ville[4] for the part he has had in this transaction.

I hope, dear Madam, you will throw me at the Prince of Conti's feet. My sense of his goodness to me will be indelible, as well as my personal regard to him.

L'Abbé le Bon[5] gave me lately an account of the Prince's

[1] The bribery and corruption of this election in 1768 is said to have exceeded anything known before in England, even in the great days of Newcastle and his Secret Service funds. £30,000 a side was spent on Northamptonshire alone.

[2] With Amélie Puchot, daughter of the comte des Alleurs. The marriage did not take place, however, till Dec. 1768.

[3] According to Mme du Deffand (*Lettres à Walpole*, i. 419 and 462) she was seventeen, pretty, and possessed of an income of twenty-two or twenty-three thousand livres.

[4] Antoine de Ferriol (1697–1774), comte de Pont-de-Veyle; author of two comedies, *Le fat puni* and *Le complaisant*; one of Mme du Deffand's oldest friends. She confirms the fact that he 'made' this marriage.

[5] The Abbé Bon (or Le Bon, for his friends called him by both names) was an old friend of Turgot's at the Sorbonne, and a regular frequenter of the salons of Mme de Boufflers, Mme Geoffrin, and Mlle de Lespinasse. Turgot

benevolent disposition, in taking himself a journey to Trie, that he might accommodate some quarrels, which Jean Jacques had had with some of his neighbours.[1]

I think that this philosopher now speaks less of his return to this country; which indeed does not well suit him, as he would here be neither courted nor persecuted. He does well to enjoy his pension at a distance from us.

I could wish it were proper for me to present my respects to Madame de Luxembourg; but I am told that I have incurred her displeasure by my unlucky quarrel with the above-mentioned personage.

This is the only subject of regret it leaves me; and I could wish to be justified in her eyes, as I am in those of all Europe. Nobody can have a greater regard for her than I have, nor a greater desire of recovering her good graces. I hope Madame de Mirepoix allows me the honour of saluting her, as also Madame de Bussi, whose situation, I am sorry to hear, is not more agreeable than formerly.[2]

The Archbishop of Toulouse,[3] I am told, has distinguished himself at the head of a commission for examining into the regulations and laws of convents; and it is resolved that henceforth nobody shall be allowed to take the vows before one-and-twenty years of age. In that case, this prelate will be the greatest reformer that has arisen since Luther.

I beg my compliments to him, as well as to the Bishop of Lavaur, whose funeral panegyrics I have read with some regret: they were so well wrote, that I wished to see his pen employed on some better subject. I am in Madame de Barbantane's debt, and shall answer her in a few days, as soon as I have fully executed her commission. Be so good as to mention my name to her, and to Madame de Vierville. I bid you adieu, dear Madam, and kiss your hands, with all the sincerity possible. I should be sorry to forget Miss Becket on this occasion.

wrote a not very flattering character of him (Turgot, *Œuvres*, i. 107 f.), but seems to have liked him, and in March 1768 made him the bearer of a letter to Hume. The abbé was then visiting England in company with M. de Boisgelin.

[1] This visit took place in the end of September 1767. Rousseau, who was still haunted by his delusions of persecution, imagined that certain of the Prince's servants were plotting against him on Hume's behalf; and the Prince went down to Trye to attempt, not with much success, to allay his fears. (See Streckeisen-Moultou, ii. 9 ff.)

[2] She was at loggerheads with her husband.

[3] Loménie de Brienne.

* 416. *To the* MARQUISE DE BARBENTANE

London, 24 May, 1768.

I should not have delayed so long, dear Madam, the answering your very obliging letter, had I not thought it essential to answer a part of it to your satisfaction. I mentioned to Lord Ossory the debt due by poor Tavistock to M. de Puységur: he told me that he knew of it already, that Lady Tavistock had told him of it, and desired him to remit the money; but his indolence and forgetfulness had hitherto prevented him; he would however give immediately orders to that purpose: these immediate orders did not follow immediately; but at last, by my reminding him frequently, the affair is executed. The twenty louis-d'ors are sent over to M. Panchaud the banker; and M. de Puységur has nothing to do but send for them to Panchaud, or draw upon him to that amount, only desiring him to place the money to the account of Mr Coutts, banker, in London. I hope, when you give this information to M. de Puységur, you will not fail to let him know how much I desire a place in his memory.

Nothing gives me greater pleasure than your telling me, that I am not forgot by my friends at Paris. I cannot but recollect with great satisfaction, the agreeable society which I enjoyed there; and shall ever reflect on it as the happiest period of my life. I have not, however, any great prospect at present of settling there, as once was my intention, though I hope still to pay you frequent visits. I find the chains, which attach me to this country, multiply upon me. The King has given me a considerable augmentation of my pension, expressing at the same time his expectation, that I am to continue my History. This motive, with my habits of application, will probably engage me in this undertaking, and occupy me for some years.

I am glad you see, from time to time, our friend at the Temple. I find by her letters that she is not quite happy in her present condition, and yet her farther elevation would be the source of greater chagrin to her. I hear she has found an advantageous marriage for her son, which will be a real and durable satisfaction to her. I am told the little Count is well spoken of, and our friend, I find, is much in conceit with him; which is a very happy turn; for she used not formerly to be over-partial in his favour. Be so good as to inform her of the King's goodness to me.

* *Priv. Corr.*, 260 ff.

I hear less mention, than formerly, of the establishment of your young princess; which I wish earnestly, on your account. Your way of life is much too confined for a person accustomed to so much liberty. But the solidity of your character enables you to enjoy yourself in any situation, and to accommodate yourself to every course of life. I should only be afraid that, were I to pay you a visit at Paris, I should have much more difficult access to your company than formerly. Pray, is not your son a very fine young gentleman? He promised very much when I saw him; and in spite of the partiality of a mother, I can almost rely on your judgment.

There have been this spring in London a good many French gentlemen, who have seen the nation in a strange situation, and have admired at our oddity. The elections have put us into a ferment; and the riots of the populace have been frequent:[1] but as these mutinies were founded on nothing, and had no connexion with any higher order of the state, they have done but little mischief, and seem now entirely dispersed. I believe most of your countrymen return very happy, that they are born under a government not liable to these inconveniences; which is a fortunate way of thinking. You ask me about M. de Chatelet:[2] he lives very splendidly; behaves obligingly to all the world; and would, I believe, be very popular, were it not for the prepossession entertained that he does not like us. The truth is, no foreign minister has much reason to like us. We are so taken up with our own cabals, and projects, and societies, that scarce any of them ever get into intimacy with any of us; and they leave the country, after having been strangers in it for several years. M. de Guerchy overcame these difficulties as much as possible, and was beloved. I hear some people are displeased with the present Ambassador, for speaking, as they pretend, disrespectfully of M. de Guerchy's memory.

Allow me to take this opportunity of renewing my compliments to Madame de Vierville and Madame de Mauri; and I beg of you to believe me, with the most sincere attachment,

Dear Madam,

Your most obedient and most humble servant,

DAVID HUME.

[1] The 'Wilkes and Liberty' riots of the Middlesex Election. For a vivid and full description see Horace Walpole's letter to Mann of 31 March and 1 April 1768.

[2] The French Ambassador.

*417. [To ANNE-ROBERT-JACQUES TURGOT]

I have delayed answering your Letters,[1] that I might be able to do it to purpose, and give you Satisfaction. The Offer, you make from Parma, is certainly very alluring to a young Man, who has Curiosity and Ambition: But it requires so many Qualities in the Person, that I found it difficult to discover one that cou'd correspond to your Expectations. Some that I thought of, I found engaged in other pursuits; but having wrote to a young Man in Edinburgh,[2] I received the enclosed Answer, which I use the Freedom to transmit to you. You see there are Objections; but to find a Person entirely satisfactory, is not easy; I am perswaded, that Mr Liston's Objection, with regard to his not having a full Acquaintance with English Authors, is founded less on reality than on his own Modesty. He is a young Man of very good Conduct and Morals and of an excellent Disposition. He lived about a Year and a half at Paris; and had the Care of Sir Gilbert Elliot's two Sons, whom I settled at Abbé Croquar's[3] Academy, Barriere St Dominique: So that,

* MS. in Bibliothèque municipale, Caen; hitherto unpublished.

[1] Of 8 March 1768 (MS., R.S.E.; *Eminent Persons*, 162 f.) and 11 May 1768 (MS., R.S.E., unpublished). In the latter, Turgot says:

'On veut a Parme profiter de la circonstance du renvoy des Jesuites pour donner a la jeunesse une education un peu meilleure et des connoissances plus etendues. Il entre dans le plan du nouveau college d'y etablir des professeurs pour y enseigner la litterature des principales nations modernes, et en particulier la litterature de la langue Angloise. On voudroit donc un sujet dont les mœurs et la probité fussent connues, qui fut bien au fait de la litterature Angloise et qui put enseigner la langue avec succès. On voudroit aussi qu'il sut bien le françois, mais surtout très bien l'italien. On desire qu'il soit Anglois et non Irlandois, et on insiste pour qu'il soit non seulement capable d'enseigner la langue, mais encore au fait de la litterature en sorte qu'on puisse l'employer comme homme de lettres.

'On lui donnera d'appointmens 20,000^ll du pays qui equivalent a 5000^ll de france, des distinctions flateuses dans le pays, comme de porter une fourure ou mante pareille a celle que portent les magistrats et certaines entrées a la cour. On ajoute que l'état de professeur est très honorable et que plusieurs gentilshommes l'embrassent et professent, l'épée au coté.

'Mr D'Argental de qui je tiens ce memoire et qui m'a prié de vous en ecrire ne dit rien sur l'article de la religion. Mais il ne doute pas que l'on ne donne des assurances de la plus grande liberté sur cet article. . . .

'Je vous seray très obligé de vouloir bien chercher quelque homme de lettres qui veuille accepter ce parti. Personne n'est plus a portée que vous d'en faire le choix. . . .'

[2] Robert Liston.

[3] *Sic* in MS. The name was Choquart.

if you will take the Trouble of calling on the Abbé, you may hear a more particular Account of him. I shall only add, that being a Scotsman, it is impossible but he must have something of the Accent of that Country; but he lived several Years in England, and has, I believe, a very tolerable Pronounciation. On the whole, the sooner he sets out the better; that he may perfect himself in the Italian without Loss of time.

Dr Tucker [1] is in the Country, and I wrote to him long ago, desiring him to give you Satisfaction on all the Points, concerning which you desire to be informed. I have received no Answer from him; which makes me conclude, that he is not at his own house. As soon as I hear from him, I shall be sure to inform you.

I know you are one of those, who entertain the agreeable and laudable, if not too sanguine hope, that human Society is capable of perpetual Progress towards Perfection, that the Encrease of Knowlege will still prove favourable to good Government, and that since the Discovery of Printing we need no longer Dread the usual Returns of Barbarism and Ignorance. Pray, do not the late Events in this Country appear a little contrary to your System? Here is a People thrown into Disorders (not dangerous ones, I hope) merely from the Abuse of Liberty, chiefly the Liberty of the Press; without any Grievance, I do not only say, real, but even imaginary; and without any of them being able to tell one Circumstance of Government which they wish to have corrected: They roar Liberty, tho' they have apparently more Liberty than any People in the World; a great deal more than they deserve; and perhaps more than any men ought to have. The same Perfection of our Government, carryed to an Extreme, has a bad Influence on our Ministers: There is too little Difference between the Governors and Governed. A Minister here can amass no Fortune, being checked in every Abuse; he can very little give Employments to his own Friends, Favourites and Flatterers, but must bestow all Offices on those who by their Votes and Credit may support Government; and he can revenge himself on none of his Enemies; because every one is so entrenched in Laws and Privileges, as to be able to set all the World at Defiance. Hence men of great Rank and Fortune are very indifferent about being

[1] Dean Tucker. The first work of Turgot to be printed was a translation (1755) of Tucker's *Reflections on the Expediency of a Law for the Naturalisation of foreign Protestants*. He had now addressed certain questions on economic subjects to Tucker, through Hume.

Ministers; being sensible, that they are more exposed to Obloquy on account of their power, and derive no consideration from it. They either decline high Offices, or behave negligently in them; and express every moment their Wishes of being free of the Trouble and Subjection, attending them. These Sentiments loosen the Attachment of their Inferiors. You will say, perhaps, either that all these Evils are Trifles: So perhaps they are; but they tend to great Mischiefs: Or that they proceed from the still imperfect State of our Knowlege: That is very true; but will Men ever reach a much more perfect State; while the rich have so many more alluring Appetites to gratify than that for Knowlege, and the poor are occupyed in daily Labour, and Industry. I mention not the Disturbances arising from foreign Wars, an incurable Evil, which often springs from the greatest & most unexpected Absurdity, and discourages every Project for serving or improving human Society. You see, I give you freely my Views of things, in which I wish earnestly to be refuted: The contrary Opinion is much more consolatory, and is an Incitement to every Virtue and laudable Pursuit.

Since I wrote the above, I have seen Sir Gilbert Elliot, who tells me, that Mr Liston has a remarkable Talent for Languages; so that he will certainly, in a very little time, render himself Master of the Italian. My compliments [to] L'Abbé Le Bon, my old Antagonist. I beg of you to believe me, with the most sincere Regard, My dear Sir,

Your most obedient and most humble Servant

David Hume

London 16 of June 1768

* 418. *To* Sir Gilbert Elliot of Minto

Dear Sir Gilbert

I beg of you to direct the enclosd to poor Liston, who will be disappointed in the Scheme for Parma: They will have nothing but a Papist.[1] Such Fools! Let the Pope excommunicate them on the one hand: I will do so on the other.

I have seen a Book newly printed at Edinburgh, calld

* MS. at Minto House; Burton, ii. 414 f.

[1] In a letter dated 3 July 1768 Turgot announces that the professor to be found for Parma must be a Catholic (MS., R.S.E., passage omitted by Burton in printing the letter in *Eminent Persons*, 163).

Philosophical Essays.[1] It has no manner of Sense in it; but is wrote with tolerable Neatness of Style: Whence I conjecture it to be our Friend, Sir David's.[2] I am obligd to him for the Treatment which he destines me, to be lock'd up for five Years in a Dungeon, then to be hangd, and my Carcass to be thrown out of Scotland. He supports himself, indeed, by the Authority of Plato, whom I own to be truly divine. Pray, have you seen the Book? Is it Sir David's? I think it has not so many Attempts at Humour, as that pious Gentleman woud employ.

We are all very quiet here, as quiet as you at Minto, tho' perhaps not so busy: No more noise of Wilkes and Liberty. Lord Mansfield said to me, that it was impossible for him to condemn him to the Pillory, because the Attorney-General did not demand it. Yesterday he represented to the Spanish Ambassador that moderate Sentence, as a Refinement in Politics, which reduc'd the Scoundrel the sooner to Obscurity. It woud be a strange Cause, which he coud not find plausible Reasons to justify.

I beg to be rememberd to Lady Elliot, and to any of your Family who may be at Minto. I ever am Dear Sir Gilbert

Yours sincerely
DAVID HUME.

London 5 of July
1768

* 419. *To* ANNE-ROBERT-JACQUES TURGOT

I have given, my dear Sir, to M. Francis [3] three Books sent me by Dr Tucker,[4] who desired me to make his Compliments

* MS. in bibliothèque municipale de Caen; hitherto unpublished.

[1] Published anonymously in Edinburgh in this year. It was by James Balfour of Pilrig, and attacked both Hume and Kames on the subject of liberty and necessity.

[2] Sir David Dalrymple.

[3] Bathaile de Francès-Daville, a friend of Turgot's, Secretary of the French Embassy in London under du Châtelet, and then Chargé d'affaires. Mme de Deffand called him 'très-turgotin'.

[4] Writing to Hume from Gloucester on 25 June 1768, Tucker says: '. . . To comply with your Request I sent a Parcel by ye Glocester Coach (wch stops at the Green Man & Still in Holbourne) containing Six Pamphlets, Viz The Elements of Commerce, Instructions for Travellers, 3 Copies of the Case of going to War, and the Letter from a Merchant to his Nephew concerning y[e] Colonies. Your Friends abroad are very welcome to make what Use of them they shall judge proper: And if they will honour Me with their Remarks, Amendments, & Corrections, I shall thank them for the Honour

to you. When he was in France, he had frequently enquired concerning his Translator; but cou'd meet with no-one, that cou'd give him Information. He is very proud, that he has so much reason to value himself on that head. The thin Quarto,[1] which he sends you, was never published; tho' the Author printed off about a hundred Copies near fifteen Years ago: He sent Copies about to his Friends and to Persons for whom he had an Esteem; and he desired them to return the Copy with their Remarks on the Margin, which was left large on Purpose. He desires the same Favour of you, and does not limit you to any time. On my Suggestion, he permits you to communicate the work to M. de Montigny and to the Abbé Morrellet, who, he hopes, will also be so good as communicate their Remarks. I think there are Passages, which may be useful to the Abbé in his Dictionary.

I am sorry to find, that Dr Tucker has little Intention of finishing and giving to the Public this valuable Work. He was extremely discouraged with the bad Reception given to this Pamphlet against War, of which he sends you two Copies.[2] There were not fifty Copies of it sold; tho' surely it merited a much better Fate. But it was wrote, as I told him, when the Public were intoxicated with their foolish Success; and a Pamphlet, if it does not take during the first Moment, falls soon into Oblivion, and very often indeed, tho' it does take. But this is not the Case with a greater Work to which the Public always, sooner or later, does Justice. You will see, that Dr Tucker is no friend to the new Theory of Finances, which has made so many respectable Proselytes in France. I have a Purpose of visiting my Friends in France this Autumn; when we shall talk over these Subjects; and if you have then finished Dr Tucker's Book, you will restore it to me. If not, it may be sent me afterwards. I am with great Truth and Sincerity My dear Sir

Your most obedient humble Servant

London 8 of July
1768

DAVID HUME

done Me, tho I much Question, Whether I shall ever proceed any farther in the Work' (MS., R.S.E., unpublished).

The parcel, however, never reached Turgot; for the Post Office in Paris lost it. (See letter from Turgot to Tucker, 12 Sept. [1770], in *Œuvres de Turgot*, iii. 422.)

[1] *The Elements of Commerce*, privately printed, 1755.

[2] Turgot translated this pamphlet, but put off printing it; and the MS. cannot now be found (*Œuvres de Turgot*, iii. 421 n.).

* 420. *To* Sir Gilbert Elliot of Minto

Dear Sir Gilbert

I send you my Letter enclosd to Mr Stewart,[1] which I hope is calculated to encourage a young Man of Merit, without overstraining the Compliment. It were better, however, for him, and for every body, to pursue, in Preference to the idle Trade of Writing, some other lawful Occupation, such as Cheating like an Attorney, Quacking like a Physician, Canting & Hypocrising like a Parson &c &c &c. It is for very little Purpose to go out of the common Track. Does he expect to make Men wiser? A very pretty Expectation truly!

I fancy the Ministry will remain; tho' surely their late Remissness or Ignorance or Pusillanimity ought to make them ashamd to show their Faces, were it even at Newmarket. These are fine doings in America. O! how I long to see America and the East Indies revolted totally & finally, the Revenue reduc'd to half, public Credit fully discredited by Bankruptcy, the third of London in Ruins, and the rascally Mob subdu'd. I think I am not too old to despair of being Witness to all these Blessings.

I approve of your farming Scheme; notwithstanding the Expence: Tho' your Situation, as well for Markets as Means of Improvement, is not advantageous. My Brother's Advice may be of Use; but you are always to remember that he is of the Sect of the *Medecin tant pis*. Had he possess'd Enterprise proportiond to his Industry, and Skill, he might have gone far in that way.

I continue my parasitical Practices, that is, of dining at all the great Tables that remain in London. We are likely to be plagu'd with this King of Denmark;[2] tho' not so much as

* MS. at Minto House; Burton, ii. 416 ff.

[1] Gilbert Stuart (1742–86), son of an Edinburgh professor; a young man who promised much and performed little of value; author of *Historical Dissertation on the Antiquity of the English Constitution*, 1768, for which he received the degree of LL.D. from Edinburgh, and a copy of which he had just sent to Hume; hack writer in London, 1768–73; editor of *Edinburgh Magazine and Review*, 1773–6.

[2] Christian VII, King of Denmark, 1766–1808; married Princess Caroline Matilda, George III's sister. He arrived in London early in August 1768. Hume's word *plagued* is probably an echo of Lord Hertford's, who, as Lord Chamberlain, had to make the arrangements for receiving this royal visitor.

formerly with Canute the Great. I have some Thoughts of paying a visit to France this Autumn; that is, if I can collect enough of Resolution to leave the present place of Abode.

When I wrote last, I did not know that Lady Elliot[1] had elop'd. That Practice continues very fashionable here; and it is to be hop'd, will spread itself more and more every day.

I thought Sir David had been the only Christian that coud write English on the other Side of the Tweed: I did not think of Balfour: It is very true: He woud fain, I see, be candid, and civil, as in his other Book; if his Zeal for the House of the Lord woud permit him.

Lord Bute certainly sets out this day sennight,[2] and it is said, is in a very bad State of Health.

Lord Chatham is a greater Paradox than ever: Is seen at home by no human Creature, absolutely by none! Rides twenty Miles every day: Is seen on the Road and appears in perfect good Health: But will now speak to no Creature he meets. I am much perswaded all is Quackery; he is not mad; that is, no madder than usual.

22 of July
1768

* 421. *To* TOBIAS SMOLLETT

Ragley,[3] September 21, 1768.

My dear Sir,

I did not see your friend, Captain Stobo,[4] till the day before I left Cirencester, and only for a little time; but he seemed to be

* *Scots Magazine*, 1807, p. 248 f.; Burton, ii. 419 f.

[1] I presume this is a joke and refers to Elliot's wife, Lady Elliot-Murray.

[2] He was going abroad.

[3] Lord Hertford's seat in Warwickshire.

[4] Captain Robert Stobo (born 1727), who is believed to have been Smollett's original for Lismahago in *Humphry Clinker*. Writing to Hume from London on 31 Aug. 1768, Smollett says: 'Perhaps I overrate my own consequence when I presume to recommend to your acquaintance & good offices, the Bearer Capt Rob[t] Stobo, a man, whose very extraordinary services & sufferings in America, have merited and obtained the most ample & honourable testimonials which he will gladly submit to your Perusal. I can safely say from my own knowledge, that he is not less modest & sensible in the conversation & occurrences of civil life, than enterprizing & indefatigable in his military capacity. All these good qualities united to an extensive knowledge of our American concerns, cannot fail to engage the Friendship and Regard of Mr David Hume, from what quarter so ever they may come recommended' (MS., R.S.E.; Burton, ii. 418 f.).

a man of good sense, and has surely had the most extraordinary adventures in the world. He has promised to call on me when he comes to London, and I shall always see him with pleasure.

But what is this you tell me of your perpetual exile, and of your never returning to this country?[1] I hope that as this idea arose from the bad state of your health, it will vanish on your recovery; which, from your past experience, you may expect from those happier climates to which you are retiring; after which the desire of revisiting your native country will probably return upon you, unless the superior cheapness of foreign countries prove an obstacle, and detain you there. I could wish that means had been fallen on to remove this objection; and that at least it might be equal to you to live anywhere, except where the consideration of your health gave the preference to one climate above another. But the indifference of ministers towards literature, which has been long, and indeed always, the case in England, gives little prospect of any alteration in this particular.

I am sensible of your great partiality, in the good opinion you express towards me; but it gives me no less pleasure than if it were founded on the greatest truth, for I accept it as a pledge of your good will and friendship. I wish an opportunity of showing my sense of it may present itself during your absence. I assure you I should embrace it with great alacrity; and you need have no scruple, on every occasion, of having recourse to me.

I am, my dear Sir,
With great esteem and sincerity,
Your most obedient and most humble servant,
DAVID HUME.

[1] Smollett's letter continues: 'With respect to myself, I am sorry I cannot have the pleasure of taking leave of you in person, before I go into perpetual exile. I sincerely wish you all health & happiness. In whatever part of the earth it may be my Fate to reside, I shall always remember with pleasure, & recapitulate with pride, the friendly intercourse I have maintained with one of the best men, & undoubtedly, the best writer of the age; if any judgement in distinguishing either character or capacity, may be allowed to, Dear Sir Your very humble serv[t]

T. SMOLLETT.

Nos patriam fugimus: tu, Tityre lentus in umbrâ
Formosam resonare doces Amaryllida silvas.

* 422. *To* Baron Mure of Caldwell

London 18 Octr 1768

Dear Baron

Immediatly upon receiving yours, I dropped a line to Graffigni,[1] who call'd on me next day. I express'd to him your Regret, that he shoud no longer have the Direction of the Academy; and told him, that you were anxious to know the Reason. He said, that the Term of his Agreement with Elin[2] was expird; that on his Proposal to renew it, with some Alteration of the Conditions, Elin had refus'd his Conditions; that in short Elin was desirous of being Master entirely, and thought his superintendance a Burthen. In the main, he spoke very decently of Elin; and said, that he believ'd the Academy, with regard to Language, and Diet and other Circumstances woud go on as before: There only was now no person who had sounded the Depths of the human Understanding, who was perfectly acquainted with all the Faculties of the Soul, and who knew how to direct, and govern, and restrain and push them at his Pleasure. As I did not think this a very material Loss, I was not much alarm'd at the Alteration. However, I drove to Norlands yesterday, and had a like Conversation with Elin: He also spoke decently of Graffigni; but he said, that the Share he demanded of the Profit, far exceeded the Share he took of the Trouble; that he came only for a few hours two days of the week yet expected half of the Profit; he expected also to govern entirely the House in every branch of it, which he (Ellin) thought inconvenient and burdensome: He had, however, offerd Graffigni the Inspection of the Classes, and a certain Share of the Profits, which he refus'd, and upon that they parted.

I need not tell you, that I saw the two boys, who are in good health, tall, handsome, pleasd and pleasing Children. They seem to speak French more naturally and familiarly than English, tho Elin assures me, that they have the English Accent perfectly. I see however a danger from this Inundation of Scots boys, of which some pour in fresh from the Caledonian Mountains, like untam'd Sarmatians, to destroy all the Arts and Civility of the South. In this respect too, the Loss of Graffigni may be felt. By his profound Study of the human Mind, he had

* MS. in possession of Mrs. Reginald Mure, Oxford; *Nineteenth Cent. & After*, xcviii. 298 f.

[1] The head master of Norlands School.

[2] The Latin master who succeeded Graffigni.

discoverd that Decency and good Manners are very proper to be inculcated in boys, and was more attentive to that point than perhaps Elin will be, who, with a sounder Understanding, has had a more vulgar Education.

I form Schemes every day of retiring to Edinburgh, and of drinking my Claret and spending my latter days among my Friends: But it requires more Resolution than I am master of, to remove from one place and go to another. No man has been more tossd about than I have been, and no man has more reluctance to changes. Had I been born to a small Estate in Scotland of a hundred a Year, I shoud have remaind at home all my Life, planted and improvd my Fields, read my Book, and wrote Philosophy: But living among the Great, and composing History have been the Lot of the later part of my Life. I believe, however, I shall write no more History, tho' some people pretend to urge me to it, and I find no Obstacle but Indolence, with the Want of any proper Object as a Motive. I have had reason to entertain such an extreme Contempt for the public, as not to think their Approbation a Motive to renounce the pleasures of sauntering and Idleness: And my Experience of the little addition, which riches give to Happiness, makes that View still more contemptible. You will think me, however, somewhat inconsistent when I tell you, that one reason of my remaining in London is the correcting a new Edition of my History,[1] which I oversee as anxiously, as if any body were concern'd about it, or ever woud perceive the Pains I take in polishing it and rendering it as accurate as possible. I can only say, that I do it for myself and that it amuses me.

Have you read any of Robertson's new History?[2] It is admirably well writ in my Opinion.

You will have heard of Chatham's Resignation:[3] His Letter to the King was decent and respectful and dutiful:[4] He only pleads his bad Health, without hinting at any Grievance, public or personal. Lord Shelburne assures me, that he was not previously acquainted with this Step, and he believes the same of the Chancellor.[5] It is however thought that these two Peers will either resign or be turnd out; and it is likely a thorough

[1] The L.P. 4to edit. in 8 vols., which appeared in 1770.

[2] *The History of Charles V*, which was in the press.

[3] On 14 Oct. 1768.

[4] It is printed in *Chatham Corr.*, iii. 343, and *Corr. of George III*, ii. 57.

[5] Lord Camden.

Alteration will ensue. Our Administration is like a Heap of loose stones, where, if you remove one, the rest will all tumble.[1] This is the least of the numberless Evils under which we labour. What do you think of our being such compleat Beggars as not to be able to subsist, and yet labouring under the Jealousy and Envy of all Europe, on account of our supposd Power and Opulence? With regard to Administrations, the present one behavd so scandalously during the late Mobs, when the Laws, and Constitution and the King and the whole Legislature were openly insulted with Impunity, that it is impossible to think we can be Losers by any Alteration.

My Compliments to Mrs Mure, and your Sister and the Captain: Remember me also to Mrs Cockburn, when you see her. I am Dear Baron

Yours very sincerely
DAVID HUME

* 423. *To the* COMTESSE DE BOUFFLERS

London, 23 December, 1768.

I am somewhat ashamed, dear Madam, but still more sorry, to be obliged to address you by letter, instead of enjoying your conversation, as I flattered myself all last autumn.[2] My intended journey was every day delayed, for different reasons, which appeared, each of them, at the time, solid and invincible; but it would be difficult for me to explain the amount of the whole. The truth is, I have, and ever had a prodigious reluctance to change my place of abode; and though this disposition

* *Priv. Corr.*, 263 ff.

[1] Cf. Burke's description of it: 'An administration checkered and speckled; a piece of joinery crossly indented and whimsically dovetailed; a cabinet variously inlaid; a piece of diversified mosaic; a tesselated pavement without cement; here a bit of black stone and there a bit of white; patriots and courtiers, King's friends and republicans; Whigs and Tories; treacherous friends and open enemies' (quoted by Basil Williams, *Chatham*, ii. 218).

[2] At least one letter of Hume's to Mme de Boufflers, written probably in June 1768, is missing; for she answers it on 15 July 1768: 'Cette visitte que vous m'annonces me fait un plaisir extrême, ce n'est point une façon de parler, prenes mes mots a la lettre, et ajoutes y la foy que merite ce que vous connoisses de ma sincerité et de mon amitié pour vous.' She then goes on to tell him what her arrangements for the summer and autumn are to be, adding: 'Telle est ma marche et vous voyes que si vous executes votre projet, je pourray ne rien perdre du sejour que vous feres icy' (MS., R.S.E., unpublished).

was more than counterbalanced by my strong desire of enjoying your society, it made me perhaps yield more easily to the obstacles which opposed my journey. For this reason I shall say nothing of my future intentions; lest I expose myself to the same reproach of irresolution, in case I do not fulfil them. But I own I have, during a long time, felt the strongest inclination of hearing from you; and knowing your situation with regard to health and domestic satisfaction. The Count, I hear, was to be married some weeks ago: I am told, that all your friends are extremely pleased with the alliance; and that the young couple were to come home and live with you; a project likely to turn out much to their advantage, and your satisfaction. I flatter myself that this arrangement will tend very much to give you more liberty in the disposal of your time—the circumstance which seemed to me chiefly wanting to your enjoyment of life: some constraint must still remain; but I hope that, besides being alleviated by your friendship for the object, it will now also admit of intervals and relaxation. It will be difficult for you ever to be so happy as I wish you; and I am more difficult to please, than you yourself would be with regard to every circumstance of your situation.[1]

I think it my duty to inform you concerning all your friends in this country. The Bedford family seem to be comforted entirely, from the shock they received on poor Lord Tavistock's death: some even reproached the Duke with being too easily comforted: but it proceeded from the ardency of his temper, which always takes itself to the present object without reserve. He begins to apprehend that he is losing his eyes again, and that he has endured a very cruel operation to no purpose.[2]

[1] Replying to this on 7 Jan. 1769, Mme de Boufflers says: 'Mon fils est marié du dix de decembre. Il a epousé une femme charmante qu'il aime et dont il est aimé. Ils ne sont point riches, mais ils peuvent vivre heureux avec ce qu'ils ont. Ma belle fille me plait, elle a des agremens de l'esprit, de la sensibilité. Elle montre beaucoup d'amitié pour moy. Mon fils paroist m'aimer aussi, je le crois honnete homme, il est né heureux, tout luy reussit, mais il n'a rien de satisfaisant pour l'amour propre. Tous les deux vivront avec moy pendant quatre ans (j'y suis engagée) et davantage, si cela me plait. Ils ne me gesnent point, parce qu'ils ne me detournent en aucun maniere de la vie que j'aime a mener et que vous vous obstines a regarder comme contrainte quelqu'effort que j'aye fait pour vous dissuader. Cette amitié a laquelle je me suis devouée, est mon premier devoir, ma principale affaire, et mon plus grand plaisir' (MS., R.S.E., unpublished).

[2] He was operated on for cataract in both eyes in Dec. 1767.

Lord and Lady Holdernesse live elegantly and sociably, as usual: my Lord is only not quite contented in being left out of the present plan of administration, and not to have any occupation. Lady Emily[1] is their great consolation, and is a fine girl; but will not prove so handsome as we expected.

I believe the Duchess of Grafton[2] was your acquaintance: her adventure cannot be unknown to you. It is not doubted but, as soon as she is divorced, she will marry Lord Ossory; and the Duke, his kept mistress,[3] who was very lately a lady of the town. These are strange scenes; and very contrary to your manners.

Lord Beauchamp is married to a young lady of family and fortune,[4] who has an entire complaisance for Lady Hertford: so that this incident, which she always dreaded, will no wise interrupt their correspondence. Lord Beauchamp makes a very good figure in Parliament; but the young people cannot endure him, on account of his want of sociableness: you remember, there was the same complaint against him at Paris; and it is a pity, considering his amiable manner in other respects.

There was a report here, which got into the newspapers, that I was going over to France in my former station: but it never had the least foundation. The truth is, I would rather pay you a visit voluntarily, than in any public character; though indeed the prospect of affairs here is so strange and melancholy, as would make any one desirous of withdrawing from the country at any rate. Licentiousness, or rather the frenzy of liberty, has taken possession of us, and is throwing everything into confusion. How happy do I esteem it, that in all my writings I have always kept at a proper distance from that tempting extreme,

[1] Lady Amelia Darcy, only child of Lord Holdernesse. She married the Marquis of Carmarthen in 1773, eloped with Captain John Byron in 1778, and was divorced the following year.

[2] Anne Liddell (died 1804), daughter of 1st Baron Ravensworth; m. (1) (1756) 3rd Duke of Grafton; left him in Aug., and was separated from him by mutual consent in Dec. 1764; divorced early in 1769; and m. (2) 2nd Earl of Upper Ossory.

[3] Nancy Parsons, otherwise known as Mrs. Horton (died *c.* 1808); she m. (1776) 2nd Viscount Maynard. It was one of the most notorious public scandals that the Duke, when Prime Minister, went about openly with her (see Junius, *passim*). He married (summer of 1769) Elizabeth (died 1822), daughter of Sir Richard Wrottesley, 7th Bart.

[4] The Hon. Alicia Elizabeth Windsor (died 1772), daughter of 1st Viscount Windsor.

and have maintained a due regard to magistracy and established government, suitably to the character of an historian and a philosopher! I find on that account my authority growing daily; and indeed have now no reason to complain of the public, though your partiality to me made you think so formerly. Add to this, that the King's bounty puts me in a very opulent situation. I must, however, expect that, if any great public convulsion happen, my appointments will cease, and reduce me to my own revenue: but this will be sufficient for a man of letters, who surely needs less money both for his entertainment and credit, than other people.

A-propos to such people, we hear that our friend Rousseau made an elopement from the Prince of Conti, and fled into Dauphiny. He tired there, and offered to return to Mr Davenport, but is now returned to Dombes, where he will not long remain.[1] He is surely the most singular and most incomprehensible, and at the same time the most unhappy man that ever was born. I have seen the copy of a paper, which he wrote in Dauphiny, containing the sentiments of all mankind with regard to him. It is certainly genuine: some marks of genius, with a great many of vanity, prove it to be no counterfeit. Did he elope from the Prince of Conti, without making a quarrel with you or his benefactor? It seems he is determined not to return to you.[2]

I beg you to lay me at the Prince of Conti's feet, and to express my inviolable regard and attachment to His Highness. May I also beg you to remember me to Mme de Vierville and Mme de Barbantane. I hope Miss Becket is well, and has the same passion, but more moderate, for you. Adieu, dear Madam. Believe me to be ever yours, with the greatest sincerity.

[1] Rousseau left Trye in June 1768, wandered from place to place for a time, lived in shabby taverns at Bourgoin from Aug. 1768 till March 1769, and then settled in Monquin till July 1770, whence he drifted back to Paris to spend the remaining eight years of his life.

[2] Replying to this on 7 Jan. 1769, Mme de Boufflers says: 'Je n'ay plus aucun commerce avec J.J. depuis votre querelle. Il a quitté l'azile qu'on luy avoit donné mais sans se brouiller avec son protecteur. Il est toujours deffiant toujours singulier, et toujours malheureux: il a epousé Mlle le Vasseur. Pourquoy a cette heure? et pourquoy pas plutot, je n'en say rien? On dit qu'il va en Angleterre. J'ay vu l'ecrit dont vous faites mention. Je doute qu'il soit de luy.'—Her statement in the first sentence is, however, not strictly true; for she wrote Rousseau two letters in the spring of 1768 (Streckeisen-Moultou, ii. 61 ff.).

* 424. *To* HORACE WALPOLE

Dear Sir,

This letter will be deliver'd to you by M. Deyverdun, a Swiss gentleman, a man of letters and of merit, whom I had occasion to know particularly, because he was in the Secretary's office, and in Mr Conway's department. He has undertaken a work, of which he has publish'd only one number, under the title of Memoires literaires de la Grande Bretagne; and he has a second in hand. He wishes to enrich it by an account of Lord Herbert's Life;[1] but not knowing where to find a copy, he uses the freedom, thro' my recommendation, to apply to you: I hope you will have no objection to the supplying him with one. I am, dear Sir,

Your most obedient & most humble Servant
DAVID HUME.

Brewers Street
11 of Novr 1768

† 425. *To* WILLIAM ROBERTSON

[Nov. or Dec. 1768][2]

I got yesterday from Strahan about thirty sheets of your History, to be sent over to Suard,[3] and last night and this morning have run them over with great avidity. I could not deny myself the satisfaction (which I hope also will not displease you) of expressing presently my extreme approbation of them. To say only they are very well written, is by far too faint an expression, and much inferior to the sentiments I feel; they are composed with nobleness, with dignity, with elegance, and with judgment, to which there are few equals. They even excel, and, I think, in a sensible degree, your *History of Scotland*. I propose to myself great pleasure in being the only man in England, during some months, who will be in a situation of doing you

* Walpole, *Letters*, Supp. vol. ii. 76.

† Stewart, *Robertson* (Coll. edit. of Stewart's *Works*), 139 ff. (incomplete).

[1] Walpole printed the *Life of Lord Herbert of Cherbury* at his private printing-press at Strawberry Hill.

[2] Robertson was in London in the early summer of 1768, to arrange for the publication of his *Charles V*. The book was published at the beginning of March 1769. The actual printing was therefore probably begun in the late autumn or early winter.

[3] Who was translating it into French.

justice, after which you may certainly expect that my voice will be drowned in that of the public.

You know that you and I have always been on the footing of finding in each other's productions *something to blame and something to commend*; and, therefore, you may perhaps expect also some seasoning of the former kind; but really neither my leisure nor inclination allowed me to make such remarks, and I sincerely believe you have afforded me very small materials for them. However, such particulars as occur to my memory I shall mention. *Maltreat* is a Scotticism which occurs once. What the devil had you to do with that old-fashioned dangling word *wherewith*? I should as soon take back *whereupon*, *whereunto*, and *wherewithal*. I think the only tolerable decent gentleman of the family is *wherein*, and I should not choose to be often seen in his company. But I know your affection for *wherewith* proceeds from your partiality to Dean Swift, whom I can often laugh with, whose style I can even approve, but surely can never admire. It has no harmony, no eloquence, no ornament, and not much correctness, whatever the English may imagine. Were not their literature still in a somewhat barbarous state, that author's place would not be so high among their classics. But what a fancy is this you have taken of saying always *an hand*, *an heart*, *an head*? Have you *an ear*? Do you not know that this *n* is added before vowels to prevent the cacophony, and ought never to take place before *h* when that letter is sounded? It is never pronounced in these words, why should it be wrote? Thus, I should say, *a history*, and *an historian*; and so would you too, if you had any sense. But you tell me that Swift does otherwise. To be sure, there is no reply to that; and we must swallow your *hath* too upon the same authority. I will see you d——d sooner.—But I will endeavour to keep my temper.

I do not like this sentence in page 149. 'This step was taken in consequence of the Treaty Wolsey had concluded with the Emperor at Brussels, and which had hitherto been kept secret.' Si sic omnia dixisses, I should never have been plagued with hearing your praises so often sounded, and that fools preferred your style to mine. Certainly it had been better to have said, 'which Wolsey &c'. That relative ought very seldom to be omitted, and is here particularly requisite to preserve a symmetry between the two members of the sentence. You omit the relative too often, which is a colloquial barbarism, as Mr Johnson calls it.

Your periods are sometimes, tho not often, too long. Suard will be embarassed with them, as the modish French style runs into the other extreme. . . .

* 426. *To* JEAN-BAPTISTE-ANTOINE SUARD

Brewer Street, 10 March 1769.

It is long since I sent off all the sheets of Charles V; and I suppose they have come safe to hand, and that the work will soon be published in Paris. It is now near a week since it has been published in London; and as far as we can judge, in so short a time, will meet with very great success. The author complains to me that he never hears from you; I excuse you on account of your indolence; but he and I will be impatient to know the sentiments of Paris with regard to the performance.

Poor Stuart[1] has lost his cause[2] which he had laboured with such assiduity, such integrity, and such capacity. Never was any sentence more unjust: but the cause had become so complicate, that it had gone beyond the comprehension of almost all our peers; and it was in the power of Lord Mansfield, who had shown a violent partiality from the beginning, to twist and turn it as he pleased and to command the plurality of votes.

If the event was in one respect disastrous and extraordinary for Stuart, it was in another as fortunate and extraordinary. On rising next morning, he found on his table a bond of annuity for 400 pounds a year, sent him by a friend, a man of sense, who had no interest in the cause, but who chose this opportunity to express his esteem and affection for Stuart. The person who has done this noble action, is Pulteney; you may have seen him at Paris with Stuart: he then bore the name of Johnstone.[3]

* Morrison, ii. 318.

[1] Andrew Stuart.

[2] The Douglas Cause. On 27 Feb. 1769 the House of Lords reversed the judgement of the Court of Session, and awarded the Douglas estates to Archibald Steuart-Douglas.

[3] William Johnstone, now Pulteney, having married the heiress of the Earl of Bath, was one of the richest men in the Kingdom.

The following draft letter, unsigned, but in Hume's handwriting, is among the MSS., R.S.E. It was printed by Burton (ii. 425) as Hume's, but I think it must have been a transcript by Hume of a letter he had received from Pulteney.

'My dear Sir

'Nothing can be more just, than the sentiment you have expressed in your letter. I am to be envied for having had it in my power to contribute to the

All the lawyers also on the side of Douglas have sent to Stuart an acknowledgment of his integrity and honour in the conduct of this cause.[1] These circumstances will give pleasure to the seiks in the Rue Royale,[2] who had an esteem for Stuart. I beg my compliments to them.

* 427. *To the* Rev. Hugh Blair

Dear Doctor Park Place[3] 28 March 1769

The *fatal Discovery* [4] succeeded, and deservd it: It has feeling, tho' not equal to Douglas, in my Opinion. The Versification of it is not enough finish'd. Our Friend escaped by lying conceal'd:[5] But the Success of all plays, in this Age, is very feeble; and the people now heed the Theatre almost as little as the Pulpit. History, I think, is the Favourite Reading, and our

* MS., R.S.E.; Mackenzie, *Home*, 157 (incomplete); Burton, ii. 421 ff.

---

happiness of the best man and the most intimate friend I have ever had in the world. There is nothing else in the possession of a fortune, that deserves the least envy or the least consideration. Every man is independent, who thinks himself so; but every man has not been blessed with such a friend, or with the power of showing, in some small degree, the value he puts upon worth, delicacy, attachment and ability like his. It adds to my happiness not a little, that your sentiments coincide so entirely with mine. You have known Stuart enough to value him as much as I do, and he has too much discernment not to put the same high value upon you, which you have commanded from every one of your friends.

'I am etc.'

[1] This is not quite the whole story. One of the barristers on the Douglas side was Edward Thurlow (Lord Chancellor, 1778–92). During the hearing of the case he attacked Stuart in such terms that Stuart called him out. They exchanged shots, were reconciled, and afterwards became close friends.

[2] Probably a reference to the *philosophes*, who were wont to assemble at the Baron d'Holbach's house in the Rue Royale.

[3] General Conway's house, near Henley-on-Thames.

[4] John Home's play, just produced at Drury Lane.

[5] 'Garrick had been justly alarmed at the jealousy and dislike which prevailed at that time against Lord Bute and the Scotch, and had advised him [John Home] to change the title of *Rivine* into that of the *Fatal Discovery*, and had provided a student of Oxford, who had appeared at the rehearsals as the author, and wished Home of all things to remain concealed till the play had its run. But John, whose vanity was too sanguine to admit of any fear or caution, and whose appetite for praise rebelled against the counsel that would deprive him for a moment of his fame, too soon discovered the secret, and though the play survived its nine nights, yet the house evidently slackened after the Town heard that John was the author' (Carlyle, *Autobiog.* 509).

other Friend, the favourite Historian. Nothing can be more successful than his last Production, nor more deservedly. I agree with you; it is beyond his first Performance; as was indeed natural to expect. I hope, for a certain Reason, which I keep to myself, that he does not intend, in his third work,[1] to go beyond his second: Tho' I am damnably afraid he will: For the Subject is much more interesting.[1] Neither the Character of Charles V, nor the Incidents of his Life are very interesting; and were it not for the first Volume, the Success of this work, tho' perfectly well writ, woud not have been so shining.

This Madness about Wilkes excited first Indignation, then Apprehension; but has gone to such a Height, that all other Sentiments with me are bury'd in Ridicule.[2] This exceeds the Absurdity of Titus Oates and the popish Plot; and is so much more disgraceful to the Nation, as the former Folly, being derivd from Religion, flow'd from a Source, which has, from uniform Prescription, acquird a Right to impose Nonsense on all Nations & all Ages: But the present Extravagance is peculiar to Ourselves, and quite risible. However, I am afraid my Mirth will soon be spoilt, and Affairs become quite serious: For I am well assurd that Lord Chatham will after the holy days creep out from his Retreat, and appear on the Scene. Depositis novus exuviis, nitidusque juventa Volvitur ad solem et linguis micat ore trisulcis.[3] (I know not if I cite Virgil exactly, but I am sure I apply him right.) This Villain is to thunder against the Violation of the Bill of Rights, in not allowing the County of Middlesex the Choice of its Member.[4] Think of the Impudence of that

[1] The History of America.

[2] Wilkes was elected for Middlesex in March 1768, and immediately afterwards surrendered himself as an outlaw and agreed to stand his trial. On 18 June 1768 he was sentenced to twenty-two months' imprisonment and fined £1,000. In Feb. 1769 he was expelled the House of Commons, and in March re-elected for Middlesex and again expelled the House. About a fortnight after the date of this letter he was again re-elected for Middlesex; whereupon the House of Commons, faced with an absurd dilemma, arbitrarily declared his opponent, Colonel Luttrel, to be the Member for Middlesex.

[3] Nunc positis novus exuviis nitidusque juventa
Lubrica convoluit sublato pectore terga
Arduus ad solem, et linguis micat ore trisulcis.
Virg., *II Aen.*, 473 ff.

[4] This was currently reported at the time, but in fact Chatham did not appear in the House of Lords after the Easter recess. He suddenly appeared at a levee in July.

Fellow; and his Quackery; and his Cunning; and his Audaciousness; and judge of the Influence he will have over such a deluded Multitude.

I was struck with a very sensible Indignation at the Decision of the Douglas Cause; though I forsaw it for some time. It was abominable with regard to poor Andrew Stuart, who had conducted that Cause with singular Ability & Integrity; and was at last expos'd to reproach, which unfortunately never can be wip'd off. For the Cause, tho' not in the least intricate, is so complicated, that it never will be review'd by the public, who are besides perfectly pleas'd with the Sentence; being sway'd by Compassion and a few popular Topics. To one who understands the Cause, as I do, nothing coud appear more scandalous than the pleadings of the two Law Lords. Such gross Misrepresentations, such impudent Assertions, such groundless Imputations never came from that place: But all was good enough for their Audience, who, bating their Quality, are most of them little better than their Brethren, the Wilkites, in the Streets.

I am very much obligd to you for giving me the Acquaintance of your Cousin, Mr Blair, who seems indeed to me a very accomplishd young Man.[1] The Death of your Brother in law [2] is a great Loss to you, and even to us all: I comprehend myself: For I intend to visit you soon, and for good and all. Indeed, I know not what detains me here, except that it is so much a matter of Indifference where I live; and I am amus'd with looking on the Scene, which really begins to be interesting. I had taken one of Allan Ramsay's Houses, but gave it up again, on the Representation of some of my Friends in Edinburgh, who said that a House on the North Side of a high Hill, in the 56 Degree of Latitude coud not be healthful: But I now repent it: Tho' I have my old House to retreat to, till I get a better. I am glad you like my Nephew: He is indeed clever, tho I am afraid a little giddy.

* 428. *To* William Robertson

28 March 1769.

. . . I find then that you are not contented without a particular detail of your own praises, and that the very short but

* Stewart, *Robertson* (Coll. edit. of Stewart's *Works*), 141 (incomplete).

[1] Robert Blair (1741–1811), Solicitor-General for Scotland, 1789–1806; Lord President of the Court of Session, 1808–11.

[2] The Rev. Hew Bannatine; ordained at Ormiston, 1747; translated to Dirkton, 1749; died, 26 Feb. 1769.

pithy letter I wrote you gives you no satisfaction. But what I say more? The success has answered my expectations: and I, who converse with the Great, the Fair, and the Learned, have scarcely heard an opposite voice, or even whisper to the general sentiment. Only I have heard that the Sanhedrim at Mrs Macaulay's condemns you as little less a friend to government and monarchy than myself. . . .

* 429. *To* Baron Mure of Caldwell

Dear Baron

If I were not the most lazy Person in the world at writing—I mean of Letters, I certainly shoud have taken an Opportunity to express to you my Indignation at the strange, tho' long expected, Issue of your great Cause.[1] I was present at it, and surely never was present at more scandalous Proceedings. If I was positive before, concerning the Justice of your Cause (and you know I was always sufficiently positive) I am much more so at present: Because formerly, tho' I cou'd not conceive how it was possible to break in upon the Solidity of your Proofs, yet, hearing frequent hints that Lord Mansfield was to be against you, I cou'd not but remain somewhat in suspence, and suspect that he might perceive some Flaw in them, unimagin'd by me. But when I heard his pleading, and found on what infamous Topics, he rested his Judgement, I then knew that no thing farther cou'd be said, and saw the whole Mystery, which is, in the most egregious Degree, a Mystery of Iniquity. He, as well as the Chancellor, had no other Ressource but to cry out perpetually, *Subornation of Perjury*, for which there is not the least Ground of Suspicion, and of which all the Douglas Lawyers before the Court of Session, both in their pleadings and Memorials, were entirely silent. Almost without a Pretence, he puff'd off, at one Breath, fifteen Witnesses, who prove the Enlevement of Mignon's Child [2] to have been about the middle of July, and he calld them all perjur'd, tho' it appears certainly, that the first time Andrew Stuart saw them, was in the presence of four Gentlemen of Character: By a like Sweep, he carryd off at once eight unexceptionable Witnesses, in order to re-habilitate Mrs

* MS. in possession of Mrs. Reginald Mure, Oxford; *Nineteenth Cent. & After*, xcviii, 303 f.

[1] The Douglas Cause.

[2] The contention of the Hamiltons was that Lady Jane Steuart procured two infants, one being Mignon's child, and passed them off as her own twin boys.

Hewit:[1] He pronounc'd Godfrey and his Wife [2] perjur'd; tho' their Evidence is irrefragably confirm'd, by every Circumstance of the fact, and by the absolute Necessity which people in their Situation lie under of keeping Books in the manner which they explain. But I need not run over points which have been fully related to you: I shall only say in a few words, that never, in one Instant, was so evidently display'd the Imbecillity of Men and their Villainy; the first in the Approbation of the Peers to such Arguments, and the second in the advancing of them by the two Law Lords.

What renders the Affair more vexatious, is, that the Question, tho' not in the least intricate, is so complicated, that it will never be review'd by the public, who, sway'd by Compassion and by a few popular Topics, are entirely satisfy'd with the Decision, and will scarce ever be perswaded to give the Matter a Revisal. The only Chance for bringing it up again, woud be by the Publication of the Speeches with a few Notes; but I despair of seeing so compleat a Copy of them as will not be disownd by the Speakers. It was to this Prejudice of the Public, together with the Complicateness of the Cause, that Mansfield trusted; and he thought, that, with the greatest Security in the world, he coud indulge his Prejudices, which, from the beginning, had been violent against you. I am afraid he has judg'd but too well, of the Nature of Mankind.

No body, Dear Baron, can be more sensible than I am of the Vexation, which you must feel, from this unfortunate Issue of your Labours and from the insolent Triumph of your Enemies; and I heartily sympathize with you upon it. But I own, there is another Person, whose Condition affects me still more sensibly; it is that of poor Andrew Stuart, who had conducted this Affair with singular Integrity and Ability, and who yet must lie under such unmerited Reproach, and for aught I can see without remedy. Pulteney's Behaviour to him [3] is noble, but is not sufficient; and yet I know not what farther can possibly be done, to throw the Infamy where it ought so justly to be laid. I see his heart is crushd by this cruel Usage; and I own, that never any Incident, which passd within my Knowledge, seems so justly the Object of Regret and Indignation.

[1] Lady Jane Steuart's faithful friend and companion in all her misfortunes.

[2] The French innkeepers at whose inn Lady Jane Steuart stayed for two or three days just before the birth of her twin boys.

[3] See note 3 on p. 195 above.

You must allow me, however, to distinguish in what I said a little above, that this Decision will never be review'd by the Public. I speak only of England, where there are always so many public and important Affairs in Agitation, that a private Cause must soon fall into Oblivion. But in Scotland, this has become, in a manner, a public Cause, and all Men of Sense are so much agreed in one Opinion, that Truth, supported by the excellent Writings on that Side, must at last triumph, over Prejudice, Clamour, and Nonsense. I know, that you have the Good sense to wait with Patience till that time; and as your Conduct, from the very Nature of your Situation, is without all Reproach, you can the more easily acquiesce in that Resolution.

My Compliments to Mrs Mure and all your Family; not forgetting the two young Gentlemen, whom you have withdrawn from us.[1] I am with great Sincerity Dear Baron

Your affectionate Friend and Servant
DAVID HUME.

Park Place
30 of March 1769.

* 430. *To the* COMTESSE DE BOUFFLERS

5 of May, 1769.

I was yesterday, dear Madam, very much alarmed, by a piece of intelligence, which I received from Madame de la Vaupalliere:[2] that having engaged your daughter-in-law to submit to inoculation, the success had appeared very doubtful: she had a great number of pustules; her face was much covered with them, her life was not out of danger, and the consequences in general were much apprehended. You may easily imagine to what degree I interest myself in this event. I foresee that, if any sinister accident happen, you will be inclined, besides regretting a person, to whom you are so much attached, to blame

* *Priv. Corr.*, 267 ff.

[1] The young Mures had gone home for a holiday. They returned to Norlands in due course.

[2] Diane-Jacqueline-Louise-Josèphe de Clermont d'Amboise (born 1733), widow of the comte de Gacé, m., 2 (1766), the marquis de la Vaupalière. She dined at Strawberry Hill and received a set of complimentary verses on 9 May 1769 (Walpole, *Letters*, vii. 274).

yourself for an advice the best founded in reason and experience. As the issue must now be perfectly known, I beg to be informed of it: I cannot forbear hoping, that your anxiety has exaggerated the danger; and that all will still end happily.[1]

We have had this winter two countrywomen of yours, very amiable persons, to whom I pay my court frequently, Madame de Chatelet[2] and Madame de Damas.[3] The manners of the latter are generally taking, and she is very popular: the former, with a very superior merit, is better calculated for every situation, than that in which she is at present engaged, namely representation, in such a crowd as this town affords, and in such a hurry as everywhere presents itself: her good sense, and her frank easy humour, with her utter inability to dissemble, render her the best companion of the world in private society. I only regret in these two ladies that, having never had much commerce with you, I have not the satisfaction of hearing your name mentioned among them so frequently as I should be inclined to.

But I am afraid, dear Madam, of entertaining you with indifferent subjects, perhaps at a time when all your attention is engaged in the most interesting event: I shall therefore conclude; but with representing to you, that there was more sharpness in your last letter, than I ever thought should have passed between us.[4] Certainly, I was not blameable in ascribing to you a great desire of liberty and leisure, both because that sentiment is natural, and even laudable; and because I am myself so much possessed with it, that I think nothing can be compared to these blessings. In all cases, my mistake was innocent; and as I never meant to offend you, I doubt not, but, upon reflection, you will again restore me to your good graces, on which I set so high a value, and which, on that account, it is impossible for me ever to deserve to forfeit.

[1] The young Countess duly recovered.

[2] Diane-Adélaïde de Rochechouart (died 1793), wife of the comte du Châtelet, the French Ambassador in London.

[3] Zéphirine-Félicité de Rochechouart (died 1776), comtesse d'Antigny-Damas, sister of Mme du Châtelet.

[4] See quotation in note 1 on p. 190 above. In continuation of the passage there quoted Mme de Boufflers says: 'A present vous connoisses mon coeur, et vous pouves conclure que les pretendues vœux que vous feres pour ma liberté, et pour mon bonheur, si vous en juges par vos idées et non par les miennes, seroient de veritables imprecations dont je souhaite que ma mort previenne l'accomplissement' (MS., R.S.E., unpublished).

* 431. *To the* Abbé Morellet

London, 10 July, 1769.

I congratulate you, dear Abbé, upon your being so far advanced in your labours. You have now a prospect of a conclusion: I expect great entertainment and instruction from your work; and your prospectus is an excellent specimen of it. I wish only you had taken care to supply M. Frances[1] with a number of receipts for subscribers. I belong to a very numerous club in London,[2] among whom I could have found many subscribers, if I had had receipts to give them, and M. Frances promised to procure them for me; but has not yet been able to make good his engagement. I hope the profit of the subscription is for yourself; and that you, as well as the public, will reap benefit by this undertaking. M. Suard would tell you what noble encouragement is given to literature in England, without the intervention of the great, by means of the booksellers alone, that is, by the public. Dr Robertson received £4000 for his Charles V, the greatest price that was ever known to be given for any book. It has been published about four months, and has met here with universal approbation. It is owned that there never was a more elegant spirited narration; and the first volume contains very curious matter, unknown to the generality of readers. But the sale to the booksellers has not quite answered expectation, in which they seem to have been too sanguine. For as the subject consists of a period, which neither interests much the present age nor this nation, the book, though perfectly well writ, does not run off so fast as they fondly imagined. There are

* *New Monthly Magazine*, original series, No. 72; Burton, ii. 426 ff. (incomplete).

This letter is in reply to one from Morellet dated 16 May 1769 (MS., R.S.E.; *Eminent Persons*, 310 ff.) sending copies of the prospectus for his *Dictionnaire du Commerce* to be presented to General Conway, Adam Smith, William Robertson, Dean Tucker, and Benjamin Franklin.

[1] Secretary to the French Embassy in London.

[2] John ('Fish') Crawford, writing to Hume from London on 9 Dec. 1766, says: 'I know not if you remember that you gave me permission to propose you as a member of a certain very infamous society in Pall Mall. In spite of all that has been said against this society, there was too much taste & sense in it for one black ball to appear against you. Ld Ossory & Ld Bolingbroke were both present when you gave me this permission, & therefore I expect that you will acknowledge them & me in what we have done' (MS., R.S.E., unpublished). And again, on 20 Jan. 1767: 'Our society is delighted to have you belong to them & much obliged to me for having procured them that honor' (MS., R.S.E., unpublished). It appears that the Club in question was Almack's.

only about 2900 sold, which yet is a great number. The translation is probably published by this time at Paris, and I hope with good success.

That part of your prospectus, in which you endeavour to prove that there enters nothing of human convention in the establishment of money, is certainly very curious, and very elaborately composed; and yet I cannot forbear thinking that the common opinion has some foundation. It is true, money must always be made of some materials, which have intrinsic value, otherwise it would be multiplied without end, and would sink to nothing. But, when I take a shilling, I consider it not as a useful metal, but as something which another will take from me; and the person who shall convert it into metal is, probably, several millions of removes distant. You know that all states have made it criminal to melt their coin; and, tho this is a law which cannot well be executed, it is not to be supposed that, if it could, it would entirely destroy the value of the money, according to your hypothesis. You have a base coin, called billon, in France, composed of silver and copper, which has a ready currency, tho the separation of the two metals, and the reduction of them to their primitive state, would, I am told, be both expensive and troublesome. Our shillings and sixpences, which are almost our only silver coin, are so much worn by use, that they are twenty, thirty, or forty per cent below their original value; yet they pass currency; which can arise only from a tacit convention. Our colonies in America, for want of specie, used to coin a paper currency; which were not bank notes, because there was no place appointed to give money in exchange: yet this paper currency passed in all payments, by convention; and might have gone on, had it not been abused by the several assemblies, who issued paper without end, and thereby discredited the currency.

You mention several kinds of money, sheep, oxen, fish, employed as measures of exchange, or as money, in different parts of the world. You have overlooked that, in our colony of Pennsylvania, the land itself, which is the chief commodity, is coined, and passes in circulation. The manner of conducting this affair is as follows:—A planter, immediately after he purchases any land, can go to a public office and receive notes to the amount of half the value of his land; which notes he employs in all payments, and they circulate through the whole colony, by convention. To prevent the public from being overwhelmed by this fictitious money, there are two means employed—first, the notes issued to any one planter, must not exceed a certain sum, whatever may be the value of his land: secondly, every planter is obliged to pay back into the public office every year one tenth part of his notes; the whole, of course, is annihilated in ten years; after which, it is again allowed him to take out new notes to half the value of his land. An account of this curious operation would enrich your dictionary; and you may have a more particular detail of it, if you please, from Dr Franklin, who will be in Paris about this time, and will be glad to see you. I conveyed to him your prospectus, and he expressed to me a great esteem of it.

I see that, in your prospectus, you take care not to disoblige your economists,[1] by any declaration of your sentiments; in which I commend your prudence. But I hope that in your work you will thunder them, and crush them, and pound them, and reduce them to dust and ashes! They are, indeed, the set of men the most chimerical and most arrogant that now exist, since the annihilation of the Sorbonne. I ask your pardon for saying so, as I know you belong to that venerable body. I wonder what could engage our friend, M. Turgot, to herd among them; I mean, among the economists; tho I believe he was also a Sorbonnist.

I sent your prospectus to Dr Tucker, but have not heard from him since. I shall myself deliver copies to Dr Robertson and Mr Smith, as I go to Scotland this autumn.

And now, my dear Abbé, what remains to me but to wish you success in your judicious labours? To embrace you, and through you, to embrace all our common friends, D'Alembert, Helvétius, Buffon, Baron d'Holbach, Suard, Mademoiselle de Lespinasse? Poor Abbé Le Bon is dead, I hear. The Abbé Galiani [2] goes to Naples: he does well to leave Paris before I come thither; for I should certainly put him to death for all the ill he has spoken of England. But it has happened, as was fortold by his friend, Caracciloli;[3] who said that the Abbé would remain two months in this country, would speak all himself,

[1] Quesnay and the Physiocrats.

[2] Ferdinand Galiani (1728–87), a Neapolitan abbé, sometime Secretary to the Neapolitan Embassy in Paris; a great friend of Mme Geoffrin, and of the *philosophes*.

[3] Dominique, marquis Caraccioli (1717–89), Neapolitan Ambassador at Paris.

would not allow an Englishman to utter a syllable; and after returning would give the character of the nation during the rest of his life, as if he were perfectly well acquainted with them.

Pray make my compliments to M. Maletête.[1] Tell him, that Prince Masserane[2] says, that he has saved much effusion of blood to this country. It is certain that M. Maletête had a great curiosity to see a riot here, and yet was resolved to keep his person in safety. For this purpose, he hired a window; and proposed to be present at one of the mad elections of Wilkes, and to divert himself with the fray. Somebody got a hint of it, and put it into the newspapers; asking the freeholders if they were so degenerate as to make themselves a laughing-stock, even to the French, their enemies, whom they despised. Prince Masserane alleges that this incident made that election so remarkably peaceable!

Are you acquainted with Crébillon?[3] I am ashamed to mention his name. He sent me over his last work, with a very obliging letter:[4] but as I must write to him in French, I have never answered him. If all the English were as impertinent as I am, the Abbé Galiani would have reason to abuse us.

I am, dear Abbé, after asking your blessing,

Yours sincerely,

DAVID HUME.

* 432. *To* ADAM SMITH

Dear Smith

I am glad to have come within sight of you, and to have a View of Kirkaldy from my Windows: But as I wish also to be

* MS., R.S.E.; *Lit. Gazette*, 1821, p. 649; Burton, ii. 429 f.

[1] Mme du Deffand describes this M. de Maletête (whoever he may have been) as 'un robin, un provincial, un suffisant, un sot' (*Lettres à Walpole*, i. 574).

[2] The Spanish Ambassador in London.

[3] Claude-Prosper Jolyot de Crébillon (1717–77), the novelist; author of *L'Écumoire*, *Le Sopha*, &c.

[4] The letter is dated 23 Nov. 1768 and begins:

'Ceux qui ne vous connoissent que par vos ouvrages, et qui ne scavent pas combien il y a de tolérance dans votre philosophie, me trouveroient bien ridicule d'oser vous adresser un Roman; mais vous m'avez prouvé qu'il n'y a rien dont le sage ne puisse tirer parti, si ce n'est pour son instruction, du moins pour son amusement. C'est donc avec toute confiance, que le frivole Crébillon adresse au Philosophe Hume, des lettre galantes, si, cependant, l'on peut donner ce titre à des lettres dans lesquelles il y a, ce me semble, fort peu de galanterie, mais où, pourtant, on parle d'amour, et dont cette passion fait le fond . . .' (MS., R.S.E.; *Eminent Persons*, 306 f.).

The novel in question was entitled *Lettres de la duchesse de *** au duc de ****.

within speaking terms of you, I wish we coud concert measures for that purpose. I am mortally sick at Sea, and regard with horror, and a kind of hydrophobia the great Gulph that lies between us. I am also tir'd of travelling, as much as you ought naturally to be, of staying at home: I therefore propose to you to come hither, and pass some days with me in this Solitude. I want to know what you have been doing, and propose to exact a rigorous Account of the method, in which you have employed yourself during your Retreat. I am positive you are in the wrong in many of your Speculations, especially where you have the Misfortune to differ from me. All these are Reasons for our meeting, and I wish you woud make me some reasonable Proposal for that Purpose. There is no Habitation on the Island of Inch-keith; otherwise I shoud challenge you to meet me on that Spot, and neither [of] us ever to leave the Place, till we were fully agreed on all points of Controversy. I expect General Conway here to morrow, whom I shall attend to Roseneath,[1] & I shall remain there a few days. On my Return, I expect to find a Letter from you, containing a bold Acceptance of this Defiance. I am Dear Smith Yours sincerely

David Hume

James's Court. 20 of Augt 1769

* 433. *To* Sir Gilbert Elliot of Minto

Dear Sir Gilbert

I am very much obligd to you for the Pains you have taken to give me an Account of your Son's Expences and Management at Oxford.[2] I found my Brother undetermind, or rather averse, to the Project. He thinks his Son [3] rather inclines to be dissipated and idle; and believes that a Year or two at Oxford woud confirm him thoroughly in that Habit, without any other Advantage than the acquiring of a little better Pronounciation: For this Reason, he rather inclind to try him a Year in the Law College here, before he makes him so much his own Master.

* MS. at Minto House; Stewart, *Robertson*, 360 f. (incomplete); Burton, ii. 430 ff.

[1] On the Gareloch, Firth of Clyde; one of the Duke of Argyll's seats. Lady Ailesbury was a Campbell, a sister of the Duke's.

[2] Hume was making such inquiries of various friends about this time. There is a long letter to him on the subject from Sir Alexander Macdonald among the MSS., R.S.E.

[3] Still the unsatisfactory Joseph.

I have been settled here two Months, and am here Body & Soul, without casting the least Thought of Regreat to London, or even to Paris. I think it improbable that I shall ever in my Life cross the Tweed, except perhaps a Jaunt to the North of England, for Health or Amusement. I live still, and must for a twelvemonth, in my old House in James's Court, which is very chearful, and even elegant, but too small to display my great Talent for Cookery, the Science to which I intend to addict the remaining Years of my Life; I have just now lying on the Table before me a Receipt for making *Soupe a la Reine*, copy'd with my own hand. For Beef and Cabbage (a charming Dish), and old Mutton and old Claret, no body excels me. I make also Sheep head Broth in a manner that Mr Keith[1] speaks of it for eight days after, and the Duc de Nivernois woud bind himself Apprentice to my Lass to learn it. I have already sent a Challenge to David Moncrief:[2] You will see, that in a twelvemonth he will take to the writing of History, the Field I have deserted: For as to the giving of Dinners, he can now have no farther Pretensions. I shoud have made a very bad use of my Abode in Paris, if I coud not get the better of a mere provincial like him. All my Friends encourage me in this Ambition; as thinking it will redound very much to my Honour.

I am delighted to see the daily and hourly Progress of Madness and Folly and Wickedness in England. The Consummation of these Qualities are the true Ingredients for making a fine Narrative in History; especially if followd by some signal and ruinous Convulsion, as I hope will soon be the Case with that pernicious People. He must be a very bad Cook indeed, that

[1] Robert Keith (died 1774), generally known as Ambassador Keith; sometime Secretary to Marshal Lord Stair; British Minister at Vienna, 1748–58; Ambassador at St. Petersburg, 1758–62; father of Gen. Sir Robert Murray Keith (1730–95), British Minister at Copenhagen, 1771, and at Vienna, 1772–92. On retiring from the Diplomatic service Robert Keith settled at the Hermitage, Leith Links, was made a member of the Poker Club, and found (to his surprise) that the Edinburgh which contained men like Robertson, Blair, 'Jupiter' Carlyle, Ferguson, Mure, and (later) Hume, was quite a tolerable place to live in.

[2] David Stuart Moncrief of Moredun, an advocate, who became a Baron of the Exchequer. 'I said Moncrieffe entertained people to flatter him, as we feed a cow to give us milk. The better the pasture, the more plentiful and richer will the milk be. Moncrieffe therefore feeds his *pecora ventri obedienta* in clover. Other comparisons may be made. He feeds people like silkworms, for their silk, or like civet cats, for their perfume' (*Boswelliana*, ed. Charles Rogers, 1874, p. 281).

cannot make a palatable Dish from the whole. You see in my Reflexions and Allusions I still mix my old and new Profession together. I am Dear Sir Gilbert

Your most obedient humble Servant
DAVID HUME.

Edinburgh
16 of Octr 1769

PS.
I beg my Respects to Lady Elliot.

* 434. *To* WILLIAM STRAHAN

Dear Sir

I never enjoyed myself better, nor was in better spirits, than since I came down here. I live as I please, spend my time according to my fancy, keep a plentiful table for myself and my friends, amuse myself with reading and Society, and find the generality of the people disposed to respect me more on account of my having been well receiv'd in greater and more renowned places: But tho' all this makes my time slide away easily, it is impossible for me to forget that a man who is in his 59th Year has not many more years to live, and that it is time for him, if he has common Sense, to have done with all Ambition. My Ambition was always moderate and confind entirely to Letters; but it has been my Misfortune to write in the Language of the most stupid and factious Barbarians in the World; and it is long since I have renounced all desire of their Approbation, which indeed coud no longer give me either pleasure or Vanity.

As to my Notion of public Affairs, I think there are very dangerous Tempests brewing, and the Scene thickens every moment.[1] The Government has, no doubt, great Resources, if they employ them with Prudence and Vigour and Unanimity. But have we any reason to think they will do so? The Parliament will certainly be . . .[2] by the Populace every day next winter. If they bear it, they degrade . . .[2] and draw on . . .[2] If they punish, they will still more enrage the Faction, and give a Pretence for the Cry that Liberty is violated. Are we

* MS. at Barnbougle Castle; Hill, 112 ff.

[1] Cf. Horace Walpole's opinion on arriving back from France in Oct. 1769. Writing to Mann on the 13th, he says: 'It [England] approaches by fast strides to some great crisis, and to me never wore so serious an air, except in the Rebellion' (*Letters*, vii. 323).

[2] MS. torn.

sure, that the popular Discontent may not reach the Army, who have a Pretence for Discontents of their own? The General in chief is a weak man, and fond of low popularity:[1] It is true, you have a very honest Chancellor[2] and a very courageous Chief Justice,[3] who will be a great Ressource in difficult times. But is it certain that Lord Bute will abstain from tampering and trying some more of his pretty Experiments? What if he take it in his head to open the Door to Pitt and his Myrmidons, who will, no doubt, chain the King for ever, and render him a mere Cypher. Our Government has become an absolute Chimera: So much Liberty is incompatible with human Society: And it will be happy, if we can escape from it, without falling into a military Government, such as Algiers or Tunis. The Matter will only be worse, if there be no shooting or hanging next Winter: This Frenzy of the people, so epidemical and so much without a Cause, admits only of one Remedy, which however is a dangerous one, and requires more vigour than has appeard in any minister of late. I have a very good Opinion of the Duke of Grafton but his Youth deprives him of Experience and still more of Authority. I dare [not ve]nture to play the Prophet, but think you are in great Danger. I see . . .[4] low: Have the People sense enough to see their Danger, and to withdraw from that precarious Security. If they coud see it in time, and catch the Alarm, it woud be a great Ressource to Government: But this is more than can reasonably be expected from them.

You say I am of a desponding Character: On the contrary, I am of a very sanguine Disposition. Notwithstanding my Age, I hope to see a public Bankruptcy, the total Revolt of America, the Expulsion of the English from the East Indies, the Diminution of London to less than a half, and the Restoration of the Government to the King, Nobility, and Gentry of this Realm. To adorn the Scene, I hope also that some hundreds of Patriots will make their Exit at Tyburn, and improve English Eloquence by their dying Speeches. I think, indeed, that no body of common Sense coud at present take the Road of Faction and Popularity, who woud not upon occasion have joind Catiline's

[1] John Manners (1721–70), Marquis of Granby; C.-in-C., 1766–70; godfather to innumerable public-houses.

[2] Lord Camden.

[3] Lord Mansfield. Needless to say, the reference here, as above to Camden, is ironical. Hume disliked both men.

[4] MS. torn.

Conspiracy; and I have no better opinion of the Gentleman you call my Friend.[1]

Pray have you seen Lord Stormont[2] since he came home? Did he enquire after you?[3]

I think, if you throw off the Errata[4] as it is printed, it will do very well. It is not long for 8 Volumes; and they are not all Errors of the Press. You mention nothing of the small Edition of my Essays, whence I conclude it is not going forward.[5] I am Dear Sir Yours sincerely and beg the continuation of your Friendship, tho' it shoud be our Lot not to pass much of our time together. I wish much to see you possessd of some Farms in this Country, where there is great Unanimity at present, and a Desire to support Government.

D. H.

Edinburgh,
25 of Octr 1769.

* 435. *To* [William Strahan]

Dear Sir

I thank you for the Copy of the Letter, which you sent me:[6] It is a mark of the Intentions of the Ministry; but according to my small Judgement it wou'd be impolitic to attack the Faction by an arbitrary Punishment of these Addresses. There is something like a Precedent for it during the Reign of Charles the second, in the punishment inflicted by the House of Commons on the Abhorrers,[7] but the House was then on the popular Side, when they may do any thing: And the Measures of that House of Commons carry less Authority with them, as they are at present condemnd by all sober People. The Ministry ought to wait with patience till some Violence or personal Insult be offerd to the Parliament, which will not be long, and will give Government great Advantages. I wish only the Army may be

* MS. in possession of the Editor; hitherto unpublished.

[1] I do not know to whom the reference is here.

[2] David Murray (1727–96), 7th Viscount Stormont; nephew of Lord Mansfield, whom he succeeded as 2nd Earl of Mansfield in 1793; Ambassador at Vienna, 1763–72; K.T., 1768; Ambassador at Paris, 1772–8. There is one letter from him to Hume among the MSS., R.S.E.

[3] Did Hume mean to write *me*, not *you*?

[4] For the 4to edition of the *History*, 1770.

[5] It was published in 1770, in 4 vols., 8vo.

[6] Neither Strahan's letter nor his enclosure is extant among the MSS., R.S.E.

[7] In 1680.

faithful, and the Militia quiet: Woud to God we had a Scotch Militia at present. This Country is almost unanimous.[1]

I like extremely the Type and paper of your new Edition.[2] I return the Sheet to you not to lose a set. If I ever see a new Edition of my History,[3] I coud wish to see [it] in a like Size; that is, under Submission to you and the Proprietors [4] who are much better Judges of these Matters. I am with great Sincerity

Dear Sir

Your most obedient humble Servant

DAVID HUME

Edinburgh
14 Novr 1769

* 436. *To* WILLIAM STRAHAN

Dear Strahan

I am extremely oblig'd to you for your account of the Debate in the House of Peers:[5] It is very judicious and accurate and impartial, as usual. I now begin to entertain strong hopes, that the King will weather this Tempest, and that the Infamy of Calumny, Faction, Madness and Disorder will at last fall on those heads, who merit it. The Ministry are much better advis'd not to give nor even to take Provocation, than they seem to have been by the Paper of Ruffhead's which you sent me last Autumn.[6] And as every obnoxious Person is turnd out,[7] the

* MS. at Barnbougle Castle; Hill, 134 f.

[1] A great part of Scotland was quite indifferent about the militia, and many towns were actively opposed to it. But perhaps he meant, 'unanimous on political questions in general'.

[2] This must refer to the 8vo edit. of the *Essays*.

[3] That is, in 8vo. It will be seen from later letters that Hume disliked the last (1763) edition of the *History* in 8vo, and was annoyed with Millar for having printed off so many copies of it.

[4] Millar being dead, the proprietors were his successors, Thomas Cadell, and William Strahan himself.

[5] Strahan, writing on 13 Jan. 1770, gave Hume a full account of the opening night of the session in the House of Lords, when Chatham spoke, principally on America and the Middlesex elections (MS., R.S.E.; *Eminent Persons*, 91 ff.).

[6] Probably the letter referred to in the preceding letter. Owen Ruffhead was appointed one of the Chief Secretaries to the Treasury in 1769, but died on 25 Oct. in that year.

[7] The most important of these were Camden, the Lord Chancellor, and Granby, the Commander-in-Chief.

King's Resolution is visible to support his Ministry, and men will either acquiesce or return to the ordinary, parliamentary Arts of Opposition. I apprehend, however, that, before the Session ends, this abandon'd Faction, not to be foild without hopes, will have recourse to the violence of the Mob, in expectation of provoking the Ministry to commit some Imprudence: Their greatest Imprudence woud be remissness on that Occasion. Open Violence gives such a palpable Reason for the severe Execution of the Laws, a thing much wanted, that it ought immediately to be laid hold of, and it will have a very salutary Effect.

The part which Chatham acts, after all the Favours and Distinctions which he has receivd from the Crown, is infamous, like himself.

I send you enclos'd an answer to one of Cadells. It is open, that you may read it, as the matter concerns you, no less than him.

I am Dear Sir Yours sincerely

Edinburgh DAVID HUME.

25 Jan. 1770

* 437. *To* SIR GILBERT ELLIOT OF MINTO

Dear Sir Gilbert

I do not know whether you be good for any thing, or at all worth the applying to: I rather suspect, not: But in case you are, I make you the following Application in favour of Christopher Tate,[1] Probationer, who was Tutor to my Nephews. The enclos'd Note gives an Account of the Parish.[2] You know, I resignd my Pretensions on the Presentation of Humbie [3] to your Nephew's Tutor; but under Promise, that you woud assist me in a like Case. This Kirk is a King's Presentation: It is within your County; and I very earnestly desire Success in this Application, and trust much to your Friendship in it.

The last unexpected Incident[4] strikes us mute with Astonishment. Either the Duke of Grafton is much to blame for leaving

* MS. at Minto House; Burton, ii. 432.

[1] Christopher Tait (1744–1813) was eventually presented by the Crown, on 3 July 1772, to the parish of Kincardine in Menteith, and was ordained there on 18 Feb. 1773.

[2] Of Roberton (see Letter 439 below).

[3] See Letter 389 above.

[4] Grafton, the Prime Minister, resigned at the end of January.

us so abruptly, in so very critical a time, or a greater than he, if he got any just Cause for it. I carry my View to very dismal Consequences, especially as I suspect the last to be the Case. I fancy we shall have curious Scenes coming, worthy the Pen of the greatest Historian. I am tird and disgusted with Conjecture. My Compliments to Lady Elliot. Believe me to be very sincerely Dear Sir Gilbert

Your affectionate humble Servant
DAVID HUME

Edinburgh
5 February 1770

* 438. *To* ADAM SMITH

What is the Meaning of this, Dear Smith, which we hear, that you are not to be here above a day or two, in your Passage to London? How can you so much as entertain a thought of publishing a Book,[1] full of Reason, Sense, and Learning, to these wicked, abandon'd Madmen?

I suppose you have not yet got over your Astonishment at this most astonishing Resignation.[2] For my part, I knew not at first whether to throw the Blame on the Duke or the King; but I now find it is entirely and compleatly the Dukes own; and I think him dishonourd for ever. Here is the Passage of a Letter, which I receivd yesterday from a very good hand.[3] 'The most 'wonderful political Event that ever happend in this Country 'happend yesterday. The Duke of Grafton, who, it seems, has 'bad Nerves, thought proper to resign on Tuesday the 30th of 'Jany at 12 of the clock forenoon. The King, who showd a 'Firmness, which few people thought he possess'd and a rage 'that no body expected from him, absolutely refus'd to treat 'with the Opposition, and calld upon Lord North to stand forth, 'assuring him, that he would never yield.[3] Lord North accord-'ingly took the Duke of Grafton's place, and yesterday met the 'house of Commons as Minister. The great danger was the 'Effect of the Pannic, and he checkt the Pannic by his Declara-'tion, that he woud never resign, and whilst his breathe was in 'his body that he woud support the King's faithful Servants, 'and the Dignity of Parliament against faction and Conspiracy:

* MS., R.S.E.; Burton, ii. 433 (incomplete).

1 Smith was working at his *Wealth of Nations*.

2 The Duke of Grafton's.

3 It is clear from George III's *Correspondence* (ii. 126 f.) that the King, in accordance with his usual practice, had concerted matters with Lord North before the Duke actually resigned.

'They renewd the same captious and popular Question about 'the Middlesex Election; and after a long and warm debate, 'they divided and Lord North carryd the Question by forty 'Votes.[1] This is reckond the most spirited Conduct that any 'man has held since the Revolution, and he is extolld to the 'Skies. The Opposition, who were parcelling out the Kingdom, 'are in despair; as there is no doubt that the new Minister will 'gather force every hour, as he has upon this critical occasion 'shown that strength of Mind, which is the precise thing hitherto 'wanting to give permanence to administration. Without doors 'there is nothing but peace and quietness; not a mouse stirring 'among the Mob; and I think the times will mend.'

So far my Friend, whose Prophesy I hope will be fulfilld; tho' for my part I am rather inclind to give myself up to despair: Nothing but a Rebellion and Bloodshed will open the Eyes of that deluded People; tho' were they alone concernd I think it is no matter what becomes of them. Be sure to bring over the Northumberland Household Book [2] and Priestley's Grammar.[3] Yours Dear Smith

DAVID HUME

Edinburgh
6 of Feby 1770
To Adam Smith Esq[r] at Kirkaldy

* 439. *To* SIR GILBERT ELLIOT OF MINTO

Dear Sir Gilbert

After all, the Minister of Roberton [4] is not dead, nor dying, for the present. He had been very ill, and reported to be dead; so that Lord Alemore [5] wrote to his Brother upon that

* MS. at Minto House; Burton, ii. 434 f. (incomplete).

[1] Writing of this speech to Mann on 2 Feb. 1770, Walpole says: 'Lord North pleased all that could bring themselves to be pleased: he not only spoke with firmness and dignity, but with good-humour . . .' (*Letters*, vii. 364).

[2] *The Regulations and Establishment of the Houshold of Henry Algernon Percy, the fifth Earl of Northumberland . . . begun Anno Domini M.D.XII*, edited by Thomas Percy, privately printed, London, 1770.

[3] *Rudiments of English Grammar*, by Joseph Priestley, London, 1769; and often reprinted.

[4] See Letter 437 above.

[5] Andrew Pringle of Haining (died 1776), Solicitor-General, 1755; raised to the Bench as Lord Alemore, 1759; one of Hume's particular friends in later years. East Alemoor is about two and a half miles north-west of Roberton.

Supposition; and many Applications were made to Lady Elliot for her Interest with you. I must therefore excuse my young Man for being misled; tho the Mistake is very unlucky, in every thing, except that it gives me a new Proof of your Desire to oblige me. I assure you I am very sensible of it. I believe I coud have accommodated matters with Lord Alemore. The Kirk is strictly speaking in the Forrest;[1] but the greatest part of the Parish is in Teviotdale.

I am glad of your Victories;[2] tho' I look upon them all as temporary and imperfect, like the fallacious Recoveries of a hectic Person who is hastening to his Dissolution. Our Government has become a Chimera; and is too perfect in point of Liberty, for so vile a Beast as an Englishman, who is a Man, a bad Animal too, corrupted by above a Century of Licentiousness. The Misfortune is, that this Liberty can scarcely be retrench'd without Danger of being entirely lost; at least, the fatal Effects of Licentiousness must first be made palpable, by some extreme Mischief, resulting from it. I may wish that the Catastrophe shoud rather fall on our Posterity; but it hastens on with such large Strides, as leaves little Room for this hope.

I am running over again the last Edition of my History in order to correct it still farther. I either soften or expunge many villanous seditious Whig Strokes, which had crept into it. I wish that my Indignation at the present Madness, encourag'd by Lyes, Calumnies, Imposture, and every infamous Art usual among popular Leaders, may not throw me into the opposite Extreme. I am, however, sensible that the first Editions were too full of those foolish English Prejudices, which all Nations and all Ages disavow.

The present firm Conduct of the King, and his manly Resentment, afford some Glimpse of hope. We at a Distance are not acquainted with these matters, and few even at London: But there still appears something mysterious in the Duke of Grafton's

[1] Ettrick Forest.

[2] That is, of Lord North's party, 'the King's Friends', to which Elliot belonged. He had apparently been somewhat lukewarm in 1769, but on a hint from the King, conveyed by Lord North, roused himself early in 1770. Writing to North on 1 Feb. 1770, the King says: 'Believe Me a little spirit will soon restore a degree of order in my Service, I am glad to find Sir Gilbert Elliot has again spoke' (*Corr. of George III*, ii. 128). The result was that on 3 Feb. Elliot was offered, and accepted, the Treasurership of the Navy, a lucrative post that he continued to hold till his death.

Resignation. I hope it proceeded only from his Discontents with Bedford House.

But I detain you too long. I shall only conclude, that, tho' I reckon myself among the *Sepoliti*,[1] I cannot forbear expressing my hearty good Wishes to your Cause and you. I am very sincerely Dear Sir Gilbert

Your obligd humble Servant
DAVID HUME.

Edinburgh
21 of Feby 1770

* 440. *To* ADAM SMITH

Extract of a Letter from London

'This Night Opposition produc'd a Motion to overwhelm Administration as they said; that no Officer, employ'd in collecting his Majestys Revenue shoud be allowd to vote in the Election of a Member of Parliament: Administration carry'd the Question 263 to 188, so administration has gained 35 since the last Division. At the same Moment the House of Lords divided 81 against 41. We look upon Opposition to be over.'[2]

Pray when do you come over to us? Do not buy any Claret to me.

D H

[February 1770.]
To Adam Smith Esq[r] at Kirkaldy

† 441. *To* WILLIAM STRAHAN

Dear Strahan

Tho' I have renouncd the World, I cannot forbear being rouzd with Indignation at the Audaciousness, Impudence, and Wickedness of your City Address.[3] To punish it as it deserves woud certainly produce a Fray; but what signifies a Fray, in

* MS., R.S.E.; hitherto unpublished.

† MS. at Barnbougle Castle; Hill, 137 ff.

[1] *Sic* in MS., perhaps intended for *sepeliti*, 'buried'.

[2] The motion was proposed by Dowdeswell in February 1770.

[3] In July 1769 the City of London presented a petition to the King, to which he returned no answer. In March 1770 the City drew up 'A Remonstrance and Petition praying for the Dissolution of Parliament and the Removal of Evil Ministers'. This the King delayed receiving, but it would appear to have been at once published in the newspapers; and finally, on 14 March 1770, the King received it on his throne. Writing the next day to Mann, Walpole says: 'In short, rebellion is in prospect, and in everybody's mouth' (*Letters*, vii. 370).

comparison of losing all Authority to Government. There must necessarily be a Struggle between the Mob and the Constitution; and it cannot come on at a more favourable time nor in a more favourable Cause. I wish therefore, (I cannot say I hope) that vigorous Measures will be taken; an impeachment immediately voted of the Mayor and his two Sherriffs for high Crimes and Misdemeanours, and the Habeas Corpus suspended till next meeting of Parliament. Good God! what abandon'd Madmen there are in England!

You have suspended my Chronicle on account of Sir Gilbert's vacating his seat.[1] I am of a Club here that get down News papers and Pamphlets from London regularly: So that you wont need to send me the Chronicle any more. Please only to let me know the Charge of it, together with other Articles I owe you.

I am sorry to hear that Dr Armstrong has printed his Tragedy [2] among his Miscellanies. It is certainly one of the worst pieces I ever saw; and totally unworthy of his other Productions. I shoud have endeavourd to dissuade him from printing it, had he been a man advisable. But I knew, that he keeps an Anger against Garrick for above twenty Years for refusing to bring it on the Stage; and he never since woud allow him to be so much as a tolerable Actor. I thought therefore it was wiser not to meddle in the Affair.

I have had a Letter from Mr Cadell, which is very obliging: I agree to the reprinting in any form you and he please, and I believe ten volumes in large Octavo will be best.[3] But I find, that I have been cutting a great way before the point, and that I am scarce ever likely to see an End of that detestable Edition.[4] I really have no reason to believe seriously, that the half of it is yet sold, or that the Book has at present any sale at all worth speaking of: Such a habit you and he have got during seven Years past of deceiving me by false Intelligence, that I am determind never to believe a word either of you says on that

[1] Elliot vacated his seat for Roxburghshire on appointment as Treasurer of the Navy, but was duly re-elected in March. Why this should cause Strahan to stop sending Hume the *London Chronicle* I do not know, unless, as Hill suggested (p. 141), Elliot franked it for him.

[2] *The Forced Marriage* (not acted) was printed in vol. ii of the *Miscellanies*, which appeared this year.

[3] For the *History*. The next edition to appear was in 8 vols., 8vo, 1773.

[4] The 8vo edit. of 1763 (see note 3 on p. 212 above, and *passim* in subsequent letters).

head.[1] For Instance you both told me when I left London, that there remaind not 700 Copies: He has since wrote me that before the meeting of Parliament he had disposd of 200 of these: In his last Letter he says, that the Sale still continues rapid. I must therefore suppose that before the month of May next, there would not be 300 in your Warehouses, which is a little enough Number (or too little) for a Book which woud take near a twelvemonth in reprinting. But he speaks still of a distant Period for beginning the new Edition. You see, therefore, that these Stories are totally inconsistent. I need only say, that I have a Copy corrected, and I believe considerably improvd at your Service, whenever you please to call for it. I am nowise impatient to have another Edition: I only show you that I had taken my Measures, in consequence of the Intelligence conveyd to me; and I shall add, that, if the Book has really any Sale, it woud probably be the Interest of the Proprietors to run the Risque of losing some of that odious Edition rather than encumber the Market any longer with it. But of this you are the best Judges.

I am Dear Strahan Yours sincerely

DAVID HUME.

Edinburgh

13 of March 1770

* 442. *To* SIR GILBERT ELLIOT OF MINTO

Dear Sir Gilbert

There is one Archibald Campbell, son of Principal Campbell of St Andrews:[2] This man has very good Parts and a great deal

* MS. at Minto House; Burton, ii. 435 (one paragraph only).

[1] It is clear that the information about the sales of the 1763 edition conveyed by Millar to Hume in Nov. 1764 was false; and that Millar had printed off more copies of this edition than he ever admitted to the author. From a letter of Strahan's to Hume, dated 14 May 1769 (MS., R.S.E.), it is clear also that Millar induced the printer to join in the deception. Strahan says: 'Do learn to put a little confidence in me; nor imagine that because I was induced to deceive you a little in regard to the number printed of the last 8vo edition, that I am to make a practise of doing so. In that, I was only the mouth of another person, who was afterwards sorry he had occasion to conceal the number of the impression from you.' But having been deceived once, Hume not unnaturally hesitated in future to believe either Strahan or Cadell when they made statements to him about sales, &c.

[2] Archibald Campbell (died 1756), sometime Professor of Ecclesiastical History at St. Andrews, and ultimately Rector; a pupil of Simson's in Glasgow; author of *An Inquiry into the Original of Moral Virtue*, *The Necessity of Revelation*, and a Discourse proving the apostles to have been no enthusiasts (which excited the horror of Wodrow).

of Learning; but has been unfortunate in his Life, and perhaps a little unhappy in his Conduct.[1] He was some Years a Purser of a Man of War, where he savd a little Money; but it is wasting daily, by his living in London, however frugally; and he has nothing before him but the Prospect of old Age and extreme Poverty. He gave to the Public not long ago two small Pieces, which are Imitations of Lucian, and which are not without Merit, *Lexiphanes*[2] and the *Sale of Authors*.[3] He had formd two plans for the Improvement of the Revenue, which seemd to me plausible and well drawn; and I carry'd him to Lord North, who expressd his Approbation of them. Lately, he wrote to me,[4] that he wishd to be appointed Purser of the Æolus, and desird me to give him a Letter of Recommendation to Lord North: But I thought, that I coud not use that Freedom with his Lordship; especially as this Office lay not immediatly in his Department. I have not mentiond to him a word of you; so that you may chuse whether or not you will send to him or take any Notice of him: A Note directed to him at the Hungerford Coffee-house in the Strand woud find him; but I woud not give him a Title to teize you, tho' I am told, that it is one of the Pleasures of Power, as well as of Beauty, to be so teizd. This I am sure of, that you will think it one of its greatest Pleasures to be serviceable to Merit in Distress; and it will be difficult to find a Man of so good Talents so little favourd by Fortune as Mr Campbell.

[1] There is one letter to Hume from Archibald Campbell the younger among the MSS., R.S.E. Its only date is 'Thursday Noon', and it seems to have been written while Hume was still in London. It speaks of enclosing a plan for raising money by taxing plays, but the enclosure is not extant; complains of ill fortune, and the bad treatment which the writer had received from his superior officers in the navy; and contains the following statements calculated to excite Hume's sympathy for the man: 'The truth is I have been from my infancy upwards a martyr to a religion which I dont remember that I ever believed. Jesus never spoke so true a word as when he said, I am come to set the father against the son, and the son against the father. You'll remember the text, and this was my case, and has given me such an inveteracy against that superstition, that were I now a man of note and independant fortune, I would give it wounds as severe but more pointed and direct than either yourself or Dr Middleton have given it, and at the same time set the clergy with all their persecuting laws at defiance. But this I need not now think of.' (See also Letter 381 above.)

This, after all, was not unlike Hume's own mental history.

[2] *Lexiphanes, a Dialogue. Imitated from Lucian* . . ., London, 1767. It was a satire on the style of Johnson, 'our English Lexiphanes', and was anonymous.

[3] *The Sale of Authors, a Dialogue in imitation of Lucian's Sale of Philosophers*, London, 1767; also anonymous.

[4] The letter is not extant.

I am sorry to inform you, that all we Statesmen in this Town condemn loudly the Conduct of you Statesmen in London; especially in allowing those insolent Rascals, the Mayor and Sherriffs, to escape with Impunity. We were much disappointed not to find them impeach'd, and a Bill of Pains and Penalties pass upon them. The Tumults which might have ensu'd in London, we thought rather an Advantage, as it woud give Government an Opportunity of chastizing that abominable Rabble. But you have thought otherwise; and it is pretended that these lenient Maxims are succeeding; that Faction abates, the Tide turns, and the Heroes of Opposition are in Despair. I am heartily glad of it: But this is a new Experiment to reconcile such extreme Licence with Government: And if in a case, where popular Complaints had not the smallest Shadow of Pretence, the King and Parliament have prevaild after a long Struggle and with much Difficulty, what must it be, where there is some plausible Appearance, and perhaps some real Ground of Complaint, such as it is natural to expect in all Governments? However, I repeat it, I am glad of the present Appearance of Tranquillity; and, indeed, distant Dangers are not to be too anxiously provided against.[1]

I ask your pardon again for the Freedom of mentioning Campbell to you; but as you belong to the Admiralty, I thought it might be easy for you in your present Situation, to slip him into some Office, such as his humble Pretensions may make him be contented with. And if you look into his Performances, you will, I believe, allow, that such a Man ought not to perish for Want, in a Country where there is so much Opulence, and so little literary Merit.[2] I am Dear Sir

Your most obedient humble Servant

DAVID HUME.

Edinburgh
5 of April 1770

[1] Writing to Mann on 23 March 1770, Walpole says: 'Lord North's temper and prudence has prevailed over much rash counsel; and will, I hope, at last, defeat the madness of both sides. There has not been much heat in the House of Commons' (*Letters*, vii. 372).

[2] It would seem that Elliot either could not, or would not, do much for the unfortunate Campbell; of whom Ramsay of Ochtertyre says: 'His morals were as bad as his principles, so that he died wretched and unlamented' (*Scotland and Scotsmen*, i. 268 n.).

* 443. *To* John Crawford[1]

Dear Crawford Edinburgh 21 of May 1770

I find, that you take the first word of *fliting*, that is of scolding, since I must interpret to you your mother tongue. I ought to abuse you for staying so little time here, for departing so abruptly, and for allowing yourself, even before I cou'd see you, to be so much pre-engaged in mixt Companies, and to have contracted for more dinners & suppers than you cou'd fulfill, even if you had stayed much longer. And yet you pretend to abuse me: I can only say in reply, very seriously and very sincerely, that no-one, either in this place or anywhere else, loves your company better; and I regret very much, that I am likely to have so little of it. I cou'd also wish that you had a prospect of your being happier in your absence, than your State of health seems to permit.

Davy Ross[2] dined with me yesterday, who tells me, that your father[3] is far from being well, and he does not think that he will be able to travel to Bath this Season.

I have made out my Letter to Monsr Francis.[4] It is a strong proof of my Reluctance to writing, when I shoud protract answering the Letter of a Man, whose Company is so agreeable to me. Please deliver my Letter to the Ambassador,[5] to whom I desire my Respects; as also in a particular manner to the Ambassadress.

I am Dear Crawford
Yours sincerely
David Hume

† 444. *To* William Strahan

Dear Sir Edinburgh, 22 May, 1770.

A few days ago, Lord Home[6] told me, that, in consequence of a new Arrangement of his Affairs, he shou'd stand in need

* MS. lately in the possession of Mr. Thomas F. Madigan, New York City; hitherto unpublished.

† MS. at Barnbougle Castle; Hill, 143 ff.

[1] 'Fish' Crawford, the friend of Horace Walpole and Mme du Deffand.

[2] David Ross (1727–1805), admitted advocate, 1751; one of the Principal Clerks of Session, 1763; raised to the Bench as Lord Ankerville, 1776. He lived at No. 3 St. Andrew's Square.

[3] Patrick Crawford of Auchenaimes. John was on bad terms with his father.

[4] The Secretary to the French Embassy in London.

[5] The French Ambassador, du Châtelet.

[6] Alexander (died 1786), 9th Earl and 14th Baron Home. He was one of the witnesses to Hume's will.

of a large Sum of Money, which he propos'd to bring from England at lower than legal Interest;[1] and he hop'd his Friend, Strahan, woud be able to assist him on that Occasion. I said, that, tho' Mr Strahan was a rich Man, yet he had such great Enterprizes in hand, that I did not believe he had much ready Money to lend. My Lord replyed, that he expected more your good Offices than your Money, and that he was too well acquainted with the Opinion, entertained by the World of his Situation, to hope for borrowing Money at low Interest upon his own Security: But that Mr Hay of Drumelzier [2] and Mr Gavin of Langtoun [3] propos'd to bind with him: Upon which he took my Promise, that I shoud write to you upon the Subject. It is certain that Mr Hay is a Man of above 4000 pounds a year clear, and Mr Gavin above 5000; and both of them frugal Men, so that there cannot be better Security in Britain; and that they intend to bind with him, My Lord's Writer, who is a man of Character, assur'd me. I think, therefore, that the Scheme is far from being *inadmissible*. I wish really, (as you no doubt do yourself) that you coud assist him on this Occasion; but in all cases, I must beg the favour of you to write me an ostensible Letter, which may satisfy him that I have not neglected his Request.

I find, that your great Reluctance to write me on a certain Subject proceeds from your Unwillingness to retract every thing that you have been telling me these seven Years: But your silence tells me the Truth more strongly than any thing you can say. Besides, I know not why you shoud have a Reluctance to retract. What you told me was for a good End, in order to excite my Industry, which might be of Advantage both to myself and the Proprietors of the former Volumes. And if there has been any Misconduct with regard to the Octavo Edition, you are entirely innocent of it. So that I see not any Reason why I may not now be told the Truth; especially as you see, that I am fully determind never to continue my History, and have indeed put it entirely out of my power by retiring to this Country, for the rest of my Life. However, this is as you think

[1] The legal rate of interest was 5 per cent. Adam Smith in the *Wealth of Nations* says that private persons in Great Britain could borrow on good security at 4 or 4½ per cent.

[2] Alexander Hay of Drummelzier and Whittinghame (1701–89).

[3] David Gavin made a fortune in the Netherlands, returned to Scotland, bought the estate of Langton, near Duns, and married Lady Elizabeth Maitland, daughter of the 7th Earl of Lauderdale.

proper: Only, it is needless for Mr Cadel to give me Accounts, which are presently refuted by the Event. I say this without the least resentment against him, who is a very obliging, and I believe a very honest man.

Nothing coud be more agreeable than your political Intelligence. I have always said, without Flattery, that you may give Instructions to Statesmen. We are very happy, that this Session is got over without any notable disaster. Government has, I believe, gain'd Strength; tho' not much Authority nor Character by its long suffering and forbearance. But the Request of the Country Gentlemen, who joind them, was a very plausible Motive;[1] besides, I am told, that their Lawyers, particularly Lord Mansfield, deserted them on this Occasion. But these are Matters that very little concern me; and except from Indignation at so much abominable Insolence, Calumny, Lyes, and Folly, I know not why I shoud trouble my head about them: These Objects too, being at a distance, affect me the less. We are happily in this Country united as in a national Cause, which indeed it has become, in some measure, by the Virulence of this detestable Faction.

We expect to see Lady Grant[2] soon in this Country; and I suppose, that I must pay my Respects to her Ladyship. I intend to give her *Her Ladyship* very often, that she may at least have some Pennyworths for her Money.

I suppose that the Edition of my Essays in Twelves[3] is now finishd or nearly so. As soon as it is finishd, pray, put Mr Cadel in mind to send me six Copies in any Parcel to Balfour or Kincaid.

I am Dear Strahan Yours sincerely
DAVID HUME.

P.S. Please to tell Mr. Cadel that if a Volume of the *Dictionaire de Commerce*[4] comes over for me from Paris, he pay a Guinea for it, which I shall refund him.

[1] The country gentlemen declared that they would *not* support the Government in any violent measures against the City.

[2] Widow of Andrew Millar. On 23 May 1770 she became the 4th wife of Sir Archibald Grant of Monymusk, Bart. (1696–1778). She died in 1788.

[3] A mistake. It was 8vo.

[4] The Abbé Morellet's. Nothing more of it than the Prospectus was ever published.

* 445. *To* William Strahan

Edinburgh 5 June 1770

Dear Sir

Even according to Mr Cadel's present account, which I have not the least Reason to give any Credit to, you have copies enow to serve you for many Years' Sale; and I give over all thoughts of any new Edition. Only, if such a thing shoud happen, I think it proper to inform you, that I have a Copy by me, corrected in many places, especially in the four first Volumes. This shall be sent you on demand either by myself, if alive, or by my Brother or Heirs; and I wish that no Edition be made without following it. I shall never make any more Enquiries about the Matter: I did not even make any Enquiries at this time; but receiving from Mr Cadel some inconsistent Accounts, which he had sent me voluntarily of himself, I took Occasion to mention them to you. As he finds his Credit runs very low with me in that particular (tho' I believe him a very honest man) he may spare himself the trouble of saying any thing farther concerning it. I wish Millar had savd the Expence of this Magnificent Quarto Edition, which can serve to no purpose but to discredit the Octavo; and make the sale, if possible, still more slow.

There is a notable Error of the Press in this last Quarto of my Essays, which confounds and perplexes the Sense; and being so easily corrected, I wish you woud give orders for that purpose. It is Vol. 2. p. 395. l. 1. for *useful* read *usual*.[1] A boy with his pen in half an hour coud go thro all the Copies.[2] It is the very first Line of the third Appendix.[3] I beg of you not to forget this Request. I have writ to Cadel to the same purpose. It is in the second page of Sheet E.e.e.

I have seen Lady Grant. I am told, that she and Sir Archibald hold as much *amorous play and dalliance*, as ever Adam and

* MS. at Barnbougle Castle; Hill, 150 ff.

[1] The first sentence of the Appendix (entitled *Of some Verbal Disputes*) to the *Principles of Morals* reads: 'Nothing is more usual than for philosophers to encroach upon the province of grammarians; and to engage in disputes of words, while they imagine that they are handling controversies of the deepest importance and concern.' The substitution of *useful* for *usual* sounds almost like a deliberate joke on the part of the compositor.

[2] This may have been done in some copies, but it was not done in those now in the British Museum and the National Library of Scotland.

[3] Which afterwards became the fourth Appendix.

Eve did in Paradise; and they make every body in love with the marryd State. It will be a curious Experiment whether his sly Flattery or her tenacious Avarice will get the better: I conjecture, that the contest is begun already. I took occasion to mention to her Sir Archibald's extensive and noble Plantations; but she told me, that she thought that Planting was his Folly, and that people ought to take care, lest their concern for Posterity shoud hurt themselves. Thus she will check the poor man in the only laudable thing he has ever done.

I wish you woud be so good as to send me an account of the Debt I owe you, which, tho' it be but a trifle, I coud wish to pay.

The Madness and Wickedness of the English (for do not say, the Scum of London) appear astonishing, even after all the Experience we have had. It must end fatally either to the King or Constitution or to both.

You say nothing to me of the new Edition of my Essays in 12°, and of my desire to have six copies of it whenever it is finishd. Perhaps you have stopd short in that work, and I think you much in the right in so doing.

I am Dear Strahan Yours sincerely

DAVID HUME.

* 446. *To the* REV. JOHN DOUGLAS

Dear Sir

I was a little surprizd to hear from Mr Dalrymple,[1] that some Papers of Lord Clarendon had fallen into your hands, by which it appears, that, so early as Fouquet's [2] Administration, which ended in 1661 or 1662, Charles the second receivd a Pension from France of two Millions a Year, a Transaction known to Lord Clarendon. I own, that without the best Authority, this Fact will appear incredible: The Greatness of the Sum, which makes near 170.000 pounds Sterling, is an Objection: The King of France had at that time no Object, in

* B.M. MSS. Egerton 2182, fo. 31 f.; *Englische Studien*, Band 63, Heft 3 (1929); hitherto unpublished in England.

[1] John Dalrymple of Cranstoun. His *Memoirs of Great Britain* appeared in the following year.

[2] Nicolas Foucquet (1615–80), French statesman. His administration came to an end in 1661.

which Charles cou'd assist him: It is difficult to reconcile this Fact to many Passages which I remember in D'Estrades's Memoirs:[1] There had very near been a Squabble between France & England about that time, with regard to the trifling Object of the Flag: All these and many other Reasons make me suspect, that Mr Dalrymple had mistaken your Meaning. I must beg of you to inform me in a few Lines of the Truth; and also whether you intend to give these Papers to the Public. Perhaps, as Charles was at that time very much straitend for Money, and was really ill usd by the Parliament in point of Revenue, he might borrow some Money from Lewis, and repay it afterwards from parliamentary Grants. I beg my Compliments to Mrs Douglas: I say nothing to Mr Pulteney [2] because I will have no Intercourse with Wilkites. Good God! how can a man degrade himself to that degree? But I beg my humble Respects to Mrs Pulteney: I am Dear Sir

Your most obedient humble Servant

DAVID HUME.

Edinburgh.
16 of June 1770
To The Reverend Dr Douglas.

* 447. *To* WILLIAM STRAHAN

Dear Sir

I am not in the least angry with Mr. Cadel: On the contrary, were I to go to the press with any new work (which it is utterly impossible I ever shoud) he is one of the first persons I should apply to for publishing it. But, pray, recollect, that a few weeks before I came down, he told me in your house of his regret that he shoud ever have been forced by Mr Millar to deceive me; but that now I might entirely depend upon the Truth of his Information; there were less than 700 of the 8vo

* MS. at Barnbougle Castle; Hill, 154 f.

[1] *Lettres, mémoires et négociations de M. le comte d'Estrades* [1607–86], 5 vols., Brussels, 1709, and 9 vols., London, 1743.

[2] William (Johnstone) Pulteney. Alex. Carlyle says: 'Pulteney was unfortunate in not taking for his private secretary and confidential friend Dr John Douglas, who had stood in that relation to the late Lord Bath, and was one of the ablest men in England. But on Pulteney's succession he found himself neglected, and drew off' (*Autobiog.*, 514). He regularly spoke and voted with the opposition in the House of Commons (*Corr. of George III*, ii, *passim*).

Edition upon hand. But after a twelvemonth's rapid sale, as he pretends, he acknowledges nine hundred and fifty, and I question not but there is above double the Number.

There has been a strange Fatality to depress the reputation of that book: First the Extravagance of Baillie Hamilton, then the Rapaciousness of Mr Millar: But this last is most incurable. I suppose you will not find one book in the English Language of that Size and Price so ill printed,[1] and now since the publication of the Quarto, however small the sale of the Quarto may be, it shows, by its corrections and additions, the Imperfection of the 8vo so visibly, that it must be totally discredited. Had it been thought proper to let me know the real State of the 8vo Edition, I shoud never have consented to the printing of the Quarto. I suppose the Proprietors will at last be oblig'd to destroy all that remains of the 8vo; I mean, if there appear any hopes of the Sale's ever reviving. If Mr Millar had been alive, his own Interest, as well as the Shame for his Miscarriage, woud have brought him to that Resolution. There remains only the former Motive with the Proprietors.

I return the Sheet of the Essays which is very elegantly printed. The numerous Editions of that work, which is much less calculated for public Sale, may convince you of the Propriety of moderate Editions. I hope Mr Cadel will send me down six copies as soon as the Edition is finishd, that I may have the Satisfaction of seeing one of my Works without Disgust.

I am Dear Sir Yours sincerely
DAVID HUME.

Edinburgh,
21 of June 1770

* 448. *To the* REV. JOHN DOUGLAS

Dear Sir

I see clearly by the Extracts of the Clarendon Papers, for which I am extremely oblig'd to you,[2] that the Money, remitted by France, was entirely for the Support of Portugal, as I conjectur'd; and was not sent with a View of engaging England in

* B.M. MSS. Egerton 2182, fo. 33 f.; *Englische Studien*, Band 63, Heft 3 (1929); hitherto unpublished in England.

[1] Both type and paper in this 1763 edition are undoubtedly bad.

[2] Neither Douglas's letter nor the extracts are among the MSS., R.S.E.

any Measures which might serve the purposes of Lewis, who indeed had not at that time any Views of Conquests or Acquisitions. It was always known, that Lewis remitted Money to England for the Service of Portugal; which being directly contrary to the Treaty of the Pyrenees, it was necessary to keep it a profound Secret, though that Secret had transpird before. Indeed, I must differ widely from you; and am of Opinion, that, from the Commencement of the Reformation till the Revolution, there is not any important Secret in the English History: And, if I coud call up the Devil by any powerful Incantation and oblige him to speak Truth, I do not recollect any Questions worth the asking with regard to that Period; Nothing which cannot be known very certainly by means merely human. The Causes of the second Dutch War, even before I saw K. James's Memoirs, were not in the least doubtful to me. Some curious pretty Anecdotes of various kinds might be known by the Devil's means; but these woud only serve to the Embellishment of History, not to the Explication of any important Events.

I remember very well that I read Deageant's Memoirs [1] and the Archbishop of Embrun's Narrative;[2] tho' I cannot at present recollect particularly the Contents; I can only recollect my general Opinion on the whole; that Deageant was a pragmatical Puppy who was entirely to be disregarded; and that K. James [3] had entertaind a silly Notion, which many Protestants have adopted, of reconciling the two Churches by mutual Concessions; and in order to show the Archbishop that he himself might be an impartial Mediator, he endeavours to convince him, that he had no bigotted Animosity against the Catholics; which was a Truth we knew before. Cardinal Bentivoglio,[4] who was Nuncio in Flanders during that Period, and had all the English Missions under his Inspection, says, that the King woud not have been displeas'd with some middling Course with regard to Religion. He must indeed have been very blind, if he had not seen that the Puritans were much more dangerous Enemies than the Catholics.

[1] *Mémoires de M.* [*Guichard*] *Deageant à M. le Cardinal de Richelieu*, Grenoble, 1668; English translation, London, 1690.

[2] *Voyage en Angleterre et autres lieux*, by Guillaume d'Hugues (died 1648), Archbishop of Embrun, Paris, 1756.

[3] That is, James I.

[4] Cardinal Guido Bentivoglio (1579–1644), Archbishop of Rhodes, and papal nuncio to Flanders and France; author of *Relazioni di G. Bentivoglio in tempo delle sue nunziature di Fiandria e di Francia*, Antwerp, 1629.

I again repeat to you my thanks for the Communication of the Clarendon Papers, which I wish to see in print, and am sorry any delay shoud take place. I am

Dear Sir

Your most obedient and most humble Servant

Edinburgh DAVID HUME

5 of July 1770.

To The Revd Dr Douglas.

* 449. *To* WILLIAM STRAHAN

[August 1770][1]

Dear Strahan

I believe this is the historical Age and this the historical Nation: I know no less than eight Histories upon the Stocks in this Country; all which have different Degrees of Merit, from the Life of Christ,[2] the most sublime of the whole, as I presume from the Subject, to Dr Robertson's American History,[3] which lies in the other Extremity.

You will very soon be visited by one, who carries with him a Work, that has really Merit: It is Dr Henry,[4] the Author of the History of England, writ on a new Plan.[5] He has given to the World a Sheet or two, containing his Idea,[6] which he will probably communicate to you. I have perus'd all his Work, and have a very good Opinion of it. It contains a great deal of Good Sense and Learning, convey'd in a perspicuous, natural, and correct Expression. The only discouraging Circumstance is its Size: This Specimen contains two Quartos, and yet gives us only the History of Great Britain from the Invasion of Julius Caesar to that of the Saxons: One is apt to think that the whole, spun out to the same Length, must contain at least a hundred

* MS. at Barnbougle Castle; Hill, 155 ff.

[1] This letter can be dated by the succeeding one.

[2] There is nothing to show what particular author or projected work Hume had in mind here.

[3] Robertson's *History of America* appeared in 1777.

[4] Robert Henry (1718–90), minister of High Meeting-house, Berwick-on-Tweed, 1760, of New Grey Friars, Edinburgh, 1763, and of Old Grey Friars, Edinburgh, 1776; Moderator of the General Assembly, 1774.

[5] The new plan was to treat the history under eight separate headings, viz.: civil and military history; history of religion; history of the constitution; history of government, law, and courts of justice; history of learning; history of the arts; history of commerce; and history of manners.

[6] Henry issued a prospectus in June 1770.

Volumes:[1] And unhappily, the beginning of the Work will be for a long time very uninteresting, which may not prepossess the World in its favour. The Performance however has very considerable Merit; and I coud wish that you and Mr Cadel may usher it in to the Public.[2] I wish that Dr Robertson's Success may not have renderd the Author too sanguine in his pecuniary Expectations: I dare advise nothing on that head, of which you are the better Judge. I shoud only think, that some Plan, which woud reserve to the Author the Chance of profiting by his good Success and yet not expose the Booksellers to too much hazard, might be the most suitable. You know, that I have been always very reservd in my Recommendations; and that when an Author, tho much connected with me, has producd a Work, which I coud not entirely approve of, I rather pretended total Ignorance of the Matter, than abuse my Credit with you. Dr Henry is not personally much known to me, as he has been but lately settled in this Town, but I cannot refuse doing Justice to his Work: He has likewise personally a very good Character in the World, which renders it so far safe to have dealings with him. For the same Reason, I wish for his Sake that he may conclude with you. You see I am a good Casuist, and can distinguish Cases very nicely. It is certainly a wrong thing to deceive any body, much more a Friend; but yet the Difference must still be allowd between deceiving a man for his Good and for his Injury.

I am Dear Sir Yours sincerely

DAVID HUME.

* 450. *To* WILLIAM STRAHAN

Dear Sir

This Letter will be deliverd to you by Dr Henry, concerning whom and whose work, I have wrote you by the Post: I have rather chosen that Method of conveying my Sentiments than by a Letter of Recommendation, which are often understood to be formal things and carry less weight with them. You will there see, that my Esteem of Dr Henry and his Performance are very sincere and cordial.

I am Dear Sir

Your most obedient and most humble Servant

Edinburgh
10 of Augt 1770

DAVID HUME.

* MS. at Barnbougle Castle; Hill, 159.

[1] Six volumes of the book did appear between 1771 and 1793, bringing the history down to the death of Henry VIII. The last volume, published after the author's death, was edited by Laing.

[2] And so they did.

* 451. *To* Baron Mure of Caldwell

Dear Baron

I am sorry, that I shoud correspond so ill to your very obliging Letter, by telling you, that I cannot propose to see you till you come to town next Winter. I am engagd in the building a house,[1] which is the second great Operation of human Life: For the taking a Wife is the first, which I hope will come in time:[2] And by being present I have already prevented two capital Mistakes, which the Mason was falling into; and I shall be apprehensive of his falling into more, were I to be at a Distance. I must therefore renounce the hopes of seeing you at your own house this Autumn, which I assure [you] I do with much Regret. My Compliments to Mrs Mure & the young Ladies. Please tell Miss Kitty,[3] that my Coat is much admird even before I tell, that it is her Livery. For her Sake, I shall be careful, that it never meet with any such Accident as the last. I am Dear Baron

Yours very sincerely
David Hume

Edinburgh.
2 Octr 1770

P.S.

Mr Moore's Verses [4] are really very elegant.

† 452. *To* William Strahan

Mr Hume's Compliments to Mr Strahan. Wishes him a good New Year: He has receivd the six Copies of his philosophical

* MS. in possession of William Mure, Esq., London; MS., R.S.E. (copy); *Caldwell Papers*, II, ii. 177 f.; Burton, ii. 436.

† MS. at Barnbougle Castle; Hill, 159.

[1] At the west end of the south side of St. Andrew's Square, in the New Town. Building had not been going on very long in the extended Royalty, and Hume's house was the sixth or seventh to be built in St. Andrew's Square. It is now marked by a small stone plaque on the west gable.

[2] This sounds like four parts jest, but I think that in fact it was three parts jest and one part earnest. If Henry Mackenzie is to be believed—and there is no reason to doubt him on this point—Hume about this time was much taken with Miss Nancy Orde, daughter of the Chief Baron of the Scottish Exchequer, and 'meant to pay his addresses' to her (Mackenzie, *Anecdotes and Egotisms*, ed. H. W. Thompson, 1927, p. 170).

[3] Baron Mure's eldest daughter.

[4] John Moore (1729–1802), surgeon in Glasgow; appointed by Mure as travelling governor to Douglas, Duke of Hamilton, 1772; author of *Zeluco*, and other novels; friend and patron of Burns, and father of Sir John Moore of Corunna.

Pieces, for which he thanks him: They are very elegantly printed, and correctly, tho' there are some few unavoidable Errors. He has sent him an Errata, which he desires Mr Strahan to annex if not inconvenient.

Edinburgh
5 of Jany 1771.

* 453. *To* William Strahan

Dear Sir

I am very glad to have heard from you, and have sent you my Letter to Lord Hertford under a flying Seal. I wish you good Success in your Project; tho' I cannot easily imagine how an Estate on the Ohio can ever turn to great Account.[1] The Navigation down the Mississipi is indeed expeditious and safe, except at the Mouth; but the return is commonly so slow, by the violence of the Current, that the Communication of that Country with the rest of the World, will always be under great Obstructions, and be carry'd on under considerable Disadvantages. But these Matters you have undoubtedly weighd and calculated, from better Information than I have had access to.

There was an Error in the page in the Errata I sent you, which I have corrected and I return you the Copy. I own, that this quick Sale of my philosophical Writings is as unexpected as the slow Sale of my historical, which are so much better calculated for common Readers. But this proves only, that factious prejudices are more prevalent in England than religious ones. I shall read over several times this new Edition;[2] and send

* MS. at Barnbougle Castle; Hill, 160 ff.

[1] From Strahan's reply, dated 1 March 1771 (the first letter of his since 13 Jan. 1770 that is extant among the MSS., R.S.E.), it appears that the scheme he laid before Lord Hertford was 'no less than the forming a new government on the Ohio'. He says that Lord Hertford was very fond of the idea of having a large tract of country in America, 'and is otherwise very attentive to the improvement of his fortune'. (This noble lord always was.)

The history of this project is curious. Benjamin Franklin, a London banker called Thomas Walpole, and others, had petitioned the King in 1769 for permission to purchase some 2,400,000 acres between the Ohio River and the Alleghanies. In 1771 the Lords Commissioners for Trade and Plantations, under the chairmanship of Lord Hillsborough, reported adversely on the scheme to the Privy Council. Franklin made a full reply to this report; the Privy Council granted the permission to purchase; and Lord Hillsborough at once resigned from the Secretaryship of State for America. But the American Revolution smashed the whole scheme.

[2] The new 4to edit. of the *Essays and Treatises*.

you a corrected Copy[1] by some safe hand. With regard to the History, I only desire to hear from you three or four Months before you put it to the Press.

Dr Henry's History is undoubtedly liable to the Objection you mention. It will be of enormous Size; and he himself, tho' a laborious Man, never expects to finish it. I think also the Price he demanded exorbitant.[2] It is however writ with Perspicuity and Propriety of Style, as I told you; but neither sprightly nor elegant; and it is judicious, but not curious: There is danger of its appearing prolix to ordinary Readers: The Subject of his next Volume will be still more uninteresting than that of his first.

I am totally detachd from all concern about public Affairs; and care not tho all the Ministry were at the Devil. This Spanish War[3] is so enormously absurd, unjust, and unreasonable that I think it never had its parralel. If we be savd from it, it will not be owing to our own prudence, but to the determind Resolution of the King of France, who acts a very laudable part: But his Brother of Spain is as freakish and as obstinate as a Mule; and our Ministry are more afraid of the despicable London Mob than of all Europe: Had they punishd that insolent Rascal, Beckford,[4] as he deserved; we shoud have been in no danger of a Spanish War; or rather of a general War: For Hostilities never continue limited between two Nations; but soon draw in all their Neighbours: In which case, France begins with declaring a public Bankruptcy;[5] and we make it the third

[1] For a new 8vo edit. Replying on 1 March, Strahan says: 'You will send up the copy of your *Essays* with your first conveniency, as the octavo edition is quite sold off.'

[2] In the same letter Strahan says of Henry and his *History*: 'The price he expected for it, was, in my estimation, so much beyond its value, that I carefully avoided making him an offer at all.'

[3] The dispute over the Falkland Islands, which never came to war. It was a three-cornered affair between England, Spain, and France. England made all preparations for war: 40,000 seamen and large additions to the army were voted, and the land tax was raised to 4*s*. in the £. But the disgrace of the Duc de Choiseul in France changed the situation, and an agreement between the high contracting parties was reached on the very day of Hume's letter.

[4] Alderman William Beckford (1709–70), twice Lord Mayor of London; M.P., City of London, 1754–70; a friend of Chatham, and an ardent supporter of Wilkes.

[5] Horace Walpole, writing to General Conway from Paris on 30 July 1771, says: 'The distress here is incredible, especially at court. The King's tradesmen are ruined, his servants starving, and even angels and archangels cannot

Year of the War. An Event which is indeed inevitable; but might have been delay'd, had it not been for this Quarrel about Falkland Island. You think we shall have peace: I am glad to hear it; but cannot allow myself to think, that any Chance will save Men so infatuated as our Ministry. It is a pleasure however that the Wilkites and the Bill of Rights-men [1] are fallen into total and deservd Contempt. Their Noise is more troublesome and odious than all the Cannon that will be fird on the Atlantic.

I am here employ'd in building a small House: I mean a large House for an Author: For it is nearly as large as Mr Millar's in Pall-mall. It is situated in our new Square; where I hope to receive you, on your first Excursion to this Country. I beg my Compliments to Sir John Pringle: I think you are not likely to send us anything worth reading this Winter.

I am Dear Strahan Yours sincerely

Edinburgh DAVID HUME

21 of Jany 1771.

* 454. *To* WILLIAM STRAHAN

Dear Sir

You will have a Copy of my philosophical Pieces corrected in a few weeks by a safe hand, who will deliver them to Miss Elliot. She will inform you by a Penny post Letter of their Arrival. I have perusd them carefully five times over; yet the Corrections I make are not of Importance. Such is the Advantage of frequent Impressions!

It vexes me to the last Degree, that, by reason of this detested Edition of my History, I shoud have so distant or no prospect of ever giving a correct Edition of that Work. I assure you, if Mr Millar were now alive, I shoud be tempted to go over to Dublin, and to publish there an Edition, which I hope woud entirely discredit the present one.[2] But as you are entirely

* MS. at Barnbougle Castle; Hill, 172 ff.

get their pensions and salaries, but sing "Woe! woe! woe!" instead of Hosannahs' (*Letters*, viii. 61).

[1] The Society of the Supporters of the Bill of Rights, formed in Feb. 1769 to 'raise an effectual barrier against such oppression [as Wilkes had suffered], to rescue him from his present incumbrances, and to render him easy and independent'.

[2] Ireland was not then under the Copyright Law that regulated publication in England and Scotland, and Irish editions of English books could be brought into England and sold there, to the detriment of the English publishers. This was done twice over in 1776 with the 1st volume of Gibbon's *Decline and Fall*. See note 3 on p. 210 of Vol. i above.

innocent in the Conduct of this Affair, I scruple to take that Resolution. The worst of it is, that Affairs have been so manag'd as to leave me in entire Ignorance of the State of the Sale; tho' I am now confident, that, as you see evidently I am resolv'd never to engaged again with the public, you will no longer have any Scruple to tell me the whole Truth of the Matter.

But to leave this Subject, which is so very vexatious, and to talk of public affairs; I am much inclind to have the same good opinion of Lord North, which you express:[1] His taking the Helm in such a Storm, and conducting it so prudently, prepossess one much in his favour: I am also assurd, that he was the last in the Ministry who woud give up the Resolution of punishing that insolent Fellow, Beckford, and the City of London. But to me, his Conduct of the Spanish Affair appears rash, insolent and unjust. The publication of the Spanish Papers confirms me farther in that Opinion. It appears, that the Spaniards had never abandond the Settlement, made by the French, which was prior to ours;[2] and consequently that their right was in every respect undisputable. And as the Court of Spain offerd from the first to disavow the Governor of Buenos Ayros,[3] if we woud disavow Hunt,[4] to run the Danger of a War which woud have thrown all Europe, and

[1] In his letter of 1 March 1771 Strahan had said: 'You seem to think we are in a much worse way than we really are. I admit the inexcusable Timidity of the Ministry, in suffering so many and so great insults, which no Government ought to overlook. But notwithstanding all our Follies and all our Misconduct, the nation in general is actually in a thriving condition.——The Opposition is melting away to nothing, and every day falling more and more into contempt.——Wilkes is hardly ever heard of, but in a way very little to this credit. The boldest of his adherents are either tired out and have deserted him, or they are no more. In short, a steady, able, honest Minister (and such I hope Lord North may prove to be) may yet support this country long in Honour and Credit.——Wealth pours in upon us from a thousand Channels, particularly the East Indies, which adds perhaps too much to our Luxury; and that may at length prove fatal. But this is a Poison which operates slowly, and many events may occur to check its progress, without endangering the general Welfare and Security of the State' (MS., R.S.E.; Hill, 177 n.).

[2] The French settled in East Falkland in Feb. 1764, the British in West Falkland not till Jan. 1766. In 1766 the French ceded their settlement to the Spanish.

[3] Buccarelli by name. He forcibly expelled the British from the islands in 1770.

[4] Captain Hunt of the Tamar frigate warned a Spanish schooner off the coast of the islands in Nov. 1769.

almost the whole Globe into a Ferment, must be regarded as an unpardonable Temerity. We were savd from that Disaster by nothing but the extreme Love of Tranquillity in the French King, an Incident which no Human Prudence coud forsee. But what must we think of the Effrontery of the Patriots, who rail at Lord North for Tameness and Pusillanimity? They did not probably know the secret, otherwise they woud have exclaimd with better Reason against his Rashness and Imprudence.

I wish I coud have the same Idea with you of the Prosperity of our public Affairs. But when I reflect, that, from 1740 to 1761, during the Course of no more than 21 Years, while a most pacific Monarch sat on the Throne of France, the Nation ran in Debt about a hundred Millions;[1] that the wise and virtuous Minister, Pitt, could contract more Incumbrances, in six months of an unnecessary War, than we have been able to discharge during eight Years of Peace; and that we persevere in the same frantic Maxims; I can forsee nothing but certain and speedy Ruin either to the Nation or to the public Creditors. The last, tho' a great Calamity, woud be a small one in comparison; but I cannot see how it can be brought about, while these Creditors fill all the chief Offices and are the Men of greatest Authority in the Nation.[2] In other Respects the Kingdom may be thriving: The Improvement of our Agriculture is a good Circumstance; tho' I believe our Manufactures do not advance; and all depends on our Union with America, which, in the Nature of things, cannot long subsist.[3] But all this is nothing in comparison of the continual Encrease of our Debts, in every idle War, into which, it seems, the Mob of London are to rush every Minister. But these are all other Peoples Concerns; and I know not why I shoud trouble my head about them.

[1] Only a slight exaggeration. The National Debt stood at about 50 millions in 1736, and at 139 millions in 1763.

[2] Cf. Hume's note to his essay *Of Public Credit*: 'I have heard it has been computed, that all the creditors of the public, natives and foreigners, amount only to 17,000. These make a figure at present on their income; but, in case of a public bankruptcy, would, in an instant, become the lowest, as well as the most wretched of the people. . . .'

[3] This is the first expression by Hume of a view that it will be seen from later letters he consistently maintained. He was almost alone in maintaining it. As late as 1775 even Burke spoke of the proposal to give up the Colonies as 'nothing but a little sally of anger; like the frowardness of peevish children, who, when they cannot get all they would have, are resolved to take nothing' (*Speech on Conciliation with America*).

I maintaind and still maintain that Henry's History has merit; tho' I own'd and still own, that the Length of the Undertaking is a great Objection to its Success; perhaps an insuperable one. But what shall we say to Sir John Dalrymple's new History,[1] of which, I see, you are one of the publishers? He has writ down that he has been offerd 2000 pounds for the Property of it: I hope you are not the Purchasers; tho' indeed I know not but you might be a Gainer by it: The ranting, bouncing Style of that Performance may perhaps take with the Multitude. This however I am certain of, that there is not one new Circumstance of the least Importance from the beginning to the End of the Work. But really I doubt much of his Veracity in his Account of the Offer: I shoud be much obligd to you for your Information on that head.[2] Never let the Bargain made by Dr Robertson [3] be thought extravagant, if this be true. I shoud add a great Number of Cyphers to bring up the Knight's Performance to an equal Value with that of the Doctor.

I very much regret with you Sir Andrew Mitchels [4] Death: He was a worthy, well-bred, agreeable man. If the Prince, at whose Court he resided, us'd him ill of late Years,[5] he richly deserves the Epithet you give him.[6] Sir Andrew's chief Fault was his too great Attachment to that prince.

I am Dear Sir Yours sincerely

Edinburgh DAVID HUME.

11 of March 1771.

* 455. *To* WILLIAM STRAHAN

Dear Sir

This will be deliver'd to you, along with a corrected Copy of my philosophical Pieces by Dr Robertson. I remind you to

* MS. at Barnbougle Castle; Hill, 182 ff.

[1] The *Memoirs of Great Britain.*

[2] Replying on 25 May 1771, Strahan says: 'The offer of £750 to Sir J. D. proves to have been more than the real value of it, as the sale of it seems to be already over here.'

[3] See Letter 431 above.

[4] British Ambassador at the Court of Frederick the Great. He died in Berlin on 28 Jan. 1771.

[5] Mitchell had been a great favourite with Frederick for many years, but in Dec. 1769 complained that at a public levee the King passed him without addressing a word to him—the very first time this had happened during the whole course of his diplomatic service in Berlin.

[6] Speaking of Frederick in his letter of 1 March, Strahan says: 'Mayhap there never existed a greater scoundrel.'

send me six Copies, as usual. This is the last time I shall probably take the pains of correcting that work, which is now brought to as great a degree of accuracy as I can attain; and is probably much more labour'd (I know not with what degree of success) than any other production in our Language. This power, which Printing gives us, of continually improving and correcting our Works in successive Editions, appears to me the Chief Advantage of that Art. For as to the dispersing of Books, that Circumstance does perhaps as much harm as good: Since Nonsense flies with greater Celerity, and makes greater Impression than Reason; though indeed no particular Species of Nonsense is so durable. But the several Forms of Nonsense never cease succeeding one another; and Men are always under the Dominion of some one or other, though nothing was ever equal in Absurdity and Wickedness to our present Patriotism.

I long much for an Opportunity of bringing my History to the same degree of Accuracy. Since I was settled here, I have, from time to time, given Attention to that Object; though the Distance and Uncertainty of the new Edition threw a damp on my Industry: But I shall now apply seriously to the Task; and you may expect the Copy about August. I beseech you do not make this Edition too numerous, like the last. I have heard you frequently say, that no Bookseller woud find profit in making an Edition which woud take more than three Years in selling. Look back, therefore, and learn from Mr Millar's Books what has been the Sale for the last six Years; and if you make the usual Allowance for a Diminution during the ensuing three, from the Number of Copies already sold, I am persuaded you will find 1500, a number large enough, if not too large. Be not over-sanguine. An Error on the one hand is more easily corrected than one on the other. I am perhaps the only Author you ever knew, who gratutiously employ'd great Industry in correcting a Work, of which he has fully alienated the Property; and it were hard to deny me an Opportunity of exercising my Talents; especially as this practice turns so much to the Advantage of the Bookseller.

I have another Proposal to make you in the same View. I have found by Experience that nothing excites an Author's Attention so much as the receiving the Proofs from the Press, as the Sheets are gradually thrown off. Now I have had an Opportunity of passing the last four Volumes of my History more than once through this Scrutiny, the most severe of any:

The first four Volumes have only been once reviewd by me in this manner. I shall send you the whole Copy about the time above mention'd, and the last four Volumes you may throw off at your Leizure: But the Sheets of the first four, I shoud wish to receive by the Post five times a week.[1] They will make about 250 Sheet and might be finishd in thirty weeks. For this Purpose I shall apply to Mr Fraser, my former Collegue in the Secretary's Office,[2] who will supply you with Franks, and such as are not confind to the usual Weight of two Ounces.[3] The corrected Copies I shall send under his Cover;[4] and you will only have to send for them to the Secretary's Office, the same as if I were in London. Mr Fraser is as regular as an astronomical Clock, and will never disappoint you. I am almost as regular; and you may give Orders to your People to be the same.

This Affair, therefore, being, I presume, settled to mutual Satisfaction, I come to give you thanks for the Perusal of Mr Johnson's Pamphlet,[5] which is a good one, and very diverting from the Peculiarity and Enormity of the Style. One sees he speaks from the Heart, and is movd with a cordial Indignation against these Ruffians. There is, however, one material Circumstance, which either he did not know, or did not think fit to mention; namely, that the French had regularly settled Falkland Island full three Years before us, and upon Remonstrances from the Court of Madrid, gave up their Right and Colony to the Spaniards, who never had abandond that Settlement.[6] Their Right, therefore, was prior and preferable to ours. For as to our ridiculous Right from the first Di(*s*)covery, allowing the Facts to be true; will any one say, that a Sailor's seeing a Mountain from the Top mast head, conveys a Title to a whole Territory, and

[1] There were only five posts a week from London to Edinburgh, viz., one every day except Wednesday and Sunday.

[2] William Fraser was Under-Secretary of State, Northern Dept., 1765–79; and in the Foreign Office, 1782–9.

[3] The limitation of 2 oz. for a franked letter had been put on by Act of Parliament in 1764. By the same Act it was ordained that the M.P. (or other authorized person) franking the letter must also write the whole of the address himself.

[4] Because the privilege of free postage worked for both sending and receiving.

[5] *Thoughts on the late Transactions respecting Falkland's Islands*, which Johnson wrote at the request of the Ministry to justify their action in not going to war.

[6] Replying on 25 May, Strahan says: 'The circumstance you mention about the prior settlement of Falkland Island by the French is not at all known here, as far as I can find, to this moment' (MS., R.S.E.; Hill, 198 n.).

a Title so durable, that even tho' it be neglected for two Centuries, it still remains with the Nation?[1] Our Ministry, therefore, have acted a Part most unjust, most insolent, and most imprudent; and which the Spaniards will deservedly remember long against us. But this Conduct proceeds entirely from the Timidity of our Ministry, who dread more the contemptible Populace of London than the whole House of Bourbon. I am curious to see how they will get out of the present Scrape;[2] though their past Measures prognosticate nothing good for the future. I say still, had they punishd Beckford, disfranchisd the City, and restord the Negative to the Court of Aldermen,[3] they woud have prevented the present and many future Frays: But still it is not too late; tho it may very soon become so.

When I blame the Insolence of our Ministry with regard to Spain, I must at the same time confess, that we do right to swagger and bounce and bully on the present Occasion: For

[1] Johnson in his pamphlet referred to Captain Davis, who was supposed to have been the first to sight Falkland Island, during the voyage of Cavendish in 1592.

[2] Writing to Mann on 22 March 1771, Horace Walpole says: 'The horizon is overcast again already; the wind is got to the north-east and by Wilkes; and without a figure, the House of Commons and the City of London are at open war. It is more surprising that Wilkes is not the aggressor—at least folly put new crackers into his hand. Two cousins, both George Onslow by name, the son and nephew of the old Speaker, took offence at seeing the debates and speeches of the House printed, and the more as they had both been much abused. They complain, and the House issues warrants for seizing the printers, and addresses the King to issue a proclamation for apprehending them. Out comes a proclamation, and no Great Seal to it. The City declares no man shall be apprehended contrary to law, within their jurisdiction. The printers are seized; Wilkes, as sitting alderman, releases one: the Lord Mayor, Wilkes, and another alderman deliver another, and commit the messenger of the House of Commons to prison. The House summons the Lord Mayor to appear before them and answer for his conduct, but as he is laid up with the gout, allow him to come on Monday last, or to-day, Friday. . . . Wilkes is summoned too: writes a refusal to the Speaker, unless he is admitted to his seat. The Speaker will not receive his letter, nor the House hear it, though read, and again ordered him to attend . . .' (*Letters*, viii. 16 f.). Some days later the Lord Mayor was committed to the Tower. But the struggle faded out, Parliament was prorogued earlier than usual, on 8 May, and the Lord Mayor automatically became free again. Writing again to Mann, on 8 May, Walpole says: '. . . but, in truth, that whole business has been wofully conducted, and has heaped nothing but disgrace on the House of Commons; who, instead of vindicating their authority, have betrayed the utmost pusillanimity' (ibid., viii. 31).

[3] That is, restored to the Court of Aldermen the power to veto decisions made by the Court of Common Council.

we have not many Years to do so, before we fall into total Impotence and Languor. You see, that a much greater and more illustrious People, namely the French, seem to be totally annihilated in the midst of Europe; and we, instead of regarding this Event as a great Calamity, are such Fools as to rejoice at it. We see not that the same Catastrophe or a much worse one is awaiting us at no distant Period. The monarchical Government of France (which must be replac'd) will enable them to throw off *their* Debts; ours must for ever hang on our Shoulders, and weigh us down like a Millstone.

I think that Mr Johnson is a great deal too favourable to Pitt, in comparing him to Cardinal Richelieu. The Cardinal had certainly great Talents besides his Audacity: The other is totally destitute of Literature, Sense, or the Knowledge of any one Branch of public Business. What other Talent indeed has he, but that of reciting with tolerable Action and great Impudence a long Discourse in which there is neither Argument, Order, Instruction, Propriety, or even Grammar? Not to mention, that the Cardinal, with his inveterate Enmities, was also capable of Friendship: While our Cut-throat never felt either the one Sentiment or the other. The Event of both Administrations was suitable. France made a Figure during near a Century and a half upon the Foundations laid by the one: England—as above; if I be not much mistaken, as I wish to be.

I was pretty sure that Sir John Dalrymple was an *Historian*, with regard to the Price offerd him for his Book. So then, his Pride is interested in being esteem'd as good a Writer as Dr Robertson! I am diverted with conjecturing what will be the Fate of this strange Book: Will it run a few Years? Or fall at once *dead born from the Press*? I think the last Event more probable, notwithstanding the Precedent of Mrs Macaulay, and notwithstanding the Antitheses and Rant and Whiggery of which it is full. After you have offerd him 750 pounds, my Pride, in case I shoud write another Volume, woud make me demand the Equivalent of a parliamentary Subsidy: I think without Vanity, my Book will at least be equal in Value to Falkland Island.[1]

[1] Replying on 25 May, Strahan says: 'If you write another volume, which the best Judges of writing are daily enquiring after, you may demand what you please for it. It shall be granted. We cannot indeed afford a sum equal to a Parliamentary Subsidy, but you shall not be offered so little as the

But I have writ you a Letter as long as an Essay; and for fear of making it a Treatise, I shall conclude by telling you, that I am with great Sincerity

Dear Sir Your most obedient humble Servant

Edinburgh DAVID HUME.

25 of March 1771.

* 456. *To* WILLIAM STRAHAN

Edinburgh, 25 of June, 1771.

Dear Sir

I have receivd both your favours,[1] for which I am oblig'd to you. I shall be able to send off by the Waggon, in less than a Month, a corrected Copy of my History; and shall write you at the time, that you may send for it, if it be not immediatly sent to you. It gives me a sensible pleasure, that I shall now have an Edition of that work, corrected nearly to my mind. I have taken incredible pains on this Edition. It puts me in mind of a saying of Rousseau's, that one half of a man's life is too little to write a Book and the other half to correct it. Most of my Corrections fall upon the Style; tho' there are also several Additions and Amendments in the Subject and in the facts.

I have got about a hundred Franks directed to you; and we shall proceed in the manner you desire. I think, however, it will not be amiss to have some of Mr Fraser's, for large Parcels; and for this purpose you may send him the enclos'd, with twenty Covers, which he will not grudge to frank to you. The rest you may get from your Acquaintance or mine, Lord Beauchamp,[2] Mr Wedderburn,[3] Mr Pulteney,[4] Mr Adam,[5] Mr Stewart of Buckingham Street[6] &c, informing them by a short Note of the reason of your applying to them.

* MS. at Barnbougle Castle; Hill, 199 ff.

Value of Falkland Islands, which in my mind is a mere Trifle. I heartily wish you would seriously think of setting about it. It is the only thing wanting to fill up the measure of your Glory as the Great Historian and Philosopher of the Eighteenth Century. . . .'

[1] Only one of these, Strahan's letter of 25 May, is extant among the MSS., R.S.E.

[2] He was M.P. for Lostwithiel, 1766–8, and for Orford, 1768–94.

[3] Having suddenly deserted his party, Wedderburn had been made Solicitor-General in Jan. 1771.

[4] He was now M.P. for Cromarty and Nairn.

[5] Robert Adam, the architect. He was M.P. for Kinross and Clackmannan.

[6] John Stewart was M.P. for Arundel, 1771–4.

I return you Warburton's Letter,[1] which diverted me. He and all his gang, the most scurrilous, arrogant, and impudent Fellows in the world, have been abusing me in their usual Style these twenty Years, and here at last he pretends to speak well of me. It is the only thing from them, that coud ever give me any mortification. We have all heard of the several Schools of Painters and their peculiar manners. It is petulance, and Insolence and abuse, that distinguish the Warburtonian School, even above all other Parsons and Theologians. Johnson is abusive in Company, but falls much short of them in his writings. I remember Lord Mansfield said to me that Warburton was a very opposite man in company to what he is in his Books; then, replyd I, he must be the most agreeable Companion in Europe, for surely he is the most odious Writer.[2]

I wish to tempt you into a Discourse of Politics, because I get Information from you. I own, that I am inclind to have a good Opinion of Lord North, but his Insolence to the House of Bourbon, and his Timidity towards the London Mob appear unaccountable. Only consider how many Powers of Government are lost in this short Reign. The right of displacing the Judges was given up;[3] General Warrants are lost;[4] the right of Expulsion the same;[5] all the co-ercive Powers of the House of Commons

[1] Seemingly a private letter from Warburton to Strahan; perhaps the letter that Alexander Gerard saw, and in which Warburton said that one half of the Scottish clergy were fanatics and the other half infidels. (See Boswell's *Tour*, Ch. III.)

[2] Replying on 23 July 1771, Strahan says: 'What his [Warburton's] Reasons may be I know not, but I have heard much of his launching out in your Praise, for some time past; sometimes indeed, in my hearing, and with much more seeming Cordiality and Heartiness than I ever heard him bestow on any other writer. . . . As a *companion* he is certainly one of the most tractable men I ever saw. So far from being insolent or overbearing, you can hardly get him to contradict you in anything' (MS., R.S.E.; *Eminent Persons*, 98).

[3] One of the first acts of George III was to confirm an Act of William III whereby judges were to hold office *quamdiu se bene gesserint*. Previously, this statement had been interpreted by some curious jugglery to mean that judges went out of office and might be replaced on the death of a Sovereign.

[4] On the Wilkes case. Lord Camden then, as Lord Chief Justice, declared general warrants to be 'unconstitutional, illegal, and absolutely void'.

[5] Wilkes again. When Hume wrote this letter, however, it might have seemed premature to say that the right of expulsion was lost; for Wilkes *had* been expelled the House of Commons, and by a vote of the House was kept out of it. But when he was again elected for Middlesex in 1774, he was allowed

abandon'd;[1] all Laws against Libels annihilated;[2] the Authority of Government impair'd by the Impunity granted to the Insolence of Beckford,[3] Crosby,[4] and the common Council: the revenue of the civil List diminishd.[5] For God's sake, is there never to be a stop put to this inundation of the Rabble? We shall have fine work next Elections, if the people above and below continue in the same dispositions, the one insolent and the other timid. For my part, I can account for Lord North's Conduct only by one supposition. He will not expose himself even in the best cause to the Odium of the populace, because he feels that he has no sure hold of the Cabinet, but depends for all his power on some invisible secret Being, call him Oberon, the fairy or any other,[6] whose Caprices can in a moment throw him off, and leave him no Resources either in popularity or authority. In this Light his caution is excusable: He bullies Spain and France and quakes before the Ward of Farringdon without;[7] because, if he shoud be suddenly displaced, he will still retain it in his power to become popular and formidable. But all these Inconveniences are slight, in comparison of our public Debts, which bring on inevitable Ruin, and with a Certainty which is even beyond geometrical, because it is arithmetical. I hope you have more Sense than to trust a shilling to that egregious bubble.

I am Dear Sir Yours sincerely
DAVID HUME.

to take his seat without opposition; and in 1782, on his motion, the House ordered all its own previous resolutions with regard to the Middlesex election 'to be expunged from the Journals of this House, as being subversive of the rights of the whole body of electors of this kingdom'. Hume was not far wrong.

1 A reference to the recent dispute with the City.

2 Lord Mansfield maintained that it was the duty of the judge to decide whether a document was libellous or not, and that all the jury had to pronounce upon was whether the libel was in fact published. The result, according to Horace Walpole (*Memoirs of George III*, iv. 168), was that hardly any jury would find the rankest satire libellous.

3 See note 4 on p. 234 above.

4 Brass Crosby (1725–93), M.P. for Honiton, and Lord Mayor of London. It was he who was committed to the Tower by the House of Commons on 27 March of this year (see note 2 on p. 241 above).

5 In 1763 George III gave up the hereditary revenues of the Crown and accepted a fixed grant of £800,000 a year. But in 1769 the debt on the Civil List was over £500,000.

6 Lord Bute.

7 For which Wilkes was alderman.

* 457. *To* William Strahan

Edinburgh, 22 of July 1771.

Dear Sir

On Saturday last, the 20th of the Month, I deliverd to the Newcastle Waggon the eight corrected Volumes of my History, directed to Mr Cadell. I chose to direct the parcel to him rather than to you, because his Shop was easier found,[1] and the Waggoner told me, that he often carry'd up Parcels to him. Please to tell Mr Cadel, that he may call for it, if it be not deliverd to him about three Weeks hence. You will see that I have made many considerable Improvements, most of them in the Style; but some also in the matter. I fancy you might be able to send me a proof Sheet about a month hence; and I shoud have been here ready to receive it; But I am assurd that Lady Aylesbury and Mr Conway are to be with the Duke of Argyle [2] this Summer; which will oblige me to leave the Town for a fortnight and go to Inverara.[3] But I shall fix to you precisely the day when I shall be ready to receive the first proof Sheet; and you may depend upon my punctuality afterwards. Mean-while, you may proceed to print the last four Volumes at your own convenience. You told me that you proposd to make this new Octavo Edition in ten Volumes.[4] Each four of the Quarto must therefore be divided into five, and you may cast them accordingly. I woud have you mind nothing but to finish the Chapter with each Volume, without forgetting the Index. You may send me down the Quarto Sheet with the Proof Sheet; and where it contains any Note that it is to be printed at the End I shall return it by the Post. I hope the Sale of the Quarto is pretty well advancd: For this new Edition may a little discredit it. I know not whether the former purchasers may complain of my frequent Corrections; but I cannot help it, and they run mostly upon Trifles; at least they will be esteemd such by the Generality of Readers, who little attend to the extreme Accuracy of Style. It is one great advantage that

* MS. at Barnbougle Castle; Hill, 212 ff.

[1] Cadell's shop was in the Strand; Strahan's printing-house was in New Street, Fetter Lane.

[2] John Campbell (1723–1806) succeeded his father as 5th Duke of Argyll in 1770. Lady Ailesbury was his sister.

[3] Inveraray Castle, on Loch Fyne, the principal seat of the Duke of Argyll.

[4] It was made in 8 vols.

results from the Art of printing, that an Author may correct his works, as long as he lives. But I have now done with mine for ever, and never shall any more review them, except in a cursory manner. I expect for my pains six Copies, over and above the six that are due me by Agreement. I believe I coud have writ more than a Volume with much less trouble than I have bestow'd on these. If you have leizure to peruse the Sheets, and to mark on the Margin any Corrections that occur to you, it will be an Addition to the many Obligations of the same kind, which I owe to you. But this I cannot expect, considering the many Avocations which you have, unless it prove an Amusement to you in this dead time of the Year. I fancy this Edition will not be publishd till after the New Year.[1] As soon as the new Edition of my philosophical Pieces is printed,[2] I shall be obligd to you to have six Copies of it. It is a great Relief to my Spirits, that I have at last a near Prospect of being fairly rid of that abominable Octavo Edition of my History.

I am Dear Sir Your most obedient humble Servant

DAVID HUME.

* 458. *To* WILLIAM STRAHAN

Dear Sir

I have now the Prospect of being settled, so as to be able to attend the Correction of the Proof Sheets. If you can, therefore, contrive to send me one which will arrive on Saturday Sennight the 31 of August, you shall have it returnd by Course of Post; and I shall never after fail to return one every post, which will be five times a week. I am oblig'd to you for humouring me in this particular.

I have receiv'd a Present of a new Book, from the Author, *The Principles of penal Law*. The Direction of it seems to be writ in your hand; and Cadel is one of the Publishers. If the Author

* MS. at Barnbougle Castle; Hill, 216 f.

[1] It was not published till 1773, probably because Cadell had a still greater number of the 'detestable edition' of 1763 on his hands than he would even now admit to Hume.

[2] This new edition of the *Essays and Treatises* is somewhat mysterious. Writing on 27 Feb. 1772, Strahan says that the six copies Hume asked for would soon be sent to him; and from Hume's letter of 3 June in that year to Cadell it appears that they were sent, and received. But I have not been able to trace any edition of the *Essays* between 1770 and 1777. Neither could Birkbeck Hill (see his note on p. 252 of his *Letters to Strahan*).

does not propose to keep his Name a Secret, I shoud be glad to know it:[1] For the Book is very ingenious and judicious. In all cases, if you know the Author, make him my Compliments and give him my Thanks. I did not imagine, however, that so ingenious a Man woud in this age have had so much weak Superstition, as appears in many passages. But these perhaps were inserted only from Decency and Prudence: And so the World goes on, in perpetually deceiving themselves and one another.

I am always oblig'd to you for your political Speculations: But I cannot agree with you, that, if matters came to a fair and open Strugle between the Land-holders and the Stock-holders, the latter woud be able to reduce the former to any Composition.[2] The Authority of the Land-holders is solidly establishd over their Tenants and Neighbours: But what Stock-holder has any Influence even over his next Neighbour in his own Street? And if public Credit fall, as it must by the least Touch, he woud be reduc'd to instant Poverty, and have authority nowhere. My only apprehensions are, with regard to the public, that this open Struggle will never happen, and that these two Orders of Men are so involvd with each other by Connexions and Interest, that the public Force will be allowd to go to total Decay, before the violent Remedy, which is the only one, will be ventur'd on. But this Event will depend much on Accidents of Men and times; and the Decision will not probably be very distant: The first War will put the Matter to a tryal, I fancy about the third or fourth Year of it, if we exert ourselves with our usual Frenzy. You may judge, from our late Treatment of the House of Bourbon, whether we can regard the present Peace as very durable.

I am Dear Sir Yours sincerely

Edinburgh DAVID HUME.

19th of Augt 1771

[1] It was by William Eden (1744–1814), afterwards 1st Baron Auckland, who was appointed in 1778 as one of the three commissioners to treat with the American colonists.

[2] In his letter of 23 July Strahan says: 'But supposing what you seem to apprehend to be unavoidable, if matters come to a Public Bankruptcy . . . I think I may venture to say, that the Stockholders will not tamely submit to be the *only* sufferers. The Debt is in fact a Debt upon the lands of Gr: Britain, these are the real security, supported by the Faith of the Legislature. It is impossible to conceive that the Public Creditors would suffer the landholders to enjoy their full Property, and undiminished by Taxes too, whilst they were robbed of their *all*' (MS., R.S.E.; Hill, 218 n.).

* 459. *To* WILLIAM STRAHAN

Inverara, 23 Augst 1771.

Dear Sir

I own, that I am, at this time, very much out of humour, and with you. Near two Years ago, I wrote to Lady Aylesbury, that I had orderd a new Edition of my History and Essays to be sent her: You wrote to me, that they were sent; but she tells me, that she never receiv'd them, and was continually in expectation of them. By what Accident this has happen'd, appears to me totally unaccountable; and the more so, as I know, that a Copy which I desird to be sent to Lord Hertford came safe to hand. I beseech you to send a Copy immediatly to Mr Conway in little Warwick Street Charing Cross, and to enquire how the former Mistake happend: For I am certain, that it proceeded not from your Fault, notwithstanding the ill-humour with which I begun my Letter. But I desird, at that time, that a Copy shoud also be sent to Lady Holderness; and I am also suspicious that this Copy has miscarryd by the same Accident; and the more so, as she never wrote me that she had receivd it, which she woud naturally have done. If you be not sure, that this Copy has been deliverd, please to inform me, that I may enquire; or rather, send a new Copy, relating the former Accident, and desiring that this Copy be returnd, in case the former Copy was deliver'd. I shall be in Town at the time which I appointed, and ready to receive the Proof Sheets.[1]

I am Dear Sir Your most obedient humble Servant

DAVID HUME.

† 460. *To* WILLIAM STRAHAN

Dear Sir

I write you in a great hurry; and can only tell you, that I like the Paper and Type very much, only I think that this Size of Type woud have suited better a Duodecimo than a large Octavo: However it will do very well.

I see the Cause of the Mistake with regard to Lady Aylesbury's

* MS. at Barnbougle Castle; Hill, 221.

† MS. at Barnbougle Castle; Hill, 223.

[1] At the end of the autograph there is written in another hand: 'Decr 6th 1769:' which I conjecture to have been the date of Hume's letter ordering the copies to be sent to Lady Ailesbury, &c.

Copy. Some body by Mistake has substituted Dr Hunter [1] in her place: But I never thought of making the Doctor a present, tho I have a great regard for him. Let Lady Aylesbury's Copy therefore be sent to her at Little Warwick Street Charing Cross.

I return the Sheet corrected; and am very sorry, that you cannot promise me to be regular: I dedicate my time entirely to it, and coud wish to have a Sheet regularly every post.

I find that any other Frank except Mr Fraser's will not suffice, both for the Proof Sheet and the Sheet of the Quarto; especially if you return the corrected Sheet, which I wish, though it be not absolutely necessary.

Edr. I am Dear Sir Yours sincerely
4 of Septr 1771 DAVID HUME.

* 461. *To* WILLIAM STRAHAN

Dear Sir Edr. 18 of Septr 1771.

I thank you for your Corrections, which are very judicious; and you see that I follow them for the greatest part. I shall be obligd to you for continuing them as far as your Leizure will permit. For tho' I know, that a man might spend his whole Life in correcting one small Volume, and yet have inaccuracies in it, I think however that the fewer the better, and it is a great Amusement to me to pick them out gradually in every Edition.

I had a Letter lately from a Bookseller in Lausanne,[2] who tells me, that he intends to publish a Translation of some of my philosophical Pieces; and desires to know the best Edition. If the last in large Octavo be finishd,[3] I shoud point it out to him; and shoud likewise be willing to send him a Copy of it, if any of our Booksellers have any Communication with Geneva or Lausanne. I shoud be glad to learn from you what answer I can make him.

I am Dear Sir Yours sincerely
DAVID HUME.

P.S.

I wish you coud come up to our Agreement of a Sheet every post.

* MS. at Barnbougle Castle; Hill, 224 f.

[1] Probably William Hunter, M.D. (1718–83), the leading obstetrician in London, and founder of the Hunterian Museum, now in Glasgow University. But perhaps his younger brother, John Hunter (1728–93), the great surgeon and anatomist.

[2] This letter is not extant among the MSS., R.S.E.

[3] See note 2 on p. 247 above.

* 462. *To* William Strahan

Dear Sir

You will see by the franking of my Letter whom we have with us.[1] I was so happy as to prevail on the Doctor to be my Guest during his Stay here, which we hope will be for ten days or a fortnight. He got over from Ireland in a short Interval between two Hurricanes by a particular Providence. At least I hope that he considers it in that Light. I am Dear Strahan

Yours &c

D. H.

29 Oct^r [1771]

† 463. *To* William Strahan

Dear Strahan

Your remarks are always very judicious and just; and I am much obligd to you. You see I have adopted all of them this sheet. Dr Franklin left me a few days ago for the west; but I expect him again in a few days.

Yours &c.

D. H.

12 of Nov^r [1771]

‡ 464. *To* William Strahan

Dear Sir

I have writ this Post to Fraser, whose Conduct has very much disappointed me. But if he delays a moment, we can easily do without him. You need only send me the Proof Sheet under any Frank, Dr Franklin's or Mr Pulteneys or Mr Wedderburn's or Lord Beauchamps or Mr Conway's (Who I hope, by the bye, has receivd the Copy of my History). The other Sheets [2] are in a great measure superfluous: Especially as I have a Copy of the Edition, from which this is taken.

I am glad to find, that the abominable Faction in England is declining. The People never tire of Folly, but they tire of the

* MS. recently in the possession of Messrs. Maggs Bros., London; hitherto unpublished.

† MS. at Barnbougle Castle; Hill, 225.

‡ MS. at Barnbougle Castle; Hill, 226 f.

[1] Benjamin Franklin. He stayed three weeks with Hume, five days with Lord Kames at Blair Drummond, and two or three days in Glasgow.

[2] That is, the 4to sheet from which the new 8vo edition was being printed. (See Letter 457 above.)

same Folly: And if their Leaders fall into the Contempt they deserve, it will be very great indeed. I hope that Pitt will have the Gout this whole Session and I pray it may be a hearty and sincere one.

I do not think, that you will be able to publish this Session; unless the printing of the four last Volumes be well advancd. But as I have at last been able to get one correct Edition of that work, I am more indifferent. I am sensible, it is an idle Amusement; but still it is an Amusement to think that Posterity will do me more Justice than the present Age, whose Suffrage indeed coud not have given me great Vanity.

I wish you saw (as I hope you will) my new House and Situation in St Andrews Square: You woud not wonder that I have abjurd London for ever.

I am Dear Sir Yours sincerely

2d Jany 1772. DAVID HUME.

P.S.

Lord Lyttleton has been so good as to send me the two last Volumes of his Henry II.[1] It woud flatter his Lordship to say that it is truly a Christian Performance.

* 465. *To* WILLIAM STRAHAN

Dear Sir

I have called on Dr Millar [2] and he on me; but have never met with him, because tho' this place be not large, I live in a manner out of Town, and am very seldom in it. My Sister also has been dangerously ill of late, which has kept me more out of Company. But I am told by a Friend, that Dr Millar said to him, there was a Bookseller in London, who had advertisd a new Book, containing, among other things, two of my suppress'd Essays.[3] These I suppose are two Essays of mine, one

* MS. at Barnbougle Castle; Hill, 230 f.

[1] Published in 1771.

[2] Probably John Millar (1735–1801), Professor of Law at Glasgow. Millar had first met Hume when the former was tutor to Lord Kames's son; and he followed Hume in metaphysics, while violently disagreeing with him in politics. His *Historical View of the English Government*, 1787, was intended to be the answer to Hume's Tory *History*.

[3] I have not been able to trace either the book or the advertisement. So

on Suicide another on the Immortality of the Soul, which were printed by Andrew Millar about seventeen Years ago, and which from my abundant Prudence I suppress'd and woud not now wish to have revivd. I know not if you were acquainted with this Transaction. It was this: I intended to print four Dissertations, the natural History of Religion, on the Passions, on Tragedy, and on the metaphisical Principles of Geometry. I sent them up to Mr Millar; but before the last was printed, I happend to meet with Lord Stanhope,[1] who was in this Country, and he convincd me, that either there was some Defect in the Argument or in its perspicuity; I forget which; and I wrote to Mr Millar, that I woud not print that Essay; but upon his remonstrating that the other Essays woud not make a Volume, I sent him up these two, which I had never intended to have publishd. They were printed; but it was no sooner done than I repented; and Mr Millar and I agreed to suppress them at common Charges, and I wrote a new Essay on the Standard of Taste, to supply their place. Mr Millar assurd me very earnestly that all the Copies were suppress'd, except one which he sent to Sir Andrew Mitchell, in whose Custody I thought it safe. But I have since found that there either was some Infidelity or Negligence in the case; For on Mr Morehead's[2] Death, there was found a Copy, which his Nephew deliverd up to me.[3] But there have other Copies got abroad; and from one

far as I know the first publication in England of the two suppressed essays was in 1777, when they appeared by themselves as *Two Essays*, without author's or publisher's name.

[1] Philip Stanhope (1717–86), 2nd Earl Stanhope, one of the best mathematicians of his day. He married (1745) the Hon. Grizel Baillie (died 1811), sister of the 7th Earl of Haddington. She was some kind of cousin of Hume's (or so he reckoned), and a great friend. There are several letters from her among the MSS., R.S.E. (See No. XXX in Appendix K.)

[2] He would appear to be the Mr. Muirhead mentioned in the following note.

[3] There used to be, in the Advocates' Library in Edinburgh, a bound copy of the proof-sheets of *Five Dissertations*, containing the essay *Of the Immortality of the Soul* but not that *Of Suicide*. To this book a note had been added, signed 'A.R.' and believed to have been written by Allan Ramsay the painter. It read: 'This book contains a piece of Mr D. Hume's, of which there is, I believe, but another copy existing. Having printed the volume as it here stands, Mr Hume was advised by a friend, to suppress the Dissertation upon Suicide; which he accordingly did. A copy, however, had somehow got into the hands of Mr Muirhead, a man of letters, who had made a very valuable collection of books. Mr Hume, after the death of Mr Muirhead, employed me to beg that copy from his nephew, who very politely delivered it up. Upon this Mr Hume gave me leave to keep the present

of these, some rascally Bookseller is, it seems, printing this Edition. I am not extremely alarmd at this Event, but if threatening him woud prevent it, I woud willingly employ that means. I am afraid all will be in vain; but if you know him, be as good as try what can be done; and also learn from what hand he had the Copy. I believe an Injunction in Chancery might be got against him; but then I must acknowledge myself the Author and this Expedient woud make a Noise and render the Affair more public. In a post or two, I may perhaps get you more particular Intelligence of the Booksellers Name.

I am extremely obligd to you for the Pains you take about correcting my Sheets; and you see that I almost always profit by it.

Yours sincerely
DAVID HUME.

Jany 25, 1772.

* 466. *To the* COMTESSE DE BOUFFLERS

Edinburgh, 25 of January, 1772.

I am truly ashamed, dear Madam, of your having prevented me in breaking our long silence; but you have prevented me only by a few days: for I was resolved to have writ to you on this commencement of the year, and to have renewed my professions of unfeigned and unalterable attachment to you. While I was at London, I had continual opportunities of hearing the news of Paris, and particularly concerning you; and even since I had settled here, I never saw any body who came from your part of the world that I did not question concerning you. The last person to whom I had the satisfaction of speaking of you, was Mr Dutens.[1] But there were many circumstances of your

* *Priv. Corr.*, 269 ff.

copy, which he had lent me: I promising not to show it to any body.' This interesting document was apparently seen by Grose when he was preparing his *History of the Editions* prefixed to vol. i of Hume's *Essays* (Green and Grose). Unfortunately it cannot now be found in the National Library of Scotland (formerly the Advocates'), and no one can tell what has become of it.

The National Library of Scotland has, however, recently acquired a valuable proof copy, corrected in Hume's handwriting, of the *two* suppressed Essays, bound up with the rest of the *Four Dissertations*. This copy belonged to Hume himself and was bequeathed by him, as a MS., to Strahan.

[1] Author of *Mémoires d'un voyageur qui se repose*.

situation which moved my anxiety, and of which none but yourself could give me information. You have been so good as to enter into a detail of them, much to my satisfaction; and I heartily rejoice with you, both on the restoration of your tranquillity of mind, which time and reflection have happily effected, and on the domestic satisfaction which the friendship and society of your daughter-in-law afford you. These last consolations go near to the heart, and will make you ample compensation for your disappointments in those views of ambition which you so naturally entertained, but which the late revolutions in France might perhaps have rendered more full of inquietude than satisfaction.

For my part, I have totally and finally retired from the world, with a resolution never more to appear on the scene in any shape. This purpose arose, not from discontent, but from satiety. I have now no object but to

Sit down and think, and die in peace—

What other project can a man of my age entertain? Happily, I found my taste for reading return, even with greater avidity, after a pretty long interruption: but I guard myself carefully from the temptation of ever writing any more; and though I have had great encouragement to continue my history, I am resolved never again to expose myself to the censure of such factious and passionate readers as this country abounds with. There are some people here conversible enough: their society, together with my books, fills up my time sufficiently, so as not to leave any vacancy; and I have lately added the amusement of building, which has given me some occupation.

I hearken attentively to the hopes you give me of seeing you once more before I die. I think it becomes me to meet you at London; and though I have frequently declared that I should never more see that place, such an incident, as your arrival there, would be sufficient to break all my resolutions. I only desire to hear of your journey as soon as it is fixed, and as long before it is executed as possible, that I may previously adjust matters so as to share the compliment with others of my friends, particularly the Hertford family, who may reasonably expect this attention from me.

Can I beg of you to mention my name to the Prince of Conti, and assure him that the world does not contain any person more devoted to him, or more sensible of the obligations which he imposed on me? I suppose Madame de Barbantane is very agreeably situated with her pupil, the Duchess of Barbantane.[1] Will she be pleased to accept of the respects of an old friend and servant? I beg to be remembered to Madame de Vierville. If Miss Becket be still with you, I wish to make her my compliments. I am, with the greatest truth and sincerity,

Ever yours,
DAVID HUME.

* 467. *To* ADAM SMITH

Edinburgh 28 of Jany 1772

Dear Smith

I shoud certainly, before this time, have challengd the Performance of your Promise, of being with me about Christmas, had it not been for the Misfortunes of my Family. Last Month, my Sister fell dangerously ill of a Fever; and though the Fever be now gone, she is still so weak and low, and recovers so slowly, that I was afraid it woud be but a melancholy House to invite you to. However, I expect, that time will re-instate her in her former Health, in which case, I shall look for your Company. I shall not take any Excuse from your own State of Health, which I suppose only a Subterfuges invented by Indolence and Love of Solitude. Indeed, my Dear Smith, if you continue to hearken to Complaints of this Nature, you will cut Yourself out entirely from human Society, to the great Loss of both Parties.

The Lady's Direction is M^{e} la Comtesse de B. Douairiere au Temple. She has a Daughter in law, which makes it requisite to distinguish her

Yours sincerely
DAVID HUME

P.S.

I have not yet read Orlando inamorato;[2] but intend soon to do it. I am now in a course of reading the Italian Historians, and am confirmd in my former Opinion that that Language has not producd one Author who knew how to write elegant, correct Prose, though it contains several excellent Poets. You say nothing to me of your own work.

To Adam Smith Esqr at Kirkaldy.

* MS., R.S.E.; hitherto unpublished.

[1] This must be a misprint for 'Duchess (or perhaps 'Princess') of Orleans.'

[2] By Matteo Maria Boiardo (*c.* 1430–94).

* 468. *To* William Strahan

Dear Sir 7 of Feby 1772

I suppress'd these Essays,[1] not because they coud give any Offence, but because, I thought, they coud neither give Pleasure nor Instruction: They were indeed bad Imitations of the agreeable *Triffling* of Addison. But if any one think otherwise, and chuse to preserve them, I have no Objection.

Pray, recollect: Did not I send you up a Passage to be inserted in the Reign of Henry VIII, and which I desird you to pin upon the Leaf of the Volume? It ought to have been printed in the last Sheet, and is now too late: But it may be added as a Note. Or is the whole an Illusion of mine, founded on my intending to send it you. The Passage contains a short Extract from an Act of Parliament, concerning the Marriage of the King with Jane Seymour, whom the Parliament recommends to him as a Piece of pure Flesh and Blood, very proper to bring him Heirs. If you have not this Passage, I shall send you another Copy of it.[2]

Yours sincerely
David Hume.

† 469. *To* Benjamin Franklin

Dear Sir, Edinburgh, 7 February 1772.

I was very glad to hear of your safe arrival in London, after being exposed to as many perils as St Paul, by land and by water, tho to no perils among false brethren; for the good wishes of all your brother philosophers in this place attend you heartily and sincerely, together with much regret that your business would not allow you to pass more time among them.

Brother Lin [3] expects to see you soon, before he takes his little

* MS. at Barnbougle Castle; Hill, 233 f.

† Franklin, *Works*, viii. 5.

[1] Hill assumed that the reference was to the two essays discussed in Letter 465 above. But I think Strahan must have written to Hume asking about some of the lighter essays (e.g., *Of Love and Marriage* and *Of Impudence and Modesty*) which had appeared in the early editions and been dropped since (see Letter 78).

[2] It was inserted as a note to vol. iv, p. 459 of this edition, and remained as a note in subsequent editions (Ch. XXXI, A.D. 1536).

[3] I conjecture that this refers to Adam Ferguson, who was hoping to be appointed Secretary to the Select Committee of Inquiry into East Indian Affairs.

trip round the world. You have heard, no doubt, of that project. The circumstances of the affair could not be more honourable for him, nor could the honour be conferred on one, who deserves it more.

I really believe, with the French author of whom you have favoured me with an extract,[1] that the circumstance of my being a Scotchman has been a considerable objection to me. So factious is this country! I expected, in entering on my literary course, that all the Christians, all the Whigs, and all the Tories, should be my enemies. But it is hard that all the English, Irish and Welsh, should be also against me. The Scotch likewise cannot be much my friends, as no man is a prophet in his own country. However, it is some consolation that I can bear up my head under all this prejudice. I fancy that I must have recourse to America for justice. You told me, I think, that your countrymen in that part of the world intended to do me the honour of giving an edition of my writings, and you promised that you should recommend to them to follow the last edition, which is in the press. I now use the freedom of reminding you of it.

Pray make my compliments to Sir John Pringle, and tell him how much I wish for his company; and be so good as to give him a description of the house I reserve for him in this square. If you really go over to America, we hope you will not grudge us Sir John as a legacy.

I am, dear Sir, with great truth and regard,
Your most obedient humble servant,
David Hume.

* 470. *To* William Strahan

Dear Sir

The Sheet you mention I deliverd with my own Hands on Friday the 31 of Jany to John Balfour,[2] who promis'd to send it with his own Letters to the Post house. It is by his unpardonable Negligence it is lost. I shall rate him about it; but if you do not receive it this post or the next, you will be so good as [to]

* MS. at Barnbougle Castle; Hill, 234 f.

[1] Neither Franklin's letter nor the extract is extant among the MSS., R.S.E.

[2] The Edinburgh bookseller.

send me another copy which I shall not entrust to him in returning it.

I am Dear Sir Yours most faithfully
D. H.

Feby 11, 1772.

P.S.

I am very well pleas'd that the Sheet is found; and also, that I did not know it, till I had writ a very scolding Letter to John Balfour for his losing it.

* 471. *To* WILLIAM STRAHAN

Edinburgh, 22 of Feby 1772.

Dear Sir

As we are drawing near a Conclusion,[1] I cannot forbear giving you many and hearty thanks, both for your submitting to so troublesome a Method of printing and for the many useful Corrections you have sent me. I suppose, since the days of Aldus,[2] Reuchlin,[3] and Stevens,[4] there have been no Printers who could have been useful to their Authors in this particular. I shall scarcely ever think of correcting any more; tho' I own that the receiving of the Sheets regularly by the post has been an Amusement and Occupation to me, which I shall have a Difficulty to supply. I fancy I must take to some kind of Composition in its place.

Pray, have you gone any length in printing the other Volumes, or are you now to begin? In this case, you can scarcely publish this Season. But as you have probably a very large fount of this Type, I hope you are pretty well advancd. I need not put you in mind of sending me a dozen Copies of the History, and half a dozen of the philosophical Pieces.

Your Encomium on the Princess Dowager[5] is elegantly written, and contains a very proper and spirited Reprehension of the

* MS. at Barnbougle Castle; Hill, 235 f.

[1] In the reprinting of the first four vols. of the *History*.

[2] The founder of the Aldine Press in Venice was Aldus Manutius (died 1515).

[3] Johann Reuchlin (1455–1522), better known as a philologist and Hebraist. In his youth he helped the printer Amorbach.

[4] Henri Estienne (1460–1520) and Robert Estienne (1503–59), printers first at Paris, then at Geneva.

[5] George III's mother. She died on 8 February of this year. Strahan's encomium was published in his paper, the *London Chronicle*, on 11 Feb.

scurrillous and scoundrel Patriots who had so long abus'd her. I wonder what they will now do for a Pretence to their Sedition.

I have lately heard a Story, extremely to the King's Advantage; which I shoud be glad to find confirmd. I am told, that this parliamentary Enquiry into the Proceedings of the East India Company did not originally proceed from the Ministry, but from the King himself, who was shockd with the Accounts he receivd of the Oppressions exercisd over the poor Natives, and demanded a Remedy.[1] I wish it may be possible to provide any, that will be durable. I trust much in the Integrity of Andrew Stuart (who, they say, will certainly be one of the Supervisors [2]) for the carrying of such a Plan into Execution.

I hear also that there is an Intention of appointing Professor Ferguson Secretary to the Commission.[3] Surely there is not a man of greater Worth in the World. If you have a Vote or Interest, I beseech you, employ it all in his favour, as well for his Advantage as for that of Humanity.

I am Dear Sir Faithfully Yours

DAVID HUME.

* 472. *To* WILLIAM STRAHAN

Dear Sir

If the Press has not got further than the 160th page of the sixth Volume, Line penult., there is a Passage which I shoud desire to have restord. It is this: *The full prosecution of this noble Principle into all its natural Consequences has, at last, through many*

* MS. at Barnbougle Castle; Hill, 247.

[1] The King's Speech on opening Parliament on 21 Jan. 1772 contained the following reference to affairs in India: 'The concerns of this country are so various and extensive as to require the most vigilant and active attention, and some of them, as well from remoteness of place as from other circumstances, are so peculiarly liable to abuses and exposed to danger that the interposition of the Legislature for their protection may become necessary.' This must have been interpreted prophetically by Hume; for the Select Committee of Inquiry into the affairs of the East Indian Company was not set up till 13 April.

[2] Andrew Stuart's name seems to have been often mentioned in this connexion; but George III was not very favourably disposed, and Lord North considered that the *Letters to Lord Mansfield* which Stuart had written should be counted as an objection to his appointment (*Corr. of George III*, ii. 496 and 498).

[3] Ferguson appears to have offered himself (ibid., ii. 498), but he was not appointed.

contests, produced that singular and happy *Government which we enjoy at present.*

I own that I was so disgusted with the Licentiousness of our odious Patriots, that I have struck out the words *and happy*, in this new Edition; but as the English Government is certainly happy, though probably not calculated for Duration, by reason of its excessive Liberty, I believe it will be as well to restore them: But if that Sheet be already printed, it is not worth while to attend to the matter. I am as well pleas'd that this Instance of Spleen and Indignation shoud remain.[1]

I am Dear Sir Yours sincerely

Edinburgh DAVID HUME.

3 of March 1772.

* 473. *To* WILLIAM STRAHAN

Dear Sir

I am much oblig'd to you for your Attention in returning me the Proof Sheets: But I never doubted of your Exactness in following my Corrections which were also, in part, your own. I had unfortunately bespoke most of the Smith Work of my new house; but I still found a small Job to give Mr Richardson, who seems to me a clever young Fellow. I remove in little more than two Months. If I find my Time lie heavy on my hands, I may, for my Amusement, undertake a reign or two after the Revolution. But I believe, in case of my composing any more, I had better write something that has no Reference to the Affairs of these factious Barbarians.

I am Dear Sir Yours sincerely

5 of March 1772. D. H.

† 474. *To* WILLIAM STRAHAN

Dear Sir

You will please to send this Letter[2] to Mr Cadel, which I have left open for your Perusal.

There is a Friend of mine, Cap^{n} Braiden,[3] who has writ, in

* MS. at Barnbougle Castle; Hill, 248.

† MS. at Barnbougle Castle; Hill, 249.

[1] The words were restored.

[2] Next letter.

[3] Patrick Brydone (1736–1818) married William Robertson's eldest daughter. His *Tour through Sicily and Malta, in a Series of Letters to William Beckford Esq., of Somerly in Suffolk* was published by Strahan next year. He was Controller of the Stamp Office, 1779–1818.

the form of Letters, his Travels thro Sicily and Malta: They are very curious and agreeable; and I as well as others of his Friends have advisd him to publish them; and I also advisd him, to carry them to you. If you read them I hope we shall agree in Opinion. I conjecture they may make one Volume a little less than a Volume of the Spectator.

I am Dear Sir Yours sincerely

DAVID HUME.

St Andrews Square
3 of June 1772.

* 475. *To* THOMAS CADELL

Edinburgh, 3 of June 1772.

Dear Sir

I have receivd a Copy of the new Edition of my Essays[1] and the four first Volumes of my History, with both which I am very well pleasd with regard to the Paper and Print. I have carefully perusd the Essays, and find them very correct, with fewer Errors of the Press, than I almost ever saw in any book; and I give you, as well as Mr Strahan, thanks for the care that has been taken of them. The four Volumes of history passd thro' my own hands; so that nothing needs be said of them. I fancy the other Volumes will not be finishd; so as to be publish'd this Season; but they will be ready early in the Winter.

I am Dear Sir Your most obedient humble Servant

DAVID HUME.

† 476. *To* ADAM SMITH

St Andrews Square 27 of June 1772

Done ere you bade: I receivd a Letter from Clason[2] himself, and immediatly wrote to Lord Chesterfield.[3] Baron Mure told me of the good Behaviour of Mr Clason, in attending Sir Thomas

* MS. at Barnbougle Castle; Hill, 252.

† MS., R.S.E.; Burton, ii. 459 ff. (incomplete).

[1] See note 2 on p. 247 above.

[2] Patrick Clason, afterwards schoolmaster of the parish of Logie Walloch, Stirlingshire. The letter Hume mentions is not extant among the MSS., R.S.E.; but another letter, from Clason to Adam Smith, is preserved.

[3] Lord Chesterfield was actively superintending the education of his godson, Philip Stanhope, who succeeded him as 5th Earl in 1773. Presumably Clason was trying to get himself appointed as one of the many tutors to this young man.

Wallace, of which I also informd his Lordship. I hope the young Man will meet with Success.

We are here in a very melancholy Situation: Continual Bankruptcies, universal Loss of Credit, and endless Suspicions.[1] There are but two standing Houses in this Place, Mansfield's [2] & the Couttses: For I comprehend not Cummin,[3] whose dealings were always very narrow. Mansfield has pay'd away 40.000 pounds in a few days; but it is apprehended, that neither he nor any of them can hold out till the End of next Week, if no Alteration happen.[4] The Case is little better in London. It is thought, that Sir George Colebroke [5] must soon stop; and even the Bank of England is not entirely free from Suspicion. Those of Newcastle, Norwich, and Bristol are said to be stopp'd: The Thistle Bank [6] has been reported to be in the same Condition: The Carron Company [7] is reeling, which is one of the greatest Calamities of the whole; as they gave Employment to near 10.000 People. Do these Events any-wise affect your Theory? Or will it occasion the Revisal of any Chapters?

Of all the Sufferers I am the most concern'd for the Adams, particularly John. But their Undertakings were so vast that nothing coud support them:[8] They must dismiss 3000 Workmen, who, comprehending the Materials, must have expended above 100.000 a Year. They have great Funds; but if these must be dispos'd of, in a hurry and to disadvantage, I am afraid the Remainder will amount to little or nothing. People's [Compa]ssion, I see, was exhausted for John in his last Calamity,[9] and every body asks why he incurr'd any more hazards. But

[1] The financial crisis in Scotland was brought about mainly by the wild conduct of the Ayr Bank (Douglas, Heron & Co.), which was founded in 1769 and which, after issuing credits in the most lavish way, stopped payment on 22 June 1772.

[2] This solid firm of Edinburgh bankers dated from 1738. At this period it was known as Mansfield, Ramsay & Co.

[3] William Cuming & Sons, a private bank in Edinburgh, founded between 1750 and 1760.

[4] Only four private banks in Edinburgh weathered this storm—Mansfields' and Cumings' among them.

[5] Head of a London bank, and in 1769 chairman of Directors of the East India Company.

[6] A Glasgow bank, founded in 1761. It lasted till 1836, when it was merged with the Glasgow Union Bank.

[7] Founded in 1760 by Dr. Roebuck. It weathered this storm.

[8] The Adam brothers were engaged at this time on the Adelphi Scheme in London. It failed financially.

[9] The failure of Adam and Thomas Fairholme in March 1764.

his Friendship for his Brothers is an Apology; tho' I believe he has a projecting Turn of his own. To me, the Scheme of the Adelphi always appeard so imprudent, that my wonder is, how they cou'd have gone on so long.

If Sir George Colebroke stop, it will probably disconcert all the Plans of our Friends, as it will diminish their Patron's Influence; which is a new Misfortune.

On the whole, I believe, that the Check given to our exorbitant and ill grounded Credit will prove of Advantage in the long run, as it will reduce people to more solid and less sanguine Projects, and at the same time introduce Frugality among the Merchants and Manufacturers:[1] What say you? Here is Food for your Speculation.

Shall we see you again this Summer?

To Adam Smith Esqr [at] Kirkaldy

* 477. *To* William Strahan

Edinburgh 6 of August 1772

Dear Strahan

Having mentiond to Sir Robert Keith how useful and agreeable Lord Stormont and Sir Andrew Mitchel, as well as Lord Hertford and myself, found your Correspondence[2] while abroad, he express'd the greatest Desire of enjoying the same Advantages while employd at Vienna,[3] and beg'd my Interest with you to procure him the favour. I own, that I cou'd not perswade myself to refuse him in so earnest a Request, both because he is as worthy and agreeable a Man as I know, and my very good Friend. I also thought, that, tho' the Encrease of your Business leaves you less Leizure than formerly, this Occupation wou'd only be a Relaxation from your usual Labours, the same Information wou'd equally serve for Lord Stormont, and Sir Robert, and you cou'd not be displeas'd to contribute in this Shape to the public Service. For all these Reasons, I cannot forbear

* B.M. Addit. MSS. 35350 (Hardwicke Papers, ii), fol. 18 ff.; *Englische Studien*, Band 63, Heft 3 (1929); hitherto unpublished in England.

1 Hume's judgement is upheld by historians of eighteenth-century Scotland. Scottish bankers learned prudence from the spectacular failure of the Ayr Bank.

2 On home politics.

3 Stormont was leaving Vienna and going as Ambassador to Paris, and Keith, after some exciting adventures in Copenhagen, was succeeding him at Vienna.

recommending Sir Robert to your Friendship and good Offices; and doubt not but your Correspondence will be agreeable to both: Tho' I own, that all the Advantages will be on his Side, while he is abroad, as the Trust repos'd in him, will not permit him to be equally communicative to you of the Transactions of his Department. I am very sincerely

Dear Strahan

Your most obedient humble Servant

DAVID HUME

To William Strahan Esqr. King's Printer

* 478. *To* [ADAM SMITH]

[October 1772.]

My dear Sir

Yours came to hand, while I was in the Country[1] where I should have been still, had it not been for a Letter of the French Ambassador, who expected to see me here in Town: He is lookd for to morrow Evening. As soon as I came to Town, I ask'd the Question you proposd; and was told by Sir William Forbes,[2] that tho' they did not commonly take the Air Notes,[3] yet he woud upon your Account: You may therefore send them over by the first Opportunity. I think that Bank more discredited by the last Step than by all their former Operations. They pretend to open at Air, in order to have a Pretence for striking off any farther Interest but as soôn as great Sums are demanded, they pretend, that they are only to change small Notes for the Circulation of the Country; & so refuse Payment: This is in effect shutting up again: They do not seem to have forseen, that it was the Interest of the two Banks here and of all the Bankers to make a Run upon them; for which they ought to have been prepar'd. As far as I can learn, the Duke of Queensberry[4] alone signs the Bonds of Annuity in his own Name; but

* M.S., R.S.E.; hitherto unpublished.

[1] Hume paid a visit to Ninewells and Minto in the autumn of 1772. He hurried back to Edinburgh from Minto because he heard that the duc de Guines (1735–1806), the French Ambassador, was expected.

[2] Sir William Forbes (1739–1806), banker in Edinburgh; apprenticed to Messrs. Coutts, 1753; partner, 1761; formed Messrs. Forbes, Hunter & Herries, 1763, which became Forbes, Hunter & Co., 1773; author of *Life of James Beattie*, 1806.

[3] See note 1 on p. 263 above.

[4] Charles (1698–1778), 3rd Duke of Queensberry, Keeper of Great Seal of Scotland, 1761; Lord Justice General, 1763.

it is imagind that the Duke of Buccleugh, Mr Douglas[1] &c, have enterd into an Agreement to bear their Share: Otherwise it were Madness in him; & indeed not very wise in him & them in any case. I had last post a Letter from Andrew Stuart: I do not like the present Situation of that Supervisorship.[2] Six to go from Europe, three to join them in the Indies: Corruption will get in among them; and probably Absurdity & Folly. And at best nine Persons can never do any Business. He tells me, that Ferguson is sure of going out Secretary. I wish it may be so. It will be a great Vexation and Disappointment to him to return to his Office with which he was before somewhat disgusted.

Yours

D H

* 479. *To* Adam Smith

Dear Smith St Andrews Square 23 of Novr 1772

I shou'd agree to your Reasoning,[3] if I coud trust your Resolution. Come hither for some weeks about Christmas; dissipate yourself a little; return to Kirkaldy; finish your Work before Autumn; go to London; print it; return and settle in this Town, which suits your studious, independant turn even better than London: Execute this plan faithfully; and I forgive you.

I was apply'd to, a few days ago, by poor Roby Arbuthnot,[4] in favour of his Son, now 13 years of Age, and a promising boy, as I am told, whom he intends to send to Glasgow, in a view of procuring him an Exhibition at Oxford. You know the State of that Family; and have probably heard that both the Parents of the boy are unfortunate People of Merit. I own, that, trusting to your Humanity, I promisd them your Interest and Advice in that Scheme: I hope you are not pre-engaged for any other Person: Otherwise I cannot doubt of your Concurrence.

Ferguson has return'd, fat and fair; and in good humour, notwithstanding his Disappointment,[5] which I am glad of.

* MS., R.S.E.; Burton, ii. 461 (incomplete).

1 Archibald, afterwards Lord Douglas, of the Douglas Cause.

2 See Letter 471 above.

3 Smith's letter is not extant among the MSS., R.S.E.

4 Probably Robert Arbuthnot of Kirkbraehead (1708–73); he left three sons, but what became of them I do not know. Or possibly a member of the private banking firm of Arbuthnot & Guthrie, which failed in June 1772.

5 I presume, at not having been appointed Secretary to the Committee of Inquiry on East Indian Affairs.

He comes over next week, to a house in this neighbourhood. Pray, come over this winter, and join us.

I am My Dear Smith Ever yours

DAVID HUME

To Adam Smith Esq[r] at Kirkaldy.

* 480. *To* COL. ALEXANDER DOW[1]

[1772]

My compliments to Ossian. He has given us a work last winter, which contains a great deal of genius and good writing; but I cannot assent to his system.[2] I must still adhere to the common opinion regarding our origin, or rather your origin; for we are all plainly Danes or Saxons in the low countries. But these subjects I reserve to a discussion over an evening fire on your return. I charge you not to think of settling in London, till you have first seen our New Town, which exceeds anything you have seen in any part of the world.

† 481. *To* WILLIAM STRAHAN

Edinburgh 16 of Jany 1773

Dear Sir

You have been guilty of a small Indiscretion in allowing a Copy of my new Edition to go out before the Publication: For I had a Letter yesterday from Mr Piercy,[3] complaining tho' in obliging terms, of the Note with regard to the old Earl of Northumberland House-hold Book; as if it were a Satyre on that particular Nobleman, which was by no means my Intention: I only meant to paint the manners of the Age. I reply'd to him, that I fancy'd it was too late to correct my Expressions; for that the Work was probably in the hands of the public.

* Burton, ii. 462 (probably incomplete). Burton gives as his reference the *Edinburgh Monthly Magazine* for Sept. 1810, but this magazine did not begin till 1817, and I have failed to trace the letter.

† MS. at Barnbougle Castle; Hill, 252 f.

[1] Alexander Dow (died 1779), soldier, historian, and dramatist; joined army in India; Captain, 1764; Lieut-Col., 1769; author of *History of Hindostan, translated from the Persian*, 1768, and *Zingis*, a tragedy, acted at Drury Lane, 1769.

[2] James Macpherson published his *Introduction to the History of Great Britain and Ireland* in 1772.

[3] Thomas Percy. His letter is extant among the MSS., R.S.E., and was printed by Burton in *Eminent Persons*, 317 ff.

I hope it is; or at least beg it may be soon. I know I have no right to demand any account of your Sales: I only entreat you to tell me precisely, as far as you can, the time of your publication; and also when you can send off the Copies for me. You told me in a former Letter that you heard I was continuing my History: I beg of you to believe that such an extravagant and absurd Idea never once enterd my head.

I am very sincerely Yours

D. H.

* 482. *To* William Strahan

Edinburgh 30 Jany 1773

Dear Sir

I find you must reprint all that Note about the Northumberland House-hold Book. The Alterations I make are very little material; but being requir'd in a very obliging manner by Dr Piercy, and, I suppose, by the Family, I could not now refuse them, without giving them great Offence, which I wish to avoid.[1]

I have likewise sent you one Addition to the Errata. The Passage at present is Nonsense, tho' I find it has escaped me in three Editions, notwithstanding it was printed right at first.[2] Be so good as to insert it in its proper place; as I suppose the Errata is not printed.

I never, that I remember, mention'd to Cap^{n} Braidon any particular Sum which he might expect, as I receivd his Manuscript in Parcels and coud form no Estimate of its Bulk.[3] His

* MS. at Barnbougle Castle; Hill, 255 f.

[1] The note appears as Note O to Ch. XXVI of the Collected edition. It is too long to quote in full, but even in its amended form cannot have been altogether pleasing to the sensitive Dr. Percy and 'the Family'.

[2] Hill very plausibly conjectured that the reference here is to the passage, on almost the last page of the *History*, in which Louis XIV and Charles II are compared as patrons of literature. The first edition reads 'ingenious part of mankind', and so does the Collected edition. But the 1770 edition reads 'ingenuous part of mankind'.

[3] Writing to Hume on 25 Jan. 1773, Strahan had said: 'I have at length agreed, but after much Difficulty with Capt. Brydon. You had raised his expectations so very high, and so much beyond the real worth of the Book, which will hardly make two octavo volumes very loosely printed, that he could not be satisfied with the very utmost the size and nature of the Book

Journey over Mount Etna is the most curious part of it; and I wish it be not anticipated by a late German Work which is translated,[1] but I have not read it. I recommended to Mr Braidon to obliterate some Levities, too much in the Shandean Style, which he promis'd to do. I do hope with these Corrections, it will be thought a good readable Book and curious.

Considering the Treatment I have met with, it woud have been very silly for me at my Years to continue writing any more; and still more blameable to warp my Principles and Sentiments in conformity to the Prejudices of a stupid, factious Nation, with whom I am heartily disgusted. I wish my Continuators good Success;[2] tho' I believe they have sence enough not to care whether they meet with it or not. Macpherson has Style and Spirit; but is hot-headed, and consequently without Judgement. The Knight has Spirit, but no Style, and still less Judgement than the other. I shoud think Dr Douglas, if he woud undertake it, a better hand than either. Or what think you of Andrew Stuart? For as to any Englishman, that Nation is so sunk in Stupidity and Barbarism and Faction that you may as well think of Lapland for an Author. The best Book, that has been writ by any Englishman these thirty Years (for Dr Franklyn is an American) is Tristram Shandy, bad as it is.[3] A Remark which may astonish you; but which you will find true on Reflection.

I admire very much this Work of Andrew Stuart;[4] tho I was

would admit of. You spoil all young authors by leading them to expect Prices only due to Veterans in Literature, and men of established Reputation' (MS., R.S.E.; Hill, 257 n.). None the less, Strahan probably did pretty well out of Brydone's book, which was widely read, and ran through several editions in the next twenty years.

[1] *Travels through Sicily and Part of Italy*, by Baron Riedesel, English trans. by John Forster, London, 1773.

[2] In his letter of 25 Jan. Strahan had said: 'After what you now tell me, I altogether despair of seeing a continuation of your History from yourself; but I have some notion it may be done by some other hand; perhaps Sir John Dalrymple or Mr. Macpherson.'

[3] Hume had seen a good deal of Sterne in Paris in the spring of 1764, and apparently got on with him very well (see Cross, *Sterne*, especially vol. ii). *Tristram Shandy* appeared at intervals between 1760 and 1767. Sterne died in 1768.

[4] Andrew Stuart, having brooded since 1769 over the House of Lords' decision on the Douglas Cause, had composed an attack on Lord Mansfield in the form of Four Letters. Writing to Baron Mure on 23 Jan. 1773, he says: 'This address . . . was completely printed only last week. So soon as it was completed, I sent the first copy to Lord Mansfield himself, and with it wrote

at first exceedingly alarmd at the Imprudence of the Attempt. I am less so, after perusing it; tho still it appears imprudent, according to the vulgar Rule of estimating these Matters.

I woud have you publish this new Edition as soon as it is ready; and rather submit to some Loss than allow the Book to be any longer discredited by that abominable Edition, which has given you and me so much Vexation, and has been one Cause why I have thrown my Pen aside for ever.

Believe me ever Yours
D. H.

* 483. *To* Andrew Stuart

Horse Wind 4 of Feby 1773

Honoured Sir

You need not doubt, that I, as your Deputy, was extremely pleas'd with your successful Attack on your capital Enemy,[1] and with the Approbation, which it meets with here from all the best Judges, both in Style and Argument. However, if one in my humble Station may presume to give my Opinion to a man so much superior to me in every respect, I shoud think, that almost all between the 11th and 22d Pages of the third Letter had better be retrench'd, or at least reduc'd to one Paragraph which shoud indicate in general the Contents of the whole. That passage is really too minute as well as intricate, and throws a Languor on that part of your performance. The

* B.M. MSS. 24023, fo. 50 f.; hitherto unpublished. This letter is endorsed by Andrew Stuart: 'A letter of pleasantry from D.H. under the feigned name of David Stuart Moncrieff. 9th February 1773.' For the real David Stuart Moncrief see note 2 on p. 208 above.

to him a letter, of which you have, inclosed, a copy. After an interval of some days, a considerable number of copies were distributed to other persons of the first consideration, and to particular friends. You cannot imagine what a noise it makes here at present. . . . While at the printer's this day, I met accidentally with Mr Mackenzie, attorney in Exchequer [author of the Man of Feeling], who told me he was to set out for Scotland to-morrow, and expected to get there in four days. . . . He carries along with him two other copies directed for Mrs Binning, whereof one is for our friend Mr Hume. I have wrote so to Mrs Binning, and desired her immediately to forward it to him. I need not desire you to recommend him a careful perusal of these Letters; the name at the bottom of them will sufficiently secure that point; but if he can spare so much time, either from his whist parties or from his entertainments, I expect that he will send me his criticisms and observations. . . .' (*Caldwell Papers*, II. ii. 212 f.).

[1] Lord Mansfield.

word *circumstantiate* wou'd also be better supply'd by *circumstantial.*

I am sorry to tell you, honoured Sir, that David Hume, whom perhaps you look on as your Friend, goes about railing at you in every Company: Son of a Whore and Son of a Bitch are the best Appellations he can afford you. He says, that it is intolerable, that this damnd Fellow, who was bred to nothing but drawing of Bonds and Leases, or at best Settlements and Entails, which are the sublime of his former Profession, shoud turn Author, and at once surpass him and all his Brethren: I am told that he has engag'd the Principal,[1] who, I hear, has the same Opinion of your Performance, to speak the same Lan[guage.] [2] Such is the base Envy and Malignity of these low Minds!

I am told by one who saw your Manuscript in London, that there was a Passage in your last Letter concerning the Change of Topics, both at the Bar and on the Bench, and the throwing out Suspicions above with regard to Subornation and Perjury which had never dard to be mentiond here. This Passage my Friend thought very much to the purpose, and ought not to have been omitted. But I ask pardon for pretending to give Advice to a man so much above me. I am sensible, that my Talents are better fitted to arrange a Dinner or Supper than a Discourse; and tho' Paullus Emilius in Plutarch, says that the same Genius which can marshal an Army will qualify a Man for disposing a Meal and vice versa, I am conscious, that there is a great Difference between the Cases. I have the Honour to be, with the greatest Deference and Regard, Honoured Sir,

Your most humble and most obedient Servant and Deputy

David Stuart-Moncrief.[3]

P.S.

I beg Pardon for writing on so bad paper to your Honour.

To Andrew Stuart Esqr Berkeley Square London.

[1] William Robertson. [2] MS. torn.

[3] Replying to this letter on 11 March 1773, Stuart says: '... The criticisms in the character of Deputy received soon after the publication, were of such a nature that there was no danger of my mistaking the author of them, I acknowledge the justness of all your observations and if there had been an opportunity of showing you those parts of the manuscript before they were printed, all due attention would have been paid to the criticisms with which you have now favoured me. . . .

'I was told yesterday that a very eminent Critick here who upon the whole is very partial to these Letters, has been at pains however to select the

* 484. *To* SIR JOHN PRINGLE

St. Andrew's Square, Edinburgh,
Feb. 10, 1773.

My dear Sir,

That the present Pretender was in London in the year 1753, I know with the greatest certainty;[1] because I had it from Lord Marischal, who said, it consisted with his certain knowledge. Two or three days after his Lordship gave me this information, he told me, that the evening before, he had learned several curious particulars from a lady (who I imagined to be Lady Primrose),[2] tho my Lord refused to name her. The Pretender came to her house in the evening, without giving her any preparatory information; and entered the room, when she had a pretty large company with her, and was herself playing at cards. He was announced by the servant under another name. She thought the cards would have dropped from her hands on seeing him. But she had presence enough of mind, to call him by the name he assumed; to ask him when he came to England, and how long he intended to stay there. After he and all the company went away, the servants remarked how wonderfully like the strange gentleman was to the Prince's picture, which

* *St. James's Chronicle*, 1–3 May, 1788; *Edin. Mag.*, May 1788, p. 340 f.; Burton, ii. 462 ff.

Scotticisms which appear in them, and that the number of them is very considerable. The person who acquainted me of this is at my desire to get me a compleat list of them which shall be forwarded to you that I may have the benefit of your Decision from which I shall make no appeal whatever the judgment be. In a company of English Criticks where I happened to dine to-day and to mention this discovery of the Scotticisms, I pleaded in my defence that it was not easy, scarce possible for an Inhabitant of the North of Tweed to avoid them, but this plea was overruled, and for the purpose of refuting me, the works of two of my best friends on the North of Tweed were appealed to as evidence against me, I mean Dr Robertson's and your own. I hope the fact is not true and therefer if you are conscious of any Scotticisms in your own works or in Dr Robertson's it would be a kind thing to me upon this occasion to favour me with a communication of them. If I can but suffer in good company I shall have no regret at being condemned for an offence of this nature. . . .' (MS., R.S.E.; *Eminent Persons*, 328 f.).

[1] It now seems to be reasonably well established that Prince Charles Edward visited London in 1750, and there declared himself a Protestant. He probably returned to London twice before 1755, but the exact dates of his visits seem to be uncertain.

[2] Anne Drelincourt (died 1775) m. (1740) Hugh, 3rd Viscount Primrose (died 1741).

hung on the chimney-piece, in the very room in which he entered. My Lord added (I think from the authority of the same Lady), that he used so little precaution, that he went abroad openly in daylight, in his own dress; only laying aside his blue riband and star; walked once through St. James's, and took a turn in the Mall.

About five years ago, I told this story to Lord Holdernesse, who was Secretary of State in the year 1753; and I added, that I supposed this piece of intelligence had at that time escaped his Lordship. 'By no means', said he, 'and who do you think first told it me? It was the King himself, who subjoined, "And what do you think, my Lord, I should do with him?"' Lord Holdernesse owned that he was puzzled how to reply; for if he declared his real sentiments, they might savour of indifference to the Royal Family. The King perceived his embarassment, and extricated him from it, by adding, 'My Lord, I shall just do nothing at all; and when he is tired of England, he will go abroad again.' I think this story, for the honour of the late King, ought to be more generally known.

But what will surprise you more, Lord Marischal, a few days after the coronation of the present King, told me, that he believed the young Pretender was at that time in London; or at least had been so very lately, and had come over to see the show of the coronation, and had actually seen it. I asked my Lord the reason for this strange fact. 'Why,' says he, 'a gentleman told me so that saw him there; and that he even spoke to him, and whispered in his ears these words: "Your Royal Highness is the last of all mortals whom I should expect to see here."—"It was curiosity that led me," said the other; "but I assure you," added he, "that the person who is the object of all this pomp and magnificence is the man I envy the least."' You see this story is so near traced from the fountain head, as to wear a great face of probability. Query, What if the Pretender had taken up Dymock's gauntlet? I find that the Pretender's visit in England, in the year 1753, was known to all the Jacobites; and some of them have assured me, that he took the opportunity of formally renouncing the Roman Catholic religion, under his own name of Charles Stuart, in the new church in the Strand; and that this is the reason of the bad treatment he met with at the Court of Rome. I own that I am a sceptic with regard to the last particulars.

Lord Marischal had a very bad opinion of this unfortunate

prince; and thought there was no vice so mean or atrocious of which he was not capable; of which he gave me several instances.[1] My Lord, tho a man of great honour, may be thought a discontented courtier; but what quite confirmed me in the idea of that prince, was a conversation I had with Helvétius at Paris, which I believe I have told you. In case I have not, I shall mention a few particulars. That gentleman told me, that he had no acquaintance with the Pretender; but some time after that prince was chased out of France, 'A letter', said he, 'was brought me from him, in which he told me that the necessity of his affairs obliged him to be at Paris; and, as he knew me, by character, to be a man of the greatest probity and honour in France, he would trust himself to me, if I would promise to conceal and protect him. I own,' added Helvétius to me, 'altho I knew the danger to be greater of harbouring him at Paris than at London; and altho I thought the Family of Hanover not only the lawful sovereigns in England, but the only lawful sovereigns in Europe, as having the full and free consent of the people; yet was I such a dupe to his flattery, that I invited him to my house; concealed him there, going and coming, near two years; had all his correspondence pass through my hands; met with his partisans upon Pont Neuf; and found, at last, that I had incurred all this danger and trouble for the most unworthy of all mortals; in so much that I have been assured, when he went down to Nantes to embark on his expedition to Scotland, he took fright and refused to go on board; and his attendants, thinking the matter gone too far, and that they would be affronted for his cowardice, carried him, in the night time, into the ship, pieds et mains liés.' I asked him, if he meant literally? 'Yes,' said he, 'literally. They tied him, and carried him by main force.' What think you now of this hero and conqueror?

Both Lord Marischal and Helvétius agree, that with all this strange character, he was no bigot; but rather had learned from the philosophers at Paris to affect a contempt of all religion. You must know that both these persons thought they were ascribing to him an excellent quality. Indeed, both of them used to laugh at me for my narrow way of thinking in these particulars. However, my dear Sir John, I hope you will do me the justice to acquit me.

[1] In two unpublished fragments of autobiography among the MSS., R.S.E., the Earl Marischal censures the Prince pretty severely.

I doubt not but these circumstances will appear curious to Lord Hardwicke, to whom you will please to present my respects. I suppose his Lordship will think this unaccountable mixture of temerity and timidity, in the same character, not a little singular.

I am, Yours very sincerely,
DAVID HUME.

* 485. *To* JEAN-BAPTISTE-ANTOINE SUARD

[21 February 1773.]

Dear Sir,

I join my request to that of my friend, Dr Robertson, in favour of Mr Jardine,[1] as well as of his young pupils, that you would admit them sometimes to pay their court to you, and would afford them your countenance and protection.[2] You will find M. Jardine a man of sense and knowledge; and in that light I have ventured to recommend him to M. d'Alembert's acquaintance, but as I know that M. d'Alembert never goes to our friend Baron d'Holbach's, where my countryman would have access to see the best company, I would farther request, that, if you find him worthy of that society, which I make no doubt of, you would, in my name as well as your own, present him to the Baron. I suppose that the Baron's house is on the same footing as formerly, a common receptacle for all men of letters and ingenuity. But there have so many alterations happened in Paris since I was there, that I cannot blindly make this request; and I leave the matter entirely to your own discretion. I only desire, that you would assure the Baron of my sincere and inviolable attachment to him, and of my entire sense of his worth, as well as of the obligations I owe him for his friendship. I am with great regard Dear Sir,

Your most obedient and most humble servant
DAVID HUME.

* *New Monthly Magazine and Universal Register*, vol. xiii, Pt. I (Jan. to June, 1820), p. 8. It appears from *Caldwell Papers*, II. ii. 319, that this note of Hume's was really a postscript to a letter from Robertson to Suard, dated 21 Feb. 1773. Robertson's letter is also printed in the *New Monthly Magazine*, *loc. cit.*

[1] George Jardine (1742–1827), a graduate of Glasgow; appointed tutor to the two sons of Baron Mure, 1771; remained with them in Paris, 1771–3; Professor of Logic and Rhetoric, Glasgow, 1774–1824.

[2] Jardine had written to Mure from Paris, asking for letters of introduction to Suard.

* 486. *To* William Strahan

Dear Sir Edinburgh 22 of Feby 1773

On reviewing your last Letter and recollecting my Answer to it,[1] I am afraid some mistake might arise between us. No doubt, any body, either from their own Inclination or from your Application, may undertake to write any part of English History they please; and I can have no Objection to it: But that this work should be publishd as a Continuation of mine, I see liable to considerable Objections; and it is necessary for me to deliberate well upon it. If it be either much better or much worse than mine, it might be improper, for my own credit, to consent to it; and as long as both the Performance and the Author are unknown to me, I cannot without farther deliberation go so far. I beg, therefore, that this Matter may be fully understood between us, and that nothing I have said may be interpreted as my Approbation of a Scheme, which is totally unknown to me.

I desire much to ask you a Question, which, if the Matter depended solely on you, I know you coud answer me in a moment. But as it is, you can easily, by consulting your Partners, be able to give me Satisfaction in it. In short, I wish to know precisely, whether you intend to publish the new Edition this Season or the Season after, or any subsequent Season. It is needless to say anything about the Index which coud have been ready long ago. I beg it of you, I even conjure you, to give me at last some Answer which I can depend on. I promise you, that this is the last time I shall write to you on the Subject.

I am Dear Sir

Your most humble and most obedient Servant

David Hume

† 487. *To* Adam Smith

St Andrews Square 24 of Feby 1773

Dear Smith

There are two late Publications here which I advise you to commission. The first is Andrew Stuarts Letters to Lord Mans-

* MS. at Barnbougle Castle; Hill, 261 f.

† MS., R.S.E.; Burton, ii. 466 f. (incomplete).

[1] See Letter 482 and note 2 on p. 269 above.

field which they say have met with vast Success in London: Andrew has easd his own Mind, and no bad Effects are to follow: Lord Mansfield is determind absolutely to neglect them. The other is Lord Monboddo's Treatise on the Origin and Progress of Language,[1] which is only part of a larger work. It contains all the Absurdity and malignity which I expected; but is writ with more Ingenuity and in a better Stile than I look'd for.

Surge et inhumanæ senium depone Camenæ.[2] Yours

D. H.

P.S.

I shoud save you Expence, by sending you over both these works, if I knew how.

To Adam Smith Esqr at Kirkaldy

* 488. *To* William Strahan

Edinburgh 15 of March 1773

Dear Sir

The Number of Copies of my History, which I desir'd to have, was twelve. I agreed with Mr Millar verbally to reserve six on every new Edition; but as I had taken uncommon Pains on this Edition, I proposd twelve, which you very frankly agreed to: I desire one copy to be sent to Lord Beauchamp with my Compliments, and the rest to be shipt off to this Place with the first convenient Opportunity.

You and Mr Cadel had so much lost all faith with me, that indeed I thought it was impossible for you any longer to deceive me: Yet when you mention'd a new Edition, I own I was so simple as to believe, that all the old one was nearly sold off. This woud have been very blameable in you, if you had proposd any other End than that of seducing me into the continuing of my work, which you thought, and probably with Reason, woud have been for my own Advantage in more respects than one. But however the Consequence is, that I am

* MS. at Barnbougle Castle; Hill, 262 f.

[1] Only the first volume of this book appeared in 1773, the remaining five being published at intervals up to 1792. In this first volume Monboddo was much helped by his secretary, John Hunter, afterwards Professor of Humanity at St. Andrews. It has even been said that Hunter wrote the volume.

[2] Horace, *Epist.* i. 18, l. 47.

now at a Loss, and ever shall remain so, what I am to think and believe: And many Questions, interesting to me, which I wishd to ask you, woud, I find, be entirely vain and fruitless; and therefore I shall forbear them, since I can give no manner of credit to the Answers. A very little time will make me totally indifferent about these Matters, which is the State of Mind that I have nearly attain'd already. I only desire that before you begin any new Edition of any of my Writings, you give me Information some time beforehand.

I am Dear Sir Your most obedient Servant

DAVID HUME.

* 489. *To* WILLIAM STRAHAN

Dear Sir Edinburgh 20 of March 1773

I have read twice over all Sir John Dalrymple's new Publication,[1] which contains many curious Papers; but it gives me great Satisfaction to find, that there is not one single Mistake in my History, either great or small, which it gives me occasion to correct. I could only wish to have an Opportunity of adding one Note in order to correct a mistake into which Sir John is very anxious to lead his Readers, as if the French Intrigues had had a sensible Influence in the Determinations of the English Parliament: And I believe it is not too late even yet to annex it.[2] I remember Mr Millar added a similar Note to the last Octavo Edition drawn from K. James's Memoirs; and it was inserted in more than half the Copies. I have sent you the Note, which I beg may be printed on a Leaf apart, and annexd to all the Copies afterwards disposd of, and even sent to all the Booksellers that have purchasd any considerable Numbers, as well as joind to my own Copies.

I hear you have given Sir John 2000 pounds for the Property of this Volume, which I scarcely believe. The Book is curious, but far from being agreeable Reading; and the Sale will probably be all at first. I again repeat my Entreaties that this Note may be annexd.

I am Dear Sir Very sincerely yours

DAVID HUME.

* MS. at Barnbougle Castle; Hill, 264.

[1] Vol. ii of the *Memoirs of Great Britain and Ireland*, vol. i having been published in 1771.

[2] See Note to Ch. LXVI of *History* (A.D. 1678).

* 490. *To* William Strahan

Edinburgh 24th of March 1773

Dear Sir

If my Letter [1] surprizd you, I assure you yours [2] no less surprizd me; and gave me no little Concern. You know, that I have frequently accus'd you no less than Mr Millar and Mr Cadell, of always representing the fair side of things to me; and you have frequently remarkd that I was totally incredulous concerning the Representations you made me. If your End has been to circumvent me, or take any Advantage of me to my Loss, you would have been very blamable. But as your Purpose plainly was and coud be no other, than to put me in good humour with the Public, and engage me into what must prove both profitable and amusing to me, I thought the Crime very venial; as I told you in my Letter: And though I wishd that the Truth had always been told me, I neither was disobligd at you nor entertaind in the least a bad opinion of you. On the contrary, there is no man of whom I entertain a better, nor whose Friendship I desire more to preserve, nor indeed any one to whom I have owd more essential Obligations. You may judge then of my Uneasyness when I found that I had unwittingly and unwillingly given you so much Disgust. But how coud you take it amiss, that I had told you in a Letter what I had so often told you without offence by words? Your protracting of this Edition, which you told me two Years ago was demanded, was a sure means of renewing my former Jealousy.—But I shall not enter into any farther Detail on this Subject which is needless: But what I think extremely needful for my own Peace of Mind is to renew my Professions of that Friendship and Esteem, which I do and always will bear to you; and to beg of you very earnestly a Renewal of those Sentiments which you always professd towards me, and whose Sincerity I have seen in a hundred Instances. I do not remember any Incident of my

* MS. at Barnbougle Castle; Hill, 270 ff.

[1] No. 488 above.

[2] Strahan's letter, dated 19 March 1773, is not among the MSS., R.S.E.; but he kept a copy of it, which Hill printed from the Barker MSS. He says: 'Yours of the 15th I received to-day, which does not a little surprise me. After having been most unfeignedly attached to you . . . I did not, I could not expect to be told by you, after all, that I was a lying scoundrel, who had constantly deceived you, to whom you could give no manner of credit. . . .' (For the whole letter see Appendix C below.)

Life, that has given me more real Concern, than your Misapprehension of me, which, I hope, a little Reflection without any Explication on my part woud have sufficd to remove. Sick People and Children are often to be deceivd for their Good; and I only suspected you of thinking that peevish Authors, such as I confess I am, are in the same Predicament. Was the reproaching you with this Idea, so great an Offence, or so heavy an Imputation upon your Faith and moral Character? I again beg of you to be assurd of my sincere Sentiments on this head, and entreat the Continuance or rather the Renewal of your Friendship; a Word which I once hop'd woud never have enter'd into our Correspondence.

I am with great Truth & Regard Dear Sir
Your most obedient humble Servant
DAVID HUME [1]

* 491. *To* ADAM SMITH

St Andrews Square 10 of April 1773.

To day News arriv'd in town that the Air Bank had shut up; and as many people think for ever.[2] I hear that the Duke of Bucleugh is on the Road: The Country will be in prodigious distress for Money this term. Sir G. Colebroke's Bankruptcy is thought to be the immediate Cause of this Event.

Have you seen Macpherson's Homer?[3] It is hard to tell whether the Attempt or the Execution be worse. I hear he is employd by the Booksellers to continue my History: But in my Opinion, of all men of Parts, he has the most anti-historical Head in the Universe.

Have you seen Sir John Dalrymple?[4] It is strange what a Rage is against him, on account of the most commendable Action in his Life.[5] His Collection is curious but introduces no new Light into the civil, whatever it may, into the biographical & anecdotical History of the times.

* MS., R.S.E.; Burton, ii. 467 (incomplete).

[1] There is nothing to show how Strahan took this eirenicon.

[2] See Letter 476 above.

[3] Macpherson's translation of the *Iliad* into Ossianic prose, published this year.

[4] See note 1 on p. 278 above.

[5] Dalyrymple's book enraged the Whigs.

Have you seen Alonzo?[1] Very slovenly Versification, some pathetic, but too much resembling Douglas.

I expect to see you soon. Have you been busy, and whether in pulling down or building up?

D. H.

To Adam Smith Esqr Kirkaldy

* 492. *To* JOHN CRAWFORD

[Nov. or Dec. 1773][2]

Dear Sir

I use the Freedom of sending you Mr Bradshaw's [3] Note to me, which I mentiond to you and which was written soon after Mr Conway's Resignation. In answer to your Question, why I have so long neglected an Affair of so great Consequence,[4] I reply, that I have not altogether neglected it: Some time after the Duke of Grafton's Resignation, I wrote to Mr Bradshaw, desiring him to lay my Claim before Lord North: He sent my letter to Mr Robinson,[5] who wrote to me, that he wou'd take a proper time of laying it before his Lordship: As this Letter was dated from My Lord's Country-house, I concluded, that he had previously laid it before him, and that the Answer was a civil Evasion or Denial.

You seem to think that I may possibly be mistaken; and that

* MS., R.S.E.; Burton, ii. 149 (incomplete). The autograph is obviously a draft; it has been much corrected, and the second paragraph appears in alternative forms, only the second of which is reproduced in the text above.

[1] Another of John Home's tragedies, produced at Drury Lane this year.

[2] The date is a guess. The letter must have been written some time before No. 494 below. We learn from a letter of Mme du Deffand to Walpole, dated 17 Nov. 1773, that Crawford had recently been staying with Hume (*Lettres à Walpole*, ii. 551). I therefore conjecture that the subject of this letter was discussed with Crawford while he was in Edinburgh, and that, after he returned to London, Hume sat down to put on paper the substance of their conversation.

[3] Thomas Bradshaw (died 1774), sometime Private Secretary to the Duke of Grafton; Lord of Admiralty, 1772; one of the men made notorious by the attacks of Junius. He was known as 'the cream-coloured Parasite' (Wraxall, *Memoirs*, 286).

[4] Apart from this letter and No. 542 below, there is nothing to show what the 'Affair of so great Consequence' was. It would seem that Hume was trying to obtain some sinecure more lucrative and more secure than the pension he had been awarded on vacating office as Under-Secretary of State.

[5] John Robinson, Secretary to the Treasury under Lord North.

as the Affair may never have been expo[sed] [1] in a proper manner to Lord North, I shoud do wisely to have it fairly represented to him. Perhaps, you are in the right; but I own, that, for one reason or other, I have ever found myself at some loss how to proceed in that Matter. The Duke of Grafton was the Minister who was so good as to take the Engagement with me, and who woud naturally incline to see it [fulfilled]:[1] But though there is no Person in England to whom I woud more willingly owe an Obligation, I have so little the honour of being known to his Grace, that I coud not presume to trouble him for a favour which it did not immediatly lie in his power to confer.[2] My Obligations to Lord Hertford and Mr Conway are so great and essential; that I scruple to give them any farther Trouble, tho I can entirely rely on their Goodness to me, and tho this Reversion was voluntarily procurd by them without the least Sollicitation on my part. You may tell me, that my case may here appear somewhat peculiar. I have a Claim or a sort of Claim of Justice in my favour: The civil List will save 200 pounds a Year by its being complyd within: And few Persons have been placd in that trust of Under-Secretary who have not retird with greater Emoluments than have been bestowd on me; for the Pension with Deductions amounts only to about 150 pounds a Year. Perhaps these Considerations ought to give me more Courage in sollicitng this Claim; Yet, if no Incident happen to overcome my Reluctance, there is danger, I own, of its lying for ever in its present neglected State. I only thought it requisite to explain to you in a few words the Motives of my Conduct, in expectation of your Approbation, at least of your Indulgence. Though I shoud not wonder, if you, as a Man of the World, laugh a little at the Scruples, which sometimes direct the Conduct of a recluse and Philosopher.

[1] Blots in MS.

[2] In the alternative version, afterwards struck out, Hume says: 'You still insist, why I acquiesc'd in this Evasion; and why I did not appeal to the Duke of Grafton, who wou'd have thought himself oblig'd to see his engagement fulfilld by his Successor. To tell you the Truth, Dear Crawford, I made it a rule from the beginning of my Life never to ask a Favour of any man; and this Humour, which, if you be very indulgent to me, you will call Modesty, if less so, Pride. I was unwilling to relinquish, after having maintain'd it thro my Youth, and during more difficult Circumstances, than those in which I am at present plac'd thro the Friendship of Lord Hertford and Mr Conway. Besides, I had so little the Honour of being known to his Grace, that . . .'

* 493. *To* William Strahan

Dear Strahan St Andrews Square 25 of Jany 1774

I write to you in a great hurry and with great Earnestness: It is to beg your Vote and Interest in the India house for Coll. Stuart,[1] Brother to our Friend, Andrew, whose Appointment to command in Bombay is in danger of being over-haul'd by the Court of Proprietors.[2] This woud be a most invidious Measure, very cruel to the Collonel and all his Friends. I know that on Andrew's Account, you woud interest yourself against it; but as he thinks, that my Entreaties woud add something to your Zeal, I hereby join them in the most earnest manner, tho' indeed rather to satisfy him, than that I think they will be any-wise necessary.[3]

I am &c

David Hume.

† 494. *To* John Crawford

St. Andrew's Square, 28 Jan. 1774.

I was told yesterday by Mr Ross [4] that he had just come from your father, who regretted very feelingly his never hearing from you, which he ascribed, not to your indolence, the true cause, but to your neglect of him and your prejudices against him.[5] In the fullness of his heart he opened up all his friendly intentions towards you, and declared that, except a reasonable provision for your sister, and a small annuity to your brother after purchasing his commission, he intended you to be the sole heir of all his remaining property. He wanted nothing from you

* MS. at Barnbougle Castle; Hill, 273. † Morrison, ii. 318 f.

[1] James Stuart (died 1793), younger brother of Andrew Stuart of Torrance.

[2] The Court of Proprietors in the East India Co. was composed of all those holding not less than £1,000 of stock. It elected the Directors.

[3] On 1 Feb. 1774 the Court of Proprietors recommended the Directors to cancel the appointment of Colonel Stuart as C.-in-C. of the Forces in the Bombay Presidency, and to appoint Colonel Robert Gordon instead. But the following year Stuart entered the Company's service as Second-in-Command on the Coromandel Coast. In 1776 he arrested the Governor of Madras, Lord Pigot, was suspended by the Directors, and applied for trial by court-martial. He was honourably acquitted in 1780, and the next year appointed C.-in-C. at Madras.

[4] See note 2 on p. 222 above.

[5] John Crawford, who was a dissipated, extravagant young man about town, had been on bad terms with his father for some years.

except your friendship, which he was sorry he could not obtain, and it was the circumstance that embittered his remaining days. I was really so much affected by Mr Ross's account of the conversation, that I promised to write to you on this head, which I hope you will take in a friendly part. Your father at this time is more particularly jealous on account of some late transactions;[1] but as your vehemence must be abated by success, I hope you will now regard them with more indulgence, indeed with that indulgence which the common maxims of the world (I mean of the prudent and discreet world) will allow them. In all cases it is your duty, as well as your interest, to write to him frequently, and with all possible marks of confidence and friendship. Humanity as well as duty (and humanity is duty) should lead you to adopt this measure. Let not indolence be an obstacle. But I trust that I need say no more on this head.

Yesterday Baron Mure told me that, by your directions, he was to make me a voter in the county of Renfrew.[2] Had you ever mentioned to me this intention, I could have given you invincible objections against it, the least of which is, the taking a journey which I am always averse to, and the living either in Mr Ross's house or the Baron's at the most disagreeable time, that of an election; and all this for no manner of purpose, as any other person (and the Baron or you must have great choice) can equally do the business. I could have got over all objections were it to be of any service to you, but as the matter is a mere formality, I know you will have no difficulty to excuse me.[3]

[1] John Crawford, writing to Baron Mure on 17 Feb. 1773, says, speaking of his father: 'I have been wearied by his persecutions into an entail of my estate along with his, which I know I shall repent all the rest of my life. We shall both be in Scotland this summer, and then if, upon a fair explanation of all that has passed between us, you shall not think me unreasonable in wishing to undo what has been done, I hope you will not refuse to pass some tedious hours in endeavouring to bring this about.' (*Caldwell Papers*, II. ii. 217.) This may explain what Hume calls 'some late transactions'.

[2] That is, by turning him for the time being into a 'parchment baron'. The franchise in the counties was in the hands of the landowners, and by a process of open and acknowledged fraud they created extra voters for an election by dividing up some of their land among their friends, who, of course, handed it back again immediately the election was completed. It was calculated that, in 1790, 1318 out of the 2,655 voters in the Scottish counties were fictitious; in Renfrewshire, the county in question, 82 out of 114 were fictitious (Mathieson, *Awakening of Scotland*, 19 f.).

[3] Crawford had. Writing to Mure in a letter dated only 'Saturday', he says: 'As to David Hume, I can only say that he promised me very positively

In the business which I entrusted to you in my last letter,[1] I must entreat you to proceed with all manner of —— of (what do you think I was going to say) with all manner of indifference. It cannot be less than my concern about it, or than my hopes of success. Let it be just proposed, and then dropped, if it be not immediately gone into. I have already reaped the most agreeable circumstance of the affair, your entering into it with friendship and alacrity.

Pray is it true that Lord Holland has paid Charles Fox's[2] debts? And will Charles now draw the line and reform, and be frugal and virtuous? I hope you excuse the prolixity of my style, in employing synonimous terms, I shall make you amends in my subscription, for I shall neither be your humble, nor obedient, nor obsequious, nor devoted servant, but yours sincerely

DAVID HUME.

Write to your father; I excuse your not writing to me.

* 495. *To* ADAM SMITH

Dear Smith St Andrews Square 13 of Feby 1774

You are in the wrong for never informing me of your Intentions and Resolutions, if you have fix'd any.[3] I am now oblig'd to write to you on a Subject, without knowing whether the Proposal, or rather Hint, which I am to give you, be an Absurdity or not. The Settlement to be made on Ferguson is a very narrow Compensation for his Class, if he must lose it: He wishes to keep it, and to serve by a Deputy in his Absence. But besides that this Scheme will appear invidious and is really

* MS., R.S.E.; Burton, ii. 471 (incomplete).

the last time I saw him to take a vote. It was very kind in him to make me such a promise. But he had better not have done it, because, by forgetting it afterwards, and by finding a thousand inconveniences at present which he did not think of before, he exposes me to the real inconvenience of not having whom to name in his place. His good nature and desire to oblige me got the better of his irresolution and laziness at the moment when I made this proposal to him. But now when he sees the prospect of some little trouble, he pretends not to recollect that I ever spoke to him on the subject.' (*Caldwell Papers*, II. ii. [237]).

Nevertheless, Crawford was duly elected for Renfrewshire without Hume's vote.

[1] No. 491 above.

[2] Charles James Fox (1749–1806), third son of Henry Fox, Lord Holland.

[3] Adam Smith was at this time in London.

scarce admissible, those in the Town Council, who aim at filling the Vacancy with a Friend, will strenuously object to it; and he himself cannot think of one who will make a proper Substitute.[1] I fancy, that the chief Difficulty wou'd be remov'd, if you cou'd offer to supply his Class, either as his Substitute or his Successor, with a Purpose of resigning upon his return. This notion is entirely my own, and shall never be known to Ferguson, if it appear to you improper. I shall only say, that he deserves this friendly Treatment, by his friendly Conduct, of a similar kind, towards poor Russel's [2] Family.

Pray, what strange Accounts are these we hear of Franklyn's Conduct?[3] I am very slow in believing that he has been guilty in the extreme Degree that is pretended; tho' I always knew him to be a very factious man, and Faction, next to Fanaticism, is, of all passions, the most destructive of Morality. How is it suppos'd, he got Possession of these Letters? I hear that Wedderburn's Treatment of him before the Council, was most cruel, without being in the least blameable. What a Pity!

* 496. *To* William Strahan

Dear Sir Edinburgh 1 March 1774.

I have heard of the Event of your great Cause concerning literary Property,[4] which is indeed no other than I expected:

* MS. in possession of Historical Society of Maine, Portland, Maine, U.S.A.; hitherto unpublished.

[1] Adam Ferguson had gone off abroad as travelling governor to Philip Stanhope, 5th Earl of Chesterfield, at a salary of £400 a year and a pension of £200 a year for life. The Town Council in Edinburgh were annoyed with him for leaving his Chair, and in 1774 cancelled his appointment. When he returned in 1776 he took legal proceedings against them, won his case, and was reinstated.

[2] James Russel.

[3] Benjamin Franklin was accused before the Privy Council on 29 Jan. 1774 of having by underhand means obtained possession of certain letters relating to public affairs, which he transmitted to Boston, and on the strength of which the Massachusetts Assembly petitioned the King to remove the Governor and Lieutenant-Governor. Alexander Wedderburn, as Solicitor-General, attacked him with scurrilous vigour, and he was deprived of his office of Deputy Postmaster-General of the Colonies. From that moment war with the American Colonies became inevitable.

[4] In the spring and early summer of 1774 the London booksellers were deep in litigation on the question of literary copyright. The question at

For the former Decision of the King's Bench was certainly contrary to the natural Sense of the Act of Queen Anne, and was deriv'd entirely from a groundless, tho' well-meant Subtlety of Lord Mansfield. I am sorry to hear, that the Triumph of his Enemies has been so great on the Occasion. Were it possible to revive another Cause[1] you wot of, their Triumph woud be much greater and much better founded.

I shoud be glad to know, whether you think your Interest will be much affected by this Decision, or the Interest of such as may be my Successors in the barren and perilous Adventure of Book-making. As to my Writings, I think it will be possible for me to prolong your Lease of them, even according to the Statute. I have never made a new Edition without Alterations, and even Additions, sometimes of considerable Length. If it were thought worth while, I coud transfer to you anew the Property of these; and if no Body can reprint these passages during fourteen Years after the first Publication, it woud effectually secure you so long from any pyrated Edition. I have writ a new Essay,[2] which I intended to add to the Collection; and shoud give it you in the same manner. Pray, ask of Mr Cadell, if there be any prospect of a new Edition of these pieces.

I think you ought, both for your own Interest and that of Learning, to apply for a new Law; as the Penalties, granted by the Statute of Q. Anne, are quite insufficient for your Protection.

I hope you can tell me something in justification, at least in alleviation of Dr Franklyn's Conduct. The factious Part he has all along acted must be given up by his best Friends: But I flatter myself there is nothing treacherous or unfair in his Conduct; though his Silence with regard to the method, by which he came by these Letters, leaves room for all sorts of malignant Surmizes. What pity, that a man of his Merit shoud have fallen into such unhappy Circumstances!

I remember, one day, at Lord Bathurst's,[3] the Company, among whom was his Son,[4] the present Chancellor, were speak-

issue (Donaldson *v.* Beckett) was whether this copyright was perpetual or expired after the book had been published fourteen years.

[1] The Douglas Cause.

[2] Presumably *Of the Origin of Government*, which appeared for the first time in the 1777 edition.

[3] Allen, 1st Earl Bathurst (1684–1775).

[4] Henry, 2nd Earl Bathurst (1714–94), Lord Chancellor, 1771–8; created Baron Apsley of Apsley, 1771.

ing of American Affairs; and some of them mention'd former Acts of Authority exercisd over the Colonies. I observd to them, that Nations, as well as Individuals, had their different Ages, which challeng'd a different Treatment. For Instance, My Lord, said I to the old Peer, you have sometimes, no doubt, given your Son a Whipping; and I doubt not, but it was well merited and did him much good: Yet you will not think proper at present to employ the Birch: The Colonies are no longer in their Infancy. But yet I say to you, they are still in their Nonage; and Dr Franklyn's[1] wishes to emancipate them too soon from their mother Country. I am Dear Sir

Your sincere Friend and humble Servant

David Hume

* 497. *To* William Strahan

[March 1774]

Dear Sir

I have writ you an ostensible Letter on the Subject of literary Property, which contains my real Sentiments, so far as it goes.[2] However, I shall tell you the truth; I do not forsee any such bad Consequences as you mention from laying the Property open. The Italians and French have more pompous Editions of their Classics since the Expiration of the Privileges than any we have of ours: And at least, every Bookseller, who prints a Book, will endeavour to make it as compleat and correct as he can. But when I said, that I thought Lord Mansfield's Decision founded on a vain Subtlety, I did not consider the matter in that Light, but only on a simple Consideration of the Act of Q. Anne. The Essay I mentioned is not so considerable as to [be] printed apart; yet any pyrated Edition woud be reckond incompleat that did not contain it.[3]

Yours

D. H.

* MS. at Barnbougle Castle; Hill, 274 f.

[1] *Sic* in MS.

[2] This 'ostensible' letter appears to have been handed to the booksellers' counsel, Mansfield by name, who declared at the Bar of the House of Commons on 13 May: 'I have by me letters of Mr Hume, Dr Robertson, etc., containing the warmest wishes to the petitioners, lamenting the late decision of the House of Peers as fatal to literature, and hoping that the booksellers might get speedy relief.' (*Parl. Hist.*, xvii. 1098, as quoted by Hill, 278.)

[3] *Of the Origin of Government*; see preceding letter.

* 498. *To* William Strahan

St Andrews Square 2 of April 1774

Dear Sir

There is a Subject which I was desird to mention to you, but which I delay'd, till your Application to Parliament were finish'd, that you might know on what footing your literary Property was to stand: It is with regard to Dr Wallace's manuscript, which was certainly finishd for the Press and which I think a very good Book:[1] I told his Son[2] about four or five months ago, before the Decision of the House of Peers, that he ought not to expect above 500 pounds for it; and he has return'd so far to my Sentiments, as to leave the Matter entirely to me; I shoud wish to know, therefore, what you think you cou'd afford.[3] I imagine this Decision will not very much alter the Value of literary Property; For if you coud, by a tacite convention among yourselves, make a Property of the Dauphin's Virgil,[4] without a single Line in Virgil's hand, or Ruæus's or the Dauphin's, I see not why you may not keep Possession of all your Books as before. However, this Decision throws you into some Uncertainty, and you may be cautious for some time in entering on any considerable Purchase.

Lord Kaims's Sketches[5] have here been published some weeks; and by the Reception it has met with, is not likely to be very popular, according to the prodigiously sanguine Expectations of the Author. But after his Elements of Criticism met with some Success, I shall never venture to make any Prophecy on

* MS. at Barnbougle Castle; Hill, 280 f.

[1] I conjecture that this is the book, *Advice to all true Patriots*, referred to in Letter 414 above. Robert Wallace died in 1771.

[2] George Wallace (1730–1805), admitted advocate, 1754; author of *A System of the Principles of the Law of Scotland*, &c.

[3] Strahan declined to pay £500 for the book, on the grounds that the subject was not promising and that none of Wallace's other books had enjoyed much sale. He offered, however, to print the book, take all risk of paper, print, &c., and give George Wallace half the net profits. (Letter to Hume dated 9 April 1774, quoted by Hill, 283 f., presumably from the Barker MSS.) This offer does not seem to have been accepted, nor the book published anywhere.

[4] *P. Virgilii Maronis Opera; Interpretatione et Notis illustravit Carolus Ruaeus, Soc. Jesu: Jussu Christianissimi Regis, ad Usum Serenissimi Delphini*, Paris, 1675 and 1682; 1st English edit., London, 1686.

[5] *Sketches of the History of Man*. It was published jointly by William Creech in Edinburgh, and Strahan and Cadell in London.

that head. I am glad to hear, that in your Bargain with him, you had a saving Clause to ensure you against Loss. Cou'd any such Clause be devis'd with regard to Dr Wallace's Book? In the mean time, I ask 500 pounds for it; as you desire that a positive Demand shoud always be made, which is indeed but reasonable. It is about half the Size of Lord Kaims's Sketches; and is better writ.

I am Dear Sir Yours sincerely
DAVID HUME.

* 499. *To* ANTHONY GREGSON [1]

Edinburgh St Andrews Square
5 of May 1774

Sir

I believe all the Payments which your Brother made to mine were at a time when I was abroad, and had left a Factory or Powers of Attorney with my Brother to receive Payment of all my Rents and Interest: But as these Powers have expir'd on my settling here, I believe it will be necessary for you to find a way of remitting the Money to this Place, which, I hope, it will not be difficult for you to do. As you seem to think it indifferent for your Nephew's Interest, whether the Money be pay'd once a Year or in the two Years, I shall consider it as an Obligation, if it be pay'd once a Year. I am

Sir

Your most obedient humble Servant
DAVID HUME

To Mr Anthony Gregson at Learmouth near Cornhill by Berwick

† 500. *To* JOHN HOME [2]

St. Andrew's Square, 4 June 1774.

Dear John,

The enclosed came to hand to-day, and as I take it to be directed to you, I have sent it you. If on opening it you find otherwise, you may return it to me, that I may find the true owner.

* MS. in Nat. Lib., Scotland (Watson Bequest, 609); hitherto unpublished.

† *Scots Mag.*, N.S. i, 1817, p. 9 f.; Burton, ii. 471 f.

[1] I know nothing more of this man than appears from the letter.

[2] The author of *Douglas*, not Hume's brother.

You have seen, no doubt, the specimen of a Scotch review.[1] My first conjecture was, that Carlyle was the author; but Dr Blair has convinced me that it is much more probably the production of your spiritual guide, Tom Hepburn;[2] but, whoever be the father, the child has a great deal of salt, and spirit, and humour. I wish he would continue, tho at the hazard of my getting a rap over the knuckles from time to time: for I see in this hero the spirit of a Drawcansir, who spares neither friend nor foe. I think I can reckon about twenty people, not including the King, whom he has attacked in this short performance. I hope all his spleen is not exhausted. I should desire my compliments to him, were I not afraid that he would interpret the civility as paying blackmail to him.

I am, dear John,
Yours sincerely,
DAVID HUME.

* 501. *To the* COMTESSE DE BOUFFLERS

Edinburgh, 7 of January, 1775.

Dear Madam,

I venture to write you a letter on the new year, in confidence of your goodness, that you will forgive me my long and very blameable silence.

As often as any of my acquaintance arrived from France, who I thought had a chance of giving me any information, I never failed to find them out, and make inquiries concerning you. But of late I have not been so fortunate as to meet with any satisfaction on that head; and I could no longer forbear applying to yourself, to learn every circumstance that interests me so much. There are certain seasons allotted to sinners for making their peace with Heaven. May I hope that the new year will be equally propitious to me; and obtain me, on my sincere penitence, the pardon of all past offences? I often think of you with the same attachment as ever; and though nothing extinguishes all passions so effectually as despair, I do not find

* *Priv. Corr.*, 272 and 281 f. (the pagination of this book went wrong, though the signatures of the different sheets follow at the right intervals).

[1] Burton speaks of this as a very scarce pamphlet published in 1774. It was entitled *The Scots Review* and ridiculed the antagonists of 'that great necromancer and magician David Hume'.

[2] The Rev. Thomas Hepburn (died 1777), minister of Athelstaneford, 1771–7. He is supposed to have been joint author with S. Haliburton of another satire, *Memoirs of Magopico*, which ridiculed a minister at Dunbar.

that my wish to enjoy again your amiable society, is a whit abated by that consideration, though aided by absence, time, and distance. Give me the consolation to think, that, though unworthy, I still retain some place in your memory.

I find by the public papers, that an incident has happened in the Royal Family, which, I know, could not fail to interest you. If it pave the way for your obtaining that end, which you long so naturally expected, and which from a very laudable fortitude you at last renounced, I shall rejoice. If it only rouze your sleeping hopes, it will serve to disturb that peace of mind, which is the chief, and, with health, the only blessing in human life. I would fain hope that your ideas of resignation are so fixed, as not to be disturbed even by this incident. I never write to you of public affairs, which are no object of concern between us: yet I cannot forbear expressing my joy, from the general aspect of things as it appears to us at a distance, that your friend is likely to have a shining theatre opened to his virtues, which have too long been suppressed by the malignity of fortune.[1] I congratulate you upon it. Durst I venture to address himself, I should also congratulate him. My profound regard to him, and my sense of his goodness, gives me a title which I hope you will plead in my favour. But even to those who are placed at a distance, it must appear a beautiful and interesting spectacle, to see so firm and steady and uniform a conduct crowned at the last with the success which it has so well merited.

From so great an object to descend to myself, would form a very abrupt transition. I cannot, however, forbear informing you, that I am settled here in peace and tranquillity and opulence; and except that I am beginning to feel some of the infirmities of old age, in all other respects my situation may pass for tolerable. I hope yours is better than tolerable, though to be perfectly desirable is never to be expected.

* 502. *To* [James *or* Thomas Coutts]

Edinburgh 14 of Feby 1775

Dear Sir

An Affair of considerable Importance has occurr'd in which I beg your Assistance and Good Offices. There is a Prospect

* MS., R.S.E.; hitherto unpublished.

[1] A reference to the recall of the Parlement of Paris in Nov. 1774.

that my Nephew, Cornet Hume,[1] of Lord Townsend's Dragoons, may have the Offer of a Lieutenancy in the same Regiment, upon Payment of the Difference, which, I believe, is rated at 250 pounds. But be it more or less, I am very desirous of accepting the Offer. Be so good, therefore, as to send to Cox and Mair, the Agents of the Regiment, and tell them that the Money for the Purchase, is in your hands and ready to be pay'd. Perhaps, the Money you may have of mine, may not amount to the whole Sum; but whatever it is, be pleas'd to advance it in case of a demand from the Agents, and draw on me at Sight for the Remainder; if you do not rather chuse, that this small Debt shou'd lie on me, till the Payment of my next quarterly Pension. You know how important the gaining of a Step is to a young Officer; so that, as I do not question your Exactness in any thing, I can still less doubt of it on this Occasion. I am Dear Sir

Your most obedient humble Servant
DAVID HUME

* 503. *To* COLONEL JAMES EDMONSTOUNE

Edinburgh, 23 March 1775.

Caro Giuseppe,

No request can be more obliging than yours;[2] and no party could have been proposed to any place, or with any company, more agreeable to me. But you remember what a plague I was to every body and to myself on my last journey; and you may recollect that I made a vow, in the bitterness of my distress, never more to leave my own house, nor lie out of my own bed. This vow I have religiously kept, except two or three days last autumn, when I went to my brother's; and tho I could scarcely there esteem myself from home, I resolved never more to pay them a visit. You have not a bed cool enough for me, which proceeds not from any distemper or disorder, but from a peculiarity of constitution, that has been gradually increasing on me these last twelve years. I am in very good health: but let me tell you, that you express yourself strangely when you say I have been *complaining*. How could you imagine that I could ever complain, even tho *fractus illabatur orbis*? I beseech you, know

* Burton, ii. 473.

[1] Joseph Home.

[2] Edmonstoune's letter, to which this appears to be a reply, is not extant among the MSS., R.S.E.

better the people to whom you speak, and the force of the terms you make use of. Miss Keiths [1] desired me to tell you, that some time ago they had a letter from Sir Basil,[2] by which they learn that your request with regard to Maillet's [3] friend, is complied with.

My compliments to Mrs Edmonstoune; embrace Jean Jacques in my name.

Dear Guidelianus, I am ever yours,

DAVID HUME.[4]

* 504. *To* MESSRS. JAMES *and* THOMAS COUTTS

Dear Sir Edinburgh 5 of April. 1775

Please pay to Cornet Hume, my Nephew, the Sum of a hundred and ten pounds, either in Money or by Letters of Credit on France,[5] and place it to my Account.

I have directed him to give you a Letter of Attorney on the Agents of the Regiment, Cox and Mair, for ten Months pay; and in consequence of this Letter of Attorney, I beg the favour of you to draw his Pay, and to give him presently an additional Letter of Credit for one hundred and twenty pounds. Whatever his pay shall fall short of this Sum of one hundred and twenty pounds, please place to my Account. I am Dear Sir

Your most obedient & most humble Servant

To Mess[rs] James & Thomas Coutts in Co[y] DAVID HUME

† 505. *To the* COMTESSE DE BOUFFLERS

Edinburgh, 17 April, 1775.

Your entering, dear Madam, into so particular a detail of your situation, was very satisfactory and agreeable to me; and

* MS., R.S.E.; hitherto unpublished. † *Priv. Corr.*, 282 ff.

[1] Jenny and Anne Murray Keith, daughters of Ambassador Keith. Anne (1736–1818), the younger daughter, was a friend of Walter Scott's, and was used by him as the prototype of Mrs. Bethune Baliol in the *Chronicles of the Canongate*. She was a great favourite in Edinburgh society.

[2] Sir Basil Keith (died 1777), second son of Ambassador Keith; served in the navy and died Governor of Jamaica.

[3] *Sic* in Burton's text. The reference is probably to Paul-Henri Mallet (1730–1807), a native of Geneva, author of *Introduction à l'Histoire de Dannemarc*. He accompanied Edmonstoune and Lord Mountstuart on a tour through Italy, and came with them to England.

[4] Edmonstoune's reply is given in Appendix C below.

[5] Joseph Home was going to France for some months (see next Letter).

I give you my sincere thanks for it.[1] I applaud extremely your way of thinking. It is both generous and discreet, and will contribute no less to your honour than your tranquillity of mind. I thought that the event you hint at, had been public and avowed. The lady I cannot recollect, though it is probable I did know her, either more or less. I should be sorry to see you even seemingly put on a level with such a person. Your letter came safely to hand, and untouched: it was conveyed under a frank of Lord Stormont's;[2] and no private letters are ever opened here. I have observed your orders with regard to it.

You are mistaken, my dear Madam: I am sufficiently of an age to feel the decline of life, and I feel it sensibly. I have, however, been always and still am very temperate. The only debauches I ever was guilty of, were those of study; and even these were moderate; for I was always very careful of my health, by using exercise. I own that this country does not entirely please me, particularly the climate. I sometimes entertain the notion of returning to France; but as I could not now, at my years, bear the tumult of Paris (and all provincial towns are unknown to me), I shall never probably carry this idea into execution.[3]

You make me prick up my ears, and lend attention, when you speak of coming over to England. I beseech you, inform me some time before you put that design in execution. I should endeavour to meet you there; which would be much better than your taking so long a journey to so remote a part of the world, where there is little worthy your curiosity.

I have a nephew, a brother's son,[4] who will pass through

[1] Mme de Boufflers's letter, to which this is an answer, is not extant among the MSS., R.S.E. The last sentence of the first paragraph in the text above probably means that she had asked Hume to destroy it, and that he did so.

[2] British Ambassador at Paris. He left Paris for London in the middle of March.

[3] Replying to this on [28 May 1775], Mme de Boufflers says: 'Seroit-il possible en effet, que vous eussies quelque legere idée de revenir en France? En verité vous ne devies pas me la communiquer, a moins de vouloir la realiser. Ce mot que vous m'en dites a renouvellé tous mes regrets, en me faisant concevoir des esperances. Vous me rendries la plus heureuse personne du monde, si vous prenies cette resolution, et je me flatte que vous vous trouveries heureux vous meme. Il y a dans le Temple une maison fort jolie que vous pourries louer. Le jardin est separé du mien par un mur, ou l'on feroit une porte. Nous nous verrions a tous momens. Nous dinerions tous les jours ensemble. Vous series seul ou en compagnie selon votre volonté . . .' (MS., R.S.E.; *Eminent Persons*, 246).

[4] Joseph Home (see preceding letter).

Paris some time in the month of June. I have given him orders to pay his respects to you. He is an officer of cavalry; and, in the interval of his duty, proposes to pass eight or nine months in a garrison town in France, for his improvement in the language and in his profession. Metz is the place fixed on. He has, as you will see, an agreeable figure; and if he could speak the language, his behaviour and conversation is very good; so that I doubt not but he will be acceptable to the good company of the place. But, in order to his reception, it will be necessary to have him recommended to the governor of the province, who, I hear, is M. Darmentieres,[1] and to the governor of the town, M. de Conflans.[2] The former I know but a very little; the second not at all. I use the freedom to apply to you for procuring him letters of recommendation. Be so good as to ask them of any of your acquaintance, if the governors be not known to you. In case you should not be at Paris, when my nephew passes, I have directed him to leave a letter for you. When you receive it, be so good as to send him up the letters; and I have directed him to call again at your hotel in the Temple, where he may receive them. He will be so little time at Paris, and speaks the language so imperfectly, that I dare not recommend him to your more particular notice, though I am persuaded you would like him very much, upon farther acquaintance. He is a piece of a scholar too, and passes for a prodigy of learning in his regiment. I doubt not but he will make a figure in that respect among the young officers.

You never mention to me Madame de Barbantane. Does she live with her pupil, and has she much satisfaction in that course of life? I beg my best respects to her.

* 506. *To* [JAMES *or* THOMAS COUTTS]

[Edinburgh, Spring of 1775.]

. . . I see by the Gazette, that he[3] is now a Lieutenant. I suppose you have been so good as to advance the Money

* MS., R.S.E.; hitherto unpublished. There is only a fragment of the autograph left, the rest having been torn away.

[1] Louis de Conflans de Brienne (1711–74), marquis d'Armentières. Hume's information was out of date: M. d'Armentières had been in command at Metz, but had died on 18 Jan. 1774. Actually it was Marshal the duc de Broglie who was in command at Metz at this time.

[2] Hubert de Brienne (1690–1777), comte de Conflans.

[3] Joseph Home.

to the Agent. My Intention was that the Fees of the Commission shoud also be advanced to him; and I shoud be glad to know the Amount of the whole. I suppose, that the whole Money, which you have advanced by my Order, exceeds my Money in your hands; and you may either draw on me for the Ballance at sight, or wait till my funds shall re-imburse you. I am Dear Sir

Your most obedient humble Servant
DAVID HUME

* 507. *To* DAVID HUME THE YOUNGER

Dear Davy. St. Andrews Square 30 of Augt 1775.

Your Letter gave me Satisfaction, and I approve very much of your Course of Study: But I think you are unreasonably diffident of Yourself with regard to the *Copia verborum*: You are not wanting in that particular, [consider][1]ing you as a Beginner; and the Course you take will tend very much to [produce gr][1]eater Facility, as well as Correctness of Expression. *Stylus est optimus [mágis][1]ter eloquentiæ.*[2] These, if not the Words, are the Sense of Quinctilian. For I cite from Memory. You know that the Roman *Stylus* was the same as the Pen.

I had a Letter to day from Mr Millar,[3] who tells me, that he expects to see you in the first Monday of November.

I do not go to Inverara so soon as I proposd: It will be next week before I set out.[4] I think I am the better for Jaunting; though in the main I shoud better like better[5] to stay at home.

My Compliments to your Mother: I am glad she has heard from Josey; but I wonder what has detain'd him so long at Paris.

I fancy you and Jock are very happy at present in your Field Sports: And your Father will not be displeasd to see the favourable Progress of the Harvest.

I am Dear Davy Your affectionate Uncle
DAVID HUME

Mr David Home at Ninewells with a great Coat

* MS., R.S.E.; Burton, ii. 474 f.

[1] MS. torn.

[2] The correct quotation is: 'Stylus optimus et praestantissimus dicendi effector ac magister.' And it occurs, not in Quintilian, but in Cicero, *de Or.*, i. 33. 150.

[3] Professor John Millar of Glasgow.

[4] The letters of Baron Mure to Hume given in Appendix C below throw light on this visit to Inveraray and on Hume's reluctance to leave home for any reason at all.

[5] *Sic* in MS.

* 508. *To* John Home

St. Andrew's Square, Sept. 20, 1775.

Dear John,

Of all the vices of language, the least excusable is the want of perspicuity; for, as words were instituted by men, merely for conveying their ideas to each other, the employing of words without meaning is a palpable abuse, which departs from the very original purpose and intention of language. It is also to be observed, that any ambiguity in expression is next to the having no meaning at all; and is indeed a species of it; for while the hearer or reader is perplexed between different meanings, he can assign no determinate idea to the speaker or writer; and may, on that account, say with Ovid, 'Inopem me copia fecit.' For this reason, all eminent rhetoricians and grammarians, both ancient and modern, have insisted on perspicuity of language as an essential quality; without which, all ornaments of diction are vain and fruitless. Quinctilian carries the matter so far, as to condemn this expression, *vidi hominem librum legentem*; because, says he, *legentem* may construe as well with *librum* as *hominem*; though one would think, that the sense were here sufficient to prevent all ambiguity. In conformity to this way of thinking, Vaugelas, the first great grammarian of France, will not permit, that any one have recourse to the sense, in order to explain the meaning of the words; because, says he, it is the business of the words to explain the sense—not of the sense to give a determinate meaning to the words; and this practice is reversing the order of nature; like the custom of the Romans (he might have added, the Greeks), in their saturnalia, who made the slaves the masters; for you may learn from Lucian, that the Greeks practised the same frolic during the festival of Saturn, whom they called *Χρονος*.

Now, to apply, and to come to the use of this principle, I must observe to you, that your last letter, besides a continued want of distinctness in the form of the literal characters, has plainly transgressed the essential rule above-mentioned, of grammar and rhetoric. You say, that Coutts has complained to you of not hearing from me; had you said either James or Thomas, I could have understood your meaning. About two months ago, I heard that James complained of me in this respect; and I wrote to him, tho then abroad, making an

* Mackenzie, *Home*, 158 ff.; Burton, ii. 475 f.

apology for my being one of the subscribers of a paper which gave him some offence. I was afraid he had not received mine. The letter of Thomas, I conceived to be only a circular letter, informing me of a change in the firm of the house: and having answered it a few days ago, by giving him some directions about disposing of my money, which proved that I intended to remain a customer to the shop; it happens, therefore, luckily, that I had obviated all objections to my conduct on both sides.

In turning over my papers, I find a manuscript journal of the last Rebellion, which is at your service.[1] I hope Mrs Home is better, and will soon be able to execute her journey. Are you to be in town soon?

Yours, without ambiguity, circumlocution, or mental reservation,

DAVID HUME.

* 509. *To* WILLIAM STRAHAN

Dear Sir Edinburgh 26 of Octr 1775

I have often regreted the Interruption of our Correspondence: But when you ceas'd to be a speculative Politician and became a practical one,[2] I coud no longer expect you woud be so communicative or impartial as formerly on that head; and my object with regard to Authorship, was, for a time, at an End. The Reason of the present Trouble is of a different kind: Dr Trail,[3] the Professor of Divinity at Glasgow, is dead; and Dr Wight, the present Professor of Church History, is a Candidate for the Office: The place is filled by a Vote of the Professors: You are understood to have great influence with Wilson, the Professor of Astronomy: And I interest myself extremely in Dr Wight's success: These are my Reasons for writing to you. But I must also tell you my Reasons for interesting myself so much in Dr Wight's Behalf. He is a particular Friend of mine: He is very much connected with all mine and your particular Friends in the Church: He is a very gentleman-like agreeable Man: And above all, he is (without which I shoud not interest

* MS. at Barnbougle Castle; Hill, 287 ff.; printed in part in the *London Chronicle*, 12–14 June, 1777.

[1] Possibly John Home's own MS. His *History of the Rebellion* did not appear till 1802, but he began to gather the materials for it many years before.

[2] Strahan became M.P. for Malmesbury in 1774.

[3] Robert Trail was appointed Professor of Oriental Languages in Glasgow in 1761, and promoted to be Professor of Divinity the same year.

myself for him) a very sound and orthodox Divine. The case of Dr Trail, (his predecessor, as I hope) was somewhat particular with regard to Orthodoxy: He was very laudably a declar'd Enemy to all Heretics, Socinians, Arians, Anti-Trinitarians, Arminians, Erastians, Sabellians, Pelagians, Semi-pelagians: In short, of every Sect, whose name terminated in *ian*, except Presbyterian, to whom he had a declar'd and passionate Attachment. He said, that it signify'd nothing to pick out a little straggling Absurdity, here and there, from the System; while the whole immense Chaos, sufficient to over-whelm Heaven and Earth, still remain'd entire, and must still remain. But in Prosecution of these Views (which one cannot much blame) he mix'd a little of the Acrimony of his own Temper; and, perhaps undesignedly, sent away all the Students of Divinity very zealous Bigots, which had a very bad Effect on the Clergy of that Neighbourhood. Now, I shall answer for Dr Wight, that his Pupils shall have all the Orthodoxy, without the Bigotry, instill'd into them by his Predecessor. I believe Dr Robertson will write you on the same Subject; and I beg you woud not lose any time in applying to Mr Wilson, in case he shoud take any other Engagements, tho we do not yet hear of any other Candidate.

I must, before we part, have a little Stroke of Politics with you, notwithstanding my Resolution to the contrary. We hear that some of the Ministers have propos'd in Council, that both Fleet and Army be withdrawn from America, and these Colonists be left entirely to themselves. I wish I had been a Member of His Majesty's Cabinet Council, that I might have seconded this Opinion. I shoud have said, that this Measure only anticipates the necessary Course of Events a few Years; that a forced and every day more precarious Monopoly of about 6 or 700,000 Pounds a year of Manufactures, was not worth contending for; that we shoud preserve the greater part of this Trade even if the Ports of America were open to all Nations; that it was very likely, in our method of proceeding, that we shoud be disappointed in our Scheme of conquering the Colonies; and that we ought to think beforehand how we were to govern them, after they were conquer'd. Arbitrary Power can extend its oppressive Arm to the Antipodes; but a limited Government can never long be upheld at a distance, even where no Disgusts have interven'd: Much less, where such violent Animosities have taken place. We must, therefore, annul all the Charters;

abolish every democratical Power in every Colony; repeal the Habeas Corpus Act with regard to them; invest every Governor with full discretionary or arbitrary Powers; confiscate the Estates of all the chief Planters; and hang three fourths of their Clergy. To execute such Acts of destructive Violence twenty thousand Men will not be sufficient; nor thirty thousand to maintain them, in so wide and disjointed a Territory. And who are to pay so great an Army? The Colonists cannot at any time, much less after reducing them to such a State of Desolation: We ought not, and indeed cannot, in the over-loaded or rather over-whelm'd and totally ruin'd State of our Finances. Let us, therefore, lay aside all Anger; shake hands, and part Friends. Or if we retain any anger, let it only be against ourselves for our past Folly; and against that wicked Madman, Pitt; who has reducd us to our present Condition. *Dixi.*[1]

But we must not part, without my also saying something as an Author. I have not yet thrown up so much all Memory of that Character. There is a short Advertisement,[2] which I wish I had prefix'd to the second Volume of the Essays and Treatises in the last Edition. I send you a Copy of it. Please to enquire at the Warehouse, if any considerable Number of that Edition remain on hands; and if there do, I beg the favour of you, that you woud throw off an equal Number of this Advertisement, and give out no more Copies without prefixing it to the second volume. It is a compleat Answer to Dr Reid [3] and to that bigotted silly Fellow, Beattie.[4]

1 Replying on 30 Oct. 1775, Strahan says he differs *toto cælo* from Hume on the subject of America. '. . . I am entirely for coercive Methods with those obstinate madmen: and why should we despair of success? Why should we suffer the Empire to be so dismembered, without the utmost Exertions on our Part? I see nothing so very formidable in this Business, if we become a little more unanimous, and could stop the mouths of domestic Traitors, from whence the Evil originated. Not that I wish to enslave the Colonists, or to make them one jot less happy than ourselves; but I am for keeping them subordinate to the British Legislature, and their Trade in a reasonable Degree, subservient to the Interest of the Mother Country; an advantage she well deserves, but which she must inevitably lose, if they are emancipated as you propose. I am really surprised you are of a different opinion. . . .' (MS., R.S.E.; *Eminent Persons*, 100; Hill, 304.)

2 This is the famous Advertisement disowning the *Treatise* as a juvenile production, complaining that critics have quoted it against him, and asking that in future only the *Essays and Treatises* be taken to represent his philosophical opinions.

3 Thomas Reid, author of *Inquiry into the Human Mind.*

4 James Beattie (1735–1803), Professor of Moral Philosophy, Marischal

I believe that I have formerly mention'd to you, that no new Editions shoud be made of any of my Writings, without mentioning it to me; I shall still have some Corrections to make. By Calculation, or rather Conjecture from former Sales, the last Edition of my History shoud be nearly sold off: Pray inform yourself whether it be not so: And how many remain on hand.[1]

I am with great Sincerity Dear Sir
Your affectionate humble Servant
DAVID HUME.

* 510. *To* BARON MURE OF CALDWELL

St David's Street[2] 27 of Octr 1775

Oh! Dear Baron, you have thrown me into Agonies and almost into Convulsions by your Request.[3] You ask what seems reasonable, what seems a mere trifle; yet am I so unfit for it, that it is almost impossible for me to comply. You are much fitter yourself. That Address, by which you gain'd immortal honour, was done altogether without my Knowledge, I mean, that after the Suppression of the late Rebellion.[4] Here is Lord

* MS., R.S.E.; *Lit. Gazette*, 1821, p. 637; *Caldwell Papers*, II. ii. 259 f.; Burton ii. 478 f. (incomplete).

College, Aberdeen, 1760; author of *Original Poems and Translations*, 1760, 2nd edit. enlarged, 1766; *Essay on the Origin and Immutability of Truth* (his attack on Hume), 1770; and *The Minstrel*, 1771–4.

[1] Strahan replied that there were 400 copies in stock, and that he intended to reprint the book next summer. But the next edition did not appear till 1778.

[2] This is now called South St. David Street; it runs from Princes Street to the south-west corner of St. Andrew's Square. Tradition says that it was named, as a joke against Hume, by Nancy Orde, daughter of Chief Baron Orde; that she chalked up the name on the gable of Hume's house during the night; and that when Hume's servant, much incensed, reported to him what had been done, he told her good-humouredly that many a better man had been called a saint before.

[3] Mure's letter is not extant among the MSS., R.S.E.; but it is clear from Hume's that Mure had asked him to draft a loyal address to the King from the freeholders of Renfrewshire, recommending forcible measures against the American Colonists. Such addresses were pouring in at this time from many parts of the country.

[4] *The Humble Address of the Justices of the Peace, Freeholders, and Gentlemen of the County of Renfrew to the King's Most Excellent Majesty*, 1746; a document prepared by Mure, and printed in *Caldwell Papers*, II. i. 79 f.

Home teizing me for an Address from the Merse; and I have constantly refus'd him. Besides, I am an American in my Principles, and wish we woud let them alone to govern or misgovern themselves as they think proper: The Affair is of no Consequence, or of little Consequence to us. If the County of Renfrew think it indispensably necessary for them to interpose in public Matters, I wish they woud advise the King first to punish those insolent Rascals in London and Middlessex, who daily insult him and the whole Legislature, before he think of America. Ask him, how he can expect, that a form of Government will maintain an Authority at 3000 Miles distance when it cannot make itself be respected or even treated with common Decency at home. Tell him, that Lord North, tho in appearance a worthy Gentleman, has not a head for these great Operations, and that if fifty thousand Men, and twenty Millions of Money were entrusted to such a lukewarm Coward as Gage,[1] they never coud produce any Effect. These are Objects worthy of the respectable County of Renfrew, not mauling the poor infatuated Americans in the other Hemisphere.

In return for my thus sketching out to you the Object of an Address, I have a favour to ask of you. Dr Trail, the Professor of Divinity, is dead, and knows now whether there be any Truth in all those Doctrines, which he taught, and of which he did not believe a word while alive. Dr Wight is a Candidate for the Chair. I know you wish him well, and will favour him: But will you do it with sufficient Zeal? I wish you woud exert Yourself. He is a sensible, good humourd, Gentleman-like Fellow, and as sound and orthodox as you coud wish. If you can engage the Principal [2] in his Interests, it will be a great Point gaind. Wight is much connected with all our Friends here, whom I know you wish to oblige.

You are to be at Hamilton, I hear, some day next week. Tell me the day; I will meet you at Coltness, that is, Weather Health & Humour serving.

Yours

D H

To The Hon[ble] Baron Mure at Caldwal near Glasgow.

[1] The Hon. Thomas Gage (1721–87), C.-in-C. in North America, 1763–72, and again in 1775; Governor of Massachusetts, 1774; was recalled to England in Aug. 1775, but promoted in October.

[2] Leechman.

* 511. *To* William Strahan

Edinburgh 13 of Novr 1775

Dear Sir

Your Memory has fail'd you.[1] The last Quarto Edition of my philosophical Pieces in 1768 was in two Volumes, and this Advertisement may be prefixed to the second Volume. There was another Quarto Edition in one Volume six or seven Years before; but that Edition must be all sold off, as you have made four or five Editions since. Your Correction is certainly just; and I had evidently been guilty of an Error in my Pen.[2]

I am glad to find there is a Prospect of a new Edition of my History.[3] I was indeed apprehensive, that the blind Rage of Party had entirely obstructed the Sale of it. I am as anxious of Correctness as if I were writing to Greeks or French; and besides frequent Revisals, which I have given it since the last Edition, I shall again run over it very carefully, and shall send you a corrected Copy. About six Weeks hence, I shall send off by the Waggon the four first Volumes; and shall direct them to Mr Cadel's Shop, which will be more easily found than your House. The other four Volumes shall follow at Leizure. I remember an Author, who says, that one half of a man's Life is too little to write a Book; and the other half to correct it. I think, that I am more agreeably employ'd for myself in this manner, and perhaps more profitably for you, than if I were writing such Volumes as Macpherson's History,[4] one of the most wretched *Productions* that ever came from your Press.

I am sorry, that I cannot agree with you, in your hopes of subduing and what is more difficult, of governing America. Think only of the great Kingdom of France which is within a days sailing of the small Island of Corsica; yet has not been able, in eight or nine Years, to subdue and govern it, contrary to [*the*] *Sentiments of the Inhabitants. But the worst Effect of the Loss of America, will not be the Detriment to our*

* MS. at Barnbougle Castle; Hill, 307 f.

[1] Strahan, writing on 30 Oct. 1775, had said: 'The *Advertisement* (a very proper one) shall be instantly printed, and annexed to all the *Essays* that still remain. . . .' (MS., R.S.E.).

[2] This must refer to some correction made in the Advertisement itself, of which Strahan may have sent a proof. There is nothing in his letter of 30 Oct. to which it can refer.

[3] See note 1 on p. 302 above.

[4] *The History of Great Britain from the Restoration to the Accession of the House of Hanover*, by James Macpherson, Cadell, London, 2 vols., 4to, 1775.

Manufactures, which will be a mere trifle, or to our Navigation, which will not be considerable; but to the Credit and Reputation of Government, which has already but too little Authority. You will probably see a Scene of Anarchy and Confusion open'd at home, the best Consequence of which is a settled Plan of arbitrary Power; the worst, total Ruin and Destruction.

I am extremely oblig'd to you for your Letter to Professor Wilson.[1] I am afraid, however, that all Efforts in favour of Dr Wight will be in vain.[2] It seems, Dr Hunter[3] supports a Friend of his; and nothing can be refusd him by the University.

I am Dear Sir Yours most sincerely

DAVID HUME.

* 512. *To* DAVID HUME THE YOUNGER

Edinburgh 8 of Decr 1775

Dear Davy

All your Letters both to me and to your Father have [given][4] great Satisfaction, particularly your last: And in return, I must give y[ou the] Satisfaction of telling you, that Mr Millar[5] is very well pleas'd with you [ ] no less than you with him. He complains only of one thing, which [is not the] usual Complaint of Tutors against their Pupils, to wit, that he is afraid you [apply yourself too] close, and may hurt your Health by too assiduous Study. I shoud not men[tion this] if I had the least Apprehension, that a hint of this Nature woud m[ake you] relax too much: But I cannot forbear saying, that every day, fair or fou[l, you] ought to use some Exercise: Relaxation for Amusement you may use [or not] as you fancy, but that for Health is absolutely necessary. When I was [of your] Age, I was inclind to give in to Excesses of the same kind; and I remember [a Story] told me by a Friend, the present Lord Pitfour: A man

* MS., R.S.E.; Burton, ii. 480 ff.

[1] See Letter 509 above. Writing on 30 Oct., Strahan says: '. . . The character you give of Dr. Wight (for I remember not of hearing anything of him till now) is a very amiable one; but indeed I could have no objection to a Divine of your recommending, who have laboured so much all your Life to extinguish that intolerant spirit, which is the Bane of true Virtue, and of the Happiness of Society.'

[2] Dr. James Baillie was appointed to the Chair; Wight succeeded him in 1778.

[3] Almost certainly Dr. William Hunter.

[4] A strip has been torn off the edge of the autograph, and all the words, or parts of words, in square brackets are conjectures.

[5] Professor John Millar of Glasgow.

was riding, with [great] Violence, and running his Horse quite out of Wind: He stopt a moment to a[sk when] he might reach a particular Place. In two Hours, reply'd the Countreym[an, if you] will go slower: In four, if you be in such a Hurry. Bad Health, be[sides other] Inconveniences, is the greatest Interruption to Study in the World.

I cannot but agree with Mr Millar, that the Republican Form of [Government] is by far the best.[1] The antient Republics were somewhat ferocious, and torn [internally] by bloody Factions; but they were still much preferable to the Monarchies or [Aristocracies] which seem to have been quite intolerable. Modern Manners have corrected this Abuse; and all the Republics in Europe, without Exception, are so well governd, that one is at a Loss to which we shoud give the Preference. But what is this general Subject of Speculation to our Purpose? For besides, that an establishd Government [cannot] without the most criminal Imputation, be disjointed from any Speculation; [Republicanism] is only fitted for a small State: And any Attempt towards it can in our [Country], produce only Anarchy, which is the immediate Forerunner of Despotism. [Will he] tell us, what is that form of a Republic which we must aspire to? Or [will the Revol]ution be afterward decided by the Sword? [One] great Advantage of a Commonwealth over our mixt Monarchy is, that it [woud consid]erably abridge our Liberty, which is growing to such an Extreme, as to be incom[patible wi]th all Government. Such Fools are they, who perpetually cry out Liberty: [and think to] augment it, by shaking off the Monarchy.

I have not heard from Josey for some time, which you may believe, has produc'd [anxious Re]flections in some of your Friends. But to show you, that you are not forgot[ten,] I showd Mr Millar's Letter to your Mother; I am afraid, said she, that [I see] some Symptoms of a Consumption in poor Davy.

[I a]m far from thinking Mr Millar's Demands in point of Money unrea[sonable. On] the contrary, I believe that I never laid out Money to better Purpose.

[Ha]rrington[2] is an Author of Genius; but chimerical. No Laws, however rigorous, [woud ma]ke his Agrarian practicable.

[1] Millar was a noted Radical, and his later association with the Friends of the People, at the time of the French Revolution, brought him into not a little disrepute.

[2] James Harrington (1611–77), author of *Oceana*, 1656.

And as the People have only a Negative, the [Senate] woud perpetually gain Ground upon them. You remember, that Montesquieu says, that Harrington establishing his Oceana in opposition to the English Constitution is like the blind Men who built Chalcedon on the opposite [Shore] to the Seat of Byzantium. I ask you Pardon for not writing to you [sooner] but beg the Continuance of your Correspondence. My Compliments to [Mr Millar,] to whom I owe a Letter. I am Your affectionate Uncle

DAVID HUME

To Mr David Home at Mr Professor Millar's at Glasgow

* 513. *To* JOHN HOME

Edinburgh, 8th February, 1776.

Dear Tyrtæus,[1]

It is a remark of Dr Swift's, that no man in London ever complained of his being neglected by his friends in the country. Your complaint of me is the more flattering.

Two posts ago, I received, under a frank of General Fraser's,[2] a pamphlet, entitled *A Letter from An Officer Retired.*[3] It is a very good pamphlet; and I conjecture you to be the author. Sallust makes it a question, whether the writer or the performer of good things has the preference? and he ascribes the greater praise to the latter. It is happy for you, that you may rest your fame on either. I here allude to what you have done for Ferguson.[4]

But, pray, why do you say, that the post of Boston is like the camp of Pirna? I fancy our troops can be withdrawn thence without any difficulty.

I make no doubt, since you sound the trumpet for war against the Americans, that you have a plan ready for governing them,

* Mackenzie, *Home*, 160 f.; Burton, ii. 482 f.

[1] A joke against Home for his martial spirit. Tyrtaeus was the poet whose songs inspired the Lacedemonians to deeds of valour.

[2] Simon Fraser (1726–82), Master of Lovat until attainted in 1746; pardoned, 1750; raised 78th or Fraser Highlanders, 1757; Major-Gen., 1771; M.P. for Inverness-shire, 1761–82.

[3] *A Letter from an Officer, retired, to his Son in Parliament*, pp. 38, 8vo, London, 1776. This pamphlet is ascribed in Halkett and Laing to 'M. J. Home'. The authority is not stated.

[4] Clearly Adam Ferguson. But I do not know what John Home had done for him at this time, unless it was to lend him £200 on note of hand (see Mackenzie, *Home*, 59).

after they are subdued; but you will not subdue them, unless they break in pieces among themselves—an event very probable. It is a wonder it has not happened sooner. But no man can foretell how far these frenzies of the people may be carried.

Yours

David Hume

* 514. *To* Adam Smith

Dear Smith Edinburgh 8 of Feby 1776

I am as lazy a Correspondent as you; yet my Anxiety about you makes me write.

By all Accounts, your Book[1] has been printed long ago; yet it has never yet been so much as advertised. What is the Reason? If you wait till the Fate of America be decided, you may wait long.

By all accounts, you intend to settle with us this Spring: Yet we hear no more of it: What is the Reason? Your Chamber in my House is always unoccupyed: I am always at home: I expect you to land here.

I have been, am, and shall be probably in an indifferent State of Health. I weighed myself t'other day, and find I have fallen five compleat Stones. If you delay much longer, I shall probably disappear altogether.

The Duke of Bucleugh tells me, that you are very zealous in American Affairs. My Notion is, that the Matter is not so important as is commonly imagind. If I be mistaken, I shall probably correct my Error, when I see you or read you. Our Navigation and general Commerce may suffer more than our Manufactures. Shoud London fall as much in its Size, as I have done, it will be the better. It is nothing but a Hulk of bad and unclean Humours. Yours David Hume

To Adam Smith Esq[r] at the British Coffee-house, Charing cross London

† 515. *To* William Strahan

Dear Sir Edinburgh 11 of Feby 1776.

Last Monday, I sent to the Newcastle Waggon the four first Volumes corrected of my History. They are directed to Mr

* MS., R.S.E.; Burton, ii. 483 f.

† MS. at Barnbougle Castle; Hill, 311.

[1] *The Wealth of Nations.*

Cadell. You will see by the Margins, that I have not been idle: And as the Corrections have cost me a great deal of care and Attention, I am anxious that the Books be safely deliver'd. They may arrive about three Weeks hence; about which time, if Mr Cadell does not receive them, I beg, that he would take the trouble of enquiring about them; and as soon as they come to hand, let me know of it by a Line. The other Volumes will be ready, whenever the Press demands them; of which you will be so good as to inform me in time.

I hope you will employ one of your most careful Compositors in this Edition: For as it is the last, which, at my Age and in my State of Health, I can hope to see, I wish to leave it correct. I think that it will not be prudent in you, to make this Edition more numerous than the former one.

I wonder what Smith means by not publishing. I am glad to see my Friend Gibbon advertised:[1] I am confident it will be a very good Book; though I am at a Loss to conceive where he finds materials for a Volume from Trajan to Constantine. Be so good as to make my Compliments to him: The Book has not yet arrived here.

I am Dear Sir very sincerely
Your most obedient humble Servant
DAVID HUME.

* 516. *To* EDWARD GIBBON

Edinburgh 18 of March 1776.

Dear Sir

As I ran through your Volume of History with a great deal of Avidity and Impatience, I cannot forbear discovering somewhat of the same Impatience in returning you thanks for your agreeable Present, and expressing the Satisfaction which the Performance has given me. Whether I consider the Dignity of your Style, the Depth of your Matter, or the Extensiveness of your Learning, I must regard the Work as equally the Object of Esteem; and I own, that if I had not previously had the Happiness of your personal Acquaintance, such a Performance, from an Englishman in our Age, woud have given me some Surprize.

* B.M. Addit. MSS. 34886 (Gibbon Papers, XIII), fo. 65; Gibbon, *Autobiographies*, 312 f., n.; Burton, ii. 484 f.

[1] The first volume of the *Decline and Fall of the Roman Empire* was published on 20 February.

You may smile at this Sentiment; but as it seems to me that your Countrymen, for almost a whole Generation, have given themselves up to barbarous and absurd Faction, and have totally neglected all polite Letters, I no longer expected any valuable Production ever to come from them. I know it will give you Pleasure (as it did me), to find that all the Men of Letters in this Place concur in their Admiration of your Work, and in their anxious Desire of your continuing it.

When I heard of your Undertaking (which was some time ago), I own I was a little curious to see how you woud extricate yourself from the Subject of your two last Chapters.[1] I think you have observ'd a very prudent Temperament; but it was impossible to treat the Subject so as not to give Grounds of Suspicion against you, and you may expect that a Clamour will arise. This, if anything, will retard your Success with the Public; for in every other respect your Work is calculated to be popular. But, among many other marks of Decline, the Prevalence of Superstition in England, prognosticates the Fall of Philosophy and Decay of Taste; and though no body be more capable than you to revive them, you will probably find a Struggle in your first Advances.[2]

I see you entertain a great Doubt with regard to the Authenticity of the Poems of Ossian.[3] You are certainly right in so doing. It is, indeed, strange, that any men of Sense coud have imagin'd it possible, that above twenty thousand Verses, along with numberless historical Facts, could have been preservd by oral Tradition during fifty Generations, by the rudest, perhaps, of all European Nations; the most necessitous, the most turbulent, and the most unsettled. Where a Supposition is so contrary to common Sense, any positive Evidence of it ought never

[1] The famous 15th and 16th chapters, on 'The Progress of the Christian Religion, and the Sentiments, Manners, Numbers and Condition of the Primitive Christians', and on 'The Conduct of the Roman Government towards the Christians, from the Reign of Nero to that of Constantine'.

[2] So accurate was this forecast that within three years Gibbon felt called upon to publish a *Vindication* of his two chapters on Christianity against the horde of orthodox pamphleteers who had attacked him for them.

[3] 'Something of a doubtful mist still hangs over these Highland traditions; nor can it be entirely dispelled by the most ingenious researches of modern criticism: but if we could, with safety, indulge the pleasing supposition that Fingal lived, and that Ossian sung, the striking contrast of the situation and manners of the contending nations [Caledonians and Romans] might amuse a philosophic mind.' (*Decline and Fall*, Ch. VI, Bury's edit., i. 129.) Cf. also note in Ch. XV (Bury's edit., ii. 64).

to be regarded. Men run with great Avidity to give their Evidence in favour of what flatters their Passions, and their national Prejudices. You are, therefore, over and above indulgent to us in speaking of the Matter with Hesitation.

I must inform you, that we are all very anxious to hear that you have fully collected the Materials for your second Volume, and that you are even considerably advanc'd in the Composition of it. I speak this more in the Name of my Friends than in my own; as I cannot expect to live so long as to see the Publication of it. Your ensuing Volume will be more delicate than the preceding, but I trust in your Prudence for extricating you from the Difficulties; and, in all Events, you have Courage to despise the Clamour of Bigots. I am with great Regard Dear Sir

Your most obedient and most humble Servant

DAVID HUME.[1]

* 517. *To* ADAM SMITH

Edinburgh 1 April 1776

Euge! Belle! Dear Mr Smith: I am much pleas'd with your Performance;[2] and the Perusal of it has taken me from a State of great Anxiety. It was a Work of so much Expectation, by yourself, by your Friends, and by the Public, that I trembled for its Appearance; but am now much relieved. Not but that the Reading of it necessarily requires so much Attention, and the Public is disposed to give so little, that I shall still doubt for some time of its being at first very popular:[3] But it has Depth and Solidity and Acuteness, and is so much illustrated by curious Facts, that it must at last take the public Attention. It is probably much improved by your last Abode in London. If you were here at my Fireside, I shoud dispute some of your Principles. I cannot think, that the Rent of Farms makes any part of the Price of the Produce, but that the Price is determined altogether by the Quantity and the Demand.[4] It appears to

* MS., R.S.E.; Stewart, *Smith*, 75 f.; Burton, ii. 486 f. (incomplete).

[1] Of this letter Gibbon says: '. . . A letter from Mr Hume overpaid the labour of ten years.' (*Autobiographies*, 311.)

[2] *An Inquiry into the Nature and Causes of the Wealth of Nations* was published on March 9.

[3] It was not noticed at all in the *Gentleman's Magazine*, and received only a two-page review in the *Annual Register* for 1776.

[4] In Bk. I, Ch. VI, 'The Component Parts of Price', Smith states that the rent of land constitutes a third part of the price of most kinds of goods. Hume's shrewd criticism is a striking anticipation of Ricardo.

me impossible, that the King of France can take a Seigniorage of 8 per cent upon the Coinage. No body would bring Bullion to the mint:[1] It woud be all sent to Holland or England, where it might be coined and sent back to France for less than two per cent. Accordingly Neckre [2] says, that the French King takes only two per cent of Seigniorage. But these and a hundred other Points are fit only to be discussed in Conversation; which, till you tell me the contrary, I shall still flatter myself with soon. I hope it will be soon: For I am in a very bad State of Health and cannot afford a long Delay.

I fancy you are acquainted with Mr Gibbon: I like his Performance extremely and have ventured to tell him, that, had I not been personally acquainted with him, I shoud never have expected such an excellent Work from the Pen of an Englishman. It is lamentable to consider how much that Nation has declined in Literature during our time. I hope he did not take amiss the national Reflection.

All your Friends here are in great Grief at present for the Death of Baron Mure,[3] which is an irreparable Loss to our Society. He was among the oldest and best Friends I had in the World.

I wrote you about six Weeks ago,[4] which I hope you received: You may certainly at present have the Subject of a Letter to me; and you have no longer any very pressing Occupation. But our Friendship does not depend on these Ceremonials.

D H

To Adam Smith Esqr

[1] In Bk. IV, Ch. VI, 'Treaties of Commerce', Smith states, on the authority of Bazinghen's *Traité des Monnoies*, that the coinage in France 'increases the value of a mark of standard gold bullion, by the difference between 671 livres 10 deniers, and 720 livres; or by 48 livres 19 sous and 2 deniers'. This works out at a seignorage of slightly over 7 per cent. (not 8 per cent., as Hume stated). But Hume's criticism was again just; for Garnier, in his edition of the *Wealth of Nations*, points out that Bazinghen was not a reliable authority, that the mint price quoted by Smith remained in force only for a very short time, and that in fact it had the effect indicated by Hume—it failed to bring bullion to the mint—and was therefore lowered to some 3 per cent.

[2] Jacques Necker (1732–1804), finance minister to Louis XVI, 1776–81 and 1788–9; author of *Essai sur la législation et le commerce des grains*, 1775. Smith quotes this book in Bk. V, Ch. II, Pt. II, Art. IV, 'Consumable Commodities'.

[3] Baron Mure died at Caldwell on 25 March 1776, of gout in the stomach.

[4] Letter 514 above.

* 518. *To* William Strahan

Dear Sir Edinburgh 8 of April 1776.

I am employed in finishing the Corrections of the four last Volumes of my History, and these Volumes will probably be sent you by the Waggon next week. You have certainly Occupation enough on the four first till their Arrival. I beg that after the four first are printed off a Copy of the new Edition of them may be sent me by the Waggon, that I may return you the Errata.

I am very much taken with Mr Gibbon's Roman History which came from your Press, and am glad to hear of its success. There will no Books of Reputation now be printed in London but through your hands and Mr Cadel's. The Author tells me, that he is already preparing a second Edition. I intended to have given him my Advice with regard to the manner of printing it; but as I am now writing to you, it is the same thing. He ought certainly to print the Number of the Chapter at the head of the Margin, and it woud be better if something of the Contents coud also be added. One is also plagued with his Notes, according to the present Method of printing the Book: When a note is announced, you turn to the End of the Volume; and there you often find nothing but the Reference to an Authority: All these Authorities ought only to be printed at the Margin or the Bottom of the Page.[1] I desire, that a Copy of my new Edition shoud be sent to Mr Gibbon, as wishing that a Gentleman, whom I so highly value, shoud peruse me in the form the least imperfect, to which I can bring my work.

We heard that yours and Mr Cadell's Warehouses had been consumed by fire: I intended to have written you on the Occasion, but as I received a Letter from you a few Posts after, in which you mentioned nothing of the Matter, I concluded the Rumor to be false. Dr Robertson tells me, that there was some Foundation for the Report; but that your Loss was inconsiderable; and that your Copies were insured.[2] I shoud not have

* MS. at Barnbougle Castle; Hill, 314 f.

[1] In the 3rd edition (1777) the footnotes were transferred to the bottom of the page.

[2] There had been a fire, on 2 March. It broke out in a warehouse belonging to Cox & Bigg, printers, in the Savoy, and destroyed their warehouse, printing-office, and dwelling-houses, along with two other warehouses in the Strand, one of which belonged to Cadell.

been sorry, if some Bales of my Essays had been in the Number; as I think I coud make some Improvements in a new Edition.

Dr Smith's Performance is another excellent Work that has come from your Press this Winter; but I have ventured to tell him, that it requires too much thought to be as popular as Mr Gibbon's.

If your Ministry have as much Reflection and Combination of thought as to make a successful Expedition on the other Side of the Atlantic with 40,000 men, they will much disappoint my Expectations. They seem to have gone wrong already by the Lateness of their Embarkations. But we shall see, which is the utmost that can be said in most Affairs of this Nature.[1]

I am Dear Sir Yours sincerely

DAVID HUME.

* 519. *To* JOHN HOME

Edinburgh April 12 1776

Dear John

The loss which both of us, and I in particular, have sustained is irreparable. The Baron [2] was the oldest and best friend I had in the World. I should be inconsolable did I not see an Event approaching, which reduces every thing to a Level.

Our news is that Lord George Germaine [3] has given that Office to his own Son. I wish this News may not prove too true.

I never had thoughts of being in London. Dr Black [4] (God bless him) tells me that nothing is so improper for me as leaving my own house, jolting about on the Road, lying in inconvenient Inns, and being disordered in my Diet; and that I shall dye with

* Copy in possession of William Mure, Esq., London; *Caldwell Papers*, i. 35.

[1] Replying on 12 April 1776, Strahan says: '. . . If the Ministry cannot land the number of men you mention in America, or very near that number, which from the great Difficulty of procuring Transports for that purpose I am afraid they will not; and if the army there is not able to make a very considerable impression this summer, we shall be in the most awkward and disagreeable situation that can be conceived. *Delay* amounts to *Defeat*. . . .' (MS., R.S.E.; Hill, 318.)

[2] Mure.

[3] George Sackville Germain (1716–85), known as Lord George Sackville, 1720–70, and as Lord George Germain, 1770–82; 1st Viscount Sackville, 1782–5; appointed Secretary of State for the Colonies, 1775.

[4] Joseph Black (1728–99), M.D. Edinburgh, 1754; Professor of Medicine, Edinburgh, 1756–66, and of Chemistry, 1766–99; famous for his work on latent heat. He was Hume's physician in his last illness.

much greater tranquillity in St. David's Street than any where else. Besides where can I expect spiritual Assistance so consolatory as from Dr Blair & Dr Robertson? Not to mention a casual Exhortation from Carlysle or from you. Even Mr Ferguson might be called on difficult emergencies.

When are you to be down? Bring Smith with you.[1]

Yours

DAVID HUME.

* 520. *To* WILLIAM STRAHAN

Edinburgh 20 of April 1776.

Dear Strahan

My Body sets out to-morrow by Post for London; but whether it will arrive there is somewhat uncertain. I shall travel by slow Journies. Last Monday, I sent off by the Waggon, directed to Mr Cadel, the four last Volumes of my History. I bring up my philosophical Pieces corrected,[2] which will be safe, whether I dye by the Road or not.

I am Dear Sir Yours sincerely

DAVID HUME.

† 521. *To* WILLIAM STRAHAN

Brewer Street 2 of May 1776.

Dear Sir

I arrived here yesterday[3] very much improved by my Journey. I have seen no body but Sir John Pringle, who says that he sees nothing alarming in my Case; and I am willing, and consequently ready to believe him. I intend to call on you this forenoon, and shall leave this in case I miss you. I know not yet what Sir John intends to do with me; so am ignorant how long I shall remain in London: But wish much to have

* MS. at Barnbougle Castle; Hill, 319.

† MS. at Barnbougle Castle; Hill, 321 f.

[1] This is exactly what happened. Smith and Home travelled down from London together, and met Hume at Morpeth on his road up. Smith went on to Kirkcaldy to see his mother, who was ill; and Home turned back with Hume, and accompanied him to London, Bath, Buxton, and so back to Edinburgh.

[2] Strahan had asked for these in his letter of 12 April; stating that he hoped to publish a new edition the following winter.

[3] He had travelled all the way by very easy stages, having had great difficulty in persuading post-boys to drive only five miles an hour.

a Conversation with you; I shall never eat a meal from my own Fireside: but all the Forenoons and Afternoons will be at my Disposal. It will do me Service to drive to your House; so that you need only appoint me by Message or Penny Post an hour any day.

I am Dear Sir Yours sincerely
DAVID HUME.

P.S.

I lodge at Mrs Perkins, a few doors from Miss Elliots, and next door to Mr Forbes the Surgeon. The Afternoons, if equally convenient for you, will rather be more convenient to me, to call on you.

* 522. *To* ADAM SMITH

London 3d of May 1776

My dear Friend

I send you enclosed an ostensible Letter,[1] conformably to your Desire. I think, however, your Scruples groundless.[2] Was Mallet any wise hurt by his Publication of Lord Bolingbroke? He received an Office afterwards from the present King and Lord Bute, the most prudish Men in the World; and he always justify'd himself by his sacred Regard to the Will of a dead Friend. At the same time, I own, that your Scruples have a specious Appearance. But my Opinion is, that, if, upon my Death, you determine never to publish these papers, you shoud leave them, seal'd up with my Brother and Family, with some Inscription, that you reserve to Yourself the Power of reclaiming them, whenever you think proper. If I live a few Years longer, I shall publish them myself. I consider an Observation of Rochefoucault, that a Wind, though it extinguishes a Candle, blows up a fire.

You may be surpriz'd to hear me talk of living Years, considering the State you saw me in, and the Sentiments which both I and all my Friends at Edinburgh entertaind on that Subject. But though I cannot come up entirely to the sanguine Notions of our Friend, John, I find myself very much recovered

* MS., R.S.E.; Burton, ii. 491 f.

[1] Next letter.

[2] As will be seen from subsequent letters, Smith could not bring himself to accept the responsibility of publishing the *Dialogues concerning Natural Religion*.

on the Road, & I hope Bath Waters, and farther Journeys may effect my Cure.

By the little Company I have seen, I find the Town very full of your Book, which meets with general Approbation. Many People think particular Points disputable; but this you certainly expected: I am glad, that I am one of the Number; as these points will be the Subject of future Conversation between us.

I set out for Bath, I believe on Monday, by Sir John Pringle's Directions who says that he sees nothing to be apprehended in my Case. If you write to me, hem! hem! I say, if you write to me, send your Letters under Cover to Mr Strahan, who will have my Direction.

I regret much, in leaving Edinburgh, that I shall lose much of your Company, which I shoud have enjoy'd this Summer. I am Dear Smith

Yours sincerely and affectionately
DAVID HUME

To Adam Smith Esqr at Kirkaldy

* 522A. *To* ADAM SMITH

London 3d of May 1776

My dear Sir

After reflecting more maturely on that Article of my Will by which I left you the Disposal of all my Papers,[1] with a Request that you shou'd publish my *Dialogues concerning natural Religion*, I have become sensible, that, both on account of the Nature of the Work, and of your Situation, it may be improper to hurry on that Publication. I therefore take the present Opportunity of qualifying that friendly Request: I am content, to leave it

* MS., R.S.E.; Burton, ii. 493. The 'ostensible' letter referred to in No. 522 above.

[1] The article reads: 'To my friend Dr Adam Smith, late Professor of Moral Philosophy in Glasgow, I leave all my manuscripts without exception, desiring him to publish my Dialogues concerning Natural Religion, which are comprehended in this present bequest; but to publish no other papers which he suspects not to have been written within these five years, but to destroy them all at his leisure. And I even leave him full power over all my papers, except the Dialogues above mentioned; and though I can trust to that intimate and sincere friendship, which has ever subsisted between us, for his faithful execution of this part of my will, yet, as a small recompense of his pains in correcting and publishing this work, I leave him two hundred pounds, to be paid immediately after the publication of it.' (*Register of Testaments*, in Register House, Edinburgh.)

entirely to your Discretion at what time you will publish that Piece, or whether you will publish it at all. You will find among my Papers a very inoffensive Piece, called *My own Life*, which I composed a few days before I left Edinburgh, when I thought, as did all my Friends, that my Life was despaired of. There can be no Objection, that this small piece shoud be sent to Mess[rs] Strahan and Cadell and the Proprietors of my other Works to be prefixed to any future Edition of them. I am My Dear Sir

Your most affectionate Friend and Servant

Dr Adam Smith DAVID HUME

* 523. *To* WILLIAM STRAHAN

My dear Sir Bath 10 of May 1776.

I was very sorry not to see you again before I left London, both because I did not see you again and because of the Cause, your being confin'd. I arriv'd here on Wednesday Evening; improv'd, as before, by the Journey; And the short Trial which I have made of the Waters, seems to succeed wonderfully. Dr Gustard,[1] with whom I am much taken, says, that he never saw a Case so much what may be calld a Bath Case, and in which he is more assur'd of the Patients Recovery. To tell the Truth, I feel myself already so much reliev'd, that, for the first time these several Months, I have to day begun to open my Mind to the Expectations of seeing a few more Years: But whether this be very desirable at my Age I shall not determine. I have not ventur'd to write any thing to Sir John Pringle till we have made a further Trial.

You have probably or soon will have some Letters directed to me under your Cover. Please direct them to this Place. I hope you will be able to give me the same good Accounts of your Health that I have given you of mine. I believe, I told you, that I had sent to the Newcastle Waggon at Edinburgh, near four Weeks ago, the corrected Copy of the four last Volumes of my History, directed to Mr Cadell. The great Pains, that these Corrections cost me, make me anxious to hear of their safe Arrival.

When we pass'd by Spine Hill near Newbury we found in

* MS. at Barnbougle Castle; Hill, 323 ff.

[1] A Scots physician, son of an Edinburgh minister; 'being of good ability and a winning address, [he] had come into very good business' (Alex. Carlyle, *Autobiog.*, 534). John Home's wife, before he married her, had been a patient of Dr. Gustard's.

the Inn Lord Denbigh,[1] who was an Acquaintance of my Fellow Traveller. His Lordship inform'd him, that he, Lord Sandwich,[2] Lord Mulgrave,[3] Mr Banks,[4] and two or three Ladies of Pleasure had pass'd five or six Days there, and intended to pass all this Week and the next in the same Place; that their chief object was to enjoy the trouting Season; that they had been very successful; that Lord Sandwich in particular had caught Trouts near twenty Inches long, which gave him incredible Satisfaction; but that for his Part, being a great Admirer of Sea Fish, in which Bath abounded, and hearing that Friday was the great Market day there for Fish, he commissiond my Friend to send him up by the London Fly a good Cargo of Soles, John Dories, and Pipers, which wou'd render their Happiness compleat. I do not remember in all my little or great Knowlege of History (according as you and Dr Johnson can settle between you the Degrees of my Knowlege) such another Instance; and I am sure such a one does not exist: That the First Lord of the Admiralty, who is absolute and uncontrouled Master in his Department, shou'd, at a time when the Fate of the British Empire is in dependance, and in dependance on him, find so much Leizure, Tranquillity, Presence of Mind and Magnanimity, as to have Amusement in trouting during three Weeks near sixty Miles from the scene of Business, and during the most critical Season of the Year. There needs but this single Fact to decide the Fate of the Nation. What an Ornament woud it be in a future History to open the glorious Events of the ensuing Year with the Narrative of so singular an Incident.

I am Dear Sir Yours sincerely

DAVID HUME.

* 524. *To the* REV. HUGH BLAIR

My dear Doctor

Bath 13 of May 1776

You have frequently heard me complain of my physical Friends that they allowed me to die in the midst of them without

* MS., R.S.E.; Mackenzie, *Home*, 162 f. (incomplete); Burton, ii. 504 ff. (incomplete).

[1] Basil Fielding (1719–1800), 6th Earl of Denbigh, Master of the Foxhounds, 1761–82.

[2] First Lord of the Admiralty.

[3] Constantine John Phipps (1744–92), 2nd Baron Mulgrave, an officer in the Navy, and at this time a junior Lord of Admiralty.

[4] Joseph Banks (1743–1820), created Bart., 1781; accompanied Captain Cook on a voyage to the South Seas, returning in 1771.

so much as giving a Greek Name to my Disorder; a Consolation which was the least I had reason to expect from them. Dr Black, hearing this Complaint, told me, that I shou'd be satisfy'd in that particular, and that my Disorder was a Hæmorrhage, a word which it was easy to decompose into *αιμος* and *ρηγνυμι*. But Sir John Pringle says, that I have no Hæmorrhage; but a Spincture [1] in the Colon, which it will be easy to cure. This Disorder, as it both contained two Greek Appellations and was remediable, I was much inclined to prefer, when behold! Dr Gustard tells me that he sees no Symptoms of the former Disorder, and as to the latter, he never met with it and scarcely ever heard of it. He assures me, that my Case is the most common of all Bath Cases, to wit, a bilious Complaint, which the Waters scarcely ever fail of curing; and he never had a Patient of whose Recovery he had better hopes.[2] Indeed, the Waters, in the short trial which I have made of them (for I have been here only four days) seem to agree very well with me; and two days ago I found myself so well, that, for the first time, I began to entertain hopes of a Reprieve. Yesterday I was not so well, from a Misunderstanding, in new Lodgings, with regard to my Bedding: My whimsicalness in this particular surprizes Dr Gustard, and he knows not what to make of it. By the bye, this Dr Gustard is an excellent kind of Man, very friendly and I believe very intelligent: He assures me (as do several others) that the Summer is the best time for Bath Waters; and if they continue to agree with me, I shall probably pass here that Season. I promised to General Conway and Lady Aylesbury, that, if I had recovered so much Health as to venture myself in Company, I shoud pass some weeks of the Autumn at Park-place: this is the only Retardment I can forsee to my return to Scotland before winter. My wishes carry me thither; though the grievous Loss we have suffered in Friends makes the Abode in that Countrey less pleasing to my Fancy than formerly.

You must have heard of the agreeable Surprize, which John Home put upon me. We travelled up to London very cheerfully together, and thence to this place, where we found Mrs Home almost quite recovered. Never was there a more friendly Action, nor better placed: For what between Conversation and Gaming (not to mention sometimes squabbling) I did not pass

[1] *Sic* in MS., but Pringle probably said *stricture*.

[2] Actually, Hume seems to have been suffering from cancer of the large intestine, with secondary cancer of the liver.

a languid Moment; and his Company, I am certain, was the chief Cause, why my Journey had so good an Effect; of which, however, I suppose he has given too sanguine Accounts, as is usual with him. My good Spirits and tolerable Appetite are capable of deceiving any body, even my Physicians, who, though able, are, I am perswaded, still groping in the dark. If I have any secret Disorder, it has not yet betrayed itself by any Symptoms, that are quite decisive.

But to leave this disagreeable Subject of my own Ails, about which, however, I know, you are interested, I learn that Willie Robertson is Candidate for the Office of Procurator to the Kirk. How I lament my Absence at so critical a time! Yet I allow you to employ my Name and Interest, in all Sollicitations with the Members of the Assembly, which will, I hope, have the same Effect as my personal Applications. Be so good as to read this Letter to Dr Black and to Mr Ferguson. When I write to one, I suppose myself writing to all my Friends; and I also wish to comprehend the Principal in the Number. Pray tell him, that Mrs Macaulay is settled in Bath; and though her Muse seems now to be mute, she is, if not a more illustrious, yet a more fortunate Historian, than either of us. There is one Dr Wilson, a man zealous for Liberty, who has made her a free and full Present of a House of £2000 Value, has adopted her Daughter by all the Rites of Roman Jurisprudence, and intends to leave her all his Fortune, which is considerable.[1]

Two Ladies of my Acquaintance have laid a Scheme of bringing Lady Huntingdon [2] and me together for her or my Conversion. I wish I may have Spirits to humour this Folly.[3]

I beg my sincere Compliments to Mrs Blair; and am [Dear] Doctor

Yours usque ad aras.

David Hume

To The Reverend Dr Blair Argyle Buildings

[1] Thomas Wilson was Rector of St. Stephen's, Walbrook, and erected a statue of Mrs. Macaulay within the altar rails. Walpole calls him 'that dirty disappointed hunter of a mitre' (*Letters*, x. 206). When Mrs. Macaulay married again, Wilson quarrelled with her and sold the statue.

[2] Selina Hastings (1707–91), Countess of Huntingdon; the friend and patron of the Wesleys, Whitefield, and many other Methodists.

[3] Replying in an undated letter from Edinburgh, Blair says: 'I would not wish you to have any thing to do with that tribe [the Methodists] either in joke or earnest. You can have no sort of intercourse with them that will not be misrepresented. You are too conspicuous a figure to be let pass without their fathering some foolish story on you.' (MS., R.S.E.)

* 525. *To* William Strahan

Bath 8 of June 1776.

My dear Sir

You will be sorry to hear, that I must retract all the good Accounts, which I gave you of my Health. The Waters, after seeming to agree with me, have sensibly a bad Effect, and I have entirely dropped the Use of them. I wait only Sir John Pringle's Directions before I leave this place;[1] and I shall, I believe, set out for the North in a few days. If any Letters for me come under your Cover, be so good as to detain them, till I can inform you of my Route.

I am glad to find, that you have been able to set about this New Edition in earnest. I have made it extremely correct; at least I believe that, if I were to live twenty Years longer, I shoud never be able to give it any further Improvements. This is some small Satisfaction to me in my present Situation; and I may add that it is almost the only one that my Writings ever afforded me: For as to any suitable Returns of Approbation from the Public, for the Care, Accuracy, Labour, Disinterestedness, and Courage of my Compositions, they are yet to come. Though, I own to you, I see many Symptoms that they are approaching. But it will happen to me as to many other Writers: Though I have reached a considerable Age, I shall not live to see any Justice done to me. It is not improbable, however, that my Self-conceit and Prepossessions may lead me into this way of thinking.

As soon as this Edition is finished, please to send a Copy of all the ten Volumes [2] to Sir John Pringle, the same to Mr Gibbon, a Copy of the History to Mistress Elliott in Brewer Street; six Copies of the whole to me in Edinburgh or to my Brother there in case of my Death.

If this Event shall happen, as is probable, before the Publication of this Edition, there is one Request I have to make to you:

* MS. at Barnbougle Castle; Hill, 328 ff.

[1] Pringle wrote on 7 June advising Hume not to leave Bath till both his physician and himself were persuaded that the waters were doing him no good.

[2] That is, 8 volumes of the *History*, and 2 of the *Essays*.

Before I left Edinburgh, I wrote a small piece (you may believe it woud be but a small one) which I call the History of my own Life: I desire it may be prefixed to this Edition:[1] It will be thought curious and entertaining. My Brother or Dr Adam Smith will send it to you, and I shall give them Directions to that Purpose.

I am also to speak to you of another Work more important: Some Years ago, I composed a piece, which woud make a small Volume in Twelves. I call it *Dialogues on natural Religion*: Some of my Friends flatter me, that it is the best thing I ever wrote. I have hitherto forborne to publish it, because I was of late desirous to live quietly, and keep remote from all Clamour: For though it be not more exceptionable than some things I had formerly published; yet you know some of these were thought very exceptionable; and in prudence, perhaps, I ought to have suppressed them. I there introduce a Sceptic, who is indeed refuted, and at last gives up the Argument, nay confesses that he was only amusing himself by all his Cavils;[2] yet before he is silenced, he advances several Topics, which will give Umbrage, and will be deemed very bold and free, as well as much out of the Common Road. As soon as I arrive at Edinburgh, I intend to print a small Edition of 500, of which I may give away about 100 in Presents; and shall make you a Present of the Remainder, together with the literary Property of the whole, provided you have no Scruple, in your present Situation, of being the Editor: It is not necessary you shoud prefix your Name to the Title Page. I seriously declare, that after Mr Millar and You and Mr Cadell have publickly avowed your Publication of the *Enquiry concerning human Understanding*, I know no Reason why

As the publication of the new edition of the *History* was delayed till 1778, Strahan and Cadell published Hume's autobiography separately in 1777. It was thus given more prominence than Hume ever meant it to have. (See Appendix M below.)

[2] 'I must confess', says Philo the Sceptic, 'that I am less cautious on the subject of Natural Religion than on any other; both because I know that I can never, on that head, corrupt the principles of any man of common sense, and because no one, I am confident, in whose eyes I appear a man of common sense, will ever mistake my intentions. . . . No one has a deeper sense of religion impressed on his mind, or pays more profound adoration to the Divine Being, as he discovers himself to reason, in the inexplicable contrivance and artifice of Nature. A purpose, an intention, a design strikes everywhere the most careless, the most stupid thinker; and no man can be so hardened in absurd systems, as at all times to reject it.' (*Dialogues*, Pt. XII.)

you shoud have the least Scruple with regard to these Dialogues. They will be much less obnoxious to the Law, and not more exposed to popular Clamour. Whatever your Resolution be, I beg you wou'd keep an entire Silence on this Subject. If I leave them to you by Will, your executing the Desire of a dead Friend, will render the publication still more excusable.[1] Mallet never sufferd any thing by being the Editor of Bolingbroke's Works.

Two posts ago I sent you a Copy of the small Essay which I mentioned.[2]

I am Dear Sir with great Regard and Sincerity

Your most obedient humble Servant

David Hume.

* 526. *To* John Home of Ninewells

Bath 10 of June 1776

Dear Brother

You woud see by my Letter to our Sister dated the 8th in what State my Health I was [and][3] that the Bath Waters did not agree with me, and that I intended to set out for Edinburgh, as to morrow. Since that time, I have been prevailed on by Importunity and Teazing, contrary to my Reason, and very much contrary to my Inclination, to delay my Departure some time. It seems Dr Gusthart, whom I consult here, had suspected from the first that all my Disorder proceeded from a Vice in my Liver; but not caring directly to oppose Sir John Pringle, he said nothing of the Matter, to me at least. But John Hunter, who marry'd our Cousin Roby Hume's Daughter,[4] coming accidentally to

* MS. in Nat. Lib., Scotland; hitherto unpublished.

[1] By a codicil to his will, dated 7 Aug., Hume cancelled the clause quoted in note 1 on p. 317 above, and left all his manuscripts to Strahan, adding: 'I desire, that my Dialogues concerning Natural Religion may be printed and published any time within two years after my Death' (MS., R.S.E.). Still later, he added another paragraph to this codicil (see note 1 on p. 334 below).

[2] *Of the Origin of Government*, published for the first time in the posthumous edition of 1777.

[3] Written and then struck out in MS.

[4] John Hunter married, in 1771, Anne (1742–1821), daughter of Robert Boyne Home, an army surgeon and afterwards of Greenlaw Castle, Berwickshire. She was famous for her literary parties and wrote several songs, some of which were set to music by Haydn.

Town, and expressing a very friendly Concern about me, Dr Gusthart proposed that I shoud be inspected by him: He felt very sensibly, as he said, a Tumor or Swelling in my Liver; and this Fact, not drawn by Reasoning, but obvious to the Senses, and perceived by the greatest Anatomist in Europe, must be admitted as unquestionable, and will alone account for my Situation. They kept, very foolishly, this Opinion of Mr Hunter's a secret from me till Yesterday; and now they pretend, that the Tumor, being small, may be discussed by Medicines and Regimen: A very silly Expectation, that an inveterate Disease of long Standing and in a vital Part, will yield to their feeble Remedies, in a man of my Years. To avoid however the Reproach of Obstinacy, I delayed my Journey, even though I feel myself declining every day, and am uncertain, whether at last I shall be able to make out the Journey. You made me promise, that I shoud write you sincerely the true State of my Health, than which really nothing can be worse. I hope however to set out in 8 or 10 days; and tis probable, that travelling, which seems not to disagree with me, may give me Force to reach my own Fireside, from which I shall never more depart, a safe Resolution, as it will require very short Perseverance to carry it into full Execution. I am Dear Brother

Very affectionately Yours

DAVID HUME

To John Home Esqr of Ninewells[1]

* 527. *To* WILLIAM STRAHAN

Bath 12 of June 1776.

My dear Sir

I leave not this Place so soon as I had intended; and shall remain long enough to hear from you. I am sensibly obliged to you for undertaking to execute my Will with regard to my Manuscripts; and I have this same day made a Codicil by which I make you entirely Master of them. It is an idle thing in us to be concerned about any thing that shall happen after our Death; yet this is natural to all Men,[2] and I often regretted

* MS. at Barnbougle Castle; Hill, 337.

[1] Not in Hume's handwriting.

[2] Strahan fastened on this statement. Writing to Hume on 19 Aug. 1775, in a mood made solemn by the thought of his friend's imminent death and

that a Piece, for which I had a particular Partiality, should run any hazard of being suppressed after my Decease.

The Cause of my Distemper is now fully discovered: It is a Tumour in my Liver, which Mr John Hunter first felt, and which I myself can now feel: It seems to be about the Bigness of an Egg, and is flat and round. Dr Gusthart, who had conjectured some other Cause, flatters me, that he now entertains better hopes than ever, of my Recovery; but I infer, that a Disorder, of so long standing, in a vital Part, will not easily be removed in a Person of my Years: It may linger some Years, which would not be very desirable. The Physicians recommend Motion and Exercise and even long Journies: I think, therefore, of setting out for Edinburgh some time next week; and will probably see you in London before the End of the good Season. I am with great Sincerity Dear Sir

Your most obedient humble Servant

DAVID HUME.

* 528. *To* JOHN CRAWFORD

Bath, 15 June, 1776.

Your very friendly letter,[1] dear Crawford, gave me much satisfaction. I should have been very happy in your company here, and to have improved you (and myself at the same time) in health, in philosophy, and in whist; but I leave this place in a few days, as the waters do me no service, and all the company are gone or going. I am, however, rather better than when you saw me, and the true cause of my distemper is now discovered.

* Morrison, ii. 319; Hill, 338 (incomplete).

---

dissolution, he quotes it, and adds: 'Now I would eagerly ask, If it is *natural to all men* to be interested in futurity, does not this strongly indicate that our existence will be protracted beyond this life?

'Do you *now* believe, or suspect, that all the Powers and Faculties of your own mind, which you have cultivated with so much care and success, will cease and be extinguished with your Vital Breath?

'Our Soul, or immaterial part of us, some say, is able, when on the Brink of Dissolution, to take a Glimpse of Futurity; and for that Reason I earnestly wish to have your *last Thoughts* on this important subject. . . .' (MS., R.S.E.; Burton, ii. 512 f.)

But Strahan's question arrived too late for Hume to answer it.

[1] Not extant among the MSS., R.S.E.

It lies in my liver, not in my bowels. You ask me how I know this; I answer, John Hunter, the greatest anatomist in Europe, felt it with his fingers, and I myself can now feel it. The devil's in it if this do not convince you. Even St. Thomas, the infidel apostle, desired no better authority than the testimony of his fingers. They tell me that I have gained a great deal by this change of the seat of war, from the bowels to the liver; but however able the generals, I expect little from this campaign, still less from our American hostilities. They also tell me that motion and exercise are my best remedies, and here I believe them, and shall put the recipe in practice.

The same remedy would serve you. Will you meet me positively, and as a man of honour, this day month, the 15th July, at Coventry, the most central town in England, and let us wander during the autumn throughout every corner of that kingdom, and throughout the Principality of Wales? You will find me in as good spirits as ever you knew me, if not in better, and resolute to set all the doctors and parsons at defiance. We may quarrel sometimes, but shall never tire of each other, I shall not travel above two or at most three stages a day, which will be an admirable trial of your patience. But your only real substantial grievance will be, that in this way of living you will not be able to spend as much a day as a fine gentleman ought to do, but you may lose as much to me in the evening at picket as is proper, which will be some compensation, for a sudden costiveness after a violent flux may be dangerous.

Pray send me two or three franks directed to Dr Gusthart at Bath. All the Members have left this place. Lord Abingdon [1] took his leave of me to-day; I found to my grief that he has become a great man for the Turf, for which his caution, cunning, sagacity, secrecy, avidity, and selfishness so eminently qualify him. He told me that the place in Europe (for he did not comprise America) in which there is the most honour and truth and fair dealing assembled is Newmarket and the neighbouring fields during the season. Pray is Lord Ossory of the same opinion?

Yours most sincerely, and with even more than Newmarket faith,

DAVID HUME.

[1] Willoughby Bertie (1740–99), 4th Earl of Abingdon; author of the pamphlet *Thoughts on Mr Burke's Letter to the Sheriffs of Bristol on the Affairs of America*, 1777.

* 529. *To the* Rev. Hugh Blair

Doncaster 27 of June [1776]

Mr John Hume, alias Home, alias the Home, alias the late Lord Conservator,[1] alias the late Minister of the Gospel at Athelstoneford, has calculated Matters so as to arrive infallibly with his Friend in St David's Street on Wednesday Evening. He has ask'd several of Dr Blair's Friends to dine with him there on Thursday, being the 4th of July; and begs the favour of the Doctor to make one of the Number.

To The Revd Dr Blair at his house near the Hermitage on the Links of Leith

† 530. *To* John Home

My Dear John Edinburgh 9 of July 1776

I offer'd to give you a Letter along with you, informing you how I shoud be on Tuesday thereafter, viz weaker and more infirm than when you saw me: This indeed woud have savd Postage, and I can do no more at present than confirm the same Truth, only that the Matter seems more to proceed with an accelerated Motion. I had yesterday a grand Jury of Physicians who sat upon me, the Doctors Cullen,[2] Black [3] and Home.[4] They all declare the Opinion of the English Physicians, absurd and erroneous. They own a small Tumour in my Liver; but so small and trivial that it coud never do me any material Injury; and they say that I might have liv'd twenty Years with it, and never have felt any Inconvenience from it: Each of them has had Patients who have had Tumours in that part ten times larger without almost complaining for Years together. They have thoroughly perswaded me to be of their Opinion; and according to their united Sentiments, my Distemper is now a Hæmorrhage as before, which is an Illness, that I had as Lief

* MS., R.S.E.; Mackenzie, *Home*, 161 f.; Burton, ii. 506 f.

† MS. in possession of Mr. W. S. Lewis, Farmington, Conn., U.S.A.; hitherto unpublished.

[1] Conservator of the Privileges of Campvere, a sinecure, worth £300 a year, to which John Home had been presented in 1763. Campvere, in Holland, had once contained a large and flourishing Scots colony, but in the eighteenth century the only duty to be fulfilled by the Conservator was to sit in the General Assembly as a ruling elder from a kirk no longer in existence.

[2] William Cullen. [3] Joseph Black. [4] Francis Home.

dye of as any other. The First Part of the Text being now discuss'd, we proceed to the second viz the Cure, which I leave to another Opportunity. I send you enclosed a Letter, which my Nephew[1] opend by Mistake, but finding, after he had read a few Lines, that it was not meant for him, he proceeded no farther. Yours sincerely

DAVID HUME

To John Hume Esq at Kilduff near Haddington

* 531. *To* WILLIAM STRAHAN

Dear Sir Edinburgh 27 of July 1776.

I arriv'd here about three weeks ago in a very shattered Condition: The Motion of the Chaise, especially during the last days, made me suffer very much; and my Physicians are now of Opinion (which was always my Sentiment) that all Exercise is hurtful to me. I am however in very good Spirits during the Intervals of my Colics; and employ myself in my usual Occupations. As a proof of it, I send you three Leaves of the sixth Volume of my History, which you will please to substitute, instead of the three correspondent Leaves as they stand at present. They contain some Corrections, or rather Omissions, which I think Improvements.[2] You will wonder, that, in my present Situation I employ myself about such Trifles, and you may compare me to the modern Greeks, who, while Constantinople was besieged by the Turks and they themselves were threatened with total Destruction, occupyed themselves entirely in Disputes concerning the Procession of the holy Ghost. Such is the Effect of long Habit! I am Dear Sir

Your most obedient humble Servant

DAVID HUME.

† 532. *To* WILLIAM STRAHAN

Dear Sir Edinburgh 30 of July 1776.

I must give you the trouble of making a new Correction, which however will be easily done. It is in the second Volume

* MS. at Barnbougle Castle; Hill, 339.

† MS. at Barnbougle Castle; Hill, 341.

[1] Presumably the youngest nephew, John.

[2] The three passages deleted dealt with the meeting of the Scottish clergy at St. Andrews in 1617, the negotiations between Philip IV of Spain and the Earl of Bristol in 1624, and Charles I's message to the House of Commons as delivered by Sir Edward Coke in 1628.

of my philosophical Pieces: That whole Passage from Page 231 till Page 239 line 3 must be thrown into an Appendix under the Title *Of Self-love*: It must be the second Appendix;[1] consequently the second Appendix becomes the third, and the third Appendix, the fourth. In like manner, what is called in Page 239, Part 2 must be Part 1, as also that in Page 241 must be Part 2. Let the Printer observe this Alteration with regard to the Appendixes in the Table of Contents.

I feel myself a good deal better since I am settled here, and never stir abroad except in a Chair. My Physicians say everywhere that they have cured me, which is very agreeable Intelligence, though somewhat new to me.

I am glad to hear, that you and Dr Robertson are fully agreed:[2] It gives me pleasure on his account, and I hope, in the Issue, upon yours. I am dear Sir

Yours sincerely
DAVID HUME.

P.S. The Title of the Section in Page 231 remains the same as before, viz *Of Benevolence.*

* 533. *To* JOHN HOME

Edinburgh, 6 August, 1776.

My dear John,

I shall begin with telling you the only piece of good news of the family, which is, that my nephew,[3] in no more than two days that he has stayed here, has recovered so surprisingly, that he is scarcely knowable, or rather is perfectly knowable, for he was not so on his first arrival. Such are the advantages of youth! His uncle declines, if not with so great rapidity, yet pretty sensibly. Sunday, ill; half of yesterday the same; easy at present; prepared to suffer a little to-morrow; perhaps less the day after. Dr Black says, I shall not die of a dropsy, as I imagined, but of inanition and weakness. He cannot, however, fix, with any probability, the time, otherwise he would frankly tell me.

Poor Edmonstoune and I parted to-day, with a plentiful

* Mackenzie, *Home*, 64 f.; Burton, ii. 507 f.

[1] To the *Enquiry concerning the Principles of Morals*.

[2] Presumably about the publication of Robertson's *History of America*, which appeared in two volumes in 1777.

[3] Joseph Home.

effusion of tears;[1] all those *Belzebubians* [2] have not hearts of iron. I hope you met with everything well at Foggo,[3] and receive nothing but good news from Buxton.[4] In spite of Dr Black's caution, I venture to foretell that I shall be yours cordially and sincerely till the month of October next,

DAVID HUME.

* 534. *To* WILLIAM STRAHAN

Dear Sir Edinburgh 12 of August, 1776

Please to make with your Pen the following Correction. In the second Volume of my philosophical Pieces, p. 245, l. 1, and 2, eraze these words, *that there is such a sentiment in human nature as benevolence.*[5]

This, Dear Sir, is the last Correction I shall probably trouble

* MS. at Barnbougle Castle; Hill, 342 f. and facsimile.

[1] Edmonstoune's last letter to Hume, written from Linlithgow on Wednesday [7 Aug. 1776], is worth quoting:

'My Dear Dear David

'My Heart is very full. I could not see you this Morning; I thought it was better for us both. You can't die, you must live in the Memory of all your ffriends and Acquaintances and your Works will render you immortal. I could never conceive that it was possible for any one to dislike you or hate you, he must be more than savage who could be an Enemy to a Man of the best Head and Heart and of the most amiable Manners.

'O Toi qui de mon Ame
Est la chere Moitie
Toi qui joins la delicatesse
Des sentimens d'une Maitresse
A la Solidité d'une sure Amitié
David, il faut bientot que la Parque cruelle
Vienne rompre des si beaux Noeuds
Malgré nos Cris & nos Vœux
Bientot nous essuyerons une absence eternelle.
'Adieu Adieu.

'J. E.

'What I mention'd to you about Hume Castle in Joke I now intend in Earnest. I shall dedicate it to you and Baron Mure; I want an Inscription. I wish you would cause some of your ffriends to compose a short one. Once more Adieu.' (MS., R.S.E.; Burton, ii. 510 (incomplete).)

[2] Probably members of the Beelzebub Club, though I have not been able to find out anything about such a club.

[3] In Berwickshire, not far from Ninewells.

[4] Where John Home seems to have left his wife.

[5] The sentence as it stood, and from which the erasure was to be made, ran: 'Upon the whole then it seems undeniable *that* there is such a sentiment in human nature as benevolence; *that* nothing can bestow more merit on

you with: For Dr Black has promised me, that all shall be over with me in a very little time: This Promise he makes by his Power of Prediction, not that of Prescription. And indeed I consider it as good News: For of late, within these few weeks, my Infirmities have so multiplyed, that Life has become rather a Burthen to me. Adieu, then, my good and old Friend

PS. DAVID HUME

My Brother will inform you of my Destination with regard to my Manuscripts.

Another Correction.

In the same Page l. 4, instead of *possession of it* read *sentiment of benevolence* [1]

* 535. *To* JOHN HOME OF NINEWELLS

Dear Brother 13 of August 1776.

Dr Black tells me plainly, like a man of Sense, that I shall dye soon, which was no disagreeable news to me: He says, I shall dye of weakness & Inanition; & perhaps give little or no warning. But tho I be growing sensibly weaker every day, this period seems not to be approaching; & I shall have time enough to inform you, & to desire your Company, which will be very agreeable to me: But at this time, your presence is necessary at Ninewells, to settle Josey & comfort his mother. Davie will be also very useful with you: I am much pleased with his Tenderness & friendship. I beg therefore that neither you nor he may set out; & as the communication between us, is open & frequent, I promise to give you timely information.

† 536. *To* SIR JOHN PRINGLE

Dear Sir Edinburgh 13 Aug. 1776

You saw me to great Advantage when I was at London, the Journey had a little revived me; which with some remains of

* Copy (in John Home's handwriting), MS., R.S.E.; *Lit. Gazette*, 1821, p. 746; Burton, ii. 508.

† *Corr. of George III*, iii. 389. This letter was probably shown to George III by Pringle; the King made a copy of it with his own hand; and it was printed from this copy by Sir John Fortescue in the *Corr.*, *loc. cit.*

any human creature than the possession of it in an eminent degree; and *that* a part, at least, of its merit arises from its tendency to promote the interests of our species, and bestow happiness on human society.' (*Principles of Morals*, Sect. II, Pt. II; Clarendon Press edit., 81.)

[1] Consequential on the former correction.

Health and Strength, made you hope that a Cure was still practicable; But Affairs change, every day and rapidly, to the worse: My Appetite is totally gone, my Strength decays, and every bad Symptom visibly augments; so that I can now look only for a near approaching Dissolution. One would little regret Life, were it not the Experience of such good Friends, as you, whom one must leave behind them. *Mais, helas! on ne laisse que des mourans:* as Ninon l'Enclos[1] said on her Death-bed. Death appears to me so little terrible on his Approaches, that I scorn to quote Heroes and Philosophers as Examples of Fortitude: a Woman of Pleasure, who, however, was also a Philosopher, is sufficient. I embrace you, Dear Sir, and probably for the last time.

DAVID HUME.

* 537. *To* DAVID HUME THE YOUNGER

Edinburgh 15 of Augt 1776

Dear Davy

You need not doubt but your Company, as well as your Father's, woud have been very agreeable to me, especially at present, for the Consolation of your Company: But I see the immediate Inconvences[2] that attend it: You cannot be well spard from Josey, whose State of Health, I am sorry to find, is still somewhat precarious: And there is no immediate Call for your being here. For besides, that you woud but pass a melancholy time with me; however your Affection might cover it, and relieve it; I am weakening very gradually, and am not threaten'd with any immediate Incident. I shall probably have more warning; in which case I shall not fail to summon you; and I shall never dye in Satisfaction, without embracing you. I doubt not but my Name woud have procured you Friends and Credit, in the Course of your Life, especially if my Brother had allowd you to carry it: For who will know it, in the present Disguise?[3]

* MS., R.S.E.; Burton, ii. 509.

[1] Ninon de Lenclos (1615–1705), the famous courtesan.

[2] *Sic* in MS.

[3] The old family dispute on the spelling of the name—Home or Hume. On 7 Aug. Hume added another codicil to his will: 'I leave to my Friend, Mr John Home of Kilduff, ten dozen of my old Claret at his Choice; and one single Bottle of that other Liquor called Port. I also leave to him six dozen of Port, provided that he attests under his hand, signed John *Hume*, that he has himself alone finished that Bottle at two Sittings. By this Concession, he will at once terminate the only two Differences, that ever arose between us, concerning temporal matters.' (MS., R.S.E.)

But as he is totally obstinate on this head, I believe we had better let him alone. I have frequently told him, that it is lucky for him he sees few things in a wrong Light; for where he does he is totally incurable. I am very much at my ease to day. I beg my Compliments to all your Family.

Your affectionate Uncle
DAVID HUME

To Mr David Home at Ninewells

* 538. *To* ADAM SMITH

Edinburgh 15 of Augt 1776

My dear Smith

I have orderd a new Copy of my Dialogues to be made besides that which will be sent to Mr Strahan, and to be kept by my Nephew.[1] If you will permit me, I shall order a third Copy to be made, and consignd to you. It will bind you to nothing, but will serve as a Security. On revising them (which I have not done these 15 Years) I find that nothing can be more cautiously and more artfully written. You had certainly forgotten them. Will you permit me to leave you the Property of the Copy, in case they shoud not be published in five Years after my Decease? Be so good as to write me an answer soon. My State of Health does not permit me to wait Months for it.

Yours affectionately
DAVID HUME[2]

To Adam Smith Esqr at Kirkaldy

* MS., R.S.E.; Hill, 364 n.

[1] The latest modification about the *Dialogues* introduced into Hume's will (see note 1 on p. 324 above) reads: 'I also ordain, that if my Dialogues, from whatever cause, be not publishd within two years and a half after my Death, as also the account of my Life, the Property shall return to my Nephew, David, whose Duty, in publishing them as the last Request of his Uncle, must be approved of by all the World.' (MS., R.S.E.)

[2] Replying from Kirkcaldy on 22 Aug.—Hume's letter had been delayed in transit, through having been sent by the carrier instead of by the post—Smith says that he will be happy to receive a copy of the Dialogues, but adds: 'With regard to leaving me the property in case they are not published within five years after your decease, you may do as you think proper. I think, however, you should not menace Strahan with the loss of anything in case he does not publish your work within a certain time. There is no probability of his delaying it, and if any thing could make him delay it, it would be a clause of this kind, which would give him an honourable pretence for doing so. It would then be said that I had published, for the sake of an Emolument, not from respect to the memory of my friend, what even

* 539. *To the* Comtesse de Boufflers

Edinburgh, 20 August, 1776.

Tho I am certainly within a few weeks, dear Madam, and perhaps within a few days, of my own death, I could not forbear being struck with the death of the Prince of Conti [1]—so great a loss in every particular. My reflection carried me immediately to your situation in this melancholy incident. What a difference to you in your whole plan of life! Pray write me some particulars; but in such terms that you need not care, in case of decease, into whose hands your letter may fall.

My distemper is a diarrhoea, or disorder in my bowels, which has been gradually undermining me these two years; but, within these six months, has been visibly hastening me to my end. I see death approach gradually, without any anxiety or regret. I salute you, with great affection and regard, for the last time.

David Hume.[2]

† 540. *To* Adam Smith

Ed[r] 23 August 1776

My Dearest Friend

I am obliged to make use of my Nephews hand in writing to you as I do not rise to day.

There is No Man in whom I have a greater Confidence than

* *Edin. Review*, xvii, 306; *Priv. Corr.*, 285; Burton, ii. 513 f.

† MS., R.S.E.; Burton, ii. 515 (incomplete).

a printer for the sake of the same emolument had not published. That Strahan is sufficiently zealous you will see by the enclosed letter, which I will beg the favour of you to return to me, but by the Post and not by the carrier. . . .' (MS., R.S.E.) (The enclosure referred to was probably Strahan's letter to Smith of 10 June 1776, which is still among the MSS., R.S.E.)

[1] He died on 2 Aug. 1776.

[2] Writing to Walpole on 7 Sept. 1776, Mme du Deffand says: 'L'Idole me donna à lire avant-hier une lettre de M. Hume, à l'occasion de la mort du Prince; il lui disait adieu, comme n'ayant plus que quelques jours à vivre. Cette lettre m'a paru de la plus grande beauté; je lui en ai demandé une copie, et je l'aurai.' (*Lettres à Walpole*, iii. 253.)

One other tribute is worth quoting: 'Certes, la femme qui inspirait à un sage mourant de tels sentiments suprêmes d'intérêt et d'amitié n'était point une âme ordinaire; et ce seul témoignage, qui rattache son souvenir à celui d'une des plus belles morts que la philosophie nous offre, suffirait pour empêcher son nom à elle-même de mourir.' (Sainte-Beuve, *Nouv. Lundis*, 2 Feb. 1863.)

Mr Strahan, yet have I left the property of that Manuscript to my Nephew David in case by any accident it should not be published within three years after my decease. The only accident I could forsee, was one to Mr Strahans Life, and without this clause My Nephew would have had no right to publish it. Be so good as to inform Mr Strahan of this Circumstance.

You are too good in thinking any trifles that concern me are so much worth your attention, but I give you entire liberty to make what Additions you please to the account of my Life.[1]

I go very fast to decline, & last night had a small fever, which I hoped might put a quicker period to this tedious Illness, but unluckily it has in a great measure gone of. I cannot submit to your coming over here on my account as it is possible for me to see you so small a Part of the day but Dr Black can better inform you concerning the degree of strength which may from time to time remain with Me.[2]

Adieu My dearest Friend DAVID HUME

P.S. It was a strange blunder to send your Letter by the Carrier.

Adam Smith Esqr Kirkaldy

FOUR UNDATABLE LETTERS

* 541. *To* MICHAEL RAMSAY

Dear Mich.

There has no Correspondence past betwixt us, for some weeks past, John having alwise occasion to write to you, about

* MS., R.S.E.; hitherto unpublished. The handwriting, style, and spelling are early, and there seems little doubt that this letter was written from Ninewells about 1730.

[1] In his letter of the day before, Smith had said: 'If you will give me leave I will add a few lines to your account of your own life, giving some account, in my own name, of your behaviour in this illness, if, contrary to my own hopes, it should prove your last. Some conversations we had lately together, particularly that concerning your want of an excuse to make to Charon, the excuse you at last thought of, and the very bad reception which Charon was likely to give it, would, I imagine, make no disagreeable part of the history. You have, in a declining state of health, under an exhausting disease, for more than two years together, now looked at the approach, or what you at least believed to be the approach of Death with a steady chearfulness such as very few men have been able to maintain for a few hours, tho otherwise in the most perfect Health. . . .' (MS., R.S.E.)

In consequence of the permission Hume gave him, Smith added to *My Own Life* the extracts from his own, Hume's, and Joseph Black's letters, as shown in Appendix L below.

[2] Hume died about 4 o'clock in the afternoon, two days later.

some Business or other. I cannot think it was upon this Account, & for want of an Invitation that you have taken a Resolution to go to Lawers [1] this Vacance contrary to a kind of promise you made me of coming here. Perhaps you was afraid, that you would have no Conveniency in this little House, or that you would disturb us. For my Share, the State of my Health is such, & Indolence makes such Progress o'er me for want of being resisted, that wtout the least Scruple, I shall give you my room, & be contented to share one with John. This I can assure you, will be no manner of Loss to me, & I hope it will make you as easy as you cou'd wish. At Lawers I can never conceive, you can live to your Satisfaction, or according to the Projects you have form'd. I wish however you had informd me of your Designs and the State of your Health. For my Share I have so little confortable in these respects to tell you, that I believe it will be no Pleasure to you to hear it. But I hope you are in a contrary Case. Bring out with you or send with the Carrier Pelisson's History,[2] & the last Volume of Rapin. I am afraid James Home come shortly to the countrey, & then I would be obligd to restore him his Book.

My Nephew [3] & your Godson arrivd here safely from Dudiston [4] where I am afraid it has been but very indifferently guided.

July 30 Michael Ramsay Esq. to be left at Mr Davidson Wigmaker's house in the first Story of Smith's Land. Edin^r.

* 542. *To* [Thomas Bradshaw]

During the hurry of your Business, while the Parliament was sitting, I forbore giving you or Ld North any trouble: But at present, while you may have a little more Leizure, I hope you will excuse my putting you in mind of that Note, which you wrote

* MS., R.S.E.; hitherto unpublished. This is a rough draft, and may be dated any time between Jan. 1770, when the Duke of Grafton resigned, and 1774, when Thomas Bradshaw died. It should be compared with Letter 491 above.

1 Presumably the village on Loch Tay.

2 Either *Histoire de l'Académie françoise jusqu'en 1652* (1563), or *Histoire de Louis XIV* (1749), both by Paul Pellisson-Fontanier (1624–93); probably the former.

3 Hume had no nephew, strictly so called, at this time; but *nephew* was a term loosely used for various relationships, and he may have been referring to one of his first cousins, the sons of the Rev. George Home of Chirnside.

4 Probably Duddingston, to the south-east of Edinburgh.

me by the Duke of Graftons Direction, and of which I use the Freedom of enclosing you a Copy. You then said, that the Duke woud recommend me to his Successor; but perhaps it has been forgot during the Tumult of Business which ensud upon his Grace's Resignation. I hope you will be so good as to lay my Case before Lord North who will be pleasd to consider the Circumstances of my Claim. I resign myself entirely to his Lordship's Wisdom, and shall hold this Office,[1] if it fall vacant, from his Favour, without making any new Applications either to the Duke of Grafton or Lord Hertford or Mr Conway. I am fully sensible of their Goodness to me; but Sollicitations of every kind, I have ever carefully avoided, even when the State of my Fortune seemd more to warrant them than at present. Perhaps, some Office of an equivalent Value may fall vacant in this Country; and as my receiving it woud be a saving to the civil List, I hope that his Lordship woud admit my Application with Indulgence and not consider it as any Impropriety.

* 543. *To* [William Strahan]

Sir

Since my other Letter was put into the Post house, I made the Clerks of the Office search more exactly. They found your Letter so spoilt by Rain Water, that the Direction was not legible: And the corrected Sheet, Letter Z, was entirely spoilt. I must therefore beg of you to send me another Copy of that Sheet: As also a Copy of Sheet R, which I have never yet receivd. Please order the enclosd half Sheet to be inserted in the Manuscript, at the proper Place. I am Yours

D H

† 544. *To* Adam Smith

Mr Hume is very unhappy in never meeting with Mr Smith. He desires to remind him of his Engagement to dine with him to morrow. If Mr Smith chuses to pass this Evening with the Chief Baron, he will there meet with Mr A. Stuart and Mr Hume.

Wednesday 3 of June

* MS. lately in the possession of Messrs. Maggs Bros., London; hitherto unpublished. This letter might be given almost any date between 1756 and Hume's death.

† MS., R.S.E.; hitherto unpublished.

[1] Apparently Hume was applying for some sinecure, but there is nothing anywhere in his correspondence to show which one it was.

APPENDIXES

APPENDIX A

ENCLOSURE TO LETTER 69

TO THE RIGHT HON^BLE the LORD-CHIEF-JUSTICE REASON, and the HON^BLE the JUDGES, DISCRETION, PRUDENCE, RESERVE, and DELIBERATION,
THE PETITION of
THE PATIENTS of WESTMINSTER against
JAMES FRASER, apothecary

Most humbly showeth,

THAT your Petitioners had put themselves and Families under the Direction & Care of the said James Fraser, & had so continu'd for several Years, to their great mutual Benefit & Emolument.

THAT many of your Petitioners had, under his Management, recover'd from the most desperate & deplorable Maladies, such as Megrims, Toothakes, Cramps, Stitches, Vapours, Crosses in Love, &c. which wonderful Success, after the Blessing of God, they can ascribe to nothing but his consummate Skill & Capacity; since many of their Neighbours, labouring under the same Distresses, dy'd every day, by the Mistakes of less learned Apothecaries.

THAT there are many disconsolate Widows among your Petitioners, who believ'd themselves, & were believ'd by all their Neighbours, to be dying of Grief; but as soon as the said James Fraser apply'd Lenitives, & proper topical Medicines, they were observ'd to recover wonderfully.

That in all hypocondriacal Cases he was Sovereign, insomuch that his very Presence dispell'd the Malady, cheering the Sight, exciting a gentle Agitation of the Muscles of the Lungs & Thorax, & thereby promoting Expectoration, Exhileration, Circulation, and Digestion.

That your Petitioners verily believe, that not many more have dy'd from amongst them, under the Administration of the said James Fraser, than actually dye, by the Course of Nature, in Places where Physic is not at all known or practic'd: Which will scarcely be credited in this sceptical & unbelieving Age.

That all this Harmony & good Agreement betwixt your Petitioners & the said James Fraser had lately been disturb'd, to the great Detriment of your Petitioners, & their once numerous Families.

That the said James Fraser associating himself with —— Carey Surgeon,[1] & William Guthrey Esqr[2] & other evil intention'd Persons,

[1] Horace Walpole (*Letters*, i. 149) refers to a certain Carey, a surgeon, as an Opposition agent in the Westminster Election of 1741. He was probably engaged in the same capacity ten years later.

[2] Of William Guthrie (1708–70), Jacobite and hack-writer, opinions vary considerably. Samuel Johnson, with whom he worked on the *Gentleman's Magazine*, thought well enough of him; Ramsay of Ochtertyre thought very ill of him.

not having the Fear of God before their Eyes, had given himself entirely up to the Care of Dame PUBLIC, and had utterly neglected your Petitioners.

That the Lady abovementiond was of a most admirable CONSTITUTION, envy'd by all who had ever seen her or heard of her; & was only afflicted sometimes with Vapours, & sometimes with a Looseness or Flux, which, not being of the bloody kind, those about her were rather pleas'd with it.

That, notwithstanding this, the said James Fraser uses all Diligence & Art to perswade the said Lady, that she is in the most desperate Case imaginable, & that nothing will recover her but a Medicine he has prepard, being a Composition of *Pulvis pyrius*[1], along with a Decoction of northern Steel[2], and an Infusion of southern *Aqua sacra* or holy Water.[3]

That this Medicine or rather Poyson was at first wrapt up under a Wafer, markt Patriotism; but had since been attempted to be administrated without any Cover or Disguise.

That a Doze of it had secretly been pour'd down the Throat of the said Dame Public, while she was asleep, & had been attended with the most dismal Symptoms, visibly heightening her Vapours, & encreasing her Flux, & even producing some Symptoms of the bloody kind. And had she not thrown it up with great Violence, it had certainly prov'd fatal to her.

That the said James Fraser & his Associates now finding that this *Catholicon* does not agree with the Constitution of the said Dame, prescribe to her large Dozes of *Phillipiacum*[4], *Cottontium*[5], & *Vandeputiana*[6], in order to alter her Constitution & prepare her Body for the Reception of the said Catholicon.

That he had even been pleas'd to see *Lovitium*[7] apply'd to her, tho known to be a virulent Caustic, and really no better than *Lapis infernalis*.

That while the Medicines, Goveriacum[8] and Trentuntium[9], were very violent, resembling sublimate or *high-flown* Mercury, he also much approv'd of them; but since they were mollify'd by late Operations, and made as innocent as Mercurius Dulcis, they were become his utter Aversion.[10]

That the said James Fraser, thro' his whole Practice on the said

[1] Gunpowder. [2] The Highland Host in the 'Forty-Five'.

[3] James Fraser was probably a Catholic. Most of the Frasers were.

[4] Probably a reference to Sir John Phillips of Picton Castle, Pembrokeshire, Horace Walpole's cousin, a noted Jacobite and a turbulent person.

[5] A reference to Sir John Hinde Cotton, 3rd Bart. (died 1752), also a Jacobite.

[6] A reference to Vandeput, one of the candidates in the election.

[7] A reference to the Lovats, with probably a special reference to Simon Fraser, Lord Lovat, who was executed in 1747.

[8] A reference to Earl Gower.

[9] A reference to Lord Trentham, the successful candidate.

[10] It was a common taunt that Lord Gower and his son had turned their coats.

Dame Public, entirely rejected all Lenitives, Soporifics, Palliatives, &c, tho approv'd of by the regular & graduate Physicians, as Dr Pelham, Dr Fox, Dr Pitt; and that he prescrib'd nothing but Chymical Salts & stimulating Medicines, in which Regimen, none but Quacks & Empirics, who had never taken their Degrees, will agree with him.

That your Petitioners remember the Story of an Irish Servant to a Physician, which seem fitted to the present Purpose. The Doctor bid Teague carry a Potion to a Patient, & tell him it was the most innocent in the World, & if it did him no good, coud do him no harm. The Footman obeys, but unluckily transposing a Word, said that if it did him no Harm, it cou'd do him no Good: And your Petitioners are much afraid, that the Catholicon abovemention'd is much of the same Nature;

May it therefore please your Worships to discharge the said James Fraser from any farther Attendance on the said Dame Public, & to order him to return to the Care & Inspection of your Petitioners & their Families.

APPENDIX B

HUME'S EARLY FRENCH TRANSLATORS

1. *The 'Political Discourses'.*

This was the first of Hume's works to appear in a foreign translation. The earliest translation of it was published as:

Discours politiques de Mr David Hume, traduits de l'Anglois par M. de M***. A Amsterdam, chez J. Schreuder, & Pierre Mortier le Jeune. MDCCLIV. [16mo, pp. ii + 355.]

The translator was Eléazar de Mauvillon, of whom Le Blanc gives an unfavourable and probably an unfair account in his letter to Hume of 25 Dec. 1754 (see extract in vol. i, p. 207, note 3). There is nothing to show that Hume ever established touch with Mauvillon; and there is much to show that he did not. As soon as we put together Letters 94, 97, 97 A, 101, 113, 114, and 137, we see that they must have been all addressed to the same person; and as the replies to some of them are extant among the MSS., R.S.E., and are all from Le Blanc, we can establish the identity of Hume's correspondent with certainty. Hume wrote all these letters to Le Blanc, and as far as we can tell, wrote no letters to Mauvillon. The entries in the Brit. Mus. Catalogue of Autograph Letters for Letters 94, 97, 101, and 113 (all among Egerton MSS. 21) should be revised accordingly.

The Abbé Le Blanc's translation appeared first as:

Discours politiques de Monsieur Hume, traduits de l'Anglois. Amsterdam; et se vend à Paris, chez M. Lambert, 1754. [2 vols., 12mo.]

The following year a second edition appeared as:

Discours politiques de Monsieur Hume. Traduits de l'Anglois. Nouvelle Edition Par Monsieur L'Abbé Le Blanc Historiographe des Batimens du Roi de France . . . Avec Privilège du Roi. A Dresde, chez Michel Groell, Libraire et Marchand d'Estampes. M.DCC.LV. [2 vols., 8vo.]

2. *Other Philosophical Works.*

In 1758, J. H. Schneider, an Amsterdam bookseller, began the publication of what he later on entitled *Œuvres philosophiques de Mr. D. Hume.* His translators were J.-B. Mérian, J.-B.-R. Robinet de Châteaugiron and Mlle de la Chaux; and 5 vols. appeared, 1758–60, as follows:

I–II. *Essais philosophiques sur l'entendement humain . . . Avec les Quatres* [sic] *philosophes* [The Epicurean, the Stoic, the Platonist, and the Sceptic].

III. *Histoire naturelle de la Religion . . . avec un examen critique et philosophique de cet ouvrage.*

IV. *Dissertation sur les passions, sur la tragédie, sur la règle du goût.*

(Only III and IV bear on the half-title *Œuvres philosophiques de Mr. D. Hume.*)

V. *Essais de morale, ou Recherche sur les principes de la morale.*

In 1759 the same bookseller brought out:

Œuvres philosophiques de M. D. Hume [2 tomes in 1 vol., 8vo.], which contained the same works as III and IV above, in the same translations, and with the same accompaniments.

In 1764 he brought out what he called a second edition of *Œuvres de M. Hume*, in 2 vols., 8vo. This contained:

I. *Essais moraux et politiques.*

II. *Essais philosophiques sur l'entendement humain.*

On 5 Dec. 1763, Schneider wrote to Hume:

'Il y a près de quatre ans que j'ai cherché à me procurer votre adres, pour avoir l'honneur de vous présenter un exemplaire de vos Essais en Français, que j'ai fait traduire dans cette Langue & dont je vais dans peu publier le 6e volume de la premiere Edition, et le 1e de la seconde Edition . . . . Les tomes 1. 2. 3. & 4 sont traduit à Berlin, & le 5e à Paris. La traduction de tomes 3 4 & 5, je les ai payé deux fois; pour en avoir seul le fond de l'Edition Française; il me fallais faire ce Sacrifice, pour empecher qu'on n'en fit pas une edition à Geneve.

'Si vous publiez Monsieur, encore quelque chose, oserai-je vous prier, de me le faire parvenir d'abord, afin que je le puisse joindre sans delais.

'Un de mes Confrere ici, a fait traduire un volume, en français, dont je ne peux pas encore avoir le Droit de copie, mais j'ai esperance d'en faire l'acquisition dans peu, pour le faire imprimer d'un même caractere & format. La Traduction est fait par Mr Mauvillon à Dresde; Mr L'Abbé le Blanc en a fait aussi une de ce volume, qui à mon avis, me semble beaucoup mieux que l'autre . . .' (MS., R.S.E., unpublished.)

J.-B.-R. Robinet, author of the book, *De la Nature*, which made some stir in its day and which Hume mentions to Blair in Letter 237, may have made Hume's acquaintance in France, but I think this is unlikely. At any rate he wrote to Hume from Amsterdam on 17 Dec. 1765, addressing his letter to Dublin on the assumption that Hume had gone there with Lord Hertford. This letter went astray, and on 2 Sept. 1767 Robinet sent another copy of it to Hume. He says that he is proposing to bring out a complete edition of Hume's works in French, and he asks for Hume's opinion on the comparative merits of Mauvillon's and Le Blanc's translations of the *Political Discourses*. He continues:

'On a imprimé en Hollande 6 petits volumes sous le titre d'Œuvres

Philosophiques contenant les Essais sur l'entendement Humain, les Essais de Morale, l'histoire naturelle de la Religion &c. Cette traduction ou plutot ces traductions sont de plusieurs mains. Il y a quelque peu de Voltaire dans les essais de morale, au moins j'ai vu des corrections de sa main sur une mauvaise traduction des premiers Essais, qui m'a passé manuscrite sous les yeux, & qui est entrée dans les 6 petits volumes dont je vous parle . . . Les traducteurs ont joint quelques notes dans lesquelles ils prétendent refuter le texte: ils me semblent de pigmées qui vont heurter étourdiment un colosse, ou des enfans qui veulent enchaîner un géant avec un cheveu. Toutes ces notes seront supprimées. . . . On vous attribue un *Traité de la Nature humaine* imprimé à Londres en 1739 & dont je ne connois point de traduction françoise. On imprime actuellement ici la traduction d'un Ouvrage Anglois intitulé: *Tableau Philosophique de l'histoire du Genre humain, depuis l'origine du monde jusqu'à Constantin.* Le traducteur vous l'attribue.' (MS., R.S.E., unpublished.)

Apparently Hume answered this letter on 26 Sept. 1767, and either then or a little later sent Robinet a copy of the *Essays and Treatises.* There are two further letters from Robinet, both dated from Bouillon, among the MSS., R.S.E. He speaks of pushing on with his edition of Hume's works, and of having it ready by the spring of 1769; but all that seems ever to have appeared is *Le Temple du Bonheur* noted below.

Meanwhile Andrew Millar's friend, David Wilson, the London bookseller who visited Paris in the later summer of 1764 and was presented by Hume to Lord Hertford (see letter 250 above), had reprinted Schneider's translations as:

Œuvres philosophiques de M. Hume, traduites de l'Anglois . . . Nouvelle Edition, Londres, D. Wilson, 1764, in 6 vols., 8vo:
I. *Les huits* [sic] *premiers Essais sur l'entendement humain.*
II. *Les quatre derniers Essais sur l'entendement humain et les quatre philosophes.*
III. *Histoire naturelle de la religion.*
IV. *Les Dissertations sur les passions, sur la tragédie et sur la règle du goût.*
V. *Les Recherches sur les principes de la morale.*
VI. *Les Essais moraux et politiques.*

This was probably a pirated edition.

Three other publications about this time may be noted:

(*a*) Essais sur le commerce; le luxe; l'argent; l'intérêt de l'argent; les impôts; le credit public; et la balance du commerce; par M. David Hume. Traduction nouvelle, avec des Réflections du Traducteur. Et Lettre d'un négociant de Londres à un de ses amis . . . A Paris, chez Saillant . . . A Lyon, Chez Aimé De la Roche . . . M.DCC.LXVII. [8vo, pp. 232.]

(*b*) Pensées philosophiques, morales, critiques, littéraires et politiques de M. Hume . . . A Londres. Et se trouve à Paris, chez la Veuve Duschesne . . . M.DCC.LXVII. [12mo, pp. xii + 416.]

(*c*) Le Temple du Bonheur, ou Recueil des plus excellens Traités sur le

Bonheur, extraits des meilleurs auteurs anciens et modernes, Tome premier. A Bouillon, Aux Dépens de la Société Typographique. Et se trouve à Paris, chez Lacombe. M.DCC.LXIX. [8vo.]

3. *The Suppressed Essays.*

Copies of Hume's two suppressed essays, *Of Suicide* and *Of the Immortality of the Soul*, found their way early into France. Perhaps Hume himself lent them to some of his philosophical friends in Paris and allowed copies to be taken; perhaps they were shown as curiosities by John Wilkes, who had a proof copy in his possession at one time. However it may have been, they appeared for the first time in a French translation in a book entitled *Recueil Philosophique*, 2 tom. in 1 vol., Londres, 1770. Tome II of this publication contains, *inter alia*:

(i) Sentences des Philosophes sur la nature de l'âme, par M. Mirabaud.
(ii) Dissertation sur l'immortalité de l'âme, traduit de l'anglois.
(iii) Dissertation sur le suicide, traduit de l'anglois.
(iv) Problème important. La religion est-elle nécessaire à la morale et utile à la politique? par M. Mirabaud.
(v) Pensées sur la religion. Anonyme.

(ii) and (iii) are Hume's essays. The 'Mirabaud' given as the author of (i) and (iv) is a pseudonym for the Baron d'Holbach, and Lanson definitely gives d'Holbach as the translator of Hume's essays, I do not known on what authority.

I imagine Hume never heard of these translations and would have been somewhat annoyed if he had.

4. The '*History*'.

These have all been referred to in the Notes above. (See especially Vol. i, pp. 258, 302, 415, 494.)

APPENDIX C

MISCELLANEOUS LETTERS TO HUME

* I. *From* Mme Dupré de St. Maur (see Letter 137 above)

A Paris ce 15 x[bre] 1757

Quelles expressions Monsieur pouroient suffire a vous peindre ma reconnoissance du beau present dont vous m'avez honnorée, je scais que c'est a Mons L'abbé Le Blanc que je dois cette faveur, il a été temoin de mon admiration pour vos ouvrages, il a scu m'en faire un merite aupres de vous, vous n'avez point dedaigné un homage peu flatteur mais bien sincere, tous les gents eclairez de notre nation vous en rendent un plus honorable, pour moy il me semble que je represente pour les ignorants, si leur classe n'est pas la plus estimable, elle est du moins la plus nombreuse, et la premiere en datte disoit notre ami Fontenelle, c'est a ce titre là que vos productions m'ont charmée; peu versée dans la Langue Angloise vous me l'avez rendue facile par la Clarté et par la beauté de votre Stile et de vos idées, j'ay trouvé dans votre histoire un traitté de philosophie appliquée a des faits bien interessans, jamais lecture ne ma tant attachée, et jamais je n'ay eu si bonne opinion de moy que lorsque je vous ai lu, j'ose Monsieur vous renvoyer a votre dissertation sur les passions pour en trouver la raison, mon amour propre vous est donc un sur garant de mon admiration de ma reconnoissance et de mon extreme desir qu'une heureuse paix retablisse pour jamais une libre communication entre deux nations dignes d'une estime reciproque, et vous engage a venir recueillir ici les fruits de la reputation que vous vous y êtes acquis, je serai bien empressée a proffitter du sejour que vous y ferez et ne perdrai aucune occasion de vous prouver la parfaitte Consideration avec laquelle je suis pour la vie Monsieur votre tres humble et tres obeissante servante

Alleon Du pré de St. Maur.

* II. *From* John Stewart (see Letter 164 above)

Paris 1st March 1759

My Dear David

My Father has probably communicated to you a part of two letters I have wrote him from this place. If he has not, tell him I beg he may, as he knows I hate writing much, and it will save me some pages. The principal motive I have for troubling you with an epistle is to express my gratitude for the obligations I owe to your friendship, for under the title of your friend I have been more caressed here than ever stranger was by people of distinguished merit

* MS., R.S.E., unpublished.

and a high rank in life. I hinted at your intention of one day paying them a visit and I assure you it gave a most general & unfeigned satisfaction to a great number of People you would like to live with and who, as far as my penetration goes, would be very happy to have you amongst them. If you have any thoughts of making a trip this Summer or Autumn, you need only say the word, and your Passport will be sent you by the return of the Post.

Madame Dupres your friend is a woman of fortune, fashion, and great good sense remarkably well behaved & generally esteemed. At her house you will see a great deal of the Politest & genteellest Company. Monsr de Trudaine who is equally desirous to see you & to have you at his Country house is a man so well known that I need not tell you the advantages of being acquainted with him. His son is one of the most amiable Characters in Paris. He has made a translation of your natural History of Religion which is too bulky to send you by the Post but I shall convey it to you by a private hand. To each of these you must send a Copy of your last Volume of the History as also to Monsr Turgot a man of very good sense great knowledge and one of your Admirers. You may add one too for the Chevalier de Chatlus [Chastellux] whom you'll wish to know when you come here. He learned the English language on purpose to read your works in the Original. All these may be directed to Mr de Trudaine, who being a Minister has every thing brought to him from the different parts of the kingdom very carefully & free of Charges. Pray don't forget our old friend Helvetius too who says he'll come to England to see you if you dont come to Paris. He lives in friendship with the above set because they love his aimiable Character at the same time that they have no very high idea of his Philosophy. He certainly is one of the best men ever was formed.

I am charged to make many Compliments to you from Mr Crebillon, Mr du Hamel, the Abbé du Renel [Raynal] & many many more who look for your coming amongst them with the same anxiety & impatience that ——[1] look for ——[1] Pray indulge them & me and come next winter. I'll meet you here soon after the Vintage is over & if you don't like the Place we'll return together.

The following books must be purchased & sent at the same time & an Acc^t of the charge transmitted to me.

Two copies of Robinson's [Robertson's] History
Johnson's Dictionary in Octavo
D^o in Folio
Shakespears Works
Popes Illiad
Tom Jones
Memoires of a woman of pleasure 2 Volumes printed for G. Fenton in the Strand 17[?]

[1] *Sic* in MS.

Miscellaneous Tracts by Middleton
Human Nature in 3 volumes by Dav: Hume
An Introduction to Languages Literary & Philosophical by H. Bailey 2 vols 8vo
Gerard Malines on Money

The whole may be sent to the care of Mr. Crawford at Rotterdam with orders to forward them to Mr de Trudaines Intendant General des finances & du commerce.

If an Cartel ship is going from Dover to Calais it will save Charges. My father will know by writing a line to Messrs Minet at Dover or sending to the Sick & Wounded Office on Tower Hill.

Messrs Minet will consign the Parcell to their friend at Calais.

Adieu my Dear Sir I won't tire you any longer. Believe me always most sincerely & respectfully Yours

JOHN STEWART

Please add to the list of books to be purchased & sent here.
The Bible in the Erse & in the Welsh languages
The best Grammar (if there ever was one) in these two languages.
D° as to the Dictionarys in D° languages

No matter whether the Grammars are wrote in Latin or English but the Dictionarys must be double viz Erse & English or Latin and English or Latin & Erse. The same as to the Welsh Dictionary. This commissn is for Mr Turgot who's a great Etymologist.

Madame du Pres husband is an Antiquarian & wishes to know from Bob Wood the dimensions of the three Pyramids in Egypt in case he measured them.

Mr Dupres also wishes to know if there is any book published giving an Acct of the Ancient English moneys & particularly their weights which he says Ld Pembroke has carelessly omitted & which he's very angry at.

The Principal of the Scots Colledge here is also very angry at your friend Robinson [Robertson] for publishing his book before he came or sent somebody to examine 18 Volumes in folio of Manuscripts & records in the reign of Mary Queen of Scots which they have in this Colledge here.

To David Hume Esqr
London.

* III. *From* JOHN STEWART (see Letter 164 above)

My Dear Sir [undated]

I wrote to you about a fourthnight ago by the Post. The present goes by a Servant I had brought with me from England who chuses to return because his health does not well bear the fatigue of posting.

I send you herewith Mr Montigny de Trudaine's Translation of

* MS., R.S.E., unpublished.

your N.H. of R. He's a very fine Young fellow, a rising man here and a great admirer of yours.

Besides the books I formerly begged of you to get I must trouble you for some more to be sent with the same address.

For Mr Turgot

The Peerage of England   D^o of Scotland   D^o of Ireland
Robinson's [Robertson's] history of Scotland
Baskerville's Milton 2 Volumes
second volume of Hume's History of England
Essays & Treatises on various subjects by David Hume
one Volume in quarto
Four Dissertations by Ditto in Duodecimo

For President de Brosses

Baskerville's Milton and Ditto for Mr de Trudaine le fils

I'm not sure whether Mr Turgot does not mean by the second Volume of your History what we commonly call the first because he reckons that of the House of Tudor to be really the first.

This is a deal of trouble I give you but 'tis to serve men who would go to the Indies to serve you, for I'm in great earnest when I tell you that you're the man of the world they hold in the highest esteem.

Pray remember to write either to Monsr or Mad^e du Pre de St Maur about the different things I recommended in my last & you should also write a short line to Mr Montigny de Trudaine after you have read his translation. A letter from you will at all times give great Satisfaction here. The few you have wrote have been much talked of. I once more repeat to you that your Correspondent Mad^e du Pre de St Maur is without exception the most accomplished woman I ever saw and I also think the most rational & sensible.

I have sent you inclosed Proposals for publishing that fine Map of France you have heard so much of. Tis under the direction of the Academy and there are 31 Sheets already struck off. These I have seen and they are inimitably well done. Pray communicate these proposals to the curious for they are vastly surprized here in having as yet had only 25 subscriptions from Great Britain. Adieu.

J. S.

[Written in Hume's hand:
The Irish Bible
A Grammar & Dictionary of Irish
Harris instead of Gerrard de Malines]

* IV. *From* Gilbert Elliot (see Letter 232 above)

So, my Dear Sir, you have at last with no small reluctance, & after many struggles prevaild with yourself to acquaint some of your friends, that Lord Hertford means to desire that Government woud

* MS., R.S.E.; Burton, ii. 278 (incomplete).

be graciously pleas'd to bestow the character & emoluments of the Secretaryship upon the person who actually performs the functions of it. At your time of life, with so much independency about you, & so unlike your former conduct—indeed I am not at all surpris'd that it cost you near two pages of apology & explanation before you woud even intrust me with the secret. Were you less deep in the study of Human nature, & somewhat more an adept in the ways of men, I am apt to think, you woud rather have fill'd your letter with excuses for not having sooner made this application. However, to take up this gravely & in your own way, I am very sincerely of opinion that Lord Hertford in making a point of this request is doing the properest thing in the world, both with regard to his friendship for you, his own character, & the particular Station he fills. You say your hope of success is but moderate, & this to be sure is a very proper disposition of mind, & yet I can hardly agree with you, for I am really of opinion that Lord Hertford must prevail, & that some other arrangement must be found for Mr Bunbury. As to what collateral assistance your friends here can give, or how necessary their efforts may be I cant pretend to judge. It is enough for me that Lord Hertford wishes that your friends shoud assist as far as they can. Upon this principle I lost no time, in stating & inforcing the propriety of your demand, in all the ways and thro all the channels to which my little interest had any access. But tho I lost no time I had however the satisfaction to find Lord Hertford had been before hand with me, even where I lest expected to find him. As to the success I shall pretend to say nothing of it, as you must learn it more authentically, by the regular dispatches, but it is really my opinion that you will succeed, & I found this opinion both upon the reasonableness of the thing, & upon the manner I found it was receivd.

As to *Ingrata patria ne ossa quidem habebis*. Dont be at all uneasie, here I can speak more peremtorily, & notwithstanding all your errors mistakes & Heresys, in Religion Morals, & Government, I undertake, you shall have at least Christian Burial, & perhaps we may find for you a niche in Westminster Abey, besides. Your Lokes, Newtons & Bacons, had no great matter to boast of during their lives, & yet they were the most orthodox of men, they required no Godfather to answer for them, while on the other hand did not Lord Hertford spread his sevenfold shield, over all your transgressions, pray what pretentions have you either in Church or State, for you well know you have offended both. But I know what is the matter with you, the French Ladys as much as the French Philosophers have contributed to render you vain, & when successful with the fair & flattered by the learned, I know what sport you will make of all our grave admonitions. I long thought you woud have been content with a reversionary estate on fame not to take full effect till after your death, but since you are corrupted by bad company we must even assist you to grow rich & lazy like other men. To my Dear Sir

I am ever Yours very truly
GILB: ELLIOT.

London 25th Apl 1764

* V. *From the* REV. JOHN JARDINE (see Letter 237 above)

Edinr Augt [?] 1764

. . . I have attempted 4 or 5 times to write to you, But this poor Church has for some time past been in such Danger, that I could never find time for it. She has imployed all my Thoughts & Care for these 12 months past. The Enemy had kindled such a flame that the old burning bush was like to have been consumed altogether. I know it will give you pleasure to hear, that my Endeavours to preserve her, have been crownd wt Successe. She begins to shine furth wt her antient Lustre, & will very soon be, not only fair as the Sun, but to all her Enemies, terrible as an Army wt Banners. Ever since you left us all your Brn in the Regency have been in a state of Persecution; but God be thanked, the Tables are changed. It is in our Power now to persecute, which like orthodox Churchmen we shall not fail to do wt the outmost Rigor.

I beg you will notify this Resolution of ours to the Archbishop of Paris & the other Leaders of the Gallican Church. This will tend much to remove their prejudices against an Union wt our Church which we suppose is already in great forwardness in consequence of your Labours among them; of which we hear every day most favourable accounts.

The Regency here are of opinion, that you ought not to be too rigorous in your Terms of Accomodation. Proceed on the plan of Compromise. E. G. Tell them, if they will give up the Worship of Images, they shall be left at full Liberty to persecute. If they will part wt four or five Sacraments we will give up as many Commands. And wt respect to the Sacrament of Matrimony particularly, if they will renounce that, the Clergy by way of Indemnification shall be allowed to commit Adultery as often as they see it for their Edification or Amusement. From these few hints, you will easily percieve, in what manner we wish this Treaty of Union between the two Churches may be carried on . . .

If they insist on having a Long Creed or Confession of Faith, consisting of many articles, I have no objection to it, provided that each of those articles be expressed so as not to be understood, and will affoord sufficient Matter of altercation among the Learned.

You know that my admonitions heretofore have done you much

* MS., R.S.E., unpublished.

good. You often stood in need of them, and I am sorry to observe from some Passages in your Letters to the Brethrn here, you stand very much in need of them at present. I clearly perceive, tho' you dont seem to have the least apprehension of it yourself, that you are in great danger of being seduced to the Commission of the Sin of Uncleannesse. An inordinate Love of the fair Sex, as I have often told you with Tears, is one of those Sins, that always, even from your earliest Years, did most easily beset you. This is your weak Side, Satan has at last discovered it, & on this unguarded Quarter, he is now making his assault. He makes love to you, by assuming the most ensnaring of all Forms, viz That of a fine Lady. Believe me, all those fine Ladys of Wit & Beauty, you speak of with so much Rapture, are all Devils. I dont say, that they have that antient visible Symbol of the demoniacal presence, by which Satan was discovered in former times, viz the Cloven foot; The Devil is grown a great deal more cunning than he was in the Days of our Forefathers, and therefore that this diabolical Mark, may be the better concealed, he has placed it more out of Sight; but tho' it is not now so easily seen as it was, yet it may be as easily felt, if you make diligent Search for it. I beseech you consider seriously, what Dishonour it will reflect on your Character as an apostle sent from the purest Church on Earth to convert the idolatrous Papists, if it shall hereafter appear that during the Course of your Mission, you have been carrying on a criminal Correspondence with French Succuba's. The great Reformer Luther has written very learnedly on this Subject in his Book called *Table Talk.* I desire you to peruse the Chapter on Incubus & Succuba. . . .

* VI. *From* JAMES EDMONSTOUNE (see Letter 238 above)

Geneva 26 March [1764]

My Dear Secretary

I have delay'd for some Time answering your Letter in Expectation of being able to tell you what is to become of me, whether I am to return Home or to remain abroad some years longer; tho I believe the latter will happen I cannot speak of it with Certainty, as I left it to Lord B[ute] to determine for me and he has not as yet given me any Answer. I write to you at present to consult you about an Acquaintance of yours Mr Vivian who is here with Lord Abingdon and who thinks of returning to England May next. You'll be so good as to determine for him what Character he is to assume on his Arrival, whether that of a Clergyman or a Layman. I suppose you know he is in Orders, but he is very very low Church, to speak plain Language, I believe him to be [a] Sort of Disciple of your own and tho he does not carry Matters quite so far as you yet you have given

* MS., R.S.E.; Burton, ii. 185 ff.

him Notions not very consistent with his Priestly Character, so that you see you are somewhat bound to give him your best Advice. Vivian is a very good naturd sensible honest Fellow without any ffortune. My young man [Lord Mountstuart] has a great Liking for him and has all the Inclination in the World to serve him, but he neither knows what to ask for him, and is not sure if his ffather would ask any Thing at present. We are as much in the Dark as to what passes in England as if we liv'd in Siberia. As you know probably something of the Matter, without entering into Politicks you may give us some Hints to direct us in what Manner to act, and whether we may not be of more Use to our Friend in acting as Auxiliaries than Principals. Youll determine whether a Man of Probity can accept of a Living a Bishoprick that does not believe all the 39 Articles; for you only can fix him, he has been hitherto irresolute. If [I am not] mistaken he seems rather inclind not to be a Clergyman but you know better than I do how difficult it is to get any tolerable civil Employment. I mean any patent Place. Write as soon as you can conveniently and if you should determine for his being a Clergyman throw in something consolatory on his being oblig'd to renounce white Stockings the rest of his Life. I wait with Impatience to hear of your being made Secretary to the Embassy. Shall a Descendant of Gospatrick Earl of Northumberland remain in the Character of Under Secretary I hope not, tho I am afraid our cursed Politicks at Home will occasion some Delay . . .

* VII. *From* ANDREW MILLAR (see Letter 267 above)

London 26 Nov 1764

. . . I shall not make any new Edition of the Stewarts till I inform you, but I am perswaded next Spring or Summer I shall. Their Sale have [*sic*] been more than the others. They came out first and ye rest some years after w^{c} was the cause, but there are above 2500 compleat Setts sold in the 4to of ye lowest sale vols, but upwards of 3000 of the Stewarts. Of y^{r} 8vo history near 2000 and y^{r} 8vo Essays 400. These things I wrote from Kew about 3 m^{ts} ago, and also y^{t} they were in daily Sale. Sure this is full encouragement for y^{o} to go on. Y^{r} Essays 8vo were only published in May, what has been sold of y^{m} of all ye different editions I cannot recollect. I was asked y^{t} question at St James's the other day, when I said I considered y^{r} Works as Classicks, that I never numbered ye Editions as I did in Books We wished to puff. This I said before many Clergy.

I am not a little surprized to see one of y^{r} excellent Understanding and merit so anxious about the Sale when the Bookseller intirely concernd never complained, but on the Contrary, would be ready to give you to y^{r} utmost wish any encouragement to proceed in y^{r}

* MS., R.S.E., unpublished.

History, and in Truth considering the N° of Enemies from particular Essays have risen from *Interest*, Bigottery, folly and knavery not less than one hundred Thousand It is rather astonishing, y^r Works have sold so much. While *Men* are *Men* this is to be expected and you are the last man I should ever [have] thought could [have] paid ye least attention to such Things. beleive me D S the furder you go in y^r History the more it will sell, wrote with the same Spirit of impartiality as that published, and Therefer confirm my hopes and y^t of all y^r friends with y^r Intention of carrying it on.

I wrote also to you from Kew that the Edition of y^r Essays of duodecimo are out of print, pray shall they be reprinted from ye 8vo?

I am now going thro' a course of Advert^s of y^r Works, &:c: a copy of w^c I inclose you. . . .

* VIII. *From* MADAME GEOFFRIN (see Letter 270 above)

[16 mars 1765]

Vous croiéz donc, quant qualité, de gros, et D'aimable Drôle, avoir acquis le Droit, de faire toutes les Drôleries possible. Vous vené mon beau Monsieur, D'en faire une un peu trop forte.

elle ressemble plus a une méchanceté, qu'a une galanterie. l'etat D'humiliation, ou se trouve mes pauvres Livres, a côté de La magnificence des vôtre, perce le coeur. ils ont tous l'aire de vieux Bouquins, qui arrivent de dessu les quais

de plus c'est l'acte de La vanité, la plus forte, dont dont on est jamais entendu parler. Il faut que vous ayéz une furieuse opinion de vos ouvrages, pour leur avoir donné un aussi bel habit. depuis que ce nouvel astre Brille sur mes planches, je n'ose plus lever les yeux dessu, tant la laideur de leur anciens citoyens m'afflige.

non je ne vous pardonnerai jamais La Révolution que vous vené de faire dans ma Bibliotheque. hélas je l'aimois telle qu'elle etoit. Aprésen elle fait mon malheur. et elle feroit ma ruine, si le Diable de La superbe me montoit a la tête, au point, de vouloir etre, aussi magnifique que l'est, vôtre fatal présen.

vanités, des vanités dit le Sage.

je répêterai, cette maxime toute la journée, pour me préserver de La folie, de vouloir vous imiter.

ce Samedy matin.

M^de La princesse de Beauvau soupe se soir chez moi. Ouy, ouy, ouy.

† IX. *From* JAMES OSWALD OF DUNNIKIER (see Letter 276 above)

13th June 1765.

Dear Hume,

Your letter of the 2d instant, gave infinite pleasure, by assuring me that Lord Hertford was using the warmest solicitations for your

* MS., R.S.E.; *Eminent Persons*, 287 f. † Oswald, 84 ff.

succeeding Bunbury: that circumstance alone is, I think, sufficient to secure success, which, notwithstanding *your incredulity*, I might almost venture to wish you joy of. The news here, before I received your letter, were, that the ministry intended to make an offer of the Secretaryship to Lord Hertford's son. If that was so, the matter is out of doubt. But if not, his application, in the present circumstances cannot, I should imagine, fail of success. My good wishes, as well as my opinion on this subject, are perfectly well known and understood by everybody. How far any interposition on my part, in any quarter whatever, could be useful to my friend, on the present occasion, you will judge by what you must have heard by this time of our situation in England. I am satisfied, however, that your success is certain, and therefore that I may wish you joy, which I do most sincerely.

Your queries I will take what pains I can to answer, and wish I could do so accurately, but that, I'm afraid, is impossible. It will take some time, and a good deal of inquiry, to do it with any degree of precision in most of your queries; to do it otherwise, would only mislead; and therefore in such cases I shall say so, and assign reasons, which, I hope, will be satisfactory. . . .

* X. *From the* EARL OF HOLDERNESSE (see Letter 283 above)

London July 2d. 1765.

Dear Sir

I received on Saturday last the letter you have favoured me with of the 24th Past which I observe to have been wrote with the knowledge of a Prince for whom I have the utmost respect and veneration, & upon a subject of the utmost delicacy & consequence to the future ease of that great personage and of another for whom you know I have the most devoted attachment. I must premise in the first place that I shall observe the most inviolable Secresy even to the person concerned unless she brings with her a suspicion of my having been wrote to & should tax me with it in which case I cannot deceive her.

I confess I think it unlikely that she will open herself at all to me upon so nice a point, I have no right to expect such unbounded confidence from her, & I am sure you will agree with me that it would be highly improper for me to touch upon so tender a subject unless she herself begins it, such a step could only create the suspicion you and the Prince wish to avoid, render all I could say of no effect, diminish her good opinion of me, without forwarding what you both wish. but if she should deign to consult me, the use I could be of to her would be to help her to think aloud, to arrange those thoughts with coolness, and method; & to draw the true conclusions

* MS., R.S.E.; *Eminent Persons*, 73 f.

after a candid examination of the different situations that occur for consideration namely

1st. continuing when a widow her former connexions.

2dly breaking those connexions and continue a widow.

3dly to marry the person with whom she has been connected.

The two first points depending upon herself must first be scrutinized and the examination of them will lead to consider how far it may be adviseable for her to push the last, and to fix her resolution in case she fails in the attempt.

It is impossible for me to determine my own opinion till I hear her reasons, my wish leads me to facilitate what the Prince desires, as far as may be consistent with the duty of a friend consulted upon a most nice and difficult conjuncture. all I can now promise is that if she does speak to me upon the affair you shall soon hear from me again upon the subject. . . .

* XI. *From* LAMOIGNON DE MALESHERBES (see Letter 308 above)

[undated]

On cherche des pretextes, Monsieur, pour se rappeller dans vôtre Souvenir quand on a eu le bonheur de vous connoitre et qu'on a le chagrin d'en estre separé. Celuy que je saisis aujourdhuy est une petite affaire que j'ay à arranger avec M. Rousseau et dont je voudrois que vous vous meslassiés. La voicy. Je luy ay donné un certificat sur une circonstance de sa vie que je crois peu interessante, mais dont il ne pense pas de même. Je suis très sur que ce certificat ne peut luy être bon à rien. Mais il s'occupe du projet d'écrire son histoire pour quelle soit imprimée après sa mort et il le régarde comme une piece justificative. Ce certificat a été Ecrit de memoire, et j'estois bien sur de ne m'être pas trompé sur le fait Essensiel que le livre n'avoit été imprimé à Paris que malgré l'auteur. Mais je me suis amusé depuis à rélire les notes qui me sont restées sur cette affaire, et je trouve qu'il y a une circonstance, fort indifferente a la verité dont la fausseté se trouve prouvée par des lettres que j'ay entre les mains, et peut l'etre par d'autres lettres qui sont je ne scais ou.

Il faut convenir que la foy due à mon certificat seroit beaucoup affoiblie si cette erreur venoit à se découvrir. Mais le moyen de tout réparer est faite. Je vous en envoye un autre ou les faits sont rétablis. Je vous prie de rétirer celuy qui est entre les mains de M. Rousseau en luy en disant la raison qu'il trouvera surement très bonne et d'y substituer celuy cy. La difference consiste en ce qu'il y a dans le premier certificat, *cette liste fut communiquée a M. Rousseau et ce fut par là qu'il apprit qu'on se proposoit d'imprimer son livre à Paris*, au lieu qu'il y a dans celuy cy, *cette liste fut communiquée à M. Rousseau*

* MS., R.S.E.; *Eminent Persons*, 219 ff.

à qui on avoit appris quelque tems auparavant qu'on avoit commencé à imprimer son livre à Paris.

Cela est bien indifferent puisque le réproche qu'on fait à nôtre pauvre ami n'est point d'avoir fraudé les loix de la Librarie de France, mais d'avoir Ecrit contre la réligion, et puisqu'il a esté poursuivi en Hollande, à Geneve et a Berne comme en France. Mais puisque ce certificat L'amuse et qu'il se repait de l'Espoir d'une apologie posthume, il ne faut pas luy refuser un si petit plaisir, il faut seulement n'y rien insérer qui ne soit vrai.

Vous me demanderés peut estre pourquoi je m'adresse a vous et non pas directement a luy, en voicy la raison. Je ne sçais s'il ne garde pas les lettres qu'on luy Ecrit. Si cela est, il est sur qu'elles seront toutes imprimées apres sa mort. Or s'il veut que mon certificat soit rendu public il ne faut pas y joindre une lettre qui apprenne qu'il a été fait à deux fois, et qui feroit croire à bien des lecteurs que M'étant trompé sur une circonstance, j'aurois pu me tromper également sur le reste.

En voila bien assés de dit, Monsieur, sur cette affaire. Mandés moy je vous prie comment nôtre ami trouve le sejour d'Angleterre, s'il a pris l'habitation que vous luy aviés choisie, ce qu'il devient, s'il a quelques besoins, s'il y a quelque moyen de luy rendre service.

Mandés moy aussi, je vous en suplie, ce qui m'interesse encore plus, ce sont des nouvelles de vous personnellement. Si vos projets de retour en France se réalisent et surtout si l'execution en approche. Vous avés tant d'amis dans ce pays cy, que vous n'auriés jamais fini s'il falloit répondre a tous ceux qui vous feroient les mêmes questions. Mais quelque interest que les autres y prennent, je vous assure que je le dispute à tout Le monde.

Récevés je vous prie, les assurances du sincère et inviolable attachement avec lequel j'ay l'honneur d'estre, Monsieur

Votre très humble et très obeissant Serviteur,

DE LAMOIGNON DE MALESHERBES.

* XII. *From* MLLE DE LESPINASSE (see Letter 317 above)

A Paris ce 23 fevrier 1766.

Je vous avois promis, Monsieur, de ne point vous ecrire, mais je sens que j'ai promis plus que je ne peux tenir et je ne puis resister au desir qui me presse de vous demander de vos nouvelles, quoique je sois obligée de me servir pour cela d'une main etrangere mes yeux n'etant pas encore retablis du mal que la petite verole leur a fait. J'ai le plaisir de m'entretenir souvent de vous avec M. D'Alembert qui aspire ainsi que moi au moment ou nous aurons le plaisir de vous

* MS., R.S.E.; *Eminent Persons*, 179 f., where the enclosure, the character of the Dauphin, is also printed at length.

As the enclosure remained among Hume's papers, it is probable that he failed to pass Mlle de Lespinasse's suggestion on to Rousseau.

revoir. Mad[e] de Boufflers me donne souvent de vos nouvelles et me fait esperer que vous ne tarderez pas a revenir. Je voudrois en hâter le moment et vous posseder sans avoir a craindre de vous perdre.

Ma lettre a encore un autre objet que de sçavoir comment vous vous portez; c'est de vous engager a proposer à M[r.] Rousseau un ouvrage qui pourra lui être honorable et utile. Je voudrois que M[r.] le Dauphin fut loué comme il le merite, et je ne connois sans exception personne en France qui en soit capable. M. Rousseau seul peut metre dans cet éloge la chaleur et l'interêt qui peuvent le rendre agreable aux ames sensibles, et dont nos orateurs nos poëtes et nos philosophes ne se doutent pas. M. Rousseau a d'ailleurs quelques raisons, qu'il ignore peut etre, pour cherir la mémoire de M. le D'auphin; car il est constant que ce Prince peu de jours avant que de mourir à [*sic*] témoigné s'interesser beaucoup à M. Rousseau et desapprouvé extremement les persecutions qu'on lui fait souffrir. Enfin, Monsieur, j'imagine que cet éloge seroit un moyen de faciliter le retour de M. Rousseau en France, et de le rendre a ses amis et a une nation qui le regrette. Si vous gouttez cette idée et que vous la fassiez gouter à M. Rousseau, je joins ici a tout hasard un petit mémoire qui vient de bonne main, et qui pourra servir a M. Rousseau de matiere pour les belles choses qu'il sçaura dire. Adieu, Monsieur, échaufféz si vous le pourez M. Rousseau sur cette besogne; je connois vôtre paresse à écrire, je ne vous demande donc point de réponse directe, je vous prie seulement de me dire un mot de ma proposition dans la prémiere lettre que vous écrivez à Mad[e] de Boufflers; mais je vous prie surtout de revenir au plutôt me dire vous même de vos nouvelles. . . .

* XIII. *From* William Strahan (see Letter 490 above)

London, March 19, 1773.

Dear Sir

Yours of the 15th I received to-day, which does not a little surprise me. After having been most unfeignedly attached to you ever since I had the pleasure of your acquaintance; after having done every thing in my power to oblige you; after having given the most careful attention to your works when under my press, for which I received your repeated acknowledgements; and after having behaved to you in the most open, candid, and ingenuous manner upon every occasion since I became a proprietor in your works; I did not, I could not expect to be told by you, after all, that I was a lying scoundrel, who had constantly deceived you, to whom you could give no manner of credit.

Such it seems, is now your deliberate opinion both of Mr. Cadell

* Barker MSS.; Hill, 266 ff. Hill speaks of the 'manly indignation' displayed in this letter (p. xlv). Other readers may think that Strahan protested with unnecessary vehemence and with self-betraying rhetoric.

and myself. Produce, I call upon you, and have a right so to do, one single instance to support the heavy charge you bring against us; concealing from you, at the desire of the late Mr. Millar, the number of the 8vo edition of your History alone excepted; which we did purely at his request, having then no interest, nor the least shadow of interest, to deceive you in that or any other particular.

I own that I am quite astonished at the style of your last letter, which is such as should be directed to one of the most worthless of the human race, and to such only.

Do not imagine, however, that I mean to enter into a laboured defence of myself. Far from it. I have nothing to apologize for; nothing have I said or done respecting you, that I now wish unsaid or undone.—Some recent cause of disgust, however groundless, you have conceived; but as my whole conduct respecting you has all along be[en] so more than blameless, this cause, whatever it may be, is to me a perfect mystery.—I told you faithfully, from time to time, how many were left on hand of the 8vo edition. You told me in a late letter *that we had better submit to some loss, than allow the book to be discredited by that abominable edition.*—All proper haste was made to finish and publish it. In my last I told you not above 100 Copies were left; this was so very true, that upon enquiry today, I find they are exactly 76, which we can either destroy, or sell abroad; they are no object. But why do I trouble either you or myself to give you any detail upon this or any other subject; which, as you very politely tell me, *is entirely vain and fruitless, as you can give no manner of credit to my answers.*

Had not Mr. Cadell and I, from the moment we were free agents and concerned in your works, done everything we could devise for your satisfaction and honour; had we not invariably refused to have any interest in any thing that had a tendency to discredit or displease you; in particular Dr. Beattie's book; had we not on many occasions—But I scorn to instance more particulars—we might have looked for this treatment from you, from which the most blameless conduct on our part has not been able to defend us.

True it is (and this does not depend on my veracity else I would not have mentioned it) that I have said and done every thing in my power to persuade (or, if you please, to *seduce*) you to continue your History, from a full conviction, as you express it in your last, *that it would have been for your own advantage in more respects than one.* Your answer was constantly in the negative; of late, *that such an absurd and extravagant idea never entered your head;* and *that you had thrown your pen aside for ever.*—Whether I did well in thus repeatedly obtruding my advice upon you, and you in as repeatedly rejecting it, time only can discover. I know I meant well; that to me is great cause of satisfaction.—And now I cease to trouble you on this head for ever.

I had forgot that you desired 12 copies of this edition. They shall be directly sent you; and as many more as you shall hereafter desire are at your service. Your request respecting future editions of your Works shall be duly attended to. I shall only add, that at no period of my life could I have patiently borne the unmerited treatment you have given me; you will not therefore wonder, that having now, by my own industry, attained to a state of independence, and I will venture to say by a conduct unimpeachable, it should not sit very easy upon my stomach.

Some time or other you will perhaps discover with certainty, whether I am or not

Your faithful and Obedt Servt

W. S.

* XIV. *From* JAMES EDMONSTOUNE (see Letter 503 above)

Dear obstinate David

Pravum et tenacem propositi virum
Non Civium Ardor recta jubentium
Non Vultus instantis Baronnæ
Mente quatit Stolida.

Will nothing move you, you obdurate Philosopher, Your Reasons are not worth a Straw, and Ill prosecute you for scandalizing my House. The Room next to your last is as cool as any Room ought to be, it looks to the North, and you was putt into a South Room merely because it was thought that the Sun's vivifying Ray would be of Use to a Man that had been worn out and so much epuisé in ffrance. Besides you Scrub, have I not seen you basking for Hours together in the Sun, contemplating Shellie, and burning with Envy at his Prowess, and I heard Nothing about your being heated till we came to Killin, and that was Crichen's doing, to season you for still a hotter Place. It is pleasant to hear a Man reputed to be a Contemptor Divum, talk of Vows and religiously keeping them. You know what Benedict the 14 said to Madame Capello, the Venetian Ambassadress whom you saw at London in the same Quality, she it seems had receivd a very fine Watch from the Cardinal Sciarra Colonna, and wanted to show it to the Pope, but could not readily unhook it, upon which he said to her, Lasciate, laciate [*sic*], deve sempre il Voto esser di rempello [?] al Santo; Now David, what thing have you vow'd and to what Divinity have you dedicated it. Have you after all your Fatti d'arme and all your Triumphs grown tird of Conquest and hung up your Arms in some poor Chapel, for one that was only armé a la legere, cant furnish any more. As you don't seem to have your usual Clearness about Vows if youll come with Mrs Mure on Wednesday the 19th the Baron & she will give [you] more distinct Ideas about them. . . .

Newtoun 12 April 1775

* MS., R.S.E.; Burton, ii. 474 (incomplete).

* XV. *From* Baron Mure (see Letter 507 above)

Caldwell Sunday 27th Augt. [1775].

My Dear David

You mistake the Matter entirely; the Duchess's[1] Proposal was not that we should come to Inverary immediately for she mentioned her Daughter Lady Betty[2] being to be down next Month, as an inducement to us. Mrs. Mure in Answer told her Grace, that we had concerted the whole Matter before we received her obliging Invitation; that you had gone a jaunt into the North of England, were to return the west Road, and be here; and that then, in about two Weeks hence, we were to set out together to wait on her, and the Duke. Now why alter that Plan? Why dont you proceed in your English Expedition, and let me keep my Word to Lady Betty Stanley, when I saw her at London, of not going to Inveraray till she came? I would really have you still to pay your Visit to John Bull, you^{ll} be the better for it. Make it as short as you please, and when you come here, stay the longer. You shall get any Bed you please on the Floor you like. Write me your Notions. Yours while Will Mure.

† XVI. *From* Baron Mure (see Letter 507 above)

What new Change is this. Mrs Mure says you should have been a Girl, for you are never two minutes of one mind; and I say you are as credulous as any Girl, and believe every Report you hear. I wish you had but half the Faith for what you ought, and are bound, to believe.

We saw Lady Betty and Lord Stanley, at Hamilton on Thursday last, they expect no more Company from England. The Bishop Lord North's Brother[3] with his Wife, were to have come but were stoped, and have laid aside their Intention, upon Account of Lord Gilford's being taken ill. I hope he^{ll} recover. Lady Betty heard from the Duchess, that there were no Body there but Miss Sempill.[4] You dont call that Company sure. Ld and Lady Eglingtown[5] are since gone there, but will be gone before we arrive. We told Lady Betty, we, that is you as well as ourselves, were to be there soon, whenever we had Notice from you. She said she would play at Whist with you

* MS., R.S.E.; *Caldwell Papers*, II. ii. 247 f.

† MS., R.S.E.; *Caldwell Papers*, II. ii. 250 f.

[1] The Duchess of Argyll, formerly Duchess of Hamilton.

[2] Lady Betty Hamilton (1753–97) married (1774) Edward, Lord Stanley (1752–1834), afterwards 12th Earl of Derby.

[3] The Hon. Brownlow North (1741–1820), Bishop of Lichfield 1771–4, Worcester 1774–81, and Winchester 1781–1820.

[4] Probably Jean Sempill (died 1800), daughter of Hew, 11th Lord Sempill.

[5] Archibald Montgomerie (1726–96), 11th Earl of Eglintoun, married (1772) Jean Lindsay (1756–78), eldest daughter of George, 21st Earl of Crawford.

from Morning to Night, was become of late so fond of it, that she had played with Andrew Stuart lately from one at Noon till one in the Morning, without ever rising, but for a few Minutes, to answer the Calls of Hunger. How can I give your strange Reason to the Duke and Duchess, in an empty House, that because it was full, you would not keep your Promise. In short we propose to go some Time next Week, what Time of it is indifferent, and we shall be determind by you, but you must decide and say when you^{ll} go along with us, for the Sake of your own Character, as well as of your Friends who wish your Company. Fix a day when you^{ll} be at Rouats, and we^{ll} meet you there, he has been here we have promised to be with him, and answered for you too. You cant get off now, so dont think of making Excuses. Yours while

W. M.

Caldwell Monday 4th Sept [1775]

On telling Kattie what I had wrote, she offers an Amendment, which I much approve; that you should come here the End of the Week, or the very Beginning of the next, or as soon as you like, and that we should set out from hence for Inveraray together, whenever we find ourselves inclined. As travelling is your Business now, this should suit you better, than coming directly to Rouat's.

APPENDIX D

LETTERS FROM GEORGE KEITH, 10TH EARL MARISCHAL OF SCOTLAND, TO DAVID HUME

* I. (See Letter 199 above.)

Jean Jaques Rousseau persecuted for having writ what he thinks good, or rather, as some folks think, for having displeased persons in great power who attributed to him what he never meant, came here to seek retreat, which I readily granted, and the King of Prussia not only approved of my so doing, but gave ne orders to furnish him his small necessarys, if he would accept them; and tho that King's philosophy be very different from that of Jean Jaques, yet he does not think that a man of an irreprochable life is to be persecuted because his sentiments are singular, he designs to build him a hermitage with a little garden which I find he will not accept, nor perhaps the rest which I have not yet offered to him. He is gay in company, polite, and what the french call *aimable*, and gains ground dayly in the opinion of even the clergy here; his enemys elsewhere, continue to persecute him, he is pestered with anonimous letters, this is not a country for him, his attachement and love to his native Towne is a strong tye to its neighbourhood, the liberty of England and the character of my good and honored friend D. Hume F——i D——r (perhaps more singular than that of J. Jaques, for I take him to be the only historian impartial) draws his inclinations to be near to the F——i D——r, for my part, tho it be to me a very great pleasure to converse with the honest savage, yet I advise him to go to England, where he will enjoy *Placidam sub libertate quietem.* He wishes to know, if he can print all his works, and make some profit, merely to live, from such an edition. I entreat you will let me know your thoughts on this, and if you can be of use to him in finding him a bookseller to undertake the work, you know he is not interested, and little will content him. If he goes to Brittain, he will be a treasure to you, and you to him, and perhaps both to me (if I were not so old). I have offered him lodging in Keith hall. I am ever with the greatest regard your most obedient servant M.

Oct: 2d 1762

† II. (See Letter 223 above.)

Touch 28 Oct: 1763

. . . Your advice of creeping nearer to the Sun is most agreable to an old Spaniard, and a sort of a Guebre by religion, but 600£ a year

* MS., R.S.E.; Burton, ii. 105 f.

† MS., R.S.E.; Burton, *Eminent Persons*, 57 ff.

will not do in London, neither in Paris, tho better there than in London; in Paris étant deja reconnu pour *hibou*, je pourrois aisement meriter aussi le titre de *Loup*, alors je serois en repos; et je ne verrois que ceux qui me plairoient; c'est terrible a ma campagne d'etre obligé de recevoir des visites sans relache; et bien de ces gens dont Alliotus pourroit dire, *Id genus Demoniorum non ejicitur nisi jejunio.* M[r] d'Alembert vous expliquera ceci; et pour vous dire la verité, je conte par *jejunio vini* me debarrasser de plusieurs. Il y une autre incommodité dans notre pays, la bigoterie et je crois aussi un peu d'hipocrisie . . . quand j'ay passé par Aberdeen les Eglises retentissoient des anathemes contre ceux qui retireroient leurs lettres de la poste le dimanche, Mr Campbell étoit un des plus zelé Predicateurs. . . .

* III. (See Letter 323 above.)

29 Aprile [1766]

In answer to your question, the Donquixotisme you mention never entered my head. I wish I could see you to answer honestly all your questions, for tho I had my share of follys with others, yet as my intentions were at bottom honest, I should open to you my whole budget, and lett you know many things which are perhaps ill represented, I mean not truly. I remember to have recommended to your acquaintance Mr Floyd, son to old David Floyd, at St Germains, as a man of good sense, honor, and honesty: I fear he is dead, he would have been of great service to you in a part of your history since 1688. A propos of history, when you see Helvetius, tell I desired you to enquire of him concerning a certain history; I fancy he will answer you with his usuall Frankness.

I do believe Mr Rousseau will find it impossible to live where he finds nobody who understand a word of what he sais, there occurs so often occasion, even of trifling things necessary, that it is a vexation not to understand the language of the country; I feel it often, tho I understand many words of German, such as kleigh, Nigh Noch, ter mighter Teyfel, and others, high sounding as here pronounced, and of which the Ter Tunder would I believe put to flight the delicate ears of the whole Town of Sienna.

I hear you are going to France this summer, if you will come to Frankfort on Mein, I will meet you there the end of July, and stay with you a fourtnight. Bon jour.

N.B. You have better roads than I, you are strong as a giant, and I am growing ten years older every month, so I think my offer fair.

* MS., R.S.E.; Burton, ii. 104 f.

APPENDIX E

LETTERS OF MME LA COMTESSE DE BOUFFLERS TO HUME

* I. (See Letter 184 above.)

Depuis longtems Monsieur je suis combattuë par des sentimens contraires. Ladmiration que me cause votre sublime ouvrage et lestime quil minspire pour votre personne vos talens et votre vertu, m'ont fait naitre souvent le desir de vous ecrire, pour vous exprimer les sentimens dont je suis profondement penetrée. D'un autre coté, considerant que je vous suis inconnuë, le peu de prix que doit avoir mon suffrage, la reserve et lobscurité meme, qui convient a mon sexe: j'ay craint detre accusée de presomption, et de me faire connoistre a mon desavantage, dun homme de qui je regarderay toujours la bonne opinion comme le bien le plus flatteur et le plus pretieux. Neanmoins, quoique les refflexions que j'ay faites a cet egard me paroissent avoir beaucoup de force un penchant irresistible les rend infructueuses, et je vais ajouter mon exemple a mille autres pour justifier la verité de cette remarque que j'ai luë dans votre histoire de la Maison de Stuard.

Men's views of things are the result of their understanding alone: their conduct is regulated by their understanding, their temper, and their passions.

Puisque quand ma raison me dit que je devrois me tenir dans le silence l'enthousiasme ou je suis m'empeche de le pouvoir garder.

Quoique femme et dans un age qui n'est pas encore avancé, et malgré la dissipation de la vie qu'on tient dans ce pays, ayant toujours aimé la Lecture, il est peu de bons livres en quelque langue et en quelque genre que ce soit que je naye lu, ou dans loriginal ou dans les traductions, et je puis vous assurer Monsieur avec une sincerité qui ne doit pas vous etre suspecte, que je n'en ay trouvé aucun qui reunit a mon jugement autant de perfections que le votre. Je ne say point de termes qui puissent vous rendre ce que jeprouve en lisant cet ouvrage. Je me sens attendrie, transportée, et l'émotion quil me cause est en quelque façon penible par sa continuité. Il eleve l'ame, il remplit le coeur de sentimens dhumanite et de bienfaisance. Il eclaire lesprit, et en luy montrant la veritable felicité intimement liée a la vertu, il luy decouvre par le meme rayon le seul et unique but de tout etre raisonnable. Au millieu des calamités qui environnent de toutes parts le Roy Charles 1 er, l'on voit la paix et la serenité briller avec eclat, et laccompagner, sur lechafaud: tandis que le trouble et les remords, cortege inseparable du crime, suivent les pas

* MS., R.S.E.; Burton, ii. 97 ff.

de Cromwell et s'asseyent sur le trone avec luy. Votre livre apprend encore combien l'abus est voisin des meilleures choses, et les refflexions quil fait faire a ce sujet, doit augmenter la vigilance et la defiance de soi meme. Il anime d'une noble emulation, il inspire lamour de la liberté, et instruit en meme tems a se soumettre au gouvernement sous lequel on est obligé de vivre, en un mot c'est une source feconde de morale et dinstructions, presentées avec des couleurs si vives qu'on croit les voir pour la premiere fois.

La clarté, la majesté, la simplicité touchante de votre stile, me ravit. Ses beautés sont si frappantes, que malgré mon ignorance dans la langue angloise, elles n'ont pu mechapper. Vous etes Monsieur un peintre admirable. Vos tableaux ont une grace, un naturel, une energie qui surpasse ce que l'imagination meme peut atteindre.

Mais quelles expressions employeray-je, pour vous faire connoistre leffet que produit sur moy votre divine impartialite? J'aurois besoin en cette occasion de votre propre eloquence, pour bien rendre ma pensée. En verité je crois avoir devant les yeux louvrage de quelque substance celeste degagée des passions, qui pour lutilité des hommes a daigné ecrire les evenemens de ces derniers tems.

Je n'ose ajouter que dans tout ce qui sort de votre plume vous vous montres un philosophe parfait, un homme detat, un historien plein de genie, un politique eclairé, un vray patriote.

Toutes ces sublimes qualites, sont si fort au dessus des connoissances d'une femme, quil me convient peu d'en parler: et j'ay dejà grand besoin de votre indulgence, pour les fautes que j'ay commises contre la discretion et la bienseance par lexces de ma veneration pour votre merite. Je vous la demande Monsieur, et en meme tems le plus profond secret. La demarche que je fais a quelque chose d'extraordinaire, je craindrois qu'elle ne m'attirat le blame, et je serois fachée que le sentiment qui me la dictée put etre meconnu. J'ay lhonneur d'être Monsieur Votre tres humble et tres obeissante servante

Hippolyte de Saujon Comtesse de Boufflers

Lon me dit Monsieur que vous avies envie de venir en france a la paix, je souhaite bien vivement que vous executies cette resolution, et pouvoir contribuer a vous en rendre le sejour agreable.

Ce 13 mars 1761 a paris

* II. (See Letter 195 above.)

a paris ce 14 juin 1762

[The letter opens with a long preamble on Hume's great merits.]

. . . Jean Jaques Rousseau citoyen de Geneve, et auteur de plusieurs ecrits, qui vous sont vraisemblablement connus; vient de composer un

* MS., R.S.E.; Burton, ii. 107 f.

traité sur leducation en quatre volumes ou il expose plusieurs principes contraires aux notres, tant sur la politique que sur la religion. Comme nous ne jouissons pas icy de la liberté de la presse, le parlement par un arret, juste s'il est comme je n'en doute pas conforme aux lois du royaume, mais neanmoins rigoureux, la decreté de prise de corps, et lon pretend, que s'il navoit pas pris la fuite, il auroit eté condamné a la mort. J'ay de la peine a croire qu'on eut pu aller si loin vu sa qualité detranger, mais quoiquil en soit, il eut eté imprudent a luy de rester en france dans de pareilles circonstances. Il est donc parti, incertain quel azile il choisiroit. Je luy ay conseillé de se retirer en angleterre, luy promettant des lettres de recommandation pour vous Monsieur et pour dautres personnes de mes amis. Je macquitte de ma promesse, et je ne puis pas a mon avis, luy choisir dans tout leurope un protecteur plus respectable par ses lumieres, et plus recommandable par son humanité. Mr Rousseau passe chez la pluspart des gens en ce pays pour un homme singulier. A prendre cette epithete selon la vraye signification, elle luy est justement donnée, car il differe a beaucoup degards de la façon dagir et de penser des hommes d'a present. Il a le coeur droit, lame noble et desinteressée. Il craint toute espece de dependance, et par cette raison, il a mieux aimé etant en france, gagner sa vie en copiant de la musique, que de recevoir les bienfaits de ses meilleurs amis, qui s'empressoient de reparer sa mauvaise fortune. Cette delicatesse peut paroistre excessive, mais elle n'a rien de criminelle, et meme elle suppose des sentimens eleves. Il fuit le commerce du monde, il ne se plait que dans la solitude, ce gout pour la retraite luy a fait des ennemis, lamour propre de ceux qui l'ont recherché s'est trouvée blessé de ses refus. Mais malgré sa misantropie apparente, je ne crois pas quil y ait nulle part un homme plus doux plus humain plus compatissant aux peines des autres et plus patient dans les siennes, en un mot sa vertu paroist si pure, si constante, si uniforme, que jusqu'a present, ceux qui le haissent, n'ont pu trouver que dans leur propre coeur des raisons pour le suspecter. Pour moy avec des apparences aussi avantageuses, j'aimerois mieux en etre trompée que de me deffier de sa sincerité.

D'apres l'opinion que j'en ay Monsieur, je l'ay jugé digne detre connu de vous et en luy procurant cet honneur, je crois luy donner la preuve la plus marquée du cas que je fais de luy. . . .

* III. (See Letter 200 above.)

July 30 [1672]

. . . Perhaps Sir, I confess it with ingenuity, had I been doom'd to be never personally acquaint'd with you, I should not have generosity enough, to correct your judgement of me. But in this particular occasion, as in all other, according my humble opinion, Right and

* MS., R.S.E.; Burton, ii. 110 ff.

good are closely united. What a Shame indeed for me, and disapointement for you: in place of the object, your imagination has adornd with such shining qualifications, to find a person, to whom nature has granted but indifferent ones. A great part of my youth is over. Some delicacy in features, mildness and decency in countenance, are the only exterior advantages, I can boast of. And as for interior, common sense, improved a little, by early good reading, are all I possess. My knowledge of the English language also, is confined as you can easily perceive. I have indeed acquir'd whithout assistance, that which I know of it; but if I am intitled to some elegancy I owe it to the repeated readings of your admirable works.

After this true picture of myself, in which I have struggled to exert the noble impartiality and candour which shine in all your writings, my first care is Sir, to acknowledge the infinite obligations you have conferr'd upon me by your kind letter. I have translat'd the P. S. to send it to my friend [Rousseau]. The esteem of such a man, must be the best balm, for his wound'd heart. But I am afraid he will not accept the glorious support, you are so good as to offer him. I fear, that the weight of his calamities has impair'd his health, and he cannot sustain, the fatigues of a long journey. In his last letter to me, he expresses a resolution, never to see England, upon that account. Nevertheless I am inform'd since, that new persecutions, may possibly determine him to alter his mind. An irregular trial has depriv'd him of the natural rights in his own country. . . .

Is it possible Sir, that this late unhappy event [the prosecution of Rousseau], could deprive of the honour of your presence, a country filled with your fervent admirers, and where every one, will endeavour, to outdo each other, in expressing the veneration and regard you so justly deserve? I hope you will not keep this severe resolution. If we want a liberty you think an advantage, t'is a reason to pity, and not to punish us. Besides your case and that of Mr Rousseau, tho' both foreigners in france, are quite different. . . .

Since I have gone so far, permit me Sir, to ask your opinion upon the last Book of Mr. Rousseau. . . .

* IV. (See Letter 244 above.)

ce 6 juillet [1764]

[The letter begins, and continues through several pages, with an elaborate and severe criticism of John Home's tragedy of *Douglas*. This part of the letter is printed in full in *Eminent Persons*, 223 ff.]

J'en etois a cet endroit de ma lettre, et je voulois vous faire quelqu'excuse, dune critique si franche et si severe, lorsque j'ay recu celle que vous mecrivies de Compiegne. Jaime mieux y repondre que de continuer.

* MS., R.S.E., unpublished.

Sil y a de la ressemblance dans nos occupations actuelles ce n'est pas la seule qui soit entre nous, car il y en a beaucoup aussi dans nos resolutions. Vous voules vous detacher de moy, je n'en say pas le motif, mais je say bien du moins celuy qui m'oblige aussi a vouloir me detacher de vous. Il n'est pas desobligeant et je ne prendray pas grande tournure pour vous le declarer, c'est que vous aves une droiture et une bonté de coeur que jestime un genie que jadmire, et une bonne humeur qui me plait, et que vous etes etranger, vous vous en ires tot, ou tard, et vous ne seres venu icy que pour me degouter de la pluspart des gens avec qui je dois vivre. Sil n'y avoit encore que cet inconvenient j'y trouverois remede, des livres tiennent lieu de bien des choses, mais le pire est que je ne puis m'en tenir a une simple estime ni a une froide admiration. Des qu'on minspire ces sentimens, on touche en même tems ma sensibilité et lon engage mes affections, d'ou il sensuit une veritable peine pour moy, lorsque les circonstances me forcent de me separer de ceux qui ont merité de faire ce progres sur mon coeur. J'ay deja plusieurs amis, dont je suis necessairement eloignée, avec peu de probabilité de les revoir jamais. C'est un malheur que je sens, plus que je ne le temoigne, et qui m'obligera a des precautions pour lavenir. Je me regarde comme une foible arbrisseau qui a jetté des racines trop loin de soy, et qui par la est exposé a plus dinjures, et de risques. A la verité je crains que mes refflexions, et ma prudence, ne me soient inutiles a present avec vous, et quil ne soit un peu tard pour commencer a les mettre en oeuvre. Mais si vous travailles si fructueusement de votre coté cela pourra me donner courage. . . .

Adieu mon cher Maitre, je vais me depecher de ne vous plus aimer, afin de navoir pas la honte detre la derniere a terminer cette utile entreprise. Mais comme je ne lay pas encore commencee je puis me permettre pour aujourdhuy, de vous assurer, que je vous aime de tout mon coeur.

* V. (See Letter 246 above.)

ce 21 Juillet [1764].

Je suis fachée davoir eté si longtems sans vous repondre. Javois beaucoup daffaires, et je ne voulois pas vous ecrire seulement pour deux lignes. Jespere que cette raison vous contentera.

Je veux vous faire une question, avant que d'entrer en matiere. Me croyes vous un coeur tendre, bienfaisant, et sensible a l'amitié? Je vous donne quelque momens pour y penser . . .[1]

Maintenant, sachant ce que je dois paroistre, par ceque je suis reellement, aux yeux d'un homme a qui de tels sentimens ne sont pas etrangers, je suppose, que votre reponse, m'est favorable; et

* MS., R.S.E.; *Eminent Persons*, 226 ff.

[1] *Sic* in autograph.

c'est de cette opinion, que vous avez de moy dont je me sers, pour vous faire comprendre, la satisfaction extreme que j'ay ressentie en aprenant de vous, celle que vous a causés, ma lettre. Si j'ay jamais eté sensible au plaisir d'obliger, si mon ame est susceptible, detre emuë par la douleur, ou la joye d'un ami, vous pouves juger, de leffet de ces dispositions naturelles, par rapport a vous. En meme tems, je ne puis me deffendre d'une refflexion, qui m'afflige. Il semble de la maniere dont vous vous exprimez, que vous ayez eu du doute sur mon amitié, et que vous ayez souffert quelque peine, dont j'ay eté loccasion. Le fond de mon coeur etant tel que vous pouvez le souhaiter, la gayeté et la vivacite, peutetre excessives, de mon caractere, doivent seules en etre accusées, et cet effet, si contraire au desir, que j'ay de vous convaincre du retour sincere dont je reconnois vos sentimens, seroit capable, de me faire hair, des qualites, dailleurs avantageuses.

Vous dites que vous etes sujet a la jalousie, meme en amitié. Vous avoueray-je que jay ce defaut aussi, mais que du sexe dont je suis, je croirois mabaisser, de le temoigner jamais, et je ne say a vray dire, si ma jalousie, ne seroit pas mieux caracterisée, en la nommant exces de delicatesse, puisquelle en veut de preference et singulierement a lestime, tant quelle na pas eté profanée. Car je pardonne que le coeur se trompe quelquefois, il est suceptible de certaines affections tout a fait, aveugles et involontaires. Mais que le plus flatteur de tous les sentimens, la baze et le soutien des autres soit honteusement deshonoré, par lapplication qu'on en fait, c'est ce que je ne puis souffrir, sans en etre blessée d'abord, et a la fin entierement detachée. J'ay quelque droit de penser de la sorte; n'ayant a offrir a mes amis, qu'une tendresse inutile, et une estime peu flatteuse par elle meme, je me suis efforcée, d'augmenter la valeur de cette derniere, en ne l'accordant, quavec precaution. Vous m'en rendrez, encore plus avare a lavenir. Mais pourquoy montrez vous toujours du repentir de votre attachement, pour moy, qui vous en temoigne un si veritable et si bien etabli? J'avoue quil sera contrarié quelquefois, par labsence, et par les devoirs, qu'un autre plus ancien a imposé sur ma reconnoissance. Ces devoirs sont sacres. Ils exigeroient le sacrifice de moimeme, si loccasion s'en presentoit. Mon inclination meme, me porte a les remplir, et ils n'auroient rien que de satisfaisans, si la religion, si le devouement, avec lesquels je m'en acquite, etoient toujours reconnus. Neanmoins, tels quils sont, et tels que je les considere, ils ne mabsorbent pas toute entiere, ils laissent place dans mon coeur pour dautres sentimens, et je puis disposer de la plus grande partie de mon tems, et vous le donner. Examinez vous pourtant, car quoiquil m'en coutat, et quelque prix que je mette a votre amitié, jaimerois mieux en arreter les progres que de les confirmer, si vous en deviez souffrir, ou que je dusse en prevoir la fin.

Cest bien un effet de cette amitié que vous voulez combattre, de vous etre attendri en vous rappellant les voeux que je fais pour ne pas vivre longtems. Mais vous vous trompez sur leurs causes. Vous attribuez a quelque peines secretes, ce qui nait seulement de linstabilité attachée aux biens que lon possedoit. Je le disois, il y a quelque tems, dans une de ces vivacités que vous me connoissez, *Il faudroit etre bien mal dans ce monde, pour ne pas desirer de mourir*. Cela a tout l'air d'un paradoxe!

En un mot, puisque votre bonté vous donne de linquietude pour moy, apres vous avoir dit que j'en suis touchée jusqu'a l'ame, je dois vous rassurer, et vous eclaircir ma situation. J'ay toutes les peines que peuvent procurer trop de sensibilité, et trop de delicatesse: Mais j'en ay aussi les avantages, et avec eux une bonne santé un heureux caractere, de la flexibilité dans l'humeur, du gout pour letude et les plaisirs simples, nulle ambition, et un peu de philosophie. Si je puis ajouter a tant de bonheur, celuy de conserver, daugmenter votre amitié, et de detruire les doutes que vous formez sur la mienne, en verité je ne vois pas comment je me plaindrois raisonablement de mon sort. Il faut m'arreter icy. . . .[1] [Then follow two pages omitted.]

Adieu, je me flatte que vous ne serez pas moins content de cette lettre que de lautre. Il faudroit que j'eusse bien peu d'art, pour avoir mal exprimer une amitie que mon coeur ressent si vivement.

* VI. (See Letter 247 above.)

ce 30 juillet [1764]

. . . Voules vous me confirmer dans l'idée ou je suis, que votre sexe, aime a etre maltraité, quil paye les rigeurs, dempressement, et les bontés de negligence, car pour vous avouer mon opinion des hommes, la pluspart me paroissent avoir naturellement lame servile. Lon peut etre seduite par eux, mais lon ne peut gueres ce me semble les estimer. Leurs hommages sont receus, et ne peuvent flatter. Tantot cest le discernement qui leur manque, tantot la delicatesse, et presque toujours la generosité. J'en ay cru voir deux ou trois qui meritoient detre exceptés. Une plus parfaite connoissance peutetre meut decouvert mon erreur. Pour vous vers qui linclination ne ma porteé qu'a la suite de lestime, je vous separe de cette foule desclaves, et je vous attribue un caractere tout-a-fait differend. Si je metois trompée, mon affection, et la base sur laquelle elle sappuye principalement, seroit bientot detruite: car, que lon me trouve une deffense contre les coups du sort, que lon m'assure le bonheur et la vie de ceux que j'aime, et je pourray repondre de n'etre jamais malheureuse par les sentimens du coeur. Je suis de mon naturel, aussi fiere que sensible, aussi portée au dedain qua la tendresse, et quiquonque ne repond pas a mon amitié, m'en paroist aussitot indigne. Je veux me

* MS., R.S.E.; *Eminent Persons*, 230 f.

[1] *Sic* in autograph.

flatter mon cher Maitre que je n'auray a exercer envers vous, que le plus doux de ces deux sentimens, et que vous ne me forceres pas duser de cette triste prudence, qui nous oblige souvent a contraindre et a renfermer les affections les plus agreables et les plus innocentes dans la crainte de faire des ingrats. Neamoins je ne puis m'empecher de le dire, j'ay attendu longtems votre lettre, je lay attendue avec impatience, et je n'en ay point eté satisfaite. Nous verrons quelle excuse vous me donneres!

* VII. (See Letter 322 above.)

ce 18 avril [1766] a Montmorency.

Votre lettre est arrivée a propos pour dissiper la colere ou jetois contre vous de votre silence. Elle ma fait grand plaisir quoiqu'elle mannonce une absence plus longue que je ne lavois prevuë. Je vois qu'elle est indispensable, et c'est le moins que vous puissiez faire pour Mylord Hertford. Non que je ne le trouve bien payé par limmortalité quil s'est assuré, en rendant votre fortune un peu moins disproportionnée a votre merite, mais c'est une recompense quil tire de laction meme, ainsi quil arrive toujours, et qui ne vous acquite pas. Je ne say si je vous ay dit que je changeois de maison. Par mon nouvel arrangement, nous logerons ensemble et pourtant separés, en sorte que nous aurons tout lagrement de la proximité, sans gesne et sans inconvenient. J'approuve fort le projet que vous faites de changer votre maniere de vivre, il est avantageux pour le public que vous reprennies vos anciennes occupations, mais il ne l'est pas moins pour vous meme. Je n'approuverois pas que vous vous abandonnassies a l'oisiveté. Lame et lesprit y perdent de leur ressort, je lay trop eprouvé, et dans peu vous ne series plus lhomme a qui lestime ma lié dune si forte amitié. Vous aures liberté entiere de mener la vie que vous voudres, je vous en assure, et vous saves qu'en chose importante je n'avance rien legerement. J'ay receu une lettre de J. J. Il me paroist content mais vous maffliges en me disant que vous ne croyes pas quil le soit longtems. Lord Tavistock a remis a Miss Becquet la boite. Elle vous remercie de votre souvenir. Tous nos amis vous font des complimens. Ceux avec qui vous aves tort vous pardonnent. Ainsi vous pouves revenir sans crainte de trouver des visages ennemis. Je vais aux eaux de Pougues avec M. le prince de Conty M^{e} la Ctesse De la Marche et d'autres personnes. J'y seray du 20 juin au 20 de juillet. Au commencement d'aoust mon fils part pour litalie et passe par paris. Je me suis beaucoup occupée de ce voyage depuis que vous etes absent, et de larrangement de mes affaires. Encore un an et je pourray mourir quand il me plaira ayant asses bien rempli tous les devoirs importans que j'avois dans ce monde.

* MS., R.S.E.; unpublished.

Il y en a eu a lile Adam un voyage fort brillant ou je me suis asses divertie. Mr Walpole *en signe de paix* en avoit ete prié, mais la goutte l'a empeché d'y venir. Sa maudite lettre est dans les papiers anglais. Est-il vray qu'on a voulu enlever Mr deon?

Me Geoffrin part pour la pologne au mois de may elle me la dit. Beaucoup de personnes se mocquent de ce voyage. Je ne suis pas du nombre, et ne pense pas que lorsque les princes se montrent capables d'amitié on doivent les traiter plus mal que dautres. Tomber dans l'ingratitude dans la crainte detre taxé de bassesse me paroist la plus grande bassesse qui y ait au monde. Sacrifier la reconnoissance a la crainte du ridicule est un tort de même espece. L'amitié du Roy de pologne pour Me Geoffrin fait honneur a tous deux, et leurs sentimens reciproques sont assurement bien desinteressés.

Apportes moy ou bien envoyes moy je vous prie par la premiere occasion le voyage ditalie par Mr Addison. Mylord Tavistock me la promis mais je crains quil ne l'oublie. Adieu.

APPENDIX F

HUME'S QUARREL IN PARIS WITH THE HON. ALEXANDER MURRAY

The Hon. Alexander Murray (d. 1777), fourth son of the fourth Lord Elibank, was a man of impetuous, choleric temperament and strong Jacobite sympathies. Having taken an active part in the Westminster Election of 1750, in support of Sir George Vandeput, he was summoned by the House of Commons to answer a complaint by the High Bailiff that he had incited the electioneering mob to violence. He appeared on 1 February 1751, and on 6 February the House committed him to Newgate. Summoned thence to receive their rebuke from the Speaker, he declined to kneel, saying: 'Sir, I beg to be excused; I never kneel but to God'; and was thereupon committed again to Newgate. He remained there till June, when Parliament was prorogued and he was released by the London sheriffs, who accompanied him in a triumphal procession through the streets to the house of his brother, Lord Elibank, in Henrietta St. Before Parliament met again in November, he betook himself to France, where he remained for the next fifteen years. In his absence the House of Commons ordered his re-committal to prison, and offered a reward of £500 for his apprehension.

In Paris he associated openly with the Jacobites, but was willing enough to treat with the British Government for a pardon. He was more or less intimate with Mme de Boufflers, and forwarded her first and second letters to Hume. His own letters doing so are dated 18 mars [*sic*] 1761 (MS., R.S.E.; Burton, ii. 94, incomplete and wrongly dated) and 20 Jully [*sic*] 1761 (MS., R.S.E.).

On Hume's arrival in Paris Murray hastened to claim acquaintance and cousinhood, partly because he liked Hume and partly, one suspects, because he thought Hume would be able to help him in the matter of his pardon. The following undated letter, written probably soon after Hume's arrival, indicates the footing they were on.

* I. Murray *to* Hume

My dear Hume

The great desire that several french Gentlemen of my acquaintance have of being known to You, which happiness I have promised to procure them, makes me ardently beg the favour of You to do me the honour to dine with me any day next week (Monday excepted) that You please to appoint. Your recountres with the men my dear friend gives me no sort of pain, but I freely own to You I am under some uneasiness how you will acquit Yourself with the fair sex whose

* MS., R.S.E.; Burton, ii. 168 f.

impatience of knowing You is not to be expressed. The day You dine with me You will meet some folks who admire Your productions as much as any of Your own countrymen, and perhaps comprehend Your sublime Ideas as well as they do. I beg leave to assure You that no body loves and admires You more than Your Most sincere friend and humble Servant A: MURRAY

Saturday morning [autumn 1763]

It would appear from Letter 259 above that Hume was discreet enough, and did not overdo his civilities to one who was virtually an outlaw. Meantime, Murray involved himself in fresh troubles, which ended in a lawsuit. The details are obscure and do not matter; enough may be gathered of them from the following letters.

* II. MURRAY *to* HUME

My dearest Cousin

. . . My affair ought to be determin'd this week, and nothing can prevent it, but some infernal hibernian cabal. The judges have hitherto, I will venture to say, paid too much regard to their intrigues and lyes; first in permitting such an unparallel'd process, secondly after an information of fifteen months, to grant them a delay of three months to produce further proofs or rather falsehoods; that time being now expired, and my enemy's not having dared to alledge any new proofs, knowing that the letters, and different receipts of Bankiers, which by a miracle I found amongst my papers, put my affair in so clear a light that any additional lyes could not have any manner of effect. I must therefore now intreat my dearest cousin and most generous of friends to write a letter to M. Le Noir and beg him to be the rapporteur of my affair, and to render me that reparation of honneur, which the enormity of the injury and insult done to a man of my birth demands, and I really think I might say character, this being the first thing that was ever laid to my charge, and being perfectly conscious never to have done any one action that could make Your cousin or a descendant of my family blush. As You are no stranger to the important and delicate transactions I have been intrusted with, the superior sentiments of Your soul must make You feel more sensibly, than all others, the most unexpressible agony I have suffered these eighteen months past in languishing under such an imputation. I am fully convinced You will write in the Strongest terms to M. Le Noir, and take such other measures as You think most probable to engage him to charge himself with the rapport of my process and press him to finish it. . . .

3 July 1764

Hume probably declined to take any part, for or against Murray, and the latter promptly ranked him among his enemies. The following undated letter is among the Laing MSS. in the University of

* MS., R.S.E., unpublished.

Edinburgh. It was obviously addressed to Hume, and it is practically certain that this is the letter which Hume forwarded to Mme de Boufflers about 13 August 1764 (see Letter 249 above).

* III. Murray *to* [Hume]

[End of July, 1764.]

As former friend of my brother Lord Elibank I send you this letter to inform you that my proces was judged last tuesday to the great discontentment of my Enemys, notwithstanding the low and indecent cabals begun by the Duke of B——, continued by a troop of Irish, etc., etc., etc. This surely must give you a very high idea of the integrity of the French judges; and the more so, when I tell you that no body appear'd in my behalf, but the Countess of Boufflers, who from a nobleness of soul, and elevation of sentiments so very peculiar to herself, assisted me to oppose the torrent of oppression that was rushing on to overwhelm me in a country I had retired to when drove from my own and where, I will venture to say, I have lived for these 14 years in such a manner as did honour to my country, name, and family. The generous and inexpressible friendship of My Lady Boufflers upon this occasion, does infinitely more than recompence all the pain my Enemys have given me; as I prefer her good opinion, to that of all those who have so shamefully join'd against me in this most infamous scheme to ruin my reputation in a country I have every sort of reason to love and consider as my own.

I should not, indeed, have wonder'd at your credulity and partiality in my affair; after having read that part of your history where you treat the character of the most lovely, and the most unfortunate Queen Mary. As a Scotchman you certainly ought at least to have endeavour'd to have render'd her justice, and as Lord Elibank's friend you should not undoubtedly have join'd in destroying his Brother's honour; if Mary had not been butcher'd by the false and unrelenting Elizabeth, who brib'd all the historians, particularly your favourite and countryman Buchanan to traduce that most divine and amable creature, my brother would not have had the honnour and happiness of justifying her injur'd fame, which he most effectually has done, by the testimony of authentick records, to the eternal shame and confusion of the Venal tribe who have loaded her with infamy. If I had died before this affair had been *judged* the dull, heavy, and false reasonings of my enemy's might have injur'd my character, and probably, no body would have given themselves the trouble to have justified me. As a proof, Sir, I am not a revengefull man, if you marry that worthy Lady Mrs Blake or obtain from her letters wrote with the same warmth and friendship, as one I was obliged in my own vindication to produce to my judges in order to destroy a manifest lye she and her Nephew publish'd in one of their printed libels, you

* *Laing MSS.*, ii. 503.

was so very obliging to distribute amongst the English, I will from the bottom of [my] soul pardon the injury's you have attempt'd to do me, if not I shall ever consider you as the most credulous and partial of all men.

I send you the traduction of Mrs Blake's letter, notwithstanding of which she makes her nephew sign a libell in which he affirms his father never apply'd to me for money.

Hume immediately wrote the draft of a letter to Lord Elibank, with whom, it will be recalled, he and Robertson had had a brush in 1759 over the character of Queen Mary. He then sent both his draft and Murray's letter to Mme de Boufflers. She replied in the following undated letter:

* IV. Mme de Boufflers *to* Hume

[? 14 Aug. 1764.]

Votre pacquet que je recois en cet instant contient mon cher Maitre deux lettres, qui ont produit en moy des effets bien differend. Celle a my Lord Elibank est digne de lhomme pour qui je me sens prevenuë dune si tendre et si forte estime, celle de Mr Murray est dune violence qu'on peut appeller folle, et qui m'irrite contre luy au dernier point. Je suis fort eloignée de vouloir vous rien prescrire a son egard, quoique je pense qu'apres son honneur que j'ay deffendu par compassion et par justice je ne puisse luy rendre un plus signale service que de luy procurer votre amitié, mais c'est son affaire plus que la mienne. S'il lestime ce quelle vaut il doit sefforcer de la meriter. Je lexcuse pourtant de la chaleur quil temoigne. Son sang doit etre aigri par tout ce quil a souffert depuis dix huit mois et sa sensibilite dans cette affaire est a son avantage. Elle prouve quil say le prix de lhonneur et la valeur de votre suffrage, et sil a cru trop legerement que vous favorisez ses ennemis cela peut venir ou de la preoccupation de son esprit, ou de son impatience naturelle, ou des faux rapports de ces memes ennemis, a qui comme vous lavez eprouvé tous moyens sont bons, absurdes ou vraisemblables, injustes ou legitimes. Adieu faites mes complimens au chevalier Mackdonalt, il a un merite infini, je sens que je l'aime.

ce 15. Par refflexion je trouve quil y a dans votre lettre a my Lord Elibank quelques expressions que jaimerois mieux qui n'y fussent pas.

At the same time she wrote to Murray, calling for an explanation from him; to which he seems to have replied somewhat as follows:

† V. Murray *to* [Mme de Boufflers]

[16 or 17 Aug. 1764. A draft letter, much corrected.]

I am this moment favour'd with your Ladyship's letter, in which you desire an explication of my complaints against Mr Hume. As it

* MS., R.S.E., unpublished. † *Laing MSS.*, ii. 503.

never was my custom to complain of injuries I had received, or thought to have received but to the persons themselves; I therefore beg to be excused from entering into any detail upon that subject; Mr Hume is the properest person to inform Your Ladyship, if there is any misunderstanding betwixt us, all I say upon that matter is that I declare to you upon my honour I love and esteem Mr Hume at present as much as ever.

I declare to your Ladyship notwithstanding of the many and vast obligations I owe you, that if your Brother, who I loved and admired beyond every manner of expression was alive, and did any thing that I thought an injury I should think it incumbent upon me to call him to an account; the augmentation of the number of my enemy's nor no earthly consideration shall ever hinder me from resenting injury's, as I would much rather the half of mankind declared themselves against me, than suffer any thing I thought an insult. If these sentiments are disagreeable to you I am heartily sorry for it. But so I was form'd, so I have lived, and so I flatter myself I shall die. I proposed doing my self the honour of waiting on you to day to consult with you in regard to the letter you wrote to Cours les vaux [?] but shall not attempt seeing you. Whatever pain it may give me, however, nothing can ever eraze out of my soul the many and great obligations I owe.

Hume, as soon as he received Mme de Boufflers's letter (IV above), sat down and wrote a pacific letter to Murray; which the latter answered as follows:

* VI. Murray *to* Hume

Dear Sir

Yesterday, I was favour'd with Yours, which made me feel two very opposite passions; pleasure beyond expression to be assured by Yourself that what I had been told was not true; pain to a great degree at seeing Your superiority over me, in point of coolness and politeness. I shall always be overjoy'd to see You, but I flatter my self You will spare me the uneasyness I must necessarly suffer if You talk on a subject, I confess to You I have been so much in the wrong. I beg You will believe me as much as ever dear Sir

Your Most obedient and most humble Servant

A: Murray

19 August 1764

Meanwhile, some one had told Hume that Mme de Boufflers was the real cause of the quarrel, and he wrote her Letter 249 above. To this she replied as follows:

* VII. Mme de Boufflers *to* Hume

ce 18 aoust [1764.]

Je ne puis en verité comprendre ce que Mr Murray peut dire, tenir de moy. Je nay pas en general de frequentes conversations

* MS., R.S.E., unpublished.

avec luy, et la difference de nos caracteres interdit toute confiance de ma part. Il est donc fort difficile que je me justifie ne sachant ce dont on m'accuse, mais je crois quil mest au moins permis de dire que je suis rarement dans le cas dune accusation fondée, et encore plus rarement dans la volonté de me deffendre des choses, qu'on mimpute faute de me bien connoistre, je m'en remets toujours au tems a cet egard et je ne me presse dobtenir une justice qui ne peut me manquer, que de la part de ceux que lenvie ou la haine aveuglent. Je n'ay a craindre ni lun ni lautre, dun homme qui me surpasse en tout ce qui est estimable, et qui dailleurs est rempli de prevention et damitié pour moy. Ainsi je ne doute pas quapres deux minutes dexplications il ne me soit facile de me disculper des torts que vous m'attribuez. Je n'ay donc nulle inquietude sur un point qui men donneroit beaucoup si je n'etois assurée de leclaircir a la satisfaction de tous deux mais en attendant je suis affligée que vous m'ayez soupconnée, non pas tant parce que vous m'avez fait injure que parce [que] cette injustice est retombée sur vous meme, et vous a donné le chagrin que vous dites. Si lon savoit avec quelle douceur je supporte un procédé assez facheux, de la part dun ami qui me doit quelquestime, on me trouveroit sans doute trop indulgente, mais m'ayant une fois convaincuë de la sincerité de votre affection, vous avez acquis tout pouvoir sur moy, vos interets vont avant les miens, et je sacrifie volontiers de la dignité qui me convient, a votre satisfaction. Je nimagine pas que vous puissies desirer des preuves plus fortes de mes sentimens, et je me flatte que vous en serez content et que le trouble que vous me depeignez, en sera au moins suspendu.

Vous avez mal diviné au sujet de la lettre que vous ecrives a my Lord Elibank, je n'ay point pretendu blamer ce que vous luy dites de son frere, parce que j'ay supposé que vous eties a portée de luy parler ainsi. Mon intention etoit de designer lepithete dont vous serves a la fin, quoique lamour de my Lord pour Marie Stuart soit une veritable extravagance, etant son ami vous deves eviter de le choquer en la traitant avec mepris.

Hume's letter to Lord Elibank is not extant, but we have evidence enough that it irritated that noble lord not a little. Elibank's reply (to which Hume's of 3 Nov. 1764 is again a reply) is not extant either; but the following extract from a letter of Sir James Macdonald indicates the tone in which it must have been composed.

* VIII. Sir James Macdonald *to* Hume

London April 26. 1765.

. . . Now that I have troubled you with all the public news, let me enter into something that regards yourself. I am sorry to see

* MS., R.S.E.; *Eminent Persons*, 53.

Lord Elibank so much out of humour in regard to you. He showed me a letter you had written to him and his answer. If I could disapprove of any thing you ever wrote it would be of th[e spir]it of that letter, though I am much [?] [1]approving of his answer. In short [I] wish that neither of these letters had ever been written, as I do not like to see old friendship's break up, especially between men of merit and who have been mutually obliged to each other. I wish you could come to understand each other better than at present you seem to do. He goes from hence to Scotland in a few days, and I think carries with him some degree of acrimony against you which I should wish greatly to see sweetened. . . .

The final letter is from Elibank, in answer (I think) to Hume's of 3 Nov. 1764. It seems to have closed the incident.

* IX. Lord Elibank *to* Hume

Balancrief July 9th 1765

Dear Sir

I have the Pleasure to understand, by yours of the —— that I have never been altogether in disgrace with you—I choose rather to pass for Dull as Mad, and it would have been the highest proof of the latter, if I had taken any thing ill of you, that I had not thought ill meant.

I own the Compliment you say you intended me in your former Letter, was too refined for my genius. I really mistook it for an intention to break with me; and as there is hardly any thing I set a greater value on than your friendship, and I was not conscious of having ever entertained a single Idea inconsistent with it, I could not resign it without pain and resentment. Diffident of my self, I showed your letter to several of our common friends, who all understood it as I did. Had my affection for you been more moderate, my answer to yours, would have been cool in proportion.

I am still mortified to think you could suspect me of siding with my Brother against you. I know the distinction between Relationship and friendship. I have ever thought those Connections incompatible; and if I was dull enough to mistake the meaning of your Letter, I have not more reason to blush, than you have for suspecting that any thing my Brother could say, was capable of influencing my sincere regard for a friend of 30 years standing, or that my Zeal for the Reputation of any Prince, Dead or alive, could draw any sentiment or expression from me, inconsistent with that admiration of your Talents as an Author, and merit as a man, I have constantly felt in my self, and endeavoured to excite in others. I am Dr Sir your sincerely obedient humble Servant

Elibank

* MS., R.S.E.; Burton, ii. 260.

[1] Autograph torn.

APPENDIX G

LETTERS FROM JEAN-JACQUES ROUSSEAU TO HUME

* I. (See Letter 196 above.)

A Motiers-travers le 19 fevrier 1763.

Je n'ai receu qu'ici, Monsieur, et depuis peu, la Lettre dont vous m'honoriez à Londres le 2 Juillet dernier, supposant que j'étois arrivé dans cette Capitale. C'étoit, sans doute, dans vôtre Nation et le plus près de vous qu'il m'eut été possible que j'aurois cherché ma retraite, si j'avois prévu l'accueil qui m'attendoit dans ma Patrie; il n'y avoit qu'elle que je pusse préférer à l'Angleterre, et cette prévention, dont j'ai été trop puni, m'étoit alors bien pardonable. Je n'ai trouvé que des affronts et des outrages où j'espérois des consolations et même de la reconnoissance. Que de choses m'ont fait regretter l'azile et l'hospitalité philosophique qui m'attendoient près de vous! Toutefois mes malheurs mêmes m'en ont rapproché en quelque maniére. La protection et les bontés de Mylord Mareschal vôtre illustre et digne Compatriote m'ont fait trouver, pour ainsi dire, l'Ecosse au milieu de la Suisse; il vous a mis entre nous par ses entretiens; il m'a fait faire avec vos vertus la connoissance que je n'avois faite encore qu'avec vos talens; il m'a inspiré la plus tendre amitié pour vous et le plus ardent desir de la cultiver, même avant que je vous susse disposé à m'honorer de la vôtre. Non, Monsieur, je ne vous rendois que la moitié de ce qui vous est dû quand je n'avois pour vous que de l'admiration. Vos grandes vües, vôtre étonante impartialité, vôtre génie vous éleveroient trop au dessus des hommes, si vôtre bon coeur ne vous en rapprochoit. Mylord Mareschal, en m'apprenant à vous voir encore plus aimable que sublime, me rend tous les jours vôtre commerce plus désirable, et nourrit en moi l'empressement qu'il m'a fait naître de finir mes jours près de vous. Monsieur, qu'une meilleure Santé qu'une situation plus comode ne me met-elle à portée de faire le voyage comme je le desirerois! Que ne puis-je espérer de nous voir un jour rassemblés près de Mylord dans vôtre commune Patrie, qui deviendroit la mienne! Je bénirois dans une Société si charmante les malheurs par lesquels j'y fus conduit, et je croirois n'avoir commencé de vivre que du jour qu'elle auroit commencé. Puisse venir cet heureux jour plus desiré qu'espéré! Avec quels transports de joye je m'écrierois en touchant l'heureuse terre où sont nés David Hume et le Mareschal d'Ecosse!

Salve satis mihi debita tellus!
Hîc domus, hac patria est.——

J. J. Rousseau.

* MS., R.S.E.; unpublished in this form. Cf., however, *Corr. gén. de Rousseau*, ix. 103 f.

* II. (See Letter 294 above.)

A Strasbourg. le 4. xbre 1765.

Vos bontés, Monsieur, me pénétrent autant qu'elles m'honorent. La plus digne réponse que je puisse faire à vos offres est de les accepter, et je les accepte. Je partirai dans cinq ou six jours pour aller me jetter entre vos bras. C'est le conseil de Mylord Mareschal mon protecteur mon ami mon pére; c'est celui de Madame de Verdelin dont la bienveillance éclairée me guide autant qu'elle me console; enfin j'ose dire que c'est celui de mon coeur qui se plait à devoir beaucoup au plus illustre de mes contemporains dont la bonté surpasse la gloire. Je soupire après une retraite solitaire et libre où je puisse finir mes jours en paix. Si vos soins bienfaisans me la procurent, je jouirai tout ensemble et du seul bien que mon coeur desire, et du plaisir de le tenir de vous. Je vous salue, Monsieur, de tout mon coeur

J. J. Rousseau.

† III. (See Letter 311 above.)

Ce Lundi soir.

Je vous supplie, mon très cher Patron, de vouloir bien m'excuser auprès de Myladi Ailesbury et de M. le General Conway. Je suis malade et hors d'état de me présenter, et Mlle le Vasseur très bonne et très estimable personne, n'est point faite pour paroitre dans les grandes compagnies. Trouvez bon, mon très cher Patron, que nous nous en tenions au premier arrangement et que j'attende dans l'après midi le Carrosse que M. Davenport veut bien envoyer. J'arrive suant et fatigué d'une longue promenade, c'est pourquoi je ne prolonge pas ma lettre; vous m'avez si bien acquis et je suis à vous de tant de maniéres que cela même ne doit plus être dit. Je vous embrasse de toutte la tendresse de mon coeur

J. J. Rousseau.

‡ IV. (See Letter 316 above.)

A Wootton le 22. Mars 1766.

Vous voyez déja, mon cher Patron, par la date de ma lettre que je suis arrivé au lieu de ma destination. Mais vous ne pouvez voir tous les charmes que j'y trouve; il faudroit connoitre le lieu et lire dans mon coeur. Vous y devez lire au moins les sentimens qui vous regardent et que vous avez si bien mérités. Si je vis dans cet agréable azile aussi heureux que je l'espére, une dės douceurs de ma vie sera

* MS., R.S.E.; *Corr. gén. de Rousseau*, xiv. 315, where the name of Mme de Boufflers is incorrectly substituted for that of Mme de Verdelin.

† MS., R.S.E. ‡ MS., R.S.E.

de penser que je vous les dois. Faire un heureux, c'est mériter de l'être. Puissiez-vous trouver en vous-même le prix de tout ce que vous avez fait pour moi. Seul j'aurois pu trouver de l'hospitalité, peut-être; mais je ne l'aurois jamais aussi bien goûtée qu'en la tenant de vôtre amitié. Conservez-la moi toujours, mon cher Patron; aimez-moi pour moi qui vous dois tant; pour vous-même; aimez-moi pour le bien que vous m'avez fait. Je sens tout le prix de votre sincere amitié, je la desire ardemment; j'y veux répondre par toute la mienne, et je sens dans mon coeur dequoi vous convaincre un jour vous même qu'elle n'est pas non plus sans quelque prix. Comme pour des raisons dont nous avons parlé je ne veux rien recevoir par la poste, Je vous prie, lorsque vous ferez la bonne œuvre de m'écrire, de remettre votre lettre à M. Davenport. L'affaire de ma voiture n'est pas encore arrangée, parce que je sais qu'on m'en a imposé: c'est une petite faute qui peut n'être que l'ouvrage d'une vanité obligeante quand elle ne revient pas deux fois. Si vous y avez trempé, je vous conseille de quitter une fois pour toutes ces petites ruses qui ne peuvent avoir un bon principe quand elles se tournent en piéges contre la simplicité. Je vous embrasse, mon cher Patron, avec le même coeur que j'espére et desire trouver en vous.

J. J. Rousseau.

* V. (See Letter 331 above.)

A Wootton le 23 Juin 1766.

Je croyois, Monsieur, que mon silence interprété par votre conscience en disoit assez; mais puisqu'il entre dans vos vues de ne pas l'entendre, je parlerai. Vous vous étes mal caché, je vous connois, et vous ne l'ignorez pas. Sans liaisons antérieures, sans querelles, sans démelés, sans nous connoitre autrement que par la réputation litteraire, vous vous empressez à m'offrir vos amis et vos soins; touché de votre générosité je me jette entre vos bras, vous m'amenez en Angleterre, en apparence pour m'y procurer un azile, et en effet pour m'y deshonorer. Vous vous appliquez à cette noble oeuvre avec un zèle digne de votre coeur, et avec un succés digne de vos talens. Il n'en falloit pas tant pour reussir; vous vivez dans le monde et moi dans la retraite, le public aime à être trompé, et vous étes fait pour le tromper. Je connois pourtant un homme que vous ne tromperez pas; c'est vous-même. Vous savez avec quelle horreur mon coeur repoussa le prémier soupçon de vos desseins. Je vous dis en vous embrassant les yeux en larmes que si vous n'étiez pas le meilleur des hommes il faudroit que vous en fussiez le plus noir. En pensant à votre conduite secrette vous vous direz quelquefois que vois n'étes pas le meilleur des hommes, et je doute qu'avec cette idée vous en soyez jamais le plus heureux.

* MS., R.S.E.; *Œuvres de Rousseau*, 1826, xxiii. 350 f.

Je laisse un libre cours aux manoeuvres de vos amis, aux vôtres, et je vous abandonne avec peu de regret ma reputation durant ma vie, bien sur qu'un jour on nous rendra justice à tous deux. Quant aux bons offices en matiére d'intérest avec lesquels vous vous masquez, je vous en remercie et vous en dispense. Je me dois de n'avoir plus de commerce avec vous, et de n'accepter, pas même à mon avantage, aucune affaire dont vous soyez le médiateur. Adieu, Monsieur, je vous souhaite le plus vrai bonheur, mais comme nous ne devons plus rien avoir à nous dire, voici la derniére lettre que vous recevrez de moi.

J. J. ROUSSEAU.

* VI. (See Letter 337 above.)

A Wootton le 10 Juillet 1766.

Je suis malade, Monsieur, et peu en état d'ecrire; mais vous voulez une explication, il faut vous la donner. Il n'a tenu qu'à vous de l'avoir depuis longtems; vous n'en voulutes point alors, je me tus; vous la voulez aujourdui, je vous l'envoye. Elle sera longue, j'en suis fâché; mais j'ai beaucoup à dire, et je n'y veux pas revenir à deux fois.

Je ne vis point dans le monde, j'ignore ce qui s'y passe, je n'ai point de parti, point d'associé, point d'intrigue; on ne me dit rien, je ne sais que ce que je sens; mais comme on me le fait bien sentir, je le sais bien. Le premier soin de ceux qui trament des noirceurs est de se mettre à couvert des preuves juridiques; il ne feroit pas bon leur intenter des procés. La conviction intérieure admet un autre genre de preuves qui réglent les sentimens d'un honnête homme: vous saurez sur quoi sont fondés les miens.

Vous demandez avec beaucoup de confiance qu'on vous nomme vôtre accusateur. Cette accusateur, Monsieur, est le seul homme au monde qui déposant contre vous pouvoit se faire écouter de moi; c'est vous-même. Je vais me livrer sans réserve et sans crainte à mon caractère ouvert, ennemi de tout artifice; je vous parlerai avec la même franchise que si vous etiez un autre en qui j'eusse toute la confiance que je n'ai plus en vous: je vous ferai l'histoire des mouvemens de mon ame et de ce qui les a produits, et nommant M. Hume en tierce personne, je vous ferai juge vous-même de ce que je dois penser de lui. Malgré la longueur de ma lettre, je n'y suivrai point d'autre ordre que celui de mes idées, commençant par les indices, et finissant par la démonstration.

Je quittois la Suisse, fatigué de traitemens barbares, mais qui du moins ne mettoient en péril que ma personne, et laissoient mon honneur en sureté. Je suivois les mouvemens de mon coeur pour aller joindre Mylord Mareschal, quand je receus à Strasbourg de M. Hume l'invitation la plus tendre de passer avec lui en Angleterre,

* MS., R.S.E.; *Œuvres de Rousseau*, 1826, xxiii. 358 ff.

où il me promettoit l'accueil le plus agréable, et plus de tranquillité que je n'y en ai trouvé. Je balançai entre l'ancien ami et le nouveau; j'eus tort: je préférai ce dernier; j'eus plus grand tort: mais le desir de connoitre par moi-même une nation célébre dont on me disoit tant de mal et tant de bien l'emporta. Sur de ne pas perdre George Keith, j'étois flatté d'acquerir David Hume. Son mérite, ses rares talens, l'honnêteté bien établie de son caractére, me faisoient desirer de joindre son amitié à celle dont m'honoroit son illustre compatriote, et je me faisois une sorte de gloire de montrer un bel exemple aux gens de lettres dans l'union sincére de deux hommes dont les principes étoient si différens.

Avant l'invitation du Roi de Prusse et de Mylord Mareschal, incertain sur le lieu de ma retraite, j'avois demandé et obtenu par mes amis un passeport de la Cour de France, dont je me servis pour aller à Paris joindre M. Hume. Il vit, et vit trop, peut-être, l'accueil que je receus d'un grand Prince, et j'ose dire, du public. Je me prêtai par devoir mais avec répugnance à cet éclat, jugeant combien l'envie de mes ennemis en seroit irritée. Ce fut un spectacle bien doux pour moi que l'augmentation sensible de bienveillance pour M. Hume que la bonne oeuvre qu'il alloit faire produisit dans tout Paris. Il devoit en être touché comme moi, je ne sais s'il le fut de la même maniére.

Nous partons avec un de mes amis qui presque uniquement pour moi faisoit le voyage d'Angleterre. En débarquant à Douvre, transporté de toucher enfin cette terre de liberté et d'y être amené par cet homme illustre, je lui saute au cou, je l'embrasse étroitement sans rien dire, mais en couvrant son visage de baisers et de larmes qui parloient assez. Ce n'est pas la seule fois ni la plus remarquable où il ait pu voir en moi les saisissemens d'un coeur pénétré. Je ne sais ce qu'il fait de ces souvenirs s'ils lui viennent: j'ai dans l'esprit qu'il en doit quelquefois être importuné.

Nous sommes fêtés arrivant à Londres. On s'empresse dans tous les états à me marquer de la bienveillance et de l'estime. M. Hume me présente de bonne grace à tout le monde; il étoit naturel de lui attribuer comme je faisois la meilleure partie de ce bon accueil: mon coeur étoit plein de lui, j'en parlois à tout le monde, j'en écrivois à tous mes amis, mon attachement pour lui prenoit chaque jour de nouvelles forces; le sien paroissoit pour moi des plus tendres, et il m'en a quelquefois donné des marques dont je me suis senti très-touché. Celle de faire faire mon portrait en grand ne fut pourtant pas de ce nombre. Cette fantaisie me parut trop affichée, et j'y trouvai je ne sais quel air d'ostentation qui ne me plut pas. C'est tout ce que j'aurois pu passer à M. Hume s'il eut été homme à jetter son argent par les fenetres, et qu'il eut eu dans une gallerie tous les portraits de ses amis. Au reste j'avouerai sans peine qu'en cela je pouvois avoir tort.

Mais ce qui me parut un acte d'amitié et de générosité des plus vrais, des plus estimables, des plus dignes en un mot de M. Hume, ce fut le soin qu'il prit de solliciter pour moi de lui même une pension du Roi, à laquelle je n'avois assurément aucun droit d'aspirer. Témoin du zèle qu'il mit à cette affaire j'en fus vivement pénétré: rien ne pouvoit plus me flatter qu'un service de cette espéce, non pour l'intérest assurément, car trop attaché peut-être à ce que je posséde, je ne sais point desirer ce que je n'ai pas, et ayant par mes amis et par mon travail du pain suffisament pour vivre, je n'ambitionne rien de plus: mais l'honneur de recevoir des témoignages de bonté, je ne dirai pas d'un si grand Monarque, mais d'un si bon pere, d'un si bon mari, d'un si bon maitre, d'un si bon ami, et surtout d'un si honnête homme m'affectoit sensiblement, et quand je considerois encore dans cette grace que le Ministre qui l'avoit obtenue étoit la probité vivante, cette probité si utile aux peuples, et si rare dans son état, je ne pouvois que me glorifier d'avoir pour bienfaiteurs trois des hommes du monde que j'aurois le plus desirés pour amis. Aussi, loin de me refuser à la pension offerte, je ne mis pour l'accepter qu'une condition necessaire, savoir un consentement dont sans manquer à mon devoir je ne pouvois me passer.

Honoré des empressemens de tout le monde, je tâchois d'y répondre convenablement. Cependant ma mauvaise santé et l'habitude de vivre à la campagne me firent trouver le séjour de la ville incommode. Aussi-tôt les maisons de campagne se présentent en foule; on m'en offre à choisir dans toutes les provinces. M. Hume se charge des propositions, il me les fait, il me conduit même à deux ou trois Campagnes voisines; j'hésite longtems sur le choix; il augmentoit cette incertitude. Je me détermine enfin pour cette province, et d'abord M. Hume arrange tout; les embarras s'applanissent; je pars, j'arrive dans cette habitation solitaire, commode, agréable: le maitre de la maison prévoit tout, pourvoit à tout, rien ne me manque. Je suis tranquille, indépendant; voila le moment si desiré où tous mes maux doivent finir. Non, c'est là qu'ils commencent, plus cruels que je ne les avois encore éprouvés.

J'ai parlé jusqu'ici d'abondance de coeur, et rendant avec le plus grand plaisir justice aux bons offices de M. Hume. Que ce qui me reste à dire n'est-il de même nature! Rien ne me coûtera jamais de ce qui pourra l'honorer. Il n'est permis de marchander sur le prix des bien faits que quand on nous accuse d'ingratitude, et M. Hume m'en accuse aujourdui. J'oserai donc faire une observation qu'il rend necessaire. En appreciant ses soins par la peine et le tems qu'ils lui coûtoient ils étoient d'un prix inestimable, encore plus par sa bonne volonté: par le bien réel qu'ils m'ont fait ils ont plus d'apparence que de poids. Je ne venois point comme un mendiant quester du pain en Angleterre; j'y apportois le mien; j'y venois seulement chercher un azile, et il est ouvert à tout étranger. D'ailleurs je n'y étois point tellement inconnu qu'arrivant seul j'eusse manqué d'assistance et de services. Si quelques personnes m'ont recherché pour M. Hume, d'autres aussi m'ont recherché pour moi; et par exemple, quand M. Davenport voulut bien m'offrir l'azile que j'habite, ce ne fut pas pour lui qu'il ne connoissoit point, et qu'il vit seulement pour le prier de faire et d'appuyer son obligeante proposition. Ainsi quand M. Hume tâche aujourdui d'aliener de moi cet honnête homme, il cherche à m'ôter ce qu'il ne m'a pas donné. Tout ce qui s'est fait de bien se seroit fait sans lui à peu près de même, et peutêtre mieux; mais le mal ne se fut point fait; car pourquoi ai-je des ennemis en Angleterre? Pourquoi ces ennemis sont-ils précisément les amis de M. Hume? Qui est-ce qui a pu m'attirer leur inimitié? Ce n'est pas moi qui ne les vis de ma vie et qui ne les connois pas; je n'en aurois aucun si j'y étois venu seul.

J'ai parlé jusqu'ici de faits publics et notoires, qui par leur nature et par ma reconnoissance ont eu le plus grand éclat. Ceux qui me restent à dire sont, non seulement particuliers mais secrets, du moins dans leur cause, et l'on a pris toutes les mesures possibles pour qu'ils restassent cachés au public: mais, bien connus de la personne intéressée, ils n'en opérent pas moins sa propre conviction.

Peu de tems après notre arrivée à Londres, j'y remarquai dans les esprits à mon égard un changement sourd qui bientot devint très sensible. Avant que je vinsse en Angleterre, elle étoit un des pays de l'Europe où j'avois le plus de réputation, j'oserois presque dire, de considération. Les papiers publics étoient pleins de mes éloges, et il n'y avoit qu'un cri contre mes persecuteurs. Ce ton se soutint à mon arrivée; les papiers l'annoncérent en triomphe; l'Angleterre s'honoroit d'être mon réfuge, elle en glorifioit avec justice ses loix et son gouvernement. Tout à coup, et sans aucune cause assignable ce ton change, mais si fort et si vîte que dans tous les caprices du public on n'en voit guéres de plus étonnant. Le signal fut donné dans un certain magasin aussi plein d'inepties que de mensonges, où l'Auteur bien instruit ou feignant de l'être me donnoit pour fils de musicien. Dès ce moment les imprimés ne parlérent plus de moi que d'une maniére équivoque ou malhonnête. Tout ce qui avoit trait à mes malheurs étoit déguisé, altéré, présenté sous un faux jour, et toujours le moins à mon avantage qu'il étoit possible. Loin de parler de l'accueil que j'avois receu à Paris et qui n'avoit fait que trop de bruit, on ne supposoit pas même que j'eusse osé paroitre dans cette ville, et un des amis de M. Hume fut très surpris quand je lui dis que j'y avois passé.

Trop accoutumé à l'inconstance du public pour m'en affecter encore je ne laissois pas d'être étonné de ce changement si brusque, de ce concert si singulierement unanime que pas un de ceux qui m'avoient tant loué absent ne parut, moi présent, se souvenir de mon existence. Je trouvois bizarre que précisement après le retour de

M. Hume qui a tant de credit à Londres, tant d'influence sur les gens de Lettres et les Libraires, et de si grandes liaisons avec eux, sa présence eut produit un effet si contraire à celui qu'on en pouvoit attendre; que, parmi tant d'Ecrivains de toute espéce, pas un de ses amis ne se montrât le mien; et l'on voyoit bien que ceux qui parloient de moi n'étoient pas ses ennemis, puisqu'en faisant sonner son caractére public ils disoient que j'avois traversé la France sous sa protection, à la faveur d'un passeport qu'il m'avoit obtenu de la Cour, et peu s'en falloit qu'ils ne fissent entendre que j'avois fait le voyage à sa suitte et à ses fraix.

Ceci ne signifioit rien encore, et n'étoit que singulier; mais ce qui l'étoit davantage fut que le ton de ses amis ne changea pas moins avec moi que celui du public. Toujours, je me fais un plaisir de le dire, leurs soins leurs bons offices ont été les mêmes et très grands en ma faveur; mais loin de me marquer la même estime, celui surtout dont je veux parler et chez qui nous étions descendus à notre arrivée, accompagnoit tout cela de propos si durs et quelquefois si choquans qu'on eut dit qu'il ne cherchoit à m'obliger que pour avoir droit de me marquer du mépris. Son frére, d'abord très accueillant, très honnête, changea bientot avec si peu de mesure qu'il ne daignoit pas même dans leur propre maison me dire un seul mot, ni me rendre le salut, ni aucun des devoirs que l'on rend chez soi aux étrangers. Rien cependant n'étoit survenu de nouveau que l'arrivée de J. J. Rousseau et de David Hume; et certainement la cause de ces changemens ne vint pas de moi; à moins que trop de simplicité, de discretion, de modestie, ne soit un moyen de mécontenter les Anglois.

Pour M. Hume, loin de prendre avec moi un ton révoltant, il donnoit dans l'autre extrème. Les flagorneries m'ont toujours été suspectes. Il m'en a fait et de toutes les façons,[1] au point de me forcer, n'y pouvant tenir davantage, à lui en dire mon sentiment. Sa conduite le dispensoit fort de s'étendre en paroles; cependant puisqu'il en vouloit dire, j'aurois voulu qu'à toutes ces louanges fades il eut substitué quelque fois la voix d'un ami; mais je n'ai jamais trouvé dans son langage rien qui sentit la vraie amitié, pas même dans la façon dont il parloit de moi à d'autres en ma présence. On eut dit qu'en voulant me faire des patrons il cherchoit à m'ôter leur bienveillance, qu'il vouloit plustot que j'en fusse assisté qu'aimé, et j'ai quelquefois été surpris du tour révoltant qu'il qu'il donnoit à ma conduite près des gens qui pouvoient s'en offenser. Un exemple éclaircira ceci. M. Penneck du Museum, ami de Mylord Mareschal et pasteur d'une parroisse où l'on vouloit m'établir vient nous voir. M. Hume, moi présent, lui fait mes excuses de ne l'avoir pas prévenu.

[1] J'en dirai seulement une qui m'a fait rire; c'étoit de faire en sorte, quand je venois le voir, que je trouvasse toujours sur la table un Tome de l'Heloïse; comme si je ne connoissois pas assez le gout de M. Hume pour être assuré que, de tous les Livres qui existent, l'Héloïse doit être pour lui le plus ennuyeux.

Le Docteur Maty, lui dit-il, *nous avoit invités pour Jeudi au Museum ou M. Rousseau devoit vous voir; mais il préféra d'aller avec Made. Garrick à la Comedie. On ne peut pas faire tant de choses en un jour*. Vous m'avouerez, Monsieur, que c'étoit une etrange façon de me capter la bienveillance de M. Penneck.

Je ne sais ce qu'avoit pu dire en secret M. Hume à ses connoissances; mais rien n'étoit plus bizarre que leur façon d'en user avec moi de son aveu, souvent même par son assistance. Quoique ma bourse ne fut pas vuide, que je n'eusse besoin de celle de personne, et qu'il le sut très bien, l'on eut dit que je n'étois là que pour vivre aux dépens du public, et qu'il n'étoit question que de me faire l'aumône de maniére à m'en sauver un peu l'embarras. Je puis dire que cette affectation continuelle et choquante est une des choses qui m'ont fait prendre le plus en aversion le séjour de Londres. Ce n'est surement pas sur ce pied qu'il faut présenter en Angleterre un homme à qui l'on veut attirer un peu de considération: mais cette charité peut être benignement interprétée, et je consens qu'elle le soit. Avançons.

On répand à Paris une fausse lettre du Roi de Prusse à moi addressée et pleine de la plus cruelle malignité. J'apprends avec surprise que c'est un M. Walpole ami de M. Hume qui répand cette lettre; je lui demande si cela est vrai; pour toute réponse il me demande de qui je le tiens. Un moment auparavant il m'avoit donné une carte pour ce même M. Walpole afin qu'il se chargeât de papiers qui m'importent, et que je veux faire venir de Paris en sureté.

J'apprens que le fils du Jongleur Tronchin mon plus mortel ennemi est non seulement l'ami le protégé de M. Hume, mais qu'ils logent ensemble, et quand M. Hume voit que je sais cela il m'en fait la confidence, m'assurant que le fils ne ressemble pas au pere. J'ai logé quelques nuits dans cette maison chez M. Hume avec ma Gouvernante, et à l'air à l'accueil dont nous ont honoré ses hôtesses qui sont ses amies, j'ai jugé de la façon dont lui ou cet homme qu'il dit ne pas ressembler à son pere ont pu leur parler d'elle et de moi.

Ces faits combines entre eux et avec une certaine apparence générale me donnent insensiblement une inquietude que je repousse avec horreur. Cependant les lettres que j'écris n'arrivent pas; j'en reçois qui ont été ouvertes, et toutes ont passé par les mains de M. Hume. Si quelqu'une lui échape, il ne peut cacher l'ardente avidité de la voir. Un soir je vois encore chez lui une manœuvre de lettre dont je suis frappé.[1] Après le soupé, gardant tous deux le silence au coin de

[1] Il faut dire ce que c'est que cette manoeuvre. J'écrivois sur la table de M. Hume en son absence une réponse à une lettre que je venois de recevoir. Il arrive, très curieux de savoir ce que j'écrivois et ne pouvant presque s'abstenir d'y lire. Je ferme ma lettre sans la lui montrer, et comme je la mettois dans ma poche, il la demande avidement, disant qu'il l'enverra le lendemain jour de poste. La lettre reste sur sa table, Lord Newnham arrive, M. Hume sort un moment; je reprends ma lettre, distant que j'aurai le tems de l'envoyer le lendemain. Lord Newnham

son feu je m'apperçois qu'il me fixe, comme il lui arrivoit très souvent, et d'une maniére dont l'idée est difficile à rendre. Pour cette fois son regard sec ardent moqueur et prolongé devint plus qu'inquiétant. Pour m'en débarrasser j'essayai de le fixer à mon tour: mais en arrêtant mes yeux sur les siens je sens un frémissement inexplicable, et bientot je suis forcé de les baisser. La physionomie et le ton du bon David sont d'un bon homme, mais où, grand Dieu, ce bon homme emprunte-t-il les yeux dont il fixe ses amis?

L'impression de ce regard me reste et m'agite; mon trouble augmente jusqu'au saisissement: Si l'épanchement n'eut succédé, j'étouffois. Bientôt un violent remords me gagne; je m'indigne de moi-même. Enfin dans un transport que je me rapelle encore avec délices, je m'élance à son cou, je le serre étroitement; suffoqué de sanglots, inondé de larmes je m'écrie d'une voix entrecoupée: *Non non, David Hume n'est pas un traître; s'il n'étoit le meilleur des hommes il faudroit qu'il en fut le plus noir.* David Hume me rend poliment mes embrassemens, et tout en me frappant de petits coups sur le dos me repette plusieurs fois d'un ton tranquille. *Quoi, mon cher Monsieur? Eh mon cher Monsieur! Quoi donc, mon cher Monsieur?* Il ne me dit rien de plus; je sens que mon coeur se resserre; nous allons nous coucher, et je pars le lendemain pour la province.

Arrivé dans cet agréable azile où j'étois venu chercher le repos de si loin, je devois le trouver dans une maison solitaire commode et riante dont le maitre, homme d'esprit et de mérite n'épargnoit rien de ce qui pouvoit m'en faire aimer le séjour. Mais quel repos peut-on gouter dans la vie quand le coeur est agité? Troublé de la plus cruelle incertitude, et ne sachant que penser d'un homme que je devois aimer, je cherchois à me délivrer de ce doute funeste en rendant ma confiance à mon bienfaiteur. Car, pourquoi, par quel caprice inconcevable eut-il eu tant de zèle à l'exterieur pour mon bien-être, avec des projets secrets contre mon honneur? Dans les observations qui m'avoient inquietté chaque fait en lui-même étoit peu de chose; il n'y avoit que leur concours d'étonnant, et peut-être, instruit d'autres faits que j'ignorois, M. Hume pouvoit-il dans un éclaircissement me donner une solution satisfaisante. La seule chose inexplicable étoit qu'il se fut refusé à un éclaircissement que

m'offre de l'envoyer par le paquet de M. l'Ambassadeur de France, j'accepte. M. Hume rentre tandis que Lord Newnham fait son enveloppe; il tire son cachet, M. Hume offre le sien avec tant d'empressement qu'il faut s'en servir par préférence. On sonne. Lord Newnham donne la lettre au Laquais de M. Hume pour la remettre au sien qui attend en bas avec son carrosse, afin qu'il la porte chez M. l'Ambassadeur. A peine le Laquais de M. Hume étoit hors de la porte que je me dis; je parie que le maitre va le suivre; il n'y manqua pas. Ne sachant comment laisser seul Mylord Newnham j'hesitai quelque tems avant que de suivre à mon tour M. Hume; je n'apperçus rien, mais il vit très bien que j'étois inquiet. Ainsi quoique je n'aye receu aucune réponse à ma Lettre je ne doute pas qu'elle ne soit parvenue; mais je doute un peu, je l'avoue, qu'elle n'ait pas été lue auparavant.

son honneur et son amitié pour moi rendoient également necessaire. Je voyois qu'il avoit là quelque chose que je ne comprenois pas et que je mourois d'envie d'entendre. Avant donc de me décider absolument sur son compte je voulus faire un dernier effort et lui écrire pour le ramener s'il se laissoit séduire à mes ennemis, ou pour le faire expliquer de maniére ou d'autre. Je lui écrivis une lettre qu'il dut trouver fort naturelle[1] s'il étoit coupable, mais fort extraordinaire s'il ne l'étoit pas: car quoi de plus extraordinaire qu'une lettre pleine à la fois de gratitude sur ses services et d'inquiétude sur ses sentimens, et où, mettant pour ainsi dire ses actions d'un côté et ses intentions de l'autre, au lieu de parler des preuves d'amitié qu'il m'avoit données, je le priois de m'aimer à cause du bien qu'il m'avoit fait? Je n'ai pas pris mes précautions d'assez loin pour garder une copie de cette lettre; mais puis qu'il les a prises, lui, qu'il la montre, et quiconque la lira, y voyant un homme tourmenté d'une peine secrette qu'il veut faire entendre et qu'il n'ose dire, sera curieux, je m'assure, de savoir quel éclaircissement cette lettre aura produit, surtout à la suite de la scéne précédente. Aucun, rien du tout. M. Hume se contente en réponse de me parler des soins obligeans que M. Davenport se propose de prendre en ma faveur. Du reste, pas un mot sur le principal sujet de ma lettre, ni sur l'état de mon coeur dont il devoit si bien voir le tourment. Je fus frappé de ce silence encore plus que je ne l'avois été de son flegme à notre dernier entretien. J'avois tort, ce silence étoit fort naturel après l'autre, et j'aurois du m'y attendre. Car quand on a osé dire en face à un homme, *je suis tenté de vous croire un traître*, et qu'il n'a pas la curiosité de vous demander *sur quoi*, l'on peut compter qu'il n'aura pareille curiosité de sa vie, et pour peu que les indices le chargent, cet homme est jugé.

Aprés la reception de sa lettre, qui tarda beaucoup je pris enfin mon parti et resolus de ne lui plus écrire. Tout me confirma bientot dans la résolution de rompre avec lui tout commerce. Curieux au dernier point du détail de mes moindres affaires, il ne s'étoit pas borné à s'en informer de moi dans nos entretiens, mais j'appris qu'après avoir commencé par faire avouer à ma Gouvernante qu'elle en étoit instruite, il n'avoit pas laissé échaper avec elle un seul tête-à-tête sans l'interroger jusqu'à l'importunité, sur mes occupations, sur mes ressources, sur mes amis, sur mes connoissances, sur leurs noms leur état leur demeure, et avec une addresse jésuitique il avoit demandé séparément les mêmes choses à elle et à moi. On doit prendre intérest aux affaires d'un ami, mais on doit se contenter de ce qu'il veut nous en dire, surtout quand il est aussi ouvert aussi confiant que moi, et tout ce petit cailletage de commére convient, on ne peut pas plus mal, à un philosophe.

[1] Il paroit par ce qu'il m'écrit en dernier lieu qu'il est très content de cette lettre et qu'il la trouve fort bien.

Dans le même tems je reçois encore deux lettres qui ont été ouvertes. L'une de M. Boswell, dont le cachet étoit en si mauvais état que M. Davenport en la recevant le fit remarquer au Laquais de M. Hume, et l'autre de M. d'Ivernois dans un paquet de M. Hume, laquelle avoit été recachetée au moyen d'un fer chaud qui, maladroitement appliqué, avoit brulé le papier autour de l'empreinte. J'écrivis à M. Davenport pour le prier de garder par devers lui toutes les lettres qui lui seroient remises pour moi, et de n'en remettre aucune à personne sous quelque prétexte que ce fut. J'ignore si M. Davenport, bien éloigné de penser que cette précaution put regarder M. Hume lui montra ma lettre, mais je sais que tout disoit à celui-ci qu'il avoit perdu ma confiance, et qu'il n'en alloit pas moins son train sans s'embarrasser de la recouvrer.

Mais que devins-je lorsque je vis dans les papiers publics la prétendue lettre du Roi de Prusse que je n'avois pas encore vue, cette fausse lettre imprimée en françois et en anglois, donnée pour vraie, même avec la signature du Roi, et que j'y reconnus la plume de M. D'Alembert aussi surement que si je la lui avois vu écrire?

A l'instant un trait de lumiére vint m'éclairer sur la cause secrette du changement étonnant et prompt du public anglois à mon égard, et je vis à Paris le foyer du complot qui s'executoit à Londres.

M. Dalembert, autre ami très intime de M. Hume, étoit depuis longtems mon ennemi caché, et n'épioit que les occasions de me nuire sans se commettre. Il étoit le seul des gens de lettres d'un certain nom et de mes anciennes connoissances qui ne me fut point venu voir ou qui ne m'eut rien fait dire à mon dernier passage à Paris. Je connoissois ses dispositions secrettes, mais je m'en inquietois peu, me contentant d'en avertir mes amis dans l'occasion. Je me souviens qu'un jour, questionné sur son compte par M. Hume, qui questionna de même ensuite ma gouvernante, je lui dis que M. D'Alembert étoit un homme adroit et rusé. Il me contredit avec une chaleur dont je m'étonnai, ne sachant pas alors qu'ils étoient si bien ensemble, et que c'étoit sa propre cause qu'il défendoit.

La lecture de cette Lettre m'allarma beaucoup, et sentant que j'avois été attiré en Angleterre en vertu d'un projet qui commençoit à s'executer mais dont j'ignorois le but, je sentois le péril sans savoir où il pouvoit être ni de quoi j'avois à me garantir; je me rappellai alors quatre mots effrayans de M. Hume, que je rapporterai ci-après. Que penser d'un écrit où l'on me faisoit un crime de mes miséres, qui tendoit à m'ôter la commisération de tout le monde dans mes malheurs, et qu'on donnoit sous le nom du Prince même qui m'avoit protégé, pour en rendre l'effet plus cruel encore? Que devois-je augurer de la suite d'un tel début? Le peuple anglois lit les papiers publics, et n'est pas déja trop favorable aux étrangers. Un vétement qui n'est le sien suffit pour le mettre de mauvaise humeur. Qu'en doit attendre un pauvre étranger dans ses promenades champêtres, le seul plaisir de la vie auquel il s'est borné, quand on aura persuadé à ces bonnes gens que cet homme aime qu'on le lapide? Ils seront fort tentés de lui en donner l'amusement. Mais ma douleur, ma douleur profonde et cruelle, la plus amére que j'aye jamais ressentie, ne venoit pas du péril auquel j'étois exposé. J'en avois trop bravé d'autres pour être fort ému de celui-là. La trahison d'un faux ami dont j'étois la proye étoit ce qui portoit dans mon coeur trop sensible l'accablement la tristesse et la mort. Dans l'impétuosité d'un prémier mouvement dont jamais je ne fus le maitre, et que mes adroits ennemis savent faire naitre pour s'en prévaloir, j'écris des lettres pleines de desordre où je ne déguise ni mon trouble ni mon indignation.

Monsieur, j'ai tant de choses à dire qu'en chemin faisant j'en oublie la moitié. Par exemple, une rélation en forme de lettre sur mon séjour à Montmorency fut portée par des Libraires à M. Hume qui me la montra. Je consentis qu'elle fut imprimée; il se chargea d'y veiller; elle n'a jamais paru. J'avois apporté un exemplaire des Lettres de M. du Peyrou contenant la rélation des affaires de Neufchâtel qui me regardent; je les remis aux mêmes Libraires à leur priére pour les faire traduire et réimprimer; M. Hume se chargea d'y veiller; elles n'ont jamais paru.[1] Dès que la fausse lettre du Roi de Prusse et sa traduction parurent, je compris pourquoi les autres écrits restoient supprimés, et je l'écrivis aux Libraires. J'écrivis d'autres lettres qui probablement ont couru dans Londres; enfin j'employai le crédit d'un homme de mérite et de qualité pour faire mettre dans les papiers une déclaration de l'imposture. Dans cette déclaration je laissois paroitre toute ma douleur et je n'en déguisois pas la cause.

Jusqu'ici M. Hume a semblé marcher dans les tenébres; vous l'allez voir desormais dans la lumiére, et marcher à découvert. Il n'y a qu'à toujours aller droit avec les gens rusés: tôt ou tard ils se décélent par leurs ruses mêmes.

Lorsque cette prétendue lettre du Roi de Prusse fut publiée à Londres, M. Hume, qui certainement savoit qu'elle étoit supposée, puisque je le lui avois dit, n'en dit rien, ne m'écrit rien, se tait, et ne songe pas même à faire en faveur de son ami absent aucune déclaration de la vérité. Il ne falloit pour aller au but que laisser dire et se tenir coi; c'est ce qu'il fit.

M. Hume ayant été mon conducteur en Angleterre y étoit en quelque façon mon protecteur mon patron. S'il étoit naturel qu'il prit ma deffense, il ne l'étoit pas moins qu'ayant une protestation publique à faire je m'addressase à lui pour cela. Ayant déja cessé de lui écrire, je n'avois garde de recommencer. Je m'addresse à un autre. Prémier soufflet sur la joue de mon patron. Il n'en sent rien.

[1] Les libraires viennent de me marquer que cette édition est faite et prette à paroitre. Cela peut être, mais c'est trop tard, et qui pis est, trop à propos.

En disant que la lettre étoit fabriquée à Paris, il m'importoit fort peu lequel on entendit de M. D'Alembert ou de son prête-nom M. Walpole; mais en ajoûtant que ce qui navroit et déchiroit mon coeur étoit que l'imposteur avoit des complices en Angleterre, ej m'expliquois avec la plus grande clarté pour leur ami qui étoit à Londres, et qui vouloit passer pour le mien. Il n'y avoit certainement que lui seul en Angleterre dont la haine put déchirer et navrer mon coeur. Second soufflet sur la joue de mon patron. Il n'en sent rien.

Au contraire il feint malignement que mon affliction venoit seulement de la publication de cette lettre, afin de me faire passer pour un homme vain qu'une Satyre affecte beaucoup. Vain ou non, j'étois mortellement affligé; il le savoit et ne m'écrivoit pas un mot. Ce tendre ami qui a tant à coeur que ma bourse soit pleine se soucie assez peu que mon coeur soit déchiré.

Un autre écrit paroit bientôt dans les mêmes feuilles de la même main que le prémier, plus cruel encore, s'il étoit possible, et où l'Auteur ne peut déguiser sa rage sur l'accueil que j'avois receu à Paris. Cet écrit ne m'affecte plus; il ne m'apprenoit rien de nouveau. Les libelles pouvoient aller leur train sans m'émouvoir, et le volage public lui-méme se lassoit d'être longtems occupé du même sujet. Ce n'est pas le compte des complotteurs qui ayant ma réputation d'honnête homme à detruire, veulent de maniére ou d'autre en venir à bout. Il fallut changer de batterie.

L'affaire de la pension n'étoit pas terminée. Il ne fut pas difficile à M. Hume d'obtenir de l'humanité du Ministre et de la générosité du Prince qu'elle le fut. Il fut chargé de me le marquer, il le fit. Ce moment fut, je l'avoue, un des plus critiques de ma vie. Combien il m'en couta pour faire mon devoir! Mes engagemens précédens, l'obligation de correspondre avec respect aux bontés du Roi, l'honneur d'être l'objet de ses attentions, de celles de son Ministre le desir de marquer combien j'y étois sensible, même l'avantage d'être un peu plus au large en approchant de la vieillesse accablé d'ennuis et de maux, enfin l'embarras de trouver une excuse honnête pour éluder un bienfait déja presque accepté; tout me rendoit difficile et cruelle la necessité d'y renoncer; car il le falloit assurément, ou me rendre le plus vil des hommes en devenant volontairement l'obligé de celui dont j'étois trahi.

Je fis mon devoir, non sans peine. J'écrivis directement à M. le Général Conway et avec autant de respect et d'honnêteté qu'il me fut possible, sans refus absolu, je me défendis pour le présent d'accepter. M. Hume avoit été le négociateur de l'affaire, le seul même qui m'en eut parlé. Non seulement je ne lui répondis point, quoique ce fut lui qui m'eut écrit, mais je ne dis pas un mot de lui dans ma lettre. Troisiéme soufflet sur la joue de mon patron, et pour celui-là s'il ne le sent pas, c'est assurément sa faute. Il n'en sent rien.

Ma lettre n'étoit pas claire et ne pouvoit l'être pour M. le General Conway qui ne savoit pas à quoi tenoit ce refus, mais elle l'étoit fort pour M. Hume qui le savoit très bien. Cependant il feint de prendre le change, tant sur le sujet de ma douleur que sur celui de mon refus, et dans un billet qu'il m'écrit il me fait entendre qu'on me ménagera la continuation des bontés du Roi si je me ravise sur la pension. En un mot, il prétend à toute force et quoiqu'il arrive demeurer mon patron malgré moi. Vous jugez bien, Monsieur, qu'il n'attendoit pas de réponse, et il n'en eut point.

Dans ce même tems à peu près, car je ne sais pas les dates, et cette exactitude ici n'est pas necessaire, parut une lettre de M. de Voltaire à moi addressée avec une traduction angloise qui rencherit encore sur l'original. Le noble objet de ce spirituel ouvrage est de m'attirer le mépris et la haine de ceux chez qui je me suis réfugié. Je ne doutai point que mon cher patron n'eut été un des instrumens de cette publication, surtout quand je vis qu'en tâchant d'aliener de moi ceux qui pouvoient en ce pays me rendre la vie agréable, on avoit omis de nommer celui qui m'y avoit conduit. On savoit sans doute que c'étoit un soin superflu et qu'à cet égard rien ne restoit à faire. Ce nom si maladroitement oublié dans cette lettre me rappella ce que dit Tacite du portrait de Brutus omis dans une pompe funébre, que chacun l'y distingoit, précisement parce qu'il n'y étoit pas.

On ne nommoit donc pas M. Hume; mais il vit avec les gens qu'on nommoit. Il a pour amis tous mes ennemis, on le sait. Ailleurs les Tronchin, les D'Alembert, les Voltaires; mais il y a bien pis à Londres; c'est que je n'y ai pour ennemis que ses amis. Eh pourquoi y en aurois-je d'autres? pourquoi même y ai-je ceux-là? Qu'ai-je fait à Lord Littleton que je ne connois même pas? Qu'ai je fait à M. Walpole que je ne connois pas davantage? Que savent-ils de moi, sinon que je suis malheureux et l'ami de leur ami Hume? Que leur a-t-il donc dit puisque ce n'est que par lui qu'ils me connoissent? Je crois bien qu'avec le rolle qu'il fait il ne se démasque pas devant tout le monde; ce ne seroit plus être masqué: Je crois bien qu'il ne parle pas de moi à M. le Général Conway ni à M. le Duc de Richemond comme il en parle dans ses entretiens secrets avec M. Walpole et dans sa correspondance secrette avec M. D'Alembert; mais qu'on découvre la trame qui s'ourdit à Londres depuis mon arrivée, et l'on verra si M. Hume n'en tient pas les principaux fils.

Enfin le moment venu qu'on croit propre à frapper le grand coup, on en prépare l'effet par un nouvel écrit satyrique qu'on fait mettre dans les papiers. S'il m'étoit resté jusqu'alors le moindre doute, comment auroit-il pu tenir devant cet écrit, puisqu'il contenoit des faits qui n'étoient connus que de M. Hume, chargés, il est vrai, pour les rendre odieux au public.

On dit dans cet écrit que j'ouvre ma porte aux Grands et que je la ferme aux petits. Qui est-ce qui sait à qui j'ai ouvert ou fermé ma porte que M. Hume avec qui j'ai demeuré et par qui sont venus à moi tous ceux que j'ai vus. Il faut en excepter un Grand que j'ai receu de bon coeur sans le connoitre, et que j'aurois receu de bien meilleur coeur encore si je l'avois connu. Ce fut M. Hume qui me dit son nom quand il fut parti. En l'apprenant j'eus un vrai chagrin que daignant monter au second étage, il ne fut pas entré au prémier.

Quant aux petits, je n'ai rien à dire. J'aurois desiré voir moins de monde; mais ne voulant déplaire à personne je me laissois diriger par M. Hume, et j'ai receu de mon mieux tous ceux qu'il m'a présentés sans distinction de petits ni de Grands.

On dit dans ce même écrit que je reçois mes parens froidement *pour ne rien dire de plus*. Cette généralité consiste à avoir une fois receu assez froidement le seul parent que j'aye hors de Genève, et cela en présence de M. Hume. C'est necessairement ou M. Hume ou ce parent qui a fourni cet article. Or mon Cousin, que j'ai toujours connu pour bon parent et pour honnête homme, n'est point capable de fournir à des satyres publiques contre moi. D'ailleurs borné par son état à la societé des gens de Commerce il ne vit pas avec les gens de lettres ni avec ceux qui fournissent des articles dans les papiers, encore moins avec ceux qui s'occupent à des satyres. Ainsi l'article ne vient pas de lui. Tout au plus puis-je penser que M. Hume aura tâché de le faire jaser, ce qui n'est pas absolument difficile, et qu'il aura tourné ce qu'il lui a dit de la maniére la plus favorable à ses vues. Il est bon d'ajoûter qu'après ma rupture avec M. Hume j'en avois écrit mon sentiment à ce Cousin-là.

Enfin on dit dans ce même ecrit que je suis sujet à changer d'amis. Il ne faut pas être bien fin pour comprendre à quoi cela prépare.

Distingons. J'ai depuis vingt cinq et trente ans des amis très solides. J'en ai de plus nouveaux mais non moins surs, que je garderai plus longtems si je vis. Je n'ai pas en général trouvé la même sureté chez ceux que j'ai faits parmi les gens de lettres. Aussi j'en ai changé quelquefois, et j'en changerai tant qu'ils me seront suspects; car je suis bien déterminé à ne garder jamais d'amis par bienseance: je n'en veux avoir que pour les aimer.

Si jamais j'eus une conviction intime et certaine, je l'ai que M. Hume a fourni les matériaux de cet écrit. Bien plus; non seulement j'ai cette certitude, mais il m'est clair qu'il a voulu que je l'eusse: car comment supposer un homme aussi fin assez maladroit pour se découvrir à ce point, voulant se cacher.

Quel étoit son but? Rien ne m'est plus clair encore. C'étoit de porter mon indignation à son dernier terme, pour amener avec plus d'éclat le coup qu'il me préparoit. Il sait que pour me faire faire bien des sotises il suffit de me mettre en colére. Nous sommes au moment critique qui montrera s'il a bien ou mal raisonné.

Il faut se posseder autant que fait M. Hume, il faut avoir son flegme et toute sa force d'esprit pour prendre le parti qu'il prit, après tout ce qui s'étoit passé. Dans l'embarras où j'étois écrivant à M. le General Conway je ne pus remplir ma lettre que de phrases obscures dont M. Hume fit, comme mon ami, l'interprétation qu'il lui plut. Supposant donc, quoiqu'il sut très bien le contraire, que c'étoit la clause du secret qui me faisoit de la peine, il obtient de M. le General qu'il voudroit bien s'employer pour la faire lever. Alors cet homme stoique et vraiment insensible m'écrit la lettre la plus amicale où il me marque qu'il s'est employé pour faire lever la clause; mais qu'avant toute chose il faut savoir si je veux accepter sans cette condition, pour ne pas exposer S. M. à un second refus de ma part.

C'étoit ici le moment décisif, la fin l'objet de tous ses travaux. Il lui falloit une réponse, il la vouloit. Pour que je ne pusse me dispenser de la faire il envoye à M. Davenport un duplicata de sa lettre, et non content de cette précaution il m'écrit dans un autre billet qu'il ne sauroit rester plus longtems à Londres pour mon service. La tête me tourna presque en lisant ce billet. De mes jours je n'ai rien trouve de plus inconcevable.

Il l'a donc enfin cette réponse tant desirée, et se presse déja d'en triompher. Déja écrivant à M. Davenport il me traite d'homme féroce et de monstre d'ingratitude. Mais il lui faut plus. Ses mesures ont bien prises, à ce qu'il pense; nulle preuve contre lui ne peut échaper. Il veut une explication; il l'aura et la voici.

Rien ne la conclud mieux que le dernier trait qui l'amene. Seul il prouve tout et sans réplique.

Je veux supposer par impossible qu'il n'est rien revenu à M. Hume de mes plaintes contre lui; il n'en sait rien, il les ignore aussi parfaitement que s'il n'eut été faufilé avec personne qui en fut instruit, aussi parfaitement que si durant ce tems il eut vécu à la Chine. Mais ma conduite immédiate entre lui et moi, les derniers mots si frappans que je lui dis à Londres, la lettre qui suivit pleine d'inquiétude et de crainte, mon silence obstiné plus energique que des paroles, ma plainte amére et publique au sujet de la lettre de D'Alembert, ma lettre au Ministre qui ne m'a point écrit, en réponse à celle qu'il m'écrit lui-même, et dans laquelle je ne dis pas un mot de lui, enfin mon refus, sans daigner m'addresser à lui, d'acquiescer à une affaire qu'il a traitée en ma faveur, moi le sachant, et sans opposition de ma part; tout cela parle seul du ton le plus fort, je ne dis pas à tout homme qui auroit quelque sentiment dans l'ame, mais à tout homme qui n'est pas hébêté.

Quoi! après que j'ai rompu tout commerce avec lui depuis près de trois mois, après que je n'ai répondu à pas une de ses lettres quelque important qu'en fut le sujet, environné des marques publiques et particuliéres de l'affliction que son infidélité me cause, cet homme éclairé, ce beau génie naturellement si clairvoyant et volontairement si stupide, ne voit rien, n'entend rien, ne sent rien, n'est ému de rien, et sans un seul mot de plainte, de justification, d'explication, il continue à se donner malgré moi pour moi les soins les plus grands les plus empressés, il m'écrit affectueusement qu'il ne peut rester à Londres plus longtems pour mon service, comme si nous étions d'accord qu'il qu'il y restera pour cela! Cet aveuglement cette impassibilité, cette obstination ne sont pas dans la nature; il faut expliquer cela par d'autres motifs. Mettons cette conduite dans un plus grand jour, car c'est un point decisif.

Dans cette affaire il faut necessairement que M. Hume soit le plus grand ou le dernier des hommes, il n'y a point de milieu. Reste à voir lequel c'est des deux.

Malgré tant de marques de dédain de ma part, M. Hume avoit-il l'étonnante générosité de vouloir me servir sincérement? Il savoit qu'il m'étoit impossible d'accepter ses bons offices tant que j'aurois de lui les sentimens que j'avois conçus. Il avoit éludé l'explication lui-même. Ainsi me servant sans se justifier il rendoit ses soins inutiles; il n'étoit donc pas généreux.

S'il supposoit qu'en cet état j'accepterois ses soins, il supposoit donc que j'étois un infame. C'étoit donc pour un homme qu'il jugeoit être un infame qu'il sollicitoit avec tant d'ardeur une pension du Roi. Peut-on rien penser de plus extravagant?

Mais que M. Hume suivant toujours son plan se soit dit à lui-même. Voici le moment de l'execution: car, pressant Rousseau d'accepter la pension, il faudra qu'il l'accepte ou qu'il la refuse. S'il l'accepte, avec les preuves que j'ai en main je le deshonore complettement. S'il la refuse après l'avoir acceptée, on a levé tout prétexte, il faudra qu'il dise pourquoi. C'est là que je l'attends; s'il m'accuse, il est perdu.

Si dis-je M. Hume a raisonné ainsi, il a fait une chose fort consequente à son plan, et par là-même ici fort naturelle, et il n'y a que cette unique façon d'expliquer sa conduite dans cette affaire, car elle est inexplicable dans toute autre supposition. Si ceci n'est pas démontré, jamais rien ne le sera.

L'état critique où il m'a reduit me rappelle bien fortement les quatre mots dont j'ai parlé cy-devant, et que je lui entendis dire et repéter dans un tems où je n'en pénétrois guéres la force. C'étoit la prémiére nuit qui suivit notre depart de Paris. Nous étions couchés dans la même chambre, et plusieurs fois dans la nuit je l'entendis s'écrier en françois avec une véhémence extrême. *Je tiens J. J. Rousseau.* J'ignore s'il veilloit ou s'il dormoit. L'expression est remarquable dans la bouche d'un homme qui sait trop bien le françois pour se tromper sur la force et le choix des termes. Cependant je pris et je ne pouvois manquer alors de prendre ces mots dans un sens favorable, quoique le ton l'indiquât encore moins que l'expression: c'est un ton dont il m'est impossible de donner l'idée, et qui correspond très bien aux regards dont j'ai parlé. Chaque fois qu'il dit ces mots je sentis un tressaillement d'effroi dont je n'étois pas le maitre; mais il ne me fallut qu'un moment pour me remettre et rire de ma terreur. Dès le lendemain tout fut si parfaitement oublié que je n'y ai pas même pensé durant tout mon séjour à Londres et au voisinage. Je ne m'en suis souvenu qu'ici où tant de choses m'ont rappellé ces paroles, et me les rappellent, pour ainsi dire, à chaque instant.

Ces mots, dont le ton retentit sur mon coeur comme s'ils venoient d'être prononcés, les longs et funestes regards tant de fois lancés sur moi, les petits coups sur le dos avec des mots de *mon cher Monsieur* en réponse au soupçon d'être un traitre; tout cela m'affecte à tel point après le reste, que ces souvenirs fussent-ils les seuls, fermeroient tout retour à la confiance, et il n'y a pas une nuit où ces mots, *je tiens J. J. Rousseau* ne sonnent encore à mon oreille, comme si je les entendois de nouveau.

Oui, Monsieur Hume, vous me tenez, je le sais, mais seulement par des choses qui me sont extérieures: vous me tenez par l'opinion, par les jugemens des hommes; vous me tenez par ma réputation, par ma sureté peut-être; tous les préjugés sont pour vous; il vous est aisé de me faire passer pour un monstre, comme vous avez commencé, et je vois déja l'exultation barbare de mes implacables ennemis. Le public, en général, ne me fera pas plus de grace. Sans autre éxamen, il est toujours pour les services rendus, parce que chacun est bien aise d'inviter à lui en rendre, en montrant qu'il sait les sentir. Je prévois aisément la suite de tout cela, surtout dans le pays où vous m'avez conduit, et où, sans amis, étranger à tout le monde, je suis presque à votre merci. Les gens sensés comprendront, cependant, que, loin que j'aye pu chercher cette affaire, elle étoit ce qui pouvoit m'arriver de plus terrible dans la position où je suis: ils sentiront qu'il n'y a que ma haine invincible pour toute fausseté, et l'impossibilité de marquer de l'estime à celui pour qui je l'ai perdue, qui aient pu m'empêcher de dissimuler quand tant d'intérets m'en faisoient une loi: mais les gens sensés sont en petit nombre et ce ne sont pas eux qui font du bruit.

Oui, Monsieur Hume, vous me tenez par tous les liens de cette vie; mais vous ne me tenez ni par ma vertu, ni par mon courage, indépendant de vous et des hommes, et qui me restera tout entier malgré vous. Ne pensez pas m'effrayer par la crainte du sort qui m'attend. Je connois les jugemens des hommes, je suis accoutumé à leur injustice, et j'ai appris à les peu redouter. Si votre parti est pris, comme j'ai tout lieu de le croire, soyez sur que le mien ne l'est pas moins. Mon corps est affoibli, mais jamais mon ame ne fut plus ferme. Les hommes feront et diront ce qu'ils voudront, peu m'importe; ce qui m'importe est d'achever comme j'ai commencé, d'être droit et vrai jusqu'à la fin quoi qu'il arrive, et de n'avoir pas plus à me reprocher une lâcheté dans mes miséres qu'une insolence dans ma prospérité. Quelque opprobre qui m'attende et quelque malheur qui me menace, je suis prêt. Quoiqu'à plaindre je le serai moins que vous, et je vous laisse pour toute vengeance le tourment de respecter malgré vous l'infortuné que vous accablez.

En achevant cette lettre je suis surpris de la force que j'ai eue de l'écrire. Si l'on mouroit de douleur j'en serois mort à chaque ligne. Tout est également incompréhensible dans ce qui se passe. Une conduite pareille à la vôtre n'est pas dans la nature, elle est contradictoire, et cependant elle m'est démontrée. Abyme des deux côtés! je péris dans l'un ou dans l'autre. Je suis le plus malheureux des humains si vous étes coupable, j'en suis le plus vil si vous étes innocent. Vous me faites desirer d'être cet objet méprisable. Oui, l'état où je me verrois prosterné foulé sous vos pieds, criant miséricorde et faisant tout pour l'obtenir, publiant à haute voix mon indignité, et rendant à vos vertus le plus éclatant hommage, seroit pour mon coeur un état d'épanouissement et de joye, après l'état d'étouffement et de mort où vous l'avez mis. Il ne me reste qu'un mot à vous dire. Si vous étes coupable ne m'écrivez plus; cela seroit inutile, et surement vous ne me tromperez pas. Si vous étes innocent, daignez vous justifier. Je connois mon devoir, je l'aime, et l'aimerai toujours, quelque rude qu'il puisse être. Il n'y a point d'abjection dont un coeur qui n'est pas né pour elle ne puisse revenir. Encore un coup, si vous étes innocent daignez vous justifier: si vous ne l'étes pas, adieu pour jamais.

J. J. Rousseau.

APPENDIX H

MISCELLANEOUS LETTERS OF JEAN-JACQUES ROUSSEAU

* I. *To* General Conway (see Letter 322 above)

A Wootton, ce 12 mai 1766.

Monsieur,

Vivement touché des grâces dont il plaît à Sa Majesté de m'honorer, et de vos bontés qui me les ont attirées, j'y trouve dès à présent ce bien précieux à mon coeur d'intéresser à mon sort le meilleur des Rois, et l'homme le plus digne d'être aimé de lui. Voilà, Monsieur, un avantage, dont je suis jaloux, et que je ne mériterai jamais de perdre. Mais il faut vous parler avec la franchise que vous aimez. Après tant de malheurs, je me croyois préparé à tous les évènemens possibles. Il m'en arrive pourtant que je n'avois pas prévus, et qu'il n'est pas même permis à un honnête homme de prévoir. Ils m'en affectent d'autant plus cruellement; et le trouble où ils me jettent, m'ôte la liberté d'esprit nécessaire pour me bien conduire. Tout ce que me dit la raison dans un état aussi triste, est de suspendre mes résolutions sur toute affaire importante, telle qu'est pour moi celle dont il s'agit. Loin de me refuser aux bienfaits du Roi, par l'orgueil que l'on m'impute, je le mettrois à m'en glorifier; et tout ce que j'y vois de pénible est de ne pouvoir m'en honorer aux yeux du public, comme aux miens. Mais lorsque je les recevrai, je veux pouvoir me livrer tout entier aux sentimens qu'ils m'inspirent, et n'avoir le coeur plein que des bontés de Sa Majesté, et des vôtres. Je ne crains pas que cette façon de penser les puisse altéré. Daignez donc, Monsieur, me les conserver pour des tems plus heureux. Vous connoitrez alors que je n'ai différé de m'en prévaloir, que pour tâcher de m'en rendre plus digne.

Agréez, Monsieur . . .

†II. *To the* Author of the St. James's Chronicle (see Letter 322 above)

Wootton, le 7 avril 1766.

Vous avez manqué, Monsieur, au respect que tout particulier doit aux têtes couronnées, en attribuant publiquement au Roy de Prusse une lettre pleine d'extravagance et de méchanceté, dont par cela seul vous deviez savoir qu'il ne pouvoit être l'auteur. Vous avez même osé transcrire sa signature comme si vous l'aviez vue écrite de sa main. Je vous apprends, Monsieur, que cette lettre a été fabriquée

* *Priv. Corr.*, 165 f.; *Œuvres de Rousseau*, 1826, xxiii. 334 f.

† *St. James's Chronicle*, April 8–10, 1766; *Œuvres de Rousseau*, 1826, xxiii. 297.

à Paris, et, ce qui navre et déchire mon coeur, que l'imposteur a des complices en Angleterre.

Vous devez au Roy de Prusse, à la vérité, à moi, d'imprimer la lettre que je vous écris et que je signe, en réparation d'une faute que vous vous reprocheriez sans doute si vous saviez de quelles noirceurs vous vous rendez l'instrument. Je vous fais, Monsieur, mes sincéres salutations.

* III. *To* RICHARD DAVENPORT (see Letter 331 above)

ce 28 Juin au soir.

L'impossibilité où je suis, Monsieur, de vous faire parvenir autrement la lettre ci-jointe, m'oblige à vous envoyer un exprès dont le voyage ne sera pas perdu pour moi, s'il me rapporte de bonnes nouvelles de vôtre santé.

La Lettre ci-jointe de M. Hume a été ouverte en ma presence par M. Walton, parce que nous étions persuadés l'un et l'autre que le contenu étoit pour moi. Mais à son ouverture j'ai vu la copie d'une lettre que j'ai écrite la semaine dernière en réponse à M. Hume. J'ai conclu de là que son intention étoit que vous vissiez le pacquet avant moi, et pour ce que cette intention ne fut trompée j'ai recacheté sur le champ le pacquet en présence de Mr Walton sans en lire un seul mot, et je vous l'envoye.

Il seroit long de vous faire par lettres le recit de ce qui s'est passé. Nous en causerons quand j'aurai l'honneur de vous voir. En attendant, lisez pesez et voyez ce qu'il vous convient de penser sur cette affaire. J'attends de vos nouvelles avec la plus grande impatience, et j'aspire au moment où sans vous incommoder vous pourrez m'en donner de bouche.

Je joins ici une autre lettre que j'avois fermée ce matin croyant la faire partir par la poste, mais on m'a dit que cela ne se pouvoit pas. Je vous fais, Monsieur, mes plus tendres salutations.

J. J. ROUSSEAU.

L'exprès est payé.

* B.M. Addit. MSS. 32491; Courtois, 114 f.

APPENDIX J

HUME AS BRITISH CHARGÉ D'AFFAIRES IN PARIS

Among *State Papers 78* (*France*), in the Public Record Office, there are sixteen dispatches to H.M. Secretary of State (General Conway), signed by Hume as British *Chargé d'Affaires* in France. The first of these is dated from Compiègne on 28 July 1765, the last from Paris on 13 November 1765. The subjects mainly dealt with are the Canada Bills, the Demolition of the Fortifications at Dunkirk, and a squabble at Dunkirk in which certain British subjects thought themselves ill-used by the French authorities. But the first dispatch, which is somewhat shorter than the majority, deals with another matter altogether: I print it in full, as a specimen.

A.

To [H.M. Secretary of State]

Compiegne 28th of July 1765

Sir

In obedience to your Excellency's Commands of the 14th Instant, which I receivd not till the 25th, I went to the Duke of Praslin, and declar'd to him, conformable to your Excellency's Instructions, that His Majesty, tho' he had chang'd his Administration at home, persever'd still in the same Disposition with regard to the several Powers in alliance with him abroad, and that his Intention and Inclination were to maintain and preserve inviolable the Peace lately concluded, and to cultivate and improve the Harmony thereby happily establish'd. The Duke of Praslin made me the same Declaration on the Part of his most Christian Majesty.

Yesterday, I receiv'd a Visit from the Count de Bernis, Nephew to the Cardinal, who apply'd to me in his own Name and in that of his Uncle. The Object of their Application was this: Lately, the King of France had sent against the Sallee Rovers a small Squadron, consisting of a few Frigates, which were so happy as to execute the Object of their Expedition. By means of Boats, which they sent up the River, they burnt, at Harache, some Privateers of that Nation; but in this Action, it unfortunately happen'd, that the Chevalier de Narbonne, a young Man of Quality, Nephew to the Cardinal and Brother in Law to the Count, was wounded and taken Prisoner by the Moors. His Relations in France are much at a Loss how to convey to him any Assistance and to make a Bargain for his Ransom; and they think, that the readiest Means is to have Recourse to the Friendship and Generosity of the English Nation. They are inform'd, that His Majesty has a Consul at Sallee (a Point that I neither coud contradict nor confirm) and they are willing to hope, that your Excellency, if acquainted with the Case, wou'd convey Orders to him, to give all manner of Protection and perform every kind of good Office to the young Gentleman, who must at present stand so much in need of Assistance. They also wish, that he wou'd conclude some Bargain with the Moors, for the Ransom of the Chevalier; and as soon as they are inform'd of the Terms, they will take care to remit the Money to the Consul, in any Method which he will direct, together with such Money as he might otherwise have expended in assisting the Prisoner. They think, that, in this Transaction, it were better, the Moors did not know any thing farther of the Quality of the Person, except that he was Ensign of the Terpsichore; for such is the Name of the Frigate to which he belongs. If His Majesty has no Consul at Sallee, they flatter themselves, that any other English Consul on that Coast or the Governor of Gibraltar, may, from your Excellency's Instructions, be willing to perform this good Office. I have us'd the Freedom of giving you a Detail of this Affair; being sensible, that your Excellency wou'd gladly lay hold of an Occasion, both of performing an Act of Humanity and of obliging so many Persons of Distinction in this Country.

I take this Opportunity, S^{ir}, of congratulating you on the late Mark which you have receiv'd of His Majesty's Favour, and of recommending myself to your Excellency's Protection. I have the Honour to be, with the greatest Esteem and Regard S^{ir}

Your Excellency's Most obedient & Most humble Servant

DAVID HUME.

Two other specimens of Hume's official correspondence are given: both of these are unpublished, and were recently in the possession of Messrs. Maggs Bros., of London.

The specimen marked B is a draft memorandum in Hume's handwriting; that marked C is a draft of his letter to the Duc de Praslin to accompany this memorandum. Both are altered and corrected as shown.

B.

Memoire

Mr H. has receivd Orders from his Court to lay before the Court of France the Proposals of the English Merchants ~~concern'd~~ concern'd in the Paper Money of Canada &c.

These Proposals are made by the English Merchants, in order to conform themselves, as much as possible to the Arret, issu'd by the Court of France. They still insist, however, that as that Arret was fram'd without consulting the Court of England, it is liable to great Objections, and exposes them ~~and their~~ to great Injustice. They insist that all the Paper Money of Canada ought to have been pay'd in full, ~~both~~ because the Faith of the French Government is doubly plighted to that purpose both by their original Engagements in Canada, and by the strong Declaration annexd to the late Treaty.

They insist, that, even if a Reduction was to have place, the ~~Liquidation of 50~~ payment of 50 per cent for the Bills of Exchange preceding ~~17~~ Oct[r] 1759 was too low, as well as that of 25 per cent for the Cards & Billets of Ordonnance; because there was so considerable a Difference made between Paper and Money in Canada.
during the years 1759 & 1760

Allowing, that such a Difference had been made in Canada; yet as
Court
the Arret of the French was not issud till July 1764, the Proprietors of the Paper Money had been great Losers, by so late a Payment.

This Hardship is greatly aggravated by the Terms of Payment: The very 25 per cent granted them cannot be disposd of but at 35 or 36 per cent Discount, ~~which is a palpable~~ a Circumstance, which the Court of France itself, reasoning upon its own Principles, must allow to be a great Hardship & Injustice.

besides ~~over and above~~ the Payments requird as above
For all these Reasons, the English Merchants insist that ‸ the Sum of 120.000 Pounds Sterling shall be pay'd them in four quarterly Payments as a Reparation of their Losses. | This Sum is proposed to be distributed among the Proprietors of the Cards & Billets d Ordonnance. The Court of England, sensible of the Justice of this Demand, support it with | the utmost Force, and demand, as soon as possible, a precise ~~and categorical~~ Answer from the Court of France. ~~The former~~ If the Demand is comply'd with, as [*erasure illegible*] the former
from the good Intentions of H.M. Christ Majesty
Court has reason to expect, she also offers to acquit the latter of all Claims, which the Canadians may have, for the unequal Taxations
of Provisions made by last
~~of~~ ‸ the French Intendant and which the ‸ Arret ~~of the~~ promis'd to
and many others of a like Nature
redress. These Claims ‸ are very considerable; and this Consideration is an additional Reason for yielding to the present Demand.

Paris 25 of Septr 1765

HUME

C.

Monsieur Le Duc

J ai l'honneur d'envoier a vot E le memoire inclus sur le papier
de Canada papiers
~~inclus~~ sur les ~~affaires~~ de Canada. Je prens la liberté de l'envoier en Anglois; parceque je sçais vous avez de si bons traducteurs qu'il vous est egal en quelle langue on vous ecrit.

V.E.
Je suis obligé ~~de vous~~ avertir que la cour d Angleterres 'attende d avoir une reponse au memoire que j ai eu l'honneur de vous
il y a quelque tems
presenter ‸ sur la peche de la terre neuve.

APPENDIX K

LETTERS TO HUME ABOUT HIS QUARREL WITH ROUSSEAU

* I. *From* Richard Davenport

. . . The receipt of Your two last gave me much uneasiness; which was augmented by some letters rec[d] yesterday from Rousseau along with Yours directed to me at Wootton. Surely there must have been some excessive great mistakes, it appears to me an heap of confusion of which I can make neither head nor tail; his letter to you is perfectly astonishing, never any thing, was, so furious, so——I protest I dont know what to call it. . . . Good God he must be most excessively out of the way, about this pension in short I have not patience to add one word more, till I hear what he can possibly have to say; & then Ill immediately acquaint you. . . .

Davenport Monday
June 30, 1766.

† II. *From* Richard Davenport

I went over to Wootton on Tuesday, had a long Conference with Mr Rousseau on the Subject of your last letters, gave into his hands yours address'd to him (which he had not read before) shew'd him those I rec[d] from you, & in the most earnest manner insisted upon his giving you an open answer, to all your questions, which I told him you had certainly a right to ask, & he could not have any pretence whatever to refuse. His spirits seem'd vastly flutterd, however he told me a long History of the whole affair, I said, that as my knowledge of the French Language was very imperfect, I might easily misrepresent things, so begg'd him to write down the whole matter.

Before he began his discourse, I could not help speaking a deal to him on the Subject of the Pension, & Express'd my astonishment, at his even having had the least thought of refusing the favours of the Greatest King in the World, to my infinite Surprize he directly return'd this answer, that he never had refus'd, nor any thing like it, spoke with the greatest respect & veneration of his Majesty, & with all sort of Acknowledgements of Gratitude to Generall Conway &c. You may well imagine my Surprize encreas'd—he then began his Story—but that I intirely leave to his pen, as he has faithfully promis'd to perform. I am really sorry for him, he's uneasy, frets perpetually, & looks terribly—tis almost impossible to conceive the

* MS., R.S.E.; Burton, ii. 335 f.
† MS., R.S.E.; Burton, ii. 336 f.

odness of his extreme Sensibility, so that I conclude when he's Guilty of an error, his nerves are more in fault, than his heart—things vex him, to the utmost extent of vexation which would not even move such a dull Soul as mine is. In short I perceive his disorder is Jealousy, he thinks you are fond of some Savant Hommes, who he unfortunately thinks his Enemys.

It will give me the Greatest Satisfaction to hear, that you have received a Satisfactory answer, & that every thing is set right again.

Davenport. 6th of July 1766.

* III. *From* MLLE DE LESPINASSE *and* D'ALEMBERT

ce 6 juillet [1766]

[Mlle de Lespinasse begins:]

He mon dieu Monsieur qu'est il donc arrivé entre vous et Rousseau; quelle noirceur vous a t il donc faite? Suivant la lettre que vous avés ecrite au baron il n'y a rien qu'on ne doive craindre; vos amis sont encore plus afligés qu'etonés; il est inconcevable qu'un homme qui vous a tant d'obligation ait pu se resoudre a vous manquer. La douceur de vos moeurs et lhoneteté de votre caractere forment un grand prejugé contre lui avant meme qu'on sache en detail de quoi il est question. Si je ne craignois pas de vous etre importune je vous suplierois de vouloir bien me dire le precis des noirceurs que vous avés eprouvées; ce n'est point du tout par curiosité que je vous le demande, car je vous crois sur votre parole, mais permetés moi de vous le dire cest par interet pour vous et pour etre a porté de vous deffendre contre les fanatiques de Rousseau dont plusieurs meritent de l'estime. Je suis veritablement afligée de voir que tant de procedés vertueux vous aient reussi si mal. Je suis cependant bien sure qu'ils ne vous degouteront pas de faire le bien. Mr dalembert ne s'en raporte pas a moi pour vous dire tout l'interet qu'il prend a votre situation. Je lui cede la plume.

[d'Alembert continues:]

Oui, mon cher ami, j'ai grande envie de savoir, ainsi que Mlle de lespinasse, le sujet qui vous afflige et qui vous tourmente. Je vois d'ici Voltaire triompher, et dire; *de quoi diable aussi se meloit il?* Pour moi je me contente de vous plaindre, et de desirer passionément d'etre mieux instruit, pour pouvoir persuader à tout le monde ce dont je suis déja persuadé d'avance, que Rousseau a grand tort avec vous. Cependant je vous conseille d'y penser à deux fois avant que de mettre vos griefs sous les yeux du public, parceque ces sortes de querelles ne font souvent qu'échauffer davantage les fanatiques obstinés, et parceque les indifferens en prennent occasion de dire du mal des gens de lettres. Mais je m'apperçois que c'est une mauvaise tête qui donne des conseils à une bonne, mon amitié excusera ma

* MS., R.S.E.; *Eminent Persons*, 184 f.

sottise; dites nous donc si c'en est une de vous attendre dans ce pays-ci; c'est un sentiment bien naturel que de vous desirer . . .

* IV. *From* ADAM SMITH

My dear friend

I am thoroughly convinced that Rousseau is as great a Rascal as you, & as every man here believes him to be; yet let me beg of you not to think of publishing any thing to the world upon the very great impertinence which he has been guilty of to you. By refusing the Pension which you had the goodness to sollicit for him with his own consent, he may have thrown, by the baseness of his Proceeding, some little ridicule upon you in the eyes of the Court & the ministry. Stand this ridicule, expose his brutal letter, but without giving it out of your own hand so that it may never be printed, & if you can, laugh at yourself, & I shall pawn my life that before three weeks are at an end, this little affair, which at present gives you so much uneasiness, shall be understood to do you as much honor as any thing that has ever happened to you. By endeavouring to unmask before the Public this hypocritical Pedant, you run the risk, of disturbing the tranquillity of your whole life. By letting him alone he cannot give you a fortnights uneasiness. To write against him, is, you may depend upon it, the very thing he wishes you to do. He is in danger of falling into obscurity in England & he hopes to make himself considerable by provoking an illustrious adversary. He will have a great party. The church, the Whigs, the Jacobites, the whole wise English nation, who will love to mortify a Scotchman, & to applaud a man who has refused a Pension from the King. It is not unlikely too that they may pay him very well for having refused it, & that even he may have had in view this compensation. Your whole friends here wish you not to write, the Baron, D'Alembert, Madame Riccaboni, Mademoiselle Riancourt, Mr Turgot &c, &c. Mr Turgot, a friend every way worthy of you, desired me to recommend this advice to you in a Particular manner, as his most earnest entreaty & opinion. He & I are both afraid that you are surrounded with evil counsellours, & that the Advice of your English literati, who are themselves accustomed to publish all their little gossiping stories in Newspapers, may have too much influence upon you. Remember me to Mr Walpole & believe me to be with the most sincere affection ever yours

ADAM SMITH.

Paris 6 July 1766

† V. *From* BARON D'HOLBACH

à Paris le 7 Juillet [1766]

J'ai reçu avec peine vos deux Lettres du 27 de Juin et du premier de ce mois. Je conçois facilement que votre ame tranquile et

* MS., R.S.E.; Burton, ii. 350 f. † MS., R.S.E.; *Eminent Persons*, 256 ff.

remplie de droiture a dû etre vivement troublée par l'assaut imprévu qu'elle vient de recevoir. Un homme comme vous n'est point accoutumé à des tracasseries, elles sont indignes d'un philosophe et ne conviennent qu'à ces Esprits inquiets et rétrécis qui ont besoin de petits mouvements pour annoncer leur existence. Il n'en est pas de même du respectable David Hume; il est comptable de son tems au Genre humain, l'Europe attend de lui la continuation d'une histoire qu'elle admire et non des pamphlets et des brochures destinées à châtier des Ingrats que l'on ne corrige jamais. Un grand homme auroit il jamais fini, s'il vouloit relever toutes les injustices qu'on lui fait? Maintenant que les premiers mouvements de votre indignation sont peut être calmés vous penséz, sans doute, comme moi et comme tous ceux de vos amis à qui j'ai fait part de votre Situation; nous Jugeons qu'une guerre littéraire dont vous ne prévoyez point la fin ni les désagréments ne convient aucunement à un Sage fait pour éclairer le monde et non pour l'amuser par de futiles querelles. Il est beau de faire des ingrats et de mépriser l'ingratitude; vous ne devéz point rougir d'avoir été la dupe de votre bon coeur; le public Juge communément trés mal des querelles dont on le rend l'arbitre; laisséz les Ecrits polémiques à ceux qui ne scavent point employer mieux leur tems. Vous voyéz donc, mon trés honoré philosophe, que les avis de vos amis Parisiens sont pour que vous conserviéz le repos et le tems, deux biens trés prétieux pour des hommes tels que vous; c'est un conseil que quelques uns d'entre eux ont suivi pour eux mêmes; attaqués, noircis dénoncés au public par celui dont vous vous plaignéz aujourdhui, ils n'ont point répondu, sans perdre pour celà rien de l'Estime des personnes éclairées, et non prévenues, les seuls Juges dont un galant homme desire les Suffrages. Vous avéz travaillé à procurer une pension à M Rousseau, il y consentoit, dites vous; Eh bien, vous avéz agi comme un trés bon ami; M Rousseau a changé d'avis et ne veut plus de cette pension; il faut y consentir; il vous insulte et vous outrage, il est grand de se mettre audessus de ces choses. S'il est quelqu'un dans le monde auprès de qui vous ayéz à vous Justifier, ce sont les personnes que vous avéz Employées pour obtenir cette pension; quand elles seront éclaircies sur votre conduite, le public doit être parfaitement content. Tel est l'avis unanime de tous vos amis en ce paÿs, tel sera sûrement le votre quand la sérénité sera rentrée dans votre ame. Hélas quand vous flatteriéz vous de l'y voir rétablie, si vous commenciéz une fois à guerroyer; une brochure en ameneroit une autre, et vous n'auriéz jamais fini. Au bout de deux ans, peut être, la paix ne seroit pas faite, et à beaucoup de chagrins vous Joindriéz celui d'avoir perdu votre tems.

Un ami de Mr. Rougement à sçû de lui qu'un nommé La Roche, valet de chambre de Mr le maréchal de Luxembourg, lui avoit remis à 3 ou 4 remises à peu près la somme dont on vous a parlé, et nommément 10 000 ll. en une fois; cette somme a été remise à M Rousseau dans le tems qu'il etoit à Môtiers travers. Voilà tout ce que mes amis ont pu découvrir sur cette affaire qui n'est point faite pour vous intéresser, si vous suivéz le conseil que Je prens la liberté de vous donner, et que vous auriéz pris de vous même si votre ame eut été dans une position plus tranquile.

Adieu, Mon très cher Monsieur; souvenéz vous que vous êtes David Hume; que votre nom est connu et respecté, et qu'il ne dépend de personne de nuire à votre réputation. Si malgré notre avis vous publiéz quelque chose, adresséz le a *Mr Suard au bureau de la Gazette de france*, et prescrivéz nous l'usage que nous devons en faire. . . .

* VI. *From* Mme de Meinières (formerly Mme Belot)

. . . Etoit-ce votre intention Monsieur que le Baron publiât la lettre qu'il a reçue de vous à ce Sujet? Est ce votre intention de faire imprimer vos griefs? Toute la france les attend avec avidité. Il faut qu'ils soyent aussi forts que vos expressions. Personne ne doute que Rousseau ne soit un extravaguant; mais on ignoroit qu'il fut *the Blackest and most atrocious Villain that Ever disgraced human nature*, et qu'on pût lui prodiguer les épithetes *of the lying, the ferocity, of the Rascal.* Vous êtes son bienfaiteur; ce titre lui impose des devoirs vis à vis de vous, mais vous prescrit des menagemens vis à vis de lui. On sait qu'il est ingrat, attrabilaire, violent, captieux, vain; on sait aussi que vous êtes prudent, circonspect, modéré; il a sans doute suivi le fil de son caractére, et sans doute que vous ne perdés pas le fil du votre. Ainsi le public présume, que vous auriés méprisé l'ingratitude, et ri de l'arrogance, de l'orgueil, de la folie du personnage, sans vous élever hautement contre lui, s'il n'avoit pas attaqué ou votre honneur ou votre sureté. On veut que l'indignation d'un homme tel que vous, n'éclate qu'a propos d'un crime réel, et qu'elle dédaigne les fautes, les singularités, les ridicules. Chacun forme des conjectures et les débite. On ne parle d'autre chose dans Paris. Les dévots de Jean Jaques prétendent que ses torts se réduisent à n'avoir pas voulu accepter une pension de votre cour, que votre bienfaisance lui procuroit, et à l'avoir refusée avec sa hauteur ordinaire, même en vous reprochant ce bienfait comme une injure. Vos amis pensent et disent que ce refus a eu des suites répréhensibles et graves; que Rousseau l'a accompagné de quelques noirceurs. Donnés moi des écclaircissemens et des armes [?], en attendant que votre manifeste paroisse. Je suis fachée de ce trouble dans la république des lettres. Votre personnel écrasera le personnel de Jean Jacques; je suis convaincue qu'il vous a manqué de la maniere la plus outrageante. Mais il est malheureux que les gens les plus éclairés de l'europe, donnent prises contr'eux aux sots, et s'entredechirent avec scandale.

* MS., R.S.E., unpublished.

Vous étiés au milieu d'eux tous, comme un colosse inébranlable, et vous voila en mouvement. Je me console cependant de ce que l'esprit philosophique peut perdre à ces fermentations, parceque j'y gagne le plaisir de causer avec vous. Si vous me faites l'honneur de me répondre avec confiance sur l'évenement du jour, je ne ferai de votre réponse que l'usage qu'il vous plaira. Peut être que si j'eusse été votre premiere confidente je vous aurois invité à faire pendre Rousseau, ou à n'en rien dire du tout. . . .

ce 7 juillet 1766.

* VII. *From* Hugh Blair

Your Letter Astonished me beyond measure. How or about what should Rousseau have had the Occasion to show Malignity towards you, his Guide and his Benefactor? . . . He must be a very sad fellow; and it gives me great pain that he should turn out so. But for Gods sake do not be in a haste in publishing any thing about him. Nothing but Necessity should oblige you to this. You know the ill natured pleasure the world enjoys in a Paper war between two persons of such fame and eminence as you & him. Both parties often suffer in such personal Contests; & how clear soever the right may be on your Side, yet Envy to you will raise Partizans for him. You will see many reasons for deliberating very cooly concerning this Step; and perhaps too you may in part have been imposed upon by reports which may have aggravated some thing in his Conduct. . . .

Edinb. 10 July 1766

* VIII. *From* Richard Davenport

I have not since I wrote, seen Rousseau, I fear you form a true Judgment of him, to mention Dreams, Suspicions &c Good God, in one half quarter of a small sheet I could have easily summ'd up all, but fairly own I was asham'd to put em upon paper, if I have the pleasure of Seeing you perhaps you'll hear Some Anecdotes that will (I cant say after what he has wrote) Surprize you, for in troth they are quite of the same stamp. They are some small Altercations which happened between him Mad^lle^ & our Women.

Davenport July 19th 1766.

† IX. *From* d'Alembert

à Paris ce 21 juillet [1766]

Vous n'avez point perdu de temps, mon cher et digne ami, pour repondre à la lettre que j'ai eu l'honneur de vous écrire il y a 8 jours, et je n'en perds point non plus, comme vous voyez, pour repondre

* MS., R.S.E., unpublished.

† MS., R.S.E.; *Eminent Persons*, 186 ff.

à celle que vous venez de m'adresser. Je commence par vous faire tous mes remercimens du détail ou vous voulez bien entrer avec moi sur l'affaire qui vous interesse et qui interesse tous vos amis, et sur la confiance que vous voulez bien me marquer. Je vais tacher de m'en rendre digne en vous faisant part de mes réflexions. D'abord je vous observerai que vous n'avez pas bien compris le sens du conseil que je vous donnois dans ma première lettre; je ne vous conseillois pas, comme vous paroissez l'avoir cru, *d'attendre que Rousseau vous attaquât*, et de rester en attendant *les bras croisés*; je vous conseillois, si je m'en souviens bien, d'y *regarder a deux fois* avant que de rendre cette histoire publique, c'est à dire, de ne rien faire précipitamment et qu'après avoir bien réflechi, parce qu'il est toujours désagreable, et souvent nuisible, d'avoir un procès par écrit devant cette bête appellée le *public*, qui ne demande pas mieux que d'avoir du mal à dire de ceux dont le merite lui fait ombrage. Je crois par votre lettre que vous avez pensé à peu près comme moi, et que vous n'avez point voulu prendre de parti extrême qu'avec réflexion. Si votre querelle avec Rousseau n'avoit pas fait tant de bruit, si vous ne vous etiez pas plaint de lui de la manière la plus vive, et ce me semble, la plus juste, je persisterois encore dans ma premiere opinion, qui seroit de ne rien imprimer. Mais le public est aujourd'hui trop occupé de votre querelle, et les choses sont trop avancées, pour que vous ne rendiez pas les faits absolument notoires. Le hasard a voulu que la plus part de vos amis, & surtout ceux à qui vous me conseillez de lire votre lettre, se soient trouvés rassemblés chez Mlle de lespinasse presque au moment que je l'ai recue; M^{r}. Turgot, M^{r}. l'abbé Morellet, M^{r}. Roux, M^{r}. Saurin, M^{r}. Marmontel, M^{r}. duclos. Tous unanimement, ainsi que Mlle de lespinasse et moi sommes d'avis que vous devez donner cette histoire au public avec toutes les circonstances. Voici ce que nous vous conseillons, je dis nous, car je parle ici au nom de tous. Vous commencerez d'abord par dire que vous savez que Rousseau travaille à ses memoires, qu'il y fera sans doute mention de sa querelle avec vous, qui a fait trop de bruit pour qu'il ne cherche pas à la tourner à son avantage, que ses memoires pourront paroitre ou après votre mort ou après la sienne; que dans le 1er cas, comme vous l'observez vous meme, personne ne pourra vous justifier; que dans le second votre défense seroit sans force; que vous avez donc cru devoir donner vous meme toute cette histoire au public, afin que M^{r}. Rousseau reponde, s'il le peut. Ensuite vous entrerez dans le detail, et dans le plus grand détail, mais surtout, et c'est une chose absolument essentielle & que nous vous recommandons tous, vous vous bornerez aux faits, exposés simplement et nettement, sans aigreur, sans la moindre injure, sans même des réflexions sur le caractere de Rousseau et sur ses écrits; vous rapporterez vos lettres et les siennes; celle qu'il vous a ecrite le 23 juin suffiroit seule pour le faire condamner; vous ne direz point du moins trop souvent que vous etes son bienfaiteur, tout le monde le sait assez; enfin mon cher ami, nous vous recommandons et nous vous conjurons de mettre dans cette brochure la plus grande moderation, mais en meme temps la plus grande clarté et le plus grand détail. Si vous pouvez avoir la lettre qu'il a ecrite à Milord Maréchal, il ne faudra pas manquer de l'inserer dans cette histoire; il ne faudra pas manquer non plus d'expliquer en détail et bien nettement ce que vous me mandez, que vous avez decouvert par differentes circonstances, que depuis deux mois Rousseau avoit formé ce dessein contre vous. Il faudra vous abstenir de parler des autres querelles qu'il a eues avec d'autres personnes, parceque le sujet de ces querelles n'est pas connu du public, que Rousseau chercheroit à le rendre obscur, et à se donner par là de l'avantage dans la reponse, s'il en fait une. Nous pensons aussi que comme le public est actuellement fort occupé de cette affaire, vous ne devez point perdre de temps pour imprimer, et que le plutôt sera le mieux; c'est même en partie pour cette raison que je me hâte de vous repondre au nom de nous tous. Je ne dois pas vous laisser ignorer une chose, c'est qu'on dit que Rousseau vous soupconne d'avoir eu part, ou du moins d'avoir eu connoissance de la lettre sous le nom du Roi de Prusse que Mr. Valpole a écrite contre lui, en quoi je ne puis approuver Mr. Valpole, parcequ'il y a de la cruauté à tourmenter un malheureux qui ne vous a point fait du mal; il est donc essentiel que vous tiriez cette affaire au clair, et que vous prouviez, comme je n'en doute pas que vous n'avez point eu de part à cette méchanceté.

Voilà, mon cher ami, ce que nous pensons et ce que pensent, ce me semble, tous les gens de lettres et les gens raisonnables. Tout le monde ne vous donnera peut être pas le meme conseil, mais vous devez vous défier de trois choses, de la foiblesse des uns qui vous conseilleront le silence par lacheté, de la fausse generosité des autres qui vous conseilleront de demeurer en repos contre vos interêts, enfin des fanatiques de Rousseau qui ne voudroient pas que vous missiez sa conduite et son caractere au grand jour. Vos veritables amis, au nombre desquels je me flatte que vous me comptez, penseront autrement, et vous conseilleront ce qu'ils croyent le plus convenable à votre reputation. Tout ce que je vous dis là, mon cher ami, je le dirois en presence de Rousseau lui même; je n'ai aucune raison, au moins que je sache, de me plaindre ni de me louer personnellement de lui; mais je dois à votre amitié qui me demande conseil, de lui dire ce que je ferois si j'etois à votre place, et si j'avois en main comme vous, de quoi rendre ma justification plus claire que le jour.

Mlle de lespinasse, à qui j'ai lu toute votre lettre, et ma reponse, et qui prend à vous le plus grand interêt, me charge de vous dire combien elle vous aime, et combien elle est persuadée que vous devez imprimer. Elle ne pense pas, non plus que moi et tous vos amis, qu'il suffise d'envoyer cinq ou six copies de cette histoire à differentes personnes, comme vous paroissez en avoir le dessein, cela auroit l'air d'une justification ténébreuse, d'une demarche obscure, enfin de ce que nous appellons un *coup fourré*, qui n'est pas digne de vous, et qui ne suffiroit pas pour mettre Rousseau absolument dans son tort. Mr. duclos en particulier me charge de vous dire que quoiqu'il ait eté jusqu'à present ami de Rousseau, il trouve que sa conduite avec vous est inexcusable, qu'elle est pleine de noirceur, et qu'il est nécessaire de la devoiler. J'ai eu l'honneur de voir Mr. Smith, nous avons beaucoup parlé de vous et de votre affaire, et je ne manquerai pas de lui faire part de votre lettre, comme vous me le recommandez. Tous vos amis, et surtout Mlle de lespinasse et moi, sont très affligés de voir que votre retour à Paris n'est pas aussi prochain que nous l'esperions. . . .

* X. *From* Mme de Boufflers

a Pougues ce 22 juillet 1766

Quelque raison que vous me puissiez dire pour ne mavoir pas instruite de letrange evenement qui occupe a cette heure langleterre et la france, je suis convaincue que par reflexion vous sentirez, si vous ne l'avez deja senty, quil n'y en peut avoir de valable. Le chagrin que vous pretendes avoir voulu m'eviter ne pouvoit etre que retardé, et letat dincertitude ou vous mavez laissée, etoit plus penible sans doute que la pleine connoissance du fait. Concevez, sous les motifs que javois de croire lhistoire fabuleuse combien ma surprise et mon ignorance que jexprimois naivement dans mes lettres, devoit contribuer a la faire paroistre telle aux personnes qui concluoient ainsi que moy que le baron dOlback neut pas du etre votre premier confident, enfin le deplaisir que vous m'avez causé par une conduite qui deroge un peu ce me semble a lamitié que vous m'avez promise.

En tout cela vous trouverez je pense de quoy contrebalancer les foibles motifs qui vous ont engagé au silence avec moy.

Persuadée que vous etes incapable de vous refuser a levidence, ou de nier une verité reconnuë, je tiens ce point pour accordé, et je le conclus en vous assurant que si j'ay commencé par vous expliquer mes sentimens a cet egard: ce n'est pas que mon mecontentement soit considerable. C'est pour agir avec plus dingenuité, pour quon ne me soupconne pas daffecter de la moderation, enfin pour traiter les choses dans lordre quil convient, en reservant le plus important pour le dernier.

Voicy maintenant la question qui se presente. Avez vous recommandé au Baron dolback de taire ou de repandre les plaintes que vous faites du procedé de Rousseau? Le public non encore instruit les trouve ameres, et juge que le Baron en servant votre indignation

* MS., R.S.E.; *Eminent Persons*, 239 ff.

dans sa premiere chaleur vous a mal servi vous meme. Votre douceur votre bonté l'indulgence que vous avez naturellement, font attendre et desirer de vous des efforts de moderation qui passe le pouvoir des hommes ordinaires. Pourquoy se hater de divulguer les premiers mouvemens d'un coeur grievement blessé que la raison n'a pu encore dompter! Pourquoy vous derober la plus noble vengeance qu'on puisse prendre dun ennemi, dun ingrat, ou plutot d'un malheureux que ses passions et son humeur attrabilaire egare, (souffrez cet adoucissement), celle de laccabler de votre superiorité, de leblouir par leclat de cette vertu meme quil veut meconnoistre.

Mais venons au fond de laffaire. La lettre de Rousseau est atroce, c'est le dernier exces de lextravagance la plus complete. Rien ne peut lexcuser, et limpossibilité deffacer une telle faute fera leternel tourment de sa vie. Ne croies pas pourtant quil soit capable d'artifice ni de mensonge, quil soit un imposteur ni un scelerat. Sa colere n'est pas fondée mais elle est reelle je n'en doute point. Voicy le sujet que j'en imagine.

J'ay ouy dire, et on le luy aura peutetre mandé, qu'une des meilleures phrase de la lettre de Mr Walpole etoit de vous. Que vous aviez dit en plaisantant et parlant au nom du Roy de Prusse, "Si vous aimes les Persecutions, je suis Roy et je puis vous en procurer de toutes les especes. Que depuis Mr Walpole avoit employé la phraze en disant quelle etoit de vous pour ne pas saproprier un bon mot dont il n'etoit pas lauteur. Si ce fait est vray et que Rousseau l'ait scu, sensible, fougueux melancholique, orgueilleux meme, comme on dit quil est, faut il s'etonner quil soit devenu fol de douleur et de rage. Cette lettre si peu digne de son genie, quil addresse au Gazetier Anglois temoigne sa disposition et en indique la cause. Tel est indubitablement le vray principe de son deplorable egarement, que j'ay deviné trop tard. Car de laccuser comme vous faites de premeditation de dessein formé de vous nuire et de vous deshonorer, cest ce qui n'est nullement vraisemblable. Tous les interets humains se reunissent pour len detourner. Estime til la gloire, la reputation, seroit ce un moyen dacquerir ou de conserver lun et lautre de se montrer ingrat. Il est sans appuy sans ressource sans consolation quelquonque si vous labandonnes, et vous imagines que c'est de sens froid avec toute sa raison, quil sexpose a tant de malheurs. Non cela n'est pas possible. On m'assure que vous avez ecrit, qu'il vouloit se ranger du coté de lopposition. Je ne puis croire que vous ayez une telle idée. Rousseau dans lopposition! Connoist il les differens interests du Pays. Darbishire est il un lieu propre aux intrigues! Tirera til plus davantages des seigneurs du parti, quil n'en a pu tirer sil leut voulu de votre amitié de la protection de Mr Conway et des bontes du Roy Dangleterre! Mais c'en est trop la dessus. Je le repete, je ne me persuaderay qua la derniere extremité, quil ait formé un projet infame, et nuisible a luy meme avec lentier usage de sa raison. Mais cette raison une fois troublée par ses passions ardentes, il n'a pu s'en servir pour les commander. Il a oublié toute decence, il a cru contre toute apparence, ce quil ne devoit jamais penser, ce que la rectitude de son propre coeur avoit du empecher quil pensat jamais. C'est qu'un homme connu, estimé, comme vous letes, dont la probité est confirmée par un long exercise ait put tromper tant dannées, ou changer en un instant. Quelque preuve qu'on luy ait donné contre vous, il a du les rejetter, dementir ses yeux memes, et sexpliquer sur ses soupçons, avec honte detre assez foible pour les avoir conçus. Au reste si ses plaintes ne sont fondées que sur la phraze qu'on vous attribuë, on peut dire que son amour propre est trop facile a blesser puisque cette phraze est plutot une satire contre le pouvoir arbitraire que contre luy. Se laisser aller a cette violence sur une simple raillerie, passer toute borne oublier tout devoir, c'est un exces dorgueil bien criminel. Sil vous a cru de moitié de toute la lettre, cela lexcuse un peu plus, mais non pas assez. Mais vous au lieu de vous irriter contre un malheureux qui ne peut vous nuire, et qui se ruine entierement luy meme, que n'avez vous laisse agir cette pitié genereuse dont vous etes si susceptible. Vous eussiez evité un eclat qui scandalise, qui divise les esprits, qui flatte la malignité qui amuse aux depens de tous deux les gens oisifs et inconsideres, qui fait faire des refflexions injurieuses, et renouvelle les clameurs contre les philosophes et la philosophie. J'ose croire que si vous eussiez eté aupres de moy, lorsque cette cruelle offense vous a eté faite, elle vous eut inspiré plus de compassion que de colere. Mais dans letat ou sont les choses, il ne faut soccuper du passé qui est irremediable, qu'autant quil en est besoin pour regler votre conduite presente et future. Vous me demandez mon avis sur une question delicate, scavoir, si vous devez instruire le public de cette avanture par un ecrit, ou lensevelir dans l'oubli. Cest a quoy j'ay besoin de refflechir. Je vais me reposer, mais avant de conclure cette premiere partie de ma lettre, je dois vous declarer que c'est par le devoir que vous men imposes et selon ce que lamitié exige de moy, que je hazarde mon opinion, et que jentreprens de vous dire ce que je ferois, mais non pas peut etre ce que vous devez faire, car il est difficile de se mettre entierement a la place dautruy. Qu'en consequence, soit que vous suiviez soit que vous rejettiez mon avis je seray contente si vous l'etes, et si le public vous approuve. Je n'ay pas la presomption de me croire la capacité qu'il faudroit pour bien conseiller un homme tel que vous, qui a sa gloire a soutenir, et sur lequel tous les yeux vont se fixer. Votre prevention en ma faveur ne peut aller jusqu'a me la supposer. Vous faites bien neanmoins dans la crise ou vous etes de ne negliger aucune precaution decouter tous les avis. Le mien en particulier sans estre decisif ne peut etre meprisable, et les sentimens qui le dicteront doivent sans doute luy donner quelque poids.

ce 25 a Paris.

Ma lettre a eté interrompuë trois jours pendant lesquels j'ay fait soixante et quatre lieues. En arrivant a Paris, j'ay trouvé la votre a M[r] D'A . . . quil avoit envoyé chez moy pour que je la lusse. J'avouë quelle ma surprise et affligée au dernier point. Quoy vous luy recommandez de la communiquer non seulement a vos amis de paris, denomination bien vague et bien etendue, mais a Mr de Voltaire avec qui vous avez peu de liaison et dont vous connoissez si bien les dispositions? Apres ce trait de passion, apres tout ce que vous avez dit et ecrit, les refflexions que je vous communiquerois, les conseils que je pourrois vous donner, seroient inutiles. Vous etes trop confirmé dans votre opinion trop engagé trop soutenu dans votre colere pour mecouter. Peu s'en faut que je ne brule ce que j'ay dejà ecrit.

Au reste vous aurez icy un parti nombreux composé de tous ceux qui seront charmés de vous voir agir comme un homme ordinaire. Ce n'est pas un mediocre avantage pour ceux qui ne pouvoient atteindre jusqua votre hauteur, de vous rapprocher tant soit peu de la leur. Pour moy je suis penetrée de cette evenement. Je n'ay pas la force decrire rien de plus sur ce triste sujet, et je najouteray que quelques lignes parce que ma conscience et mon amitié m'y obligent. Si les choses sont telles que je me les figure, le trouble de Rousseau en ecoutant Mr Davenport, et en lisant votre lettre, n'est point la conviction dune noirceur meditée. Il nait dun trait de lumiere, qui luy aura fait entrevoir labime ou son fol orgueil la precipité, il aura commencé a douter de la realité de ses griefs, il en aura eté accablé. Nous verrons quel effort il fera pour se tirer de ce mauvais pas.

Autre article auquel je dois repondre. M. le prince de Conty, a qui je n'ay pas montre votre lettre, parce quil est absent depuis dix jours, setoit chargé de linformation chez Mr de Rougemont. Il la differé dun jour a lautre, ensuite il a passé luy meme chez ce Banquier qui s'est trouvé sorti. Le Banquier voyant un tel nom auroit du venir sur le champ demander quels ordres on avoit a luy donner. Il n'en a rien fait. Bref tantot par une raison, tantot par une autre, ce que nous voulions savoir n'a pas eté scu.

Vous ne me connoissez point quand vous imaginez que je puisse vous avoir caché le resultat des recherches que nous faisons de concert. Mais que pretendez vous faire des nouvelles informations dont vous chargez Mr Dolback. Vous n'avez pas dessein apparemment de rien ecrire contre ce malheureux homme qui soit etranger a votre cause. Vous ne serez pas son delateur, apres avoir eté son protecteur. De semblables examens doivent preceder les liaisons et non pas suivre les ruptures. Au nom de ce que vous vous devez, au nom dune amitié dont lestime fut la baze, prenez garde a ce que vous allez faire. Que craindries vous? Ni Rousseau, ni personne ne peut vous nuire. Vous etes invulnerable si vous ne vous blesses vous meme.

J'ay fait prier votre ami Mr Smith de venir chez moy. Il me quitte a linstant. Je luy ay lu ma lettre. Il aprehende aussi bien que moy que vous ne vous soyez trompé dans la chaleur dun si juste ressentiment. Il vous prie de relire la lettre de Rousseau a Mr Conway. Il ne nous paroist pas quil refuse la pension, ni quil desire qu'elle soit publique, il demande quelle soit differée jusqua ce que la tranquilité de son ame atterée par un violent chagrin soit retablie, et quil puisse se livrer tout entier a sa reconnoissance. Dans la mauvaise humeur ou il etoit, votre meprise quil aura cru volontaire aura achevé de laigrir et de luy renverser la raison.

[With the above letter should be compared the following, written almost at the same time, to Rousseau:

MME DE BOUFFLERS *to* ROUSSEAU

Paris, 27 juillet 1766.

M. Hume m'a envoyé, Monsieur, la lettre outrageante que vous lui avez écrite. Je n'en vis jamais de semblable. Tous vos amis sont dans la consternation et reduits au silence. Eh, que peut-on dire pour vous, Monsieur, après une lettre si peu digne de votre plume qu'il vous est impossible de vous en justifier, quelque offense que vous puissiez vous croire! Mais quelles sont donc ces injures dont vous vous plaignez? Quel est le fondement de ces horribles reproches que vous vous permettez? Ajoutez-vous foi si facilement aux trahisons? Votre esprit par ses lumières, votre coeur par sa droiture, ne doivent-ils pas vous garantir des soupçons odieux que vous avez conçus? Vous vous y livrez contre toute raison, vous qui eussiez dû vous refuser à l'évidence même, et démentir jusqu'au témoignage même de vos sens. M. Hume un lâche! un traitre! Grand Dieu! Mais quelle apparence qu'il eut vécu cinquante ans passés, aimé, respecté au milieu des ses compatriotes, sans en être connu! Attendait-il votre arrivée pour lever le masque, pour ternir une vie glorieuse plus qu'à moitié passée? Et pour quel intérêt? Ce ne peut être ni jalousie, ni rivalité: vos génies sont différents, ainsi que vos langages, ainsi que les matières que vous avez traitées. Il n'envie pas non plus votre bonne fortune, puisque de ce côté il a toutes sortes d'avantages sur vous. Ce serait donc le plaisir de faire le mal et de se déshonorer gratuitement qui lui auraient inspiré les noirceurs dont vous l'accusez? Qui connut jamais de pareils scélérats, de pareils insensés? Ne sont-ce pas des êtres de raison? Je veux néanmoins supposer un moment qu'il en existe; je veux de plus supposer que M. Hume soit un de ces affreux prodiges, vous n'êtes pas justifié pour cela, Monsieur. Vous l'avez cru trop tôt; vous n'avez pas pris des mesures suffisantes pour vous garantir de l'erreur. Vous avez en France des amis et des protecteurs, vous n'en avez consulté aucun,

* Streckeisen-Moultou, ii. 59 ff.

et quand bien même vous eussiez fait tout ce que vous avez omis, quand vous auriez acquis toutes les preuves imaginables de l'attentât le plus noir, vous eussiez dû encore modérer votre emportement contre un homme qui vous a réellement servi. Les liens de l'amitié sont respectables même après qu'ils sont rompus, et les seules apparences de ce sentiment le sont aussi.

Madame la maréchale de Luxembourg et moi nous attendons impatiemment vos explications sur cette incomprehensible conduite. De grâce, Monsieur, ne les différez pas, que nous sachions au moins comment vous excuser, si l'on ne peut vous disculper entièrement. Le silence auquel nous sommes forcées vous nuit plus que toute chose.]

* XI. *From* Lady Hervey

Old-Windsor the 23[d] July 1766

After the letter you showed me, S[r] and the account you gave me, when you was here, of that madman Rousseau nothing can surprise me from that quarter: but it does worse for it allarms me, his Frenzy is grown to such a height that I really think him dangerous, and that for his own sake and that of others 'tis full time he shou'd be locked up. Detestation for his malevolence, and compassion for his madness, make a sort of odd mixture in ones Sensations for him, and both prevent ones laughing at the ridiculous as well as absurd idea he has got about the conspiracy of the Triumvirate he supposes united to hurt him. You have really done by this Country, in importing him, what the late Lord Hillsborough did by Ireland, in carrying them the noxious animals and insects which were not the produce of that Country, and if Jean Jaques encreases and multiplys here you will have a great deal to answer for. . . .

† XII. *From* Turgot

A Paris le 23 Juillet 1766.

. . . J'ay pris aussi bien de la part au chagrin que vous a causé l'extravagance et l'ingratitude de Rousseau. Je me trouvay dernierement chéz Mlle de L'Espinasse, lorsque M. D'Alembert reçut votre lettre, l'abbé Morellet y vint aussi. Nous nous reunimes tous dans le meme avis et d'Alembert se chargea de vous ecrire nos communes reflexions. Je vous avoue cependant que mon premier penchant avoit eté de vous confirmer dans le parti auquel vous incliniés de ne pas imprimer quant a present, et je ne suis revenu a l'avis commun que d'après la consideration que les choses n'etoient plus entieres; que votre premiere lettre au Baron d'Holbach avoit eté aussi publique qu'elle pût l'etre; qu'aux yeux de tous les partisans de Rousseau qui sont en grand nombre, vous etiés devenu son accusateur et

* MS., R.S.E.; *Eminent Persons*, 27 f.

† MS., R.S.E.; *Eminent Persons*, 130 ff.; *Œuvres de Turgot*, ii. 496 ff.

comme tel obligé de justifier les imputations et les qualifications dont vous l'aviés noirci.

Quelques personnes ont eu depuis des idées differentes. Je vous citeray en particulier M^r De Malesherbes, qui a lû l'extrait de votre lettre et celle de Jean Jacques. Vous savés l'interêt vif qu'il y a toujours pris et qu'a l'enthousiasme assés naturel qu'inspire l'eloquence de cet auteur, il joint un sentiment fondé sur la connoissance personnelle de l'homme. Il croit que les torts qu'il a eus avec vous peuvent s'expliquer par la seule violence de son caractere aussi impetueux que defiant sans etre obligé de recourir aux maneuvres reflechies dont vous l'avés cru coupable. Il a dit il vu une scene toute semblable a la votre qui s'etoit passée vis a vis du Libraire Guerin, auquel Rousseau avoit de très grandes obligations. Quelques circonstances ayant fait trainer en longueur l'impression d'Emile, Rousseau s'imagina que Guerin qui etoit assés lié avec les Jesuites leur avoit communiqué son manuscrit et s'etoit entendu avec eux pour le perdre. Il ecrivit a ce libraire son ami et son bienfaiteur une lettre toute semblable a celle qu'il vous a ecrite. Ce fut M^r De Malésherbes qui se chargea luy meme de remettre la lettre de Rousseau. Il eut toutes les peines du monde a le faire revenir de cette extravagance et alors il montra un repentir aussi vif que l'avoit eté sa fureur. M^r De Malesherbes a eté temoin de plusieurs scenes de cette nature. D'après lesquelles il est resté convainçu que Rousseau avoit la plus malheureuse facilité de se livrer aux soupçons les plus injustes et les plus insensés contre ses meilleurs amis, qu'il s'abandonnoit alors a toute l'impetuosité de son caractere, mais qu'il n'y avoit dans toute cette conduite ny manœuvre ny noirceur. D'après cette idée si Rousseau avoit seulement varié sur l'art. de la pension, si après avoir cedé a vos conseils, a ceux de Milord Marechal en consentant a l'accepter, il s'en etoit repenti, si votre crime a ses yeux etoit non d'avoir supposé un consentement qu'il nieroit avoir donné, ce qui seroit d'une mauvaise foi atroce, mais plutot de l'avoir engagé a donné ce consentement que la revolution de ses pensées luy represente comme son deshonneur, il y auroit ce semble dans son fait plus de folie que de noirceur. Sa lettre ne desavoue pas son consentement, ainsi seule elle n'etablit pas sa manœuvre odieuse. Vous croyés avoir des preuves que plusieurs mois auparavant il preparoit cette scene et lors meme qu'il paroissoit le plus gay. C'est la le point decisif et c'est sur quoy vous ne devés pas craindre de vous etendre, car les preuves sont d'autant plus necessaires qu'une sceleratesse aussi profonde et aussi atroce est veritablement inconcevable. On n'y voit point un interêt qui ait pu l'y determiner, celuy de se targuer du Refus d'une pension du Roy seroit l'idée du monde la plus absurde après avoir donné son consentement, avoir ecrit a Milord Marechal, remercié Mr Conway et le General Græme; peut-il dementir ces temoignages quand il n'y auroit que le votre seul, pourroit-il imaginer que dans la position ou vous etes vis a vis de luy, on ne vous croiroit pas par preference sur un fait qui se seroit passé entre vous deux. Le motif de secouer les obligations qu'il vous a n'est pas plus vraysemblable. Je le concevrois, s'il devoit vivre en societé avec vous, si son orgueil pouvoit jamais souffrir de l'espece d'avantage que vous donnoient sur luy les services que vous luy aviés rendus; mais lorsqu'il vous a insulté vous etiés deja loin de luy. Il ne devoit jamais passer sa vie avec vous et par consequent jamais il ne devoit sentir le poids de la reconnoissance, s'il est vray qu'elle pese tant a son orgueil. Voila bien des motifs qui feroient douter non de son tort vis a vis de vous, mais que ce tort ait eté precedé d'une maneuvre reflechie qui en constateroit la noirceur et l'atrocité. Vous trouverés peut-etre que nous mettons bien de la subtilité a ne trouver dans l'action de Rousseau que de la folie. Il est sur que vous qui avés presentes toutes les circonstances, vous pouvés juger beaucoup mieux que nous des principes de sa conduite mais il est bon que vous sachiés l'impression qu'a fait votre esprit sur des personnes a la verité prevenues pour Rousseau, mais qui certainement le sont encore plus pour vous, qui savent que votre caractere et votre conduite ne peuvent etre exposés au plus leger nuage et qui sur quelque fait que ce soit n'auront pas le plus leger doute lorsque vous aurés parlé. Je ne connois point du tout Rousseau que je n'ay vu que des instans dans le tems qu'il alloit chéz le Baron d'Holbach, mais je fais beaucoup de fond sur l'opinion de M. de Malesherbes qui l'a connu intimement et qui craint que votre juste indignation ne vous ait induit en erreur sur le vray principe des torts, d'un homme dont les torts les plus legers seroient inexcusables. Au reste il n'est personne dans ce pays cy qui puisse imaginer que votre reputation courre le plus leger risque dans toute cette affaire. Personne au monde n'imaginera que vous ayés demandé une pension pour Rousseau afin de le deshonorer. Parce qu'excepté luy personne ne pensera qu'une pension l'eut deshonoré. Quant a ce que le Roy d'Angleterre ou plutot Ses ministres auroient eté un peu compromis il me semble que la folie de Rousseau bien loin de vous noircir vous excuse, et qu'il est clair que si l'on peut vous blamer, ce n'est que d'avoir mis trop de zele a luy rendre service et de n'avoir pas assés craint les inconsequences de sa mauvaise tête. Quant aux accusations de Rousseau de vous etre entendu avec ses ennemis, je le repete, elles sont si extravagantes quelles ne peuvent pas trouver créance auprès de ses meilleurs amis et quelles portent leur refutation avec elles. De tout cela il resulte que l'impression et la publication de cette Histoire ne peut avoir d'objet que de vous justifier des imputations de sceleratesse, de noirceur et d'atrocité que vous avés faites a Rousseau et dont il est impossible qu'il ne soit pas instruit. Il est certain que si vous avés des preuves de la manœuvre dont vous le soupçonnés il est bon de les donner au public et quelque facheux qu'il soit de voir l'humanité deshonorée par le caractere de ceux dont les talens luy font le plus d'honneur, il est essentiel avant tout que le vray soit connu, et qu'on ote a l'hypocrite le masque qui le rend dangereux.

Je pense que d'Alembert a insisté pour que vous nous envoyiés votre manuscrit avant de rien publier. Comme les amis de Rousseau sont principalement dans ce pays cy nous serons plus a portée de connoitre exactement l'effet de l'ouvrage et de prevoir les objections. L'abbé Morellet est sur cela entierement de mon avis. Vous pourrés adresser les paquets a M^{r} De Montigny pour en eviter le port a D'Alembert. Pour moy je crains d'etre en Limousin quand vous aurés fini l'ouvrage, car je dois partir au commencement de Septembre, et il y auroit de l'indiscretion a vous en demander une seconde copie.

M^{e} Du Pré est a Montigny pour jusqu'au mois de Novembre.

Adieu, Monsieur, je vous souhaite tout le bonheur que merite la bonté de votre ame et je suis bien persuadé que le mauvais succès que vous venés d'eprouver ne vous degoutera pas de faire du bien. Vous trouverés votre recompense en vous meme, et l'estime et l'amitié de tous les honnêtes gens vous dedommageront de l'ingratitude d'un mechant ou d'un fou. . . .

* XIII. *From* HORACE WALPOLE

Dear Sr Arlington Street July 26. 1766.

Your Set of litterary Friends are what a Set of litterary Men are apt to be, exceedingly absurd. They hold a consistory to consult how to argue with a madman; and they think it very necessary for your character to give them the pleasure of seeing Rousseau exposed, not because He has provoked you, but them. If Rousseau prints, you must; but I certainly woud not, till He does.

I cannot be precise as to the time of my writing the King of Prussia's letter, but I do assure you with the utmost truth that it was several days before you left Paris, & before Rousseau's arrival there, of which I can give you a strong proof; for I not only suppressed the letter while you staid there, out of delicacy to you; but it was the reason why, out of delicacy to myself, I did not go to see him, as you often proposed to me; thinking it wrong to go & make a cordial visit to a man, with a letter in my pocket to laugh at him. You are at full liberty, dear S^{r}, to make use of what I say in your Justification, either to Rousseau or any body else. I shoud be very sorry to have you blamed on my account; I have a hearty contempt of Rousseau, & am perfectly indifferent what *the Litterati of Paris*[1] think of the

* MS., R.S.E.; Walpole, *Letters*, vii. 31 f.

[1] When using this for his *Concise Account* Hume altered *the Litterati of Paris* into *anybody*, and *think* into *thinks*. The alterations appear in the autograph, in Hume's hand.

matter. If there is any fault, which I am far from thinking, let it lie on me. No parts can hinder my laughing at their Possessor if He is a Mountebank. If He has a bad & most ungrateful heart, as Rousseau has shown in your case, into the bargain, he will have my Scorn likewise, as he will of all good and sensible men. You may trust your Sentence to Such, who are as respectable Judges, as any that have pored over ten thousand more volumes. . . .

* XIV. *From* TURGOT

A Paris le 27 Juillet 1766
au soir.

Je me crois obligé, Monsieur, de revenir sur quelques une des reflexions que je vous ay adressées dernierement sur la mauvaise querelle que Rousseau vous a faite. Les nouvelles circonstances que j'ay apprises me font voir cette affaire sous un jour un peu different qui peut etre exigera de vous des demarches plus delicates, que si elle eut eté telle que je la supposois d'abord. Vraysemblablement vos autres amis vous auront aussi fait part de leurs idées a ce sujet et que vos propres reflexions les auront prevenues, mais j'aime mieux vous dire tout ce que j'ay pensé au risque de barbouiller inutilement du papier, que de ne pas repondre pleinement a votre confiance.

Je sors de chéz le Baron d'Holbach ou etoit votre ami Mr Smith. Il m'a appris que vous aviés envoyé a Me de Bouflers la lettre de Rousseau a Mr Conway, et m'a beaucoup surpris en me disant que cette lettre ne contenoit point un refus de la pension dans le cas ou elle ne seroit pas publique, mais seulement des regrets de ce que la circonstance du secret priveroit Rousseau de la satisfaction de faire eclater sa reconnoissance. Le tout accompagné de reflexions chagrines, vagues et obscures qui paroissent relatives aux idées qu'il s'etoit formées de vos pretendus torts avec luy. Il devient clair par là que la lettre outrageuse qu'il vous a ecrite n'est pas relative au refus de la pension et ne renferme comme je l'avois deja remarqué aucun desaveu du consentement qu'il vous avoit donné. Je n'ay pas vu la lettre meme que vous avés envoyée a M^e^ De Bouflers parce qu'il y a si longtems que je n'ay eté chéz cette Dame que je ne pourrois honnêtement l'aller voir pour un sujet qui luy est etranger. Mais ce que Mr Smith m'en a dit ne me paroit nullement equivoque, quoy que peut etre le galimathias chagrin de la fin ait pu y en mettre pour Mr Conway et en consequence pour vous. D'après ce fait je crois qu'il faut chercher a la conduite de Rousseau une explication toute differente de celle qui s'etoit d'abord presentée a vous, et de celle que je vous avois communiquée par ma premiere lettre. Voici maintenant ce que j'imagine. Vous avés fait avant son depart de paris et je crois meme en sa presence une plaisanterie bien legere sur

* MS., R.S.E.; *Eminent Persons*, 136 ff.

son gout supposé pour les persecutions. Cette plaisanterie a eté inserée par Mr Walpole dans la lettre qui s'est repandue sur le nom du Roy de Prusse. Cette lettre est devenue publique en Angleterre, elle a donné lieu a une lettre de Rousseau dans les papiers publics ou il en paroit amerement affecté. Mr Walpole ou d'autres gens pour luy ont repliqué par deux ou trois plaisanteries qui certainement l'auront piqué jusqu'au vif. Or avec le caractere sombre et soupconneux de Rousseau, l'impression profonde que ces plaisanteries ont faites sur son ame, vos liaisons avec Mr Walpôle et avec la Societé du Baron d'holbach, la circonstance de cette plaisanterie employée par Mr Walpole et qu'il savoit etre originairement de vous, il n'a peut etre fallu qu'un mot, un rapport ambigu pour enflammer son imagination et luy faire regarder comme certaine la chimere la plus absurde. La petite supercherie de Mr Davenport s'etoit liée a tout l'edifice de ses soupçons, vous etiés present et l'impression s'est effacée promptement; mais quand il a eté livré a luy meme dans la solitude son ame s'est de nouveau echauffée, ses soupçons sont revenus plus violens que jamais, la fausse interpretation que vous avés donnée vous et Mr Conway a la lettre ecrite a celuy cy luy a paru une demonstration de vos trahisons et c'est alors qu'il vous a ecrit cette lettre extravagante qui vous a si cruellement agité. Si cette explication est juste, ce que vous pouvés mieux que nous reconnoitre par le detail des circonstances, Rousseau n'est assurement pas excusé, mais sa faute devient d'un genre different. Elle n'est plus l'effet d'une maneuvre premeditée de sens froid, preparée longtems a l'avance, masquée par les apparences de la reconnoissance et de l'amitié, dictée par le projet sot et noir tout a la fois de se menager la gloire du refus eclatant d'une grace a laquelle il avoit consenti par ecrit, et de se degager de toute obligation envers un bienfaiteur qu'il ne doit jamais revoir. C'est un trait de violence, de folie, une saillie de son caractere sombre, defiant, impetueux; ce n'est point une noirceur reflechie une sceleratesse atroce. Son ingratitude envers vous est réelle, mais elle n'est point premeditée.

L'Espece d'erreur ou vous avés eté sur ce point ne laisse pas d'etre affligeante, par la publicité qu'elle vous a mis dans le cas de donner a vos imputations, et je crains qu'il n'en resulte quelque embarras pour la conduite que vous avés a tenir. Toutes les accusations de Rousseau tout le systeme de perfidie que son imagination vous a preté, ne doivent pas vous causer la plus legere inquietude; quand meme il auroit l'imprudence ou l'impudence d'en porter ses plaintes au public il ne pourroit que se deshonorer en pure perte. Je ne crois pas que personne au monde imagine que vous l'ayés mené en Angleterre pour le deshonorer et fussiés vous moins connu que vous ne l'etes vous n'auriés encore suivant moy rien a craindre parcequ'un tel trait n'est point dans la nature. La seule reflexion a laquelle les accusations de Rousseau donneroient lieu c'est que vous avés eté la dupe de votre bon cœur, et cela ne vous feroit nul tort. Vous devés donc etre parfaitement tranquille sur le fond de l'affaire, et peut etre meme avant l'eclat quelle a fait Rousseau luy même auroit il retracté ses extravagances. Ce qu'il y a de facheux, c'est qu'une erreur legere jointe a l'indignation la plus juste vous ait mis dans le cas de rendre cette affaire publique dès le premier moment. Par la les Soupçons de Rousseau qu'il eut eté d'abord facile de detruire seront confirmés dans sa tête et il n'en reviendra peut etre jamais. Il pensera et dira que sa lettre a Mr Conway etoit claire et que vous n'y avés supposé de l'equivoque que pour avoir un pretexte de le deshonorer, de luy imputer une conduite bizarre, un orgueil extravagant, une mauvaise foy par laquelle il auroit compromis et vous, et Mr Conway et le Roy d'Angleterre. Il pensera et dira que par la publicité que vous avés donnée a cette avanture c'est vous qui avés manqué au Roy d'Angleterre en divulguant l'offre de cette pension qui devoit etre secrete. Si la supposition du refus et la fausse idée ou a eté en consequence Mr Conway que Rousseau ne desiroit l'offre que pour avoir la gloire du refus, a fait manquer l'affaire de sa pension, il dira encore que vous l'avés engagé a consentir a cette pension pour luy faire perdre la reputation de son desinteressement et que vous avés ensuite cherché a jetter de l'equivoque sur ce consentement pour luy faire perdre en meme tems l'avantage de la pension et le rendre meprisable et odieux au Roy d'Angleterre. Ceux qui se connoissent en honnêtes gens ne croiront pas un mot de tout cela, mais ils vous plaindront d'avoir donné prise sur vous a cet homme par une erreur et par une trop grande promptitude a laisser paroitre une indignation très naturelle et très juste contre l'outrage le plus odieux de la part d'un homme que vous avés comblé de biens. Si je ne me trompe pas dans cette façon de voir, votre position est un peu embarassante parce que vous êtes dans le cas d'avoir un tort vis a vis d'un homme qui en a de plus graves encore. Votre tort en luy meme est souverainement excusable puisqu'il est l'effet du premier mouvement le plus juste qui fut jamais. Mais ce tort joint a l'erreur qui a precedé et a la publicité qui a suivi a produit un mal très réel, et ce mal réel et cette publicité confirmeront Rousseau dans ses torts, les justifieront a ses yeux et luy fourniront l'occasion de les aggraver. Dans le premier point de vue ou nous voyions l'affaire vous n'aviés a craindre que les accusations de Rousseau et leur absurdité pouvoit et devoit vous assurer pleinement de vous dispenser de toute precaution. Dans le second point de vue ce n'est point des soupçons de Rousseau que vous avés a vous justifier c'est des accusations que vous avés repandues contre luy dans vos lettres a gens que vous savés avoir eté ses ennemis et qui ne les ont pas tenues secretes, comme en effet vous ne le desiriés pas. Dans l'eclaircissement il reste a Rousseau un tort réel et très grave, mais qui n'est ny du meme genre ny aussi noir que vous l'aviés supposé. Il est embarassant de vous donner Conseil et quoy que vous ayés desiré d'avoir mon avis, je crains qu'il n'y ait de l'indiscretion a moy de vous dire tout ce que je pense, mais je me flatte que vous n'y verrès qu'un effet de l'interêt bien sincere que je prens aux peines que vous a causées une action honnête dont vous ne deviés recueillir qu'une satisfaction pure et dont vous devés toujours recueillir une gloire qu'aucune equivoque ne ternisse.

Je crois donc que le meilleur parti a prendre est dans cette affaire comme dans toutes les autres de se tenir a la verité dans toute sa simplicité et si vous vous etes en effet trompé de le dire le premier et a Rousseau et a vos amis et meme au public. Je ne doute pas que vous ne pensiés comme moy et que vous ne vous croyiés bien plus obligé de vous expliquer si vous avés eu quelque tort que si vous aviés eu pleine et entiere raison. Vous n'etes assurément pas dans le cas de demander pardon a Rousseau, il a des torts trop essentiels avec vous et vous ne perdés rien du droit ou vous etes de luy demander compte de ses soupçons atroces. Ce que vous avés a dire a donc trois objets. 1° d'exposer l'etonnement ou vous a jette la lettre de Rousseau, de la traiter avec le mepris qu'on doit a une veritable extravagance et de le sommer de s'expliquer sur les motifs de ses soupçons absurdes. 2° d'avouer franchement la fausse interpretation que vous avés donnée a sa lettre, 3° de vous excuser sur la publicité que vous avés donné a cette affaire et assurement l'excuse n'est pas difficile. Le tout ecrit avec simplicité, moderation, et fermeté. Ce seroit a Rousseau luy meme que je voudrois envoyer ce papier et ne me decider sur la publication que d'après sa conduite. J'irois meme jusqu'a luy offrir de le publier avec ses explications ou pour mieux dire ses retractations. S'il etoit de bonne foy et qu'il revint sur ses idées, cette explication donnée au public de concert termineroit cette affaire de la maniere la plus satisfaisante pour tous deux. S'il s'obstine, alors vous imprimeriés seul, vous donneriés les pieces au public. Vous diriés la verité vous vous condamnieriés de bonne foi sur vos legeres erreurs et certainement le public vous rendroit une pleine justice sur le fond. Je suppose que l'affaire de la pension eut eté retablie en faveur de Rousseau secretement ou avec publicité, car maintenant ce seroit le secret de la comedie. Cela me paroit necessaire pour luy oter les inductions qu'il tireroit de la suppression et dût il encore payer d'ingratitude ce nouveau service vous n'etes pas a une action genereuse près. Voila des conseils données bien a la hâte, mais vous les rectifierés par vos reflexions et par une connoissance plus precise des circonstances de detail. . . .

Mercredi 30. Ma lettre n'etant point partie Lundi, je l'ouvre pour la relire. Elle est ecrite bien a la hâte, peutetre ai je mis a la chose trop d'importance. L'abbé Morellet craint que votre bonne ame n'en soit chagrinée. Je serois bien faché de vous causer le moindre amertume. J'ay suivi en ecrivant l'impression du moment. Vous la jugerés et vous me pardonnerés si j'ay eu tort. Ce qu'il y a de sur c'est qu'en quelque tems que ce soit je crois utile de dire la verité dans tout son detail. C'est le seul moyen de terminer nettement toute querelle. Je viens de voir l'extrait que l'abbé Morellet m'a montré de la nouvelle lettre de Rousseau, dont vous rendés compte a D'Alembert. Ces absurdités portent leur refutation avec elles et je crois encore que leur folie diminue beaucoup de l'atrocité. Mon principe de dire toute verité me conduiroit a penser que Mr Walpole doit a vous et a D'Alembert l'aveu de cette lettre qui est la cause primitive de cette malheureuse affaire comme nous l'avions assés bien deviné ici. Je vous reitere les assurance de l'attachement le plus sincere et du desir extreme que j'ay de meriter votre amitié.

* XV. *From* Mme de Meinières

[?aout 1766]

J'ai communiqué, selon vos intentions Monsieur, la lettre que vous m'avés fait l'honneur de m'écrire, à M. de Montigny, et rien n'est si honnête, si zèlé, et si tendre à votre égard que la réponse qu'il m'a faite a ce sujet. Il a été d'avis que je montrasse a quelques uns de mes amis la relation de votre démêlé avec ce fou de jean Jacques; je l'ai donc traduite le plus litteralement qu'il m'a été possible, et je l'ai fait lire à plusieurs personnes que je croyois à propos de mettre, ou de ramener dans vos intérets; mais je n'en ai donné, ni laissé prendre de copies.

Je ne crois pas que vous deviés craindre, surtout a présent, le personnage que M. Rousseau voudra vous donner dans ses mémoires. Votre personnel et le sien, également connus, sauveront la verité, des prestiges de son eloquence. Il n'a que ses conjectures extravagantes à vous imputer, et vous avés des faits autentiques contre lui, qui le couvrent de confusion. Tout le monde s'éleve volontiers contre les ingrats, une partie pour en avoir fait, une autre pour se dispenser d'en faire. D'ailleurs, l'on craint l'on hait ou l'on admire cet homme bisarre, mais on ne l'aime pas, et vous êtes aimé. Ses entousiastes et ses envieux cachés tiennent le même langage sur son compte lorsqu'ils parlent de ses écrits, parce que ceux là en sont yvres et ceux cy redoutent sa plume. Mais les derniers deviendront de tout leur coeur, vos troupes auxiliaires, lorsqu'ils [*sic*] ne faudra attaquer que sa conduite, et donner, pour ainsi dire, un coup de raquette à la balle partie de votre main. Voila pourquoi je souhaitois qu'on ne l'accablât de votre part que de son propre procédé. Voila pourquoi j'ai eu regret aux premieres épithetes, de *coquin, de scelérat, du plus noir de tous les hommes qui aient jamais déshonnoré la nature humaine*, parce qu'elles ont paru trop fortes, et que quand l'historique

* MS., R.S.E., unpublished

de votre querelle est venue les justifier, j'étois fachée d'entendre dire à tous les partis . . .[1] *quoi! ce n'est que cela*, au lieu que *cela* auroit été trouvé effroyable si les qualifications ne l'avoient pas précédé, et que le public les eût proportionées lui même. Je vous invite donc Monsieur, si vous faites imprimer ce qui s'est passé entre vous et M. Rousseau, à ne présenter que les faits, depuis leur commencement jusqu'à leur fin, sans y ajouter ni une réflexion ni une plainte, ni un reproche. Laissé faire toute cette besoigne au lecteur. Plus la narration sera simple, plus elle sera frappante, soyés en sur. Le comique de Moliere n'est pas dans les mots, il est dans les choses, l'odieux de l'inquisition, dans le manuel des inquisiteurs, sort du tableau naïf de l'inquisition même, et non des exclamations de l'écrivain de cet ouvrage, qui ne s'en permet point. Ne confondés pas vos amis avec les ennemis de Jean Jacques. Les uns veulent vous servir; les autres ne veulent que se servir de vous pour lui nuire. Je vis dans la retraite depuis longtems et je la préfere au tourbillon brillant du monde. Je ne connois point vos sociétés intimes de paris; je ne me suis point concertée avec les gens que vous y aimés le mieux; et je parie qu'ils ont pensé comme moi sur cette querelle. Je ne prétends point à l'honneur de vous donner des conseils; mais je crois devoir à l'estime, à l'attachement, à la reconnoissance que je vous ai voué, de vous raconter mes petites idées, et de vous rendre compte de celles d'autrui qui sont parvenues à ma connoissance. . . .

Eh! mon Dieu! soyes certain que vos ouvrages et vos qualités personnelles mettent votre gloire à couvert, pour le tems et pour l'éternité. Les sophismes de Rousseau ne passeront point aux races futures, ou n'y passeront que pour des sophismes. Le mérite de son stile n'est que superficiel, et se perdra à mesure que notre langue et notre gout varieront; or ils varieront encore. Son humeur attrabilaire; son ingratitude signalée tant de fois; son orgueil insupportable, et agresseur de tous les orgueils, lui aliennent la pluspart de ses contemporains. Au lieu que les vérités historiques et philosophiques sont immortelles; et que vos mœurs douces, votre bonté, votre sublime modestie vous rendent cher à tout ce qui vous connoit. Bon jour mon original. Je suis votre tres humble et tres affectionnée copie.

* XVI. *From* Mme de Barbentane

a Villers cotterest 3 aoust 1766

Mon attachement pour vous Monsieur, est trop vrai, et le Malheur que vous éprouvéz trop grand, pour que je ne vous dise pas combien je le partage. Il est affreux de trouver un ennemi, dans celui qu'a tant de titres on devoit croire son ami; je n'entrerai dans aucun

* MS., R.S.E., unpublished.

[1] Dots in autograph.

raisonnement sur cette étrange histoire; vous connoissiez mon enthousiasme pour le malheureux, que vous aviez secouru, j'ai paine a le croire un monstre, et plus de paine encor a le déffendre. M^de^ de Boufflers ma lû la lettre qu'elle vous a écrite, elle dit tout ce que je pense, beaucoup mieux que je ne le pourois faire. J'ai voulu seulement vous assurer Monsieur qu'il est impossible de sentir plus vivement que moi le chagrain que vous ressentéz, parce qu'il est impossible d'avoir une plus haute idée de la bonté de votre coeur. . . .

* XVII. *From* D'ALEMBERT

ce 4 aout 1766

Ah! pardieu, mon cher Jean Jacques, il n'y a pas moyen d'y tenir, quelque envie qu'on ait de respecter votre situation, et de ne se pas mocquer de vous; vous avez beau etre malheureux, vous etes aussi trop plaisant, et il faut rire malgré qu'on en ait. C'est donc moi qui suis auteur, ou tout au moins complice de la lettre de Mr. Valpole; et vous etes sur de cela comme si vous l'aviez su; et je suis depuis longtemps *votre ennemi secret*, et j'ai fait un complot avec Mr. Hume pour vous perdre; je ne me serois jamais douté de tout cela, et je vous felicite d'avoir de si bonnes lunettes.

Laissons là ce pauvre fou, mon cher ami, et parlons de la très plaisante lettre qu'il vous a écrite, et des preuves incontestables qu'il a de votre trahison. Il y en a surtout une qui m'a frappé, c'est ce *regard fixe* qui est en effet bien propre à faire *ouvrir les yeux* sur votre perfidie aux moins clairvoyans. Je me souviens qu'un jour que vous me parliez en me regardant entre deux yeux, je vous conscillois en ami de vous défaire le plutôt que vous pourriez ce regard là, et qu'il vous joueroit un mauvais tour; vous y voila prêt, et je vous l'avois bien prédit. Il ne faut jamais regarder fixement les gens à qui on parle; je l'ai oui dire à un grand philosophe qui regardoit tout le monde de travers.

Il y a dans la drôle de lettre de *ce joli petit homme*, comme vous l'appelliez autrefois, une phrase sacramentelle ou sacramentale, à laquelle vous n'avez peut être pas fait autant d'attention qu'elle le mérite; c'est que *le public, qui d'abord avoit eté fort amoureux de lui, commença bientôt apres a le négliger*. Voilà ce qui le fâche veritablement, et il s'en prend à qui il peut. Vous vous etiez chargé de montrer l'ours à la foire; sa loge qui d'abord étoit pleine, est bientôt restée vuide, et il vous en rend responsable. Il est d'ailleurs très certain, et je le scais de duclos son ami à qui il l'a dit, ainsi qu'à bien d'autres, qu'il *ne peut pas souffrir toutes les personnes à qui il a obligation*, et sur ce pied là vous avez bien des droits à sa haine. Mais il faudroit du moins être un peu plus adroit, adroit au moins comme il pretend *que je le suis*, et ne pas avoir *la betise* de vous dire entr'autres raisons de votre *déloyauté*, que votre bienfaisance envers lui est trop sur-

* MS., R.S.E.; *Eminent Persons*, 191.

naturelle pour être sincere, car quiconque lira cet endroit de sa lettre, en conclura que cette autre personnage, ce grand predicateur de la vertu dans ses écrits, ne croit donc pas à la vertu des autres; or il en resultera de facheux soupcons contre la sienne; et quand on joindra à cela ses procedés envers ses autres amis, et les cinq ou six enfans qu'il a faits à la servante, et qu'il a mis aux enfans trouvés, on dira qu'il n'a pas bonne grace à crier *vertu* aux quatre coins des rues; et tout ce qu'il a écrit sur la vertu paroitra bien froid; et toute son éloquence ne fera pas plus d'effet que le beau *Pathos* qui termine sa lettre; mon premier mouvement en le lisant a eté d'admirer sa Rhetorique; le second a ete de rire, et de dire en levant les epaules; voila un homme qui employe la force d'Hercule pour rompre un fétu.

Après tout cela, mon cher ami, vous devez sentir quel est mon avis sur le parti que nous devons prendre, c'est de ne rien publier du tout contre Rousseau, et d'attendre qu'il nous attaque. Comme je n'ai reçu votre troisieme lettre qu'hier au soir, et que le courier me presse, je n'ai pu savoir l'avis de vos autres amis; mais c'est celui de Mlle de lespinasse, et de toutes les personnes à qui j'ai pu en parler. Votre seconde lettre a entierement perdu Rousseau dans l'esprit même de ses plus zelés partisans; il n'y a absolument qu'une voix aujourd'hui pour dire que c'est un fou et un vilain fou, et un fou dangereux. Ceux qui lui font le plus de grace, mettent seulement en doute, s'il est veritablement méchant; et c'est de quoi je ne doute pas pour mon compte, mais cela ne fait rien au fond, il suffit qu'il soit déclaré unanimement fou, digne d'être mis à Bedlam, pour que nous n'ayons rien à en craindre. D'ailleurs, et c'est la réflexion que me faisoit hier un de mes amis, homme très sensé, qui voit bien Rousseau tel qu'il est; tout ce qu'il veut, c'est de faire parler de lui, à quelque prix que ce soit; et le plus mauvais tour qu'on puisse lui jouer, c'est d'empêcher le plus qu'il est possible qu'on n'en parle, et par consequent de ne rien imprimer contre lui sans nécessité. Ne laissez pourtant pas de m'envoyer copie de la grande lettre, et de toute la correspondance; c'est un recueil curieux et qu'il est bon d'avoir; si le paquet étoit trop gros et trop coûteux, vous pourriez trouver quelque occasion de me le faire tenir, par exemple, en l'adressant a Mr. de Montigny, qui me le remettroit surement, ou par le courier de l'ambassadeur.

Quant à moi, mon cher ami, quoique l'opinion et les discours d'un fou ne me touchent gueres, quoique la lettre et les complots dont il m'accuse aient tout à la fois fait rire et indigné tous ceux qui en ont entendu parler, je vous prie cependant de faire jetter à cette bête feroce au travers de ses barreaux le petit papier que je vous adresse. Vous le trouverez, je crois, décent et moderé, et pour peu qu'il reste à ce méchant fou quelque legere étincelle de pudeur et de raison, j'espère que cette déclaration, quand il l'aura lue, me vangera bien cruellement de lui. Je n'ai pu me dispenser de dire dans ce papier que j'ai désaprouvé la lettre de Mr. Valpole; vous savez ce que je vous ai dit plusieurs fois à Paris sur ce sujet. Mad^{e} de Boufflers sait que je lui ai dit la même chose, aussi bien que Mad^{e} de Luxembourg, et mille autres; et je crois que Mr. Valpole auroit pu se dispenser de cette platitude (car c'en est une, et la lettre n'est pas trop bonne) d'autant plus que l'effet de cette Pasquinade a eté de tourner tout à fait la tête à un pauvre frenetique, et de compromettre deux honnêtes gens dont l'un est de ses amis, et dont l'autre ne lui a fait aucun mal. On dit ici comme une chose très certaine, que c'est Madame du deffand qui lui a inspiré cette méchanceté (elle en est très capable, et vous le savez bien); on ajoute que c'est elle qui a revu et corrigé la lettre pour le style; Peut être Rousseau l'a-t-il entendu dire; et comme il peut ignorer que je ne vois plus Mad^{e} du deffand depuis deux ans, il a pu en conclure que j'avois travaillé à la lettre. On dit aussi que Mr. Valpole avoit porté sa lettre à lire et à corriger à Mr. Helvetius, qui le lui a refusé, quoiqu'il ait de très grandes raisons de se plaindre de Rousseau; ce procédé si noble et si honnête auroit du faire faire des réflexions à Mr. Valpole, et l'engager à remettre son papier dans sa poche pour n'en plus sortir. Il ne fait, ce me semble, que ce qu'il vous doit en vous permettant de dire qu'il est l'auteur de la lettre; il feroit mieux encore de l'écrire à Rousseau lui même, de lui dire les choses comme elles sont, en lui marquant d'ailleurs (s'il le juge àpropos) autant de mépris qu'il voudra, et en disculpant pleinement tous ceux à qui il a valu si mal a propos une tracasserie. Mais quelque parti qu'il prenne, je crois pour moi me devoir à moi même de confondre Rousseau, qui apparemment me demandera pardon de sa sottise, et qui l'obtiendra aisément, à condition de ne parler jamais de moi en bien ni en mal. C'est apparemment ma liaison avec Voltaire qui lui a fait croire que j'étois son ennemi; il est vrai que j'aime infiniment mieux la maniere d'écrire de Voltaire que la sienne; il est vrai que Rousseau m'a toujours paru un charlatan, fort éloquent à la verité, mais qui a le malheur d'employer son éloquence à des chimeres, et qui finira par être oublié; il est vrai que bien loin de le croire, comme beaucoup de gens, un adroit sophiste, je le trouve un mauvais et maladroit logicien; il est vrai enfin que je sais de science certaine que si Voltaire s'est moqué de Rousseau, Rousseau a eu les premiers torts avec lui en lui écrivant une lettre impertinente et ridicule sur les comédies qu'il faisoit jouer auprès de Geneve, et en lui disant qu'il étoit *l'empoisonneur* de sa patrie; mais ce qui est encore plus vrai, c'est que j'ai fait tout mon possible pour calmer Voltaire, et pour l'empêcher d'écrire contre ce pauvre fou là. Je me souviens que je lui écrivois un jour; *il est vrai que Rousseau a aboyé, comme vous le dites, contre les Philosophes* (dans son Emile); *mais avouez aussi qu'il a mordu les ennemis de la philosophie jusqu'au sang* (dans le Vicaire savoyard); *il faut donc*, continuois-je, *ne lui pas jetter les pierres, mais du pain, pour l'empecher d'aboyer, et pour lui donner la force de mordre.* Je lui écrivois dans une autre lettre; *Rousseau est un homme de beaucoup d'esprit, mais qui n'a d'esprit que quand il a la fièvre; il ne faut ni le guerir, ni l'outrager.* Je vous demande, mon cher ami, si ce sont la les propos d'un homme qui cherche à nuire a Rousseau; Mlle de lespinasse a lu ces lettres, et me serviroit de témoin en cas de besoin. Elle vous remercie mille fois de votre souvenir, et paroit bien revenue sur le compte de Jean Jacques. . . .

Mille pardons de cette longue lettre, mais je me flatte qu'elle ne vous ennuyera pas. Je me rejouis d'avance de lire le beau plaidoyer de 18 pages de Diogène Rousseau; je vous prie d'envoyer ce billet tout ouvert à Mr. Davenport, et d'en prendre copie auparavant, *ne varietur*; Mr. Davenport la donnera à Rousseau, après en avoir aussi pris copie; et j'en garde une autre de mon côté. Rousseau, moyennant ces précautions, ne pourra pas le falsifier.

[The enclosure, which Hume was to send to Rousseau, but which he did not send, is substantially the same as the *Déclaration* which d'Alembert later appended to Hume's *Exposé succinct*.]

* XVIII. *From* Mme de Boufflers

ce 6 aoust 1766

Les embarras et loccupation que m'ont donnez larrivée de mon fils et son depart m'ont empechée de vous ecrire et de repondre a votre lettre quoique je leusse fort desiré. Vous reconnoissez votre faute envers moy, et vous m'en demandez pardon. C'est ce que javois deja fait avant que vous m'en eussiez prié, elle na pas donné la moindre atteinte a notre amitié et si vous laviez imaginé ce seroit en ce point que consisteroit votre plus grand tort mais si je suis facile a appaiser je ne le suis pas autant a persuader et quoique j'aye pesé les considerations que vous moffrez, quoique je me sois mise a votre place, je persiste toujours a dire que vous eussiez dû garder plus de moderation, quelle eut servi a faire briller davantage, la raison, qui est incontestablement de votre coté, que vous naviez pas la moindre raison de craindre que le public se trompat dans cette querelle et que tout le mal que vous en pouviez recevoir c'est vous qui vous letes fait vous même. Heureusement il n'est pas irreparable et la bienfaisance, la bonté constante de votre caractere, peut excuser un premier mouvement de colere. M. dalembert ma fait voir la grande lettre de Rousseau. Je suis de lavis de ceux qui croyent sa tete affectée, mais je ne suis pas du votre a legard du stile, je n'y reconnois ni son genie ni son eloquence ordinaire, la conclusion exceptée. . . .

* XIX. *From* Mme du Deffand

Paris ce 13 aout [1766]

Oui Monsieur, Jay été toutes des premieres a connoitre votre merite, Jen fais vanité et J'ay desirée tres sincerement d'etre votre

* MS., R.S.E., unpublished.

amie; Je m'etois flatée d'y avoir réüssie, et c'est avec beaucoup de chagrin que Je me suis appercüe que Je m'étois trompée? N'allez pas me dire que c'est actuellement que je me trompe. Convenez que si quelqu'un de votre connoissance se lioit aujourdhuy intimement avec J. Jacques, vous ne pourriez pas le regarder comme votre ami, et vous trouveriez singulier qu'on traita *d'animosité* le Juste ressentiment que la mechanceté et l'ingratitude inspirent. Jignore si lusage authorise ou tolere les liaisons de nos amis avec nos ennemis, Je ne scay que ce que dicte l'amitié et Je serois fachée d'en scavoir davantage

Vous ne devez pas douter de ce que J'ay pensée sur les procedés de J. Jacques, J'en ay eté indignée mais peu surprise. Vous devez vous consoler de cette avanture, il ni a point de honte a etre la dupe de son bon cœur, Je suis bien persuadée que c'est l'avis de notre amy Mr Walpole, et Je suis fort trompée s'il ne lui est pas arrivé souvent d'eprouver de tels inconvenients

Pour mon petit Craufurd, ses vertus ne sont pas si actives, il pourra grace a sa paresse et à son indiference etre a Labri de tels accidents

Vous ne me parlez point de votre retour, Langleterre est elle donc comme les enfers qui ne rendent rien

Vous voyez Monsieur que Je desire de vous revoir, c'est vous dire ce que Je pense pour vous. Je crois ainsy que vous qu'il arrivera un Jour qui détruira tout ce qui soppose a notre union, Je le desire, Je l'espere, et Jauray bien du plaisir a pouvoir aimer ce que J'estime et Jadmire, mais Je vous declare que Je ne calmeray point votre jalousie sur Mr Craufurd, Je l'aimeray toute ma vie.

Adieu Monsieur, Je suis choquée des complimens qui terminent votre lettre.

* XX. *From* Earl Marischal Keith

Potsdam 15 August 1766.

I have three of yours, the last by Mr Franklin only yesterday, sent me from Utrecht by Mr Brown. I am much grieved by what happens between you and J. J., for still I can not suspect him, of black ingratitude in his heart which many now accuse him of, but I believe his warm imagination has realised to him suspicions that have not the least foundation, as I know being well informed of your warm and hearty friendship to him, and having seen with what tendernesse and regard you did all in your power to serve him; his *écart* afflicts me on his account more than yours, who have, I am sure, nothing to reproach yourself [with]. It will be good and humain in you, and like Le Bon David, not to answer; which you say is your opinion. J. J. is already attacked, and will be more so on all hands; his enemys pursued him with inveterate malice when they had nothing in truth

* MS., R.S.E.; *Eminent Persons*, 70.

to say; now he has given them hold, they are all upon him. If some body should accuse me of having murdered Henry IV of France, I should not justify myself, because the accusation would not gain the least credit. . . .

* XXI. *From* BARON D'HOLBACH

J'ai recu, Mon très cher Monsieur, avec un trés grand plaisir la Lettre que vous m'avéz fait L'honneur de m'ecrire le 5 de ce mois. J'ai Laissé à Voré des amis fort surpris et touchés de votre désagréable avanture avec Rousseau; elle a fait en ce paÿs ci un trés grand Eclat; mais Je ne connois personne qui ait balancé un instant entre vous et cet ingrat; s'il lui reste quelques partisans à Paris, ce ne peut être que parmi des opiniâtres sur qui la raison ne peut rien, ou que leur Entousiasme empêche de se rendre à l'Evidence. M D'Alembert m'a communiqué vos Lettres, elles ont vérifié une prédiction que j'avois faite à quelques uns de mes amis, que Rousseau feroit le fou pour se tirer de cette affaire; c'etoit en effet la seule porte pour en sortir; il scait bien que l'on a pitié des foux, et que l'on pardonne à ceux qui sont méchants par nécéssité. J'apprens qu'il a ecrit une Lettre à son Libraire Guy; Je ne scai ce qu'elle contient, vû qu'il lui déffend de la communiquer à personne, sinon à quelques amis qu'il lui désigne; cependant on assure qu'il n'entreprend point de se Justifier. Au reste, Mon trés cher Monsieur, Je crois que vous prenéz le bon parti en gardant le Silence, il faut y persister Jusqu'à ce que votre adversaire vous force de le rompre, ce qui pourra bien arriver, vû que ce seroit un miracle s'il se tenoit tranquile; alors une exposition simple des faits, jointe aux preuves authentiques que vous avéz en main, suffira pour vous faire triompher et pour couvrir d'infamie l'ingrat qui ne vous oppose que des soupçons insensés. Nos amis communs sont, ainsi que moi, trés fachés des rudes epreuves que votre bon coeur vient d'essuyer; il n'est personne qui ne vous rende Justice, et je ne pense point qu'il y ait un seul homme à Paris qui ose elever la voix en faveur d'un Visionnaire qui a si indignement outragé l'amitié bienfaisante; douter, comme il fait, que votre bienfaisance soit naturelle, c'est prouver Evidemment qu'il ignore cette heureuse disposition. Ainsi, Je vous le répéte, Mon trés cher Monsieur, que votre ame reprenne sa sérénité accoutumée; oubliéz, s'il se peut, celui qui l'a troublée; et soyéz sur que votre conduite a les suffrages unanimes de tous les honêtes gens qui ont entendu parler de cette affaire. . . .

Paris le 18 d'août 1766.

† XXII. *From* MME DU PRÉ DE ST. MAUR

A Montigny le 20 aoust 1766

Il ne falloit pas Monsieur vous aimer autant que je vous aime pour etre vivement affectée du bizare denouement de votre union avec

* MS., R.S.E.; *Eminent Persons*, 259 f.   † MS., R.S.E., unpublished.

J. J. Tout Paris y a pris part, les uns avec interêt, les autres par pure Curiosité. Les premiers indices de votre mecontentement ont tout d'abord excité ces deux sentimens. Avec quelle impatience n'a t'on pas attendu l'explication d'une Enigme dont il etoit impossible de deviner le mot? A peine a t'il eté connu que l'indignation contre Rousseau a eté generalle. Ses amis, c'est a dire les Amateurs de ses ouvrages ne l'ont deffendu qu'en disant qu'il est fol, les votres se sont affligez de voir un ingrat extravagant detruire en un moment le plaisir si digne de vous que vous preniez a faire son bonheur. Je vous avoue Monsieur que c'est a ce sentiment là que mon Coeur s'est arrêté. Les indifferens ont raisonné diversement ceux d'entr'eux qui se picquent de n'agir jamais que prudemment ont dit que vous vous etiez trop pressé de repandre tant de bienfaits sur J. J. avant que de vous être assuré qu'il en fut digne; ceux qui guettent les philosophes pour les trouver en faute ont eu une joye platte et maligne de voir celui qui avoit reuni tous nos suffrages trompé par un usurpateur du même titre; j'ay vû de tous ces gents là Monsieur, mais je n'en n'ay point rencontré qui vous supposassent l'ombre d'un tort vis a vis de Rousseau. Faittes vous donc l'honneur de croire que vous n'avez pas plus besoin de justification en france qu'en Angleterre. M^r. de Montigny receut avant hier au soir les papiers que vous lui avez envoyez. Nous passâmes une partie de la Nuit a les Lire. M^r. Trudaine etoit desja retiré et n'en n' apris connoissance qu'hier. M^r. et M^e. de Montigny M^rs. de Fourqueux de Tournieze, Saurin et moy etions de la premiere Lecture. Elle nous a fait a tous la même impression. Si nous differons en quelque Chose sur l'opinion qu'elle nous donne de Rousseau ce n'est que par des nuances imperceptibles. On ne peut attenuer le Vice de son coeur qu'en lui supposant plus de degrez de folie. Votre Conduite a son egard est au dessus de toutte objection. Vous avez voullu le rendre heureux, il n'en n'est pas susceptible. D'autres avant vous l'avoient tenté sans plus de succez, mais le voila bien plus Malheureux que jamais, parce qu'il est avili et degradé, parce qu'a quelque degré que se portent a present ses Malheurs il n'a plus a attendre des amis les plus sensibles que de la Compassion. Qu'a donc a redouter l'excellent David Hume d'un Etre aussi deplorable? aussi abandonné? Rien assurement. Par consequent rien a faire rien a ecrire, encore moins a imprimer, renoncer a une Chimere Charmante a la verité, se feliciter de n'avoir a rompre qu'avec un seducteur et non avec un Ami, rire même de ce que les lumieres de la plus saine philosophie combinées avec les sentimens les plus exquis ne mettent pas a l'abri d'être trompé par un fol plein de talent et d'artifice, voila ce me semble Monsieur la facon de penser de ceux de vos amies qui habitent actuelement Montigny. Les Mânes de Fontenelles invoquées nous paroissent du même avis. C'est a M^r. Trudaine qu'elles ont repondu, et avec raison, puisqu'il n'a jamais eté mieux entendu que par lui, et que vous remplissez si parfaittement dans son coeur et dans son estime le vuide qu'il y a Laissé. Je ne vous dis rien pour M.r et M.e de Montigny qui doivent vous donner incessamment de Leurs nouvelles, mais les lecteurs nommez si dessus me prient de les rappeller a votre souvenir et même a votre amitié. . . .

* XXIII. *From* TRUDAINE DE MONTIGNY

a Montigny ce 23 aoust 1766

J'ay recu ici, Monsieur, la lettre que vous m'avez fait l'honneur de m'ecrire et le pacquet qui contenoit la relation de votre commerce epistolaire avec Mr Rousseau, et de ce qui s'est passé entre vous. Je scais que Madame Dupré vous en a deja ecrit et vous a mandé avec quel empressement nous avons lu ces papiers qui contenoient les eclaircissemens les plus autentiques sur une affaire que nous connoissions deja par le bruit qu'elle a fait dans le public mais qui nous interessoit assez vivement pour que nous recussions avidement les details. Si vous etes sensible a l'opinion qu'on a de vous dans ce pays ci vous devez, Monsieur, jouir d'une satisfaction bien douce. Depuis qu'on parle de cet affaire et on en parle beaucoup il ne s'est pas ouvert une bouche que pour faire votre eloge. Les plus entousiastes des admirateurs de Jean jaques ont parlé de vous comme les autres et ont été très ardens a publier vos louanges. Les voix n'ont pas été si unanimes sur le compte de l'ecrivain Genevois les uns l'ont regardé comme un homme noir et mechant qui sacrifioit tous les sentimens honêtes au desir de faire parler de lui. Ses amis se sont contenté de le faire passer pour le plus fol et le plus deffiant des hommes. Pour moi je ne puis plus conserver pour son caractere aucune estime et eut-il été emporté par ses passions je tiens qu'on doit juger les hommes par leurs passions, et celles qu'il a montré dans cette occasion me paroissent fouler au pied l'amitié la reconnoissance l'humanité et tout ce que nous connoissons d'honête et de respectable dans les sentimens qui gouvernent le coeur des hommes. Je le crois bien malheureux aujourdhui et la reputation que ses talens lui ont acquis me paroissent bien peu capable de le consoler du bruit que font ses procedés vis a vis de vous. Que je vous ay bien reconnu! Monsieur, et que mon coeur a bien volé au devant du votre! dans la note ou vous dittes que depuis sa lettre vous avez ecrit a Mr Davenport pour lui recommender son malheureux hôte ce sont vos termes ils sont dignes de vous. Il vous a manqué de la maniere la plus cruelle mais c'est un homme et c'est un homme pour qui ses talens et ses malheurs doivent encore servir de recommendation après que ses procedés même ont devoilé son caractere. Me Dupré vous aura mandé sans doute le resultat de notre petit Areopage. Je pense puisque vous me demandez mon avis que vous n'avez pas plus de

* MS., R.S.E., unpublished.

besoin ici qu'en Angleterre d'Imprimer pour faire connoitre la droiture et la noblesse de votre conduite. J'ay trouvé votre narration parfaitement bien ecrite et fort interessante. J'en ay fait une traduction pour mon pere et si vous l'approuvez je la garderay en vous donnant ma parole qu'elle ne sortira pas de mes mains et que je ne la communiqueray qu'a vos amis qui seront bien aise de la voir. Je pense toute reflexions faites qu'il suffira que cet ecrit reste entre les mains de deux ou trois de vos amis surs qui le feront voir aux personnes auxquelles ils jugeront qu'il sera necessaire de le montrer. Je ne puis au surplus que me referer a l'avis des personnes aux quelles vous me chargez de le faire passer. Je l'envoye a Mr Dalembert et je le prie de le faire passer a Mr Turgot qui n'est pas encore parti pour son intendance. Aussitot que je seray a Paris (et ce sera dans peu de jours) j'en raisonneray avec eux et j'auray l'honneur de vous mander le resultat de nos conversations. Madame de Montigny est bien eloignée de se mocquer de vous. Elle est très affligé de cette avanture. Vous scavez combien elle aimoit Rousseau sans l'avoir jamais vu. Mais son amitié pour vous lui a fait bien veritablement partager la peine que tout cela a du vous causer. Elle n'a point entendu parler du portrait de Rousseau que vous vouliez lui envoyer et qui auroit été un present bien touchant pour elle il y a deux mois. . . .

* XXIV. *From* D'ALEMBERT

a Paris ce 1er septembre [1766]

J'ai recu, mon cher ami, votre gros paquet, dont je connoissois déjà plusieurs pieces; j'ai lu, en levant les épaules, la longue lettre de Rousseau, qu'il faudroit intituler, lettre de la *commere* Rousseau à Mr. Hume; car toute cette lettre n'est qu'un *commerage* plat et ennuyeux, digne d'une femme du peuple, mais à la verité d'une femme méchante et dangereuse. Vos amis sont partagez sur la question, si vous devez imprimer cette histoire; on dit que vous serez ici à la fin de septembre. Vous serez alors plus a portée de voir le parti qu'il est le plus à propos que vous preniez.

Je compte que vous avez envoyé à Rousseau la déclaration que je vous ai adressée pour la lui faire parvenir. Je la lui adresse par une autre voie, afin qu'il n'en pretende cause d'ignorance, & j'y joins une lettre très moderée, mais dont je crois qu'il ne se vantera pas.

Tout cela ne m'empêche pas, mon cher ami, de persister dans mon avis sur la lettre de Mr. Valpole, et d'être persuadé 1° que cette lettre ne vaut pas grand chose en elle même; 2° que Mr. Valpole n'auroit point dû attaquer un homme qui ne lui faisoit point du mal; Rousseau est un charlatan, je l'avoue, il faut se contenter de ne point acheter ses drogues, sans lui jetter des pierres. 3° que

* MS., R.S.E.; *Eminent Persons,* 200 ff.

Mr. Valpole aura eternellement à se reprocher d'avoir fait perdre l'esprit à ce pauvre diable là, et de vous avoir compromis très mal à propos, aussi que moi, qui à la verité ne m'en souci gueres. . . .

[Here follows the passage about Mme du Deffand, 'la Vipère', which is quoted on p. 432 above.]

Laissons là cette ordure, et revenons à Rousseau, qui à la verité en est une autre. Vous n'avez peut etre pas vu dans sa grande lettre de *commere*, la vraie raison de sa mauvaise humeur. C'est que l'accueil qu'on lui a fait en Angleterre a eté fort au dessous de ce qu'il esperoit; *hinc iræ, hinc lacrymæ*; il en fait l'aveu assez maladroitement, et montre bien à découvert toute la sottise et l'indiscretion de son orgueil. Je ne suis point etonné du peu de sensation qu'il a fait. Son grand merite est dans le style, et ce merite est presque perdu en angleterre; d'ailleurs on n'est pas fort empressé dans votre pays pour voir un original; l'angleterre en fourmille, et ses originaux ont meme sur Rousseau l'avantage d'être naturels; car Rousseau n'est qu'un original factice; mais je le repete, il ne falloit point le vexer comme Mr. Walpole a fait; et j'ajoute qu'apres ce qui en a resulté, Mr. Walpole devroit ecrire à Rousseau, pour l'assurer qu'il est seul auteur de cette lettre, et que surtout ni vous ni moi n'y avons aucune part. Il en fera ce qu'il voudra; quant à moi je rirai egalement de tout le monde, et des charlatans comme Rousseau, et des poltrons come Mr. Walpole qui n'osent les attaquer à découvert. . . .

* XXV. *From* BARON D'HOLBACH

Vous auréz vu, Mon trés cher Monsieur, par ma dernière que Je persistois toujours à croire que vous ne deviéz point vous engager dans une guerre ouverte avec Rousseau; mais, ainsi que vos amis d'ici, je me vois forcé de changer d'avis; quelques personnes qui ont lûe la lettre que votre Ingrat a ecrite au Libraire Guy, assure qu'elle vous est injurieuse qu'elle contient un déffi contre vous, en un mot qu'elle est ecrite de maniere à faire une impréssion défavorable sur l'Esprit de bien des gens, qui ne voient les choses que trés superficiellement. Celà posé Je trouve que la pluspart de ceux qui s'intéressent à vous, Monsieur, pensent que vous ne pourréz guères vous dispenser de publier une Justification; Elle devient nécéssaire, vû le grand nombre de partisans et même de fanatiques que votre adversaire a dans toute l'Europe et surtout ici; on assure qu'ils prétendent dejà se prévaloir de votre silence, et qu'ils disent qu'il est étrange d'intenter des accusations si graves contre quelqu'un sans les Justifier. Ainsi je me vois obligé à me départir à la fin de mes conseils pacifiques; Je persiste néantmoins à vous conseiller une modération, qui est dejà dans votre caractère et dont Je crois votre

* MS., R.S.E.; *Eminent Persons*, 261 ff.

adversaire incapable; il ne s'agit que d'une exposition simple des faits et des preuves; il est bien difficile que les sophismes et les tirades d'Eloquence parviennent à obscurcir la vérité toute nue Et exposée sans passion. Aureste c'est l'avis de M D'alembert qui compte vous Ecrire sur le même ton; les auteurs de la Gazette littéraire s'offrent d'être vos interprêtes pour ce paÿs; vous scavéz que vous ne pouvéz tomber en de meilleures mains. M Suard m'apprend que des personnes de ses amis reçoivent une quantité de Lettres de Genève et de la Suisse, par lesquelles on vous accuse, ou bien l'on exige à grands cris votre justification. Vous voyéz que ces circonstances sont de nature à vous obliger d'entrer en lice et de renoncer pour quelques tems à votre sérénité philosophique; d'ailleurs on prétend que Rousseau prépare des mémoires de sa vie, dans lesquels il est [à] craindre qu'il ne représente ses bienfaiteurs, c'est à dire ses Ennemis, sous les traits que lui suggéreront sa méchante ame et son imagination atrabilaire; il est important de le prévenir; vous sentéz qu'après sa mort, ou même après avoir fait son impréssion sur le public, il seroit trop tard ou du moins trés difficile d'y porter du remede.

Je suis bien fâché d'être ainsi forcé de vous pousser à une démarche dont vous scavéz que J'étois ci devant fort éloigné; mais il faut céder à la nécéssité; les partisans de Rousseau sont nombreux, il a pour lui la foule de ceux qui se laissent éblouir par de belles déclamations dont il est parvenu à se faire des Entousiastes; pour vous, Mon trés cher Monsieur, vous auréz pour vous les amis de la vérité, qui est faite pour triompher de la mauvaise foy et du préjugé. . . .

Malgré ce que je vous dis du grand nombre des partisans de Rousseau, soyéz pourtant persuadé que tous ceux qui ont vu vos lettres ici sont entièrement désabusés sur son compte.

rue royale bute St Roch le 1er de 7bre 1766.

* XXVI. *From* Trudaine de Montigny

A Paris ce 1 Sept 1766

. . . Soyez persuadé Monsieur que nous n'avons pu faire mauvais usage de ces papiers. Vous pouvez être bien tranquille sur la facon de penser de tout paris sur votre compte. Il n'y a qu'une seule voix. J'en ay causé avec Mr Dalembert et Mr Turgot. Ils pensent a ce qu'il me semble a peu près comme moi. Cependant Mr Dalembert pense que peutêtre seroit-il utile dans quelque tems de faire imprimer cette relation. Dans ce cas je vous proposerois quelques legers changemens, que je vous prie de me permettre a vous indiquer. Si vous vous determinez a faire imprimer, par ex. je trouverois bien quelque chose a dire a vos notes que j'adoucirois ou même que je supprimerois peutêtre en entier me contentant de restituer les faits dans les endroits ou cela seroit absolument indispensable. La force

* MS., R.S.E., unpublished.

des raisons et des procédés est si manifestement de votre coté que la plus grande moderation sera toujours ce que vous pouvez dire de plus fort contre ce malheureux fol. Mais je m'en reviens toujours a mon avis qu'il faut attendre et ecouter la facon de penser du public. Madame Dupré a du vous ecrire sur le même ton. Rapportez vous en a vos amis sur le moment ou la chose sera necessaire. En attendant soyez sur que nous ferons un si bon usage de ce que nous avons entre les mains que votre reputation est en bonnes mains. J'ose dire que vous en devriez être touché si vous en etiez temoin. Je crois que M^r D'Alembert ne vous a pas repondu parce qu'il avoit entendu dire que vous deviez arriver ici dans le courant de ce mois de Septembre. . . .

* XXVII. *From* Mme de Barbentane

a Villers cotterest 3 7bre 1766

Etant absente de paris depuis 16 semaines, je n'ai pû Monsieur suivre éxactement vôtre corespance [*sic*], et j'en ai le plus grand regret, non que jaie besoin de rien de plus, pour fixér mon opinion; quand on vous a vû autant que je l'ai fait, il est impossible d'avoir aucun doute, et malgré l'excés de mon enthousiasme pour le malheureux qui a cessé d'etre votre ami, je n'ai pas hesité un moment sur ce que je devois croire de vous. Il me paroit certain que sa tête est phisiquement ataquée; et cette idée est la moins facheuse pour moi, je puis croire au moins que lorsque je l'estimois avec tant de veneration, il en etoit digne. . . .

† XXVIII. *From* Turgot

A Paris le 7 Septembre 1766

J'ay trouvé ici, Monsieur, votre lettre du 5 Aout a mon retour d'un voyage que j'ay eté faire en Normandie. D'Alembert qui venoit alors de recevoir votre recit de l'histoire de Rousseau avec les lettres que vous y avés inserées me l'a communiqué. Je vous crois a present si ennuyé de cette affaire que je ne sais si je dois encore vous en parler. Mr de Montigni m'a cependant dit que vous desiriés de savoir ma façon de penser. Vous imaginés bien quelle ne peut pas etre douteuse sur le fond de l'affaire et je crois qu'excepté Rousseau et peut etre Mlle le Vasseur, il n'y a personne dans le monde qui s'imagine ny qui eut jamais imaginé que vous ayés mené Rousseau en Angleterre pour le trahir et a qui sa longue lettre et ses demonstrations ne fassent pitié. Mais je vous avoue que j'y vois toujours plus de folie que de noirceur. J'y vois les sophismes dont une imagination sombre se sert pour empoisonner les circonstances les plus simples et les transformer au gré de la manie qui l'occupe, mais je

* MS., R.S.E., unpublished. † MS., R.S.E.; *Eminent Persons*, 144 ff.

ne crois point que ces extravagances soyent un jeu joué et un pretexte pour secouer le poids de la reconnoissance qu'il vous doit: il paroit sentir luy meme que personne ne le croira, et qu'il se couvre d'opprobre du moins pour le moment aux yeux du public. Il avoue qu'il sacrifie et son interêt et meme sa reputation: et il est certain que cette affaire luy fait un tort irreparable, l'isole du genre humain et luy ote tout appuy contre les persecutions auxquelles ses opinions et encore plus les traits de sa misanthropie l'exposeront toujours. Je persiste donc a ne le croire que fou et je suis affligé que l'impression trop vive qu'a faite sur vous sa folie vous ait mis dans le cas de la faire eclater et de la rendre irremediable, car le bruit qu'a fait votre lettre au Baron, est pour Rousseau une demonstration que ses conjectures etoient fondées sur la verité meme. Il a bien mandé a M[e] De Bouflers qu'il ne se plaignoit pas, et que cette lettre qui vous a donné lieu a le diffamer comme le dernier des hommes n'etoit ecrite qu'a vous. L'eclat que vous avés fait luy a fait tout le mal possible et sa lettre ne vous en a fait aucun. Les gens sensés qui se mettront a votre place sentiront combien ce mouvement de vivacité etoit naturel en voyant tant de services payés par tant d'outrages, aucuns n'excuseront Rousseau d'avoir conçu des soupçons aussi atroces sur des motifs aussi frivoles, mais quelques uns de vos amis et moy en particulier regretteront que vous vous soyés laissé aller a cette premiere impression et que vous ne vous soyés pas contenté de repondre simplement a Rousseau qu'apparemment il etoit devenu fou, sans en ecrire a paris avant d'avoir vu le fond de ces soupçons.

J'ay lu avec attention la lettre de R. a Mr Conway, elle contient sans doute un refus pour le moment, mais il est certain que Mr Conway et vous, vous vous êtes trompés si vous y avés vu qu'il exigeoit que la pension fut publique, et qu'il fit de ce changement la condition de son acceptation. Votre erreur a cet egard a eté pour luy une confirmation de ces soupçons, et peut etre a t'elle contribué a vous tromper dans la suite sur les motifs de sa conduite et a vous faire substituer un systeme de noirceur reflechie, a l'extravagance sombre et soupçonneuse dont vous avés eté justement blessé, mais dont Rousseau se trouve etre cruellement la victime. Sa grande lettre explique tout. Il est clair qu'il n'a refusé la pension que parce qu'il ne vouloit pas vous la devoir, et non pour se faire aux yeux du peuple un merite de son refus. Il convient que vous l'avés demandée de son aveu; on voit evidemment que la lettre de Mr Walpole qu'il a sottement imputée a D'Alembert est cause de tout et que c'est sa publication dans les papiers publics qui a fait revivre les pueriles remarques qui remplissent sa lettre et auxquelles il n'auroit sans cela fait aucune attention serieuse.

Dans toute cette affaire il s'en faut beaucoup que je trouve Mr Walp. innocent. Je trouve la plaisanterie sur Rousseau dans le moment ou il l'a faite une chose tres malhonnête. J'en ay eu cette idée dès le premier moment et les effets quelle a produits ne sont pas propres a me faire changer d'avis. Je n'ay pas vu sans une sorte d'indignation, l'air de triomphe de cette homme sur un evenement dont il est la cause.

Après vous avoir dit aussi franchement mon avis, vous serés surpris peut etre de me voir presque revenu a l'avis de faire imprimer. La folie de Rousseau est telle qu'il a ecrit ici differentes lettres dans lesquelles il regarde votre trahison comme si constante et les demonstrations comme si terrassantes pour vous, qu'il vous defie de publier les pieces sans vous deshonorer a moins que vous ne les falsifiés; ce ne sont pas ses termes mais c'en est le sens. Si cette espece de defi devenoit public a un certain point et faisoit plus d'impression en Angleterre qu'il n'en peut faire en France, peut etre serés vous obligé d'imprimer. Mais en ce cas je voudrois retrancher tout recit, toute imputation de mensonge, toutes notes excepté quelques unes necessaires pour retablir simplement les faits, importans, comme celuy de la scene qui s'est passée la veille de son depart pour Wootton. Encore voudrois je que dans ces notes vous dissiés simplement le fait, sans traiter Rousseau de menteur, sans vous abaisser a le prouver. Vous devés etre cru sur ce que vous dirés et vous le serés. Je ne mettrois autre chose a la tete sinon que les discours repandus sur la querelle &c et l'espece de defi que Mr Rousseau vous fait de publier ce qui s'est passé vous obligent a regret a publier les accusations de Mr Rousseau contre vous, et que vous croyés leur publication une reponse suffisante. Voila quel est actuellement mon penchant. Mais comme je ne vois a cela rien de pressé, je crois que vous ferés bien de vous donner tout le tems d'y reflechir. Plus vous mettrés dans cette affaire de moderation et meme d'indifference, plus le tort de Rousseau deviendra evident. . . .

* XXIX. *From the* Abbé Morellet

Paris le 8 Sept. 1766.

. . . Je ne vous parle pas de cette affaire de Mr. rousseau avec vous. Vous deves en avoir les oreilles rompües. Mon avis sur cela est le même que celui du baron et de Mr d'alembert. Il me paroit necessaire que vous fassies imprimer les pieces du procés c'est à dire les lettres, un petit recit qui les lie semblable à celui que vous aves fait dans votre derniere grande lettre à Mr d'alembert et des remarques plus nombreuses encore que celles que vous aves faites et qui se presentent naturellement sur toutes ces lettres, le tout sans le moindre mot insultant et en affoiblissant à dessein toutes les expressions par lesquelles vous releverez les faussetés et les contradictions dont les lettres de j. j. sont pleines. Il n'y a pour vous aucun inconvenient à cette publication. Il est impossible que toute

* MS., R.S.E.; *Eminent Persons*, 309 f.

l'addresse du sophisme et toute la chaleur de l'eloquence colorent l'extravagance ou la mechanceté (je vous donne le choix) de sa conduite envers vous. Vous pouves juger par moi de la force et de l'impression que doit faire la lecture de ces pieces. Vous saves que j'etois attaché à Mr rousseau que j'estime même pour le fonds de ses idées beaucoup plus que vous en un mot que j'étois un de ses devots les plus zelés. Mais il n'y a pas d'attachement qui tienne contre des traits pareils. . . .

* XXX. *From* Lady Grizel Stanhope

[Geneva] Sep: 12 1766

Yours of the 29th of Aug: I rcd. on the 8 inst. When I first heard of your quarrel, & that you intended to publish something, I was very silent, as I wished that nothing might be said about it till the work appeared, knowing your humane disposition & that perhaps your ever good nature might make you relent, but several letters from Paris made it publickly known here in about a fortnight after. I repeat what I have said before, that I think you have gone too far to retreat with credit. His friends triumph, & the few who are impartial seem inclining to his side, but the enclosed [1] will convince you I am in the right. I hear he has wrote more letters much to the same purpose, but this is the only one I have seen, & is I think sufficient. I hope, by what you know of him, that you are now convinced that my friends are as honest & as much to be relied on as Yours. I could say a word or two of another of Yours, but I leave it to time & a Good Providence to open Your Eyes to the Truth in all Things. All I shall say, is, be less hasty in the choice of your friends. This advice to you as a man of Letters, may at this time be of use, if you follow it, for you are in many things too apt to think others as honest as yourself. I am nearer the fountain head, & know what you do not, so what I say is serious. I have lately fought your battles stoutly, I don't tell you I always do it. You may be sure my abhorrence to him adds a little to my zeal for you, but without any partiality, I can'not blame you for any thing in this affair, but for yours too great credulity (a failing one can't always accuse you of) & for your ill judged good nature. I seldom felt more pleasure than I did when I heard you had found him out so soon, for I was sure that sooner or later you would do it. Your uncommon marks of friendp hastened the discovery. Had you procured a pension of a thousand pounds, he had assassinated you, but as it was but a Hn[d] he only abuses you, & you have reason to be thankfull you have come off so well. I am convinced by all I have heard of him, that it is his maxim to use those people worse to whom he has the

* MS., R.S.E., unpublished.

[1] Not extant.

greatest obligations, he has given many proofs of it, & it is the only thing in which he has not changed his mind. I think it now depends on you to unmask Him. . . .

* XXXI. *From* D'ALEMBERT

à Paris le 6 octobre [1766]

Vos intentions, mon cher ami, seront executées ponctuellement, et le sont même déja en partie. Mr. Suard a déja traduit vos papiers, nous y avons fait, de concert avec le Baron, les changemens convenables & conformes à ce que vous desirez, nous y joindrons un petit avertissement, ou nous insisterons, comme vous le voulez avec raison, sur votre repugnance à instruire le public de cette querelle, et sur les raisons qui vous y obligent; & tout cela paroitra dans 8 à 10 jours sous le nom de vos amis, mais non pas de moi seul, precisement parce que je suis melé dans la querelle. Je donnerai à Mr. Suard, à quelques changemens près, la petite déclaration que je vous avois envoyée; elle sera imprimée avec votre factum, et se trouvera en très bonne compagnie. Cela vaut mieux que de l'avoir envoyée à Rousseau; ainsi je ne me plains pas que vous ne l'ayez pas fait, quoiqu'à dire vrai, les raisons que vous m'en donnez ne soient pas trop bonnes; avouez que la veritable est que vous n'avez pas voulu faire connoitre à Rousseau que je desaprouve votre ami Valpole; il est pourtant vrai que vous lui etes redevable de cette tracasserie. À l'égard de la Vipere ma voisine, je persiste à vous dire que c'est ce que nous appellons en grec une *bougresse*; je la plaindrai pourtant volontiers d'etre aveugle, à condition qu'elle sera muette; votre excessive bonté pour elle me fait souvenir d'un mot d'un Roi de Sparte à qui on vantoit la bonté de quelqu'un; *comment peut il etre bon*, disoit-il, *s'il n'est pas terrible aux méchans?*

Mr. de Nivernois a lu vos papiers, et en pense comme tous les gens raisonnables, ou plutôt comme tous ceux qui savent les détails de cette ridicule querelle. Madame de Boufflers ne veut pas etre nommée et ne le sera pas; Madame de Verdelin ne veut pas l'etre non plus, et on se passera bien de son nom. . . .

† XXXII. *From* SUARD

a Paris 2 9bre 1766

. . . Vous avés desiré que je fusse votre traducteur et je n'avois pas besoin de tous les sentimens qui m'attachent a vous pour me charger de ce travail avec plaisir. Votre cause me paroissoit celle des honnêtes gens et surtout celle des amis de la philosophie; Il y a longtems que je regardois Rousseau comme un profond et dangereux Charlatan, qui avoit passé sa vie a recevoir des bienfaits de tout le

* MS., R.S.E.; *Eminent Persons*, 202 f. † MS., R.S.E., unpublished.

monde et a faire tout le mal qu'il avoit pu a ceux qui lui avoient fait le plus de bien. Je crois qu'il est tres bon qu'il soit demasqué et il l'est. J'ai toujours insisté sur la necessité d'imprimer; parce que vos plaintes etant connues et ayant fait de l'eclat, le grand scandale etoit fait et il etoit juste que la peine en retombat sur l'auteur de l'iniquité. Notre brochure a fait tout l'effet qu'elle devoit faire sur tous les esprits raisonnables et non prevenues; Il y a bien dans un certain monde de ces gens, d'une sensibilité excessive sur tout ce qui blesse le moins du monde leur amour propre, et d'une moderation Stoïque sur tout ce qui interesse celui des autres, qui couperoient la gorge a leur ami pour une parole imprudente, et feroit un procés sur un manque d'etiquette, mais qui voudroit qu'un homme de lettres se laissat outrager dans ce qu'il a de plus sensible, sans se servir des armes qu'il a pour se defendre; ces gens la pretendent qu'il eut mieux valu laisser tomber cette affaire; quelques autres entousiastes de Rousseau ou ennemis entousiastes des Philosophes cherchent a excuser son procédé, mais ces gens la forment le très petit nombre, et ce n'est pas a eux qu'il faut parler raison. Aux yeux de tout le reste David hume sera toujours un homme genereux, sensible et bienfaisant, Jean Jaques Rousseau n'est qu'un visionnaire ingrat, menteur et mechant. Il n'y point d'homme honnête qui ne voulut avoir fait au même prix ce que vous avés fait pour cet ingrat. . . .

[This Appendix may be fittingly rounded off with the best of the squibs that appeared in the newspapers on the subject of the Hume–Rousseau quarrel. The following appeared as No. 3 of a series of periodical essays entitled *The Miscellany*, purporting to be written by Nathaniel Freebody, in the *St. James's Chronicle* for 13–15 Jan. 1767. Burton printed it in a footnote to *Life*, ii. 340 f., and said: 'It has the appearance of having been written by a Scottish lawyer.']

HEADS OF AN INDICTMENT LAID BY J. J. ROUSSEAU, PHILOSOPHER, AGAINST D. HUME, ESQ.

1. That the said David Hume, to the great scandal of philosophy, and not having the fitness of things before his eyes, did concert a plan with Mess. Tronchin, Voltaire, and D'Alembert, to ruin the said J. J. Rousseau for ever, by bringing him over to England, and there settling him to his heart's content.

2. That the said David Hume did, with a malicious and traitorous intent, procure, or cause to be procured, by himself, or somebody else, one pension of the yearly value of £100 or thereabouts, to be paid to the said J. J. Rousseau, on account of his being a philosopher, either privately or publicly, as to him the said J. J. Rousseau should seem meet.

3. That the said David Hume did, one night after he left Paris, put the said J. J. Rousseau in bodily fear, by talking in his sleep;

although the said J. J. Rousseau doth not know whether the said David Hume was really asleep, or whether he shammed Abraham, or what he meant.

4. That, at another time, as the said David Hume and the said J. J. Rousseau were sitting opposite each other by the fireside in London, he, the said David Hume, did look at him, the said J. J. Rousseau, in a manner of which it is difficult to give any idea: That he, the said J. J. Rousseau, to get rid of the embarassment he was under, endeavoured to look full at him, the said David Hume, in return, to try if he could not stare him out of countenance; but in fixing his eyes against his, the said David Hume's, he felt the most inexpressible terror, and was obliged to turn them away, insomuch that the said J. J. Rousseau doth in his heart think and believe, as much as he believes anything, that he, the said David Hume, is a certain composition of a white-witch and a rattlesnake.

5. That the said David Hume on the same evening, after politely returning the embraces of him, the said J. J. Rousseau, and gently tapping him on the back, did repeat several times, in a good-natured easy tone, the words, 'Why, what, my dear Sir! Nay, my dear Sir! Oh, my dear Sir!' From whence the said J. J. Rousseau doth conclude, as he thinks upon solid and sufficient grounds, that he, the said David Hume, is a traitor; albeit he, the said J. J. Rousseau, doth acknowledge, that the physiognomy of the good David is that of an honest man, all but those terrible eyes of his, which he must have borrowed; but he, the said J. J. Rousseau, vows to God he cannot conceive from whom or what.

6. That the said David Hume hath more inquisitiveness about him than becometh a philosopher, and did never let slip an opportunity of being alone with the governante of him, the said J. J. Rousseau.

7. That the said David Hume did most atrociously and flagitiously put him, the said J. J. Rousseau, philosopher, into a passion; as knowing that then he would be guilty of a number of absurdities.

8. That the said David Hume must have published Mr Walpole's letter in the newspapers, because, at that time, there was neither man, woman, nor child, in the island of Great Britain, but the said David Hume, the said J. J. Rousseau, and the printers of the several newspapers aforesaid.

9. That somebody in a certain magazine, and somebody else in a certain newspaper, said something against him, the said John James Rousseau, which he, the said J. J. Rousseau, is persuaded, for the reason above-mentioned, could be nobody but the said David Hume.

10. That the said J. J. Rousseau knows, that he, the said David Hume, did open and peruse the letters of him, the said J. J. Rousseau, because he one day saw the said David Hume go out of the room, after his own servant, who had, at that time, a letter of the said

J. J. Rousseau's in his hands; which *must* have been in order to take it from the servant, open it, and read the contents.

11. That the said David Hume did, at the instigation of the devil, in a most wicked and unnatural manner, send, or cause to be sent, to the lodgings of him, the said J. J. Rousseau, one dish of beefsteaks, thereby meaning to insinuate, that he, the said J. J. Rousseau, was a beggar, and came over to England to ask alms: whereas be it known to all men by these presents, that he, the said John James Rousseau, brought with him the means of subsistence, and did not come with an empty purse; as he doubts not but he can live upon his labours—with the assistance of his friends; and in short can do better without the said David Hume than with him.

12. That besides all these facts put together, the said J. J. Rousseau did not like a certain appearance of things on the whole.

APPENDIX L

EXTRACTS FROM LETTERS ABOUT HUME'S DEATH

* I. *From* Joseph Black *to* Adam Smith

Edinb. Monday 26 Aug[st] 1776

Dear Sir

Yesterday about 4 o'clock afternoon Mr Hume expired. The immediate approach of his Death became evident in the night between Thursday & Friday when the looseness became very excessive & was attended with vomiting now & then this continued the greater part of the time that remained & soon weakened him so much that he could no longer rise out of his bed. He continued to the last perfectly sensible & free from much pain or feelings of distress. He never dropped the smallest expression of impatience but when he had ocasion to speak to the people about him always did it with affection & tenderness. I thought it improper to write to bring you over, especially as I had heard that he had dictated a letter to you on Thursday or Wednesday desiring you not to come. When he became very weak it cost him an effort to speak and he died in such a happy composure of mind that nothing could have made it better.

Yrs affect[ly]

J. Black.

† II. *From* William Cullen *to* William Hunter

Sept. 17, 1776.

You desire an account of Mr Hume's last days, and I give it you with some pleasure, for, though I could not look upon him in his illness without much concern, yet the tranquillity and pleasantry which he constantly discovered, did even then give me satisfaction, and, now that the curtain is dropped, allows me to indulge the less alloyed reflection. It was truly an example 'des grands hommes qui sont morts en plaisantant;' and to me, who have been so often shocked with the horrors of the superstitious on such occasions, the reflection on such a death is truly agreeable. For many weeks before his death he was very sensible of his gradual decay, and his answer to inquiries after his health, was, several times, that he was going as fast as his enemies could wish, and as easily as his friends could desire. He was not, however, without a frequent recurrence of pain and uneasiness, but he passed most part of the day in his drawing-room, admitted the visits of his friends, and, with his usual spirit, conversed with

* MS., R.S.E.; generally printed, with considerable alterations, along with No. III below, as an addendum to Hume's *My own Life*.

† Thomson, *Cullen*, i. 607.

them upon literature, politics, or whatever else was accidentally started. In conversation he seemed to be perfectly at ease, and to the last abounded with that pleasantry, and those curious and entertaining anecdotes, which ever distinguished him. This, however, I always considered rather as an effort to be agreeable, and he at length acknowledged that it became too much for his strength. For a few days before his death he became more averse to receive visits; speaking became more and more difficult for him; and, for twelve hours before his death, his speech failed altogether. His senses and judgment did not fail till the last hour of his life. He constantly discovered a strong sensibility to the attention and care of his friends, and, amidst great uneasiness and languor, never betrayed any peevishness or impatience. . . .'

* III. Adam Smith *to* William Strahan

Kirkaldy, Fifeshire, Nov. 9, 1776.

Dear Sir,

It is with a real, though a very melancholy pleasure, that I sit down to give you some account of the behaviour of our late excellent friend, Mr. Hume, during his last illness.

Though in his own judgment his disease was mortal and incurable, yet he allowed himself to be prevailed upon, by the entreaty of his friends, to try what might be the effects of a long journey. . . . Upon his return to Edinburgh, though he found himself much weaker, yet his cheerfulness never abated, and he continued to divert himself, as usual, with correcting his own works for a new edition, with reading books of amusement, with the conversation of his friends; and sometimes in the evening with a party at his favourite game of whist. His cheerfulness was so great, and his conversation and amusements ran so much in their usual strain, that notwithstanding all bad symptoms, many people could not believe he was dying. 'I shall tell your friend Colonel Edmonstoune,' said Dr Dundas to him one day, 'that I left you much better, and in a fair way of recovery.' 'Doctor,' said he, 'as I believe you would not choose to tell any thing but the truth, you had better tell him I am dying as fast as my enemies, if I have any, could wish, and as easily and cheerfully as my best friends could desire.' Colonel Edmonstoune soon afterwards came to see him, and take leave of him; and on his way home he could not forbear writing him a letter, bidding him once more an eternal adieu, and applying to him, as to a dying man, the beautiful French verses in which the Abbé Chaulieu, in expectation of his own death, laments his approaching separation from his friend the Marquis de la Fare. Mr. Hume's magnanimity and firmness were such, that his most affectionate friends knew that they hazarded nothing in talking and

* Generally printed as addendum to Hume's *My own Life*.

writing to him as to a dying man; and that so far from being hurt by this frankness, he was rather pleased and flattered by it. I happened to come into his room while he was reading this letter, which he had just received, and which he immediately showed me. I told him, that though I was sensible how very much he was weakened, and that appearances were in many respects very bad, yet his cheerfulness was still so great, the spirit of life seemed still to be so very strong in him, that I could not help entertaining some faint hopes. He answered, 'Your hopes are groundless. An habitual diarrhoea of more than a year's standing would be a very bad disease at any age; at my age it is a mortal one. When I lie down in the evening I feel myself weaker than when I rose in the morning; and when I rise in the morning weaker than when I lay down in the evening. I am sensible, besides, that some of my vital parts are affected, so that I must soon die.' 'Well,' said I, 'if it must be so, you have at least the satisfaction of leaving all your friends, your brother's family in particular, in great prosperity.' He said that he felt that satisfaction so sensibly, that when he was reading, a few days before, Lucian's *Dialogues of the Dead*, among all the excuses which are alleged to Charon for not entering readily into his boat, he could not find one that fitted him: he had no house to finish, he had no daughter to provide for, he had no enemies upon whom he wished to revenge himself. 'I could not well imagine,' said he, 'what excuse I could make to Charon, in order to obtain a little delay. I have done every thing of consequence which I ever meant to do, and I could at no time expect to leave my relations and friends in a better situation than that in which I am now likely to leave them: I therefore have all reason to die contented.' He then diverted himself with inventing several jocular excuses, which he supposed he might make to Charon, and with imagining the very surly answers which it might suit the character of Charon to return to them. 'Upon further consideration,' said he, 'I thought I might say to him, "Good Charon, I have been correcting my works for a new edition. Allow me a little time that I may see how the public receives the alterations." But Charon would answer, "When you have seen the effect of these, you will be for making other alterations. There will be no end of such excuses; so, honest friend, please step into the boat." But I might still urge, "Have a little patience, good Charon, I have been endeavouring to open the eyes of the public. If I live a few years longer, I may have the satisfaction of seeing the downfall of some of the prevailing systems of superstition." But Charon would then lose all temper and decency. "You loitering rogue, that will not happen these many hundred years. Do you fancy I will grant you a lease for so long a term? Get into the boat this instant, you lazy loitering rogue."'

But though Mr Hume always talked of his approaching dissolution with great cheerfulness, he never affected to make any parade of his great magnanimity. He never mentioned the subject but when the conversation naturally led to it, and never dwelt longer upon it than the course of the conversation happened to require; it was a subject indeed which occurred pretty frequently, in consequence of the inquiries which his friends, who came to see him, naturally made concerning the state of his health. . . .

Thus died our most excellent, and never-to-be-forgotten friend; concerning whose philosophical opinions men will no doubt judge variously, every one approving or condemning them according as they happen to coincide, or disagree with his own; but concerning whose character and conduct there can scarce be a difference of opinion. His temper, indeed, seemed to be more happily balanced, if I may be allowed such an expression, than that perhaps of any other man I have ever known. Even in the lowest state of his fortune, his great and necessary frugality never hindered him from exercising, upon proper occasions, acts both of charity and generosity. It was a frugality founded not upon avarice, but upon the love of independency. The extreme gentleness of his nature never weakened either the firmness of his mind, or the steadiness of his resolutions. His constant pleasantry was the genuine effusion of good nature and good humour, tempered with delicacy and modesty, and without even the slightest tincture of malignity, so frequently the disagreeable source of what is called wit in other men. It never was the meaning of his raillery to mortify; and therefore, far from offending, it seldom failed to please and delight even those who were the objects of it. To his friends, who were frequently the objects of it, there was not perhaps any one of all his great and amiable qualities which contributed more to endear his conversation. And that gaiety of temper, so agreeable in society, but which is so often accompanied with frivolous and superficial qualities, was in him certainly attended with the most severe application, the most extensive learning, the greatest depth of thought, and a capacity in every respect the most comprehensive. Upon the whole, I have always considered him, both in his lifetime, and since his death, as approaching as nearly to the idea of a perfectly wise and virtuous man, as perhaps the nature of human frailty will admit.

I am ever, Dear Sir,

Most affectionately yours,

ADAM SMITH.

APPENDIX M

THE PUBLICATION OF THE 'DIALOGUES CONCERNING NATURAL RELIGION' AND OF HUME'S 'MY OWN LIFE'

By a codicil added to his will on 7 Aug. 1776, Hume left his MSS. to William Strahan. He says: 'I desire, that my Dialogues concerning natural Religion may be printed and published any time within two Years after my Death; to which, he [Strahan] may add, if he thinks proper, the two Essays formerly printed but not published. My Account of my own Life, I desire may be prefixed to the first Edition of my Works, printed after my Death, which will probably be the one at present in the Press. I desire that my Brother may suppress all my other Manuscripts . . . I also ordain, that if my Dialogues from whatever Cause, be not publishd within two Years and a half of my Death, as also the Account of my Life, the Property shall return to my Nephew, David, whose Duty, in publishing them as the last Request of his Uncle, must be approved of by all the World.'

On 2 Sept. 1776 Hume's brother sent Strahan the MSS. of the *Dialogues* and of *My own Life*. Three days later Adam Smith wrote to Strahan about them. As to the *Dialogues* he says: 'The latter, tho' finely written, I could have wished had remained in manuscript to be communicated only to a few people. When you read the work, you will see my reasons without my giving you the trouble of reading them in a letter. But he [Hume] has ordered it otherwise. . . . I once had perswaded him to leave it entirely to my discretion either to publish them at what time I thought proper, or not to publish them at all. Had he continued of this mind the manuscript should have been most carefully preserved and upon my decease restored to his family; but it never should have been published in my lifetime.' As to the other MS. Smith says he proposes to add 'a very well authenticated account' of Hume's behaviour during his last illness; but he particularly asks that the autobiography (together with his additions to it) should not be published along with the *Dialogues*, since he cannot have his own name associated with the publication of the *Dialogues* in any way. (Draft letter among MSS., R.S.E.)

Strahan kept quiet about the *Dialogues* for some time. But in Nov. 1776 he suggested to Smith that Hume's autobiography, even when enlarged by Smith's letter, would hardly make a volume; and that it might be well to add some of Hume's letters. (MS., R.S.E.) Smith did not think well of this proposal. He says: 'Mr Hume's constant injunction was to burn all his papers, except the Dialogues and the account of his own life. This injunction was even inserted in the body of his will. I know he always disliked the thought of his letters ever being published.' (Hill, 351). The proposal was accordingly dropped.

By the end of the year Strahan had decided to publish the new edition of Hume's Works before he published the *Dialogues*—a decision which greatly pleased Smith. (Draft letter from Smith to Strahan, undated, among MSS., R.S.E.) Early in 1777 David Hume the Younger desired to know from Strahan what precisely he was going to do about the MSS.; and Strahan replied on 13 Feb., saying that he had not yet decided whether he would ever publish the *Dialogues* or not. On 25 Feb. John Home of Ninewells wrote to Strahan protesting against: (i) the publication of the autobiography as a separate pamphlet, instead of as a preface to an edition of the *Works*; and (ii) the proposal to include letters in this publication. (MS., R.S.E.) Strahan excused himself about (i) by saying that Hume had not expressly forbidden it and that, in any case, Adam Smith had agreed to it; and as to (ii), declared that he had dropped the project altogether. (MS., R.S.E.) *My own Life* appeared as an 8vo pamphlet of 62 pages that spring.

John Home had to make the best of this, but he still wanted to known what was going to be done about the *Dialogues*. Strahan finally decided that he would not publish them; the MS. appears to have been returned to Edinburgh; and in 1779 they appeared, presumably on the responsibility of David Hume the Younger, as—

> Dialogues | concerning | Natural Religion. | By David Hume, Esq; | Printed in 1779. [4to, pp. 152.]

no publisher's name being given.

The publication seems to have made much less noise than Adam Smith had expected. Hugh Blair wrote to Strahan on 3 Aug. 1779: 'As to D. Hume's *Dialogues*, I am surprised that though they have now been published for some time, they have made so little noise. They are exceedingly elegant. They bring together some of his most exceptionable reasonings, but the principles themselves were all in his former works.' (*Rosebery MSS.*, as quoted by Hill, 364.)

INDEX OF PERSONS

The first numeral after each name indicates the page on which a biographical note about the person may be found. An italic numeral indicates the first page of a letter from Hume to the person named. Numerals following † indicate unimportant references or mere mentions of the name.

INDEX OF BOOKS AND SUBJECTS

Books are nearly always classified under their titles, but in a few cases under their authors' names. Numerals following † indicate unimportant references.